TAANACH I

STUDIES IN THE IRON AGE POTTERY

AMERICAN SCHOOLS OF ORIENTAL RESEARCH

EXCAVATION REPORTS

edited by
David Noel Freedman

EXCAVATION REPORTS
TAANACH I
STUDIES IN THE IRON AGE POTTERY
by
Walter E. Rast

TAANACH I
STUDIES IN THE IRON AGE POTTERY

by
Walter E. Rast

edited by
Albert E. Glock

The Taanach Excavations are a joint expedition of the Concordia Seminary, St. Louis, Missouri and the American Schools of Oriental Research to Tell Taʿannek, West Bank of Jordan.

Published by
AMERICAN SCHOOLS OF ORIENTAL RESEARCH

Distributed by
American Schools of Oriental Research
126 Inman Street
Cambridge, MA 02139

TAANACH I
STUDIES IN THE IRON AGE POTTERY
by
Walter E. Rast

Copyright © 1978
by
American Schools of Oriental Research

Library of Congress Cataloging in Publication Data
Rast, Walter E   1930-
    Taanach I.

    (Taanach series ; 1)(Excavation reports ; 1)
    Bibliography: p.
    Includes index.
    1. Taanach, Jordan. 2. Pottery-Jordan. 3. Iron age-Jordan. I. Title. II. Series. III. Series: Excavation reports ; 1)
DS154.9.T25R37   933   76-5474
ISBN 0-89757-201-7 (previously 0-89130-103-8)

Printed in the United States of America
1 2 3 4 5

To The Memory of
PAUL W. LAPP

TABLE OF CONTENTS

	LIST OF FIGURES	ix
	EDITORIAL PREFACE	xiii
	PREFACE	xv
I.	INTRODUCTION	1
II.	IRON I STRATIGRAPHY AT TAANACH AND COMPARATIVE SITES	3
	Relation to Late Bronze Strata	3
	Iron I Phasing	3
	Comparative Iron I Stratigraphy	4
	Date of Taanach Iron I Periods	6
III.	POTTERY GROUPS OF PERIOD I	7
	The Cuneiform Tablet Building, SW 5-1, 5-2, 6-1, 6-2	7
	The Drainpipe Structure, SW 2-25, 3-25	7
	The Twelfth-Century House, SW 5-8	7
	Primary Comparative Loci	8
	Additional Comparative Loci and Strata	9
	The Pottery	9
	Summary	14
IV.	POTTERY GROUPS OF PERIOD IIA	17
	SW 4-7, Loci 68, 53, and 44	17
	SW 6-2, Locus 68	17
	SW 5-2, Loci 60, 61	17
	SW 2-8, Locus 18	17
	SW 4-7, Loci 57, 60	17
	SW 4-7, Locus 42	18
	Primary Comparative Loci	18
	Additional Comparative Loci and Strata	18
	The Pottery	18
	Summary	21
V.	POTTERY GROUPS OF PERIOD IIB	23
	The Cultic Structure, SW 2-7	23
	Cistern L. 69, SW 2-8	23
	Cistern L. 74, SW 6-2	23
	Primary Comparative Loci	24
	Additional Comparative Loci and Strata	26
	Date	26
	Pottery from the Cultic Structure	27

		Pottery from Cistern L. 69, SW 2-8	35
		Pottery from Cistern L. 74, SW 6-2	36
		Summary	38
VI.	POTTERY GROUPS OF PERIODS III TO V		41
		Iron II Stratigraphy at Taanach and Comparative Sites	41
		Period III	41
		Period IV	41
		Period V	41
		Comparative Strata and Chronology	41
		Pottery Groups of Period III	42
		Pottery Groups of Period IV	43
		Pottery Groups of Period V	44
		Summary	44
VII.	POTTERY GROUPS OF PERIOD VI		47
		Period VIA	47
		Period VIB	47
		Comparative Strata and Date	47
		The Pottery	48
		Summary	51
VIII.	MISCELLANEOUS IRON AGE POTTERY		53
		Period IA	53
		Period IB	53
		Period IIB	53
		Periods III-VI	54
IX.	CONCLUSION		55
	BIBLIOGRAPHY		57
	INTRODUCTION TO FIGURES		63
	FIGURES 1-97		64
	INDEXES		271

LIST OF FIGURES

Fig. 1.   Pottery from the Cuneiform Tablet Building (Period IA).

Fig. 2.   Same

Fig. 3.   Pottery from the Drainpipe Structure (Period IA).

Fig. 4.   Pottery from the Twelfth-Century House (Period IA).

Fig. 5.   Same

Fig. 6.   Same

Fig. 7.   Same

Fig. 8.   Same

Fig. 9.   Pottery from the Drainpipe Structure (Period IB).

Fig. 10. Same

Fig. 11. Same

Fig. 12. Same

Fig. 13. Same

Fig. 14. Same

Fig. 15. Pottery from the Cuneiform Tablet Building (Period IB).

Fig. 16. Same

Fig. 17. Same

Fig. 18. Pottery from SW 4-7, Locus 68 (Period IIA).

Fig. 19. Pottery from SW 4-7, Locus 53 (Period IIA).

Fig. 20. Pottery from SW 4-7, Locus 44 (Period IIA).

Fig. 21. Same

Fig. 22. Pottery from SW 6-2, Locus 68 (Period IIA).

Fig. 23. Same

Fig. 24. Pottery from SW 5-2, Loci 60/61 (Period IIA).

Fig. 25. Pottery from SW 2-8, Locus 18 (Period IIA).

Fig. 26. Pottery from SW 4-7, Loci 57/60 (Period IIA).

Fig. 27. Same

Fig. 28. Pottery from SW 4-7, Locus 42 (Period IIA).

Fig. 29. Same

Fig. 30. Pottery from the Cultic Structure (Period IIB).

Fig. 31. Same

Fig. 32. Same

Fig. 33. Same

Fig. 34. Same

Fig. 35. Same

Fig. 36. Same

Fig. 37. Same

Fig. 38. Same

Fig. 39. Same

Fig. 40. Same

Fig. 41. Same

Fig. 42. Same

Fig. 43. Same

Fig. 44. Same

Fig. 45. Same

Fig. 46. Same

Fig. 47. Same

Fig. 48. Same

Fig. 49. Same

Fig. 50. Same

Fig. 51. Same

Fig. 52. Pottery from Cistern 69 (Period IIB).

Fig. 53. Same

Fig. 54. Same

Fig. 55. Pottery from Cistern 74 (Mostly Period IIB).

Fig. 56. Same

Fig. 57. Same

Fig. 58. Same

Fig. 59. Same

Fig. 60. Same

Fig. 61. Same

Fig. 62. Same

Fig. 63. Same

Fig. 64. Same

Fig. 65. Same

Fig. 66. Same

Fig. 67. Same

Fig. 68. Same

Fig. 69. Same

Fig. 70. Pottery from SW 4-7, Locus 41 (Period III).

Fig. 71. Pottery from the Northeast Outwork, NEO-2 (Period III).

Fig. 72. Pottery from SW 4-7, Locus 36 (Period IV).

Fig. 73. Pottery from SW 4-7, Locus 37 (Period IV).

Fig. 74. Pottery from SW 4-7, Locus 38a (Period IV).

Fig. 75. Pottery from SW 5-6, Locus 16 (Period V).

Fig. 76. Same

Fig. 77. Pottery from SW 4-7, Stone-Lined Pit 7 (Period VIA).

Fig. 78. Same

Fig. 79. Pottery from SW 5-7, Stone-Lined Pit 11 (Period VIA).

Fig. 80. Pottery from Pit 74 (Period VIA).

Fig. 81. Same

Fig. 82.   Same

Fig. 83.   Pottery from SW 2-25, Stone-Lined Pit 125 (Period VIB).

Fig. 84.   Same

Fig. 85.   Pottery from SW 3-25, Stone-Lined Pit 22 (Period VIB).

Fig. 86.   Same

Fig. 87.   Pottery from SW 2-25, Locus 19 (Period VIB).

Fig. 88.   Miscellaneous Pottery (Period IA).

Fig. 89.   Same

Fig. 90.   Same

Fig. 91.   Miscellaneous Pottery (Period IB).

Fig. 92.   Miscellaneous Pottery (Period IIB).

Fig. 93.   Same

Fig. 94.   Miscellaneous Pottery (Period III-VI).

Fig. 95.   Miscellaneous Pottery (Periods III-VI, except NO. 2, Period IA).

Fig. 96a.   Drainpipe Structure.

Fig. 96b.   Tablet Building.

Fig. 96c.   Twelfth-Century House.

Fig. 97a.   Cultic Structure.

Fig. 97b.   Section through SW 2-7, looking south.

Editorial Preface

With this study of the Iron Age pottery of Taanach we begin the publication of the report of the Concordia-ASOR Excavation of Tell Taᶜannek. The project was conceived and guided by the Concordia Committee for Archaeological Study in the Near East, a committee of the School for Graduate Studies of Concordia Seminary, St. Louis, Missouri, U. S. A. The organization of the project includes a core staff of A. Glock, D. Hillers, C. Graesser, D. Voelter, and W. Rast. Director was P. W. Lapp and Associate Director was A. von Rohr Sauer. The chief archeological aim of the project was a refined understanding of the stratigraphy of a site well known since the Sellin excavations in 1902-4. A necessary consequence is more control of the development of ceramic typology. The present study by W. Rast is thus one important type of benefit foreseen by the planners of the Taanach Project.

In early 1970 P. W. Lapp drowned in a tragic accident off the north coast of Cyprus. In 1972 Concordia Seminary was reorganized and two members of the core staff left the school. The appointment of a new director and the reorganization of the support system for the project necessarily has delayed the completion of the work. A final season of excavation has been postponed. There now seems reasonable hope that both the publication and excavation will be brought to completion. It would be gratuitous to offer a time limit or even a schedule of future volumes. Several research projects are under way and these will be brought out in this series when they have achieved a satisfactory form. It is our hope that the work begun with such energy by Lapp will be completed with enough solid contribution both in new knowledge of stratigraphy as well as new method of presentation that the whole will be a useful contribution to scholarship.

Since the inception of the excavation of Tell Taᶜannek in 1963 there have been significant changes in how archeologists in the Middle East approach their task. The search for history, for clues to the separation and chronology of occupation deposit has in the past dominated the aims of working field archeologists. The most significant chronological marker in Palestine has been changing ceramic styles. Increasingly, however, archeologists are affirming that history is not only chronology, art is not the only key to the human spirit and politics the only outline of significant event. The influence of the cultural anthropologist has reached the Middle East often through the work of the prehistorian. Under his influence culture is more broadly defined. Rather than emphasize fine arts, the more useful definition of culture for the archeologist includes all physical instruments developed by people to facilitate adaptation to a particular place. The artifacts that the archeologist excavates are then the key to a cultural tradition which in part must be the aim of the archeologist to reconstruct. This aim of archeological research is at present very slowly being introduced into existing programs. It remains to be seen if this is a workable objective. The present volume was conceived and in large part written before these objectives crystallized in the Taanach publication program. Nevertheless, the task of refining ceramic chronology remains fundamental in any kind of archeology of Palestine. This volume is a significant contribution to this need. Future volumes will gradually assume a wider horizon for culture history.

Albert E. Glock
Director, Taanach Excavations
Albright Institute, Jerusalem

NOTE: All dates are B.C. unless otherwise noted.

Preface

This study of the Iron Age pottery of Taanach had its beginnings after the second season of excavations in the summer of 1966. During the year 1966-1967, as James Alan Montgomery Fellow of the American Schools of Oriental Research, I had the benefit of the guidance and criticism of Paul W. Lapp, then Professor of Near Eastern History and Archaeology at the Jerusalem School. The bulk of the laboratory work on the groups chosen for special examination was carried on during that year and a first draft of the manuscript on what has been designated the Period IIB pottery was produced. The delay in the appearance of the volume was caused, in part, by the war in June of 1967, which inevitably brought some confusion into the plans for continued study of the material. More seriously, the tragic death of Paul Lapp in 1970 necessitated a reconstitution of the Core Staff and its direction. Throughout this entire period the work has benefited immeasurably from the contributions of Fouad and Issa Zoghbi. Their labors in carefully drawing the groups and preparing the plates as well as in supplying necessary information on the pottery cannot be applauded enough for helping bring the volume to completion. In the later stages of the study I have received much help from Albert E. Glock, who has taken over the directorship of the Taanach expedition and the editorship of its publications. The technical fabric and surface descriptions were supplied by him, with the assistance of Lois Glock, using a new scheme devised for the Taanach publication. It was his idea as well to include photographs of pottery with the line-drawings, a format which should ease usage of the visual sections of the volume. I am grateful to Lois Glock for preparing the indexes as well. The publication office staff of the American Schools of Oriental Research, David Noel Freedman, director, has given great assistance. James Eisenbraun especially made substantial contributions in editing the volume for publication. David Voelter is responsible for the plans and sections in Figs. 96 and 97.

The list of those who have given assistance by making the pottery of comparative sites available for examination includes the following: Messrs. Yusuf Saad and ʿAref el-ʿAref, former curators of the Palestine Archaeological Museum, the Megiddo pottery in the museum; the late Père Roland de Vaux, the Tell el-Fārʿah (N) Iron Age pottery; the late Professor Yohanan Aharoni, the Iron Age pottery from Tell Arad; Professor Yigael Yadin, Iron Age pottery from Hazor; Professors Yadin and Y. Shiloh, Iron Age pottery discovered in the new excavations at Megiddo; Professor M. Broshi, the Persian pottery from Megadim; the Israel Department of Antiquities, Iron Age pottery from Tell Goren; and Dr. Moawiyah Ibrahim, the important Iron Age pottery he has recently uncovered at Sahab in Jordan. I am also indebted to Professor Yadin who supplied unpublished copies of plans from Hazor. Professor John Holladay made available a copy of his dissertation (Harvard University) which contains much of the unpublished Shechem material, and this has been especially helpful for the study of the small amount of Iron II material from Taanach. The nearby resources of the Joseph Regenstein Library and the Oriental Institute of the University of Chicago have been indispensable for continuing the work in this country.

Others also deserve a word of thanks for the assistance and support they gave during the time this volume was in preparation. I am grateful to the American Schools of Oriental Research and its late President, Dr. G. Ernest Wright, for the appointment as a Fellow of the Schools during 1966-67. The Committee on Creative Work and Research of Valparaiso University and its director, Dr. Waldemar C. Gunther, also gave generous support during 1966-67. The late president of Valparaiso University, Dr. O.P. Kretzmann as well as its present chief officer, Dr. Albert Huegli, offered continuous encouragement. Earlier drafts of the manuscript were read and criticized by Albert E. Glock, Nancy L. Lapp, and James Sauer, and I have profited greatly from their numerous suggestions. The volume is much the better for their help, while the author bears burden of whatever weaknesses still remain. The difficult task of typing has been carried on by my student assistants, Jane Barnes, Rebecca Carino and Katherine Linder.

My greatest indebtedness is to the late director of the Taanach excavation, Paul W. Lapp, to whose memory this volume is dedicated. Lapp's broad knowledge of

Palestinian archaeology has informed the study at so many points that it is impossible to give adequate acknowledgment. Nearly all aspects of the present volume were discussed with him in one way or another. That Paul Lapp should have been taken so suddenly by accidental drowning in Cyprus on April 26, 1970 continues to sadden the memories of those who were privileged to work closely with him. The fruits of his many outstanding contributions live as an enduring challenge to those of us left behind.

Finally, I wish to express my personal indebtedness to the Aid Association for Lutherans, an insurance company supportive of many worthy cultural and social endeavors. This agency provided the bulk of the financial backing for the expedition and thus was largely responsible for converting the plans for excavation at Taanach into reality.

Walter E. Rast
15 November 1976

Chapter One
Introduction

The succession of Iron Age strata excavated at Tell Taʿannek during 1963, 1966 and 1968 contained important ceramic sequences, especially for Iron I. This volume, with an upper limit at ca. 1200 and a lower at the end of the fifth century, is based on selected pottery groups representing the best stratified examples of sequences discovered on the mound during the three seasons. The complete description of the stratigraphy on which the study rests is scheduled for a separate publication. Whereas some refinements may become necessary as the study of the stratigraphy proceeds to its final form, it does not appear that these will alter in a major way the conclusions arrived at here. The study of the stratigraphy in the present volume has relied heavily on the field books, sections and plans of the five major areas excavated, as well as on the reports for each season submitted by the area supervisors: Albert E. Glock, Carl Graesser, Delbert Hillers, Walter E. Rast and Alfred von Rohr Sauer. In addition, the preliminary reports on the three seasons have been used and may be consulted for reference (Lapp 1964; 1967a; 1969b).

Three features characterize the discussion in the following chapters. First, the study is based on representative groups of controlled, stratified pottery. The loci in which the pottery groups selected for publication were found were usually occupation levels, destruction layers, or fills from which the latest horizon could be isolated. The stratigraphic relation of the loci to the material above and below them is presented in the discussions in the ensuing chapters, and it will be possible to check these data in detail in the locus lists and discussion of the subsequent stratigraphy volume.

Second, the focus of the discussion in the following chapters is on the development of form. Whereas much valuable information other than that applying to form may be obtained from the study of ceramic remains, the present examination has concentrated on form. The goal has been that of attaining greater precision in the chronological significance of formal changes, a goal which is possible to meet, at least in part, with carefully controlled groups.

Third, the study incorporates a large amount of comparative discussion. The Iron Age pottery from Taanach is utilized as a starting point for reviewing ceramic groups from contemporary sites. This aspect of the study operates at two levels. One is the attempt to identify stratified loci at other sites for primary comparison, the other a more general comparison of the published stratigraphy from other sites.

This comparative work provides the basis for dealing with the problems of chronology which are discussed at various places in the succeeding chapters. The determination of absolute dates for the Taanach groups is not bolstered in any substantial way by non-ceramic or epigraphic material, and coins are naturally lacking for the earlier material. Apart from the alphabetic cuneiform tablet (from the so-called Cuneiform Tablet Building), whose independent chronological value is limited, only a small amount of epigraphic evidence has turned up from Iron Age Taanach. The determination of dates consequently rests heavily on comparative stratigraphy. Thus, for example, a close synchronization is made between the Cultic Structure group and several good loci at Megiddo and other sites. Similar correlations are attempted for other periods.

The chapters which follow are arranged according to six chronological periods and their subdivisions. The discussion of each period begins with a description of the Taanach loci from which the pottery came. Primary comparative loci (PCL) are then presented. In order to qualify as a PCL the stratified and uncontaminated character of a comparative locus must be clear. Parallels from non-primary loci are also utilized to clarify both Taanach and other sites. Each section concludes with a summary, consolidating the distinguishing ceramic features of the period.

Consistent with Lapp's (1969a:71-89) approach to excavation, the choice was made to line up the pottery by locus rather than by type. This procedure works well for a large group representing one period like that from the Cultic Structure (Chapter 5). It is more cumbersome when a number of differing loci are discussed together, in which case it will be necessary to refer simultaneously to several figures for the discussion. The value of the approach is that it gives primary place to the stratified provenience of the ceramic remains. The increasing care paid to carefully excavated, controlled loci in the field, pursued at Tell Taʿannek and at an ever larger number of sites, promises to produce greater refinements in pottery typology and chronology in the ancient Near East.

Chapter Two
Iron I Stratigraphy at Taanach and Comparative Sites

Relation to Late Bronze Strata

Most of the earliest Iron Age structures at Taanach were found directly above LB I remains. This was clearly the case with four major structures from this period, the Cuneiform Tablet Building, the Drainpipe Structure, the Twelfth-Century House, and Iron I Court (See Fig. 96 for plans).

That the Cuneiform Tablet Building in SW 5-1, 5-2 was constructed on LB I debris became clear in 1966 when digging proceeded to lower layers (Lapp 1967a:19-21). The foundations of Wall L. 83 were found to have been placed into L. 116, an ashy destruction layer containing sherds from LB I, and this same layer was also present under the debris layer, L. 80, associated with the first destruction of the Cuneiform Tablet Building. Elsewhere in this area there was evidence that the LB I debris had been leveled off for the construction of the Cuneiform Tablet Building.

The Drainpipe Structure similarly was built upon the remains of LB I occupation on the south summit of the tell (Lapp 1967a: 23-24). This was most evident in a probe trench below the Iron I Wall L. 164 in SW 2-25 which had stratification parallel to that of the Cuneiform Tablet Building. Directly below Wall L. 164 were layers of packed destruction debris with LB I sherds. Similar stratification elsewhere in the same building was discovered in a probe below Iron Age Wall L. 5 which had been constructed on the foundations of an earlier wall. Layers abutting these earlier foundations contained LB I pottery. The Twelfth-Century House in SW 5-7, 5-8 and 4-7 was a further example (Lapp 1969b: 34-37). The east wall of this building, SW 4-7 Wall L. 119, followed approximately the same line as the wall of an LB I building bordering on the LB I street. A section in the south part of this area showed that the Iron Age builders had trenched into the west side of this street and had laid one of the house walls directly over the line of the street wall of the LB I building. There was no evidence, however, that the street had been resurfaced or used in the Iron Age.

Just south of the later Cultic Structure in SW 2-7, an Iron I courtyard in SW 2-8 was also found to have been constructed on impacted destruction debris of LB I (Lapp 1967a:26).

A preliminary conclusion from this would be that Taanach was unoccupied between the destruction of the LB I city and the end of LB II or the beginning of the Iron Age, and this seems to have been largely the case (Lapp 1964:8; 1967a:3; 1969b:5). However, in 1968 a rather sparsely attested intervening phase dating to the last part of the fifteenth and perhaps overlapping into the fourteenth century came to light (Lapp 1969b:5). This material and some from the late thirteenth century will be discussed in the forthcoming volume on Bronze Age pottery and stratigraphy.

Iron I Phasing

Iron I at Taanach consisted of two main periods separated by a gap. The first of these was characterized in turn by two sub-phases, designated in this report as Periods IA and IB and found in the Cuneiform Tablet Building, the Drainpipe Structure, and the Iron I Court south of the Cultic Structure. The first two of these buildings are discussed below in connection with the pottery groups associated with them. The third has been described in the preliminary report of the 1966 season (Lapp 1967a:26-27). In all three, initial construction in Period IA experienced an interruption. Both the Tablet Building and Iron I Court were at least partly destroyed, and the same was true for an earlier phase of the Drainpipe Structure. Period IB began shortly after this interruption, and its builders usually made use of what remained of the earlier structures, often considerably modifying and expanding them. Despite the interruption, the continuity in the architecture of the two phases suggests a single stratum.

The Twelfth-Century House provides an exception (Lapp 1969b:34-37). It consisted of rooms surrounding a court, built near the beginning of Period IA. Sometime during Period IA it was remodeled, but it finally went out of use before the beginning of Period IB. During Period IB a house made of more massive stones was constructed in the same area following a different orientation. The latter was not well preserved and contained only a few pottery remains of Period IB type (see Fig. 91:2,4).

The main structures representing Period IB, then, are the Cuneiform Tablet Building, the Drainpipe Structure, and the Iron I Court. All three experienced a severe destruction at the end of this period, probably as a result of the same events. Following this destruction a gap occurred before the new pottery traditions of Period II began to appear.

The second major period, Period II, seems to have spread over nearly a century. The most impressive development during this period was the construction of substantial structures and installations, such as the Cultic Structure (see Fig. 97), the court and cistern built above the Cuneiform Tablet Building, and the cistern to the south of the Cultic Structure. Evidence of this same occupation, ascribed to Period IIB, was also found in many other loci.

The Period IIB phase, however, did not spring up at once. There were apparently gradual efforts somewhat earlier to reuse the site. In a number of areas, loci containing slightly earlier pottery than that from the Cultic Structure came to light, suggesting an initial phase in Period II, designated Phase IIA. The sparser architectural remains of this phase indicate a time of smaller settlement, but one in which the pottery and architectural traditions of Period II made their initial appearance.

The Period IIA groups came mostly from isolated layers, sometimes associated with stumps of walls. No whole or even partially preserved plans of structures were recovered from this phase. The best loci representing it were L. 68 of SW 6-2 and L. 60 and 61 of SW 5-2. In both cases the stratigraphy contained pottery of Period IB, followed by that of Period IIA above it, and finally by Period IIB forms.

Period IIB came to an end with a severe destruction, most clearly evident in the Cultic Structure.

Comparative Iron I Stratigraphy

The sites which have produced correlative stratigraphy are discussed briefly in what follows. The intention here is a general comparison of the Iron I phasing at Taanach with the published stratigraphy of other sites. More precise correlations of individual loci are made in the chapters following. The concluding chapter brings together in table form the results of the comparative study.

TELL BEIT MIRSIM

The phasing of Iron I in Palestine, which has achieved wide acceptance, goes back in particular to Albright's work at Tell Beit Mirsim. Here the latest phase, Stratum B3, was fixed by the destruction of Shishak I, dated now to 918 (Albright 1932:57, 74; 1943:38, n. 4; also see Chapter 5). Working back from this point, Stratum B2 was distinguished by the presence of Philistine wares, while B1 was believed to reflect a pre-Philistine culture, but one no longer associated with Late Bronze traditions. By reference to the records of Ramses III on the temple at Medinet Habu concerning the invasion of the Sea Peoples (ca. 1168/67), Albright proposed that Philistine pottery would have accompanied the Philistine spread to the inland towns of Palestine from the mid-twelfth century on (Albright 1932:53-58; Wright 1961:95-96). Stratum B1 was thus assigned to the twelfth century with a probable continuation to the end of that century. Stratum B2 was dated to the late twelfth century and seen as continuing through most of the eleventh century when it was succeeded by Stratum B3. The latter was characterized by a new tradition of hand burnishing over a red slip, attributed to the formation of the Israelite monarchy in the tenth century.

MEGIDDO

This framework has been filled out at other Palestinian sites, the most important being Megiddo. Because of problems in the original reports, the stratification of Megiddo has experienced revision in the light of a restudy of the materials (Albright 1940; Wright 1950b; Yadin 1960, 1970). Stratum VIIA is now recognized as the stratum when Philistine wares were beginning to appear. Wright (1950b:59) originally noted minimal Philistine evidence in Stratum VIIA, but subsequently pointed to the impressive Philistine pottery from this stratum (1966:77, n. 19; also Sinclair 1960:16, n. 2). Stratum VIIB apparently represents the end of the Late Bronze period with some loci transitional to the beginning of Iron I.

Taken in relation to that from Tell Beit Mirsim, the comparative evidence at Megiddo suggests a date from the late thirteenth century to ca. 1175 for Stratum VIIB, while Stratum VIIA may be dated to ca. 1175-1125 (Wright 1961:94-95; Maisler [Mazar] 1951:25). Following the destruction of Stratum VIIA a gap occurred, above which the thin Stratum VIB was found with no relation to the plan of the previous stratum (Loud 1948:33). The dating of Stratum VIB to ca. 1075-1050 has been underscored by Dothan's phasing of Philistine pottery (T. Dothan 1967:64). Stratum VIA was built as an entirely new city and seems to have been in existence during the latter half of the eleventh century (Yadin 1970:93-95). The subsequent Stratum VB followed as an early tenth-century occupation, preceding by not more than half a century the important Solomonic Stratum VA-IVB. The dating for the Megiddo Iron I strata has been challenged by Kenyon (1969:52-60) who has proposed a series of higher dates with Stratum VIIB being attributed to the destruction of Thutmose III and Stratum VIIA to the fourteenth century. Kenyon's dates are problematic, however, and it is to be doubted that they will successfully displace the more commonly accepted lower ones followed in the present study. If the presentation to follow is essentially correct, forms such as the goblet chalice from Megiddo L. 2048 (Loud 1948: Pl. 72:15) can only with great difficulty be assigned to the fourteenth century (Kenyon 1969:54, Fig. 25:7).

HAZOR

The Hazor strata important for Iron I are Strata XII, XI, and X. The discovery in Area A of a casemate wall similar to those at ᶜAin Shems, Tell Beit Mirsim and

Gezer, led the excavators to date Stratum X to the time of Solomon (Yadin and others 1960:3; Aharoni 1959). During the fourth season, excavation below Stratum X in Area B turned up an early shrine and two incense stands, ascribed to Stratum XI and dated to the eleventh century (Yadin 1959:12). Below this, there appeared remnants of poor settlement with rubble foundations for tents, hut, and many silos. This was designated Stratum XII and dated approximately to the mid-twelfth century (Yadin 1959:13-14).

TELL ABU HAWĀM, TELL ZEROR, TELL ᶜAMAL, ᶜAFULA

These four northern sites, like Megiddo, are close to Taanach and thus have special significance. At Tell Abu Hawām the destruction of Stratum V probably occurred during the first quarter of the twelfth century while the following Stratum IVA seems also to have ended in a destruction about the middle of the same century. Similar to Taanach, a gap occurred until the late eleventh century, represented by Stratum IVB. This, in turn, was succeeded by the late tenth century Stratum III (Hamilton 1935; Maisler [Mazar] 1951; Van Beek 1955). The stratigraphy at Tel Zeror needs reworking, but Stratum III is apparently late tenth century (Ohata, ed. 1966). Similarly, Tell ᶜAmal Strata IV-III are of special importance for the latest phases of Iron I (Levy and Edelstein 1972:342-43).

The separation of materials at ᶜAfula finds some assistance in the comparative discussion below. Stratum IIIB may be dated to the last half of the twelfth century while Stratum IIIA seems to be a late eleventh-century occupation with extension into the tenth century (see also T. Dothan 1967:64).

BETH SHAN

A further site of importance for Taanach because of its geographical linkage with cities in the Esdraelon Plain is Beth Shan. The publication of materials from Levels VI to IV has brought to light neglected but important comparative material. Two major phases for Iron I were found: Level VI beginning with the age of Ramses III and Lower Level V, attributed to the tenth century with the larger part being Solomonic (James 1966:149-153).

BETHEL, ᶜAI, EL-JIB, SHILOH

The final publication of the Bethel excavations defined four major phases for the Iron I period (Kelso 1968:32-35). Phases 1 and 2 were attributed to the early and late twelfth centuries respectively, corresponding to Stratum VIIB and VIIA at Megiddo. Phase 3 was essentially an eleventh-century stratum belonging to the middle division of Iron I and having some Philistine pottery. Phase 4 was subdivided into 4a and 4b in the 1954 campaign with Phase 4a representing an early tenth-century occupation while Phase 4b was credited to the Solomonic Period.

The nearby site of ᶜAi (et-Tell) contained only two phases from the earliest division of Iron I, designated as Phases I and II (Callaway 1969:5-9). Thereafter occupation ceased for the remainder of Iron I. At el-Jib a number of buildings discovered in a sounding were dated to the earliest phase of Iron I (Pritchard and others 1964:35-37), while Shiloh similarly had materials belonging to early Iron I and perhaps continuing through the second phase (Buhl and Holm-Nielsen 1969:30-35). The discussion of "collared-rim jars" in Chapter 3 pursues the matter of the incorrect date in Iron II assigned the materials in the Shiloh publication.

GEZER

The publication of the new excavations at Gezer adds considerably to the knowledge of ceramic development during Iron I. Field I has produced two published strata thus far (Strata 4 and 3), both of which continued Canaanite pottery traditions but during which Philistine pottery also appeared (Dever and others 1970:25-28). In Field II a post-Philistine phase may have been present in Stratum 7, while Stratum 6 was identified as Solomonic and destroyed possibly by Shishak (Dever and others 1970:60-63). Of special importance is the separation of phases within the Philistine period (Strata 4 and 3 in Field I) as well as the closer identification of the post-Philistine but pre-Solomonic Stratum 7.

TELL QASILE

Tell Qasile on the Yarkon has similarities to Gezer in its stratigraphy for Iron I. Strata XII and XI were characterized by the presence of Philistine wares, placing them in the middle phase of the Iron I period (Maisler [Mazar] 1951a:73-74, 125-128). Stratum X was a post-Philistine stratum which appeared also to precede the Solomonic period while Stratum IX was attributed to David and Solomon (Maisler [Mazar] 1951a:128-140, 194-195).

ᶜAIN SHEMS, ASHDOD

A number of other sites also contained strata or materials corresponding to one or more of the subdivisions of Iron I. Stratum III at ᶜAin Shems consisted of a town extending from the twelfth into the eleventh century, while Strata IIa and IIb belonged respectively to a late eleventh-early tenth and late tenth-century occupation (Grant and Wright 1939:51-84, 127-145). As would be expected, Ashdod has brought forth important Philistine materials for the second phase. Strata XII and XI were both characterized by Philistine wares while Stratum X was apparently post-Philistine (M. Dothan 1971:20-21, 27-33).

DEIR ᶜALLĀ

The publication of Deir ᶜAllā enlarges the picture to include Transjordan. Excavations showed that a Late Bronze occupation with an imposing temple ended in a massive destruction by earthquake, dated closely to between 1205 and 1194 by the discovery in the debris of a faience vase containing the cartouche of the Egyptian queen, Tausert (Franken and Kalsbeek 1969:19). Following upon this Late Bronze destruction a succession of Iron Age levels appeared. Phases A-D represented a series of occupations by a people who may have been itinerants connected with a smith industry localized at the site (Franken and Kalsbeek 1969:21). Beginning with Phase E, new and substantial buildings belonging to a small walled town emerged, and this type of architectural activity continued through Phase L (Franken and Kalsbeek 1969:44-6l). On the basis of what were designated "Philistine" wares found already in Phase A as well as the general ceramic typology, it would seem that Phases A-D should be dated between ca. 1125 and 1050 corresponding to the middle subdivision of Iron I. Phases E-J may be dated between the mid-eleventh to the late tenth century, tying in with the third phase of Iron I (Lapp 1970b).

Date of Taanach Iron I Periods

Several lines of evidence help to fix the date of the two major phases of Iron I at Taanach in relation to the sites noted. As will be seen below, the pottery of Period IA has various carry-overs from the end of the Late Bronze Age suggesting a transitional period from LB II to Iron I. Period IA thus corresponds closely to the pre-Philistine stage of comparative sites. Period IB follows slightly later and correlates with comparative strata containing early Philistine pottery. However, the lack not only of Philistine wares but also of local forms suggesting continued development during the second phase of Iron I leads to the conclusion that the site was abandoned during most of the eleventh century.

Following this gap a new pottery repertory connected with Period II comes to light, the most distinguishing feature of which is hand burnishing. The change in architectural and ceramic traditions suggests new settlers at the site. The period corresponds to the third and post-Philistine phase of Iron I. As noted, Period IIA represents the modest beginnings of this occupation, expanding into the more impressive Period IIB.

Following are the proposed dates for the periods and their subdivisions:

Period IA	ca. 1200-1150
Period IB	1150-1125
Period IIA	ca. 1020-960
Period IIB	960-918

Chapter Three
Pottery Groups of Period I

The pottery groups discussed in this chapter came from loci within three major structures.

The Cuneiform Tablet Building, SW 5-1, 5-2, 6-1, 6-2

The Cuneiform Tablet Building, named for the alphabetic cuneiform tablet discovered in it, was found in a fragmentary state (Lapp 1964:23; 1967a:19-21). Two building phases, referred to here as Periods IA and IB, were discovered in this structure.

PERIOD IA

The original building of Period IA was apparently only partially completed. To this phase belonged Walls L. 67, 68 and 69 with a doorway at the southeast corner (Fig. 96b). Wall L. 83 within the building may have served as a curtain wall in Period IA. L. 80 and 81 represent debris from the first destruction of the building. L. 80 was a yellowish-brown layer with white and black ash. It was found on the east side of Wall L. 83, running as far as the easternmost wall of the Tablet Building excavated, Wall L. 67. The Canaanite cuneiform tablet, TT 433, was discovered within L. 80 against the east side of Wall L. 83. On the west side of Wall L. 83 was a hardened, brittle layer, L. 81, apparently representing the same destruction deposit.

PERIOD IB

Sometime not long after the burning in Period IA, the building was reused, although parts of the original structure were razed and covered over by a cobblestone pavement, L. 77. That this was stratigraphically later was indicated by Wall L. 83 which was taken down in order to make way for L. 77. The fragmentary character of the later phase obscured the extent and use of the building during this period. However, in SW 6-2 there was evidence that the building extended to the west. Most of Wall L. 81 in SW 6-2 was robbed out, probably in the tenth century, but the stump remaining belonged stratigraphically to Period IB. This was suggested by the ashy and burnt brick destruction debris (L. 103, 104, 106) west of Wall L. 81. That these loci represented a second destruction during Period IB was most clear in L. 106, underneath which was L. 117, a bricky, hard soil containing Period IA pottery.

The Drainpipe Structure SW 2-25, 3-25

Two phases, corresponding to Periods IA and IB, were also discovered in the area of the south slope dominated by the Drainpipe Structure (Lapp 1964:23-26; 1967a:21-26; 1969b: 39).

Period IA was most clearly preserved in a pocket of destruction debris, L. 45, discovered directly below the east Wall L. 26 of the Drainpipe Structure where it joined with south Wall L. 164 (Fig. 96a). At this corner a large piece of drainpipe belonging to the later phase was found standing *in situ* during the 1963 season. This layer of debris thus lay stratigraphically between LB I layers below it and Wall L. 26 belonging to the Period IB Drainpipe Structure. The extent of the Period IA building was not determined since excavation did not proceed below the Period IB structure except here and in one other place.

In *Period IB* the structure consisted of a courtyard with a cistern, trough and basin, along with rooms off three sides of the courtyard. This structure was bounded by Wall L. 26 on the east, Wall L. 164 with its larger stones on the south, and Wall L. 5 on the west. A "pillared" Wall, L. 212, was found to the east of Wall L. 5, with a flagstone pavement between Wall L. 212 and Wall L. 5. A similar wall, L. 195, may have stood on the north.

The building of Period IB was covered by a layer of destruction debris which sometimes reached a thickness of 1.5 m. On the south side of the structure a heaped up mass of burnt brick showed that walls of this building were made of mud brick laid on stone foundations. At the north end of the excavated area burnt charcoal and ashy debris were abundant. Walls L. 164 and 212 both showed signs of the intensity of the burning, and both were leaning inward, suggesting battering. The pottery came from twelve loci, all of which contained this destruction debris.

The Twelfth-Century House, SW 5-8

A house with a well-preserved plan and belonging to Period IA was unearthed in SW 5-8 and 5-7 (Lapp 1969b:34-37). Room 2 was apparently a courtyard, covered in part by a roof (Fig. 96c). To the south of it was Room 3, separated from Room 2 by a "pillared" Wall L. 136. In its earliest use, Room 3 had a tamped floor with a *tabun* L. 155 set against the south wall L. 142 and a pit L. 157 to the west of the *tabun*. During this time Room 3 may thus have also served as a court.

At a slightly later time Room 3 was provided with a more substantial pavement made of large, flat stones, L. 138, carefully set in place. The partition Wall L. 147 was constructed on the east edge of this pavement, making Room 3 smaller in size and separating off the east part as an additional room. With this change Room 2 seems to have become the main courtyard, having a dirt floor L. 152, 153, another *tabun* L. 124 just to the north of Wall L. 136, as well as two deep pits.

Although two building periods are attested, they were apparently closely related in time since the pottery typology remains the same throughout. The building thus corresponds to the Period IA use of both the Cuneiform Tablet Building and Drainpipe Structure. The stratigraphy confirms this, since a few pottery remains from a later structure above the Twelfth-Century House date to Period IB.

SUMMARY OF POTTERY BEARING LOCI

	Period IA		Period IB	
	Loci	Figures	Loci	Figures
Cuneiform Tablet Building	(SW 5-2) 80,81	1-2	(SW 6-2) 103,104,106	15-17
Drainpipe Structure	(SW 2-25) 45	3	(SW 2-25) 44,49,61,62, 124,158,160, 162,171,180, 186,208	9-14
Twelfth-Century House	(SW 5-8) 155,157, 153,124, 138	4-5 6-8		

Primary Comparative Loci

The number of sealed loci excavated in Palestine corresponding to Period I at Tell Ta‛annek is relatively small. The most important correlations can be made with the following loci.

PERIOD IA

Megiddo. Locus 2131. This locus consisted of a small room, apparently one of several in a larger structure, built up against the west side of the Late Bronze Age gate which continued to be used with modifications in Strata VIIB and VIIA (Loud 1948:Fig. 383). L. 2131 was phased with the Stratum VIIB remains and these largely represent the end of LB II at Megiddo. However, while it is evident that residual Late Bronze traditions are still present in some of the pottery of this locus, it would appear that the bulk of it is either transitional to Iron I or already into the beginning of the latter. At the same time there is some apparently intrusive pottery and thus it cannot be taken as a perfectly sealed locus (Loud 1948:Pl. 65: 3). Yet its large number of forms, often whole, make it one of the more usable comparative sources for this period.

Bethel. Locus 42. A full description of this locus is lacking in the final report. It apparently consisted of debris within a room of an Iron I house (Kelso 1968:Pl. 23). L. 42 is credited to Phases 1 and 2 on the plan showing this locus (Kelso 1968:Pl. 4a), and it would seem by comparison with the Taanach pottery that it is from the earliest part of Iron I. This is supported also by the use of piers in the construction of the walls of the Bethel house, a technique nearly identical to that employed in both the Twelfth-Century House and the Drainpipe Structure at Taanach (Kelso 1968:32, §130).

Gezer. Loci of Stratum 5 in Field I. The loci attributed to Stratum 5 in Field I have the closest parallels to Period IA at Taanach. Of the five loci from which the published sherds came, L. 2012A was a pit cutting through surfaces of Stratum 6; L. 3009.1, bricky destruction debris below Surface 3009; L. 2009.1, a make-up below Surface 2009; L. 3008.1, bricky destruction debris below Surface 3008; and L. 1027.1, a make-up below Surface 1027 (Dever and others 1970:22-24, 71-81). Pottery from these loci was well sealed.

PERIOD IB

Megiddo. Locus 2048. This impressive locus in Area BB was designated a temple (Loud 1948: 102-105). It is somewhat problematic to describe it as a sealed locus since the structure was first constructed in Stratum VIII and continued in use down to Stratum VIIA. Thus we cannot be certain that the pottery from this building was always successfully separated. Yet, with some reservation, the group from this building may be used as primary comparative evidence for Period IB.

Gezer. Loci of Strata 4 and 3 in Field I. L. 1024.1 and 1025.1, phased as Stratum 4 in Field I, both had seemingly homogeneous groups (Dever and others 1970:26, 71). L. 1025.1 was a make-up for Surface 1025 while L. 1024.1 represented destruction debris on top of Surface 1025. L. 1012.1, attributed to Stratum 3 in Field I, may have some materials dating slightly later, but it also fits generally with Period IB. The locus is described as a make-up below Surface 1012 and is mostly homogeneous with one intrusive sherd (Dever and others 1970: 27-28, 70).

El-Jib. Area 10-L-5. This area consisted of a house which made use of the outer city wall for its one side on the northwest end (Pritchard and others 1964:39). The determinative locus was a plastered floor, preserved only on this northwest side of the house and abutting the city wall. The small group of pottery associated with this floor appears to be homogeneous and fits well with Period IB. Two sherds were found in the detritus above the floor; the rest came from the composition immediately below the floor.

Additional Comparative Loci and Strata

In addition to the PCL, parallels to the Period I pottery are found in the following: Hazor Stratum XII, Tell Abu Hawām Strata V and IVA, ᶜAfula Stratum IIIB, Tell Qasile Stratum XII, Ashdod Strata XIII and XII and Pit 2001, Phases A and B at Deir ᶜAllā, ᶜAi Phases I and II, ᶜAin Shems Stratum III, Shiloh, and Tell Beit Mirsim B1.

The Pottery

JARS (FIGS. 1:1-2, 4:1-5, 6:1-2, 9:1, 10:1-17, 15:1-5)

The developments in both large and medium-sized jars during Period I provide some important chronological clues. An interesting jar rim in this respect is the one found in Fig. 1:1. This heavy rim is from a pithos and represents a degenerate twelfth-century example of an LB II type of storage jar. During LB II these jar rims frequently had stepped molding which has all but disappeared on the one here. Examples of the LB II rim are abundant at Hazor (Yadin and others 1958:Pl. 88:11-12; 1960:Pls. 122, 145), while a rim assigned to Stratum XII in the twelfth century still contains considerable molding (Yadin and others 1961:Pl.168:9). At Shiloh a rim of this type from Cave S, "105," is correctly assigned to Iron I (Buhl and Holm-Nielsen 1969:Pl. 7:76). This form, then, would suggest a date very close to the end of the Late Bronze Age.

Although prominent in the thirteenth century, the stepped jar rim tradition faded out in the following century. In this period it was supplanted by the storage jar with collared rim. A good example of this can be seen by comparing Fig. 1:1 with Fig. 10:4 from Period IB. The latter has a long neck with a flaring rim like Fig. 1:1. It lacks completely any of the furrowing of the earlier rim and has a collar on the shoulder. Fig. 10:4 also possesses four handles like a similar jar at Megiddo attributed to Stratum VII B-A (Loud 1948:Pl. 68:6). A further example from Hazor has several handles, a shorter neck and a collar. Although it was dated to LB II, it should possibly be reassigned a date at the beginning of Iron I (Yadin and others 1958:Pl.113:18).

A jar which also had a heavy rim is Fig. 10:2. This jar may also have had a collar on the shoulder like the similar example from Phase I at ᶜAi (Callaway 1969:Fig. 5:1).

The most widely discussed storage jar of the period has been the one with collared rim. Examples of this type are found in both Periods IA and IB (Figs. 4:1; 9:1, TT 1810; 10:1, 3, 4). Considerable attention has been given to the significance of this jar since Albright (1934:12-13; 1940:548; 1960:118) pointed to its chronological usefulness for such sites as Bethel, Beth-zur, and Tell Beit Mirsim. More recent excavation has further clarified its range and has also shed light on its development. Present knowledge points to two main types of collared-rim store jars during Iron I representing, however, more an evolution than independent development. In its earliest form, probably still reflecting Late Bronze influence, this jar had a long neck with a thickened rim which is usually everted. The pronounced ridge at the base of the neck suggested the designation of a collar. Later the neck tended to become shorter with the ridge or collar moving closer to the rim. The rim was also thickened but usually not so massively as with the first type. These two developments are referred to below as long- and short-necked types.

The four examples published here all belong to the long-necked type. The Taanach evidence adds support to that of other sites that the long-necked type appears about 1200, at the beginning of Period IA. Apparently it also disappeared not long after the end of the third quarter of the twelfth century. The type with shorter neck begins no earlier than Period IB, and examples from this period were present in other areas excavated. In contrast to the previous type, this type survived to the end of Iron I (Fig. 35:1, TT 1866).

One of the first sites at which the collared-rim jar was observed is Bethel, and the publication of the excavations at this site shows how prominent this jar was during Iron I (Kelso 1968:Pl. 56:1-21). The collared-rim jars from PCL 42 are all of the long-necked variety, suggesting a date earlier in the twelfth century (Kelso 1968:Pl. 56:13-14, 16, 18). It is also noteworthy that cooking pot rims in the same locus are still close to the LB II form, like those of Period IA at Taanach (Kelso 1968:Pl. 57:12-14, 16, 19-20, 22). Also from Period IA is an example with long neck from Gezer PCL 3008.1 (Dever and others 1970:Pl. 28:18).

At Hazor collared store jars appeared in Stratum XII. On several the collar is long (Yadin and others 1961:Pl. 167:5-6; 168:20), while on others it has moved up the neck closer to the rim (Yadin and others 1961:Pl. 167:7). One attributed to Stratum VIIB at Megiddo has a collar medium way up the neck of the jar and is probably to be reassigned to Stratum VIIA or later (Loud 1948:Pl. 64:8; cf., 83:1, 4). The example from ᶜAfula also indicates a mid-to-late twelfth century date for Stratum IIIB at this site (M. Dothan 1955:Fig. 16:4). An example from PCL 10-L-5 at el-Jib has a collar closer to the rim which tends to support a later twelfth-century date for this group (Pritchard and others 1964:Fig. 36:10). The photograph of a storage jar from Taanach published by Sellin has a long neck and may date to Period IA (Sellin 1904:Fig. 109). A whole series of these jars from Shiloh has been dated to Iron II, but this contradicts the evidence from other Palestinian sites. Of the jars published, only several seem to be close to Iron II, and these are probably best dated to the late tenth century by comparison with the collared-rim jar from the Taanach Cultic Structure (Buhl and Holm-Nielsen 1969:Pl. 15:186; 16:192; see below Fig. 35:1, TT 1866). Two of the Shiloh jars, in fact, clearly belong to the long-necked variety and thus cannot date beyond the end of the twelfth century (Buhl and Holm-Nielsen 1969:Pl. 16:190, 191).

Among recent excavations, those conducted at ᶜAi have brought to light evidence similar to that at Taanach for the development of the collared-rim jar. Phase I was distinguished by a jar with long collar, while in Phase II the collar became shorter, although the long-collared type continued (Callaway 1968:316-317; 1969:5-9). Like Taanach in Period IA, the long-collared jar of Phase I at ᶜAi was found alongside cooking pots with everted, triangulated rim still in the tradition of LB II, which would support a date for this phase early in Iron I (Callaway 1968:316). The development toward a shortened neck and a collar closer to the rim in Phase II corresponds to the findings at Taanach and other sites (Callaway 1969: 8-9).

The evidence for collared-rim jars in Transjordan is also important. At Deir ᶜAllā two storage jars from Phase A belong to the long-necked type, indicating that this phase begins prior to the end of the twelfth century (Franken and Kalsbeek 1969:Fig. 47:1-2). Judging from the typology of the Phase A groups as a whole, this seems to be at the end of the history of the type rather than at its beginning, and thus the Phase A group probably dates not earlier than ca. 1150. Of special importance is the large number of long-collared jars of the same type discovered in a tomb at Sahab and dated by the excavator, Dr. Moawiyah Ibrahim, to the early twelfth century (oral communication). The argumentation of Y. Aharoni (1971:132-133, 135) is problematic. On the basis of an inscribed handle from Raddana, apparently from a collared-rim jar, Aharoni wishes to move the date for these jars back to the earlier thirteenth and even fourteenth centuries. The excavators at Raddana, Callaway and Cooley (1971:11), found no problems in dating the occupational stratum from which these jars came to the twelfth or late thirteenth centuries. From epigraphic evidence Cross and Freedman (1971:22) have dated the inscribed handle to about 1200.

Turning to other jars, three different types of rim are represented in Figs. 1:2 and 4:2 from Period IA, and Fig. 10:5-6 from Period IB. Fig. 1:2 has a plain rim with an inward sloping neck of medium length. No close parallels for this rim could be found. Fig. 4:2 from Period IA has a simple rim and grooved neck. That this jar rim continued into Period IB is indicated by Fig. 10:5. Jars having this type of rim at Megiddo are ascribed to a range between Stratum VIIB and VI, thus paralleling the Taanach evidence (Loud 1948:Pls. 73:7; 82:9). Finally, the jar with vertical neck and thickened rim in Fig. 10:6 is reminiscent of the jar with long collar discussed above. It is possible that it may have possessed a collar but this cannot be determined on the present sherd. A parallel is found in PCL 10-L-5 at el-Jib (Pritchard and others 1964:Fig. 36:12).

Various jar handles and bases of Period IA and IB are found in Figs. 4:3-5, 6:1-2, 10:7-17, 15:1-5. The handles may be from jars or jugs, but in either case the section is oval through the whole of Period I. Jar bases of the knobbed LB II style have virtually disappeared by the time of Period I and have been replaced by a base which is sometimes flattened, sometimes partly rounded, and sometimes slightly pointed. The partly rounded type can be seen in Fig. 10:15, a somewhat more flattened type in Fig. 10:16-17, and the base tending toward a point in Fig. 15:1. Fig. 10:15 is paralleled by a Stratum XII jar with rounded base found at Hazor as well as a slightly later example from Stratum VI at Megiddo (Yadin and others 1961:Pl. 169:2; Loud 1948:Pl. 73:8). The pointed base in Fig. 15:1 recalls a Stratum VIIA-VIA example at Megiddo as well as several jar bases at Bethel (Loud 1948:Pl. 73:6; Kelso 1968:Pl. 57:9-11). It is noteworthy that Hazor Stratum XII exemplifies an identical variety of flattened, rounded, and pointed jar bases (Yadin and others 1961:Pl. 202:16, 8 and 15 respectively) in its twelfth century groups.

JUGS AND JUGLETS (FIGS. 1:3-7, 3:1-5, 4:6-7, 6:3-18, 11:1-17, 15:6-17)

Some development in the rim forms of jugs occurs during Periods IA and IB. Several jug rim traditions continue in both phases, but an innovation in Period IB is the jug with simple rim and ridged neck. For convenience, jug rims are discussed according to three groupings: those with thickened rims; those with flattened, slightly thickened rims with a tendency to flare outward; and those with simple rims and fairly long ridged necks.

Jugs with thickened rims are represented at Taanach in both Period IA (Fig. 1:3) and Period IB (Fig. 11:1). Rims of this type were also found in Stratum B1 at Tell Beit Mirsim where Albright observed they were "like the less characteristic LB types" (1932:58, Pl. 26:10-12). The closest parallel to the Taanach examples is an LB II rim from Bethel (Kelso 1968:Pl. 54:10). This one has a straighter neck than the ones from Taanach but it has the same type of overlapped, rounded rim. Thus the Taanach rims suggest vestigial LB II forms. Figs. 1:4 and 6:3

POTTERY GROUPS OF PERIOD IA

represent a more everted variant of this rim which seems to be closer to the Tell Beit Mirsim parallels cited.

Related to the above rims, but with some variations, are those in Figs. 3:1-2 and 6:4-6 from Period IA. In these the rim is also thickened, but it is more triangular than the preceding examples. A jug in PCL 2048 at Megiddo seems to be of this type (Loud 1948:Pl. 71:1) as does a fragmentary sherd from PCL 1025.1 for Period IB at Gezer (Dever and others 1970:Pl. 27:22). The latter two examples, however, are probably later than those from Taanach.

Several other thickened jug rims are found in Figs. 1:6, 3:3-4, and 4:7, all from Period IA. Fig. 1:6 has an everted, thickened rim with dark, red, band-painted decoration, a vestige of the Late Bronze tradition. A parallel to this rim and its decoration is found in an LB II rim from Stratum IB in Area C at Hazor (Yadin and others 1958:Pl. 86:5). Though listed as belonging to a jar, the rim may well be from a jug such as the Taanach example. Fig. 4:7 apparently belongs to the same type but is unpainted. Fig. 3:3-4 are thickened on the exterior and are slightly concave on the interior of the rim. A close but slightly later parallel to this rim form is ascribed to Stratum IIIB at ᶜAfula (M. Dothan 1955: Fig.16:20).

The second general group was the most prominent type at Taanach during Period I. Rims of this type are slightly thickened and everted, and often flattened or cut on the top. Sometimes the rim is slightly concave on the interior. Examples from Period IA are found in Figs. 1:5, 4:6 and 6:7-10 while the form continued into Period IB as found in Fig. 11:2-3. A close parallel to Fig. 6:7 comes from Stratum XII at Hazor (Yadin and others 1961: Pl. 201:20).

During Period IB a variation of the main type was achieved when the rim was cut or flattened and the neck was profiled, either by making a ridge on the exterior (Fig. 11:5) or by bending the wall of the neck, providing a wavy effect (Fig. 11:4). It is noteworthy that the latter two examples are almost exactly paralleled by two rims from ᶜAfula Stratum IIIB, one of which is profiled on the exterior (M. Dothan 1955:Fig. 16:6), the other having a wavy neck (M. Dothan 1955:Fig. 16:5). An example from Hazor Stratum XII also belongs to this type (Yadin and others 1961:Pl. 201:23).

Further variants are found in both Periods IA and IB. Fig. 6:14 has the same kind of concave interior as Fig. 6:8, except that it lacks the slight thickening of the rim. Fig. 6:15, without thickened rim, displays the same slight eversion typical of many of the jug rims in this period. It is decorated with small red to black dots and bands as is a similar jug rim from Period IB in Fig. 11:6. Fig. 6:16 has a related type of decoration, which is probably a vestigial Late Bronze tradition. The two everted rims from Period IB in Fig. 15:10-11 also seem to reflect variations of the second group, but neither has marked characteristics.

The third group consists of jugs with simple rims and straight ridged necks, represented in Figs. 11:7-12 and 15:6-7. This jug rim was probably made much like the flattened cut rims of Fig. 11:4-5, the only difference being its simple, rounded form. The distinction between the two is important, however, and the form here has special chronological value. At Taanach it does not seem to appear before Period IB, unless Fig. 6:13 be taken as a precursor. It clearly is most prominent in Period IB and seems to persist even later, judging from other sites. Whole forms are found in Stratum VI at Megiddo (Loud 1948:Pl. 81:3) as well as in Tombs 1101 B Upper and 237 (Guy and Engberg 1938:Pls. 8:13, 72:12) at the same site. Although the Stratum VI example may date slightly later into the eleventh century, the examples from the two tombs could be placed in the late twelfth century judging from the Taanach evidence. A number of these rims appeared in Stratum IIIB at ᶜAfula, adding yet more evidence for the parallels between this stratum and Period IB groups at Taanach (M. Dothan 1955:Fig. 16:10-13). Finally, a good representation of the type is found in PCL 1012.1 from Stratum 3 at Gezer (Dever and others 1970:Pl. 26:14).

Jugs of both phases of the twelfth century customarily displayed ring bases as can be seen in Figs. 6:17, 11:13, and 15:13. An exception is the flat, slightly concave base of a small jug in Fig. 6:18. Like the jar handles of this period, jug handles have mostly oval sections like that in Fig. 11:14. Painted jugs are not abundant during Period I, although several examples have been noted. To these can be added the handle and fragment of the side of a jug in Fig. 15:12, which is decorated with dark red, painted bands.

The fragment of a strainer from Period IB in Fig. 11:15 is particularly interesting. If the section drawing of this fragment is compared with a fairly complete strainer jug containing Philistine decoration in Megiddo Stratum VIA, it can be seen that these are very close in form (Loud 1948:Pl. 76:1). This leads to the suggestion, which can also be seen in other vessels, that the Philistines sometimes made use of local forms to which they simply added their distinctive decorative motifs. Similar strainers are found in Stratum XII at Hazor (Yadin and others 1961:Pl. 201:24).

Several juglet fragments are also found in groups from Periods IA and IB. Fig. 11:16 is a typical juglet found at various sites in the twelfth century having a flaring rim with handle attached to the top of the rim. The range of this type at Megiddo is given from Stratum VIIB to VI and a good parallel is found in PCL 2131 (Loud 1948:Pl. 63:5; cf., Pls. 67:16 and 71:8). Fig. 15:14 is made in similar fashion, but is from a smaller juglet and has a narrower mouth.

During Period I juglet bases developed from the pointed base of the Late Bronze Age to the more rounded base which became characteristic of Iron I. This can be seen in the two examples preserved here. Fig. 1:7 from Period IA still displays the pointed base of LB II, while Fig. 11:17 from Period IB has a round base. An identical development can be noted during Stratum VII at Megiddo (Loud 1948:Pl. 63:4, 5). The three fragments of sides and handles of juglets in Figs. 3:5 and 15:15-16 also fit this development from more elongated, pointed-base juglets to those with rounder body and base. Fig. 15:15-16 from Period IB are of the rounded type. The flat base in Fig. 15:17 also has a parallel in a juglet assigned to Stratum VII at Megiddo (Loud 1948:Pl. 71:4).

CRATERS (FIGS. 1:8-12, 4:8-10, 7:1-5, 12:1-7, 16:1-5)

The earliest Iron Age crater rim in the groups presented here is Fig. 1:12 from Period IA. It has an everted, bevelled rim and is also one of several vessels from Period I which were burnished, others being Figs. 1:3, 3:7, and 8:1-2 from Period IA and Fig. 15:13 from Period IB. These few examples indicate that burnishing was rare during Period I and, when employed, was done with irregular strokes on the natural surface. The form of this crater is still in the LB II tradition, and the closest parallel to it is a crater with handles from Stratum IA-B in Area C at Hazor (Yadin and others 1960:Pl. 125:9).

The crater with slightly thickened, squared rim, and often with carinated sides is found in both Periods IA and IB. Two large examples from Period IA are in Fig. 4:8-9 while Fig. 12:1 is a smaller example from Period IB. The form is a carry-over from the Late Bronze tradition where various banded and criss-cross motifs were employed in decorating this vessel. The same type is found in both Stratum VIIB and VIIA contexts at Megiddo (Loud 1948:Pls. 66:4; 69:14, 16). An unpainted example from PCL 10-L-5 at el-Jib for Period IB is close in form to those from Taanach (Pritchard and others 1964:Fig. 36:14).

A prominent crater, which begins in Period IA and continues in Period IB, is found in Figs. 1:8-10, 4:10, 7:1-5, 12:2-7, and 16:1-5. The most distinctive characteristics of this crater are its deep body and round, folded-over rim. Sometimes these rims seem to be overlapped in rather crude fashion while at other times they are carefully smoothed. Craters with this rim form continue to late Iron I at Taanach and are still found in the early part of Iron II (see Figs. 63:3-11, 70:3-4, 72:4-5, 74:2). Numerous parallels are present at Megiddo where they are found in Strata VIIB to VI and in several tomb groups of the early Iron Age (Loud 1948:Pls. 66:1, 69:11-12, 78:14, 84:20, 22; Guy and Engberg 1938:Pls. 62:30, 68:12, 71:3, 6-16, and 73:12, 13). Few examples are present in the published pottery from Hazor, but one vessel from Stratum XII belongs to this type (Yadin and others 1961:Pl. 201:8). Noteworthy also are examples in Strata IIIB and IIIA at ᶜAfula (M. Dothan 1955:Figs. 17:12-19[IIIB], and 12:15-18, 22-25[IIIA]).

The crater with simple rim in Fig. 1:11 may be a variation of either this common type of crater or of the squared-rim type. No close parallels to this form could be found.

BOWLS (FIGS 1:13-17, 2:1, 3:6-14, 4:11, 5:1-9, 8:1-13, 13:1-14, 14:1-10, 16:6-7, 17:1-10)

Beginning with larger bowls only two are found in the present groups, both from Period IB (Fig. 16:6-7). The first has a simple, everted rim. The rim of the second is bent to the exterior, then flattened and slightly thickened on the interior. Both examples have good parallels from other sites. Fig. 16:6 seems to have been a common type during the twelfth century as can be seen in a PCL 2012A bowl rim at Gezer (Dever and others 1970:Pl. 28:7). A similar bowl at Megiddo is ascribed to a range from Stratum VIIA to VI (Loud 1948:Pl. 74:6). Parallels are also found in Hazor Stratum XII (Yadin and others 1961:Pl. 164:11-18) as well as at Tell en-Naṣbeh (Wampler 1947:Pl. 53:1155). At Deir ᶜAllā this bowl type begins to appear during Phases A and B (Franken and Kalsbeek 1969:Figs. 46:56-59 and 50:61-66). The bowl with flattened rim in Fig. 16:7 may represent a local form which again was incorporated into the Philistine repertory. Philistine craters, with a similar rim, are found in Stratum 12 at Ashdod (M. Dothan 1971:Fig. 1:9-10) and in L. 1002.1B at Gezer (Dever and others 1970:Pl. 27:26).

With few exceptions the traditions for medium and small bowls continue through Periods IA and IB. There is little variation from two main types, both of which stem from Late Bronze forms. One of these is a bowl with a shoulder and rim which are more incurved than the usual bowls of the Late Bronze Age. The rim of this bowl is sometimes slightly thickened on the interior. The whole form is found in a fragmentary bowl from Period IA in Fig. 8:1. Other examples from Period IA are found in Figs. 1:13-14, 3:6-8, and from Period IB in Figs. 13:1-3 and 17:2-3. Bowls with this form still appear occasionally in Period II (Fig. 25:7-8).

Several close parallels for this form are found in PCL at Gezer and Megiddo. The Period IA bowl in Fig. 8:1 is close in form to a bowl from PCL 2131 at Megiddo (Loud 1948:Pl. 65:9). Fig. 1:13 is identical to that found in PCL 2012A at Gezer (Dever and others 1970:Pl. 28:5). The similar forms in Period IB in Figs. 13:2-3 and 17:1-3 are paralleled by a bowl from PCL 2048 at Megiddo (Loud 1948:Pl. 71:19). Additional examples are from Silo 24 belonging to Stratum B1 at Tell Beit Mirsim (Albright 1932:Pl. 26:9), from Stratum IVA at Tell Abu Hawām (Hamilton 1935:48, no. 290) and at Hazor, where an example is given a range from Stratum X-XII (Yadin and others 1961:Pl. 164:3). Also of this type are two bowl rims from Bethel (Kelso 1968:Pl. 60:1-2).

Four additional bowls are also of this general type, but they display variations. The first three (Figs. 4:11, 13:13-14) have an incurved shoulder with a cyma profile and a thickened, rounded rim. An example from Period IA is Fig. 4:11 while the same bowl appears in Period IB as seen in Fig. 13:13-14. A similar but slightly later bowl is characteristic of Stratum 3 in Field I at Gezer (Dever and others 1970:Pl. 26:4), and the type is also found in Stratum XII at Hazor (Yadin and others 1961:Pl. 201:4-5). Further examples are present at ᶜAfula in Stratum IIIB (M. Dothan 1955:Fig. 17:23, 30) while at Deir ᶜAllā it seems to have been a common bowl during Phases A and B (Franken and Kalsbeek 1969: Figs. 46:27, 49:78-81).

POTTERY GROUPS OF PERIOD IA

The other variant with an incurved rim is the bowl sherd with bar handle in Fig. 17:4. The rim of this bowl is somewhat more inverted, with a thickening of the rim on the interior reminiscent of Late Bronze inverted bowl rims. The closest parallel is a bar-handled bowl with an almost identical rim assigned to Stratum III at ᶜAin Shems (Grant and Wright 1938:Pl. 62:16). The view has sometimes been held that the spatulate, bar-handled bowl began to appear first in the eleventh century (Sinclair 1960:21). At Taanach several other examples of the bar-handled bowl, in addition to the one published here, were found in related twelfth-century contexts, thus pushing its appearance back at least a century earlier. None are present in the Stratum XII pottery published from Hazor, but a bar-handled bowl is attributed to Stratum VIIA at Megiddo (Loud 1948:Pl. 69:6). The ones found by Albright at Tell el-Fûl were all burnished and from the latter part of Iron I (Albright 1924:14). In addition there is one among the Phase B material at Deir ᶜAllā (Franken and Kalsbeek 1969:Fig. 50:27). Numerous examples from various sites dating to the latter part of Iron I will be discussed below in connection with the whole bowl of this type found in the Cultic Structure (Fig. 47:1).

The most common bowl type represented in both Periods IA and IB is one with a plain rim and simple curved or fairly straight sides. Often this bowl had a flat base. Examples from Period IA are found in Figs. 1:15-17, 3:9-12, 5:1, and 8:2-7, while Figs. 13:4-9 and 17:1 are Period IB examples. Although this bowl is most prominent in Period I, occasional examples are still found in Period II (Fig. 25:11-12).

Close parallels to these bowls are abundant. At Gezer the general type is found from Strata 5 through 3, corresponding to the range of this bowl at Taanach (Dever and others 1970:Pls. 28:20, 27:24, and 26:11). Fig. 3:10 from Period IA is close to the form found in PCL 2131 at Megiddo (Loud 1948:Pl. 65:5) while several other parallels to the Period IA example in Fig. 1:15 exist at Megiddo and probably belong in the twelfth century (Loud 1948:Pl. 68:15; Guy and Engberg 1938:Pl. 62:5). This bowl type also represents another common form which seems to have been adapted to the Philistine repertory. The way the latter used the type can be seen in several bowls from Stratum III at ᶜAin Shems (Grant and Wright 1938:Pl. 59:29-32).

Two additional Period IA bowls with rim variations are in Fig. 8:8-9. Fig. 8:8 has a thicker rim than most of the smaller bowls of this period and is shallower as well. The rim has a groove on the exterior below the rim. Although not an exact parallel, a bowl from Stratum XII at Hazor may be similar to it (Yadin and others 1961:Pl. 201:7; see Franken and Kalsbeek 1969:Fig. 50:63). Fig. 8:9 seems to carry on the Late Bronze tradition of inverted rims and is paralleled by a rim from Stratum IIIB at ᶜAfula (M. Dothan 1955:Fig. 17:28) as well as one from PCL 3009.1 at Gezer (Dever and others 1970:Pl. 28:14).

Fig. 8:10 from Period IA and Fig. 13:10 from Period IB are from shallow bowls. Fig. 8:10 is the prototype of the shallow, burnished bowls which become prominent in Period IIB (Fig. 48:15-19). A bowl, apparently of this type, is found in Stratum IIIB at ᶜAfula (M. Dothan 1955:Fig. 17:26). A further parallel comes from Tomb 63 at Megiddo, and it is probable that the deposit in this tomb is to be assigned a date at the end of the thirteenth or early twelfth century (Guy and Engberg 1938:Pl. 60:6). Fig. 13:10 resembles the bowls with fairly straight sides found in Megiddo Stratum VIIA, but it has a distinctively thinner ware (Loud 1948:Pl. 69:2, 4).

Three bowl rims from both Period IA and IB have a slight carination of the side, apparently a vestige of LB II carinated bowls. Fig. 8:11 is an example from Period IA while Fig. 13:11-12 are from Period IB. These examples indicate that the carination has almost disappeared in favor of more simplified side walls. Similar tendencies were observed at Bethel (Kelso 1968:64 § 256). A degenerate carinated bowl attributed to Stratum VIIB at Megiddo can be cited as a parallel (Loud 1948:Pl. 65:14). Fig. 13:11 is made of thinner ware and seems also to have been slightly carinated.

Bowls in both Periods IA and IB had a variety of flat, disc, and ring bases as found in Figs. 2:1, 3:13-14, 5:2-9, and 8:12-13 for Period IA, and Figs. 14:1-10 and 17:5-10 for Period IB. The ring bases especially can be compared with those on bowls from the Cultic Structure to see the development from Period I to Period II (Figs. 45-47). During Period I ring bases were generally heavier, and the ring was usually cut flat. In contrast, the bases of the bowls in Period II were usually not so thick while the ring was often more pointed and flaring than in Period I.

COOKING POTS (FIGS. 2:2-8, 3:15, 14:11-13, 17:11-15)

Some development in cooking pots is also traceable during Period I. In Period IA the typical everted triangular rim of LB II continues as illustrated in Fig. 2:2-8. Such rims were still widely employed at the beginning of the Iron Age, and examples can be found at Bethel (Kelso 1968:57:19-21, 58:13, 15), Shiloh (Buhl and Holm-Nielsen 1969:71 and Pl. 7:68-72, 75), ᶜAi (Callaway 1968:316), and elsewhere. At Shiloh, however, the attribution to Iron II in the final report was incorrect. Fig. 2:7 is a degenerate example of this type and can be compared with an example ascribed to LB II at Hazor (Yadin and others 1958:Pl. 127:7). Fig. 14:11 shows how this rim persisted into Period IB, but by this time it began to be supplanted by a different type of rim.

This new type had a more elongated rim which was sometimes flat and at other times bent slightly upwards to form a wide groove around the rim. The latter feature became most typical of cooking pot rims in Period II (Figs. 49:1-3, 66:1-35). This elongated rim, however, apparently represented more a development from the Late Bronze triangular rim than a completely new type, as Fig. 3:15 from Period IA and Fig. 14:12-13 from Period IB suggest. These latter three rims are best viewed as transitional between the LB II triangular type and the elongated rim. The same kind of transitional forms are present in PCL 10-L-5 at el-Jib (Pritchard and others 1964:Fig. 36:9) and at Ashdod in Pit 2001 (Dothan and Freedman 1967:Fig. 34:16).

Both rims in Fig. 17:11-12 exhibit the development toward the elongated cooking pot rim of Period IB. Two rims from Ashdod Pit 2001 are close in form to these rims (Dothan and Freedman 1967:Fig. 34:14, 18), and it is noteworthy that the same development is found in PCL 1025.1 for Period IB at Gezer (Dever and others 1970:Pl. 27:19). Fully elongated rims with wide grooves are found in Fig. 17:13-15. These are the most prominent cooking pot rims in Hazor Stratum XII (Yadin and others 1961:Pl. 166:1-5, 7-8), and examples of them are again present in Pit 2001 at Ashdod (Dothan and Freedman 1967:Fig. 34:15, 21).

This picture of the development of cooking pot rims helps to clarify the situation at several other sites. The cooking pot rims in Phase A at Deir ʿAllā are of the elongated variety, suggesting again that this phase corresponds to Period IB at Taanach (Franken and Kalsbeek 1969:Fig. 46:1-4). Similar evidence is also present in Stratum XII at Hazor (Yadin and others 1961:Pls. 165:1-23, 166:1-8), and at ʿAin Shems (Grant and Wright 1938:Pl. 62:26-31 and 33-38) where a parallel development in cooking pots seems to take place during this period. Pl. 62:28-30 at ʿAin Shems suggest vestigial Late Bronze types and are thus probably early twelfth century while Pl. 62:35, 38 may be late twelfth century. The remainder are probably from eleventh-century vessels.

CHALICES (FIGS. 3:16, 8:14-15, 14:14-16, 17:16-17)

Sherds from three different types of chalice during Period I are found in Figs. 3:16, 14:14 (TT 928) and 17:16. Fig. 3:16 is from Period IA. It has simple, curved sides and a flat, thickened and grooved rim. A whole example of this type of chalice is TT 1356 in Fig. 89:4. The form is LB II, during which period it was represented at various sites (Yadin and others 1960:Pl. 141:20; Guy and Engberg 1938:Pls. 16:9-10, 19:17, 31:7, 34:11-12 and 35:28). Its presence here indicates again the transitional character of the Period IA groups. A similar chalice but without a grooved rim was found in PCL 2131 at Megiddo (Loud 1948:Pl. 67:5), while several other examples came from various loci of Stratum VIIB (Loud 1948:Pl. 65:23; Shipton 1939: Stratum VII, No. 50). One with a grooved rim was found in Stratum VIIA (Loud 1948:Pl. 70:11). The popularity of this chalice began to wane in Period IB when it was supplanted by the one discussed in the following paragraph although the type continued to be made as late as Period II (Fig. 23:11; cf. Lamon and Shipton 1939:Pl. 33:17).

During Period IB a new type of chalice was introduced (Fig. 17:16) which became the most common type down to Period IIB. This chalice had a simple everted lip which was increasingly splayed until in Period II it became almost horizontally flattened (Fig. 27:2). Evidence of this type is also found at Megiddo where a painted and burnished example was assigned a range between Strata VIIB and VIA (Loud 1948:Pl. 67:3). Another example at the latter site, ascribed to Stratum VI, is nearly identical with Fig. 17:16 (Loud 1948:Pl. 87:9).

A different type of chalice, shaped like a goblet, also appeared in Periods IA and IB (Figs. 8:14, TT 990 and 14:14, TT 928). The earlier example, TT 990, is decorated with painted bands, while TT 928 is unpainted. However, it seems that no chronological value is to be found in the painted or unpainted character of these vessels. At Megiddo, a chalice of this type was found near PCL 2048 for Period IB. It was decorated with red painted bands and had traces of burnishing on the natural surface (Loud 1948: Pl. 72: 14). Both unpainted and painted examples are found in Stratum VI (Loud 1948: Pl. 87:2-3). The form is clearly characteristic of Periods IA and IB, and evidence at other sites shows that it continued into the eleventh century as well. It seems, however, that by the tenth century its popularity had run out. The date of the example ascribed to Stratum VII at Tell Qasile is questionable, and the chalice is probably intrusive (Maisler [Mazar] 1951a: 205 and Fig. 10:a).

Summary

The general picture which emerges during Period I is one of development from LB II. This is particularly the case with Period IA which has the earmarks of a transitional period. That this is at the very end of LB II and the early part of Iron I is indicated by the many forms resembling LB II types which have run their course and have usually degenerated, yet are found side by side with newer forms.

It is helpful to pull together the examples which have been pointed out as having affinities to LB II types as well as to note common LB II types which are missing. The following can be noted: 1) Stepped jar rims have generally passed out of use by the time of Period I, though one example of a degenerate jar rim of this type was found at Taanach. 2) Jug rims in Period IA sometimes have thickened rims reminiscent of Late Bronze jugs. 3) During Period IA the most common cooking pot bears the triangulated, everted rim typical of the LB II cooking pot but now developed into its last stages. 4) Occasional burnishing is found on a few bowls. During this period this was always done on the natural surface distinguishing it from the burnishing over a red slip characteristic of Period II. 5) Squared rim craters are found in Periods IA and IB, but they are usually unpainted in contrast with some LB II examples. 6) Other vessels, especially jugs, occasionally contain vestigial painting in the tradition of LB II. 7) One type of chalice represents a continuation of a popular LB II chalice into early Iron I. 8) Several bowls still have slightly carinated sides, suggestive of the very end of the Late Bronze tradition.

Most of these carry-overs have been noted in the Period IA groups although a few persist into Period IB. It might be noted also that the earliest of all the Period IA groups

POTTERY GROUPS OF PERIOD IA

seems to be that from the Cuneiform Tablet Building (Figs. 1-2). This group has a noticeable number of relationships to LB II forms although in almost every case they are late and vestigial. Alongside these Late Bronze remnants are new developments already in Period IA—forms like the jar with collared rim, a bowl well-known from the early part of Iron I, as well as the common type of Iron I chalice with splayed lip. The picture Period IA then is that of both continuity and development so that this period seems to be related both to the end of the preceding period and the beginning of new traditions.

By the time of Period IB many of the new forms of Period IA, such as the collared-rim jar, have become developed and common while most of the Late Bronze vestiges have faded. In addition, new forms become more abundant with the introduction of several styles of jug rims, new kinds of bowls, and the cooking pot with elongated rim. This period, then, has become more distant from Late Bronze traditions and represents a fuller development of more distinctly Iron Age types.

Stratigraphically the two periods at Tell Ta'annek were separated by a destruction, the evidence for which, as noted previously, was found in several of the structures from which these groups came. On the other hand, the ceramic evidence does not seem to point to disjunctions in the population during this period. Rather, it seems that following the destruction of Period IA, the same or similar people returned to reconstruct some of the structures. Most probably these were Canaanites. This evidence, in turn, would seem to be more in accord with the description in Judg 1:27 and Josh 17:11-12 than that of Josh 12:21.

The several conflagrations in the course of a single century suggest the unsettled character of the period and correlate with similar evidence from other sites such as Megiddo. The problem of how to account for the disruption at the end of Period IA is not clear. It is possible that it simply reflected a local catastrophe. But the destruction of Period IB seems clearly to have been by means of military attack, given the devastation wrought on the Drainpipe Structure and several other buildings. The events which suggest themselves for the latter are those recorded in Judges 4 and 5, the battle between the Israelite forces in the north under Barak and those of the Canaanites under Sisera.

The problem of the date for the battle of Judges 5 is a knotty but essential one for establishing a fixed point for the chronology of the early Iron Age in Palestine. Following Lapp, who adopted Albright's (1970:117-118; Engberg 1940:4-9) proposed date of long standing, the present study accepts the date of about 1125 for these events. However, as Albright noted (1968:13, n. 35) this date may have to be raised slightly to 1150 by reference to more precise dates for Ramses II and III. In this case the dates for Periods IA and IB at Taanach would probably have to be raised slightly to fit the synchronisms with Egypt.

If the identification with Judges 4-5 has some basis, and if the battle was won by the Israelites, an enigma appears in that Taanach apparently was not occupied until the beginning of Period II, a century later. The archaeological evidence would not support a hasty occupation of the site by Israelites following the victory celebrated in the Song of Deborah (Judges 5). Perhaps this may indicate that even with the successful drive against a city of the Esdraelon Plain, the Israelites were not assured of very great security in this area and so chose not to settle. Megiddo would seem to substantiate this since the earliest attestation of an Israelite occupation at that site would have to be in Stratum VB (Wright 1961:96; Yadin (1970:95). All evidence taken together, then, points to the Canaanite character of Taanach until Period II.

Chapter Four
Pottery Groups of Period IIA

For Period IIA the stratified evidence is limited. A clear stratified sequence from Periods IIA to IIB was generally not present in the squares excavated although SW 6-2 L. 68 and SW 5-2 L. 60 and 61 were exceptions. Nonetheless, a differentiation between Period IIA and IIB must be made. Period IIB was a well-defined stratum with a distinctive pottery typology. Period IIA, on the other hand, was characterized by pockets of debris, and its pottery suggests the beginning of forms and techniques of decoration which became more widely used in Period IIB.

The evidence for Period IIA was found largely in the area to the west and northwest of the Cultic Structure where Period IIA remains were stratigraphically above those of Period I. It is noteworthy that the Period IIB Cultic Structure to the east also lay directly above Period I remains, but in this case there was no intervening material which could be attributed to Period IIA. This would suggest that Period IIA represented an initial, rather limited reuse of the mound following the gap after Period IB, and that occupation spread out over larger parts of the mound during Period IIB. The scarcity of structural remains from Period IIA, only wall stubs being preserved, suggests the tentativeness of this phase which was apparently also effaced by the operations of Period IIB. The following Period IIA loci are illustrated in this report.

SW 4-7 Loci 68, 53, and 44

These three loci were discovered in a confined area of SW 4-7. L. 68 consisted of a layer of brown and black ashy soil, probably occupational debris, on the east side of a stump of Wall L. 64. Wall L. 64 had been largely robbed by a stone-lined Arab pit L. 6. Immediately beneath L. 68 was a layer of soil L. 76 with Period I sherds, while mixed layers with Iron II forms appeared above it.

To the south of Wall L. 64 a yellow ashy, bricky soil designated L. 53 was probably the same occupational debris as L. 68. The layer beneath, L. 58, also contained Period I pottery. A small stump of Wall L. 38 found resting on L. 53 belonged to a later Iron II construction.

L. 44 was a stone-lined pit approximately 3 m. south of L. 68 and 2 m. east of L. 53. Excavation did not determine its exact relation to the occupation layers, but the pottery suggests that it was contemporary with the latter.

SW 6-2 Locus 68

This locus consisted of hard, yellow-brown soil with red, black and white flecks found underneath a plastered floor L. 42. Pottery from the latter provided the basis for assigning the floor to Period IIB. L. 68 was probably a fill used to level the area for the plaster floor. Below L. 68 was L. 71 with pottery attributed to Period IB. L. 71 thus was contemporary with the Cuneiform Tablet Building to the east.

SW 5-2 Loci 60, 61

Although separated by a wall, these two loci apparently belonged to the same building phase. Both consisted of soft brown or gray soil containing decomposed clay brick. L. 60 on the south and L. 61 on the north side of a wall stump L. 69 were contemporary with the wall. L. 48 above L. 60 and 61 contained sherds from Period IIB while underneath were loci belonging to the Period IB Cuneiform Tablet Building.

SW 2-8 Locus 18

In the southwest part of SW 2-8 a large orthostat L. 12 was the only object of any size in the Iron Age layers. Abutting this stone on the north and east sides was a yellow, ashy layer L. 18 representing a localized burning. Beneath L. 18 a fairly hard gravel layer L. 38 contained sherds of Period IB. The earliest use of the orthostat seems also to have been connected with this phase. Above L. 18 were layers with mixed sherds from Iron II and later.

SW 4-7 Loci 57, 60

These two loci were ashy layers, and several whole vessels came from them. L. 57 was below a fragmentary plaster floor L. 56 of which traces remained only in the southwest part of the square south of Wall L. 19. The pottery dated the plaster floor to Period IIB or Period III. L. 60 was found in the southeast part of the square below L. 59. The ashy soil and whole pottery in L. 57 and 60 suggest a burned structure which probably reflects a local accident rather than part of a larger destruction since there is no evidence that Period IIA was destroyed as a whole.

SW 4-7 Locus 42

This locus consisted of grayish-brown soil to the west of the stump of Wall L. 64 noted in the groups from SW 4-7 above. Above this layer, L. 40 had Period IIB sherds while L. 74 below contained sherds from Period I.

Primary Comparative Loci

Megiddo. Building 2072. This building was discovered in Area AA just west of the city gate (Loud 1948:33-37, Figs. 83, 386). It was a sizable building with a large number of whole pottery forms. Rooms 2068-2071 are especially important for comparative purposes. The building was attributed to Stratum VIA dated to the last half of the eleventh century.

ᶜAin Shems. Room 316. This room was called a storeroom in the final publication (Grant and Wright 1939:134). It contained a homogeneous group of pottery. The locus was ascribed to Stratum IIa with a date at the very end of the eleventh and the beginning of the tenth century.

Gezer. Loci of Stratum 7 Field II. A number of loci were phased as Stratum 7 and dated to the end of the eleventh and first half of the tenth century. L. 1075 was destruction debris with much mudbrick and ash found above Surface 1076. Both L. 1076.1 and L. 1085 were a makeup for Surface 1076, while L. 1077.1 was the same for Surface 1077. L. 1083P represented occupational debris from above Surface 1083 while L. 1095P was the same on Surface 1095. L. 1084 was a pit dug from Surface 1095.

Additional Comparative Loci and Strata

In addition to the PCL there are parallels for the Period IIA groups in the following: Megiddo Strata VIA and VB, ᶜAin Shems Stratum IIA, Hazor Stratum XI, the Fortress Phase at Tell el-Fûl, ᶜAfula Stratum IIIA, Tell Abu Hawām Stratum IVB, Tell Qasile Stratum X, Lachish Tomb 521 and Cave 6024, and Deir ᶜAllā Phases E through H. Tell Beit Mirsim Stratum B2 also continues to this period but would be represented only by the latest materials from this stratum. Occasional parallels are also found at Bethel in Phase 4a. Tell ᶜAmal, near Tell Taᶜannek, also has a small amount of comparative material corresponding to this period. The excavators dated Stratum IV to the first half of the tenth century while Stratum III was assigned to the last half of the same century. Very few parallels can be found, however, between the Stratum IV material and Taanach Period IIA, whereas it will be seen in the following chapter that much of the Stratum IV and Stratum III material is identical to that from Period IIB at Taanach.

The Pottery

JARS (FIGS. 19:1-3, 20:1-2, 22:1, 24:1-3, 25:1-2, 26:1, 28:1)

Although these groups contain few examples of jars, several forms represented are significant for chronological development. The storage jar TT 1864 in Fig. 20:1 is heart-shaped and has a body reaching its widest diameter just above the middle of the jar while its lower part tapers toward a pointed base. Figs. 20:2 and 24:3 apparently belong to the same type. A close parallel is found in Tomb 521 at Lachish, which Tufnell considered a rare type (Tufnell 1953:224, Pl. 94:477). However, several more examples are known and it seems certain that this jar was found at the end of the eleventh and the beginning of the tenth centuries. An example at Megiddo can thus be assigned a more precise date toward the end of the eleventh and beginning of the tenth century. (Loud 1948:Pl. 82:7). It is possible that a Phase E jar at Deir ᶜAllā may reflect a slightly earlier example of this type (Franken and Kalsbeek 1969:Fig. 60:34). This jar apparently does not continue into Period IIB, where examples are lacking, and the most prominent storage jar has a long, ovoid body (Figs. 30-31).

The jar rim in Fig. 22:1 is an anomaly. It is apparently from a neckless jar, but parallels are lacking. It may be the prototype of the cylindrical jars of Iron II. Relationships to jar TT 460 from the Cultic Structure (Fig. 35:2) suggest themselves although Fig. 22:1 has a more pouched body and does not have quite the cylindrical shape of TT 460.

The jar with small spout TT 834 in Fig. 26:1 represents an early specimen of this type which becomes common in Period IIB (Fig. 36:1-2, TT 467, TT490). During Period IIA such jars display an expansion of the body below the midpoint of the sidewalls, giving a bloated effect, while in Period IIB the body becomes more rounded. The Megiddo evidence parallels that from Taanach. Examples of the spouted jar as a general type are absent before Stratum VIA. When they begin to appear in Stratum VIA they have the greater expansion characteristic of Period IIA examples at Taanach (Loud 1948:Pl. 77:12-13) while in Stratum V the body is rounder (Lamon and Shipton 1939:Pl. 19:106). One of the Megiddo jars contemporary with Period IIA is from PCL 2070 (Loud 1948:Pl. 77:12).

Figs. 19:1-3, 24:1, 25:1-2 and 28:1 are mostly jar handles. They are generally oval in section. The incised cross on Fig. 19:3 is found at Megiddo during both Iron I and II and thus adds little to chronological precision (Lamon and Shipton 1939:Pls. 41:8, 14; 42:29, 56). However, the circular mark in Fig. 28:1 is more rare. The only parallel for it at Megiddo is a handle ascribed to Stratum V (Lamon and Shipton 1939:Pl. 42:42). The slightly flattened base of Fig. 24:2 can also be compared to a jar type found in Stratum VI at Megiddo (Loud 1948:Pl. 83:6).

JUGS, JUGLETS AND PYXIS (FIGS. 18:1, 19:4-6, 20:3, 22:2-6, 25:3-5, 26:2, 27:1)

Jugs are more plentiful than jars in these selected groups of Period IIA. Although considerable variety is found in the rim forms of this period, for convenience they are discussed according to the general features of

POTTERY GROUPS OF PERIOD IIA

thickened, profiled and thickened, bowed rims.

Jugs with thickened rims are found in Figs. 19:4-5, 22:2-3, and 25:3. As a rule the rims are rounded and the neck is fairly long, the shortest being Fig. 19:5. Similar thickened and rounded rims were also found in PCL 1076.1 at Gezer (Dever and others 1970:Pl. 35:1). A close parallel is also found in Stratum IIIA at ᶜAfula (M. Dothan 1935:Fig. 11:16).

The second general type has an incipient or developed profile on the neck. Three sherds belong to this type, Figs. 18:1, 19:6, 25:4 and whole Jug TT 631 in Fig. 26:2. Figs. 25:4 and TT 631 have an almost identical rim and one in Cistern L. 74 (Fig. 58:12) may also belong to Period IIA. TT 631 has an expanded lower body noted as a characteristic of Period IIA in Fig. 26:1 above. The same expansion in the body is found in a similar jug from Stratum VI at Megiddo which may be assigned more precisely to Stratum VIA (Loud 1948:Pl. 81:1). Gezer also has similar profiled necks in this period such as one in PCL 1084 (Dever and others 1970:Pl. 35:12).

Other contemporary sites where profiled jug rims are found include ᶜAfula where they are represented in Stratum IIIA (M. Dothan 1955:Fig. 11:6-15). The various examples from Tell el-Fûl all belong to the Fortress Phase at that site and can be dated to the end of the eleventh and the first half of the tenth century as a result of recent excavations (Albright 1924:Pl. 28:1-16; Lapp 1965: 2-3). The basic features of the profiled jug rim are thus initiated during Period IIA. During Period IIB they are further refined as seen in the jug from the Cultic Structure (Fig. 37:1 TT 103).

Jugs with thickened, bowed rims are illustrated in Figs. 20:3 and 22:4. The first has a long straight neck which is concave on the interior of the thickened rim. This rim form is common and is suggested already in twelfth-century jars and jugs such as a larger one from Hazor Stratum XII (Yadin and others 1961:Pl. 167:3), and a jug or jar from Phase B at Deir ᶜAllā (Franken and Kalsbeek 1969:Fig. 51:24). During Period IIB the exterior of the thickened rim is sometimes provided with a groove (Figs. 37:2 TT 440; 59:4-5 TT 385). The rim in Fig. 22:4 begins to appear in Period IIA, continuing into Period IIB and even into Iron II (Fig. 72:1). Since this jug resembles one type of cooking pot in this period, it is often difficult to distinguish the two except by the ware (see Lamon and Shipton 1939:Pl. 20:115; Guy and Engberg 1938:Pl. 40:2). Several from Cistern L. 74 may belong to either Period IIA or IIB (Fig. 62:2-4). The continuation of this jug into Iron II is attested by examples from Stratum A at Tell Beit Mirsim (Albright 1932:Pls. 57:14, 58:3, 6) and from Iron II contexts at Lachish (Tufnell 1953:Pl. 84:173, 185).

There are several other rim types which do not fit the three general categories. Fig. 22:5 has an inverted rim similar to Period IIB jug rims (Fig. 61:9-10). The rim and neck of a slightly smaller jug from Stratum V at Megiddo is close in form to this rim (Lamon and Shipton 1939:Pl. 7:170). The handle in Fig. 25:5 with its roughly diamond-shaped section, is common in late Iron I.

Fig. 22:6 is from a juglet with rounded base, the latter being the typical juglet base in Periods IIA and IIB. Among abundant parallels are examples from Stratum V at Megiddo, Tomb 521 at Lachish, and the Phase J pottery at Deir ᶜAllā (Lamon and Shipton 1939:Pl. 5:138-140; Tufnell 1953:Pl. 88: 302; Franken and Kalsbeek 1969:Fig. 69:8).

Pyxis TT 621 in Fig. 27:1 can be compared with several Period IIB examples (Fig. 40:12-14 TT 488, TT 372, TT 73). The one here is characterized by its squatter body, but there is apparently no chronological significance in the difference between examples thrown higher from the base in comparison to the more depressed types (cf. Fig. 92:6). TT 621 is also decorated with red painted bands like a closely parallel one from Stratum VIA at Megiddo (Loud 1948:Pl. 77:7). It is worth noting that in Period IIB the decoration of these vessels tends to change from painted bands to red wash or slip, sometimes burnished. This same development in decoration of pyxides is found at Megiddo where band-painting is common in Stratum VIA (Loud 1948:Pl. 77:7) while Stratum V introduces red slip and burnishing (Lamon and Shipton 1939:Pl. 19:96-97).

CRATERS (FIGS. 18:2-3, 19:7, 22:7-8, 24:4-5, 25:6, 28:2-4)

The most common crater of Period IIA continues the type with rolled rim which gained prominence in Periods IA and IB (Figs. 7:1-5, 12:2-7). Sometimes it is crudely formed as in Fig. 22:8. This crater apparently continues into Period IIB judging from a number of examples in Cistern L. 74 (Fig. 63:3-11), although some of the Cistern L. 74 forms could belong to Period IIA. Beyond this, the form is still present, but probably tailing off in Period III (Fig. 70:3-4) and IV (Figs. 72:4-5, 74:2).

The evidence for this crater at Megiddo and Hazor is similar to that at Taanach. At Megiddo these deep bowls or craters are ascribed to a range between Stratum VIII and Stratum VIA and, like Taanach, they continue to the latter part of the eleventh century (Loud 1948:Pl. 84:20, 22). Additional examples are associated with Stratum V at the same site (Lamon and Shipton 1939:Pls. 31:158-159, 32:162, 165, 166), and seemingly the form continues into Iron II at Megiddo (Lamon and Shipton 1939:Pl. 28:89). A crater of this type is also found at Lachish in Cave 6024 (Tufnell 1953:Pl. 82:133) as well as in Stratum XI at Hazor (Yadin and others 1961:Pl. 203:12). In addition there are abundant examples from Stratum IIIA at ᶜAfula (M. Dothan 1955:Fig. 12:15-18, 22-26). In general, the type is a stereotyped one throughout Iron I although there is some flexibility in the rim form.

In addition to the common rolled-rim type, Fig. 22:7 has a heavily thickened rim. Such heavy rims are popular in craters toward the end of Iron I as in the larger crater from the Cultic Structure (Fig. 41:1) and one from Cistern L. 74 (Fig. 63:1). Similar evidence from slightly later in the tenth century is found at Gezer (Dever and others 1970:Pl. 34:20).

BOWLS (FIGS. 18:4-6, 19:8, 21:1-4, 23:1-8, 24:6-8, 25:7-13, 28:5)

In the following discussion bowls are grouped according to those with simple rims and those with thickened, flattened rims. In addition, several bowls of thin ware make their appearance in Period IIA.

Bowls with simple rims are found in Figs. 24:8 and 25:7-8. These have sharply incurved sidewalls which are sometimes inverted as in Fig. 25:7. This bowl is a common type in Period IIA, and although the one here has an untreated pink surface, the type begins to be supplied with a red slip and burnishing. A close parallel comes from PCL 1083P at Gezer which has a red-slipped exterior (Dever and others 1970:Pl. 35:8). The same type, sometimes finished with a red slip, is very common in Stratum IIa at ᶜAin Shems (Grant and Wright 1938:Pl. 63:1-2, 5-8; 1939:135). The first two from ᶜAin Shems are from PCL 316. A decorated bowl in Stratum XI at Hazor also resembles this type (Yadin and others 1961:Pl. 203:1).

Also belonging to bowls with simple rims are those in Figs. 18:5, 23:4 and 25:11-12. The sides of this bowl are not so incurved as the previous examples, and the type may represent the continuation and development into Period IIA of a prominent bowl of Period IB (see Fig. 13:4-9). Although no examples here are so treated, this type also begins to be supplied with a red slip during this period as can be seen in a Stratum IIa parallel from ᶜAin Shems (Grant and Wright 1938:Pl. 63:9). At Deir ᶜAllā this bowl corresponds to Franken's Type 5a which is found between Phases A-G but seems to decline in use after this (Franken and Kalsbeek 1969:147-148, Fig. 64:88). Similar evidence seems to be present in Stratum IIIA at ᶜAfula (M. Dothan 1955:Fig. 13:4-5).

The deep bowl in Fig. 23:1 also has a simple rim and is hand burnished over a red slip. It resembles a slightly later bowl from PCL 2081 for Period IIB at Megiddo (Loud 1948:Pl. 89:14).

Bowls with thickened, flattened rims are found in Figs. 18:4, 21:1-3, 23:2, 25:9-10 and 28:5. Most of these are burnished with a red slip in Period IIB, but only Figs. 23:2 and 25:10 are so treated here. The unburnished forms in Fig. 21:1-3 can be compared with the same form burnished over a red-to-orange slip in Period IIB (Fig. 45:9). Parallels to these flattened bowl rims are found at several sites, including several from the Fortress Phase at Tell el-Fûl (Albright 1924:Pl. 26:18) and from Stratum IIIA at ᶜAfula (M. Dothan 1955:Fig. 13:9).

One other bowl may also be considered here although it has a somewhat different rim. It is the form in Fig. 23:3 whose rim is everted and overlapped on the exterior. The example here is hand-burnished over a red slip. The form resembles a larger vessel designated a crater from PCL 1084 at Gezer which is also red-slipped (Dever and others 1970:Pl. 35:14). In addition, a good parallel is present at ᶜAin Shems (Grant and Wright 1938:Pl. 62:12). This example was found in Room 441 and was attributed to Stratum III. However, since it was horizontally burnished over a red slip on the interior and part of the exterior, it probably should be reassigned to Stratum IIa.

During this period several smaller thin ware bowls also begin to appear like those in Figs. 23:5-6 and 24:6-7. The bowls in Fig. 24:6-7 are of special importance because they belong to the beginning of the class of "saucer bowls" which became prominent in Period IIB (Fig. 48:15-19). Noteworthy is the absence of burnishing in Period IIA, while in Period IIB and also in early Iron II, this type is commonly burnished.

Fig. 23:5 is burnished over a red slip in the tradition of Period IIB bowls suggesting that the technique of treating Period IIB bowls has its origin already in Period IIA. The type can be compared with Period IIB bowl (Fig. 45:7) as well as one from Phase G at Deir ᶜAllā (Franken and Kalsbeek 1969:Fig. 64:90). The bowl in Fig. 23:6 also has hand burnishing over a red slip. It is probably from a thin bowl with carinated side similar to one ascribed to Strata V-IV at Megiddo (Lamon and Shipton 1939:Pl. 28:93A).

Various bowl bases from this period are found in Figs. 18:6, 19:8, 21:4, 23:7-8 and 25:13. Fig. 18:6 has the same kind of heavy ring base found in the groups of Period I while Figs. 19:8, 21:4 and 23:8 have bases more like those of Period IIB. Two bases, Figs. 23:7 and 25:13, are flat and slightly concave.

COOKING POTS (FIGS. 18:7, 19:9, 21:5, 23:9-10, 24:9, 29:1-5)

The most common cooking pot of Period IIA has an elongated rim sometimes bent slightly upward at the outer tip forming a wide groove. The effect is that of a collar. This rim made its appearance already in Period IB (Figs. 14:12-13, 17:11, 13-15). In Figs. 18:7, 23:10 and 24:9 the rim is somewhat shorter like examples in ᶜAin Shems Stratum IIa and Deir ᶜAllā Phase G (Grant and Wright 1938:Pl. 63:3-5; Franken and Kalsbeek 1969:Fig. 63:72-73). The remainder have more elongated rims, and this is the most common variation in Period IIB. Similar elongated rims are found in Hazor Stratum XI (Yadin and others 1961:Pl. 203:7-10) and in Phase G at Deir ᶜAllā (Franken and Kalsbeek 1969:Fig. 63:77, 79). A further parallel is assigned to Stratum VI at Megiddo (Loud 1948:Pl. 85:16).

A somewhat different cooking pot rim is represented in Fig. 19:9. This one is also elongated but more flattened. The form is probably a continuation of an eleventh-century cooking pot rim, the example here coming from the very end of that century. Evidence at Deir ᶜAllā shows that this rim type was present at that site from the eleventh down to the early part of the tenth century (Franken and Kalsbeek 1969:Figs 49:1-4, 53:50, 63:61). The cooking pot TT 864 in Fig. 21:5 is differentiated by its deeper body and slightly carinated side, its two handles and distinctive rim. The type is not abundant, but there is a close parallel from PCL 2070 at Megiddo (Loud 1948:Pl. 79:6). This Period IIA cooking pot apparently continues in the one-handled, deep cooking vessels of Period IIB (Fig. 50:1-3).

CHALICES (FIGS. 23:11, 24:10, 27:2)

Two different types of chalices are found in these groups. The first has curved sides and a grooved, flattened rim (Fig. 23:11). This type seems to be a late vestige of the chalice prominent in Period I (Fig. 3:16). Although the form may be intrusive, there seems to be parallel evidence at Megiddo where a decorated chalice with this type of rim is ascribed to Stratum V (Lamon and Shipton 1939:Pl. 33:17).

The more common chalice has shallow, curved sidewalls and an everted rim. A whole example TT 630 is found in Fig. 27:2 while Fig. 24:10 also seems to be a rim of this type. This type begins in Period IB (Fig. 17:16), but there is some development between Period IB and IIA. During Period IB the rim is less splayed while in Period IIA it tends to be flattened out almost horizontally.

Summary

For their relative chronological position these groups must be compared with those from the succeeding Period IIB phase as well as with those of Period IB. Beginning with the latter, there are several forms from Period IB which continue into Period IIA although the majority of such forms have died out by the time of Period IIA. Forms which continue are the rolled rim craters, which are still popular in Period IIA, and the cooking pot with elongated rim, a form which originated in Period IB and continues in Period IIA. A third carry-over was also noted in the chalice with grooved rim. Forms which are conspicuous by their absence in Period IIA are storage jars with long, thickened collared rims; jugs with simple rims and ridged necks; and the general types of simple bowls characteristic of Period I as a whole.

On the other hand, Period IIA introduces an impressive range of new types and features. Those which have been noted above can be summarized as follows: storage jars whose bodies reach their largest diameter above midsection and then taper to more or less pointed bases; jars with small spouts; jars and jugs with depressed bodies; jugs with simple or profiled rims; bowls with thickened and flattened rims and with a development toward more carinated sidewalls; shallow, thin bowls; and deep cooking pots with handle or handles. These characteristics are often the very ones which become accentuated in the pottery of Period IIB. In Period IIA such features suggest initial experimentation while by the time of Period IIB they appear to have become widespread and developed. This would intimate a date for the Period IIA groups slightly preceding those of Period IIB.

The most important innovation of Period IIA is the use of a red slip on a limited number of smaller bowls along with the practice of hand burnishing. Several of the groups contained no examples of such red-slipped and burnished vessels. In the case of Loci 68, 53 and 44 of SW 4-7, this may indicate a slightly earlier date in the late eleventh century for these groups. That there are altogether only a small number of burnished vessels in Period IIA suggests that we are at the very beginning of the practice. The technique seems to have been utilized on mostly small bowls, being applied subsequently to larger bowls and other vessels.

The Taanach evidence suggests a date for the introduction of red-slip burnishing at approximately 1000 which is supported by comparative evidence. At Tell Beit Mirsim the practice was noted as the chief feature distinguishing Stratum B3. It made its main appearance at Megiddo in Stratum VA-IVB. At ᶜAin Shems it was discovered to be the most characteristic treatment of the pottery of Stratum IIb. The same may be noted of Deir ᶜAllā where red-slipped burnishing began in Phase E and then became ubiquitous, especially on bowls, by the time of Phase G.

The direction from which this new influence entered Palestine is not absolutely certain, but it seems increasingly that the flow was from north to south. Of special importance is the prominence of red-slipped, burnished wares in Phase O in the ᶜAmuq Plain (Swift 1958:124-51). The excavation of further Iron Age sites in Syria should help to clarify the probable north Syrian origin of this tradition and its relation to the Aramaean peoples. From there it seems these features made their way to northern and southern Palestine. Historically the most advantageous time for such a development would have been the reign of David which opened up new possibilities for contact with Syria. The early experiments with red-slip burnishing would seem to fit well in his reign when such cross-cultural contacts were beginning to occur. They naturally grew stronger in the days of Solomon (Van Beek 1969:356-57).

Period IIA would suggest, therefore, the very beginnings of an Israelite settlement at Taanach in the time of David. By this time the last remaining threats to Israelite occupation in the area had been nullified, and there was an increasing tendency to utilize sites along the Esdraelon Plain. These settlements were small and tentative at first, but by the time of Period IIB some, like Taanach, were provided with the opportunity of growing to substantial size.

Chapter Five
Pottery Groups of Period IIB

The pottery presented in this chapter came from one of the important Iron I buildings at Taanach, the Cultic Structure, and from two cisterns, Cistern L. 69 and Cistern L. 74.

The Cultic Structure, SW 2-7

In 1902 Ernst Sellin (1904:75-78; Figs. 102, 104, 105; Pls. 12-13) excavated to the east of SW 2-7 on the present grid. Here he discovered several significant pieces among which was the famous cultic stand now in the Museum of Classical Antiquities, Istanbul (Lapp 1969b:42 and n. 59). These discoveries were responsible in part for the decision of the recent expedition to excavate immediately to the west of Sellin's large trench. By digging adjacent to Sellin's large cut, it was hoped that additional cultic material might appear which would further clarify the earlier discoveries (see Fig. 97a, b).

Early in the 1963 season such evidence began to appear. Just west of Sellin's trench the remains of several walls emerged, belonging to two rooms of a building which had been partially demolished by the earlier excavations. The situation was complicated by the fact that later construction during Iron II had been undertaken on the north, and this phase had reused the foundations of several walls of the earlier building. Wall L. 16, a rather well-preserved wall almost 9 m. in length, represented the western wall of the Period IIB building. On the north a part of the east-west Wall L. 30 had survived, but on the east it was demolished by the trench of the earlier excavations. On the east side, only a small piece of the north-south Wall L. 38 remained, with Wall L. 15 joining it perpendicularly more than midway the preserved length of the building. Wall L. 15 served to divide the two areas in the building, designated as Rooms 1 and 2.

To the east of these remains was the large rectangular basin in which an impressive stone stele was found (Lapp 1964:29; 1967a:27-30). This installation had previously been partly excavated by Sellin who designated it an "olive-press" (Sellin 1904:76). However, the recent excavations make it probable that the basin had been employed for cultic purposes, at least in one of its phases. Although the stratification was destroyed by the earlier excavations, it is likely that the Cultic Structure extended originally to the east incorporating the basin with its stele.

The pottery came from within well-sealed destruction debris of the preserved rooms, the larger amount from Room 1. In Room 1, the destruction layer of approximately 0.75 m. in depth was discovered immediately below a loose fill, L. 14, dating to Iron II. The destruction layer itself was composed of fine, gray ash mixed with soft, burnt, red debris and pockets of packed, brown soil. The various locus numbers assigned to these layers with different textures were Loci 13, 26, 27, 33, 35, 48, 57, 59, 61 and 63, all comprising the same destruction level. Below the destruction debris of Room 1 was a floor of tamped earth, sealing the destruction layer underneath.

Room 2 was similar. The destruction level was sealed on the top by a floor, L. 25, belonging to an Iron II building. Beneath this floor, L. 28 and 36 consisted of destruction debris approximately 0.75 m. in depth like that found in Room 1. Both loci contained broken sherds and pots as well as bits and pieces of plaster. The floor in this room was also of tamped earth, sealing the destruction layer below.

Cistern L. 69, SW 2-8

A cistern only a few meters from the Cultic Structure was discovered at the beginning of the 1968 season. The shaft of this cistern had been noted by Sellin, and it was probably in this area that he had discovered the cultic stand mentioned previously. The upper part of the shaft had been demolished by a large gash, L. 156, made by the earlier excavations. Part of the cistern had collapsed, pushing several whole vessels into the soft silt of the bell of the cistern. Among these were the pieces of a cultic stand TT 1500 comparable in its importance to the earlier one found by Sellin (Lapp 1969c).

The stratigraphic relation of this cistern to the Cultic Structure could not be satisfactorily determined since the earlier excavation had destroyed much of the evidence. However, the cache belongs typologically to the same horizon as the pottery from the Cultic Structure, and it is even more likely that the cistern was part of the Cultic Structure complex.

Cistern L. 74, SW 6-2

During the 1963 season a cistern was discovered in the balk between SW 5-1 and SW 6-1 in the area slightly west of the Period I Cuneiform Tablet Building (Lapp 1964:33). Excavation indicated three major periods during which this cistern was in use. The latest was when its shaft alone was employed as a refuse pit during Period VI (see below, Chapter 7). During Period II it served as an installation in a large court area, while in LB I it was characterized by several plastered phases. It is probable, too, that it was also in use during Period I when the Cuneiform Tablet Building occupied the area since several Period I forms appeared alongside LB I sherds in the bottom of the cistern. During Period II the cistern was cleaned out so that most of the vessels remaining were associated with the period being discussed here.

The Period II courtyard, with which the cistern was associated, lay stratigraphically above the Period IB Cuneiform Tablet Building. Approximately 3 m. south of the cistern was a rectangular basin, L. 76 and 77, similar to that found in the Cultic Structure with a large stele plastered against its east wall (Lapp 1964:32, Fig. 17). Farther to the west was a second basin of square shape, L. 45. Between these two basins and to the south of them were the remains of a plastered floor L. 42 which probably belonged to the court area. The pottery found on the floor was similar to that of Cistern L. 74 and the Cultic Structure.

Primary Comparative Loci

The dating of these three groups rests on the correlation of the best defined of the three, that of the Cultic Structure, to key groups from comparative sites. Preliminary study of the Cultic Structure vessels showed their similarity to pottery from L. 2081 at Megiddo (Lapp 1964:37, n. 59). Subsequently, in preparing the pottery for publication, it has become evident that Building 10 at Megiddo also has a striking resemblance, both architecturally and in its pottery, to the Cultic Structure. Our investigation, therefore, must begin with the relation of these loci, and it will then proceed to define more broadly the relation of the Taanach and Megiddo deposits in this period. It will be observed that the cultural similarities between the two sites are more remarkable in this period than in any other, Megiddo being the richer of the two sites.

MEGIDDO. LOCUS 2081.

L. 2081 at Megiddo was an area defined by remnants of walls on the north, west and south (Loud 1948:Fig. 388). Since it was found in a fragmented state, it was not clear whether it was originally connected with a much better preserved group of rooms to the north of it. The excavators decided that it was and interpreted this locus as the forecourt of the impressive central room with two upright slabs at its south end (Loud 1948:44-45, Fig. 100). The most significant feature was the cache of cultic objects and vessels found in its southwest corner (Loud 1948:44, Fig. 102). Unfortunately the description of this locus is very brief and discussion of the stratification is lacking. Only in a general way was it assigned to Stratum VA. However, the mostly whole vessels in the locus point to a destruction layer and burning is suggested in the report (Loud 1948:43, Fig. 99). Like the pottery from Taanach's Cultic Structure, the group from L. 2081 appears to be homogeneous.

Of particular importance is the place of this locus in recent efforts to clarify stratigraphic and architectural features at Megiddo. Albright and Wright have both demonstrated that Strata VA and IVB belong together and probably comprise the Solomonic city commonly referred to as Stratum VA-IVB (see chapter 2.). More recently Yadin has carried on several follow-up excavations at Megiddo with two important results. First, Yadin observed that the six-chambered, two-towered gate discovered at Megiddo had a notable resemblance to the gate found in the center of the upper mound at Hazor (Loud 1948:48, Fig. 105; and 46, Fig. 104). In addition, a reexamination of Macalister's plans at Gezer suggested that the gate associated with the "Maccabean Castle" was of similar construction to those at Megiddo and Hazor (Yadin 1958). In the second place, Yadin's probe east of the gate led him to conclude that the wall constructed of "offsets" and "insets," and ascribed to Solomon by the excavators, may in fact have been a later wall dating to the time of Ahab. Below this he recorded remnants of a casemate wall parallel to those of Hazor and Gezer (Yadin 1960:64-67). The exact relation of this casemate wall to the city gate at Megiddo was no longer traceable since the trench cut by Schumacher in 1903-1905 had demolished the evidence in this area. However, since the casemate at Hazor adjoins the gate (Yadin 1969:56-58) and since an identical situation is apparent in Macalister's plans at Gezer (Macalister 1912: 217, Fig. 104), Yadin proposed that similar architectural features must have been present at Megiddo. Aharoni (1972) has debated the matter with Yadin (1973). However, the architectural, stratigraphic and ceramic arguments seem to lie in Yadin's favor, and his results correspond well with those at nearby Taanach.

This evidence, plus further clarification of the fort on the south end of the mound as well as the discovery of another fort on the north connected with the casemate system, led Yadin to conclude that Megiddo VA-IVB was a formidable Solomonic city. He also observed that several of the public and private buildings ascribed by the previous excavators to Stratum V, and more specifically to VA, should now be attributed to the same stratigraphic horizon as the forts, the casemate wall and the gate (Yadin 1960:68). This line of interpretation might also be applied to L. 2081 located southwest of the city gate in Square L 7.

Albright's suggestion (Wright 1950a:39-46; 1950b:59) that the "Solomonic gateway" in the plan for Stratum IV actually belongs in Stratum VA (Loud 1948:Figs. 388, 389) would link L. 2081 to the building phase represented by the gate, thus making it Solomonic. In addition, although evidence for a casemate wall is lacking on the west side of the mound, its inner face would probably have been just behind L. 2081 judging from the line of the later offset-inset wall of Stratum IV (Loud 1948:Fig. 389).

The devastating destruction characterizing Stratum VA-IVB may be credited to a serious attack which brought this city to an end. The historical problems connected with this destruction are discussed below, but it is important here to note that the L. 2081 group was well sealed in destruction debris.

MEGIDDO. BUILDING 10.

Another building at Megiddo with pottery important for comparative purposes is Building 10. It is natural that this building has been the object of considerable discussion since it is one of the more impressive structures of Stratum VA-IVB. Most of the building appeared in Squares P 13 and Q 13 in Area C on the east side of the mound (Lamon and Shipton 1939:3 and Fig. 6; May 1935:4-11 and Pl. 1). It was an elongated rectangular structure with at least seven rooms. Since a number of limestone altars were found to the south of this building, it has been interpreted as a building with cultic significance. It is not impossible that the Cultic Structure at Taanach may originally have been a similar type of building since its surviving walls suggest a building of rectangular shape with a number of rooms.

The date of Building 10 seems not to have been adequately settled. Albright (1943:29, n. 10) and Wright devoted themselves to a study of this structure and its pottery contents and came to the conclusion independently that it was a Solomonic structure belonging to Stratum VA-IVB. Albright also called attention to the great conflagration by which this building, like others in that stratum, was destroyed; and he held that this destruction could hardly be credited to any other attack than the well-known one of Shishak. More recently this building seems to have been overlooked in an attempt at synthesizing the Solomonic architecture of Megiddo. On Yadin's (1970:Fig. 2) "Plan of Megiddo in the Days of Solomon," Building 10 is dotted rather than hatched which would phase it with Stratum IVA. However, Yadin has communicated privately that this was a mistake on the plan and that this building should be taken with the Stratum VA-IVB city.

The study of the Taanach Cultic Structure pottery in comparison with that from Building 10 indicates the close affinities of the two groups. The typological similarities accord with the stratified situation at both sites in that both groups were embedded in thick destruction debris. Along with L. 2081 from Megiddo, then, Building 10 will be employed as primary comparative evidence. Of special importance are Room 6 and 7 of this building from which the greater amount of pottery came.

HAZOR. LOCI OF STRATUM X.

A second site with a clear relation to Taanach and Megiddo in this period is Hazor. As noted, Yadin's discovery of the city gate and casemate wall at this site helped to open the way for clarifying the Solomonic strata at several sites. The city gate was found to dominate the center of the upper mound, while earlier seasons of excavation had traced the casemate wall up to the gate on the south (Yadin and others 1958:10; 1960:1-3). A follow-up excavation in 1968 uncovered the same wall to the north of the gate where, at its farthest point on the north, it turned westward. This discovery confirmed the view set forth earlier by Yadin that the Solomonic city, designated Stratum X, was largely confined to the western part of the upper mound (Yadin 1969:56-58).

The pottery important for comparative purposes came from loci of the Stratum X city and can sometimes be related to the casemate wall. However, since the latter continued in use in Stratum IX, the pottery remaining from the time of its construction in Stratum X is minimal. There were, nevertheless, several good loci associated with this wall discovered in the 1956 season. These loci (Loci 64c, 116c, 118b, 159b, 174b) were all found on the surface of a pavement along the west side of the wall (Yadin and others 1960:2) and appear to be homogeneous.

During the 1957-1958 seasons, a series of walls appeared on the interior of the city west of the casemate in Squares F-15, G-14, and H-14. A considerable amount of the pottery published from these seasons came from Loci 213c, 200c, 209c, 221c, 202c and 207c, all of which were rooms or areas defined by these walls according to unpublished plans supplied by Yadin. Although discussion of the stratification is not yet available, these seem also to have contained largely homogeneous groups of pottery. The pottery from L. 92a, a structure discovered to the north of the Stratum VIII "Pillared Building" is problematical. Some of the forms suggest parallels with Taanach Period IIB pottery, but others indicate that the groups may be from a slightly later period. The burn layer over this locus was dated to the first part of the ninth century (Yadin and others 1958:10, 22). Thus the pottery from this locus, while it may be utilized for comparative purposes, must be recognized as containing later forms as well.

TELL ᶜAMAL. LOCI 26, 27, 28, 29, 33, 34.

Located near Beth Shan and having regional affinities with Taanach, Tell ᶜAmal is particularly important for comparative purposes. Of the four strata delineated in the recent excavations, Strata III and IV are of special interest. The buildings of these strata were characterized by mud-brick walls laid on foundations of stone. In Strata III and IV a number of rooms were excavated, the most important being Loci 26, 29, and 34 (Levy and Edelstein 1972:330-333, 343). The most significant feature of both strata was the thick, ashy destruction defining them. All buildings had been badly burnt with the result that the pottery groups were well sealed.

A problem arising in the interpretation of these two strata is their differentiation from each other, one which seems to hold up on neither stratigraphic nor typological grounds. Levy and Edelstein (1972:342-343) credited Stratum IV to David, with Stratum III being ascribed to Solomon and its destruction to Shishak. Historically it is difficult to conceive of a major destruction between David and Solomon, and the fact that the walls of Stratum III followed the lines of walls of Stratum IV is suspicious in this case. The pottery also presents difficulties for such a separation since many forms are found in both strata. Furthermore, the largest number of parallels cited for both Stratum III and Stratum IV come from Stratum V at Megiddo and specifically from Building 10 at that site, a PCL for our Period IIB pottery.

These factors point to the probability that much of Strata III and IV at Tell ʿAmal represents a single stratum correlating with Period IIB at Taanach. Typologically there may be several slightly earlier forms, but these do not always coincide with the divisions between Stratum IV and Stratum III as can be seen from the discussion following.

BETH SHAN. LOCUS 1024.

This locus was originally considered to be the courtyard of a fortress, but more recently has been interpreted as a temple (James 1966:33-34). Its cultic nature was emphasized, among other items, by pieces of a cylinder stand encircled by a spotted serpent, a red-burnished fragment apparently from a shrine house, and a limestone "libation tank" of Egyptian style. It is thus an interesting structure to consider in regard to other putative cultic buildings of this period, such as the one at Taanach. The pottery from L. 1024 consisted of a meager eight forms, but they provide the basic stratified group for the definition of Lower Level V at Beth Shan, and they are also closely parallel to Period IIB types at Taanach. The group was sealed under a plastered floor, and its homogeneity is thus assured.

TELL EL-FÂRʿAH (N). LOCUS 418.

The excavations at Tell el-Fârʿah (N) uncovered an occupation designated Niveau III. Of all loci from this stratum, Room 418 of House 436 was of special importance (De Vaux 1955:480). This room contained a hoard of pottery lying in destruction debris on the floor. Like much of the Niveau III pottery at this site, the group corresponds to Period IIB at Taanach, and the destruction may reflect that of Shishak (Wright 1961:111, n. 97).

Additional Comparative Loci and Strata

The sealed groups discussed above are complemented by an abundance of pottery at various sites some of which also comes from carefully defined loci. In addition to the PCL, there are numerous parallels to be found in other groups of Stratum VA-IVB at Megiddo, Stratum X at Hazor, Strata III-IV at Tell ʿAmal, Niveau III at Tell el-Fârʿah (N), and Lower Level V at Beth Shan. Also important for comparison with Taanach are Tell Abu Hawām Stratum III, Stratum IIIA at ʿAfula, and Stratum 3 at Tel Zeror. Remains from this period were also discovered at Tell Abu Qudeis off the road between Taanach and Megiddo (Stern 1969).

Further comparisons can be made with Samaria Periods I and II which have materials extending slightly later, as noted below. The publication of Gezer Stratum 6 (Field II) pottery is incomplete at this writing, but the clarification of the Solomonic gateway and adjoining casemate wall raises the expectation of important material for this period. Southern sites include Arad whose casemate wall (Stratum XI) contained a cache of whole forms (Aharoni 1968:12, Fig. 7), Tell Beit Mirsim B3, and ʿAin Shems Stratum IIb. At Deir ʿAllā in Transjordan, the Phase J material also corresponds most closely to this period. Finally, a number of tombs have comparative material, including Jericho Tomb A85, Tell en-Naṣbeh Tombs 32 and 54, and Lachish Tombs 116, 218, 223 and 521 with Tomb 218 containing pottery closest to that of Period IIB at Taanach.

Date

Because of the special importance of the cache from the Taanach Cultic Structure, the problem of the absolute date of this group demands special attention. The key site for the correlation and dating, as will be noted below, is Megiddo. The resemblance of the L. 2081 and Building 10 pottery to that of the Cultic Structure suggests a close relationship between these structures. Since all three were abruptly destroyed and their contents sealed in destruction layers, it is likely that they were brought to an end by the same series of events. The best known epigraphic evidence bearing upon this destruction is the list of cities subjugated by Shishak on the second pylon of the Amon temple at Karnak, which can be compared to 1 Kgs 14:25-26 and 2 Chr 12:9. In the Egyptian relief, Taanach appears as the first name (No. 14) in the second line while the first name in the third line is Megiddo (No. 27). Mazar has made a strong case for reading the first part of the inscription in *boustrophedon* style (Mazar 1957:60). If his proposal is accepted, Megiddo would follow directly after Taanach, and the list would seem to reflect the route chosen by Shishak as well as the succession of his destruction. The parallel destructions of the whole Stratum VA-IVB city of Megiddo, including L. 2081 and Building 10, and the Cultic Structure at Taanach, might then be credited to this well-attested invasion, just as the same events might also account for destruction levels at other sites mentioned in the list. (Albright 1943:29, n. 10; 38, n. 14). The fragment of a stele of Shishak found at Megiddo by Schumacher is also important evidence in this regard (Lamon and Shipton 1939:61). The consensus on this matter is found, for example, in Yadin (1970:95), Dever and others (1970:63), and James (1966:134-135, 152-53).

In I Kgs 14:25 the date for Shishak's invasion is given as "the fifth year of king Rehoboam." On the date of Rehoboam's accession there is not full agreement, and several solutions have been offered. An early suggestion was that of Mowinckel, who proposed a date of 930, while Begrich placed the event slightly later in 926. Albright (1932:57; 1943:37, n. 13; 1945; 1953b; 1956; also Freedman 1961:209-10) earlier accepted the date of Begrich but subsequently lowered it to 922, the bottom limit for the beginning of the dual monarchy and the date commonly followed at present. At the same time, other scholars continue to hold to a 931/930 date (Thiele 1965: 55; Horn 1967:7-8). According to the former view the attack of Shishak would have taken place about the year 918/917; according to the latter, about 926. Whereas it is recognized that final certainty on this rather small chronological difference is not yet possible, the lower date of 918 is followed in the present study.

Pottery from the Cultic Structure

JARS (FIGS. 30-36)

The Cultic Structure contained many complete as well as partially complete large storage jars. Despite the fact that remains of storage jars appear commonly at excavated Iron Age sites in Palestine, there has been little discussion of the features characterizing their development. Since the Taanach group is closely dated, it may be taken as an important index for the development in such vessels in the north around 918.

With the exception of Fig. 34:2-3 from Room 2, the collection of jars illustrated in Figs. 30-34 all came from Room 1 of the Cultic Structure. Some still contained traces of grain. These jars have either an ovoid body as in Figs. 30-32, (TT 36, 469, 474, 476, 477, 478, 481 and others) or a development toward a bag-shaped body as those in Figs. 33-34 (TT 459, 475, 482, 483 and others). The ovoid type generally has the greatest diameter slightly below the center of the body and tends toward a more pointed base (Figs. 30-31). The bag-shaped jars in Figs. 33-34 reach their largest diameter at an even lower point which is then finished with a rounded base. The tendency toward expansion below the center of the body may be taken as a typological characteristic of the storage jars of this period.

Other features of these jars are the smooth exterior of the body and oval section of the handle. On the latter, Albright pointed to the oval section as a distinguishing feature of Iron I handles in comparison with Iron II jar handles which he observed as being characteristically ribbed (Albright 1932:64, 80). However, as seen below, oval handles also continue in Periods III-IV (Fig. 73:1). Perhaps a more important feature is that in Period IIB handles the upper part of the handle projects horizontally from the carinated or rounded shoulder while in Iron II handles tend to tilt slightly upward (Loud 1948:Pl. 15:76-77; De Vaux 1952:571, Fig. 9:6).

Also noteworthy is the variety of rim forms found on these jars. There are three main rim types: a thickened rim which is cut around the lower outer edge, a profiled rim, and a simple rim. The first is illustrated in Figs. 30-32. An exact parallel to this type is found in PCL 6 of Building 10 at Megiddo (Lamon and Shipton 1939:Pl. 21:123) while similar jars also came from Tell ᶜAmal Stratum IV (Levy and Edelstein 1972:Fig. 8:4), and ᶜAfula Stratum IIIA (M. Dothan 1955: Fig. 11:1-5). The potter's marks found in Fig. 32:2-4 also have close parallels from Stratum V at Megiddo (Lamon and Shipton 1939:Pl. 42:30, 33, 51, 53, 56-58). This rim and jar type may thus be taken as especially characteristic of Period IIB.

Storage jars with profiled rims are found already in Period IIB as Figs. 33 and 34:1-3 show. The handles are the same type as those found in Figs. 30-31, and the body has an even wider diameter below the center with a tendency to a more rounded base. Profiled rim jars were prominent during Iron II down to the sixth century (Lamon and Shipton 1939:Pl. 15:75-77; Yadin and others 1961:Pl. 209:14; De Vaux 1952:571, Fig. 9:6). The examples here show that rims of this type originated by the time of Period IIB. The Period IIB examples differ from those of Iron II, however, in being heavier, rounder and of red to brown color in contrast to the more sharply cut rims on jars of slate-colored ware in the later periods. The same kind of jar is found in Strata IV-III at Tell ᶜAmal (Levy and Edelstein 1972:347, Fig. 8:5-10), and one at Tel Zeror may also belong to this earlier period (Ohata, ed., 1966:Pl. 9:2). An example attributed to Megiddo Strata IV-III is probably to be reassigned to Stratum VA-IVB by comparison with the Taanach jars (Lamon and Shipton 1939:Pl. 14:70). A further example is found in Stratum X at Hazor (Yadin and others 1960:Pl. 51:18-19) while the late tenth-century group from the casemate wall at Arad has a profiled rim on a restored bag-shaped jar (Aharoni 1968:12, Fig. 7, bottom left). Finally, at Deir ᶜAllā a whole series of such rims is found in Phase J (Franken and Kalsbeek 1969:Fig. 70:19-30).

The bag-shaped jars with simple rim, TT 475 and 459 in Fig. 34:4-5, have close parallels in two jars from PCL Room 6 of Building 10 at Megiddo (Lamon and Shipton 1939:Pl. 20:120-121). A further example assigned to Megiddo Stratum VA can be compared with TT 475 (Loud 1948:Pl. 147:1). It has a buff surface and dark core similar to the Taanach jar. A smaller example was found in Stratum IV at Tell ᶜAmal (Levy and Edelstein 1972:347, Fig. 8:3). The jar with simple rim from the casemate wall at Arad also belongs to this type (Aharoni 1968:12, Fig. 7, bottom middle).

The storage jar with collared rim, TT 1866 in Fig. 35:1, is of special importance since it came from a clearly stratified context. This jar provides firm evidence for storage jars with short collars down to Period IIB. The view that the collared rim ceased to be found after the mid-eleventh century consequently needs modification. As noted earlier (Chapter 3), two types of collared rims were found in Period I, a jar with a long collar and a thick rim, and one with a shorter collar and a less massive rim. The first apparently terminated by the end of Period IB, while the second continued into Period II, as evidenced by the example here.

These data from Taanach help to clarify information from several other sites. An example of a collared rim from Period I at Samaria is close to this example from the Cultic Structure and can be taken as a further illustration of this type at the end of Iron I (Kenyon 1957:100, Fig. 1:16). Whether and how far the collared rim continued into Iron II remains to be clarified by future excavation. One is ascribed to Stratum VIII at Tell Qasile (Maisler [Mazar] 1951a:199,Fig. 10:c). An example attributed to Strata IV-III at Megiddo is problematic and probably has to be reassigned to Stratum VIA or earlier (Lamon and Shipton 1939:Pl. 17:86). Similarly, the collared rim in Stratum V at Hazor may be intrusive, belonging more likely to Stratum X material since it is close in form to the Cultic Structure jar (Yadin and others 1958:Pl. 57:8, same as Pl. 62:3).

The cylindrical jar, TT 460 in Fig. 35:2, is the prototype of a jar which became prominent in Iron II during which time the body was not so deep as the earlier examples. The best parallel to the one here is an almost identical cylindrical jar from Tell ᶜAmal Stratum IV (Levy and Edelstein 1972:347, Fig. 8:2). Parallels from other sites are scarce, but these two examples show that this jar was present in the north by the time of Period IIB.

Small jars from the Cultic Structure are found in Fig. 36. The two spouted examples, TT 467 and 490 in Fig. 36:1-2, are similar in form, but differ in exterior decoration in that TT 467 is horizontally and vertically burnished over a red slip while TT 490 has a plain, unburnished surface. Evidence for this type of spouted jar was noted already in Period IA (Fig. 26:1), but the form becomes particularly prominent in Period IIB. The body appears to undergo some modifications during the two periods. In Period IIA, as noted above, the body tends to be more depressed while by the time of Period IIB its shape has become rounder. An example from PCL Room 6 of Building 10 at Megiddo has a rounder body in comparison with earlier Stratum VIA spouted jars with more depressed bodies (Lamon and Shipton 1939:Pl. 19:106; Loud 1948:Pl. 77:12-13). The evidence in development is thus quite similar at Megiddo. Three jars with spouts are ascribed to Stratum IV at Tell ᶜAmal (Levy and Edelstein 1972:353, Fig. 11:1-2, 4). Two are covered with a red slip, one is burnished, and a third is unburnished. All three have more rounded rather than bloated bodies suggesting a correspondence to Period IIB. An example with painted decoration is also found in Periods I and II at Samaria and is similar to the Taanach jars (Kenyon 1957:103, Fig. 2:1).

The amphora, TT 350 in Fig. 36:3, belongs to a vessel which has an interesting development. The example here is entirely preserved and has a vertically burnished pink-to-orange slip. The neck is vertical with some thickening of the rim. The base is rounded and slightly pointed.

A close parallel from PCL 418 at Tell el-Fârᶜah (N) is especially important (De Vaux 1955:577, Fig. 16:10). The latter example and the one from Taanach are nearly analogous in form, the Tell el-Fârᶜah amphora displaying similar burnishing techniques over a red slip. Both examples also have a more rounded base which may be a feature with chronological significance contrasting with more pointed or knobbed bases of Iron II amphorae. At Megiddo three amphorae were discovered in the debris of PCL Rooms 6-7 of Building 10, and all have more or less rounded bases (Lamon and Shipton 1939:Pls. 19:114, 22:130-131).

By contrast, Iron II amphorae with pointed or knobbed bases are present at many sites. An amphora from Samaria has a sharply pointed base and apparently belongs to Periods V and VI although its stratified position was not certain (Crowfoot 1957:170, Fig. 23:1). The examples at Tell en-Naṣbeh seem to be from Iron II contexts and represent this same tendency toward a knobbed or pointed base (Wampler 1947:Pls. 26:438-442, 27:443). This holds also for Lachish where amphorae from Tombs 1002 and 106 contained knobbed bases (Tufnell 1953:Pl. 91:424-425). At Tell Beit Mirsim this distinction between late Iron I and Iron II amphorae received confirmation. All the examples presented from this site are of the knobbed variety and belong to Stratum A (Albright 1932:Pls. 53:7-12, 54:5-10). Finally, in a tomb at Munshara near Samaria, dated between 850-800 on typological grounds, four amphorae were found among the tomb gifts. It is noteworthy that three of them have bases more pointed than Taanach's example, and one of them is of the knobbed type (Zayadine 1968:569, Fig. 1:3-6, Pl. 60:2-4).

A second example of an amphora is Fig. 36:4. This vessel is larger then the previous one but has the same characteristics of long neck and oval-sectioned handles attached to the body. The rim, however, is plain and thickened compared to the thickened, flat rim of Fig. 36:3. Like the latter, it is burnished horizontally and vertically over a dark red slip. Unfortunately the bottom part was not recovered, but it may have been rounded like the previous example.

Small jars of the type in Fig. 36:5 are found in late tenth-century contexts at other sites such as Stratum VA at Megiddo (Loud 1948:Pl. 89:1-2; Lamon and Shipton 1939:Pl. 19:107). Although not an exact parallel, a small jar at Megiddo is particularly interesting to compare with the Taanach example. It was found in the hoard in PCL Room 6 of Building 10 (Lamon and Shipton 1939:Pl. 22:129). It is burnished over a red slip and has a more rounded body than the one from Taanach.

JUGS (FIGS. 37-39)

An unburnished jug, TT 103 in Fig. 37:1, is a well-made vessel with rounded, thickened rim and a profiled neck. A similar jug was found in PCL Room 6 of Building 10 at Megiddo (Lamon and Shipton 1939:Pl. 7:174). Fig. 37:2, TT 440, represents the Palestinian version of the oenochoe (Crowfoot 1957:168). It is possible that the example here, and several broken specimens and rims in Cistern L. 74 (Fig. 59:4-7) are some of the earliest examples of this type of vessel to be found in Palestine.

POTTERY GROUPS OF PERIOD IIB

These vessels are found fairly frequently in Iron II at which time the neck is narrower with a more flaring rim and trefoil mouth (Lamon and Shipton 1939:Pl. 3:83-86; Crowfoot 1957:166, Fig. 22:9; Zayadine 1968:573, Fig. 3:4). The Iron Age tomb at Munshara near Samaria contained a vessel of this kind still quite close to the Taanach form but with a pronounced pinched lip more typical of Iron II (Zayadine 1968:573, Fig. 3:1). Also closer to the Taanach example is one from Megiddo assigned a range from Stratum IV-III (Lamon and Shipton 1939:Pl. 3:88). A rim attributed to Stratum X at Hazor may also come from a vessel of this type (Yadin and others 1960:Pl. 51:15). Since known examples are thus far from northern sites, it may be suggested that foreign influence in the production of this jug type was largely confined to north Palestine.

The two jugs, TT 454 and 470 in Fig. 38:1-2, are identical in form, the first being somewhat larger than the second. The globular body is like that of the profiled jug in Fig. 37:1. The rim is slightly thickened and incurved and lightly pinched. No exact parallels were found but comparisons can be made with a jug with incurved rim from Cistern L. 74 (Fig. 60:1). Several shorter incurved jug rims of this type were also found in the Cistern L. 74 group (Fig. 61:8-11). These jugs are variants of a rather common jug type, one which employed a variety of rims on a simple, globular body, during the latter part of Iron I and the beginning of Iron II. Jugs from Beth-zur (Funk 1968:Fig. 8:1), PCL Room 6 of Building 10 at Megiddo (Lamon and Shipton 1939:Pl. 8:178) and Munshara (Zayadine 1968:571, Fig. 2:3, 5) illustrate the general type.

The jug rim and handle in Fig. 39:1 is similar to the preceding two whole jugs but its neck is narrower and shorter like two rims from Cistern L. 74 (Fig. 62:2-3). These jugs resemble the cooking pot with handles from this period although the latter usually had a wider mouth (Fig. 67:3-4; Lamon and Shipton 1939:Pl. 5:118-119, probably cooking pots and not jugs). Two jugs of this general type, but with a more incurved rim, were found in the casemate wall at Arad (Aharoni 1968:12, Fig. 7, Nos. 3 and 4, second row).

Fig. 39:2, TT 468, is a well-preserved example of a jug with a red slip exhibiting both horizontal and vertical hand-burnishing. Decoration was achieved by omitting the burnish in small blocks around the bottom side of the jug. The form is striking, the body being nearly spherical. The long neck and flaring rim give the vessel an unusually graceful shape. Only one close parallel could be found for this jug elsewhere, and that was a jug from PCL 418 at Tell el-Fârᶜah (N) (De Vaux 1955:577, Fig. 16:12). In reporting on the latter jug, De Vaux (1955:580) called attention to the lack of parallels. The Taanach jug, however, provides an example of a similar vessel.

The two jugs, TT 414 and 83 in Fig. 39:4, 6, are unique. Both are hand burnished, TT 414 displaying vertical and horizontal burnishing, and TT 83 vertical burnishing. TT 414 has very thin ware much like the bowls in Fig. 48:15-19. Especially noteworthy are the unevenly spaced decorative buttons on the inside of the top part of the neck, three of which are preserved. No parallel for this vessel could be found, but its fine manufacture and design suggest that it was not an ordinary vessel. TT 83 appears to be a variant of a jug type found also in PCL 2081 at Megiddo. Here a fine, hand-burnished vessel made of thin ware like TT 414 was found in an apparently cultic context (Loud 1948:Pl. 88:1; see also 44, Fig. 102). TT 83 is quite similar except that it has a disc base in comparison to the rounded base of the Megiddo example. Similar vessels with rounded base are found in the ninth century at Samaria and the nearby Munshara tomb (Kenyon 1957:111, Fig. 5:4; Zayadine 1968:573, Fig. 3:3).

JUGLETS AND PYXIDES (FIG. 40)

Fig. 40 contains the variety of juglets found in the Cultic Structure. Of special importance is juglet TT 63 with ridged neck in Fig. 40:1. This juglet was badly weathered, but it was possible to observe the dark painted bands on the body below the rim as well as the vertical burnishing over a light red-to-tan slip. No exact parallels to this vessel could be found although it has resemblances to several somewhat larger jugs (Loud 1948:Pl. 88:15; Lamon and Shipton 1939:Pl. 7:172; Grant and Wright 1938:Pl. 65:42). The best explanation may be that it is a local imitation of the Cypriot Black-on-Red I (III) juglet found in considerable abundance at various Palestinian sites during this period. Examples of such imported juglets are found in PCL Rooms 6 and 7 of Building 10 at Megiddo (Lamon and Shipton 1939:Pl. 5:123) as well as PCL 2081 at the same site (Loud 1948:Pl. 89:6). Others were present in L. 92A at Hazor (Yadin and others 1958:Pl. 46:1), at Tell en-Naṣbeh (Wampler 1947:Pl. 43:873), and in Stratum B3 at Tell Beit Mirsim (Albright 1932:Pl. 51:9). At Taanach an actual Cypriot import of this type was also found but in a poorly stratified context (TT 604, Fig. 93:5). As a local imitation TT 63 from the Cultic Structure does not achieve the fine throw in the handle exhibited by the originals, nor is its decorative treatment as elegant. If the interpretation of this juglet is correct, it fits well as a vessel in the late tenth century.

The juglet fragment in Fig. 40:2 also represents a good late tenth-century form. It is closely paralleled by a Stratum V example at Megiddo which is also hand burnished over a red slip (Lamon and Shipton 1939:Pl. 5:137). Fig. 40:3, TT 386, has hand-burnishing over a red slip and is decorated with dark bands as TT 63. Like the latter, it also has a ridged neck. The best parallel to this juglet is one assigned to Stratum V at Megiddo (Lamon and Shipton 1939:Pl. 5:135) which also has a ridged neck and is vertically hand-burnished over a red slip, but lacks banded decoration.

The small, burnished, piriform juglets, TT 327, 306, 88 in Fig. 40:4-6 are of the same type as a black-burnished juglet from PCL 418 at Tell el-Fârᶜah (N) (De Vaux 1955:577, Fig. 16:5) and a similar one from PCL Rooms 6-7 of Building 10 at Megiddo (Lamon and Shipton 1939:Pl. 5:126). These all have their handles attached below the rim on the neck, a characteristic distinguishing them from Iron II juglets with handles nearly all the way to the rim (Albright 1932:71; De Vaux 1952:561). Besides the parallels from Tell el-Fârᶜah (N) and Megiddo, these juglets have numerous parallels from late tenth-century contexts at other sites such as Tomb 54 at Tell en-Naṣbeh and Tomb 521 at Lachish (Wampler 1947:Pl. 41:804-805, 42:843; Tufnell 1953: Pl. 88:328).

The dipper juglet, TT 62, in Fig. 40:7 has a rounded base typical of Iron I. The lip is lightly pinched in contrast to the more heavily pinched lips of Iron II. It is also continuously burnished over a red slip on the exterior. A good parallel is a juglet from Stratum VA at Megiddo which also is vertically burnished over a red slip (Lamon and Shipton 1938:Pl. 5:120). Other late tenth century parallels are found in Phase I at Deir ᶜAllā (Franken and Kalsbeek 1969:Fig. 70:52), Jericho Tomb A 85 (Kenyon 1965:488, Fig. 253:18), and Lachish Tombs 116 and 218 (Tufnell 1953:Pl. 88:285). The latter two are also hand-burnished over a red slip, and the lip is slightly pinched.

The fragment in Fig. 40:8 is the bottom of a cylindrical juglet, the closest parallel for which is a juglet from PCL 2081 at Megiddo (Loud 1948:Pl. 88:13). Fig. 40:9-11, TT 458, 466 and 484 are also dipper juglets but with squatter bodies than TT 62. The closest parallels to TT 458 are juglets assigned to Stratum VB at Megiddo and Stratum IIb at ᶜAin Shems (Loud 1948:Pl. 87:14; Grant and Wright 1938:Pl. 66:37). TT 484 is paralleled by an example from PCL Rooms 6-7 of Building 10 at Megiddo (Lamon and Shipton 1939:Pl. 5:121).

Fig. 40:12-14, TT 488, 372 and 73 are pyxides with pierced lug handles, all examples here being closely hand burnished over a brown or tan surface. These locally made vessels belong to the end of a development which, in its earliest and most original stage, was associated with the Mycenaean tradition. During the Late Bronze Age Mycenaean pyxides made their way as imports to such Palestinian sites as Tell Abu Hawām (Hamilton 1935:46, No. 283). Already toward the end of Late Bronze, local imitations were manufactured as examples from Stratum C at Tell Beit Mirsim attest (Albright 1932:Pl. 44:4, 47:9). The typical Iron I imitation is often small and more crudely constructed.

The Taanach pyxides are closely paralleled by late Iron I examples from other sites. TT 488 has a slightly out-turned rim and is most closely approximated by an example from Stratum V at Megiddo (Lamon and Shipton 1939:Pl. 19:95). The form appears earlier, however, as is apparent in an almost identical pyxis assigned to Strata VIIB-VI at Megiddo (Loud 1948:Pl. 68:7). A similar pyxis was discovered in a fill in a square next to the Cultic Structure (TT 66; Fig. 92:7). TT 372 and 73 are both characterized by a bowed neck but the body on the latter is more squat. These examples can be compared with several from Tell Beit Mirsim Stratum B3 (Albright 1932:Pl. 51:5), Tell el-Fârᶜah (N) Niveau III (De Vaux 1955:579, Fig. 17:6) as well as a number from Tombs 32 and 54 at Tell en-Naṣbeh (Wampler 1947:Pl. 74:1695, 1698, 1706).

CRATER (FIG. 41)

The large crater, TT 489, in Fig. 41 was the most spectacular vessel to come from the Cultic Structure. It was lying in the massive destruction of the building and was partly filled with a group of perforated clay balls (Lapp 1964:28). The crater has eight handles which are attached approximately at the bottom of the rim and at the carination of the shoulder. The rim is thickened and flattened and overlaps on both the exterior and interior. There is a collar on the shoulder midway between the carination and the rim, and the vessel rests on a heavy ring base.

The most striking parallel to this crater is one from PCL Room 6 of Building 10 at Megiddo (Lamon and Shipton 1939:Pl. 21:125). This vessel has a collar on the neck and a carinated shoulder, both features almost identical to the Taanach crater. Its eight handles are shaped and placed on the shoulder and neck in a fashion similar to the Taanach crater. The clearest difference between them is that the Megiddo crater is finished with incised rope and ring decoration on the neck. Similar vessels were found in Tomb 37E at Megiddo (Guy and Engberg 1938:Pl. 39:13) and at Lachish (Tufnell 1953:Pl. 82:124). A further parallel from several centuries earlier is the large crater found in an apparent cultic context at Hazor (Yadin and others 1961:Pls. 122:1, 4; 280:12; 303:9). This example was found in the "Holy of Holies," L. 2113 in Area H, ascribed to Stratum 1A and attributed to the end of LB II. It was discovered together with other cultic furniture such as an altar, a basin and a basalt libation table. It is noteworthy that the Hazor crater has the top part of its handles attached to the rim in contrast to the later Taanach crater. It also has a flat base in comparison to the ring base of the Taanach vessel.

LARGE BOWLS (FIGS. 42-44)

Figs. 42:1-4 and 43:1-4 may be taken together since they are characterized by a similar thickened rim and carinated shoulder. All examples have ring bases typical of the latter part of Iron I. At the same time, all have hand-burnished red slip on the entire interior and only on the rim on the exterior. These characteristics are also found on the smallest example, TT 451, Fig. 43:2. It is probable that this bowl type developed from the common deep bowl or crater of Period I (Fig. 7:1-5), the older type still being made in Period IIB, although not as prominently as the new red-slipped, burnished bowls of Period II. Similar evidence is present in Stratum V at Megiddo (Lamon and Shipton 1939:Pl. 31:158).

Good parallels to Figs. 42-43 are found at Megiddo. The first is an almost identical large deep bowl from PCL Rooms 6-7 of Building 10 (Lamon and Shipton 1939:Pl. 29:110). This bowl, like those from Taanach, has a red slip on the interior up to and including the thickened rim. The Megiddo bowl is closest in form to Fig. 42:4, and 43:2, TT 479 and 451. Also similar to TT 479 is a bowl from Tell el-Fârᶜah (N) which can be assigned a date in the late tenth century (De Vaux 1955:585, Fig. 19:14). A further parallel comes from Megiddo Tomb 76A, an example close to TT

POTTERY GROUPS OF PERIOD IIB

439 (Guy and Engberg 1938:Pl. 74:16; see Lamon and Shipton 1939: Pls. 31:153, 32:161, 163).

The two examples in Fig. 44:1-2 represent a variant of this bowl type in that they possess a ridge below the rim. Like the other bowls they also have a hand-burnished slip on the interior to the rim. No exact parallels for these could be found, but deep bowls from two different sites are similar to this type. The first is a bowl from Phase H at Deir ᶜAllā (Franken and Kalsbeek 1969:Fig. 68:2). The Deir ᶜAllā bowl has a thickened rim and carinated shoulder like the Taanach examples as well as a crudely fashioned ridge below the rim. A second parallel is an unburnished bowl from Megiddo Stratum V (Lamon and Shipton 1939: Pl. 29:111). The rim of this bowl is not as thick as the Taanach examples, but it has a ridge below the rim.

Fig. 44:3, TT 461, seems to be a simplified variant of the type just discussed. It has the same carinated shoulder as the former bowls, but lacks the curved neck and thickened rim. In this case the neck and rim are simply constructed. Following the surface treatment techniques typical of Period IIB, this bowl has a red slip on the interior and on the exterior shoulder to the point of carination while the shoulder only is hand burnished both on the interior and exterior. Almost the same treatment is found in a parallel bowl with simple rim from PCL 2081 at Megiddo (Loud 1948:Pl. 89:14). The red slip on the latter is carried over to only part of the exterior, and burnishing is vertical on the interior and horizontal on the exterior shoulder.

One of the most interesting bowls from the Cultic Structure is TT 487, Fig. 44:4. In contrast to the preceding types, this is a shallower bowl, but it is especially striking because of its large size. No parallels to this large bowl could be found, and it may have been strictly a local form. A vessel from Deir ᶜAllā, described as a "mensif" bowl can be compared although it is not exactly parallel (Franken and Kalsbeek 1969:Fig. 76:3, Pl. XV).

Fig. 44:5 is also a shallow bowl, but larger than the medium to small-sized bowls which follow. It has the overlapped, flat rim typical of many smaller bowls of this period and like them is hand burnished on the interior to the point of carination on the exterior shoulder. A similar bowl, lacking the overlapped rim on the interior, is found in PCL Room 6 of Building 10 at Megiddo (Lamon and Shipton 1939:Pl. 30:116). The latter example is hand burnished over a red slip on the interior and rim. That the form continued into Iron II is evidenced by an unburnished but decorated example from Stratum VIII at Hazor (Yadin and others 1958:Pl. 47:9).

MEDIUM AND SMALL BURNISHED BOWLS (FIGS. 45-48)

The Cultic Structure contained a large group of medium and small bowls, almost all of which display a distinctive form of hand burnishing. In none of these bowls is there evidence of the close parallel lines of the ring burnishing of Iron II. Rather, burnishing is done with uneven lines when it is applied horizontally or vertical or criss-cross lines when it is applied on the interior bottom of the bowl. Usually the burnishing is performed over a red slip, but occasionally the latter has a red to orange or brown color. This slip is commonly applied over the entire interior, extending over the rim to the carination or rounding on the shoulder. The majority of these small to medium bowls also has a ring base, although the smaller bowls in Fig. 48 occasionally have a disc or round base. For the sake of convenience the bowls are grouped by rim types, and five basic categories are considered: bowls with simple rims; slightly thickened rims; cut rims; thickened, flat rims; and saucer bowls with simple rims.

The two bowls, TT 485 and 445, in Fig. 45:1-2 have simple rims. That of TT 485 is bowed slightly in comparison to TT 445, and it is brought to a point at the tip. Each bowl has a hand-burnished slip on the interior over the rim to the carination of the shoulder. Close parallels to these bowls are found in PCL Room 6 of Building 10 at Megiddo (Lamon and Shipton 1939:Pl. 30:120, 126) with a close parallel to TT 485 being a Stratum IIb bowl from ᶜAin Shems (Grant and Wright 1938:Pl. 66:12). An unburnished bowl from Tomb A85 at Jericho is also of this type (Kenyon 1965:Pl. 253:2). Further examples from a slightly later time are found in Tomb 54 at Tell en-Naṣbeh (Wampler 1947:Pl. 55:1243) and at Samaria during Periods I and II (Kenyon 1957:100, Fig. 1:4 and 108, Fig. 4:10).

In Fig. 45:3-9, TT 416, 415, 464 and others, are various bowls which have slightly thickened rims. In several cases they approximate the form of the bowls in Fig. 46, the difference being that they do not have the characteristic cut rim of the latter. These bowls display the same technique of hand burnishing as Fig. 45:1-2 except that Fig. 45:3, 5 and 6 are burnished over a brown or red slip only to the top of the rim. A close parallel to TT 416 is a bowl from a silo group at ᶜAin Shems attributed to Stratum IIb (Grant and Wright 1938: Pl. 66:27). The ᶜAin Shems example has a spirally burnished red slip over the rim to the interior which is similar to the treatment of the Taanach bowl. TT 415 has slight variations but belongs to the same type. The three bowls in Fig. 45:5-7 can be compared with an example from PCL Room 6 of Building 10 at Megiddo (Lamon and Shipton 1939:Pl. 28:98). The latter has a carinated shoulder like the Taanach bowls and a similar surface treatment. The bowl sherd in Fig. 45:8 is close in form to a bowl from PCL Room 6 of Building 10 at Megiddo (Lamon and Shipton 1939:Pl. 28:106). The Megiddo bowl also has similar burnishing over a red slip on the interior to the exterior carination of the shoulder. Fig. 45:9 has close parallels in a bar-handled bowl from Hazor PCL 159b (Yadin and others 1960:Pl. 51:6) as well as a bowl from Niveau III at Tell el-Fârᶜah (N) (De Vaux 1952:563, Fig. 6:18).

The most distinguishing characteristic of the bowls in Fig. 46:1-15, 17 is that each has a sharply cut, flat rim sometimes slightly thickened. The majority of these bowls also has a marked carination on the shoulder, and is commonly hand burnished over a red slip on the interior to the exterior carination of the shoulder. Exceptions are TT 442, Fig. 46:13, which is continuously burnished over a red slip on the interior to the top of the rim, and Fig. 46:9 and 17, which are hand burnished over the entire interior and exterior.

The most striking parallel to these bowls is one from PCL 2081 at Megiddo (Loud 1948:Pl. 89:10). This carinated, cut-rim bowl has irregular burnishing over a red slip on the interior to the shoulder on the exterior. It is in every respect identical to the Taanach bowls having its closest analogies in Fig. 46:3, 7 and 12, TT 453, 450 and 455. To the same type of cut-rim bowl belongs a bowl assigned to Stratum IIb at ᶜAin Shems (Grant and Wright 1938: Pl. 66:6). This bowl is ring burnished over a red slip on the interior and rim and has grooving below the exterior of the rim. It is closest in form to Fig. 46:8, TT 441 and Fig. 46:14, TT 452. A number of unburnished bowls at Lachish represent a slightly later development of this type such as one from Cave 1002 dated between the late ninth and eighth centuries (Tufnell 1953:Pl. 79:9). Two bowls from mixed deposits at Samaria likewise fit this type and are attributed to Periods I and II (Crowfoot 1957:151, Fig. 17:4, 5). They are closest in form to Fig. 46:13, TT 442, and Fig. 46:14, TT 452 but may be slightly later since they are hand burnished over a red slip on the entire interior and exterior. A bowl with cut rim at Hazor is mistakenly attributed to Stratum III and should be reassigned a late tenth-century date (Yadin and others 1958:Pl. 76:14). The small bowl sherd in Fig. 46:17 has several important parallels. Similar forms are found in Phase J at Deir ᶜAllā (Franken and Kalsbeek 1969:Fig. 70:9), and in Stratum IIb at ᶜAin Shems (Grant and Wright 1938:Pl. 66:11). The latter has a red slip on the entire interior and exterior but is unburnished. A further red-slipped, burnished bowl sherd, assigned to Hazor Stratum IXB, may be compared with these examples (Yadin and others 1961:Pl. 175:3).

Fig. 47:1-5 contains a group of medium-sized bowls all of which have flat, thickened rims. All examples have hand burnishing over a red or red to brown slip which extends from the interior to the exterior carination. The bowls were made with great care, and the burnishing was carefully done.

Fig. 47:1, TT 449, belongs to the class of bowls with spatulate bar handles. The horizontal bar occupies more than one-third of the circumference of the bowl, and at each end is a pinched vertical knob ("nail-head") which is positioned approximately 5 mm. below the flattened top of the rim. A close parallel to this bowl is an irregularly burnished example found in PCL 2081 at Megiddo (Loud 1948:Pl. 147:8; description under Pl. 90:4). A further example at Megiddo also approximates this form and should probably be assigned to the Stratum VA-IVB horizon (Lamon and Shipton 1939:Pl. 24:39). An unburnished bar-handled bowl with a different rim form was also found on the pavement near the casemate wall in PCL 159b at Hazor (Yadin and others 1960:Pl. 51:6). At ᶜAin Shems the type was represented in a number of hand-burnished, red-slipped examples, and Wright referred to it as a typical bowl in Stratum IIa and the early part of Stratum IIb (Grant and Wright 1938:Pl. 63:15-22).

This bowl type is found at Taanach as early as the twelfth century (Fig. 17:4). Similarly in Megiddo Stratum VIIA, an unburnished bowl displays a handle of this type (Loud 1948:Pl. 69:6). Parallel evidence has also appeared at Deir ᶜAllā where unburnished bar-handled bowls begin in Phase B (Franken and Kalsbeek 1969:Fig. 50:15, 51, 86) and continue through subsequent phases until burnished examples take over in Phases H and J (Franken and Kalsbeek 1969:Figs. 66:61, 70:2-3). The distinguishing feature during the tenth century, therefore, is the continued use of this handle on new types of burnished bowls. Bar handles also continued to be used on bowls well into Iron II as evidenced at Megiddo and Hazor (Lamon and Shipton 1939:Pl. 24:36-38; Yadin and others 1958:Pls. 47:14; 51:21, 23). The suggestion made by Tufnell that earlier handles are farther from the rim and that the handles move closer to the rim on later examples does not appear to be substantiated (Tufnell 1953:265; see Sinclair 1960:21). In fact, the Period IB example from Taanach mentioned above is quite close to the rim while several Iron II examples have the bar handle considerably lower on the shoulder (Lamon and Shipton 1939:Pl. 24:37-38). The position of the handle on the bowl seems to be dictated more by local preference, and it is necessary to look to other features such as rim or body form, surface treatment and decoration for characteristics distinguishing these bowls in different periods.

Fig. 47:2-3, TT 352 and 412, represent a common bowl of the latter part of Iron I. They are closely paralleled by a bowl from PCL 2081 at Megiddo (Loud 1948:Pl. 89:9) which is nearly identical in rim and body form and in its red-slipped burnishing. The same form is present at ᶜAin Shems in Stratum IIb-c (Grant and Wright 1938:Pl. 66:15). The latter example has a brown slip inside and over the rim, but is unburnished. A similar burnished example is present among Phase K material at Deir ᶜAllā (Franken and Kalsbeek 1969:Fig. 72:11). That this type persisted into the first part of Iron II is evident from a Stratum IX bowl at Hazor which has a high ring base and is well-burnished on the interior and exterior (Yadin and others 1961:Pl. 208:27).

The slightly different bowls with out-turned, flat rims in Fig. 47:4-5 also have several good parallels. A similar bowl rim comes from PCL 221c at Hazor (Yadin and others 1961:Pl. 174:8), and a further one comes from PCL Room 6 of Building 10 at Megiddo (Lamon and Shipton 1939:Pl. 30:130). Slightly later examples are found in Stratum VIII at Hazor (Yadin and others 1960:Pl. 54:11) and in Stratum A at Tell Beit Mirsim (Albright 1932:Pl. 65:20b).

Fig. 48:1-19 contains a large collection of small bowls. Those in Fig. 48:1-14 are somewhat thicker while those in Fig. 48:15-19 are thin, delicately constructed bowls. Fig. 48:1-14 usually have flaring rims and shoulders which often have a cyma profile. They also possess a round or

POTTERY GROUPS OF PERIOD IIB

flattened and sometimes small disc bases such as Fig. 48:1-3. The most important parallel to the latter three bowls is found in PCL 2081 at Megiddo (Loud 1948:Pl. 89:13). The form of this cyma-profiled bowl at Megiddo is nearly identical to that of TT 443, Fig. 48:3, and its surface treatment is the same as that of the Taanach bowls. A decorated, unburnished example is also found in Stratum V at Megiddo (Lamon and Shipton 1939:Pl. 31:144). At ᶜAin Shems two examples were assigned to Stratum IIb both being closely burnished over a red slip on the interior to the point of carination on the exterior (Grant and Wright 1938:Pl. 63:11, 12). An unburnished rim of a smaller bowl from Phase L at Deir ᶜAllā also belongs to this type (Franken and Kalsbeek 1969:Fig. 75:8). This bowl type continues in Iron II during which time the rim is more flaring as evidenced by examples from Period VII at Samaria (Kenyon 1957:126, Fig. 11:9, 11-15) and Stratum II at Beth-zur (Lapp and Lapp 1968:Fig. 18:1-4).

The thin, plate-like bowls with tapered rims in Fig. 48:15-19 are made of fine, tan ware and are continuously burnished over a red slip on the entire interior and exterior. A close parallel is found at Megiddo in PCL 2081 (Loud 1948:Pl. 89:11), and a further example from Megiddo probably belongs to the Stratum VA-IVB horizon (Lamon and Shipton 1939:Pl. 28:93b). This type also continued into the first part of Iron II as evidenced by a bowl from Stratum IX at Hazor (Yadin and others 1961:Pl. 208:25) and one from Period III at Samaria (Kenyon 1957:108, Fig. 4:9).

COOKING POTS (FIGS. 49-50)

Two types of cooking pot are found in Figs. 49-50: one, a shallow type with open mouth and carinated side in Fig. 49:1-3, and the other a globular, jug-like type with a handle in TT 456, 472, 65, Fig. 50:1-3. The first type is characterized by the elongated rim found already in Period IB. The second is not so common judging from the smaller number of published examples. Its body is usually rounded, the handle running from the side to the rim. It resembles the one-handled jug with very similar form from the same period (De Vaux 1955:577, Fig. 16:3), but it has a longer neck, and its ware contains many tiny crystalline inclusions.

An area near L. 2081 (S=2081) at Megiddo contained a cooking pot of the same kind as Fig. 49:1 (Loud 1948:Pl. 90:5). This type is exceedingly common at various late Iron I sites in Palestine, and the group from Cistern L. 74 at Taanach contained a large number of them (Fig. 66). For the one-handled cooking pots in Fig. 50:1-3 the closest parallel comes from Tell Abu Hawām Stratum III (Hamilton 1935:22, No. 80). This pot is listed as a jug, but the description suggests it may have been a cooking vessel since it is burned on the underside. A similar example from PCL Rooms 6-7 of Building 10 at Megiddo is listed as a jug, but is probably a cooking vessel (Lamon and Shipton 1939:Pl. 5:119). A later example from Megiddo is attributed to Strata III-II (Lamon and Shipton 1939:Pl. 5:118), and it is this globular vessel that developed into the dominant type during Iron II.

LAMPS, CENSER, AND STAND (FIG. 51)

The lamps in Plate 51:1-2, TT 89 and 473, are typical for the end of Iron I. The base, common on lamps during Iron II, is flattened with some tendency toward becoming rounded. The rims of lamps in Period IIB also tend to a wider flange than in the earlier periods. An excellent parallel to these lamps comes from the two PCL at Megiddo, Room 6 of Building 10 and L. 2081 (Lamon and Shipton 1939:Pl. 38:19; Loud 1948: see under Pl. 90:9). Two further parallels are also found in Megiddo Tomb 76A (Guy and Engberg 1938:Pl. 74:23-24). Finally, a lamp from Niveau III at Tell el-Fârᶜah (N) has much the same form (De Vaux 1952:563, Fig. 6:9).

The vessel, TT 64 in Fig. 51:3, belongs to a class of small, perforated cups set on a tripod base. The Taanach example has a sharp carination at the shoulder and three lines of perforations. Many parallels are present at other sites, and these may be classified as examples with or without handles. The Taanach vessel belongs to the latter type. A good parallel to the Taanach example comes from PCL 64c at Hazor (Yadin and others 1960:Pl. 51:17). The sherd of this small vessel is listed as a jug, but it has similar lines of perforations on the shoulder. The neck resembles the one from Taanach, and it was also apparently without handles. Other examples without handles come from Megiddo Stratum V and from tombs at Lachish (Lamon and Shipton 1939:Pl. 31:146; Tufnell 1953:Pl. 90:380-381). Perforated vessels of this type with handles have been found at many sites both east and west of the Jordan River. At Tell el-Fârᶜah an example with two lug handles was found in Niveau III (De Vaux 1951:411, Fig. 10:16), and another with a single handle came from the period between Niveau III and Niveau II (De Vaux 1955:585, Fig. 19:1). Two examples at Hazor were found in Stratum XB, and one had a handle (Yadin and others 1961:Pl. 171:16-17). Other examples with handles are found well into Iron II at sites such as Megiddo (Lamon and Shipton 1939:Pl. 23:20-24) and Hazor (Yadin and others 1958:Pls. 49:31, 51:30). Several excavations have indicated the prominence of this vessel at sites to the east of the Jordan River (Glueck 1967:30-38; Pritchard 1969). A hoard of them appeared in an Iron Age tomb in the Wadi Afrit near Mount Nebo, all having handles (Saller 1966:206-207, Figs. 15, 16). An Iron II tomb near Amman also produced a group of these vessels, but apparently none of these had the typical perforations (Dajani 1966:Pls. 7:47, 129; 8:48, 56, 57). Also from Transjordan are several from the late tenth century at Tell er-Rumeith excavated by Lapp and under study for publication by J. Sauer.

The use of these vessels has posed a problem for which the Taanach example may suggest a solution. The interpretation that they were strainers was utilized for two Hazor examples (Yadin and others 1961:Pl. 171:16-17). Similarly, at Tell el-Fârᶜah (N) the suggestion was made

Table I
Cultic Structure Parallels to Locus 2081 and Building 10 Pottery at Megiddo

Cultic Structure Fig.	Megiddo Locus 2081 (Loud 1948:43-46)	Megiddo Building 10 (Lamon and Shipton 1939: Fig. 6, P-Q 13)
30-32		Pl. 21:123
34:4-5		20:120-121
36:1-2		19:106
36:3		19:114, 22:130-131
37:1		7:174
40:4-6		5:126
40:8	Pl. 88:13	
40:11		5:121
41		21:125
42:1-4, 43:1-2		29:110
44:3	89:14	
44:5		30:116
45:1		30:126
45:2		30:120
45:5-7		28:98
45:8		28:106
46:3, 7, 12	89:10	
47:1	147:8	
47:2-3	89:9	
47:4-5		30:130
48:1-10	89:13	
48:15-19	89:11	
50:1		5:119
51:1-2	90:9	38:19

that these vessels were used for cheese-making (De Vaux 1951:412). However, had they been used for straining, perforations nearer the base would be expected, whereas the examples cited are almost uniformly perforated near the shoulder and neck. On the basis of her study of vessels of this general type from the Greek Islands, Rhodes and Cyprus, G. Crowfoot proposed that they should be interpreted as censers. These vessels could accordingly represent Palestinian counterparts to similar vessels found to the northwest and could have been used for some sort of cultic purpose (Crowfoot 1940:150-53). The Taanach example lends support to this explanation in that its context is more probably cultic than not, and an interpretation of this vessel as a censer would fit well with other contents of the building from which it came. Since the same type of perforated cup has turned up recently in the excavations at Kamid el-Loz in the Beqᶜa in Lebanon, it is likely that they found their way to Palestine via Phoenicia rather than directly (Hachmann and Kuschke 1966:65, Fig. 25:1, 3).

Fig. 51:4, TT 351, is a jar stand like those found at many Palestinian sites. Its two openings on the shoulder are notable but other such examples have been found in Stratum IV at Megiddo (Lamon and Shipton 1939:Pl. 34:13) and in Cave 6024 at Lachish (Tufnell 1953:Pl. 90:389).

In summary then, the cumulative evidence for the contemporaneity of the Cultic Structure, Megiddo L. 2081, and Megiddo Building 10 groups is impressive. Nearly one out of every four or five forms in the Cultic Structure group has an identical or close parallel in one of these two groups from Megiddo. The results of the above discussion are given in Table 1.

Pottery from Cistern L. 69, SW 2-8

JARS (FIGS. 52:1-2)

The homogeneous cache from Cistern L. 69 has some forms identical to those of the Cultic Structure as well as some which expand the repertory of Period IIB. Fig. 52:1-2 provide further examples of profiled jar rims during Period IIB. Fig. 52:1 can be compared with the profiled jar rims found in the Cultic Structure and Cistern L. 74 (Figs. 34:1, TT 482 and 55:1). As noted above, a rim of this type was present in a good late tenth century context at Hazor (Yadin and others 1960:Pl. 51:19). Fig. 52:2 is also slightly profiled, but is from a jar whose body is not so large as Fig. 52:1.

BOWLS (FIG. 52:3-9)

The medium-sized bowl with handles, TT 1855 in Fig. 52:3, has several parallels from the latter part of Iron I. The best one comes from PCL 174b at Hazor (Yadin and others 1960:Pl. 51:9). The same type is found in the south at Tell Beit Mirsim at the end of Iron I (Albright 1932:Pl. 23:6).

Fig. 52:4-8 are bowls similar to those found in the Cultic Structure. Fig. 52:4 has a plain rim like a bowl from the Cultic Structure (Fig. 45:2, TT 445) as well as one from Stratum V at Megiddo (Lamon and Shipton 1939:Pl. 30:134). Fig. 52:5 is also parallel to a bowl from the Cultic Structure (Fig. 45:5) but has more incurved sidewalls. Fig. 52:6 has a carinated side as do many bowls in the Cultic Structure (Fig. 46:1-14), but it lacks the characteristic red slip and is burnished only on the rim. Fig. 52:7 has no parallels from the Cultic Structure but is similar to a bowl from PCL Room 6 of Building 10 at Megiddo (Lamon and Shipton 1939:Pl. 28:99). The latter example has a flat base in contrast to the small, ring base of the Taanach example. Fig. 52:8 is also parallel to the small bowls from the Cultic Structure (Fig. 48:1-14).

The bowl with pronounced carination, TT 1854 in Fig. 52:9, is not a common bowl in this period and could be taken as an LB I form. However, similar bowls were found at Iron Age Megiddo and Hazor. The most important parallel is from PCL Room 6 of Building 10 at Megiddo (Lamon and Shipton 1939:Pl. 32:168). The Megiddo example has a shorter, less flaring neck and is irregularly burnished over a red wash. At Hazor a "Samarian bowl" from Stratum IX has the same carinated form (Yadin and others 1961:Pl. 208:30). The Hazor bowl also has a whitish-gray, burnished slip in contrast to the orange-tan, unburnished ware of the Taanach bowl.

COOKING POTS (FIG. 53:1-4)

Fig. 53:1-4 can be compared to cooking pot rims from the Cultic Structure (Fig. 49:1-3). In Fig. 53:1, the groove around the rim has been crudely fashioned, while the tip of the elongated rim in Fig. 53:3 is also roughly made, similar to a Stratum X rim at Hazor (Yadin and others 1961:Pl. 207:9, 12-17). The general type of elongated cooking pot rim is characteristic of Stratum X at Hazor as it is of Period IIB at Taanach.

CHALICES AND LAMP (FIG. 53:5-7)

The chalice, TT 1853 in Fig. 53:5, is distinguished by its splayed lip and carinated base. Interesting as a parallel is the chalice associated with the high stand found in PCL 2081 at Megiddo (Loud 1948:Pl. 90:9). The latter also has a flattened lip, but a simple rather than a carinated base. A chalice with splayed lip was found in the recent excavation at Lachish along with several high stands like the one from Megiddo (Aharoni 1969:Pl. 32a). Wright noted the development of the more splayed and flattened chalice rim toward the end of Iron I at ᶜAin Shems (Grant and Wright 1939:135). The carinated base is also characteristic of this period, and an example is found in Tomb 76A at Megiddo (Guy and Engberg 1938:Pl. 74:25).

The lamp fragment in Fig. 53:7 is similar to those found in the Cultic Structure and Cistern L.74 (Figs. 51:1-2, 69:6).

OFFERING STAND (FIG. 54)

The partially preserved vessel, TT 1830 in Fig. 54, is of special importance for the group found in Cistern L. 69. It belongs to a class of objects commonly designated as incense or offering stands. Features which command special attention are the down-turned leaves or tabs, the pronounced ridging at three different places on the exterior, and the handles toward the lower part of the stand. The vessel is cylindrical with a smaller diameter toward the top.

A number of parallels to this vessel are impressive. Several examples were found at Megiddo including a decorated one in PCL 2081 (Loud 1948:Pl. 90:9). Further examples from Strata V-VI were discovered at the same site (May 1935:Pls. 19-20). More recently, several have turned up in a hoard of vessels at Lachish in an area identified as a sanctuary (Aharoni 1969:Pl. 32a and p. 577).

In his study of the Megiddo stands, May called attention (1935:20-23, Fig. 6) to the diffusion of vessels of this type in Mesopotamia, Egypt, and Syria already in the Late Bronze Age and even earlier. The projecting tabs on these vessels he took to be conventionalized lotus leaves deriving from Egyptian architectural detail on pillars and capitals. The example discovered at Megiddo by Schumacher seems to lend support to this interpretation. The tabs on the Taanach examples are witness to the persistence and ubiquity of this tradition.

The closest parallel to the Taanach stand comes from Megiddo in an example assigned to Stratum VI (May 1935:Pl. 20:P6056). This reconstructed form has a diminishing diameter from base to top like the one from Cistern L. 69. It also has ridging parallel to the Taanach example and possesses a single line of down-turned tabs as well. Unlike the Taanach stand it has no handles, and it has two apertures in the lower half of the vessel, a phenomenon which is impossible to determine in the case of the fragmented Taanach example. The handles on the latter, however, are paralleled by other stands from Megiddo which possess them (May 1935:Pl. 20:P6055).

With regard to the use of these vessels, they have sometimes been referred to as incense stands. This interpretation seems to be eliminated by the fact that evidence for burning is absent. A clue for their use, however, may lie in the fact that several of the stands were found with a uniquely shaped bowl or basin inserted into the hollow of the stand. The close parallel from Megiddo contained such a bowl (May 1935:Pl. 20:P6056; Lamon and Shipton 1939:Pl. 38:1). The Lachish examples also possessed accompanying bowls (Aharoni 1969:Pl. 32a). Similarly, a chalice could be inserted into the stand from PCL 2081 at Megiddo (Loud 1948:Pl. 90:9). Since the bowls and chalices would probably have been used for poured offerings, the best explanation for the stands would be that they were used for libations rather than for burning incense (Courtois 1969:96-100).

This stand, together with the more elaborate stand, TT 1500, discovered in Cistern L. 69, lends support to the interpretation of the group as a hoard of vessels probably associated with the Cultic Structure.

Pottery from Cistern L. 74, SW 6-2

JARS (FIGS. 55-57)

The large group from Cistern L. 74 contained many parallels to the Cultic Structure pottery as well as forms differing from or absent from the latter. Another example of a profiled jar rim from Period IIB is found in Fig. 55:1. Again it can be noted that the rim in Period IIB is thicker and rounder than the later Iron II examples with cut rim. The ware is also red or brown in contrast to the slate-colored ware of later Iron II vessels. A similar profiled rim is found in a good late tenth century context at Hazor (Yadin and others 1960:Pl. 51:19). Fig. 55:2 is similar to the jar with ovoid body from the Cultic Structure (Fig. 30:3 TT 477), the body being somewhat thicker.

Fig. 56:1-4 contains a group of jar bases from Cistern L. 74. Fig. 56:1 has a thicker, pointed base like TT 380 in Fig. 55:2, while Fig. 56:2 belongs to the prominent ovoid-shaped type found in the Cultic Structure (Fig. 30:1-4). Fig. 56:3 has a rounder base like the jar from PCL Rooms 6-7 of Building 10 at Megiddo (Lamon and Shipton 1939:Pl. 21:122) while the base in Fig. 56:4 may be from a jar or jug which is not quite as tall.

Spouted jars like TT 383 found in Fig. 57:1 have already been discussed in several places before (Figs. 26:1, 36:1-2). The example here has a bloated body which would suggest a closer connection with Period IIA. Fig. 57:2, TT 1856, can be compared with a similar example found in PCL Room 6 of Building 10 at Megiddo (Lamon and Shipton 1939:Pl. 22:128).

JUGS (FIGS. 58:1-62:8)

Of all the vessels from Cistern L. 74, the jug class was best represented. Some whole jugs were found as well as a number of examples of which only the lower half remained. Jugs are classed here according to those with thickened, profiled, and simple rims, and those with bowed neck and rim.

Thickened rims characterize the jugs in Fig. 58:1-7. TT 382 in Fig. 58:1 flares at the upper part of the neck and the thickened rim. A similar jug at Megiddo with globular body, flaring neck and thickened rim is probably to be assigned to Stratum VA-IVB (Lamon and Shipton 1939:Pl. 7:163). The example is vertically burnished on the neck and has some banded decoration. The rims in Fig. 58:2-3 are variants of this type while Fig. 58:4-6 are reminiscent of an early Iron I thickened jug rim (Figs. 3:1-2, 6:4, 11:3). Fig. 58:7 is similar but is rounded rather than bevelled on the rim top.

Profiled jug rims like those in Fig. 58:8-12 came into use in Period IIA and were ubiquitous during Period IIB. A well-made jug with this rim type was found in the Cultic Structure (TT 103, Fig. 37:1), and a similar one came from PCL Room 6 of Building 10 at Megiddo (Lamon and Shipton 1939:Pl. 7:174).

POTTERY GROUPS OF PERIOD IIB

Figs. 58:13 to 59:3 have only the lower halves preserved. They are especially useful in providing information on the surface treatment of jugs in this period. All have an applied slip which varies from red or pink to cream, and all are hand burnished. Three also have painted decoration. These jugs are analogous to Stratum VA-IVB examples at Megiddo. TT 1858, Fig. 58:14, is closely paralleled by a jug from PCL Room 6 of Building 10 at Megiddo (Lamon and Shipton 1939:Pl. 6:154). The latter example is vertically hand burnished and has white and dark banded decoration like the Taanach jug. The banded decoration in Fig. 59:1 is also paralleled by a jug from PCL Room 6 of Building 10 at Megiddo (Lamon and Shipton 1939:Pl. 6:147), and similar decoration is found on the bottom part of a jug from the casemate wall group at Arad (Aharoni 1968:12, Fig. 7, second from left, third row). Also at Megiddo and probably from Stratum VA-IVB is a vessel with decoration of crossed diagonal lines and hand-burnishing like TT 1860, Fig. 59:2 (Lamon and Shipton 1939:Pl. 6:151-152).

The partly preserved TT 385 as well as the fragments in Fig. 59:4-7 represent the Palestinian version of the oenochoe. This vessel and the fragments are all parallel to jug TT 440 found in the Cultic Structure (Fig. 37:2).

Jugs with various simple rims are found in Fig. 60:1-3. The fairly complete form, TT 381 in Fig. 60:1, is typical for Period IIB at Taanach. The same jug, TT 454, is present in the Cultic Structure although the rim on the latter is slightly bowed toward the interior (Fig. 38:1). It is noteworthy that the simple rims in Fig. 60:2-3 are also slightly pinched like the example just mentioned from the Cultic Structure. A similar jug was found in Stratum XB at Hazor (Yadin and others 1961:Pl. 172:2). The bases in Figs. 60:4 (TT 1857) and 61:1-4 exhibit the globular body typical of Period IIA and IIB jugs. A jug of this kind at Beth-zur is probably to be dated to the tenth century (Funk 1968:Fig. 8:1).

The nearly whole vessel, TT 1859 in Fig. 61:5, as well as the rims in Fig. 61:7 to 62:5 belong to jugs with a thickened, bowed rim. Fig. 61:6 is thickened but not bowed but probably represents a variant of the same rim type. Close parallels to TT 1859 could not be found, but it is in the same tradition of form and manufacture as jugs TT 454 and TT 470 from the Cultic Structure (Fig. 38:1-2). The latter both have similar bowed rims, but the neck is longer than TT 1859. This is also the case with the rims in Fig. 61:7-11, all of which are from jugs with shorter necks than those in the Cultic Structure. A similar bowed rim on a jug with a rounded base is attributed to Stratum V at Megiddo (Lamon and Shipton 1939:Pl. 7:170). The bowed rims in Fig. 62:1-5 are from jugs with even shorter necks. These jugs resemble the globular cooking pot of Period IIB and normally can be distinguished from the latter only by the ware of the vessel (Figs. 67:3, TT 692, 68:4). Thus a vessel from PCL Rooms 6-7 of Building 10 at Megiddo is of similar type, but its description suggests it may be a cooking pot (Lamon and Shipton 1939:Pl. 5:119). A good parallel for Fig. 62:4 is from the casemate wall group at Arad (Aharoni 1968:12, Fig. 7, third from left, second row). It also has a thickened, bowed rim as the one from Taanach. Examples of the bottoms for jugs like the ones here are probably those found in Fig. 62:6-7.

Fig. 62:8 represents a less common, narrow-necked jug type with a profile and simple flaring rim. A Stratum V jug at Megiddo has a similar form with a neck which is slightly wider and shorter (Lamon and Shipton 1939:Pl. 8:177). Both are decorated with red and black paint, and the motifs on the handles are parallel although not identical.

JUGLETS (FIG. 62:9-13)

Juglet TT 690 in Fig. 62:9 is distinguished by its rounded body in contrast to the more elongated bodies of many juglets in this period. A parallel to this form is a burnished example ascribed to Stratum VB at Megiddo (Loud 1948:Pl. 87:19). TT 691, Fig. 62:10, has a slightly more elongated body and is close to a juglet from Tomb 76A at Megiddo (Guy and Engberg 1938:Pl. 74:18). Fig. 62:11 is the typical elongated juglet of Period IIB and is parallel to an example from S=2081 at Megiddo (Loud 1948:Pl. 88:12). Several slightly later juglets of this type were found at Munshara near Samaria (Zayadine 1968:583, Fig. 8:1-8). Fig. 62:13 was crudely made with a hole bored through the side.

CRATERS (FIG. 63)

Craters with heavy rims have already been noted in the large vessel, TT 489, from the Cultic Structure (Fig. 41). Fig. 63:1-2 are from similar although somewhat smaller vessels. The first can be compared with a Stratum V crater at Megiddo as well as with a later Iron II example at the same site (Lamon and Shipton 1939:Pl. 32:167, 28:88). No close analogies could be found for the second.

The crater with folded rim like those in Fig. 63:3-11 was found as late as Period IIA at Taanach (Figs. 18:2, 19:7, 22:8, 24:4, 28:2-4). During Period IIB a burnished deep bowl or crater appeared which became the more popular vessel (Figs. 42, 43). There is some evidence that the older folded-rim type persisted into Period IIB and even into Period III (Fig. 70:3), and similar evidence seems to be present at Megiddo and Hazor (Lamon and Shipton 1939:Pl. 28:89; Yadin and others 1961:Pls. 183:2, 184:1). However, at Taanach the form seems to have tapered off in popularity after Period IIA, and it is noteworthy that no examples at all were found in the Cultic Structure group. Thus the prominence of these rims in Cistern L. 74 and the absence of deep, burnished Period IIB bowls may suggest that some forms in the cistern group date to Period IIA (see Summary following).

BOWLS (FIGS. 64-65)

Twenty-five bowl rims came from Cistern L. 74. Of these, seventeen are burnished and eight unburnished, paralleling the evidence from the Cultic Structure for the treatment of small and medium bowls in this period. Like those from the Cultic Structure, the bowls are usually burnished inside and out and on the outside most often to the carination on the shoulder of the bowl.

The bowls in Fig. 64:1-8 all have incurved sidewalls and more than half are burnished. A bowl from PCL Room 6 of Building 10 at Megiddo is of the same type (Lamon and Shipton 1939:Pl. 30:123) while Fig. 64:8 is almost identical to a bowl from PCL 2081 at Megiddo (Loud 1948:Pl. 89:12). Fig. 64:9 is larger and has a thickened rim with wavy profile. A fairly close parallel is the bar-handled bowl from PCL 159b at Hazor (Yadin and others 1960:Pl. 51:6). The two bowls in Fig. 64:10-11 display hand burnishing over a red slip in exactly the same manner as bowls from the Cultic Structure and are most closely paralleled by a bowl from the latter (Fig. 45:5). The rim in Fig. 64:12 is from a shallower bowl. A similar bowl with red slip was found in PCL 116c at Hazor (Yadin and others 1960:Pl. 51:1).

Fig. 65:1-4 are small bowls with a variety of simple rims. TT 402 in Fig. 65:1 has a close parallel in an unburnished bowl from PCL 209c at Hazor (Yadin and others 1961:Pl. 174:3). Fig. 65:3 is a smaller example of the bowls with cut rim as TT 353 found in the Cultic Structure (Fig. 46:5). Fig. 65:4 is also close to several of the shallow, thin bowls from the Cultic Structure (Fig. 48:12-13).

Fig. 65:5-6 have thickened, flat rims like those on a nearly whole bowl, TT 352, from the Cultic Structure (Fig. 47:2). Fig. 65:7 is from an unburnished bowl, but it has a close parallel in a burnished sherd from L. 92a at Hazor (Yadin and others 1958:Pl. 45:3). Fig. 65:8 again has a parallel in a smaller but similar bowl in the Cultic Structure (Fig. 45:7). Fig. 65:9 is a bowl which becomes prominent in Iron II at which time it develops straighter sides (Lamon and Shipton 1939:Pl. 24:43-44), but the one here has a slight carination, like a Stratum IX example from Hazor (Yadin and others 1960:Pl. 52:1). The bowl with thickened, grooved rim in Fig. 65:10 is close in form to a bowl from PCL Room 6 of Building 10 at Megiddo (Lamon and Shipton 1939:Pl. 30:122), while the small burnished rim in Fig. 65:11 is from a bowl with simple rim like those found in the Cultic Structure (Fig. 48:6). Fig. 65:12 is from a shallow bowl with a thickened, splaying rim. No close parallels for this rim could be found. Finally, Fig. 65:13 is from a small, shallow plate bowl like TT 444, 447 and 463 found in the Cultic Structure (Fig. 48:15-19).

COOKING POTS AND BAKING TRAYS (FIGS. 66:1-69:2)

As in the case of the Cultic Structure, two types of cooking pots are found in the Cistern L. 74 group. The first type has the elongated rim which is bent up to form a wide groove around the rim (Fig. 66:1-34). This type is ubiquitous throughout Period II and was found well represented in the Cultic Structure group (Fig. 49:1-3). Stratum X cooking pots at Hazor have the same kind of rim with similar variation (Yadin and others 1961:Pl. 207:9-17). Fig. 66:35 has a similar rim but with a slightly higher neck. Fig. 67:1 may belong to a jar but its ware suggests a cooking vessel. It is the only example of this type in the present groups and close parallels could not be found. Fig. 67:2 is also a less common type, having a shorter rim. It may be like a larger example from L. 92a at Hazor (Yadin and others 1958:Pl. 45:20).

The second type of cooking pot is distinguished by its globular body and its single or double handles as in Figs. 67:3 to 68:7. TT 692 in Fig. 67:3 has a slightly bowed neck and can be compared with a nearly complete example, TT 456, from the Cultic Structure (Fig. 50:1). Fig. 67:4 is similar, the neck being straighter. Figs. 67:5-6 and 68:1-2 also have a globular body, slightly less squat than the previous two examples. Fig. 68:2 has two handles instead of one. A close parallel to these is a one-handled example from PCL 418 at Tell el-Fârᶜah (N) (De Vaux 1955:577, Fig. 16:3). Fig. 68:3-4 have bowed rims while Fig. 68:5 can be compared to a cooking pot rim from Phase J at Deir ᶜAllâ (Franken and Kalsbeek 1969:Fig. 69:59). The latter also has a narrow mouth like the ones from Taanach. Fig. 68:8 has a thicker, flaring rim and no parallels could be found for it.

Fig. 69:1-2 are baking trays, examples of which are present at other sites in late Iron I and early Iron II. Close parallels to the ones here are found in Stratum IX at Hazor (Yadin and others 1960:Pl. 52:26-27) and Megiddo Stratum V (Lamon and Shipton 1939:Pl. 31:152).

CHALICES AND LAMP (FIG. 69:3-6)

Fig. 69:3-4 are typical chalice bases of this period (see TT 1853, Fig. 53:5) as is the rim in Fig. 69:5. Both bases and rim are exactly the kind found in two Stratum V chalices at Megiddo (Lamon and Shipton 1939:Pl. 33:18, 20). The lamp fragment in Fig. 69:6 is also nearly identical to TT 89, a lamp from the Cultic Structure (Fig. 51:1).

Summary

The Cultic Structure group is so clearly defined that a summary of the characteristics of Period IIB seems superfluous. Of all features which might be underscored, the burnishing of small jars, jugs and bowls during Period IIB is most important. The practice of hand burnishing over a red slip is easily recognizable on many of the forms from the Cultic Structure, and it likewise distinguishes some of the vessels of Cistern L. 69. Other loci from the mound including the section cut south of the Northeast Outwork also contained burnished forms of the same type (see Chapter 6). The Cultic Structure and Cistern L. 69 thus represent excellent homogeneous groups for Period IIB.

The case with Cistern L. 74 is different. Much of the material must be attributed to Period IIB by comparison with the above groups. But there appear to be some Period IIA forms and possibly an occasional Period I remnant such as the jug rims, Fig. 58:4-5. Forms which might suggest Period IIA would be TT 383, the spouted

POTTERY GROUPS OF PERIOD IIB

jar with bloated body in Fig. 57:1 and the common folded crater rims, Fig. 63:3-11. In addition, the bowls with incurved sidewalls in Fig. 64:1-8, although sometimes burnished or red-slipped, differ from the more common carinated bowls of the Cultic Structure. It is possible that this difference may also reflect a slightly earlier date, and these bowls may well belong in Period IIA rather than IIB. On this basis, Cistern L. 74 should be viewed as a moderately mixed group.

Chapter Six
Pottery Groups of Periods III to V

Iron II Stratigraphy at Taanach and Comparative Sites

Above the Period IIB structures and layers the areas excavated were found in very disturbed condition. Only fragments of walls and sporadic remnants of occupation dating to Iron II were present. The one exception was the impressive Northeast Outwork on the lower plateau of the north end of the mound, originally uncovered by Sellin and reexcavated in 1968. This building as well as other finds of the earlier excavations dating to Iron II show that there was occupation at Taanach during this period. However, later pit digging in the Persian and Arab periods, along with erosion, erased much of the evidence.

For the above reasons the groups isolated from this period are small and usually cannot be related to well-defined structures. As a result, Taanach is able to make only a minimal contribution to the ceramic sequence of Iron II. At best it can only substantiate and occasionally clarify the horizons found at other sites with richer material for this period.

Period III

SW 4-7, LOCUS 41

L. 41 was loose, dark soil largely confined to the northeast part of SW 4-7. It was a thin layer largely cut away by a stone-lined pit, L. 6, on the south end of the square. Below L. 41 a layer of fine, brown soil, L. 65, had sherds from Periods I and IIA while a hard, brown layer, L. 40, above had Iron II pottery. Although the group from L. 41 is not large, it is from a well-defined context.

NORTHEAST OUTWORK, NEO-2

The only area explored on the northern end of the mound during the recent excavations was the *Nordostvorwerk* (Sellin 1904:30-32; Lapp 1969b:39-42). During the season of 1968 the interior was reexcavated, and a section was cut against its north and south sides to determine more precisely the date and significance of this building. Since the Sellin expedition had cleared much of the western half of the interior, all traces of its debris had to be removed before excavating a new section through the interior. The latter clarified the way the building was constructed and something of its possible function. As Sellin had noted, the foundation of the structure was laid on the sloping bedrock of the lower, northern shoulder of the mound. On the north, east, and west sides, the facing was of well-cut ashlar masonry while on the south, large, roughly cut stones were laid against the sloping bedrock. The interior was filled with a core of large stones and rubble (L. 3, 5 and 36). Unfortunately only a handful of sherds turned up in this filling. Since these are crucial for the dating of the Northeast Outwork and since the stratified evidence on all sides of the exterior was destroyed by the tunnelling of the earlier excavations, the sherds from these uncontaminated loci are presented here.

Period IV

SW 4-7, LOCI 36, 37, 38a

These loci consisted of a single, black, ashy layer found over most of the east half of the square. Stratigraphically this layer was above L. 40, a compact, brown layer, and the previously discussed L. 41 of Period III. Although the loci were excavated separately, they are consolidated here. L. 36 was found below L. 31 in the northeast part of the square, L. 37 below L. 32 along the east side, south of later Wall 9, and L. 38a also below L. 32 in the center of the square. Loci above the ashy layer contained mixed pottery, the latest being from the latter part of Iron II.

Period V

SW 5-6, LOCUS 16

L. 16 was discovered at the north end of SW 5-6. It consisted of a pile of strewn rocks, probably from a demolished structure, embedded in fine, brown soil. The rocks had fallen on a small hoard of pottery, some vessels of which were mendable. Above L. 16 was a compact fill, L. 14, belonging apparently to the Persian period. Below L. 16 was L. 17 which contained a number of mostly late Iron II sherds.

Comparative Strata and Chronology

The state of Palestine ceramic chronology during Iron II is not as favorable as that for Iron I. One factor contributing to this is the greater uniformity of the age of the Israelite monarchy. In contrast to Iron I, during which a number of major cultural developments took place fostering observable changes in the ceramic tradition, the Iron II period experienced a more continuous occupation and apparently greater homogeneity. As a result, changes in the ceramic traditions are not so obvious, at least in light of our present knowledge. Interruptions do occur, such as the Assyrian conquest of the last quarter of the eighth century. The unstable political conditions during the three centuries following the breakup of the united kingdom may also be reflected in a greater degree of regional ceramic variation, but more precise information must come from other sites with a greater amount of Iron II material than excavated at Tell Ta'annek.

HAZOR

Since the Iron II material at Taanach is sparse, the method of isolating PCL is not pursued in this chapter. Comparisons are made rather with the general stratified materials of a number of sites. Of particular significance is Hazor with a succession of strata through the whole of Iron II. By correlating the archaeological evidence with that of written sources, the excavators concluded that the post-Solomonic Stratum IX was destroyed by Ben-Hadad during the reign of Baasha (1 Kgs 15:20, 2 Chr 16:4), ca. 885. Stratum VIII represented the Omri-Ahab period with its most impressive structure being the "Pillared Building" in Area A. This building was repaired in Stratum VII and was probably destroyed by Hazael, ca. 815, at the time of Jehu. Stratum VI belonged to the first half of the eighth century, and its destruction was connected with the earthquake at the time of Jeroboam II and Uzziah (Amos 1:1, Zech 14:5). Stratum V was built on the ruins remaining from this catastrophe, and this stratum was believed to have suffered a devastating blow at the hands of Tiglath-Pileser III in 732. Stratum IV was an "open city" reflecting Assyrian occupation of the site. It was dated to the latter part of the eighth and the beginning of the seventh centuries, while Stratum III was also attributed to the seventh century (Yadin and others 1958:22-23; 1960: 36-37).

MEGIDDO

Another site of importance is Megiddo. At Megiddo Stratum IVA seems to have run at least to the last quarter of the ninth century (Wright 1961:99, Chart 9; Albright 1943:2, n. 1). Stratum III represents the eighth-century city which apparently escaped destruction by the Assyrians since the succeeding Stratum II was found to be a continuation of the Stratum III city with some rebuilding of the latter (Lamon and Shipton 1939:62). Stratum II, then, was in existence through a large part of the seventh century.

SAMARIA, TELL EL-FÂR'AH (N), TELL BEIT MIRSIM, DEIR 'ALLĀ

At Samaria Periods I and II were noted by Kenyon as transitional between Iron I and II especially because of the simultaneous appearance of hand- and wheel-burnishing techniques (Kenyon 1957:94). Thus some material from Samaria is close to Taanach Period IIB while the main amount belongs to the ninth century. Periods II through VI spanned the latter part of the ninth century and continued through the following century while Period VII was ascribed to the seventh century (Kenyon 1957:95-98). At nearby Tell el-Fâr'ah (N), the period called "Niveau Intermediaire" was attributed to the ninth century with Niveau 2 being dated to the eighth and Niveau 1 to the seventh century (De Vaux 1951:412-420; 1955:583-586). At Tell Beit Mirsim Stratum A1 contained material from the ninth century while A2 was dated to the eighth and seventh centuries (Albright 1932:76-89). Finally, at Deir 'Allā, Phases K and L follow the Solomonic Phase J and probably date to the ninth century.

The correlations which can be made between Taanach and these comparative sites are based mostly on ceramic parallels. Taanach's Period III is most closely matched by the pottery of Phases K and L at Deir 'Allā, Period II at Samaria, Stratum VIII at Hazor, and the end of Stratum IV and the beginning of Stratum III at Megiddo. Taanach's Period IV has its closest parallels in Stratum VA at Hazor and Stratum III at Megiddo, while Period V at Taanach corresponds to Strata IV-III at Hazor and Stratum II at Megiddo. The dates proposed are as follows:

	Loci	Figures	Date
Period III	SW 4-7, L. 41	70	ca. 875-800
	NEO-2, L. 3, 5, 36	71	
Period IV	SW 4-7, L. 36, 37, 38a	72-74	ca. 750-732
Period V	SW 5-6, L. 16	75-76	ca. 700-650

Pottery Groups of Period III (Figs. 70-71)

Bowed jug rims of the type in Fig. 70:1 continue to be found in Period III (see Fig. 61:7-11). That the same type persisted as late as Period IV is evident from several examples below (Figs. 72:1, 74:1). Fig. 70:2 is apparently a degenerate example of the profiled jug rim for which an interesting parallel is found in Phase K at Deir 'Allā (Franken and Kalsbeek 1969:Fig. 72:96). The paucity of profiled jug rims in Period III along with a number of degenerate examples suggests that this form tapers off and eventually disappears during the ninth century. Its heyday is thus in Periods IIA and IIB.

Fig. 70:3-4 indicate that the Iron I crater with overlapped rim also continues in Period III. A similar example at Megiddo is attributed to Stratum IV and later (Lamon and Shipton 1939:Pl. 28:89) while one from Period II at Samaria closely resembles Fig. 70:4 (Kenyon 1957:105, Fig. 3:11).

Figs. 70:5 and 71:1-6 contain several bowl rims of Period III. Fig. 70:5 has straighter sidewalls than bowls from Period II, a development more characteristic of Iron II. A similar but slightly later bowl comes from Stratum VIII at Hazor (Yadin and others 1958:Pl. 47:2).

The first of the bowl rims from the Northeast Outwork (Fig. 71:1) belongs to a deep bowl with a fairly thick rim. The best parallel is on a small to medium-sized crater with handles in Hazor Stratum VIII (Yadin and others 1960:Pl. 56:6). The rim in Fig. 71:2 is from a wide-mouthed, shallow bowl. It is slightly overlapped on the interior. Close parallels are found in Stratum VIII at Hazor (Yadin and others 1960:Fig. 54:3), Strata IV-III at Megiddo (Lamon and Shipton 1939:Pl. 25:67), and in Phase L at Deir ᶜAllā (Franken and Kalsbeek 1969:Fig. 75:62). This bowl rim supports the dating of the Northeast Outwork group as a whole to the last part of the ninth century. Fig. 71:3 is from a small to medium, deep bowl with a mouth smaller than the widest diameter of the body. It has a thickened rim similar to that of a deep bowl from Stratum VIII at Hazor (Yadin and others 1958:Pl. 47:25). Fig. 71:4 represents the development during Period III of one of the bowl types of the Cultic Structure (Fig. 45:5); it is also paralleled by a bowl from Stratum VIII at Hazor (Yadin and others 1958:Pl. 47:17a). The shallow bowl with flaring sides and tapered rim in Fig. 71:5 also shows the development in Period III of the shallow bowl type as TT 443, 448, 486 of Period IIB (Fig. 48:1-4). It has good parallels from Stratum VIII at Hazor (Yadin and others 1960:Pl. 55:3, 12), Strata IV-III at Megiddo (Lamon and Shipton 1939:Pl. 24:56), and Phase L at Deir ᶜAllā (Franken and Kalsbeek 1969:Fig. 75:3). Fig. 71:6 is a simple rim of a small bowl with straight sidewalls. The larger bowl from L. 41 in SW 4-7 is close in form and represents a slightly earlier example of this type (Fig. 70:5).

Only one cooking pot rim, Fig. 70:6, is represented in these Period III groups. This rim is not as elongated as the usual cooking pot rim of Period IIB, but it apparently has developed from the latter (Fig. 66:1-35).

Pottery Groups of Period IV (Figs. 72-74)

Several types of jug rims are illustrated in Figs. 72:1-3, 73:2 and 74:1. Fig. 72:1 represents the Period IV development of the bowed jug rim. Good parallels are found in Strata III-II at Megiddo (Lamon and Shipton 1939:Pl. 5: 118) and in Stratum A at Tell Beit Mirsim (Albright 1932:Pl. 57:14). Fig. 73:2 is a jug rim not greatly different from a similar form in Period IIB (Fig. 61:6) which suggests the long life of this form well into Iron II. A similar rim is found in Stratum V at Hazor (Yadin and others 1958:Pl. 56:12). The everted, thickened rim in Fig. 72:2 also has a parallel from Stratum A at Tell Beit Mirsim (Albright 1932:Pl. 59:10); and a similar rim, slightly less thickened and listed as a jar, was found in Stratum VA at Hazor (Yadin and others 1960:Pl. 96:9). Fig. 72:3 is a further illustration of an earlier jug type which develops into Period IV. It can be compared with TT 468, a red-slipped, burnished jug with narrow neck from the Cultic Structure (Fig. 39:2). The neck and rim of the two examples are similar, but the one here has its handle attached at the rim. This jug seems to be similar to the crude jug found in Strata III-I at Megiddo (Lamon and Shipton 1939:Pl. 4:94). The oval section of the handle in Fig. 73:1 can be compared with a slightly later handle from Period V (Fig. 75:7).

Further examples of the small crater with folded rim are found in Figs. 72:4-6 and 74:2. Several other sites also have this vessel continuing well into Iron II. Figs. 72:4 and 74:2 can be compared with examples from Stratum III at Megiddo (Lamon and Shipton 1939:Pl. 27:87) and Stratum VA at Hazor (Yadin and others 1960:Pl. 83:4). Fig. 72:6 is a smaller version of this same type. Judging from its ware, Fig. 72:5 may be the rim of a cooking pot rather than a crater. A similar form from Period VI at Samaria is listed as a cooking pot (Kenyon 1957:120, Fig. 9:17; cf. 117, Fig. 7:6) while a Stratum VA example at Hazor is described as a crater (Yadin and others 1960:Pl. 83:6).

Figs. 72:7, 73:3-6, and 74:3-4 illustrate various bowl rims from Period IV. The shallow bowl in Fig. 72:7 can be compared with a similar bowl from Stratum V at Hazor (Yadin and others 1961:Pl. 251:6). Fig. 73:3 is a characteristic form of Period IV. It has short, vertical sidewalls with high carination, and the rim is tapered to a point. A smaller bowl with this kind of rim is found in Stratum VA at Hazor (Yadin and others 1960:Pl. 92:14). The two bowls in Fig. 73:4-5 have lightly carinated sidewalls, probably a continuation of the tradition of Period IIB bowls. They are, however, treated differently on the surface than Period IIB bowls. Fig. 73:5 is unburnished while Fig. 73:4 is horizontally burnished on the interior only, in more typical Iron II fashion. The small bowl with thickened, grooved rim in Fig. 73:6 is paralleled by several Stratum VA bowl rims from Hazor (Yadin and others 1960:Pls. 92:30, 93:1; 1961: Pl. 230:5) and has important chronological value for dating these groups. Fig. 74:3 is from a medium-sized, deep bowl with incurved rim. No close parallels could be found for it. Fig. 74:4 is similar to a red, wheel-burnished bowl from Stratum V at Hazor (Yadin and others 1961:Pl. 251:1).

The cooking pot rims in Fig. 72:8-9 represent the development of the Iron I elongated, grooved rim well down into Iron II. By the time of Period IV the rim is less elongated than earlier. The type survives into Period V where it continues to appear next to a new type of rim (compare Fig. 76:9 with Fig. 76:6-8). Rims similar to the ones here are found at Samaria in Period IV (Kenyon 1957:114, Fig. 6:35, 37-38).

Pottery Groups of Period V (Figs. 75-76)

Fig. 75:1 illustrates the late Iron II development of the profiled storage jar rim. In the early development of the form, the rim is more rounded (Fig. 52:1) while by the time of Period V it is usually sharply cut and sometimes slightly grooved. The ware of the later examples is also gray or pink in contrast to the brown to orange ware of Period IIB. The best parallel to Fig. 75:1 comes from Period VII at Samaria (Kenyon 1957:126, Fig. 11:24) while additional examples at Megiddo are given a range from Strata IV to I (Lamon and Shipton 1939:Pl. 15:76-77). Fig. 75:3 is another example and has parallels in Strata III-IV at Hazor (Yadin and others 1958:Pls. 77:30, 78:25) and Period VII at Samaria (Kenyon 1957:126, Fig. 11:25).

The "sausage jar," TT 1861 in Fig. 75:2, like the storage jars with profiled rim in this period, has gray or slate-colored ware. This jar appears to have become prominent in the seventh century although there is evidence at Megiddo that it existed in an earlier form (Lamon and Shipton 1939:167, and Pls. 14:72, 20:119). The type is related to the long jars of Period VI, but the latter have differences in construction and ware (Figs. 80:5, 81:1-3, 83:1-2). The example here is distinguished by a small neck and a thickened, squared rim and by a body which reaches its narrowest diameter a little below the center. The best parallel to it comes from Megiddo which is probably to be attributed to Stratum II at that site (Lamon and Shipton 1939:Pl. 17:83). The Megiddo example also has a short neck and a thickened, more rounded rim. A slightly earlier parallel comes from Hazor Stratum VA (Yadin and others 1961:Pl. 230:28).

The three handles in Fig. 75:4-6 fit well into late Iron II. Fig. 75:4 has three punch impressions, reminiscent of similar types in Period IIB (Fig. 32:2). The two handles in Fig. 75:5-6 have a somewhat more oblong section which approaches the handles of Period VI (Figs. 81:1, 82:1,3).

Two remains of jugs are illustrated in Fig. 75:7-8. The first has a long neck which bows in sharply near the rim. It is probably from a jug like the slightly earlier example found in Strata IV-III at Megiddo (Lamon and Shipton 1939:Pl. 3:88). The second can be compared with a jug found in Strata III-II at Megiddo (Lamon and Shipton 1939:Pl. 4:93).

Among the bowls, Fig. 76:1 is an anomalous, deep vessel for which no close parallels could be found. The bowl with simple rim and curved sides in Fig. 76:2 is reminiscent of much earlier Iron I bowls (Fig. 13:6). Examples of this bowl are not numerous this late in Iron II, but a bowl ascribed to Strata IV-III at Megiddo is similar although it is a bit earlier (Lamon and Shipton 1939:Pl. 24:46). A Stratum VA bowl from Hazor may also represent an Iron II example (Yadin and others 1961:Pl. 231:15). The bowl in Fig. 76:3 has a rounded rim and is grooved below the rim. It also resembles earlier Iron I forms (Fig. 13: 13-14), and it is possible that this form as well as Fig. 76:2 may be intrusive. No good parallel from late Iron II could be found for Fig. 76:3. Fig. 76:4 is from a fairly common bowl in this period. It has straight, flaring sides, and the rim is usually simple or slightly thickened. Examples of the type are also found in Period VI at Samaria (Kenyon 1957:122, Fig. 10:1), in Strata IV-II at Megiddo (Lamon and Shipton 1939:Pl. 24:41), and in Stratum VA at Hazor (Yadin and others 1961:Pl. 225:23). Fig. 76:5 suggests that ring bases like those in Period IIB continued to appear as late as Period V (Fig. 46:8, TT 441; 14, TT 452).

TT 1863 and others in Fig. 76:6-8 are several cooking pots with a new kind of grooved rim which comes into prominence in Iron II. This cooking pot type arises next to the common Iron I type with elongated rim and virtually supplants the latter already in early Iron II (Lapp and Lapp 1968:66-67). Evidence from various sites indicates that the grooved rim became prominent by at least the first half of the eighth century and continued down through the seventh century. Thus, at Samaria, the first examples are associated with Period IV, while further illustrations appear through Period VI (Kenyon 1957:114, Fig. 6:39-40, 120, Fig. 9:18, 122, Fig. 10:27; see p. 117). Megiddo examples are listed from Strata IV-I, which suggests that the type appears around the end of the ninth century and continues to the end of Iron II (Lamon and Shipton 1939:Pl. 39:1, 4-6, 8-10). Similar examples were found at Tell Beit Mirsim in Stratum A (Albright 1932:Pls. 55:2, 5, 9, 56:2). Fig. 76:8 is somewhat smaller than the other two but it represents the same type. Fig. 76:9 still has the older elongated cooking pot rim, though now modified, which survives in occasional examples in late Iron II.

The lamp fragment in Fig. 76:10 may have had a flat, rounded base as suggested in the reconstruction and thus would represent a continuation of the late Iron I lamp (TT 89, Fig. 51:1). It can be compared with two somewhat earlier examples from Stratum VA at Hazor (Yadin and others 1961:Pl. 232:3-4). Alongside this form, the lamp with flattened or footed base begins to appear in the latter part of Iron II although no examples are found in these groups from Taanach (Yadin and others 1961:Pl. 232:9-10).

Summary

None of the three periods presented here is without its problems. Perhaps the most tentative is Period III, including the small bits of evidence for the re-dating of the Northeast Outwork. The forms in Period III have a definite continuity with those of Period IIB, and it could be concluded that they represent the latter horizon. Nonetheless, the groups show some development beyond our Period IIB, and in the case of the Northeast Outwork this evidence must be taken with the architectural features of the latter building in determining a date for this building and its contents. Architecturally, the large, rectangular-faced stones employed in the construction of the Northeast Outwork were apparently hewn earlier, probably in the period of Solomon. As they were discovered, they were in a secondary positioning, a matter to be discussed in the volume on stratigraphy. This would argue for a post-Solomonic date for this impressive structure.

POTTERY GROUPS OF PERIODS III-V

Ceramic features in the pottery from the Northeast Outwork and elsewhere pointing to developments beyond Period IIB are the following: 1) Bowls seem to be developed from the Period IIB bowls although they are not far removed from those traditions. There are several new forms not found in the Period IIB groups. 2) Burnishing on a red slip is present and tends to be done on both the exterior and interior. There are no traces of bowls being burnished on the exterior to the point of carination, the marked characteristic of Period IIB. 3) The one elongated cooking pot rim found in the Period III groups also shows some development beyond the Period IIB rims. 4) Especially noteworthy is the absence of clear diagnostic forms of Period IIB which would suggest that these groups date slightly later than Period IIB. It would thus appear that Period III more properly falls in the ninth century.

Period IV is characterized stratigraphically by a phenomenon whose significance has to be considered in the light of comparative study. The several loci in SW 4-7, from which the Period IV groups came, all suggest a destruction, the loci consisting uniformly of ashy, burned material. The amount of material is insufficient to determine whether this burned debris belonged to a localized fire in the Period IV town or whether a larger attack took place at this time. The latter is a possibility if a connection is made with the Assyrian destruction of 732 which seemingly terminated Hazor Stratum V. The problem cannot be solved, but the small amount of evidence here suggests, at least, the possibility of a connection with these events.

The date for Period V in the first half of the seventh century might be contested. It could be argued that diagnostic forms such as the "sausage jars" would call for a slightly earlier date if the view is held that such jars do not appear much after the 732 Assyrian destruction. The "sausage jars" discussed by Holladay (1966:215, 397-408, Figs. 83-86b) are all from Stratum V at Hazor and thus dated to before 732 or 722. However, jars of this type are also attributed to Stratum IV at the same site thus indicating that they continued into the seventh century (Yadin and others 1960:Pl. 101:9, 10, 12-15). It is noteworthy that the excellent stratified eighth century pottery groups at Tell er-Rumeith lack these jars as well as jars with profiled rims like the one in Fig. 75:1 (oral communication from James A. Sauer). Although an argument from absence, this might lend support to a date after 732 for the Taanach group. Parallels with Period VII at Samaria cited above, however, offer additional support for a post-732 date for this material. The Period V group, then, might reflect a resumption of occupation at Taanach during the times of Assyrian control in the north. It might be noted again that more Iron II materials than those presented here could be expected at Taanach in future excavation. Sellin appears to have uncovered substantial Iron II material including a water decanter (Sellin 1904:63, Fig. 77).

Chapter Seven
Pottery Groups of Period VI

Excavation in the southwest quadrant brought to light many stone-lined pits attributed to Period VI in the phasing of the present study. There were only a few remains of structures indicating that the town was not extensively settled in this period. In SW 1-9, the remains of two rooms were apparently part of a Persian building (Lapp 1967a:30-32, Fig. 20). The building had been used in two phases, but the trench of the earlier Sellin excavations had cut through on the east side, destroying much of the architecture and contents. Another structure belonging to Period VI was the latest phase of the Northeast Outwork. Pottery from the platform pavements to the north and west indicated that this significant structure, originally constructed in Period III, continued in use into the Persian period. Unfortunately, however, the amount of pottery from these stratified buildings was sparse. The groups presented in this chapter came from pits containing a larger amount of material.

Period VIA

SW 4-7, STONE-LINED PIT L. 7

This pit was discovered on the west side of SW 4-7 not far below the surface. The stony, detritus layer, L. 4, above, had mixed pottery with the latest coming from the Arabic period. Since sherds going back as far as Period IIB were found in it, the pit seems to have been in use through most of Iron II. The larger amount of material belonged, however, to Period VIA. Below the pit was L. 69, a soft, brown layer containing mixed Iron I pottery.

SW 5-7, STONE-LINED PIT L. 11

This well-constructed pit was found in the center of the north quarter of SW 5-7. During Arab times Wall L. 3 was laid over the top of the pit, and some of the top stones of the latter were pulled off. Judging from a few sherds in the lower part, the pit appears, like the previous one, to have been used earlier in Iron II even as far back as Period IIB. Sherds presented from this pit came from approximately the middle part of its debris, L. 15. The yellow, clay layer, L. 66, below, had Iron I pottery.

SW 6-2, PIT L. 74

This locus has already been discussed in relation to the Period IIB materials found in the cistern of which it was a part. The pottery group presented in this chapter came from the final use of the cistern when its shaft was employed as a pit. Below this debris, the bell of the cistern contained Period IIB remains, and in its lowest deposits were a few LB I sherds. An Arab bath dating to the eleventh or twelfth century A.D. sealed the pit above.

Period VIB

SW 2-25, STONE-LINED PIT L. 125;
SW 3-25, STONE-LINED PIT L. 22; AND
SW 2-25, L. 19

Two stone-lined pits were discovered in the vicinity of the Drainpipe Structure on the south end of the mound. In contrast to those previously discussed, they represent pits originally constructed in Period VIB. Pits L. 125 and L. 22 were adjacent on the north end of SW 2-25 and 3-25. They were found directly underneath Arab graves which had been cut into the area and which robbed out a small part of the pits at the top. Both pits were cut into the Period IB debris of the Drainpipe Structure. SW 2-25, L. 19 was a small part of Stone-lined Pit L. 125 cleared in 1963 but completed in 1966. It is thus part of the group from SW 2-25 but is presented here separately as it was excavated.

Comparative Strata and Date

The Persian Period, designating the span between 539 and 333 (Battle of Issus), has been characterized by imprecision in ceramic typology. Although a fair number of sites have turned up materials dating to this era, there have been few efforts to define development of pottery forms (Lapp 1970a:179). The groups from Taanach offer some new data for at least part of this period.

HAZOR

As for Iron II, so also for the Persian period, Hazor is of special importance. In Area B the Stratum III Citadel, built at the end of the seventh and the early part of the sixth centuries, was reconstructed during Stratum II. The latter stratum was dated between the end of the fifth and the end of the fourth centuries (Yadin and others 1958:54-7, 65). Of special importance in this large building was Hall 3009 which contained the best group of finds, some of which provide good parallels to the groups from Taanach. Area G also produced materials of the type found in Stratum II. Above Stratum II was the uppermost stratum at Hazor representing the Hellenistic occupation of the site.

TEL GOREN, MEGIDDO, TELL ABU HAWĀM

Similar to Hazor, Stratum V at Tel Goren has been dated to the late seventh and early sixth centuries, while Stratum IV was designated as Persian and given a date during the fifth and fourth centuries. At the same time, some of the pottery listed under Stratum V may be used for comparative purposes since a number of the vessels apparently belong with the Stratum IV horizon (Mazar and others 1966:16, Fig. 16:1-2). Megiddo Stratum I has material important for this period although the broad range attributed to it, between 600 and 350, needs reexamination (Lamon and Shipton 1939:88, 91). At Tell Abu Hawām two phases were discerned in Stratum II. Stratum IIA was originally dated between 569 and 525 and Stratum IIB from 525 to the beginning of the fourth century (Hamilton 1935:2-5, 66). These dates have more recently been lowered by Stern to 538-385/83 for Stratum IIA, and 385/83-332 for Stratum IIB (Stern 1968).

ADDITIONAL SITES

In addition to the above sites, there is material from Tell en-Naṣbeh (Wampler 1947) as well as groups from the tombs at ᶜAthlit (Johns 1933). Neither of these sites, however, offers primary evidence for the chronology of the period. Better is the small amount of pottery found in the Persian Residency at Lachish, dated by the excavators between 450 and 350 (Tufnell 1953:135). Pottery found at ᶜAfula also suggested a small amount of Persian occupation between Strata II and III (M. Dothan 1955:29). The period promises to receive considerable clarification when the finds at Megadim and several other recently excavated sites such as Tell el-Ḥesi are published (Lapp 1970a:187, n. 43).

The presence of a number of imported vessels and fragments in the stone-lined pits at Taanach makes possible a closer dating of these groups. A pit similar to Pits 7, 11 and 74 and probably contemporary with the latter was found in SW 6-5, L. 28. It contained two Attic white-ground lekythoi TT 1793, 1794, which have been dated to the middle of the fifth century (Lapp 1964:43-44). Thus the above cluster of pits, located in the south-central part of the mound, may be dated to approximately 450 or slightly earlier. On the other hand, Pits L. 125 and L. 22, found on the lower south slope, appear to be slightly later. slightly later. Their dating is sharpened by a kylix found in one and a lekythos fragment in the other. As can be seen in the discussion, both the kylix (TT 848, Fig. 84:6) and the lekythos fragment (Fig. 86:4) have their best parallels from the late fifth century. Finally, the small group from L. 19 in SW 2-25 may be taken as contemporary with Pits L. 125 and L. 22.

	Loci	Figures	Date
Period VIA	Pit L. 7 (SW 4-7)	77-78	ca. 450-425
	Pit L. 11 (SW 5-7)	79	
	Pit L. 74 (SW 6-2)	80-82	
Period VIB	Pit L. 125 (SW 2-25)	83-84	ca. 425-400
	Pit L. 22 (SW 3-25)	85-86	
	L. 19 (SW 2-25)	87	

The Pottery

JARS (FIGS. 77:1-3, 79:1-3, 80:1-5, 81:1-3, 83:1-3, 85:3-7, 87:3-4)

The first jar rim to be discussed is found in Fig. 77:1. It is from a neckless jar and is distinguished by its grooved, thickened rim. The orange surface is typical of the Persian period. Since this rim type does not appear in the other groups, it is possible that it is a late example, and it may be that the form passed out of use about the middle of the fifth century. Grooving is found on late Iron II holemouth rims such as those from Lachish (Tufnell 1953:Pl. 97:550) and Tell Beit Mirsim (Albright 1932:Pl. 52:1). The same practice is also present farther to the south as attested by a jar from Umm el-Biyara belonging to about the middle of the seventh century (Bennett 1966:391, Fig. 4:5). However, the closest parallel to Fig. 77:1 comes from an unnumbered stratum between Strata II and III at ᶜAfula (M. Dothan 1955: Fig. 10:7).

A further group of jar rims is found in Fig. 80:1-4. Fig. 80:1 has a slight ridge on the neck and may be taken as a late vestige of the profiled jar rim which began in Period IIB and developed through Iron II. During the Persian period this rim is replaced by one which is more an offshoot of the profiled rim than a new form. It is represented in Fig. 80:2-4 and is slightly thickened and grooved. It appears on jars with a body like Fig. 80:4 and possibly also Fig. 83:3. A parallel to these groove-rimmed jars is found at Tell en-Naṣbeh (Wampler 1947:Pl. 20:344). Fig. 77:2 is a smaller jar related to the same general class but with thickened rim.

Two jars with thickened rims are found in Figs. 77:3 and 79:1. Fig. 77:3 has a long neck and thickened rim which flares slightly while Fig. 79:1 has a shorter neck and a more rounded rim like those on jars of the Hellenistic period (Lapp and Lapp 1968:Fig. 21:7-9). Similar rims are found in Stratum II at Hazor (Yadin and others 1961:Pl. 257:23). A somewhat earlier jar with rounded rim and a slightly longer neck comes from Tel Goren Stratum V (Mazar and others 1966:Fig. 22:3).

Another group of jars illustrates the fifth-century counterpart to cylindrical "sausage jars" of Iron II. Examples of these are found in Figs. 80:5, 81:1-3 and 83:1-2. In Iron II these jars sometimes have a short neck (Fig. 75:2), while on the Persian jars the common tendency is for the rim to be attached at the shoulder tip. Two rim types on such jars are represented here. The first is a

POTTERY GROUPS OF PERIOD VI

thickened, flat-topped rim like the one in Fig. 81:1. A good parallel is from Tell Abu Hawām Stratum II, and the Taanach example probably had a pointed base such as the whole form from this site (Hamilton 1935:4, Fig. 3). The second type has a rim which is drawn to a point at the tip like Figs. 80:5 and 81:2, or rounded like Fig. 81:3. An example from Stratum II at Hazor can be compared with Fig. 81:2 (Yadin and others 1961:Pl. 257:17). In the latter part of the fifth century the rim is drawn up to an even more vertical point as is evident in Fig. 83:1-2, and this may represent the latest modification prior to the further development of this rim in the Hellenistic period.

A variety of handles from jars and jugs is found in Figs. 79:2-3 and 85:3-7. Figs. 79:2 and 85:5 are oval-shaped like the jug handle in Fig. 83:4. Fig. 85:7 is similar and is from a smaller jug or juglet. Fig. 79:3 has a thin, painted band on the handle, while Fig. 85:3 comes from a "sausage jar" like Fig. 81:1. The handles on "sausage jars" are almost always twisted or gnarled, a characteristic feature of the period. The flattened handle in Fig. 85:6 also represents a common handle during the Persian period. It can be compared with the flattened and ribbed handle in Fig. 80:4. Similar handles are also found in Stratum II at Hazor (Yadin and others 1958:Pl. 81:10).

Finally, the large handle in Fig. 87:4 has special chronological significance. It belongs to the type of high loop handles utilized on large jars with an elongated body and having pronounced pointed bases. Several of these were discovered at Megiddo where they were attributed to Stratum I (Lamon and Shipton 1939:Pl. 12:63-64), and further examples were found in one of the ᶜAthlit tombs (Johns 1933:51, Fig. 4f) and in the Persian Residency at Lachish (Tufnell 1953:see under Fig. 96:506). There is little evidence for these vessels before about 450, and, in fact, their presence points toward the end rather than the middle of the fifth century. An unpublished handle of this type from L. 1 in the Northeast Outwork at Taanach suggests that this earlier structure was reused during Period VIB.

JUGS AND JUGLETS (FIGS. 77:4-5, 81:4-7, 83:4-5, 84:1, 85:1-2, 87:1)

Fig. 77:4 is noteworthy because it resembles somewhat the jug with bowed rim from Iron II. The ware is red, typical of many of the vessels of the Persian period. It can be compared with a Period IV rim made of tan ware (Fig. 74:1). This rim seems to disappear during Period VI since late parallels for it are scarce.

A common jug rim during Period VI is one which is thickened in a variety of ways, as in Figs. 81:4, 84:1, and 85:2. The ware in these small-to-medium-sized jugs usually has a gray color. Fig. 81:4 has a vertical neck. The rim in Fig. 85:2 is similar but flares out slightly more, displaying a slight grooving of the rim. Jugs with thickened rims are also found in Stratum II at Hazor (Yadin and others 1958:Pl. 81:7). Fig. 84:1 has a shorter neck, and its shoulder comes close to the rim.

A further group of jugs in Fig. 83:4-5 has thickened rims, though not as heavy as the previous examples. These rims seem to be from slightly larger jugs than the ones discussed above. At Megiddo a similar jug, assigned a range from Strata III to I, is probably more distinctive of the latter stratum (Lamon and Shipton 1939:Pl. 2:68). The rim in Fig. 85:1 is identical to the previous two, while the one in Fig. 87:1 has vestigial ridging on the neck. That these jugs occur only in the pit groups from the lower south slope suggests that they may have first begun to appear toward the latter part of the fifth century in Period VIB.

The handle in Fig. 77:5 probably comes from a small jug. It is formed with two coils of clay pressed together, and decoration is with horizontal black and red, painted lines. It can be compared with TT 910, the imported jug with a high-thrown handle found in the miscellaneous groups below (Fig. 94:4). The juglet fragment in Fig. 81:5 has a thickened rim with a pronounced ridge around the neck. A parallel from Stratum II at Hazor has a similar ridge with a more flaring rim than the Taanach example (Yadin and others 1958:Pl. 80:20).

In Fig. 81:6 is a small, handleless bottle with pointed base. More complete examples of the type were discovered at Tel Goren (Mazar and others 1966:Fig. 19:14, 15). Having its origin in Assyria, probably as early as the eighth century, this bottle was found both west and east of the Jordan River (Amiran and others 1970:291, 296). It continued in use during the Persian and Hellenistic periods (Yadin and others 1958:58-59). The best parallel to the one here is a bottle from Stratum II at Hazor (Yadin and others 1958:Pl. 80:22) which was also made of pink ware like the Taanach bottle. Other bottles were found in Tomb 14 at ᶜAin Shems (Grant and Wright 1938:Fig. 68:10) and at Tell en-Naṣbeh (Wampler 1947:Pl. 75:1732). The flat base in Fig. 81:7 is also from a juglet or bottle. Its cylindrical body tapered toward the top, and it probably had two handles attached close to the neck. Parallels for this smaller example are not numerous. It can be compared to an alabastron from Stratum V at Tel Goren (Mazar and others 1966:Fig. 19:16) as well as a larger jar in Stratum II at Hazor (Yadin and others 1958:Pl. 83:2).

CRATERS (FIGS. 77:6, 79:4, 86:2)

Only a few craters are represented in the Persian groups from Taanach. Fig. 77:6 can be compared to a crater from Tell el-Fûl (Sinclair 1960:Pl. 26:16). The latter example is especially noteworthy because it is decorated with chevron design in contrast to the one from Taanach. Lapp's observation that chevron design disappeared before mortaria arrived on the scene appears to hold up in this group from Taanach since the vessel here is lacking such decoration, while in the same group (Fig. 77:7-9) mortaria are present (Lapp 1970a:185). The crater rim in Fig. 79:4 has orange ware typical of Period VI. Parallels for the form, however, could not be found. The crater in

Fig. 86:2 is also unusual and may have been influenced by the shape of some of the cooking pots of this period.

MORTARIA (FIGS. 77:7-9, 79:5, 81:8-9, 84:2, 85:8-10, 86:1, 87:2)

Well represented in all of the Persian groups from Taanach are the large, shallow vessels commonly designated as mortaria. Often these vessels have a light green or yellow ware. In general, two rim types are present, one having a heavy rim on the exterior, like Figs. 77:7-8, 84:2 and 85:8-9, the other having a slightly thickened, plain rim such as Figs. 81:8 and 87:2. Two types of base are also found, one a heavy ring base as in Figs. 77:9, 79:5 and 85:10, the other a flat base as in Figs. 81:9 and 86:1. Since these variations in base type occur simultaneously, there is apparently no chronological significance in them. Parallels to these mortaria are abundantly present at comparative sites for this period. Stratum II at Hazor has examples with heavy rims (Yadin and others 1961:Pl. 257:3, 7). The plain rim is also present at the same site as is the flat base (Yadin and others 1958:Pl. 79:23; 1961: Pl. 257:2). Some examples, such as Fig. 85:9, have a rippled outer surface, and similar examples appear in Stratum II at Hazor (Yadin and others 1961:Pl. 257:7, 9). The latter feature is limited to the Persian period (Lapp 1970a:185). Fig. 85:8 has a thickened rim which is more down-turned than the other examples, and it is noteworthy that a similar example is present at Hazor (Yadin and others 1961:Pl. 257:1). In addition to Hazor, other sites with examples of mortaria are Tell Abu Hawām Stratum II (Hamilton 1935:4, Fig. 4), ᶜAfula (M. Dothan 1955:Fig. 10:14-16), Megiddo (Lamon and Shipton 1939:Pl. 23:15-17), Cave 534 and the Residency at Lachish (Tufnell 1953:Pl. 98:567-568), Ashdod Stratum 2 in Area D (Dothan and Freedman 1967:Fig. 40:10-11), and Tel Goren (Mazar and others 1966:Fig. 16:1-2). These vessels thus represent a prominent fifth-century form which continued to be popular into the Hellenistic period (Lapp 1970a:185; N. Lapp 1964:17-18).

BOWLS (FIGS. 77:10-11, 82:1-2)

Fig. 77:10 is the only shallow bowl found in the group here. It has slightly incurved sidewalls and a flat rim and, except for its orange ware, could be taken as a bowl from as early as Period IIA (see Fig. 64:10-11). No close parallels to this bowl could be found.

Deep bowls with incurved sides or vertical necks such as those in Figs. 77:11 and 82:1-2 comprise a prominent type in Period VIA. Their absence in the Period VIB groups here does not preclude the possibliity that they continued to the late fifth century. Fig. 77:11 is small and has incurved sides with a cyma profile. No close parallels to this form could be found. Fig. 82:1 is a medium-sized deep bowl with handles, incurved sides, and a shaved rim. It can be compared with a slightly earlier, handleless bowl from Tell en-Naṣbeh (Wampler 1947:Pl. 66:1502). The small bowl in Fig. 82:2 may be taken as the prototype of a bowl which was popular in the Hellenistic period and even later (Lapp 1961:Type 51.1, 2).

COOKING POTS (FIGS. 79:6, 82:3-4, 84:3-4)

A common cooking pot of this period is found in Fig. 79:6 and 84:3. This vessel has a globular body with two handles and is made of thin ware. Figs. 79:6 and 84:3 have flaring rims which overlap on the exterior. They can be compared with Stratum II examples at Hazor (Yadin and others 1961:Pl. 257:13) as well as one from Stratum II at Tell Abu Hawām (Hamilton 1935:4, Fig. 6). The neck and shoulder in Fig. 82:4 are probably also from a cooking pot of this type, the neck here being straighter and the rim shaved on the interior.

A different type of cooking pot is found in Fig. 82:3. This type, appearing here only in Period VIA, probably represents a development of the common cooking pot with grooved rim at the end of Iron II. The vessel has sidewalls sloping inwardly to the rim with virtually no neck or shoulder. Parallels from other Persian contexts were not found for this form. Finally, the small-mouthed cooking pot rim in Fig. 84:4 is evidently a late example of a type represented by a number of Stratum V examples from Shechem (Lapp 1970a:186). Those from Shechem date at least a half-century earlier, so that the Taanach rim represents the end of the life-span of this form.

LAMPS (FIGS. 78:1-3, 82:5-6, 84:5, 86:3)

Several fragments of Persian lamps belong to these pit groups. Figs. 78:1-3, 82:6, 84:5 and 86:3 are all made of orange to red ware and have flat base characteristic of the Persian period. The lamp with footed base in Fig. 82:5 is characteristic of the latter part of Iron II as can be seen in examples from Tell Beit Mirsim (Albright 1932:Pl. 70:4-8), Megiddo Stratum III (Lamon and Shipton 1939:Pl. 37:6-7), and Tel Goren Stratum V (Mazar and others 1966:Fig. 23:4-9). It might be concluded on the basis of Taanach evidence that this type disappears shortly after the middle of the fifth century. The type with flat base and wide lip is present at first alongside lamps with footed base, but then becomes the main type in Period VIB. It is noteworthy that the Persian groups of Stratum II at Hazor and Stratum II at Tell Abu Hawām have only lamps with flattened bases which suggests a date for these groups toward the end of the fifth century (Yadin and others 1961:Pls. 258:2-3, 19:16; Hamilton 1935:4, Fig. 5; Lapp 1970a:186).

IMPORTED WARES (FIGS. 82:7, 84:6, 86:4)

Several imported pieces are found in these groups. The body sherd in Fig. 82:7 is probably from an imported vessel belonging to the Cypriot White Painted V tradition (Gjerstad 1948:57; Gjerstad and others 1935: Pl. 165:7). Gjerstad discusses pottery of this kind from the end of Period 6 at Idalion and proposes a date about 470 at the latest for it (Gjerstad and others 1935:*Text*, 625). This dating is slightly higher than that attributed to Period VIA in the present study, although, as noted previously, the 450 figure for the upper limit of Period VIA is

POTTERY GROUPS OF PERIOD VI

approximate, and its range could be extended a bit earlier. This sherd thus provides general support for the dating of the Period VIA groups.

Fig. 84:6, TT 848, is an Eastern Greek version of the well-known kylix. As an imported piece it differs completely in ware, form and decoration from anything made locally during this period. Examples in Palestine exhibit the movement southward of this vessel which had its origin in the southern coastal area of Turkey. Two vessels of this type were found at Mersin and designated "Ionian bowls." They have the same kind of pink ware and red-brown paint as the ones here (Garstang 1953:Fig. 161:6-7). The best Palestinian parallel so far discovered is an unpublished example from Jaffa now in the Jaffa Museum (Museum No. 315, Reg. No. 80Y/62/J; see Lapp 1970a:180, n. 9). This example was found together with a group of late fifth-century Attic wares, providing a close date for the kylix. Another example was found in a tomb at ᶜAthlit whose shaft had been disturbed by the later intrusion of a medieval fosse (Johns 1933:101, Fig. 88; Lapp 1970a:180, n. 9). Fragments of this vessel type were also observed among the unpublished Stratum II pottery from Megadim (Lapp 1970a:183, n. 21).

The fragment of an Attic white-ground lekythos in Fig. 86:4 also found its way to Taanach as part of an import. The example here is decorated with a pattern of palmettes much like a lekythos from Athens (Haspels 1936:100, No. 2213; Pl. 36:5). These vessels were prominent during the fifth century, and the example here fits well with the Period VIB group in which it was found.

Summary

Several features characterize Period VI and point to development within it. The most obvious is the chalky, orange ware of which many vessels during this period, both at Taanach and elsewhere, are made. Other distinguishing characteristics can be summarized as follows: 1) During the entire period a "sausage jar" with a rim either rounded or pulled to a point is found. This jar is often made of red or orange ware and usually has gnarled handles. 2) The large loop handle found on some jars (Fig. 87:4) suggests the latest phase of Period VI, but examples seem to be present already in Period VIA at several other sites as well as at Taanach (Lapp 1970a:183). 3) Jugs for the period are less distinctive. The most common type has a vertical neck with thickened rim and seems to grow in its prominence during Period VIB. 4) The bottle and two-handled juglet or alabastron in Fig. 81:6-7 are both good diagnostic forms for the period. 5) Mortaria are found throughout Period VI, pointing to the prominence of this vessel during the fifth century, a feature confirmed at various comparative sites. 6) Bowls are scarce in the groups discussed above and have few distinguishing features, but cooking pots show the transition from a form still related to Iron II types in Fig. 82:3 to a thinner vessel in Fig. 84:3. Plain, undecorated craters like the one in Fig. 77:6 point to a later development than the chevron-design crater known from other sites, and the form is thus important for fixing the date of these groups. 7) Lamps with footed base are on the way out in Period VI with the flat-based lamp, again usually made of orange ware, becoming the main type. 8) Finally, as has been noted, the three imported vessels or vessel fragments in Figs. 82:7, 84:6 (TT 848), and 86:4 have special chronological value and help to undergird the dating of these groups.

Chapter Eight
Miscellaneous Iron Age Pottery

In this final section all whole or nearly whole Iron Age forms from the recent excavations are presented. Although these examples were usually discovered in mixed loci, they are important because they provide whole sections of vessels which are often seen only as sherds in the groups selected above. The discussion of the individual forms is kept to a minimum. Wherever they are parallel to pottery in the groups above, reference is made to the latter, and parallels can be consulted there. If they represent a form not discussed previously, parallels are cited from other sites utilizing wherever possible the PCL isolated at these sites.

Period IA (Figs. 88-90)

The four-handled jar, TT 1862, in Fig. 88:1 came from a fairly clear Period IA deposit in SW 2-8. The general type, which may have a ring or rounded base, continues through much of Iron I as evidenced by an example attributed to the times of Ramses II at Beth Shan (Fitzgerald 1930:Pl. 49:22) and one from Stratum VIA at Megiddo (Loud 1948:Pl. 77:1).

The two jugs, TT 1430 and TT 1281, in Fig. 88:2-3 also fit well into Period IA. TT 1430 has a thickened rim like a rim from the Period IA Tablet Building (Fig. 1:3). It is also paralleled by early Iron Age jugs at Bethel (Kelso 1948:Pl. 54:10) and ʿAin Shems (Grant and Wright 1938:Pl. 60:1). The small jug, TT 1281, has no parallels in the groups above, but it is close to a jug with more pointed base from the end of LB II at Hazor (Yadin and others 1960:Pl. 132:3).

Crater TT 832 in Fig. 89:1 is a whole example of the ubiquitous Iron I crater discussed in various places above. The small bowl, TT 1431, with sinuous profile in Fig. 89:2 is found throughout the twelfth century as seen in the groups above (Figs. 4:11, 13:13-14). A close parallel is from PCL 2131 at Megiddo (Loud 1948:Pl. 65:12).

Chalices TT 988, 1356, 1146 in Fig. 89:3-5 all fit well in Period IA. TT 988 has an interior overlapped rim and is closely paralleled by a chalice from PCL 2131 at Megiddo (Loud 1948:Pl. 67:5; cf. Guy and Engberg 1938:Pl. 68:19, and Grant and Wright 1938:Pl. 59:22). TT 1356 is similar, but the rim is grooved. It has a close parallel in Fig. 3:16. TT 1146 has a simple, bevelled rim and can be compared to a Phase B chalice at Deir ʿAllā (Franken and Kalsbeek 1969:Fig. 48:53).

The cup and saucer, TT 1157, in Fig. 90:1 also has good parallels during this period. Three examples are found in PCL 2131 at Megiddo (Loud 1948:Pl. 67:7-9). The same locus at Megiddo also has a lamp similar to TT 1054, Fig. 90:2 (Loud 1948:Pl. 66:9). Fig. 90:3, TT 945, has a parallel in a lamp assigned to Stratum III at ʿAin Shems (Grant and Wright 1938:Pl. 61:34).

Period IB (Fig. 91)

The four vessels in Fig. 91 can all be confidently assigned to Period IB. Fig. 91:1, TT 753, is the base of a jug, or possibly a cooking pot, with a globular body like one found at Megiddo (Loud 1948:Pl. 67:14). The important cache of weights from SW 2-8, L. 27, was found in this jug (Lapp 1967a:34). TT 891 in Fig. 91:2 displays the carinated body typical of cooking pots through most of Iron I. A later example from L. 2070 at Megiddo, assigned to Stratum VIA, provides a good parallel to it (Loud 1948:Pl. 79:6). TT 564, the wide-mouthed bowl with simple rim in Fig. 91:3, stands in the tradition of older Late Bronze bowls and is one of the latest of this type (Loud 1948:Pl. 71:17; Sellers and others 1933:Pl. 7:7). In Iron I these simple-rimmed bowls usually have flat or disc bases like the one in Fig. 1:15, thus the one here is unusual. Goblet chalices like TT 800 in Fig. 91:4 are a distinctive feature of Period I as are TT 990 and TT 928 (Figs. 8:14, 14:14). The one here is close to TT 928, although its profiled neck differs from the simple neck and rim of the former.

Period IIB (Figs. 92-93)

The base of TT 845 in Fig. 92:1 is found on many globular jugs of Period II. The Cistern L. 74 group contained similar examples (Fig. 61:2-4). Juglets TT 635, 127, 35 and 128 in Fig. 92:2-5 closely parallel ones in the Period IIB groups presented above. TT 635 can be compared with TT 690 in Fig. 62:9, TT 127 and 35 with TT 386 in Fig. 40:3, and TT 128 with TT 327 and 306 in Fig. 40:4-5. TT 127 in Fig. 92:3 also has a close parallel in a juglet from PCL 2081 at Megiddo (Loud 1948:Pl. 88:11) while TT 35 is paralleled by a juglet from Stratum V at the same site (Lamon and Shipton 1939:Pl. 5:135). Pyxis TT 272 in Fig. 92:6 is locally made. Its painted bands might suggest an earlier date since a similar example is found as early as Stratum VIIA at Megiddo (Loud 1948:Pl. 68:9). However, the form is closely paralleled by an unpainted pyxis from Stratum III at Tell Abu Hawām (Hamilton 1935:20, Fig. 60); and a cruder, painted example from Stratum V at Megiddo supports the interpretation that such decoration was employed on pyxides into the tenth century (Lamon and Shipton 1939:Pl. 19:100). Pyxis TT 66 in Fig. 92:7 is nearly identical to TT 488 in Fig. 40:12 from the Cultic Structure.

TT 115, TT 681 and Fig. 93:3 are all of the type found in the Cultic Structure with red-burnished slip reaching to the exterior carination (see Figs. 45:3, 47:4-5, 48:4-5). TT 551, the lamp in Fig. 93:4, also has a parallel in TT 473 from the Cultic Structure (Fig. 51:2).

The two poorly stratified Cypriot juglets TT 604, 605 in Fig. 93:5-6, are presented here under Period IIB although they could go down into Period III or possibly even Period IV as well. It is doubtful, however, that they date as late as the seventh century judging from the evidence from various Palestinian sites (Lapp 1967a:37-39). TT 604 belongs to the type designated Black-on-red I(III) while TT 605 is probably Black-on-red II(IV) (Gjerstad 1948:Figs. 25:10, 38:12). Since much of the Cypriot evidence has come from tombs, the dating of these juglets has depended more on Palestinian contexts than vice versa (Albright 1932:72; 1943:6, n. 2; 1953a:22-26; Van Beek 1951). Both types occur in PCL for the late tenth century at Megiddo. A parallel to TT 604 is found in Rooms 6-7 of Building 10 (Lamon and Shipton 1939:Pl. 5:123) while a close parallel to TT 605 was found earlier at Taanach by Sellin (Sellin 1904:Figs. 8b, 44, 97; Gjerstad 1948:250). They appear in the south in Tell Beit Mirsim Stratum B3 (Albright 1932:Pl. 51:9), as far north as Hazor (Yadin and others 1960:Pl. 52:17), and elsewhere at sites too numerous to demand mention here. There may be some development in the decoration of these juglets from a red-burnished slip earlier in the eleventh and first part of the tenth century (Yadin and others 1961:Pl. 172:1) to a lighter tan or brown slip a bit later, the latter being represented by the ones here. Discussion has frequently been devoted to these juglet types, but it cannot be said that their range and development have been fully clarified as yet. At present it seems safest to conclude that both types are found in the late tenth century and that they appear to continue for a century or a century and a half beyond that.

Periods III-VI (Figs. 94-95)

In Figs. 94-95 are found all large fragments of Iron II or Persian vessels from contexts not treated above. They are arranged according to type rather than chronologically. Fig. 94:1 is from a jar with profiled rim. It has a smoother, rounded shoulder and body than Fig. 94:2. The close parallels from Hazor Stratum VI suggest a date during the first half of the eighth century although the example here could be later (Yadin and others 1961:Pl. 219:23-24). The one in Fig. 94:2 is distinctly a late Iron II example of the profiled rim jar and can be dated to the first half of the seventh century by means of a Period V parallel above (Fig. 75:1). Close parallels for Fig. 94:3 could not be found, but its ovoid-shaped body suggests development from the Period IIB jars of the Cultic Structure (Figs. 30-31). The form may thus belong in either Period IIB or Period III. Fig. 94:4, TT 910, is an important fragment representing a Cypriot import. The example fits with Cypro-Archaic II vessels and could date anywhere between 600 and 475. Distinctive features of these jugs are the exaggerated bodies, high-thrown handles, and pinched lips (Gjerstad 1948:Fig. 41:9). Decoration is usually with dark-brown, concentric circles and lines on a buff or tan surface. TT 910 may be a late form belonging with the Period VIA groups.

Fig. 95:1-8 are all Iron II juglets of various shapes with the exception of TT 48 in Fig. 95:2 which should be placed in Iron I. TT 60 may belong to Period IV. It can be compared with a juglet from Stratum VI at Hazor (Yadin and others 1961:Pl. 184:18). TT 48 probably belongs in Period IA carrying on the tradition of Late Bronze juglets but with a more rounded base. Parallels from Stratum VII through VI at Megiddo can be compared with it (Loud 1948:Pls. 63:5, 71:8). TT 519, with its red slip, is like seventh-century juglets found at Tell Beit Mirsim and elsewhere (Albright 1932:Fig. 68:41). TT 143 also has parallels in Strata VI and V at Hazor and probably belongs with the Period IV groups at Taanach (Yadin and others 1958:Pls. 52:15, 73:6). The juglet with rounded body, TT 801, is also probably from Period IV with a parallel again being found in Hazor Stratum VA (Yadin and others 1961:Pl. 228:19). TT 546 can be compared to a more elongated Stratum V juglet at Hazor (Yadin and others 1961:Pl. 252:13). TT 802 has a more rounded body than TT 386 (Fig. 40:3) from the Cultic Structure. It is possible that it belongs with the Period IIB groups like similar examples in Stratum V at Megiddo (Lamon and Shipton 1939:Pl. 5:134, 135) and especially the one cited from PCL Room 6. Finally, the juglet TT 120 in Fig. 95:8 is from the Persian period and fits well in Period VI. Its best parallels are from Hazor Stratum II (Yadin and others 1961:Pls. 191:1, 257:15) and from Tel Goren (Mazar and others 1966:Fig. 33:2).

TT 823, the cooking pot in Fig. 95:9, is in the tradition of the globular, handled cooking pot of Period IIB (Fig. 50:1-2). This example with thickened rim may be slightly later, dating, perhaps, to Period III. Finally, the lamp in Fig. 95:10 fits well with the Period VI groups. A poorly stratified example at Megiddo is close in form (Lamon and Shipton 1939:Pl. 37:8).

Chapter Nine
Conclusion

The range of deductions it is possible to make on the basis of shifts in ceramic traditions is limited (Lapp 1961:221). Yet, caches of pottery are hardly deserving of the intricate attention paid them unless they can yield insights into their historical and cultural significance. At the same time, such interpretation is difficult. A new people moving in to occupy an old site may either bring distinctive traditions along with them, or they may adapt the localized ones in such a way that their newly acquired command of a site is barely discernible. Thus it is necessary that ceramic investigation be backed up by stratigraphy and by the indispensible references to a site and its history in ancient written texts.

Granted the need for some reserve, studies of pottery groups such as this call for a venture into interpretation. For the early part of Iron I we have observed that the close continuity between Period I ceramics and the Late Bronze tradition of Palestine would point to a stable Canaanite cultural prominence through the early part of Iron I. This does not mean that that nucleus was unchallenged. In fact, the stratigraphic evidence suggests otherwise. The conspicuous disturbance especially at the end of Period IB must certainly be attributed to an incursion which terminated the cultural pattern of the twelfth century at Taanach, even if that pattern persisted elsewhere for a longer time.

The gap in occupation following the end of Period IB is of cultural and historical importance. That Taanach was unoccupied during most of the eleventh century must be viewed in relation to the archeological history of nearby Megiddo. The latter site as well experienced a lacuna during the first quarter of the eleventh century, but occupation began again earlier and more elaborately than at Taanach. Comparative stratigraphic and ceramic study makes it impossible to interpret the relation between these two sites as contrastive. Thus it is not really accurate to conclude that during Iron I Taanach tended to be occupied when Megiddo was abandoned and vice versa (Albright 1960:117-118; Lapp 1967b:9). The patterns seem rather to run parallel and are usually simultaneous.

A second major cultural nucleus apparently arose with the innovations of Period II. The attribution of these developments to the Israelites is undergirded by comparative study, above all from Megiddo. In an important chapter Aharoni (1970) places the Israelite occupation of Megiddo and other sites in the north earlier than the late eleventh and tenth centuries. However, at several points Aharoni's argument appears weak. 1) The attribution of Stratum VI of Megiddo to Israelites is replete with difficulty; and the excavators' point, that Stratum VI was still strongly reflective of Canaanite tradition, does not appear to have been substantially disproven by Aharoni. 2) The dating of the events behind the Song of Deborah (Judges 5) may well be slightly earlier than 1125, as we have noted above; but Aharoni, in keeping with his general tendency to raise dates in Iron I, attempts to push this date too high to accommodate the evidence from Taanach. 3) The idea that collared-rim store jars are typically Israelite seems more and more to be coming under question. Contrary evidence may be found in the jars of this type from Sahab in Trans-jordan. All in all, the view that serious Israelite occupation of Megiddo began with David (Stratum VB) still appears to have the least number of problems connected with it. The data from Taanach support an interpretation of consolidated Israelite movement into sites of the Esdraelon Plain during the late eleventh and tenth centuries. Although interrupted by a serious attack at the end of Period II, the site can be pictured as having been reused by the same peoples from Period III through Period V.

The remains of Period VI have no direct continuity with those of Periods III to V. They appear, rather, as isolated pockets belonging to more temporary and spotty occupation. This fits well with the Persian occupation of many Palestinian sites when military groups or local employees of the Persian administration apparently settled at previously major sites in order to supervise the affairs of a country now greatly changed in its social and political features.

These cultural and historical inferences apply to the site of Taanach itself and are important for tracing developments during the Iron Age. The ceramics from the site are also helpful for their comparative value in opening the way for links with other sites and for providing a more integrated interpretation. Thus the present study has concentrated heavily on comparative evaluation of the remains. The results are gathered here in summary form in Table 2. It is to be hoped that the publication of future sites will contribute even greater accuracy to this necessary synthesis.

TABLE 2
Correlations Between Iron Age Taanach and Comparative Sites

Taanach		Megiddo	Hazor	Tell El-Fārʿah		Others
Period IA 1200-1150	12th Century House (SW 5-7, 5-8)	L. 2131 (STR. VIIB)	STR. XII		Tell Abu Hawām, STR. V, IVA ʿAfula STR. IIIB	Gezer, Field I, STR. 5 Bethel, Phase 1
Period IB 1150-1125	Drainpipe Structure (SW 2-25, 3-25) Tablet Building (SW 5-2, 6-1, 6-2)	L. 2048 (STR. VII A)			Tell Qasile, STR. XII Tell Beit Mirsim, STR. B₁ El Jib, Area 10-L-5 Ashdod, Pit 2001, STR. XIII-XII	ʿAin Shems, STR. III ʿAi, Phase I, II Deir ʿAllā, Phases A, B Gezer Field I, STR. 4-3
1125-1075		STR. VIB	STR. XI		Tell Beit Mirsim, STR. B₂ Tell Qasile, STR. XI	Bethel, Phase 2
1075-1050						
1050-1025		STR. VIA			ʿAfula STR. IIIA (some) Deir ʿAllā, Phases C-D	
Period IIA 1020-960	L. 68, 53, 44, 57, 60 (SW 4-7) Others	L. 2072 (STR. VIA) STR. VB	STR. XI		Tell El-Fūl, Fortress Phase Tell Abu Hawām, STR. IVB Tell Qasile, STR. X Bethel, Phase 3, 4a	Gezer, Field II, STR. 8, 7 ʿAin Shems, Rm 316 (STR. IIA) ʿAfula, STR. III A (some) Deir ʿAllā, Phases E-H
Period IIB 960-918	Cultic Structure & Cistern 69 (SW 2-7, 2-8) Cistern 74 (SW 6-2)	L. 2081 Building 10 (STR. VA-IVB)	STR. X L. 64c,116c, 118b,159b, 174b	House 436, Room 418 (Niv. III)	Tell Beit Mirsim, STR. B₃ ʿAin Shems, STR. IIb Arad, STR. XI Deir ʿAllā, Phase J Tel ʿAmal, STR. IV-III Beth-Shan, Lower Level V	Jericho, T. 85 Tell En-Nasbeh, Ts. 32, 54 Tell Qasile, STR. IX Gezer Field II, STR. 6 Tell Abu Hawām, STR. III
Period III 875-800	L. 41 (SW 4-7) Northeast Outwork (NEO-2)	STR. IV-III	STR. VIII-VII	Niv. Intermédiaire	Tell Beit Mirsim, STR. A₁ Samaria, Period I, II Deir ʿAllā, Phases K, L	
800-750		STR. III	STR. VI	Niv. II	Tell Beit Mirsim, STR. A₁ Samaria, Periods II-IV	
Period IV 750-732	L. 36,37,38a (SW 4-7)	STR. III	STR. V	Niv. II	Samaria, Periods V-VI	
732-700		STR. III	STR. IV		Samaria, Period VII	
Period V 700-650	L. 16 (SW 5-6)	STR. II	STR. IV-III	Niv. I	Samaria, Period VII	
650-450					Tell El-Fūl, Cisterns Tell Goren, Stratum V	
Period VI 450-400	L. 7 (SW 4-7) L. 11 (SW 5-7) L. 74 (SW 6-2) L. 125, 19 (SW 2-25) L. 22 (SW 3-25)	STR. I	Rebuilt Citadel (STR. II)		Tell Abu Hawām, STR. II Tell Goren, STR. V (Some) & IV ʿAthlit Tombs Lachish Residency Megadim	

Bibliography

AHARONI, Y.
1959   The date of casemate walls in Judah and Israel and their purpose. Bulletin of the American Schools of Oriental Research 154: 35-39.
1968   Arad: its inscriptions and temple. The Biblical Archaeologist 31: 2-32.
1969   Chronique archéologique: Lakish. Revue Biblique 76: 576-578.
1970   New aspects of the Israelite occupation in the north. *In* Near Eastern archaeology in the twentieth century, essays in honor of Nelson Glueck, edited by J. A. Sanders, pp. 254-267, Doubleday & Co., Inc., Garden City, N. Y.
1971   Khirbet Raddana and its inscription. Israel Exploration Journal 21: 130-135.
1972   The stratification of Israelite Megiddo. Journal of Near Eastern Studies 31: 302-311.

ALBRIGHT, W. F.
1924   Excavations and results at Tell El-Fûl (Gibeah of Saul). Annual of the American Schools of Oriental Research 4.
1932   The excavation of Tell Beit Mirsim. I: The pottery of the first three campaigns. Annual of the American Schools of Oriental Research 12.
1934   The Kyle memorial excavation at Bethel. Bulletin of the American Schools of Oriental Research 56: 2-15.
1940   Review of Megiddo I: Seasons of 1925-34, strata I-V. American Journal of Archaeology 44: 546-550.
1943   The excavation of Tell Beit Mirsim. III: The Iron age. Annual of the American Schools of Oriental Research 21-22.
1945   The chronology of the divided monarchy of Israel. Bulletin of the American Schools of Oriental Research 100: 16-22.
1953a   Correspondence with Professor Einar Gjerstad on the chronology of "Cypriot" pottery from Early Iron levels in Palestine. Bulletin of the American Schools of Oriental Research 130: 22-26.
1953b   New light from Egypt on the chronology and history of Israel and Judah. Bulletin of the American Schools of Oriental Research 130: 4-11.
1956   Further light on synchronisms between Egypt and Asia in the period 935-685 B.C. Bulletin of the American Schools of Oriental Research 141: 23-27.
1957   From the stone age to Christianity. Second edition. Doubleday Anchor Books, Garden City, N. Y.
1960   The archaeology of Palestine. Revised edition. Penguin Books, Baltimore.
1968   Yahweh and the gods of Canaan. Doubleday & Co., Inc., Garden City, N. Y.

AMIRAN, R., with P. BECK and U. ZEVULUN
1970   Ancient pottery of the Holy Land: From its beginnings in the Neolithic period to the end of the Iron Age. Rutgers University Press, New Brunswick, N. J.

BENNETT, C.-M.
1966   Fouilles d'Umm El-Biyara. Rapport préliminaire. Revue Biblique 73: 372-403.

BUHL, M.-L., and S. HOLM-NIELSEN
1969   Shiloh: The Danish excavations at Tall Sailūn, Palestine, in 1926, 1929, 1932, and 1963. The pre-Hellenistic remains. Publications of the National Museum, Archaeological-Historical Series 1, Volume 12. The National Museum of Denmark, Copenhagen.

CALLAWAY, J. A.
1968   New evidence on the conquest of Ai. Journal of Biblical Literature 87: 312-320.
1969   The 1966 ͨAi (et-Tell) excavations. Bulletin of the American Schools of Oriental Research 196: 2-16.

CALLAWAY, J. A., and R. E. COOLEY
1971   A salvage excavation at Raddana, in Bireh. Bulletin of the American Schools of Oriental Research 201: 9-19.

COURTOIS, J.-C.
1969   La maison du prêtre aux modèles de poumon et de foies d'Ugarit. *In* Ugaritica VI, edited by J.-C. Courtois, Mission de Ras Shamra 17. Bibliotheque archéologique et historique 81, pp. 91-119. Librairie Orientaliste Paul Geuthner, Paris.

CROSS, F. M., and D. N. FREEDMAN
1971   An inscribed jar handle from Raddana. Bulletin of the American Schools of Oriental Research 201: 19-22.

CROWFOOT, G. M.
1940   Some censer types from Palestine, Israelite period. Palestine Exploration Quarterly 72: 150-157.
1957   Israelite pottery, general list. *In* The objects from Samaria. Samaria-Sebaste. Reports of the Work of the Joint Expedition in 1931-1933 and of the British Expedition in 1935. No. 3, by J. W. Crowfoot, G. M. Crowfoot and K. M. Kenyon, pp. 134-198. Palestine Exploration Fund, London.

DAJANI, R. W.
1966   An Iron Age tomb from Amman. Annual of the Department of Antiquities of Jordan 11: 41-47.

DEVER, W. G., H. D. LANCE, and G. E. WRIGHT
1970   Gezer I: Preliminary report of the 1964-1966 seasons. Annual of the Hebrew Union College Biblical and Archaeological School in Jerusalem.

DOTHAN, M.
1955   The excavations at ᶜAfula. ᶜAtiqot 1, English series, 19-70.
1971   Ashdod II-III: the second and third seasons of excavations, 1963, 1965. ᶜAtiqot 9-10, English series.

DOTHAN, M., and D. N. FREEDMAN
1967   Ashdod I: The first season of excavations, 1962. ᶜAtiqot 7, English series.

DOTHAN, T.
1967   The Philistines and their material culture. (Hebrew) The Bialik Institute and the Israel Exploration Society, Jerusalem.

ENGBERG, R. M.
1940   Historical analysis of archaeological evidence: Megiddo and the song of Deborah. Bulletin of the American Schools of Oriental Research 78: 4-7.

FITZGERALD, G. M.
1930   The four Canaanite temples of Beth-Shan. Part II. The pottery. Publications of the Palestine Section of the Museum of the University of Pennsylvania 2. The University Press for the University of Pennsylvania Museum, Philadelphia.

FRANKEN, H. J., and J. KALSBEEK
1969   Excavations at Tell Deir ᶜAllā. I. Stratigraphical and analytical study of the Early Iron Age pottery. Documenta et Monumenta Orientis Antiqui 16. E. J. Brill, Leiden.

FREEDMAN, D. N.
1961   The chronology of Israel and the ancient Near East. A. Old Testament chronology. *In* The Bible and the ancient Near East: Essays in honor of William Foxwell Albright, edited by G. E. Wright, pp. 203-214. Doubleday & Co., Inc., Garden City, N. Y.

FUNK, R. W.
1968   The Bronze Age-Iron I pottery. *In* The 1957 excavation at Beth-zur by O. R. Sellers, R. W. Funk, J. L. McKenzie, P. and N. Lapp. Annual of the American Schools of Oriental Research 38: 35-53.

GARSTANG, J.
1953 Prehistoric Mersin. Clarendon Press, Oxford.

GJERSTAD, E.
1948 The Swedish Cyprus expedition, IV, Part 2. The Cypro-geometric, Cypro-archaic and Cypro-classical periods. Swedish Cyprus Expedition, Stockholm.
1953 See Albright 1953a.

GJERSTAD, E., J. LINDROS, E. SJÖQVIST, A. WESTHOLM
1935 The Swedish Cyprus expedition. II. Text and plates. Finds and results of the excavations in Cyprus 1927-1931, 2 volumes. Swedish Cyprus Expedition, Stockholm.

GLUECK, N.
1967 Some Edomite pottery from Tell el-Kheleifeh, Parts I and II. Bulletin of the American Schools of Oriental Research 188: 8-38.

GRANT, E.
1939 Ain Shems excavations (Palestine). Part V (Text). Biblical and kindred studies No. 8. Haverford College. Haverford, Pa.

GRANT, E., and G. E. WRIGHT
1938 Ain Shems excavations (Palestine). Part IV (Pottery). Biblical and kindred studies No. 7. Haverford College, Haverford, Pa.

GUY, P. L. O., and R. M. ENGBERG
1938 Megiddo tombs. Oriental Institute Publications 33. University of Chicago Press, Chicago.

HACHMANN, R., and A. KUSCHKE
1966 Berichte über die Ergebnisse der Ausgrabungen in Kāmid el-Lōz (Libanon) in den Jahren 1963 und 1964. Saarbrücker Beiträge zur Altertumskunde 3. Rudolf Habelt Verlag, Bonn.

HAMILTON, R. W.
1935 Excavations at Tell Abu Hawām. Quarterly of the Department of Antiquities in Palestine 4: 1-69.

HASPELS, C. H. E.
1936 Attic black-figured lekythoi. I. Text and II. Plates. École française d'Athènes. Traveaux et mémoires. Fasciocole 4. E. de Boccard, éditeur, Paris.

HOLLADAY, J. S., Jr.
1966 The pottery of northern Palestine in the ninth and eighth centuries B.C. Ph. D. dissertation. Harvard University.

HORN, S. H.
1967 Who was Solomon's Egyptian father-in-law? Biblical Research 12: 3-17.

JAMES, F.
1966 The Iron Age at Beth Shan: A study of levels VI-IV. Museum monographs. The University Museum, University of Pennsylvania, Philadelphia.

JOHNS, C. N.
1933 Excavations at ᶜAtlīt (1930-1): The south-eastern cemetery. Quarterly of the Department of Antiquities in Palestine 2: 41-104.

KELSO, J. L.
1968 The excavation of Bethel (1934-1960). Annual of the American Schools of Oriental Research 39.

KENYON, K. M.
1942 The summit buildings and constructions. In The buildings at Samaria. Samaria-Sebaste. Reports of the

work of the Joint Expedition in 1931-1933 and of the British Expedition in 1935. No. 1, by J. W. Crowfoot, K. M. Kenyon and E. L. Sukenik, pp. 91-139. Palestine Exploration Fund, London.
1957 Pottery: Early Bronze and Israelite. *In* The objects from Samaria. Samaria-Sebaste. Reports of the work of the Joint Expedition in 1931-1933 and of the British Expedition in 1935. No. 3, by J. W. Crowfoot, G. M. Crowfoot and K. M. Kenyon, pp. 90-134, 198-202. Palestine Exploration Fund, London.
1965 Excavations at Jericho. II. The tombs excavated in 1955-58. The British School of Archaeology in Jerusalem, Jerusalem.
1969 The Middle and Late Bronze Age strata at Megiddo. Levant I: 25-60.

LAMON, R. S., and G. M. SHIPTON
1939 Megiddo I: Seasons of 1925-34, strata I-V. Oriental Institute Publications 42. University of Chicago Press, Chicago.

LAPP, N. R.
1964 Pottery from some Hellenistic loci at Balâṭah (Shechem). Bulletin of the American Schools of Oriental Research 175: 14-26.

LAPP, P. W.
1961 Palestinian ceramic chronology: 200 B.C. - A.D. 70. American Schools of Oriental Research, Publications of the Jerusalem School 3. American Schools of Oriental Research, New Haven.
1964 The 1963 excavation at Taʿannek. Bulletin of the American Schools of Oriental Research 173: 4-44.
1965 Tell el Fûl. The Biblical Archaeologist 28: 2-10.
1967a The 1966 excavations at Tell Taʿannek. Bulletin of the American Schools of Oriental Research 185: 2-39.
1967b Taanach by the waters of Megiddo. The Biblical Archaeologist 30: 2-27.
1969a Biblical archaeology and history. The World Publishing Company, New York and Cleveland.
1969b The 1968 excavations at Tell Taʿannek. Bulletin of the American Schools of Oriental Research 195: 2-49.
1969c A ritual incense stand from Taanak. Qadmoniot 2: 16-17, 26a. (Hebrew).
1970a The pottery of Palestine in the Persian period. *In* Archäologie und Altes Testament, Festschrift für Kurt Galling, edited by A. Kuschke and E. Kutsch, pp. 179-197. J. C. B. Mohr (Paul Siebeck), Tübingen.
1970b The Tell Deir ʿAllā challenge to Palestinian archaeology. Review of excavations at Tell Deir ʿAllā I. Vetus Testamentum 20: 243-256.

LAPP, P. W., and N. LAPP
1968 Iron II — Hellenistic pottery groups. *In* The 1957 excavation at Beth-zur by O. R. Sellers, R. W. Funk, J. L. McKenzie, P. and N. Lapp. Annual of the American Schools of Oriental Research 38: 54-89.

LEVY, S., and G. EDELSTEIN
1972 Cinq années de fouilles à Tel ʿAmal (Nir David). Revue Biblique 79: 325-367.

LOUD, G.
1948 Megiddo II: Seasons of 1935-39. Text and plates. Oriental Institute Publications 62. University of Chicago Press, Chicago.

MACALISTER, R. A. S.
1912 The excavation of Gezer: 1902-1905 and 1907-1909. I. John Murray, London.

MAISLER (MAZAR), B.
1951a The excavations at Tell Qasîle, preliminary report. Israel Exploration Journal 1: 61-76, 125-140, 194-218.
1951b The stratification of Tell Abū Huwâm on the Bay of Acre. Bulletin of the American Schools of Oriental Research 124: 21-25.

MAY, H. G.
1935 Material remains of the Megiddo cult. Oriental Institute Publications 26. University of Chicago Press, Chicago.

MAZAR (MAISLER), B.
1957 The campaign of Pharaoh Shishak to Palestine. Supplements to Vetus Testamentum 4: 57-66.

MAZAR (MAISLER), B., T. DOTHAN AND I. DUNAYEVSKY
1966   En-Gedi: the first and second seasons of excavations 1961-1962. ᶜAtiqot 5, English Series.

OHATA, K. (editor)
1966   Tel Zeror I: Preliminary report of the excavation. First season 1964. The Society for Near Eastern Studies in Japan, Tokyo.

PRITCHARD, J. B.
1969   On the use of the tripod cup. *In* Ugaritica VI, edited by J.-C. Courtois. Mission de Ras Shamra 17: Bibliotheque archéologique et historique 81, pp. 427-434. Librairie Orientaliste Paul Geuthner, Paris.

PRITCHARD, J. B., W. L. REED, D. M. SPENCE, J. SAMMIS
1964   Winery, defenses, and soundings at Gibeon. Museum Monographs. The University Museum, University of Pennsylvania, Philadelphia.

SALLER, S.
1966   Iron Age tombs at Nebo, Jordan. Liber Annuus 16: 165-298.

SELLERS, O. R.
1933   The citadel of Beth-zur. Westminster Press, Philadelphia.

SELLERS, O. R., R. W. FUNK, J. L. MC KENZIE, P. AND N. LAPP
1968   The 1957 excavation at Beth-zur. Annual of the American Schools of Oriental Research 38.

SELLIN, E.
1904   Tell Taᶜannek Denkschriften der Kaiserlichen Akademie der Wissenschaften in Wien, Philosophisch-historische Klasse 50. Carl Gerold's Sohn, Wien.

SHIPTON, G. M.
1939   Notes on the Megiddo pottery of strata VI-XX. Studies in Ancient Oriental Civilization 17. University of Chicago Press, Chicago.

SINCLAIR, L. A.
1960   An archaeological study of Gibeah (Tell el-Fûl). Annual of the American Schools of Oriental Research 34-35: 1-52.

STERN, E.
1968   The dating of stratum II at Tell Abu Hawam. Israel Exploration Journal 18: 213-219.
1969   Excavations at Tel Qadesh (Tell Abu Qudeis). Qadmoniot 2: 95-97.

SWIFT, G. F., Jr.
1958   The pottery of the ᶜAmuq phases K to O and its historical relationships. Ph. D. dissertation, the University of Chicago.

THIELE, E. R.
1965   The mysterious numbers of the Hebrew kings. Second edition. Wm. B. Eerdmans Publishing Co., Grand Rapids, Mich.

TUFNELL, O.
1953   Lachish III: The Iron Age. 2 volumes. Text and plates. Oxford University Press, London.

VAN BEEK, G. W.
1951   Cypriote chronology and the dating of Iron I sites in Palestine. Bulletin of the American Schools of Oriental Research 124: 26-29.
1955   The date of Tell Abu Huwam, stratum III. Bulletin of the American Schools of Oriental Research 138: 34-38.
1969   Hajar bin Humeid: Investigations at a pre-Islamic site in South Arabia. Publications of the American Foundation for the Study of Man 5. The Johns Hopkins Press, Baltimore.

VAUX, R., de
1951　La troisième campagne de fouilles a Tell El-Far ͨ ah, près Naplouse. Rapport préliminaire. Revue Biblique 58: 393-430.
1952　La quatrième campagne de fouilles a Tell El-Far ͨ ah, près Naplouse. Rapport préliminaire. Revue Biblique 59: 551-583.
1955　Les fouilles de Tell El-Far ͨ ah, près Naplouse, cinquième campagne. Rapport préliminaire. Revue Biblique 62: 541-589.

WAMPLER, J. C.
1947　Tell en-Naṣbeh II: The pottery. The Palestine Insititute of Pacific School of Religion and the American Schools of Oriental Research, Berkeley and New Haven.

WRIGHT, G. E.
1950a　The discoveries at Megiddo, 1935-39. The Biblical Archaeologist 13: 28-46.
1950b　Review of Megiddo II: Seasons 1935-39. Journal of the American Oriental Society 70: 56-60.
1961　The archaeology of Palestine. In The Bible and the ancient Near East: Essays in honor of William Foxwell Albright, edited by G. E. Wright, pp. 73-112. Doubleday & Co., Inc., Garden City, N. Y.
1966　Fresh evidence for the Philistine story. The Biblical Archaeologist 29: 70-86.

YADIN, Y.
1958　Solomon's city wall and gate at Gezer. Israel Exploration Journal 8: 80-86.
1959　The fourth season of excavations at Hazor. The Biblical Archaeologist 22: 2-20.
1960　New light on Solomon's Megiddo. The Biblical Archaeologist 23: 62-68.
1969　The fifth season of excavations at Hazor 1968-1969. The Biblical Archaeologist 32: 50-71.
1970　Megiddo of the kings of Israel. The Biblical Archaeologist 33: 66-96.
1973　A note on the stratigraphy of Israelite Megiddo. Journal of Near Eastern Studies 32: 330.

YADIN, Y., Y. AHARONI, R. AMIRAN, T. DOTHAN, I. DUNAYEVSKY, J. PERROT.
1958　Hazor I: An account of the first season of excavations, 1955. Magnes Press, Jerusalem.
1960　Hazor II: An account of the second season of excavations, 1956. Magnes Press, Jerusalem.

YADIN, Y., Y. AHARONI, R. AMIRAN, M. DOTHAN, T. DOTHAN, I. DUNAYEVSKY, J. PERROT.
1961　Hazor III-IV: An account of the third and fourth seasons of excavations, 1957-1958. Magnes Press, Jerusalem.

ZAYADINE, F.
1968　Une tombe du Fer II a Samarie-Sébaste. Revue Biblique 75: 562-585.

Introduction to the Figures

Some explanation of the system, terms and purpose of the ware descriptions may be useful. The style of the ware descriptions has had its impact also on the format of the figures. The general purpose of both descriptions and drawings is to illustrate the process of construction as well as to provide the reader with a feel for the material. The pages of inked drawings and of photos were finished before the verbal descriptions were developed by the editor who is responsible for this section of the monograph. We are particularly grateful to Piri Yarden for adding the hundreds of details to the original drawings to indicate forming and finishing lines. The result is a heightened feel for the pottery which is usefully assisted by the juxtaposition of photos and drawings. The original photographs of sherd groups and vessels were the work of Elia Kahwadjian, intended for the plates opposite drawings usually found in archeological publications. The revision of layouts to combine drawings and photographs was undertaken by Lois Glock. In a few instances the time lapse between original work and revision resulted in gaps in the format. Also, no attempt has been made to indicate the scale of the photos since the scale of the drawing accurately indicates size.

The ware descriptions are presented in columnar form to facilitate clustering of like items and identification of unique features. Form and stratigraphic identification are followed by three divisions of description for each sherd section: Fabric Color, Core, and Non-Plastics. The working process is as follows:

Color was identified by means of the Munsell Soil Color Chart. To translate our verbal color designations into Munsell Soil Color codes requires some knowledge of the Chart. The following specifics may serve as a general guide. In general the range of Hue was 2.5YR to 7.5YR, the range of Value was 5 to 7 or reddish brown to light brown to pink, while Chroma could range from 1 to 6, generally between 2 and 4. Core color is usually a variety of gray located in the middle section of Chroma 1, which ranges from black to white. Within the Hue ranges of most of these descriptions, "dark gray" is lower in Value (3-4) while "light gray" is higher (6-7).

Non-plastics were identified on the basis of work done previously with the Bronze Age pottery from Taanach. More than 200 thin-sections of Bronze Age pottery were analyzed by Jonathan Glass. Chips of the Iron Age pottery were also presented to Glass, but the report has been delayed and was not available for final editing of these ware descriptions. If there are corrections, they will appear in future Taanach reports. Size of non-plastics generally follows a screen where "large" means 1 mm. or greater, "medium" is 0.5 mm. to 1 mm., and "fine" is 0.5 mm. or less. The "frequency" of each non-plastic is estimated on a scale where m(any) is about 40-25%, s(ome) is 25-15%, and f(ew) is 15-5%. The category "density" is parallel in terminology and percentage to "frequency" but differs in that it reflects a total of all types of non-plastics.

In addition to the three categories of sherd section included in this ware description are five categories of data on the surface, exterior and interior. The five features of the surface are also chosen to reveal information about process of manufacture. Color is based on Munsell so that "pink" is in the upper ranges of Value (7-8) and the middle range of Chroma (2-4), usually either 5YR or 7.5YR in Hue. "Voids" refer to holes, breaks, or fissures on the surface. There is also an effort to call attention to details that can be interpreted as forming features from which the process can be extrapolated. Since I am not a potter an effort was made to check my description of these details. Fifty photographs of representative details plus my descriptions were sent to Dr. Owen Rye of the Australian National University, Canberra, Australia. He is both a potter and a ceramic technologist with considerable experience in ceramic ethnography. He confirmed, corrected, or elaborated the descriptions he received so that what is here presented has had the benefit of his criticism. What errors remain are the responsibility of the editor. In a few cases where "pop-outs" is in the text, the meaning is synonymous with "spalling." "Flashing line" means a seam or join generally identified where a horizontal thickening occurs on the surface. The term "wet-smoothing" does not imply any specific tool; it may have been produced by hand, cloth, leather, or straw. Hopefully the abbreviations are self-interpreting.

Albert E. Glock

FIG. 1 POTTERY FROM THE CUNEIFORM TABLET BUILDING (PERIOD IA)

1. Identification		2. Section							3. Surface	
a.	b.	a.	b. Core		c. Non-Plastics				a. Exterior	b. Interior
Item	Square, Locus Basket	Fabric Color	Color	Extent	Type	Size	Frequency	Density	Color, n-p, voids, forming, finishing features	Same
1. Jar Rim	SW 5-2 80.158	lt br	lt gr	+50%	lms cal bas	l,m m,s m,s	m f s	med	Ex: pk wh, some n-p covered, many seen, rough texture. Thumb-wide depression forms irreg lower line of rim. Horiz marks from revolving vessel thru fingers to smooth. In: lt rd br; many lime spalls; some organic pseudomorphic voids; scaling begins 7cms below rim; irreg fold-over line 2.5cms below rim.	
2. Jar Rim	81.159	rd yl	dk gr	50%	lms bas	m,s m,s	f f	low	Ex: pk, n-p as in No. 1 but fewer; thumb-wide finger-print lined horiz depression on neck 2 cms down fr rim. In: pk, larger n-p seen but smoothed, embedded without drag lines; depression similar to ex but narrower, below rim.	
3. Jug Rim	80.155 & 157	lt br		none	lms bas	m,l m	f s	med	Ex & In: lt rd br, n-p mostly visible, grainy. Rim top burnished. Ex: wet-smoothed; In: forming ridges rise fr L to R.	
4. Jug Rim	81.159	rd yl		none	lms	s,f	s	low	Ex & In: lt pk, sm lms n-p seen, even; Ex: sharp undercut rim, wet-smooth.	
5. Jug Rim	80.155	pk		none	lms bas	s,f s	s f	low	Ex & In: pk, n-p seen, smooth usu; Ex: smoothing lines around placement zone of handle broken off below rim; In: fold-over ridge below rim.	
6. Jug Rim	81.159	pl br		none	biomic	f	m-s	med	Ex & In: pk wh slip, n-p break thru, coarse feel. Wet-smoothed. Ex: fading wk red painted bands.	
7. Juglet Base	80.158	pk	dk gr	inner 60%	lms	m	s	low	Ex: pk, n-p seen, smoothed. In: dk gray, voids due to fired veg matter. Core has many pits.	
8. Crater Rim	80.158	lt br		none	lms cal	l,m s	s f	med	Ex & In: pk white, lms n-p visible, evened. In: rim less smooth. Ex: rim folded over leaving sharp line where it reaches the neck.	
9. Crater Rim	80.158	lt br	vlt gr	50%	lms bas	l,m m	s f	low	Ex & In: pk, some l lms n-p visible on smooth ex, more covered on inner rougher surface. Ex: folded over rim separated from shoulder by sharp v-shaped undercut.	
10. Crater Rim	80.155	lt br	vlt gr	50%	lms bas	l,m s	f f	lo	Ex & In: as No. 9. Rim folded down onto neck, bottom edge tool-trimmed side has evidence of turning.	
11. Crater Rim	81.159	pk	gr	+50%	lms bas cal	l,m l,m f	f f f	lov	Ex & In: pk, more lms pop-outs on ex than in. Wet-smoothed in & ex, also on ex just below rim is thumb-wide horiz depression.	
12. Crater Rim	80.155	lt rd br	(rim & body) (base)	none +50%	bas biomic lms	s s s-m	s f vf	low	Ex & In: rd yl, few n-p seen, close horiz burnish. Ex: just below shoulder bend burnish lines slanted & vertical. 3 tooled shallow grooves where shoulder bends in. Irreg incisions on shoulder. In: join seam for coil or slab used to form upper shoulder.	
13. Bowl Rim	81.159	rd yl	lt gr	-50%	bas lms	s,f s	s f	low	Ex & In: pk, few lms n-p seen, surf even. Ex: shallow incised line just below rim, faint-line wet-smoothing. Incised lines where shoulder bends in to rim.	
14. Bowl Rim	81.159	rd yl	vlt gr	+50%	lms bas	l,m,s m,s	m s	med	Ex & In: pk, lms n-p seen, wet-smoothing has left n-p in place. In: thumb-wide depression just below rim leaves slight lower ridge ine.	
15. Bowl Rim to Base	80.158	rd yl	dk gr	+50%	lms bas	l,m,s s	m f	med	Ex: lt rd br, lower 2/3 turned, drag marks L to R, upper 1/3 lightly wet-smoothed. Fingermarks evident over turning at junct of body & base. In: wet-smooth lines base to rim, also a diagonal swipe leaving rough surf, base to rim.	
16. Bowl Rim	80.158	(Upper right corner of No. 15)								
17. Bowl Rim	80.158	lt br	vlt gr	-50%	lms bas	s l-s	f f	low	Ex & In: lt pk, wet-smoothed. Few n-p seen on inner rim edge.	

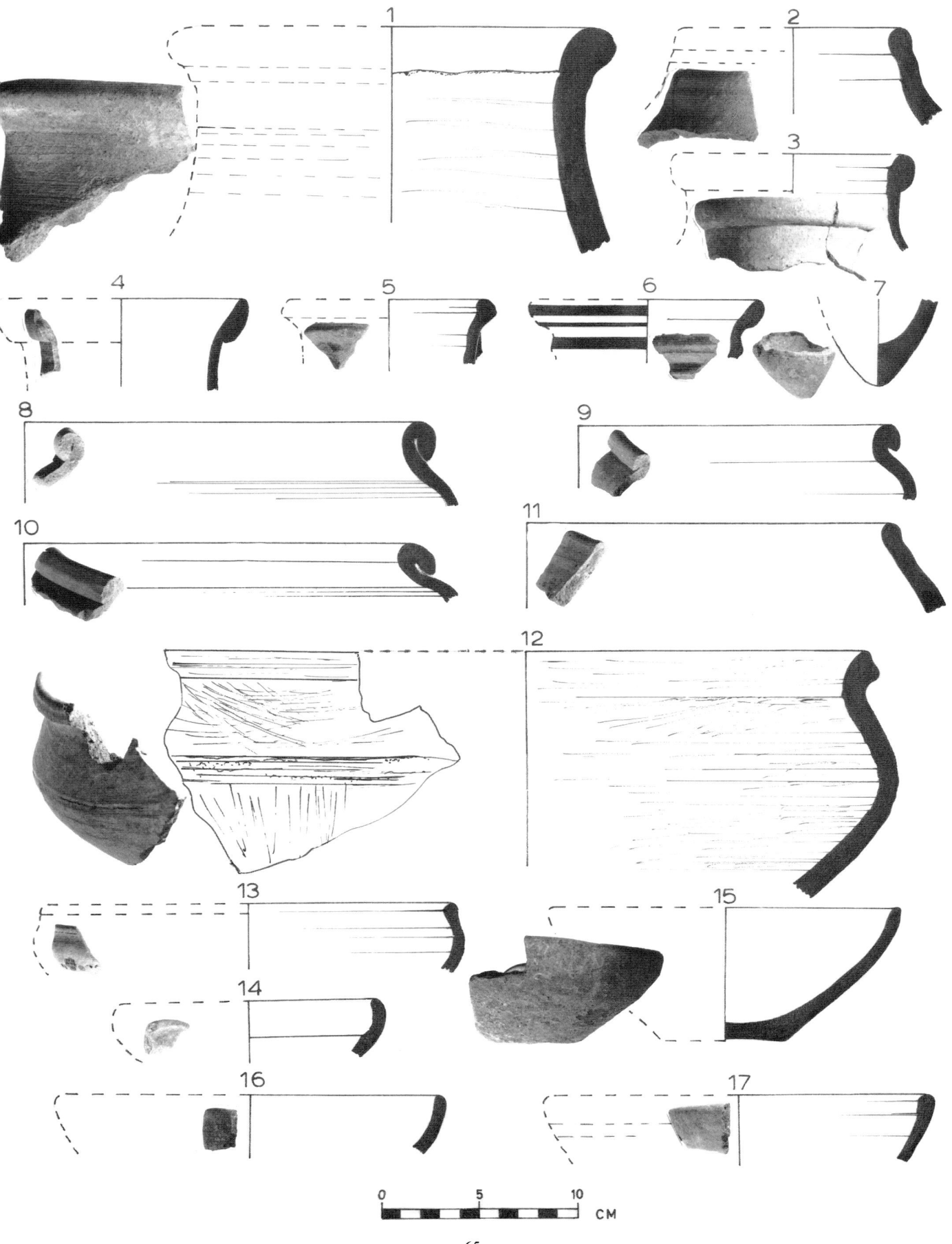

FIG. 2 POTTERY FROM THE CUNEIFORM TABLET BUILDING (PERIOD IA)

1. Identification		2. Section						3. Surface	
a. Item	b. Square, Locus Basket	a. Fabric Color	b. Core		c. Non-Plastics			Density	a. Exterior	b. Interior
			Color	Extent	Type	Size	Frequency		Color, n-p, voids, forming, finishing features	Same
1. Bowl Base	SW 5-2 80.158	lt gr (slip)	dk gr	-100%	bas lms	s s-f	s s	low	*Ex*: lt gr slip (bloom?); wet-smoothed around base, also diagonal swipe. Ring base may be from added clay coil; narrow blunted end of reed (?) tool used to trim outer edge of base; *In*: lt gr covered with gr to dk gr carbon deposit.	
2. Cook Pot Rim	81.159	lt rd	dk gr	50%	cal	s	s	low	*Ex & In*: rd br, some n-p seen, wet-smoothed; *Ex*: irreg line of fold-over just under rim edge.	
3. Cook Pot Rim	80.155	lt rd	(rim, neck) (body) gr	none +50%	cal lms	s,f m,s	m m	med	*Ex & In*: rd br, wet-smoothed; *ex*, some n-p seen but *in*, many n-p, esp lms: salty aspect. *Ex*: fold line not as in No. 2.	
4. Cook Pot Rim	80.155	lt rd	gr	50%	cal	s,f	m	med	As No. 2.	
5. Cook Pot Rim	80.157	lt rd	dk gr	50%	cal	s,f	s	low	As No. 2.	
6. Cook Pot Rim	80.157	lt rd	dk gr	50%	cal lms	s,f m,s	m m	med	As No. 3 except lt rd br.	
7. Cook Pot Rim	80.155	gr		none	lms	s,m	m	med	*Ex & In*: gr, lime spalls *ex* and fissures *in*. Trace of wet-smoothing.	
8. Cook Pot Rim	80.158	lt rd	dk gr	+50%	lms	l,m	m	high	*Ex & In*: gr, lms n-p common, grainy, wet-smoothing.	

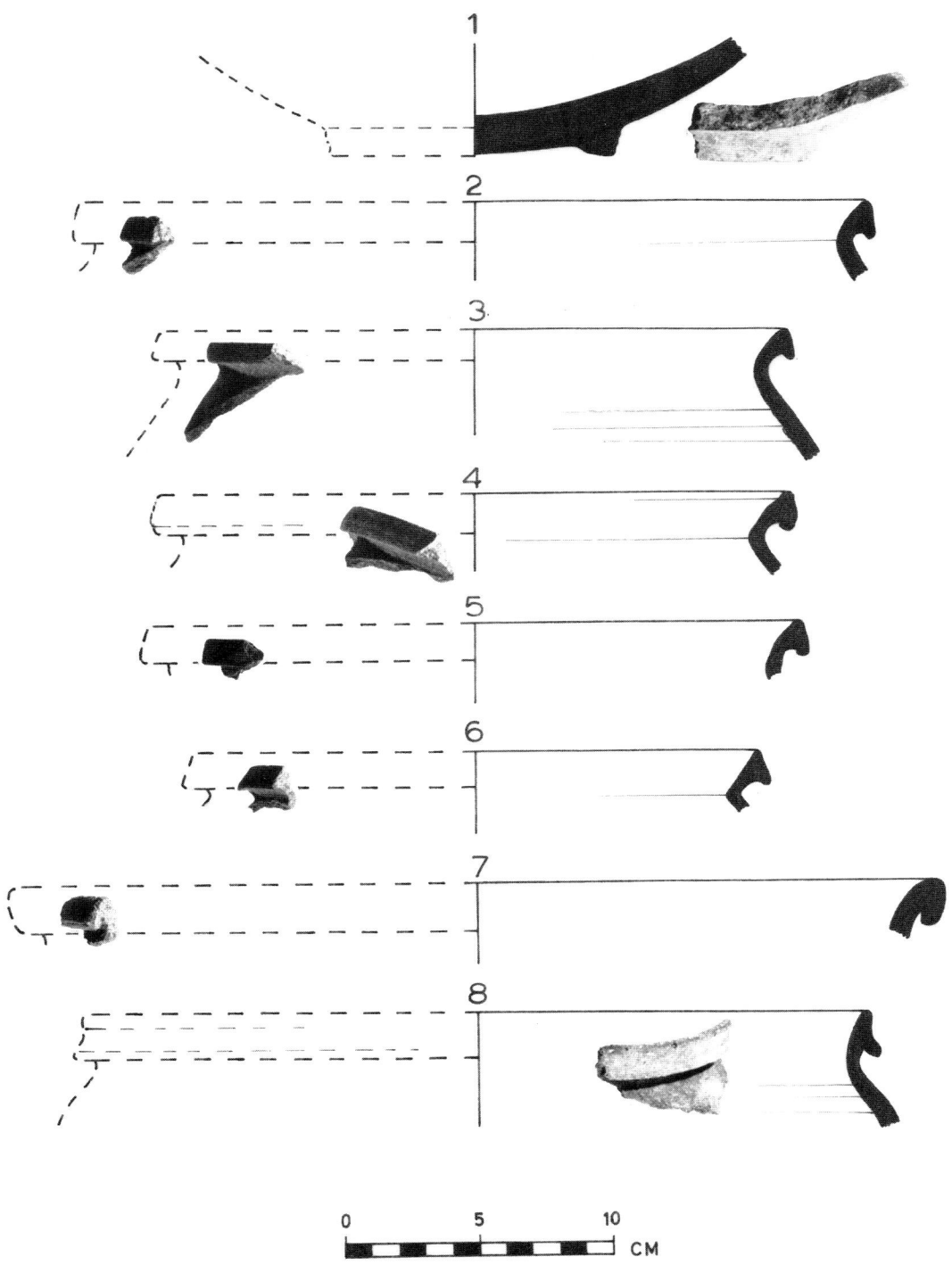

FIG. 3 POTTERY FROM THE DRAINPIPE STRUCTURE (PERIOD IA)

1. Identification		2. Section							3. Surface	
a.	b.	a.	b. Core		c. Non-Plastics				a. Exterior	b. Interior
Item	Square, Locus Basket	Fabric Color	Color	Extent	Type	Size	Frequency	Density	Color, n-p, voids, forming, finishing features	Same
	SW 2-25									
1. Jug Rim	45.79	pk		none	lms biomic	m,s / s	s / f	low	*Ex & In*: pk, wet-smoothed. Under rim irreg ridged. Some n-p seen.	
2. Jug Rim	45.79	rd yl		none	lms	m,s	s	low	*Ex & In*: pk, wet-smoothed. Very few n-p seen.	
3. Jug Rim	45.79	pk		none	lms	f	f	vlow	*Ex & In*: lt pk, lms n-p seen esp on *ex*.	
4. Jug Rim	45.79	pk		none	lms	s,f	f	low	*Ex & In*: pk, wet-smoothing on *ex* broken by lime spalls, rubbing below rim on *in*.	
5. Juglet handle &body	45.79	pk		none	lms	m,s	f	low	*Ex*: smooth, few n-p, pk. *In*: pk, forming ridges interrupted by roughness inside handle placement.	
6. Bowl Rim	45.77	pk		none	cal	l,m,s	m	med	*Ex & In*: pk; *ex* more smooth than *in*; rim top wet-smoothed.	
7. Bowl Rim	45.77	pk		none	cal	m,s	m	med	Larger sherd of same bowl rim as No. 6. 3.5 cms below rim on *ex* is incised line, irreg burnishing. *In*: narrow, generally horiz stick lines.	
8. Bowl Rim	45.79	pk		none	lms / cal / bas	l,m,s / s / s	f / m / f	med	*Ex*: pk, few lms n-p, wet-smoothed, rubbed; *In*: some bas n-p as gr spots, few small lms, wet-smoothing.	
9. Bowl Rim	45.77	rd yl		none	lms / bas	m,s / s	f	med	*Ex & In*: pk, continuous fingermarks but throwing marks not removed or smoothed in *ex*. Few n-p visible.	
10. Bowl Rim to Base	45.79	rd yl	gr	-50%	cal / bas	vf / f	vf / f	low	*Ex & In*: pk, continuous fingermarks. *Ex*: few n-p, body near base thickened by adding clay.	
11. Bowl Rim	45.77	yl rd		none	bas / lms	f / m,s	m / s	med	*Ex & In*: rd yl, wet-smoothed, many bas, some lms n-p visible.	
12. Bowl Rim	45.77	lt rd br		none	lms / bas	m,s / m,s	s / s	low	*Ex*: pk, many lms & bas n-p, smooth; *In*: covered with lt gr deposit, few n-p seen.	
13. Bowl Base	45.77	rd yl	gr	50%	bas / cal	s / m,f	m / s	med	*Ex*: pk, many lms n-p seen, several l to s pit voids, few drag mks L to R, smoothing slip, base is centered. *In*: rd yl, pitted, lt gr deposit.	
14. Bowl Base	45.77	rd yl	gr	+50%	lms / bas	l,m,s / -s	m / m	med	*Ex & In*: dk pk, n-p seen all over but *ex* body which is wet-smoothed lightly. *In*: some shallow small pits.	
15. Cook Pot Rim	45.77	rd yl	dk gr	+50%	cal	f	m	low	*Ex & In*: lt rd br, wet-smoothed, *In*: carbon deposit below rim line.	
16. Chalice Rim	45.77	pk	dk gr	50%	cal / bas	m / s,f	f / f	low	*Ex & In*: pk, wet-smoothed, some n-p roughen surf. *In*: rim folded over, bottom partly trimmed.	

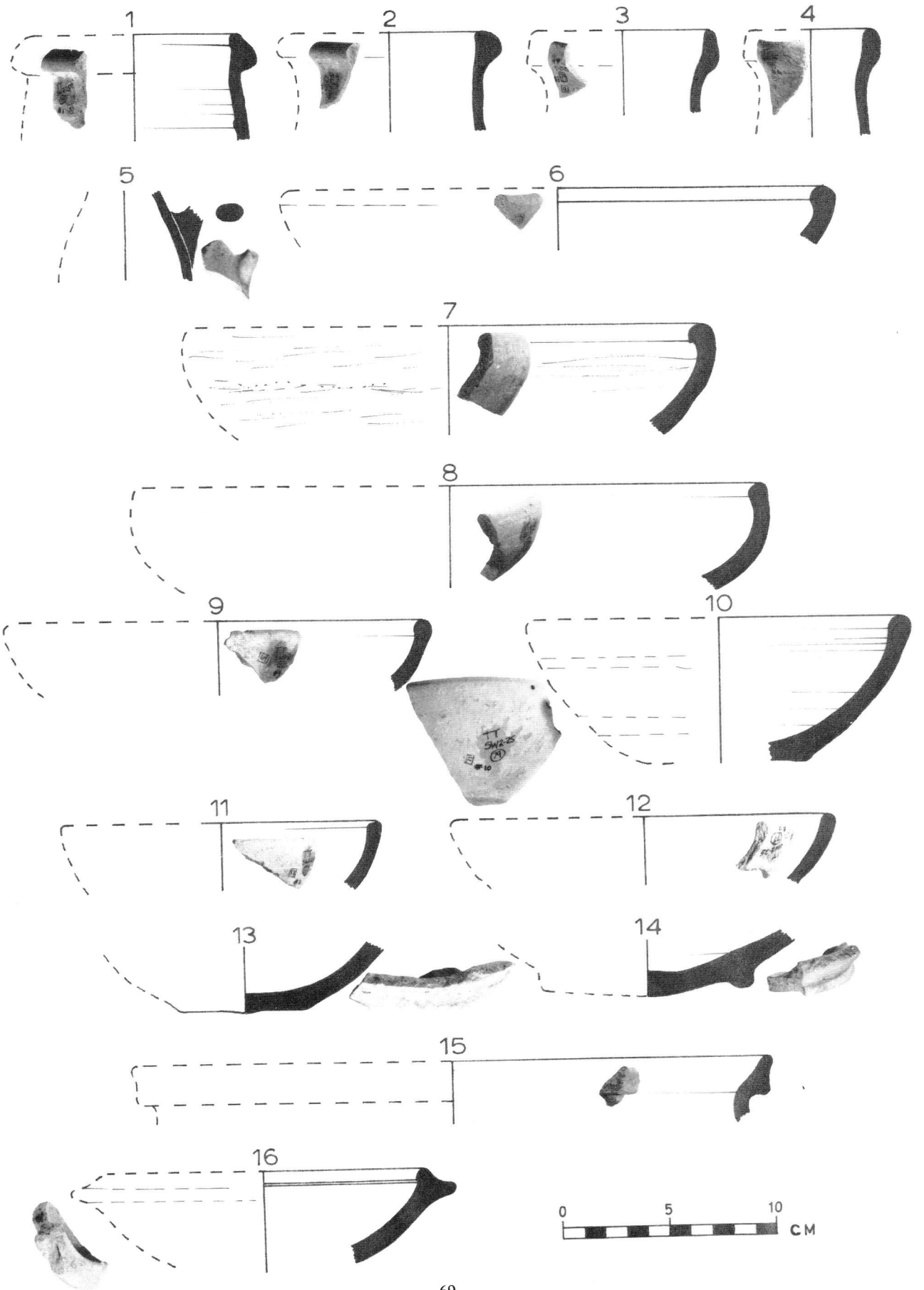

FIG. 4 POTTERY FROM THE TWELFTH-CENTURY HOUSE (PERIOD IA)

1. Identification		2. Section						3. Surface	
a.	b.	a.	b. Core		c. Non-Plastics			a. Exterior	b. Interior
Item	Square, Locus Basket	Fabric Color	Color	Extent	Type	Size	Frequency	Density	Color, n-p, voids, forming, finishing features	Same
1. Jar Rim	SW 5-8 157.208	lt rd		none	lms biomic	l,m,s s	s s	med	*Ex*: wk rd to lt rd; many n-p & pits, wet-smoothed. Dk gr & greenish encrustation. *In*: lt rd, fewer n-p than on *ex*, lime spalls, lt wet-smoothing, horiz rim to neck, diagonal below.	
2. Jar Rim	155.206	lt rd	rd yl	+50%	lms bas	m,s,f s	s s	med	*Ex*: pk, n-p roughen surf, visible. Wet-smoothed, less clear. *In*: rim top and *in* roughly rubbed.	
3. Jar Handle & Body	157.208	rd yl	pk gr (handle) (body) rd yl (body, above join)	-50% +50% 50%	lms bas	l,m,f l	s f	low	*Ex*: pk & pk gr, few lms n-p seen, many rectang straw voids; body *In*: n-p seen, pk wh, forming lines, or wet-smoothing.	
4. Jar Handle & Body	157.208	rd	dk gr	+80%	lms	l,m,s. f	s	low	*Ex* & *In*: pk to pk gr, many n-p seen, grainy, wet-smoothing on handle.	
5. Jar Handle	155.219	lt rd (body) lt rd (handle)	rd yl dk gr	+50% +50%	bas lms	s.f l,m,s	s	med to high	*Ex*: pk, many n-p seen, scaling on handle reveals lt rd fabric, wet-smoothing. *In*: body pk, horiz throwing ridges. Few protruding n-p seen.	
6. Jug Rim	155.206	pk		none	lms bas	l,s m	f vf	low	*Ex*: pk, few l, many s n-p on surf, wet-smoothing. *In*: pk, n-p seen, grainy residual clay, knuckle ridges.	
7. Jug Rim	157.208	pk	dk gr	-100%	lms lms	l,m f	s f	low	*Ex* & *In*: pk, lms n-p seen, esp *in*; wet-smoothed.	
8. Crater Rim	155.219	pk		none	lms bas	s s	f s	low	*Ex*: dk pk, many n-p seen, wet-smoothed but few fingerprint lines. *In*: lt pk, many forming ridges.	
9. Crater Rim & Handle	155.219	pk	gr	50%	lms bas	m m	s f	low	*Ex*: handle as No. 3, dk pk, also rim.	
10. Crater Rim	157.208	*In*: rd yl *Ex*: lt rd	pk br	+50%	bas lms	s,f f	f f	vlow	*Ex* & *In*: lt pk, few n-p seen, firm, smooth surf, wet-smoothed, more lines visible *ex* than *in*.	
11. Bowl Rim	155.206	rd yl		none	lms bas	m,s s	f s	low	*Ex* & *In*: much like No. 10. Lt pk, n-p seen, wet-smoothing, few fingerprint lines.	

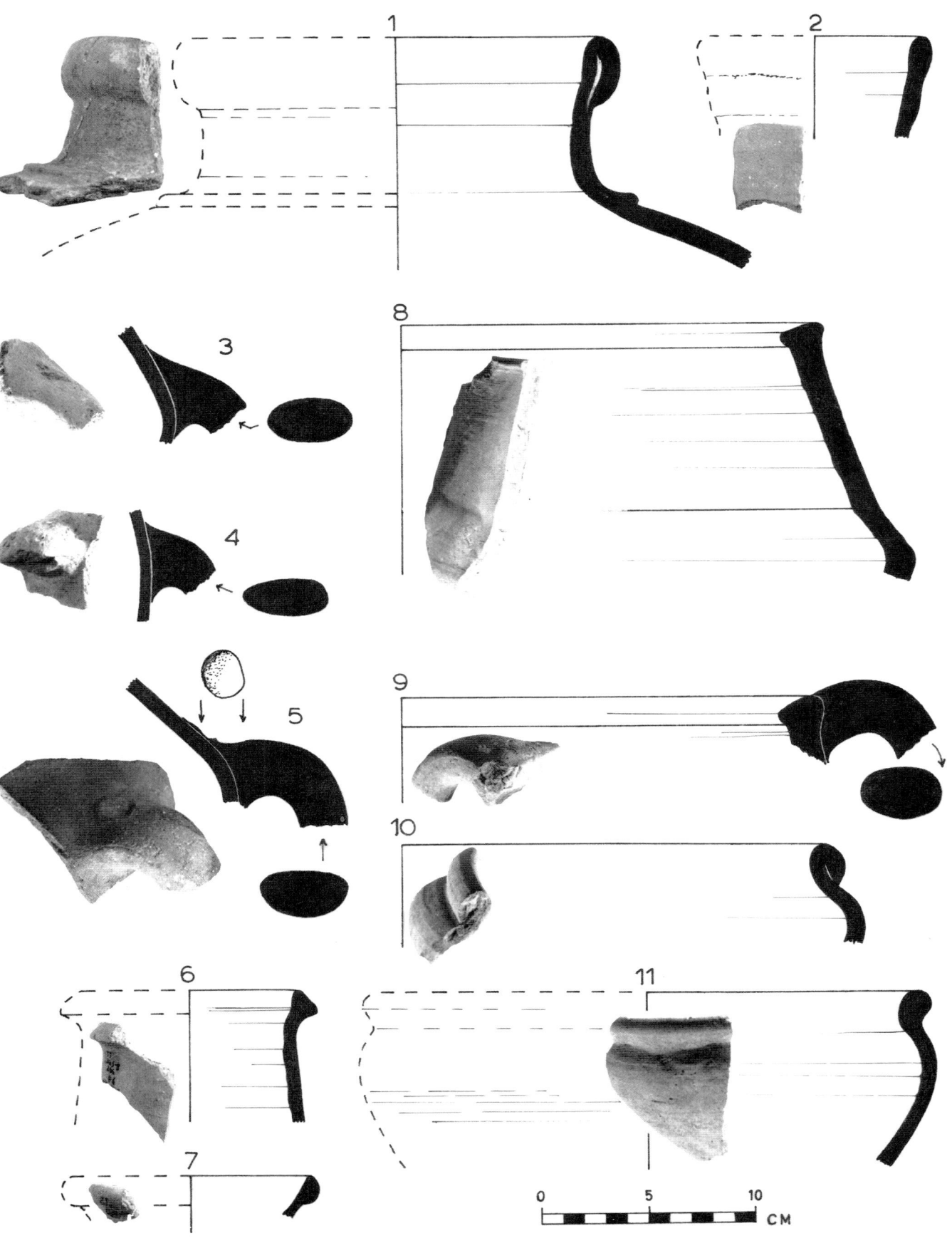

FIG. 5 POTTERY FROM THE TWELFTH-CENTURY HOUSE (PERIOD IA)

1. Identification		2. Section						3. Surface	
a.	b.	a.	b. Core		c. Non-Plastics			a. Exterior	b. Interior
Item	Square, Locus Basket	Fabric Color	Color	Extent	Type	Size	Frequency	Density	Color, n-p, voids, forming, finishing features	Same
1. Bowl Rim	SW 5-8 157.208	lt rd br	gr	none at rim to 25%	lms	l,m s	m	med-h	*Ex*: pk slip, many n-p seen, drag marks r-l, 3 cms below rim series of 1 cm wide turning ridges. *In*: pk, n-p visible, wet-smoothing lines on rim.	
2. Bowl Base	155.219	lt rd br		none	lms	l,m,s	s	low	*Ex*: pk, lightly wet-smoothed, few n-p visible. *In*: pk, shallow pits, scaling, few n-p seen.	
3. Bowl Base	155.219	lt rd br	(body) (base)gr	none -100%	lms	l,m,s	s	low	*Ex*: pk slip, few n-p seen at base. *In*: few lime spalls, some pits, carbon deposit.	
4. Bowl Base	157.208	pk	(body)gr	+50%	lms	l,m	s	med	*Ex*: pk slip, wet-smoothed on slow wheel. *In*: pk, many pits, deeper than No. 2. No finish lines. 2ndary carbon on edge.	
5. Bowl Base	157.208	lt rd br	lt gr	+50%	lms bas	m,s m	s vf	low	*Ex*: as No. 4; *In*: as No. 4, add carbon deposit.	
6. Bowl Base	157.208	pk	gr bleeds *in*	+50%	lms	m,s	s	low	*Ex*: pk, lms n-p seen, ring base added, circular finishing lines on bottom and up inside of ring. *In*: uneven finishing lines, pk darkened by carbon, few n-p visible.	
7. Bowl Base	157.208	lt rd br	(base)gr (body)gr	+50% -100%	lms	l,m,s	s	med	*Ex*: pk, lms n-p seen, ring base added, circular finishing lines on bottom and up inside of ring. *In*: uneven finishing lines, pk darkened by carbon, few n-p visible.	
8. Bowl Base	155.206	Mends with No. 3. Same description								
9. Bowl Base	157.208	pk	(base)gr (body)	+50% none	lms	l,m,s	s	med	*Ex*: pk, many n-p, deep drag marks fr wet-smoothing. *In*: lt pk, n-p seen, wet-smoothing, as *ex*, on slow wheel.	

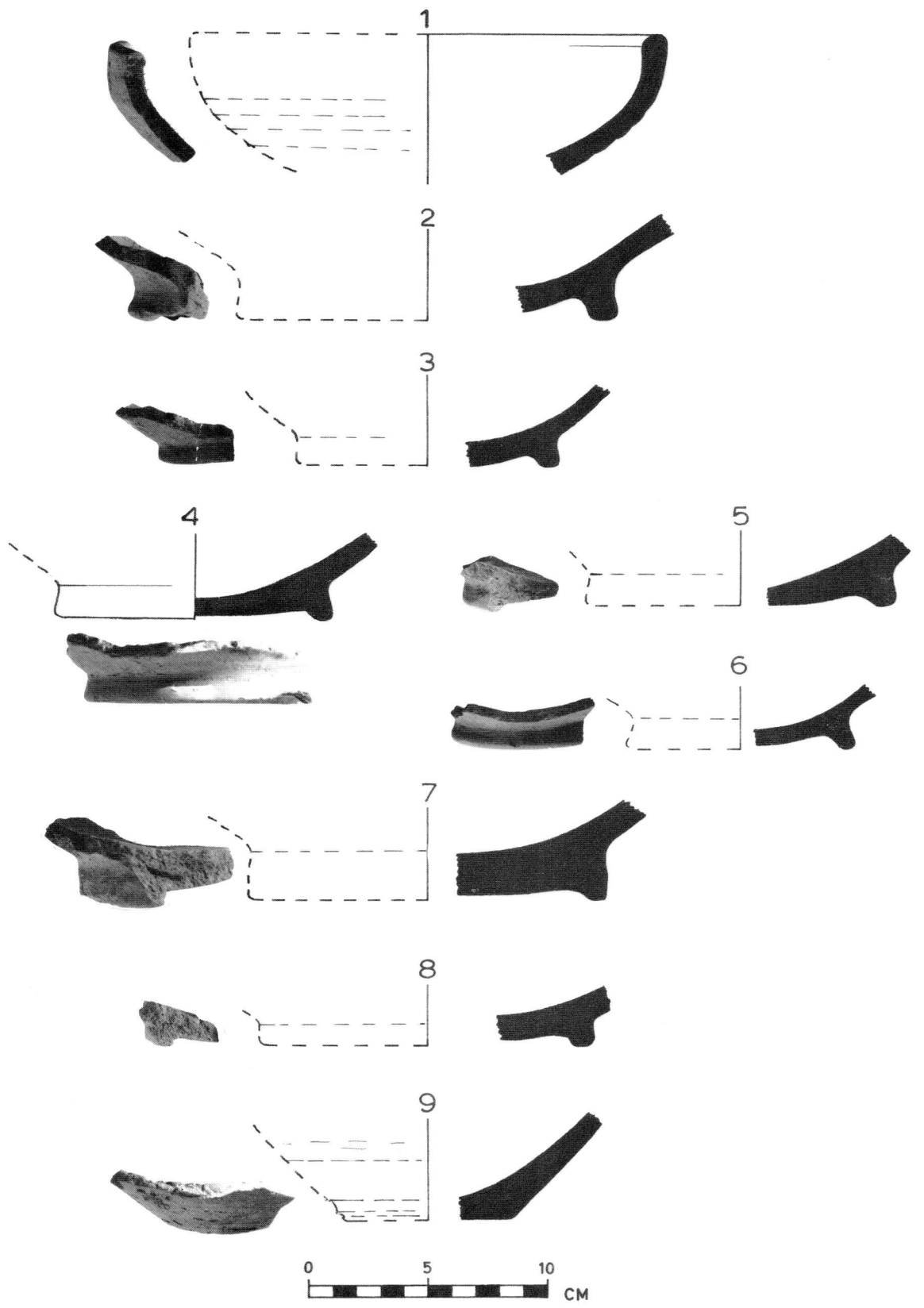

FIG. 6 POTTERY FROM THE TWELFTH-CENTURY HOUSE (PERIOD IA)

1. Identification		2. Section						3. Surface	
a. Item	b. Square, Locus Basket	a. Fabric Color	b. Core		c. Non-Plastics				a. Exterior	b. Interior
			Color	Extent	Type	Size	Frequency	Density	Color, n-p, voids, forming, finishing features	Same
1. Jar Handle	SW 5-8 153.201	rd yl	(handle) gr (body)	-100% none	lms bas	s m	f vf	vlow	*Ex*: pk gr, handle top wet-smoothed with straw leaving many long angular depressions; join is well smoothed. *In*: pk, some n-p seen lime spalls, some horiz smoothing lines.	
2. Jar Handle	153.201	rd yl	(handle) (body) dk gr	none 100%	bas lms	s,f l,m,s	s s	low low	*Ex*: pk, joining very crude, sides squeezed, join patched. Eroded round seal impression. *In*: pk gr, horiz forming lines *in* body.	
3. Jug Rim	153.200	rd gr		none	lms	s,f	s	vlow	*Ex*: wh slip, lumpy, irreg rim depression. *In*: broken wh, rough finish.	
4. Jug Rim	153.201	lt rd	lt gr	+50%	lms	s,f	s	low	*Ex & In*: lt rd, wet-smoothing more visible *ex* than *in*. *In*: few pits.	
5. Jug Rim	153.201	lt br		none	lms bas	s,f s	f vf	vlow	*Ex*: pk, vfew n-p, slight irreg ridge under rim, a tool mark. Wet smoothed. *In*: shallow parallel lines from wet-smoothing.	
6. Jug Rim	153.201	rd yl		none	lms bas	s m,s	f s	low	*Ex*: pk, tool crease under rim. *In*: pk, rough with protruding bas n-p.	
7. Jug Rim	153.201	pk		none	lms	s,f	f	vlow	*Ex*: pk, chipped, wet-smoothing. *In*: pk, n-p seen, wet-smoothing.	
8. Jug Rim	138.205	pk		none	lms	l,m,f	s	low	*Ex & In*: lt rd, n-p seen, wet-smoothed. *In*: forming ridge below rim.	
9. Jug Rim	124.163	rd yl		none	lms bas	l,m,s f	vf s	low	*Ex & In*: rd yl, n-p seen but embedded, wet-smoothed. *Ex*: bottom of rim ridge irreg tooled. *In*: vert wipe thru horiz smoothing lines.	
10. Jug Rim	124.163	pk	pk	50%	lms bas	m,s m	f vf	low	*Ex & In*: rd yl, some n-p seen, wet-smoothed.	
11. Jug Rim	153.201	pk	pk	+50% bleeds to *ex*.	lms	m,s	s	low	*Ex*: pk wh, some n-p seen, wet-smoothed, also *In*: rd yl, some n-p seen.	
12. Jug	153.201	(Joins with No. 11. Same description).								
13. Jug Rim	153.201	rd		none	lms lms bas	l f s	vf f vf	low	*Ex*: pk white, bloom, faint traces of irreg wet-smoothing. *In*: lt rd some wh granules appearing.	
14. Jug Rim & Handle	138.205	rd yl	(rim)lt gr (handle) dk gr	-50% +50%	lms	s	vf	vlow	Handle *Ex*: pk, some grass pits, slight smoothing lines, hard finish. Body *In*: pk, vfew n-p seen, forming ridge below rim, wet-smoothing.	
15. Jug Rim	124.163	lt rd br		none	lms	l,m	s	low	*Ex*: dk pk, wet-smoothing on rim, wk rd (10 R) horiz paint band horiz turning lines above paint & below rim. Lt rd paint droplets on rim to *In*: pk, wet-smoothed.	
16. Jug Rim & Handle	138.205	pk	(body) (handle) gr	none +50%	lms bas	l,m,s l,m,s	s f	med	Handle *Ex*: pk, lms n-p seen, wet-smoothed, rd (2.5YR) paint bars on L half of handle. Body *Ex*: join void where handle is fixed to body. *In*: horiz forming ridges 2cms below rim.	
17. Jug Base	138.205	pk	gr	+50%	lms cal	s,f f	vf f	vlow	*Ex*: lt pk slip, few n-p, most of wet-smoothing lines erased. *In*: lt gr, few pits, irreg wet-smoothing.	
18. Jug Base	153.201	lt br		none	lms bas	l,m,s m	s f	low-m	*In*: dk pk, n-p seen, circular forming ridges to center point. *Ex*: pk, few n-p, slight band depression where broken foot joins base. Bottom: pk, many n-p seen, some pits, roughly cut as from a mat.	

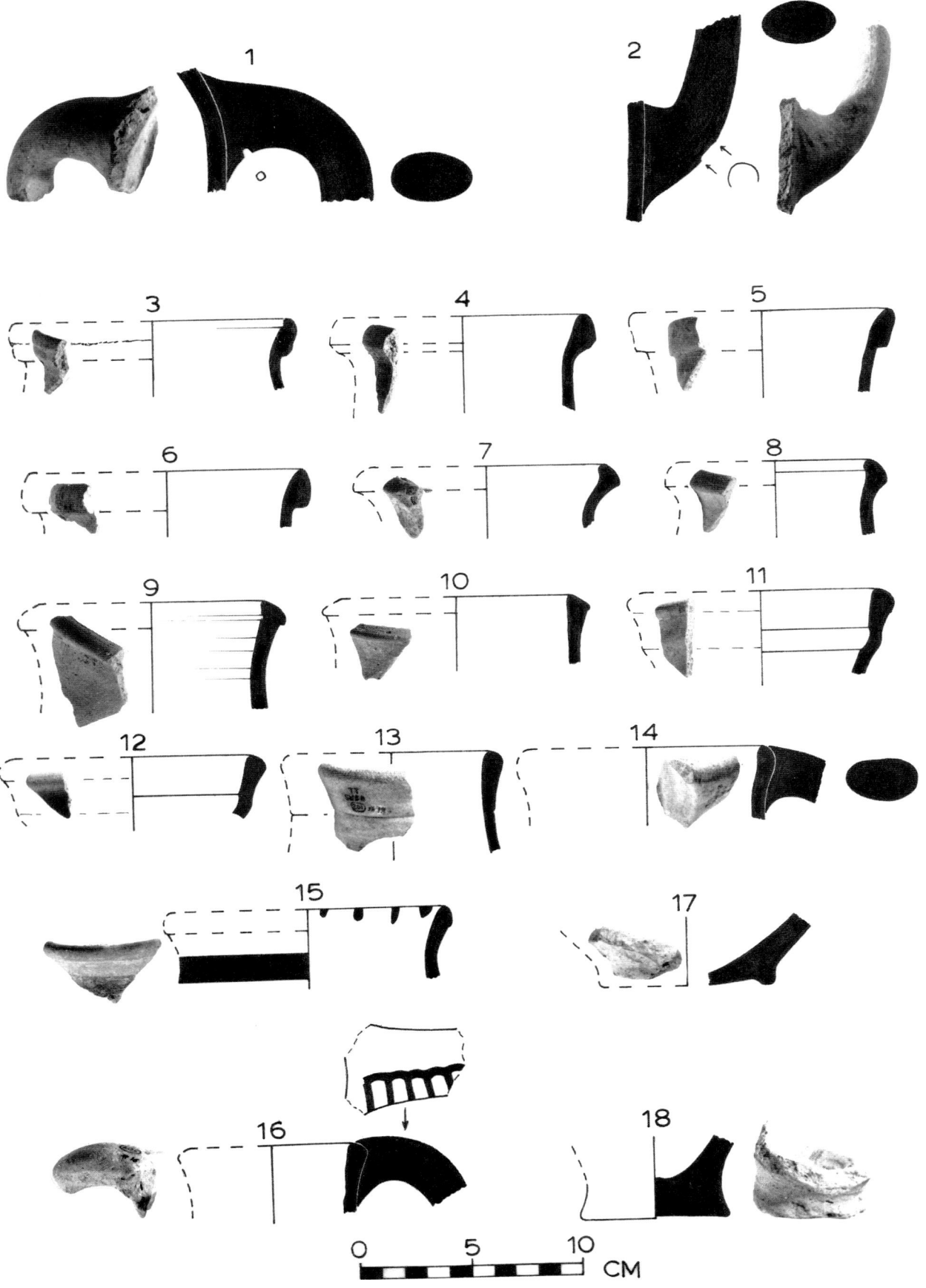

FIG. 7 POTTERY FROM THE TWELFTH-CENTURY HOUSE (PERIOD IA)

1. Identification		2. Section							3. Surface	
a.	b.	a.	b. Core		c. Non-Plastics				a. Exterior	b. Interior
Item	Square, Locus Basket	Fabric Color	Color	Extent	Type	Size	Frequency	Density	Color, n-p, voids, forming, finishing features	Same
1. Crater Rim	SW 5-8 124.163	rd yl		none	lms	l,m,s	m-s	med	*Ex*: pk, n-p seen, some large, shallow spalls, lower third of rim depressed with flat-headed tool. *In*: pk, wet-smoothed.	
2. Crater Rim	124.163	rd yl	rd yl	50%	lms bas	m,s s	f vf	low	*Ex*: pk, n-p embedded, slight traces of wet-smoothing, tooled crease at base of rim, fold void in section. *In*: as *ex*, add in knuckle depression at line of rim base.	
3. Crater Rim	124.163	rd yl	rd yl	50%	lms bas	l,m,s f l,m	s,m s	med-h	*Ex*: pk, many n-p seen, irreg smoothing. *In*: pk, large n-p visible, slight ridge raised at rim base. Generally like No. 1.	
4. Crater Rim	153.201	lt br	dk gr	none -100%	lms	m,s	s	low	*Ex*: lt rd br, smoothing lines erased but surface hard, generally as No. 2. *In*: lt rd br, finish line leaves rough surf.	
5. Crater Rim	153.201	br	(body) gr (rim)	-50% +50%	lms	m,s	s	low	*Ex*: lt rd br, carbon deposit, tooled undercut of folded-over rim, fold-over void in section. *In*: lt rd br, slight crease below rim.	

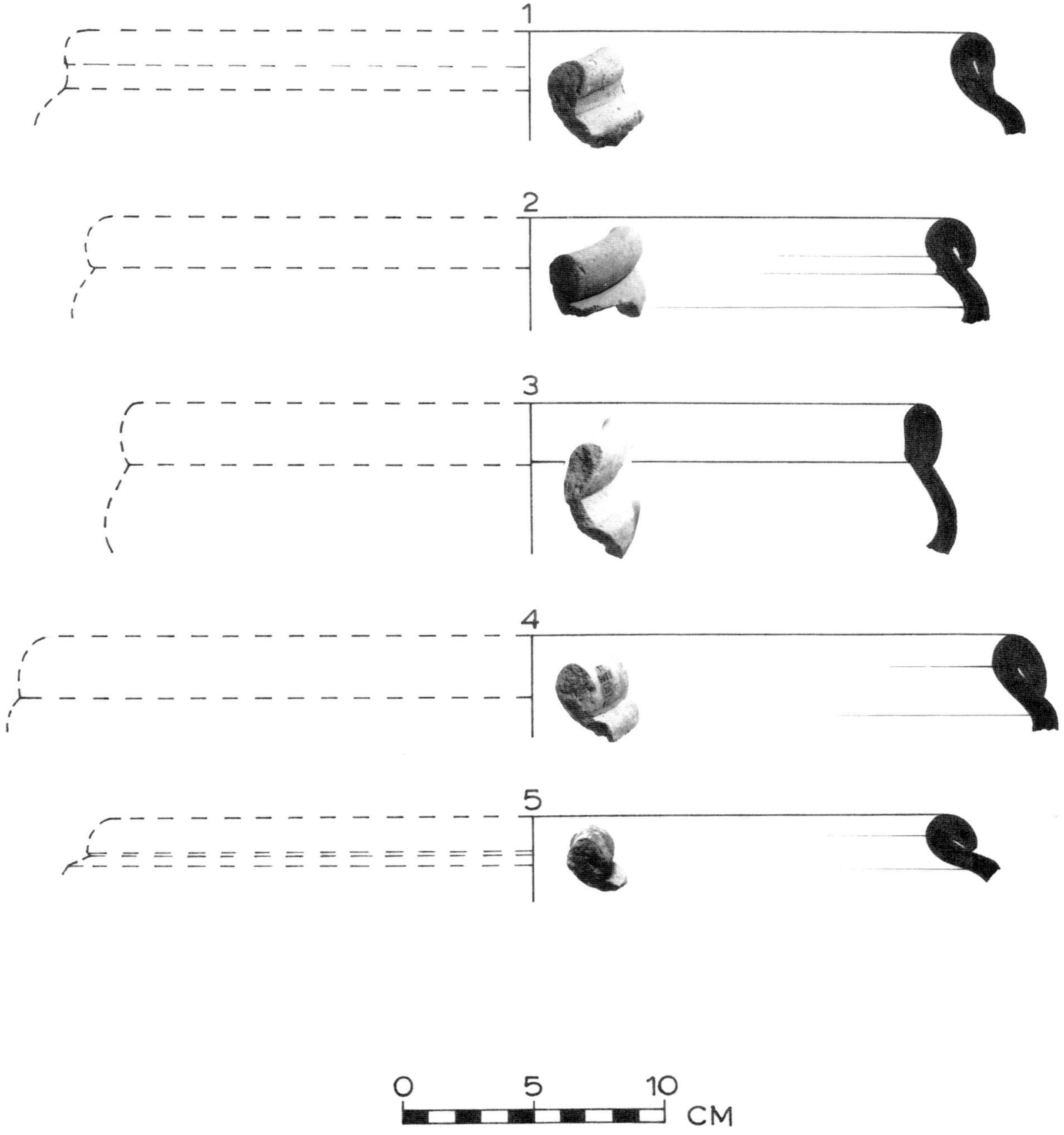

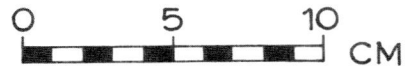

FIG. 8 POTTERY FROM THE TWELFTH-CENTURY HOUSE (PERIOD IA)

1. Identification		2. Section						3. Surface	
a. Item	b. Square, Locus Basket	a. Fabric Color	b. Core		c. Non-Plastics			a. Exterior	b. Interior
			Color	Extent	Type	Size	Frequency	Density	Color, n-p, voids, forming, finishing features	Same
	SW 5-8									
1. Bowl Rim to Base	124.195	lt br		none	lms bas	l,m,s l,m,s	m	med-h	*Ex*: dk pk slip, some n-p seen, few pit voids, irreg flat depression 4 cms below rim where coil to form rim was added; horiz spaced burnishing rim to base, eroded at the base, footring added as coil. *In*: lt pk, many n-p seen, some pits, wet-smoothing below rim.
2. Bowl Rim	124.163	lt br	gr	50%	lms bas grog	m,s s s	f f vf	low	*Ex*: pk wh, large n-p seen firing cracks. *In*: pk wh, some n-p seen, wet-smoothed, close horiz burnish.
3. Bowl Rim	153.201	rd yl		none	lms	m,s	f	vlow	*Ex & In*: dk pk, wet-smoothing on *ex* to rim.
4. Bowl Rim	153.200	rd yl		none	lms	l,s	f	vlow	Joins with No. 3 rim.
5. Bowl Rim	153.201	rd yl	lt gr	-30%	lms bas	m s	s f	low	*Ex & In*: pk wh, some n-p seen but neatly smoothed.
6. Bowl Rim	138.205	br		none	lms	f,s	f	low	*Ex*: pk wh, few n-p seen, roughened, some applied patching, wet-smoothed as also *In*: grayed, irreg edge to rim fold, excess clay patching.
7. Bowl Rim	138.205	yl rd		none	lms	m,s	s	low	*Ex*: pk, lime encrusted, few drag lines, wet-smoothed, also *In*: pk, thumbwide horiz depression below rim, few n-p seen.
8. Bowl Rim	138.205	lt br	lt gr	50%	lms	s	m,s	low	*Ex*: lt pk at rim but dk pk below, paint (?), n-p common, some smoothing; *In*: lt pk, fewer n-p seen shallow pitting, wet-smoothing.
9. Bowl Rim	153.201	yl rd	gr	50%	lms	s,f	s	low	*Ex & In*: lt pk, n-p roughed some, wet-smoothed.
10. Bowl Rim	153.201	rd gr		none	bas	m,s,f	m	med	*Ex & In*: pk gr, many n-p roughen surface, some wet-smoothing, excess clay on *ex*.
11. Bowl Rim	153.201	rd yl	gr	+50%	lms	m,s,f	m	med	*Ex & In*: pk, more n-p on *ex* seen than *in*, few drag lines on *ex*, wet-smoothed.
12. Bowl Base	138.205	lt br		none	lms bas	s s	f f	low	*Ex & In*: rd yl to dk pk, few n-p smoothed, ring base trimmed with edging tool on wheel, *ex* of base wet-smoothed.
13. Bowl Base	153.201	rd yl	lt gr	50%	lms bas	s,f s	f f	low	*Ex & In*: lt pk; trace of forming spiral *in* center, many small pits; turning traces on *ex*, 2 cms up fr base smoothed, above this surface is rough.
14. Chalice TT 990	124.163	lt pk	gr	+50%	lms	l,m,s	m	med	*Ex*: lt pk, 8.5 cm wide, rd br paint bands rim to upper shoulder, 3 more at center shoulder. Many lms n-p on neck, lime spalls, several patches of surplus clay, irreg wet-smoothing. *In*: forming ridges, depressed center with cracks.
15. Chalice Base ?	138.205	lt rd-br		none	lms bas	l,m,s s	s m	med	*Ex & In*: dk pk, many n-p, some exposed, others covered, smoothing on *in*.

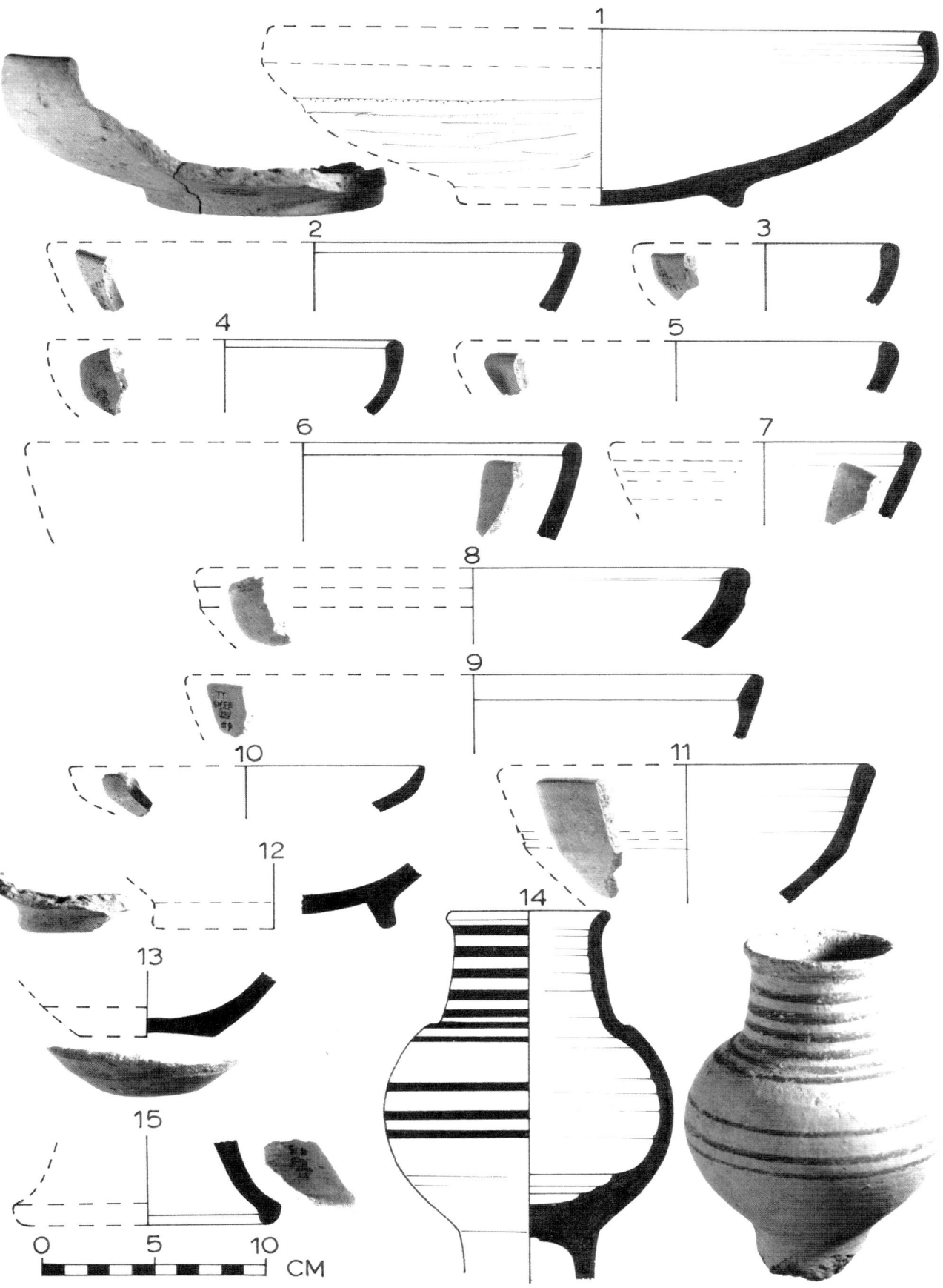

FIG. 9 POTTERY FROM THE DRAINPIPE STRUCTURE (PERIOD IB)

1. Identification		2. Section							3. Surface	
a.	b.	a.	b. Core		c. Non-Plastics				a. Exterior	b. Interior
Item	Square, Locus Basket	Fabric Color	Color	Extent	Type	Size	Frequency	Density	Color, n-p, voids, forming, finishing features	Same
1. Jar TT1810	SW 2-25 44.81,83	red to lt rd		none	lms bas grog	l,m,s s s	m f f	med-h	*Ex*: rd to rd gr, many n-p, lime spalls, below handles are rope depressions, many sherds eroded, neck depressed at one point of collar. *In*: sherds generally eroded leaving only n-p visible. Rd & gr colors are often secondary.	

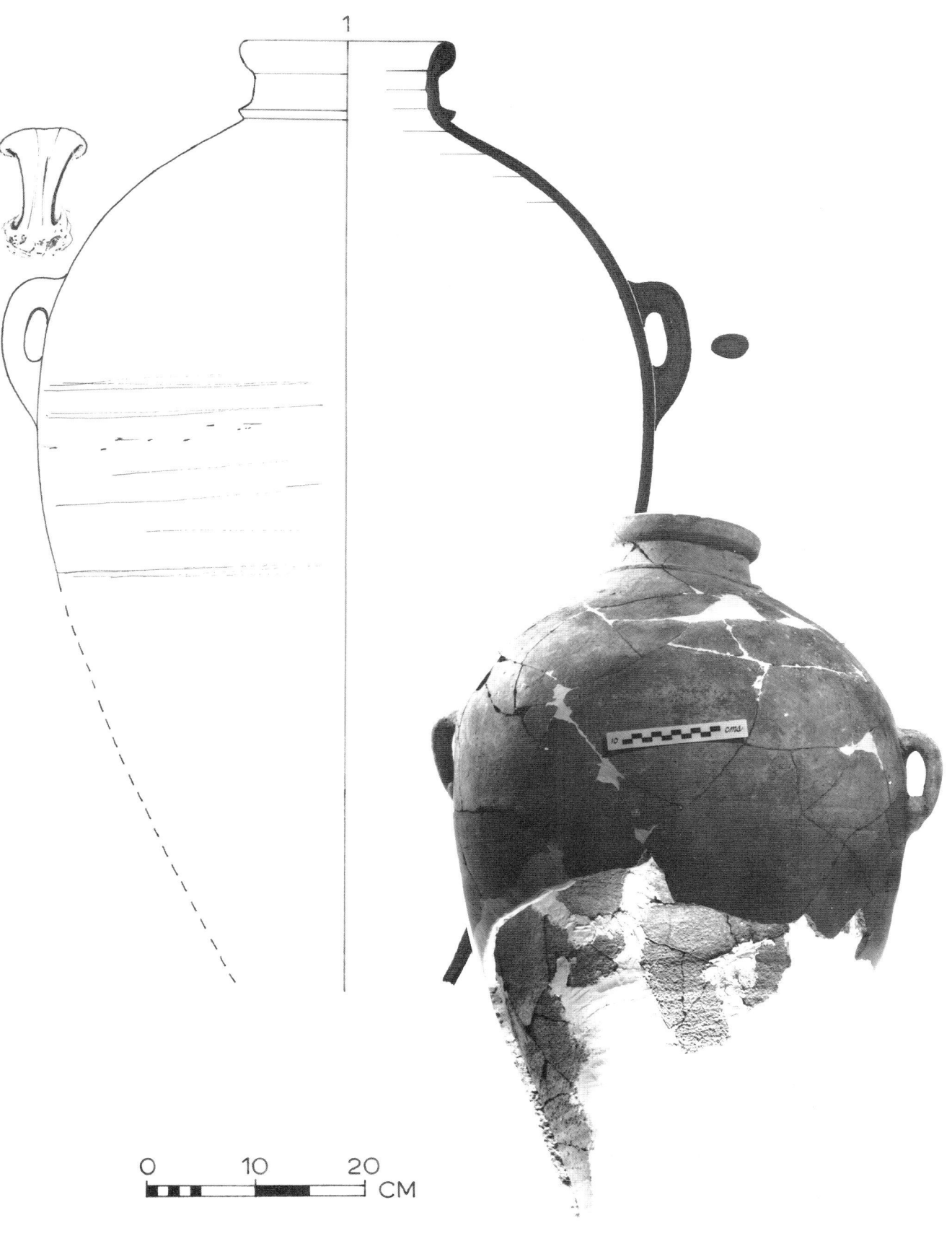

FIG. 10 POTTERY FROM THE DRAINPIPE STRUCTURE (PERIOD IB)

1. Identification		2. Section						3. Surface	
a. Item	b. Square, Locus Basket	a. Fabric Color	b. Core		c. Non-Plastics			a. Exterior	b. Interior
			Color	Extent	Type	Size	Frequency	Density	Color, n-p, voids, forming, finishing features	Same
	SW 2-25									
1. Jar Rim	124.231	rd yl		none	lms bas	s,f s	s f	low	*Ex*: very pale br slip, horiz throwing lines, many tiny, some larger, pits. *In*: rd yl many tiny pits plus lms spalls, scaling on rim.
2. Jar Rim	171.319, 341	dk pk	gr	50%	lms bas grog	l,m,s m,s s,f	s s f	med	*Ex* & *In*: pk, horiz wet-smoothing more visible on *in* than *ex*. Smoother than No. 4. Few drag lines. *In* has crude horiz ridges and smoothing at rim-neck join.
3. Jar Body	61.112	rd yl (ex. 10%)	gr	75% (in.)	lms	l,m,s	s	med	*Ex*: rd yl, many n-p seen, light vert and horiz wet-smoothing. *In*: many n-p seen, coil ridge, wet-smoothing.
4. Jar Rim & Neck	160.426	rd br	lt gr	+50%	lms cal	m,s,f m	s f	med	*Ex*: pk, wet-smoothing before handles applied, few n-p seen; *In* rd gr, coil lines, straw pitting, faint trace of wet-smoothing.
5. Jar Rim	186.424	pk gr		none	lms	l,s	f	low	*Ex*: lt pk grayed with charcoal, few n-p seen, irreg wet-smoothing lines. *In*: lt pk, some n-p protrude, wet-smoothing mostly horiz.
6. Jar Rim	158.300	pk wh	pk gr	80%	grog lms	m,s l,m	s f	med	*Ex*: pk wh, roughened by n-p covered, slight smoothing. *In*: same except that many more n-p visible.
7. Jar Handle	124.231	rd yl	lt gr	none 50% (above handle)	grog	m,s	m	med	*Ex*: very pale br slip (as No. 1), some n-p seen, tiny pits, some forming lines. Looks like pulled handle. *In*: rd yl, faint wet-smoothing, pitting.
8. Jar Handle	160.376	rd yl		none	lms bas	m,s f	s f	med	*Ex* & *In*: pk gr, surf rough from n-p protruding, clay surplus spread though handle joins are smooth. *In*: horiz wet-smoothing.

FIG. 10 (CONTINUED)

1. Identification			2. Section						3. Surface	
a.	b.	a.	b. Core		c. Non-Plastics				a. Exterior	b. Interior
Item	Square, Locus Basket	Fabric Color	Color	Extent	Type	Size	Fre-quency	Density	Color, n-p, voids, forming, finishing features	Same
	SW 2-25									
9. Jar Handle	186.424	rd yl		none	lms bas	l,m,s l,m	s s	med	*Ex*: pk, lms n-p on eroded handle, fewer on body but *In*: n-p seen in area of spalling where color is lt gr, elsewhere rd yl.	
10. Jar Handle	158.315	pk gr		none	lms bas grog	s,f s,f f	s m f	med	*Ex*: lt pk, protruding n-p give rough surf, some forming lines & smoothing. *In*: same plus more pits.	
11. Jar Handle	158.300	lt rd br		none	bas grog lms	s,f m,s s	s s f	med	*Ex*: pk wh, some n-p seen, shave lines smooth join, vert drag marks. *In*: pk wh, some n-p slightly protrude, horiz smoothing lines.	
12. Jar Handle	158.315	rd	gr	75%	grog bas cal	s m m	s f vf	med	*Ex & In*: rd, some n-p visible, rough but wet-smoothed. Some voids.	
13. Jar Handle	171.327	br	gr	75%	lms bas	l,m,s m,s	s s	med h	*Ex*: rd yl, some n-p seen, some straw voids, *In*: pk, horiz and slant wet-smoothing.	
14. Jar Handle	180.364	br	gr	-100%	lms	s,f	s	low	*Ex & In*: lt rd br, in part covered with charcoal, protruding n-p, straw voids; *In*: wet-smoothing, coil crease.	
15. Jar Base	158.315	lt rd br	gr	75% (int.)	lms bas grog	l,m,s s m,s	s f f	med	*Ex*: lt rd br, n-p seen in shallow voids, *In*: gr, wall flaked; compression ridge in center of base.	
16. Jar Base	162.341	lt rd br		none	lms bas	l,m,s s	m s	med h	*Ex*: lt pk, many n-p just under rippling surface but exposed en masse where firing cracks most visible. *In*: pk gr, light horiz forming lines, firing cracks, large spalled area.	
17. Jar Base	186.428	lt rd	gr	+50%	lms bas	l,n m,s	m m	high	*Ex*: dk pk, many n-p seen esp on base eroded, lime spalls. *In*: rd yl, n-p seen, 2 incised concentric circles around base center. Many pit voids.	

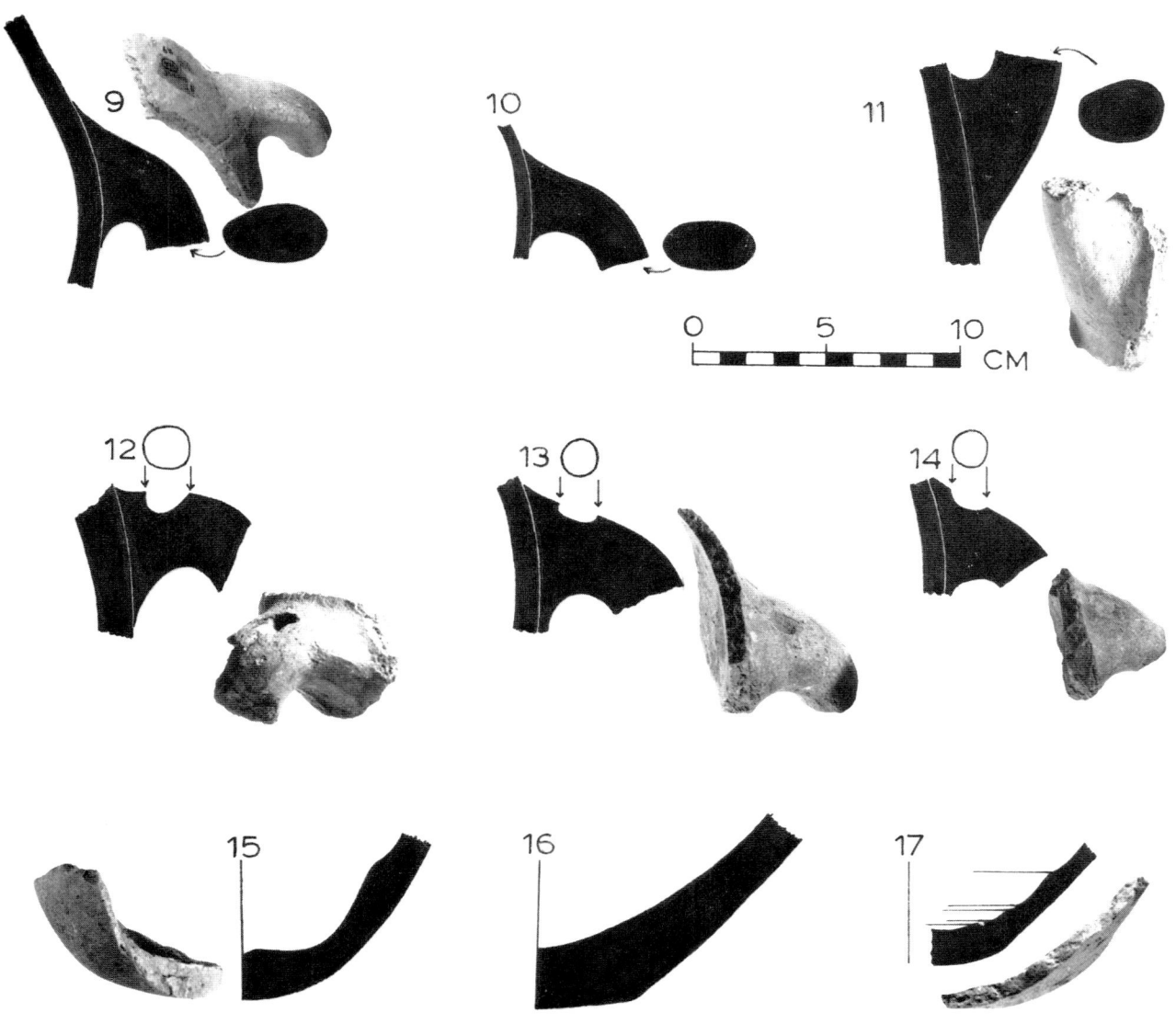

FIG. 11 POTTERY FROM THE DRAINPIPE STRUCTURE (PERIOD IB)

1. Identification		2. Section						3. Surface	
a.	b.	a.	b. Core		c. Non-Plastics			a. Exterior	b. Interior
Item	Square, Locus Basket	Fabric Color	Color	Extent	Type	Size	Fre-quency	Density	Color, n-p, voids, forming, finishing features	Same
	SW 2-25									
1. Jug Rim	208.421	lt br		none	lms bas grog	l,f s s	s f f	low m	Ex & In: rd yl, some n-p on ex, more on in which is also more pitted, ex wet-smoothed, in more coarsely finished.	
2. Jug Rim	186.428	rd gr	dk gr	100%	lms	s,f	f	vlow	Ex: pk gr, very few pits & voids, light wet-smoothing. In: br, rim base partly delineated by pointed tool, coarsely smoothed.	
3. Jug Rim	49.87	rd yl		none	lms	l,m,s	s	low	Ex & In: pk, some n-p protrude, some smoothed, surfaces a bit rough though wet-smoothed.	
4. Jug Rim	158.324	lt br		none	lms	m,s	m	med	Ex & In: pk, many n-p seen and protruding, giving rough surf. Pits, lime spalls, wet-smoothed.	
5. Jug Rim	186.425	dk gr	dk gr	100%	lms	s,f	f	vlow	Ex: pk gr, few n-p protrude but covered, wet-smoothed. In: grey, wet-smoothed, also on rim.	
6. Jug Rim	49.87	pk	gr	+50%	lms	l,m,s	s	low	Ex & In: lt pk, some n-p seen, rough crude wet-smoothing. Rd br paint band on ex neck, faint paint dots on rim.	
7. Jug Rim	160.426	lt br	gr	50%	lms	l,m,s	m	med h	Ex: lt br, many n-p seen most embedded, few voids, wet-smoothed, dark grey burn below rim. In: rd yl many n-p seen thru lime spalls, light wet-smoothing.	
8. Jug Rim	158.303	rd yl		none	lms bas grog	m,s m,s m	s f f	med l	Ex & In: pk, some n-p on surf, horiz thumb-side depression below rim in. Wet-smoothed.	
9. Jug Rim	171.319	lt br	gr	irreg spot int. rim	lms	l,m,s	m	med h	Ex: pk, some n-p seen, wet-smoothed. In: rd yl, many n-p seen, irreg ridge below rim.	
10. Jug Rim	160.426	rd yl		none	lms bas	l,m,s m,s	m s	med	Ex: pk, some large n-p protrude in part due to flaking, wet-smoothed as In: pk gr, more n-p covered but protruding than exposed, few lime spalls.	
11. Jug Rim	160.426	rd yl		none	lms	l,m,s	m	med	Ex & In: to below rim, rd yl, then pk. Many n-p seen some lime spalls, most embedded, wet-smoothed. On ex below rim two horiz thumb depressions separated by ridge.	
12. Jug Rim	180.364	pk		none	lms bas	l,m m	f f	low	Ex: very pale br, n-p seen, limespalls on rim, smoothing also In: pk, otherwise as Ex.	
13. Jug Base	186.425	lt br gr		none	lms bas	l,m,s s	s f	med	Ex: lt br, few n-p seen also protruding, wet-smoothing, turning line ex to ring base. In: lt gr, spalling, straw voids along smoothing lines.	
14. Jug Handle	158.324	dk gr	dk gr	100%	lms grog	m,s s	s f	low	Ex: lt gr, pits due to popouts, crudely smoothed & attached. In: pk gr, some pitting, wet-smoothed.	
15. Jug Strainer	49.87	lt br	gr	none (body) 50% (spout)	lms bas	m,s m	s vf	low	Ex & In: rd yl; ex badly flaked exposing few n-p; in smoothed, few n-p, excess clay ridges on inside perforations.	
16. Juglet Rim & Handle	158.315	lt br		none	lms	m,s	s	low	Ex & In: pk, some n-p visible due to spalling, straw voids due to smoothing.	
17. Juglet Base	160.376	lt br	gr	80% (int.)	lms	l,m,f	f	low	Ex: lt rd, slip (?), lm encrusted and scaled. In: lt br, deep base flaked due to burial, forming ridges on walls, pitting.	

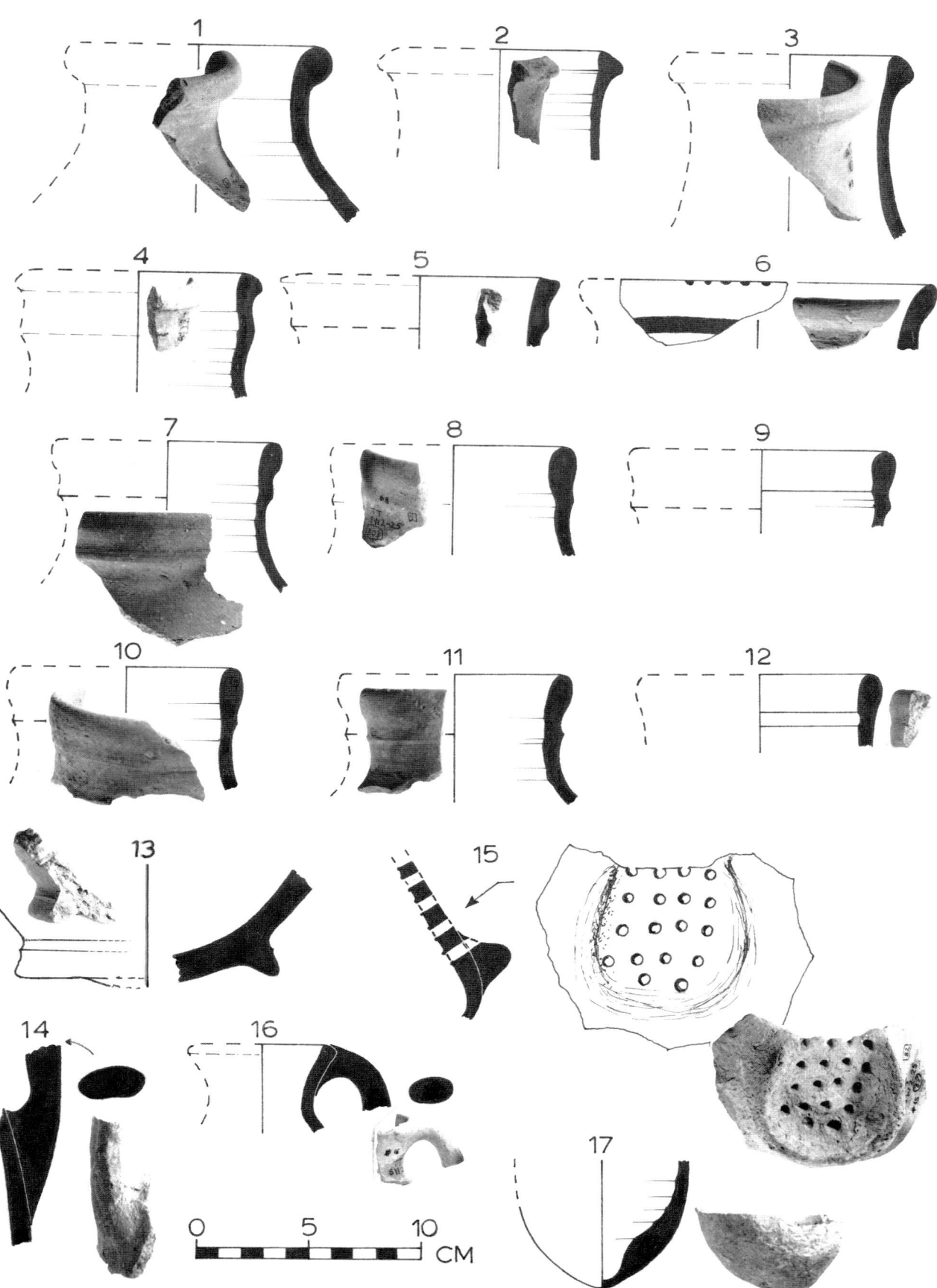

FIG. 12 POTTERY FROM THE DRAINPIPE STRUCTURE (PERIOD 1B)

1. Identification		2. Section						3. Surface	
a.	b.	a.	b. Core		c. Non-Plastics			a. Exterior	b. Interior
Item	Square, Locus Basket	Fabric Color	Color	Extent	Type	Size	Frequency	Density	Color, n-p, voids, forming, finishing features	Same
	SW 2-25									
1. Crater Rim	158.324	rd yl	dk pk	50%	lms	l,m,s	s	med h	*Ex* & *In*: rd yl, n-p seen, generally embedded, *ex* wet-smoothed, *in* pitted.	
2. Crater Rim	186.428	rd yl	lt br	+75%	lms bas	l,m,s m,s	s s	med h	*Ex* & *In*: rd yl, as in No. 1. *Ex* tooled undercut to rim.	
3. Crater Rim	158.315	rd yl	gr	+60%	lms	l,m,s	s	med l	*Ex* & *In*: rd yl, n-p protrude from surf, crudely smoothed with horiz finger strokes, *ex* rim undercut & partly covered.	
4. Crater Rim	186.425	rd	rd yl	75%	lms	l,m,s	s-m	med h	*Ex*: dk pk, protruding n-p give rough surf, *In*: lt pk, otherwise the same.	
5. Crater Rim	158.300	rd yl		none	lms bas	l,m,s l,m	s f	med	*Ex* & *In*: dk pk, protruding n-p, spalls, rough smoothing, tooled rim base sealed.	
6. Crater Rim	62.113	pk gr	lt gr	none (body) 50% (rim)	lms bas	s,f s,f	f vf	low	*Ex* & *In*: dk pk darkened by charcoal, very few n-p seen, irreg smoothed, rougher *in* below rim.	
7. Crater Rim	158.427									

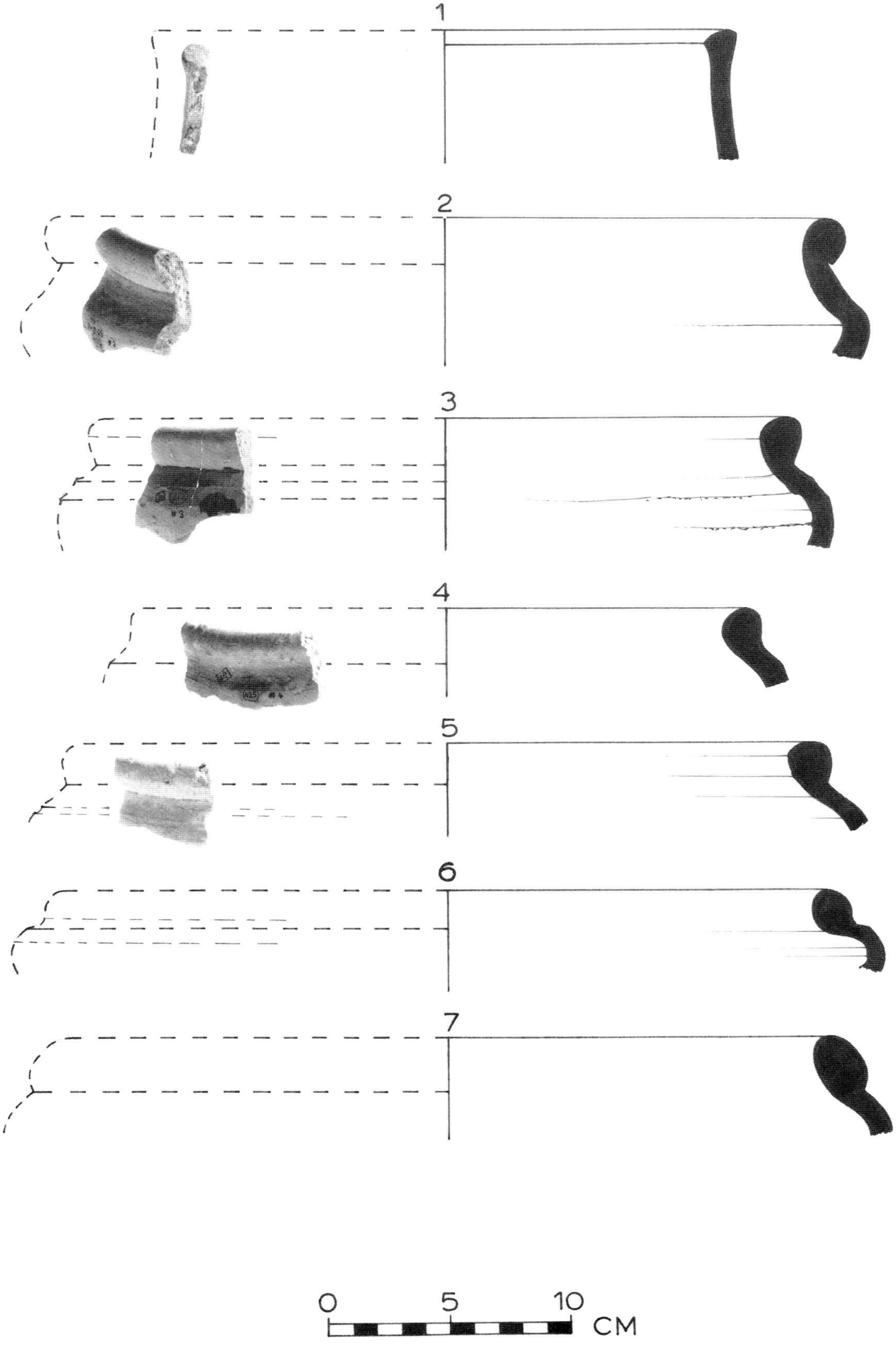

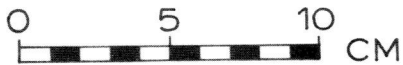

FIG. 13 POTTERY FROM THE DRAINPIPE STRUCTURE (PERIOD IB)

1. Identification		2. Section						3. Surface	
a. Item	b. Square, Locus Basket	a. Fabric Color	b. Core		c. Non-Plastics			a. Exterior	b. Interior
			Color	Extent	Type	Size	Frequency	Density	Color, n-p, voids, forming, finishing features	Same
	SW 2-25									
1. Bowl Rim	49.87	lt br	dk gr	75%	lms	m,s	f	low	*Ex* & *In*: rd br, few n-p seen, horiz straw voids, wet-smoothing.	
2. Bowl Rim	49.87	lt br	dk gr	50%	lms bas	l,m,s s,m	s s	med l	*Ex*: lt pk, n-p embedded, *In*: rd yl, n-p as *ex*, some wet-smoothing below rim.	
3. Bowl Rim	49.87	lt br		none	lms bas	s s	f f	low	*Ex* & *In*: rd yl, few n-p seen, *ex* roughly finished; *in* wet-smoothed.	
4. Bowl Rim	158.324	dk pk		none	lms	m,s	s	m low	*Ex*: dk pk, n-p seen, lime spalls, pitted under rim, shallow horiz thumb-wide depressions. *In*: rd yl, some n-p seen, wet-smoothed.	
5. Bowl Rim	186.425	dk pk	lt br	30%	lms	m,s	f	low	*Ex*: dk pk, few n-p, few pits, horiz wet-smoothing interrupted by fingerprints. *In*: rd yl, n-p protrude slightly, wet-smoothed with some drag marks.	
6. Bowl Rim	186.425	lt br		none	lms	m,s	f	low	*Ex* & *In*: dk pk, few n-p, pits, drag marks, wet-smoothing.	
7. Bowl Rim	160.376	lt br	lt gr	25%	lms	m,s	s	low	*Ex*: dk pk, straw voids, few pits, few n-p seen, esp on rim. *In*: rd yl slightly darkened by charcoal, some n-p seen, light wet-smoothing.	
8. Bowl Rim	158.303	lt br		none	lms	l,m,s	s	med	*Ex* & *In*: dk pk to rd yl, many n-p seen, *in* rough, *ex* wet-smoothing lines.	
9. Bowl Rim	171.319	dk pk	lt br	60%	lms bas grog	m,s s s	s f f	med	*Ex* & *In*: dk pk, some n-p seen, esp *ex*, wet-smoothed.	
10. Bowl Rim	171.319	rd yl	dk gr	75%	lms bas	f f	s s	low	*Ex*: rd yl grayed, clay inhomogeneous, some n-p protrude slightly, wet-smoothed, some pits. *In*: dk pk, few n-p covered, wet-smoothed.	
11. Bowl Rim	160.376	dk pk		none	lms bas	s,f s,f	s s	low	*Ex* & *In*: dk pk, few n-p covered, wet-smoothing.	
12. Bowl Rim	158.303	lt gr to pk gr	pl br	60%	lms grog	m,s m,s	s f	low	*Ex*: gray, n-p protrude, covered, horiz wet-smoothing marks as *In*: v pl br, some n-p covered, wet-smoothing.	
13. Bowl Rim	158.324	dk pk	lt br	+50%	lms	m,s	f	low	*Ex* & *In*: dk pk, few n-p covered, few drag marks, wet-smoothing.	
14. Bowl Rim	186.428	lt br	gr	50%	lms	l,m,s	s	low	*Ex* & *In*: dk pk, n-p seen on surface, straw voids most on *ex*, horiz smoothing lines sharper at rim, roughened below shoulder.	

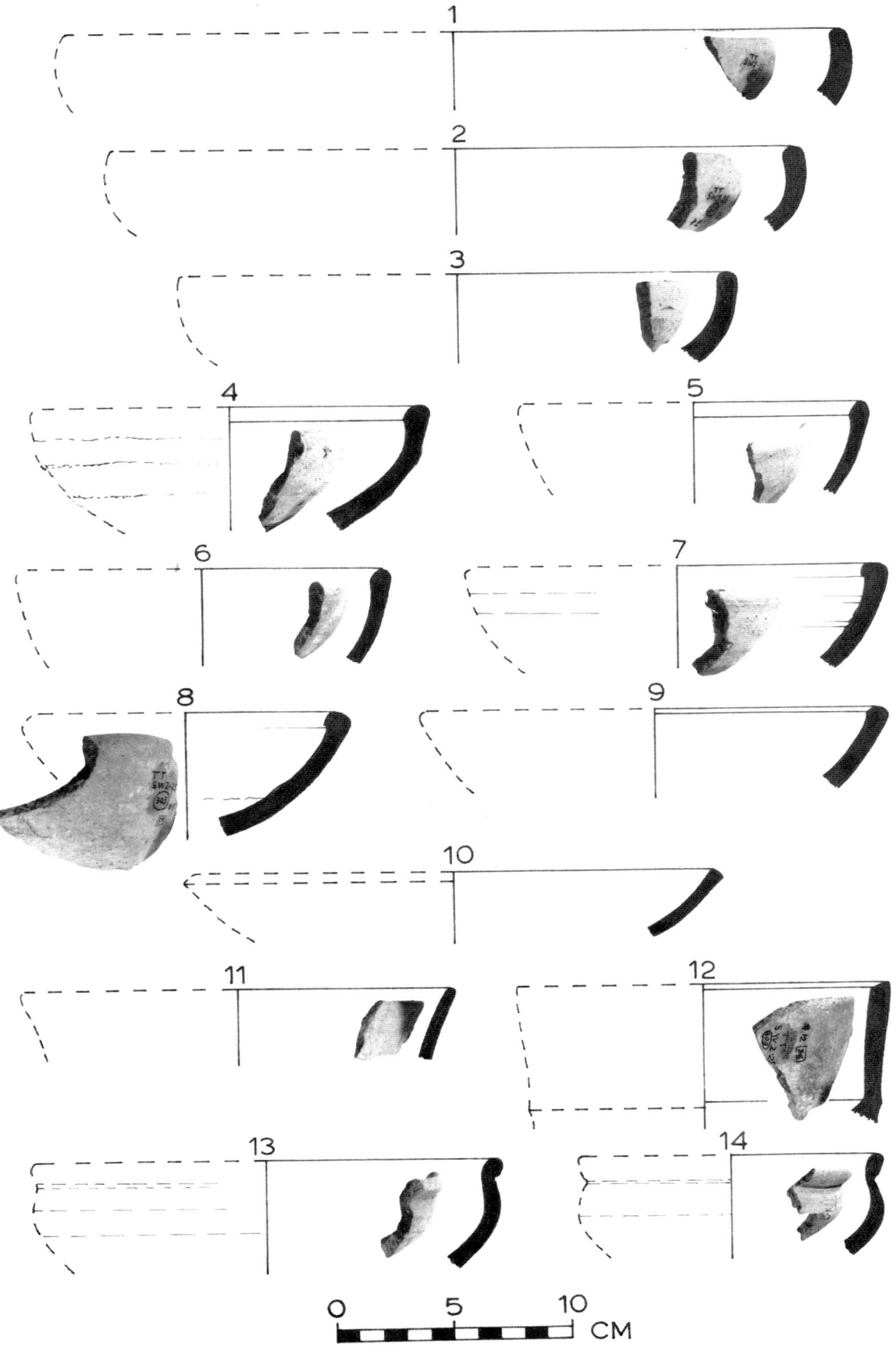

FIG. 14 POTTERY FROM THE DRAINPIPE STRUCTURE (PERIOD IB)

1. Identification		2. Section							3. Surface	
a. Item	b. Square, Locus Basket	a. Fabric Color	b. Core		c. Non-Plastics				a. Exterior	b. Interior
			Color	Extent	Type	Size	Frequency	Density	Color, n-p, voids, forming, finishing features	Same
	SW2-25									
1. Bowl Base	160.376	dk pk	gr	+75%	lms	l,m,s	s	low	*Ex*: dk pk to lt rd, few n-p, drag marks, straw voids. *In*: dk pk, n-p seen under scaling, usually tiny lms.	
2. Bowl Base	158.324	dk pk	gr to br	75%	lms	l,m,s	s	med	*Ex*: dk pk, some n-p protrude, seen in spalls, drag marks, wet-smoothing. *In*: few n-p protrude, criss-cross wet-smoothing.	
3. Bowl Base	61.126	rd yl	dk pk	inner 80%	lms	l,m,s	m	med h	*Ex*: dk pk, many n-p seen, embedded, lime spalling, drag marks, wet-smoothing. *In*: lime spalls more common, pits.	
4. Bowl Base	208.421	dk pk	lt br	80%	lms	s	f	low	*Ex*: dk pk, some n-p, spalling and drag marks. *In*: rd yl, some n-p seen thru pits, little smoothing technique visible.	
5. Bowl Base	49.87	dk pk to lt br	gr	inner 50%	lms	s,m	s	low	*Ex*: rd yl, n-p seen, few drag marks, circular wet-smoothing lines on disk base, body better covered. *In*: grayed by charcoal, flaked, some pitting.	
6. Bowl Base	160.376	rd yl	lt br	outer 75% (base) center 75% (body)	lms	l,m	s	low	*Ex*: dk pk, some n-p seen, few pits, slight wet-smoothing. *In*: rd yl, flaking exposed n-p, otherwise as No. 5.	
7. Bowl Base	171.319	dk pk	dk gr	60%	lms grog	l,m,s s	s-m f	med h	*Ex*: dk pk, some embedded n-p seen, few straw voids, wet-smoothing marks. *In*: dk pk made ashy gray, some n-p seen thru lime spalls, some shallow fissures.	
8. Bowl Base	158.300	lt br		none	lms	m,s	f	vlow	*Ex*: lt pk, some n-p seen embedded, light wipe lines, ring base not well joined. *In*: dk pk, some n-p seen, surf smooth.	
9. Bowl Base	158.324	pk gr	lt gr	inner 60%	lms	m,s	f	vlow	*Ex*: pk gr, some n-p protrude, covered, roughened, wet-smoothed. *In*: gray by burn, irreg smoothed. Wide & deep horiz void in base.	
10. Bowl Base	158.300	lt br		none	grog bas	m,s s	s s	low	*Ex*: dk pk, few n-p seen, eroded, encrusted. *In*: dk pk, wet-smoothed, but surf remains rough.	
11. Cook Pot Rim	158.427	lt rd		none	cal	m,s,f	m	med	*Ex & In*: lt rd br, n-p on surf, on *in* protruding slightly, wet-smoothing lines, untrimmed clay in tooled ridge incised below *ex* rim, drag marks, eroded *ex* lower body.	
12. Cook Pot Rim	186.425	rd br	dk gr	75%	cal	m,s,f	m	low	*Ex*: rd gr, many tiny n-p, grayed due to 2ndary firing, wet-smoothing, very slight drag marks. *In*: br, lightly wet-smoothed.	
13. Cook Pot Rim	186.424	rd br	dk gr	+75%	cal	s,f	m	low	*Ex*: rd gr, ashy fr use, n-p seen as salt sprinkle as on *In*: rd br, larger n-p seen, wet-smoothed on both sides.	
14. Chalice TT 928 Complete	160.422	pl br	gr	50%	lms	l,m,s	s	low	*Ex*: dk pk, some n-p seen & covered, wet-smoothing around neck is horiz, slants on body, two depressions on body, in one case due to mending. Much the same under base and inside vessel.	
15. Chalice Rim	158.324	lt br	gr	50%	lms	m,s	f	low	*Ex*: lt gr, few n-p on rim, wet-smoothing wipe lines. *In*: lt pk, n-p seen, few protrude slightly, wet-smoothed.	
16. Chalice Rim	171.319	pk gr	lt gr	+50%	lms bas	m,s s	s f	med	*Ex*: dk pk, rim roughened and lm encrusted, some wipe lines. *In*: lt br, wet-smoothing, lm encrusted.	

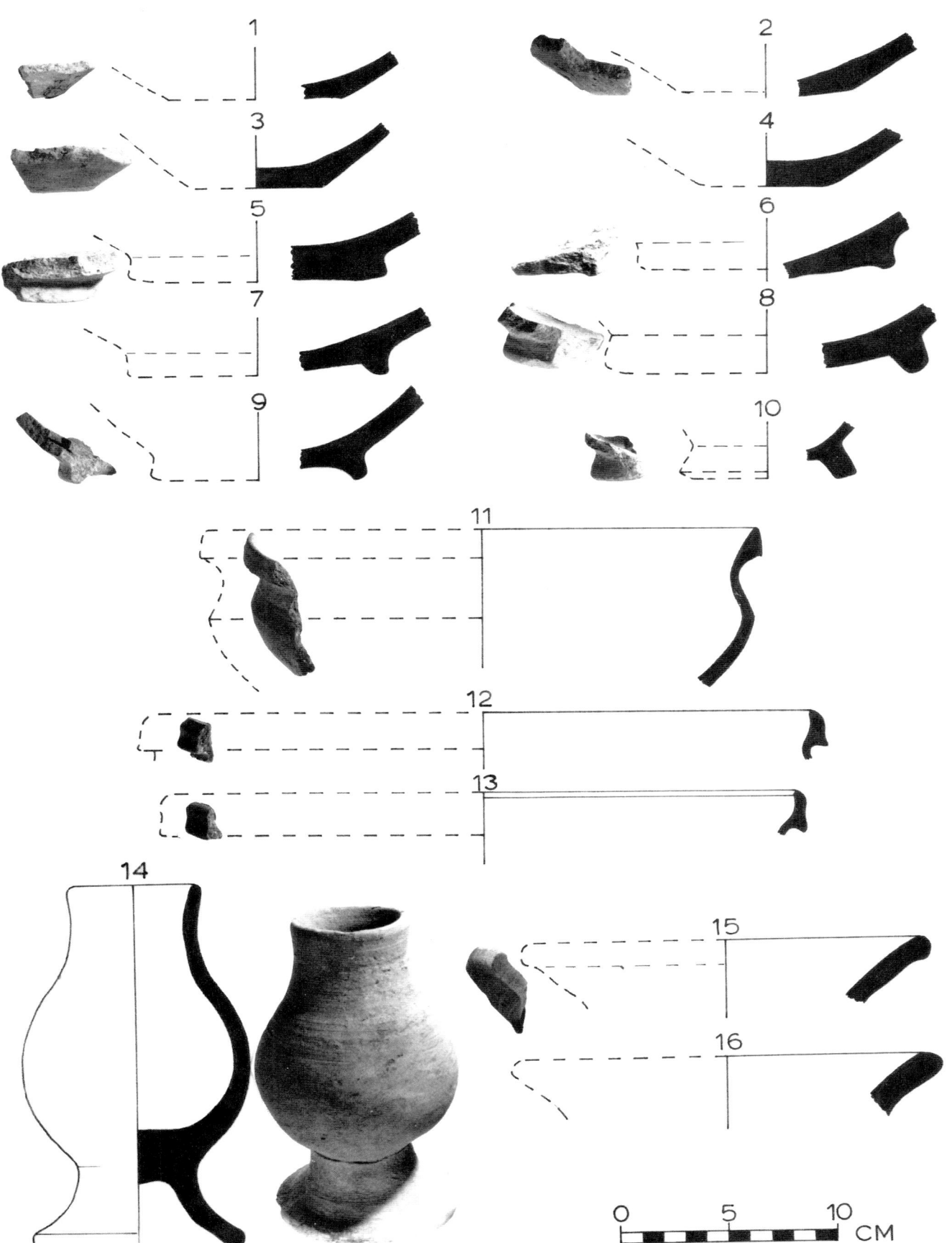

FIG. 15 POTTERY FROM THE CUNEIFORM TABLET BUILDING (PERIOD IB)

1. Identification		2. Section						3. Surface	
a.	b.	a.	b. Core		c. Non-Plastics			a. Exterior	b. Interior
Item	Square, Locus Basket	Fabric Color	Color	Extent	Type	Size	Frequency	Density	Color, n-p, voids, forming, finishing features	Same
	SW 6-2*									
1. Jar Base	104.227	l br to lt rd br	to gr	none 50%	lms grog	m,s s	f f	low	Ex: dk pk, lightly smoothed. In: lt pk, criss-cross finger lines, ridged smoothing forming heavy base.	
2. Jar Handle	103.226	rd yl	gr lt gr	80% of outer edge 40% body	lms grog	f f	f f	vlow	Ex & In: dk pk, wet-smoothed clean join on ex but more ridged under the handle. Lime encrusted. Slight join line with body.	
3. Jar Handle	103.226	dk pk	dk gr lt gr	60% handle Inner 50% body.	lms bas	l,f f	s s	low	Ex: dk pk, straw voids, smoothing lines round handle, center join ridge to L. In: pl br, also gr, wet-smoothing, deeper depression where body bends inward.	
4. Jar Handle	103.226	rd yl	gr	60% handle Inner 50% body.	lms	m,f	vf	vlow	Ex: rd yl, many straw voids, joining has slight ridges on top of each side of handle. In: pk gr, wet-smoothed.	
5. Jar Handle	103.226	lt rd br	dk gr	50% body & handle	lms grog	vf vf	vf vf	vvlow	Ex: lt pk, joined to body handle tilting up on R. In: body pk gr, wet-smoothed before handle joined. Many tiny voids in section.	
6. Jug Rim	103.226	rd yl	dk pk	+50%	lms	l,s	s	low	Ex & In: rd yl, n-p protrude, mostly covered. Excess clay interrupts crude horiz forming lines.	
7. Jug Rim	103.226	rd yl	lt rd br	Inner 60%	lms	l,m,s	s	low	Ex & In: dk pk, n-p embedded on ex, protrude in and lime spalls. Wet-smoothed.	
8. Jug Rim	104.227	lt rd br		none	lms	m,s,f	s	low	Ex: dk pk, some protruding n-p covered, wet-smoothing. In: lt rd br, otherwise the same as ex.	
9. Jug Rim	104.227	lt br		none	lms grog	m,s s	s f	med l	Ex: pk, gr, many n-p seen slightly protruding giving irreg surface, some shallow drag lines and wet-smoothing. In: dk gr pk, forming depressions with wet-smoothing lines.	
10. Jug Rim	103.226	dk pk		none	lms bas	m,s s	s f	med l	Ex: dk pk, some n-p seen, generally smoothed wet. In: rd yl, otherwise same but pitted.	
11. Jug Rim	103.226	rd yl		none	lms bas	l,m,s s	s vf	low	Ex & In: dk pk, some n-p showing, few voids on rim, wet-smoothing coated on ex, few lime spalls.	
12. Jug Handle	104.227	dk pk to rd yl	dk gr	75% (handle) 50% body)	lms bas	f m,s	s f	low	Ex: rd yl, rough finish under handle, above on body are rd and rd br horiz paint bands. In: rd yl, flaked, spalls, wet-smoothing.	
13. Jug Base	103.226	rd yl to lt rd br	gr	-50%	lms	m,s	f	vlow	Ex: lt rd br, shallow finger depression just above base ring; above that horiz close hand-burnish as on base. In: dk pk, few n-p seen, forming ridges above base, fingerprint lines parallel to ridges.	
14. Juglet Rim	106.220	lt rd br	lt br	80%	lms bas	m,s s	f f	low	Ex & In: dk pk, n-p covered, ex wet-smoothed.	
15. Juglet Handle	103.226	lt br	lt gr	-25% inner	lms	vf	vf	vvlow	Ex & In: pk gr, 2ndary rd br film, some straw voids. In: wet-smoothing.	
16. Juglet Handle & Body	103.226	lt rd br	lt br lt gr	50% inner 40% handle	lms shell	l,s,f s	vf vf	vlow	As No. 15. Ex: irreg vert burnishing, straw voids esp around handle. In: wet-smoothing to neck where wall thins, depressed band where new clay added.	
17. Juglet Base	104.227	dk pk	lt gr	40% inner	lms	s,f	f	vlow	Ex: rd yl, eroded, string cut off-center whirl, rough finish. In: dk pk, some dk n-p seen on & under flaked surface, slight circular center depression.	

*The Cuneiform Tablet Building was located in SW 6-1, but recorded as SW 6-2.

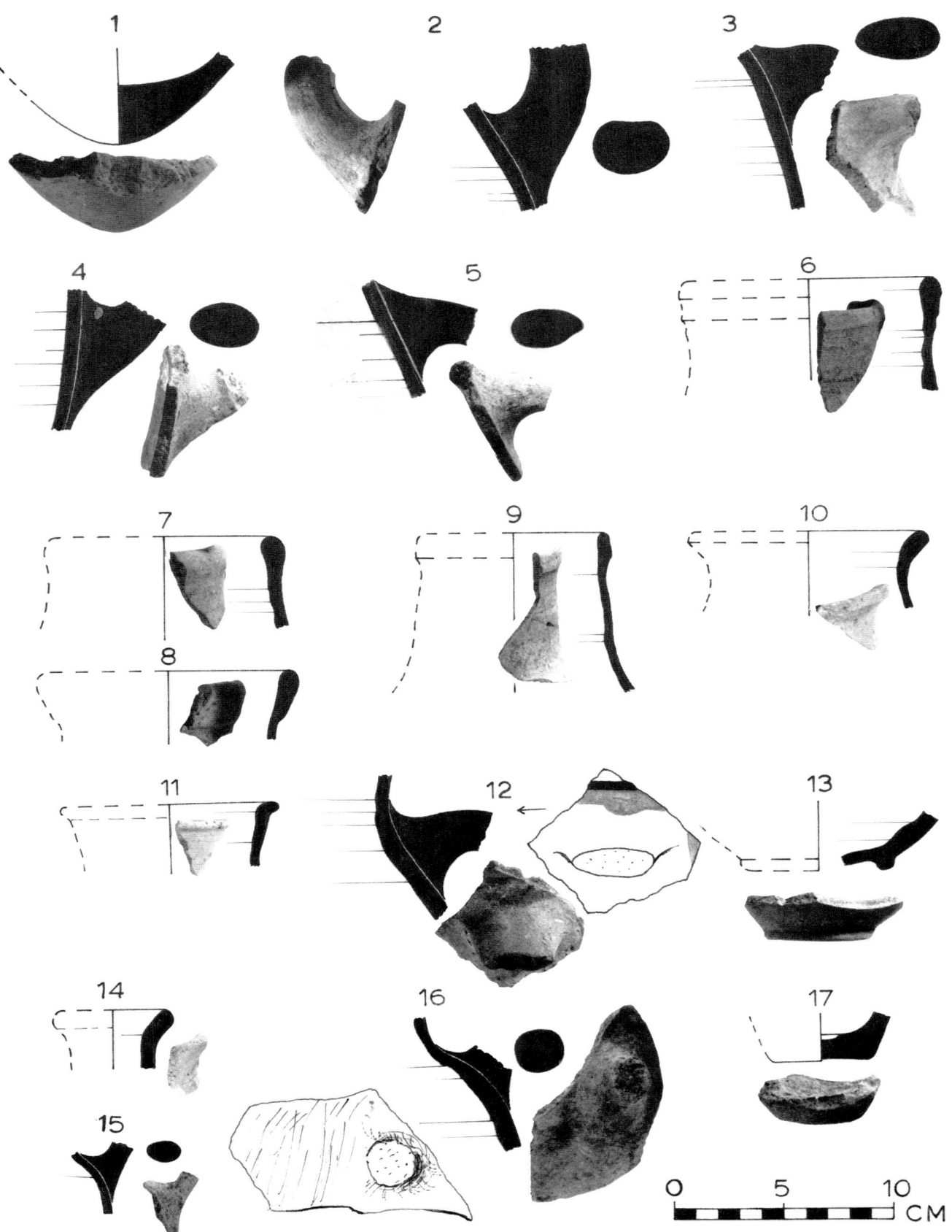

FIG. 16 POTTERY FROM THE CUNEIFORM TABLET BUILDING (PERIOD IB)

1. Identification		2. Section						3. Surface	
a. Item	b. Square, Locus Basket	a. Fabric Color	b. Core		c. Non-Plastics			a. Exterior	b. Interior
			Color	Extent	Type	Size	Frequency	Density	Color, n-p, voids, forming, finishing features	Same
1. Crater Rim	SW 6-2* 104.227	dk pk	lt gr	-50%	lms	l,m,s	m	med	*Ex*: rd yl, many n-p seen, protruding slightly, tooled trim to folded-over rim, slightly irreg surface, wet-smoothing interrupted by vert rubbing. *In*: dk pk, many n-p seen, pitted with lime spalls, horiz thumb-wide depression mid-shoulder.	
2. Crater Rim	103.226	rd yl	lt gr	50%	lms	m,s	s	low	*Ex & In*: rd yl, wet-smoothed, folded-over rim pressed into wall with tool ca .8cm wide.	
3. Crater Rim	104.227	lt br	gr	50% at rim -25% body	lms	s	s	low	*Ex & In*: dk pk, some embedded n-p seen on rim & *in* few pits, rim edge untrimmed, wet-smoothed.	
4. Crater Rim	104.227	lt rd br	lt gr	As No. 3	lms grog shell	l,m,s s m	s vf f	med l	*Ex & In*: lt br with some lt rd br *ex*, n-p seen only slightly protruding wet-smoothed.	
5. Crater Rim	104.227	rd yl	lt gr	50% at rim +30% body	lms	s,f	s	vlow	*Ex & In*: lt rd br, coated with 2ndary rd br film (as Fig. 15: 15). Wet-smoothed throwing ridges more deeply lined than usual, esp on *ex*.	
6. Bowl Rim	104.227	rd yl	gr	75%	lms	s,f	f	vlow	*Ex & In*: dk pk, some tiny n-p roughen surf, one large on *in*, wet-smoothing, slant lines below rim.	
7. Bowl Rim	104.227	rd yl to lt br	dk gr	+60%	lms	m,s	s	low	*Ex & In*: rd yl, lm encrusted, *in* esp eroded, tiny n-p seen, wet-smoothing interrupted with fingerprints.	

*The Cuneiform Tablet Building was located in SW 6-1, but recorded as SW 6-2.

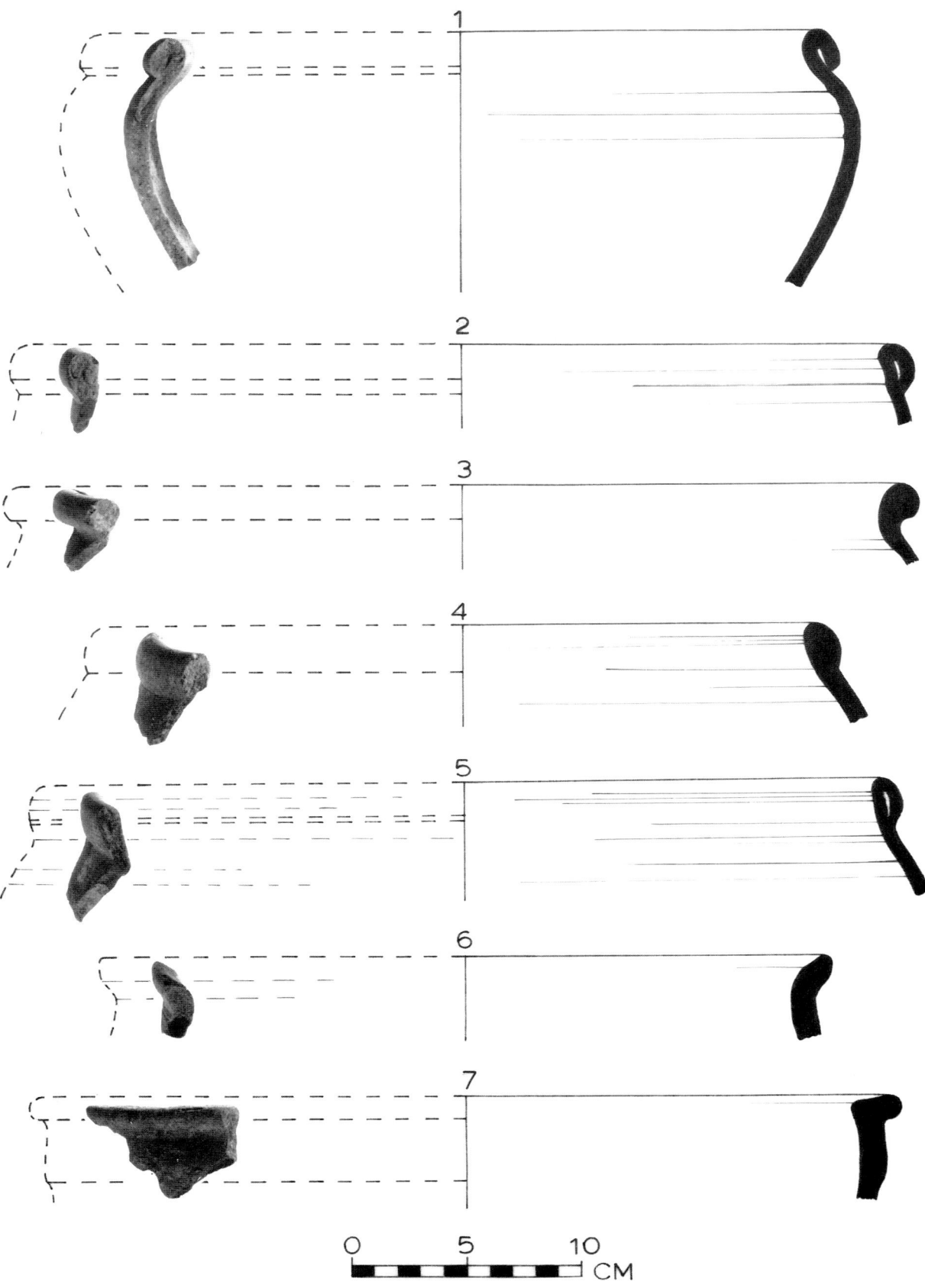

FIG. 17 POTTERY FROM THE CUNEIFORM TABLET BUILDING (PERIOD IB)

1. Identification		2. Section						3. Surface	
a. Item	b. Square, Locus Basket	a. Fabric Color	b. Core		c. Non-Plastics			a. Exterior	b. Interior
			Color	Extent	Type	Size	Frequency	Density	Color, n-p, voids, forming, finishing features	Same
	SW 6-2*									
1. Bowl Rim	103.226	lt rd br	gr	-50%	lms grog	l,m,s s	f vf	low	Ex & In: dk pk, few n-p protrude, flaking on *ex* expose more, wet smoothing.	
2. Bowl Rim	104.227	rd yl	dk gr	+50%	lms	m,s,f	f	low	Ex & In: rd yl, some n-p protrude, eroded rim exposes tiny n-p wipe lines barely visible.	
3. Bowl Rim	103.226	br	gr	30%	grog	s	f	vlow	Ex & In: rd yl, few n-p protrude on *ex*, wet-smoothing, few drag marks, 2 crudely scraped bands on *ex*.	
4. Bowl Rim & Handle	104.227	lt br		none	lms bas (sand?)	l,m,s m	s	low	Ex & In: rd yl, n-p seen on surf, wet-smoothing on *in* but on *ex* where bar handle applied joining a little rough, straw voids, some pitting.	
5. Bowl Base	104.227	lt rd br	lt br	+50%	(sand?)	m,s	s	low	Ex: lt rd br, wet-smoothed, drag marks, few n-p visible, few lime spalls, series of concentric circles form base. In: dk pk, faint wipe lines, few straw voids.	
6. Bowl Base	106.220	rd yl to lt br	gr	60%	lms cal	m,s m	f vf	vlow	Ex & In: rd yl, faint wet-smoothing lines, few n-p seen, In encrusted, mostly *in* where wipe lines criss-cross.	
7. Bowl Base	103.226	v pl br		none	lms	s,f	f	vlow	Ex & In: pk gr but *in* eroded, pitted, also gray film. On *ex* n-p seen, wet-smoothing.	
8. Bowl Base	103.226	lt rd br	gr	-90% (body) none (base)	lms	s,f	f	vlow	Ex In: rd br, 2ndary charcoal, few n-p protrude but covered, wet smoothing, more criss-crossed on *ex* body.	
9. Bowl Base	104.227	br to rd yl	lt gr	-50% (body)	lms	l,m,s	s	med l	Ex & In: lt rd br to rd yl; some n-p seen thru erosion on base ring circular wet-smoothing lines in base; *in* much pitted, few n-p seen.	
10. Bowl Base	104.227	lt br	dk gr	inner 75% (base) none (body)	lms cal	m,s f	f f	low	Ex: lt br, very few n-p seen, some circular lines crossed with wipe lines. In: heavy dk gr charcoal deposit, pits large and tiny.	
11. Cook Pot Rim	104.227	dk br	dk gr	±50%	cal	s,f	m	low	Ex & In: dk br much coated with charcoal deposit, many fine n-p seen, wet-smoothing, groove under *ex* rim sharply tooled.	
12. Cook Pot Rim	106.220	rd br		-50%	cal	s,f	m	low	Ex & In: rd br, *ex* grayed by burning, n-p give salty look, wet smoothing rim tooled as No. 11.	
13. Cook Pot Rim	104.227	lt rd br	gr	40%	cal	s,f	m	med	Ex & In: rd br with 2ndary graying, n-p seen on surf, wet smoothing, *ex* rim sharply undercut.	
14. Cook Pot Rim	103.226	rd yl	dk gr	50%	cal	s,f	m	low	Ex: rd br, much eroded so many n-p seen, In: rd yl, n-p seen though not eroded, wet-smoothing.	
15. Cook Pot Rim	103.226	rd yl	dk gr	-50%	cal	s,f	s	low	Ex: dk rd, flaked, tiny n-p seen, faint wet-smoothing. In: lt rd br 2ndary gray charcoal, many n-p covered, wet-smoothing.	
16. Chalice Rim	104.227	rd br	dk gr	inner 60%	lms	m	vf	vlow	Ex: rd yl, few pits, slight wet-smoothing lines. In: lt rd br, heavy deposit of charcoal, wet-smoothing.	
17. Chalice Rim	103.226	lt br	dk gr	inner -50%		s	f	low	Ex: rd yl, pop-outs, drag marks, crude horiz wipe lines, *in*: dk pk few pits, faint wipe lines.	

*The Cuneiform Tablet Building was located in SW 6-1, but recorded as SW 6-2.

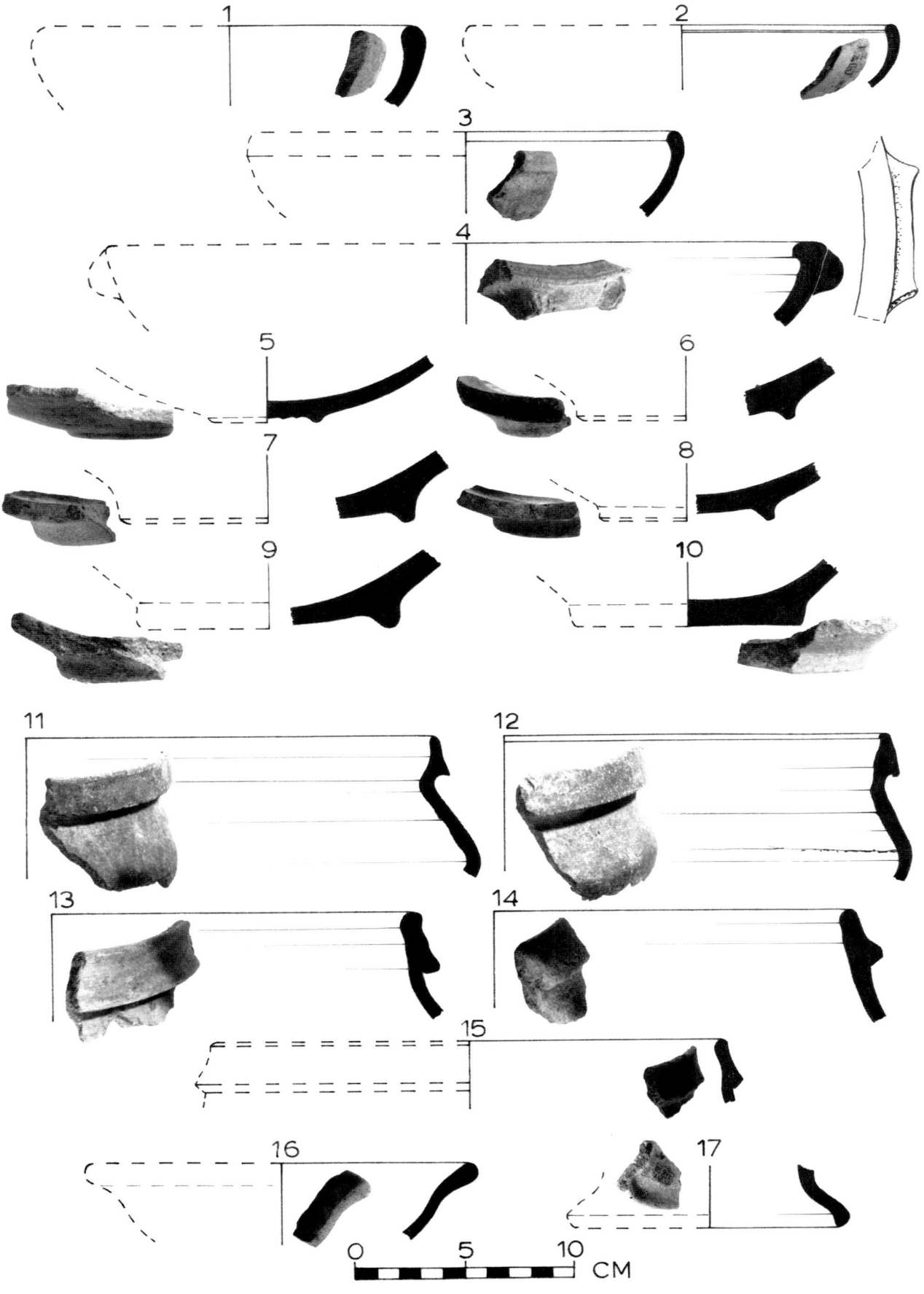

FIG. 18 POTTERY FROM SW 4-7, LOCUS 68 (PERIOD IIA)

1. Identification		2. Section						3. Surface	
a. Item	b. Square, Locus Basket	a. Fabric Color	b. Core		c. Non-Plastics			a. Exterior	b. Interior
			Color	Extent	Type	Size	Frequency	Density	Color, n-p, voids, forming, finishing features	Same
	SW 4-7									
1. Jug Rim	68.111	rd yl	lt br	+50%	lms grog cal	m,s s f	f f f	low	Ex & In: rd yl, few embedded n-p, rubbed traces of wet-smoothing.	
2. Crater Rim	68.111	lt br		none	lms	l,m,s	s	med	Ex & In: v pl br, many lime spalls, esp on rim which is also flaked, crude pressure band at bottom on rim, slightly undercut, some wipe lines.	
3. Crater Rim	68.111	dk pk to lt br	vlt gr	-10%	lms	m,s	s	low	Ex & In: dk pk, some n-p seen, few protrude, two narrow tooled ridges at ex base of rim.	
4. Bowl Rim	68.111	rd yl	lt br	-75%	lms	m,s	f	low	Ex: pk gr, some n-p seen, roughened wet-smoothing lines, thumb-wide horiz shallow depression below rim. In: rd yl, many tiny n-p below eroded rim, wet-smoothing lines, slip.	
5. Bowl Rim	68.111	lt br		none	lms	s	f	low	Ex & In: dk pk, some n-p visible, esp on in, also protrude, wet-smoothing.	
6. Bowl Base	68.111	lt rd br to lt br	gr	50%	lms	m,s	f	low	Ex: lt rd br, irreg wiping on body, circular on base. In: lt rd, some m to l n-p seen, shallow spalls, tiny voids, criss-cross wet-smoothing.	
7. Cook Pot Rim	68.111	rd br	gr	20%	cal	f	f	low	Ex & In: lt rd br, mostly tiny n-p visible, shallow wet-smoothing lines, on ex edge of rim this leaves irreg outer line.	

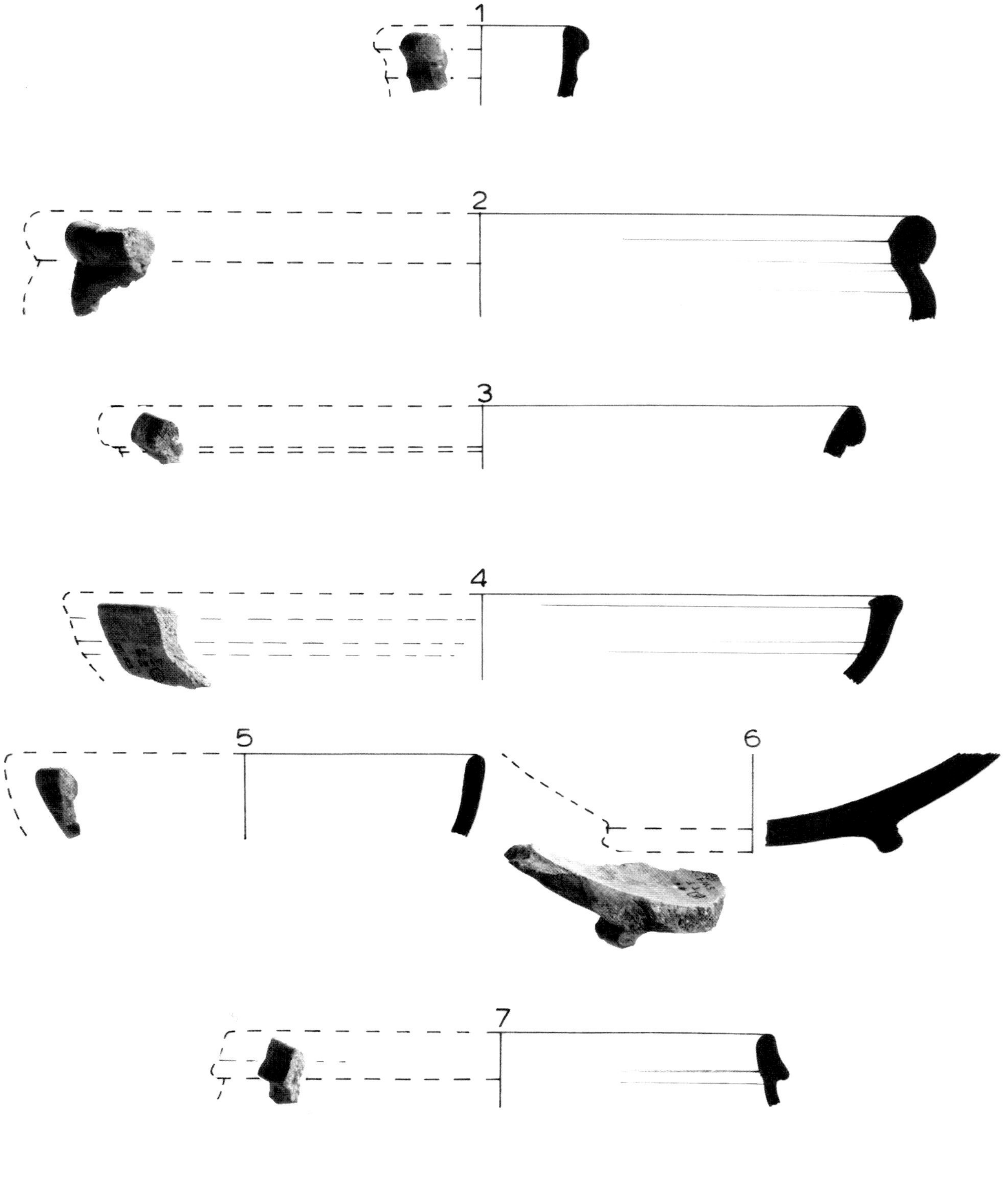

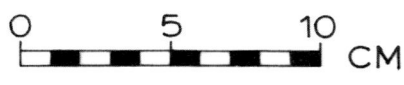

FIG. 19 POTTERY FROM SW 4-7, LOCUS 53 (PERIOD IIA)

1. Identification		2. Section							3. Surface	
a.	b.	a.	b. Core		c. Non-Plastics				a. Exterior	b. Interior
Item	Square, Locus Basket	Fabric Color	Color	Extent	Type	Size	Frequency	Density	Color, n-p, voids, forming, finishing features	Same
	SW 4-7									
1. Jar Handle	53.85	rd br	gr	inner 80%	lms	l,m,s	s	med	*Ex*: pk gr to gr, many n-p seen thru spalls, many straw voids on handle, tiny pits, horiz wet-smoothing interrupted by handle join which is slightly fissured from body. "Steam" hole to R of handle. *In*: gray, many n-p seen thru spalls, reg horiz tool marks wiped vertically.	
2. Jar Handle	53.85	yl br	lt gr	-50% (handle) none (body)	lms	m,s	f	low	*Ex & In*: dk pk, few n-p visible, straw voids common on handle, few pits also *in*, finger depressions at handle base producing ridge on L of handle. *In*: reg spaced horiz tool lines.	
3. Jar Handle	53.84	rd yl	gr gr	inner 90% (body) 80% (handle)	lms	l,m,s	s	med	*Ex*: pk wh, n-p embedded, many pits on handle, vert wet-smoothing & straw voids, cross on handle made with horiz line first, then vert. Horiz wipe marks on body. *In*: lt gr, embedded n-p, many seen in lime spalls, pits. Horiz tool marks esp below handle join.	
4. Jug Rim	53.85	lt rd br		none	lms	l,m,s	s	low	*Ex*: dk pk, n-p embedded, protruding, few voids, slight horiz wipe lines. *In*: rd br; as above except for forming ridges bottom half of neck.	
5. Jug Rim	53.86	rd yl	vlt gr	inner 40%	lms bas	l,m,f s	s vf	low	*Ex & In*: dk pk, n-p seen thru some spalls, few on surf, wet-smoothing lines clear, *in* 2ndary gray.	
6. Jug Rim	53.84	lt rd br		none	lms	l,m,f	f	vlow	*Ex & In*: rd yl, few n-p embedded, few spalls shallow, wet-smoothing, prob slipped.	
7. Crater Rim	53.85	pk gr	vlt gr	25%	lms	m,f	s	low	*Ex & In*: rd br, some lms n-p seen, some flaking, smoothing lines.	
8. Bowl Base	53.85	rd yl	lt gr	-50%	lms grog	s,f f	s s	low	*Ex*: dk pk, some n-p protruding, few embedded, few straw voids, circular wet-smoothing. *In*: pk wh, n-p below surf, shallow circular wipe lines, slip covering.	
9. Cook Pot Rim	53.86	rd br	dk gr	inner 75%	cal	f	m	low	*Ex & In*: rd gr to rd br, many tiny n-p on surf, shallow forming lines below *ex* rim as well as *in* at shoulder bend.	

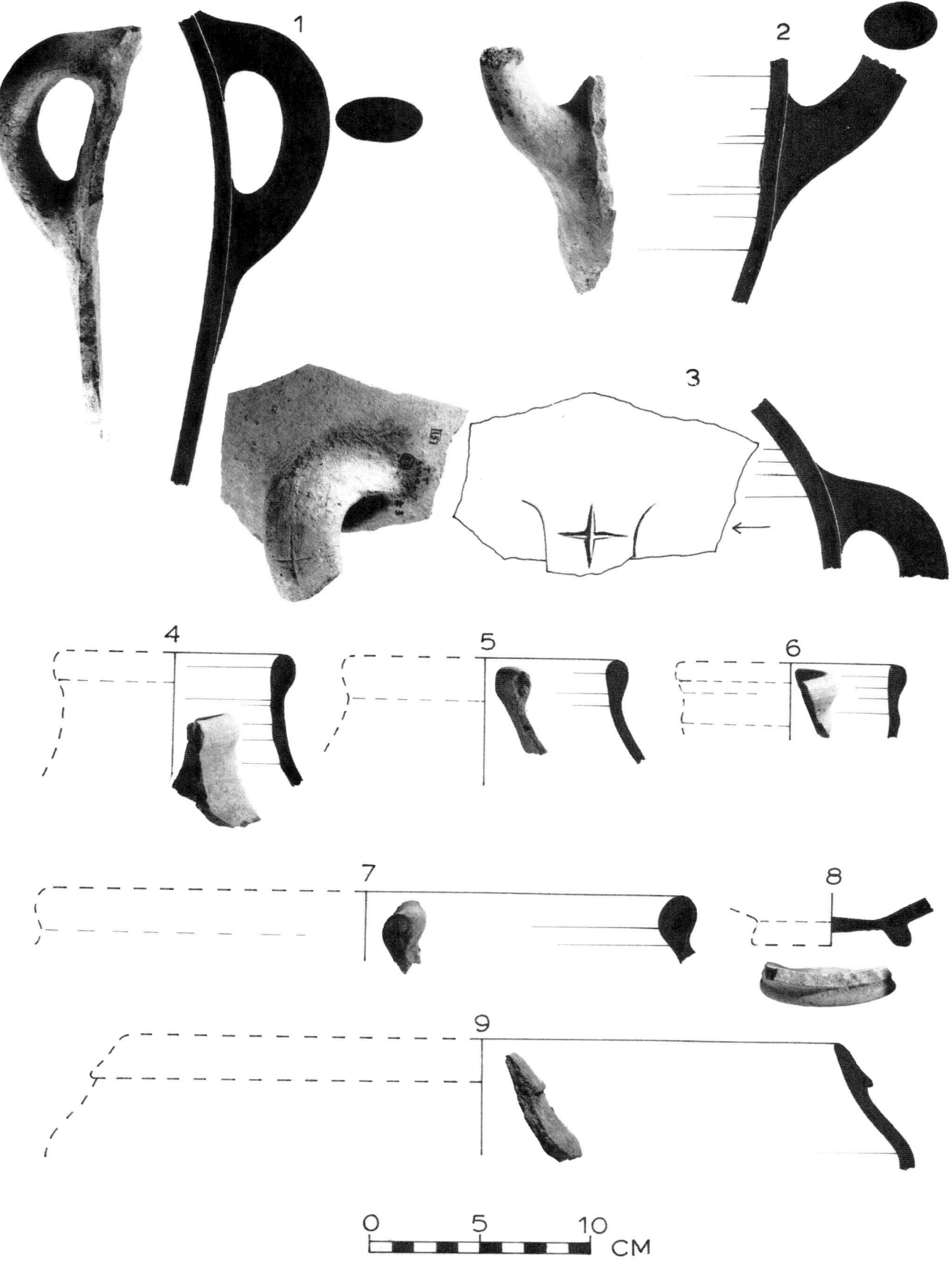

FIG. 20 POTTERY FROM SW 4-7, LOCUS 44 (PERIOD IIA)

1. Identification		2. Section							3. Surface	
a.	b.	a.	b. Core		c. Non-Plastics				a. Exterior	b. Interior
Item	Square, Locus Basket	Fabric Color	Color	Extent	Type	Size	Frequency	Density	Color, n-p, voids, forming, finishing features	Same
1. Jar TT1864	SW 4-7 44.127	rd	gr	inner +50%	lms grog	l,m,s l,s	s f	med	*Ex*: dk to lt pk, many n-p protrude slightly, some lime spalls, pits, flashing line just above handle on shoulder, grooved forming ridges on *ex* and *in* of neck, *in* join ridge, wet-smoothing lines criss-cross on body, horiz on shoulder where they appear as scraping marks. *In*: pk gr to rd br, forming ridges above base may be coil seams where wall thickens toward shoulder.	
2. Jar Rim & Neck	44.126	rd yl	lt br	75%	lms grog bas	s,f s l	s s vf	low	*Ex & In*: dk pk, some n-p protrude, few *in* pop-outs, *in* circular forming lines, *ex* wipe lines cross arc downwards on shoulder, horiz on neck. Heavy lm encrustation.	
3. Jug Rim	44.126	rd yl	lt gr	50%	lms	l,m,s f	m	med	*Ex*: dk pk, many n-p seen but embedded, some protruding, faint wipe lines. *In*: pk wh, many n-p protrude, horiz forming lines on neck, narrower finishing lines below rim.	

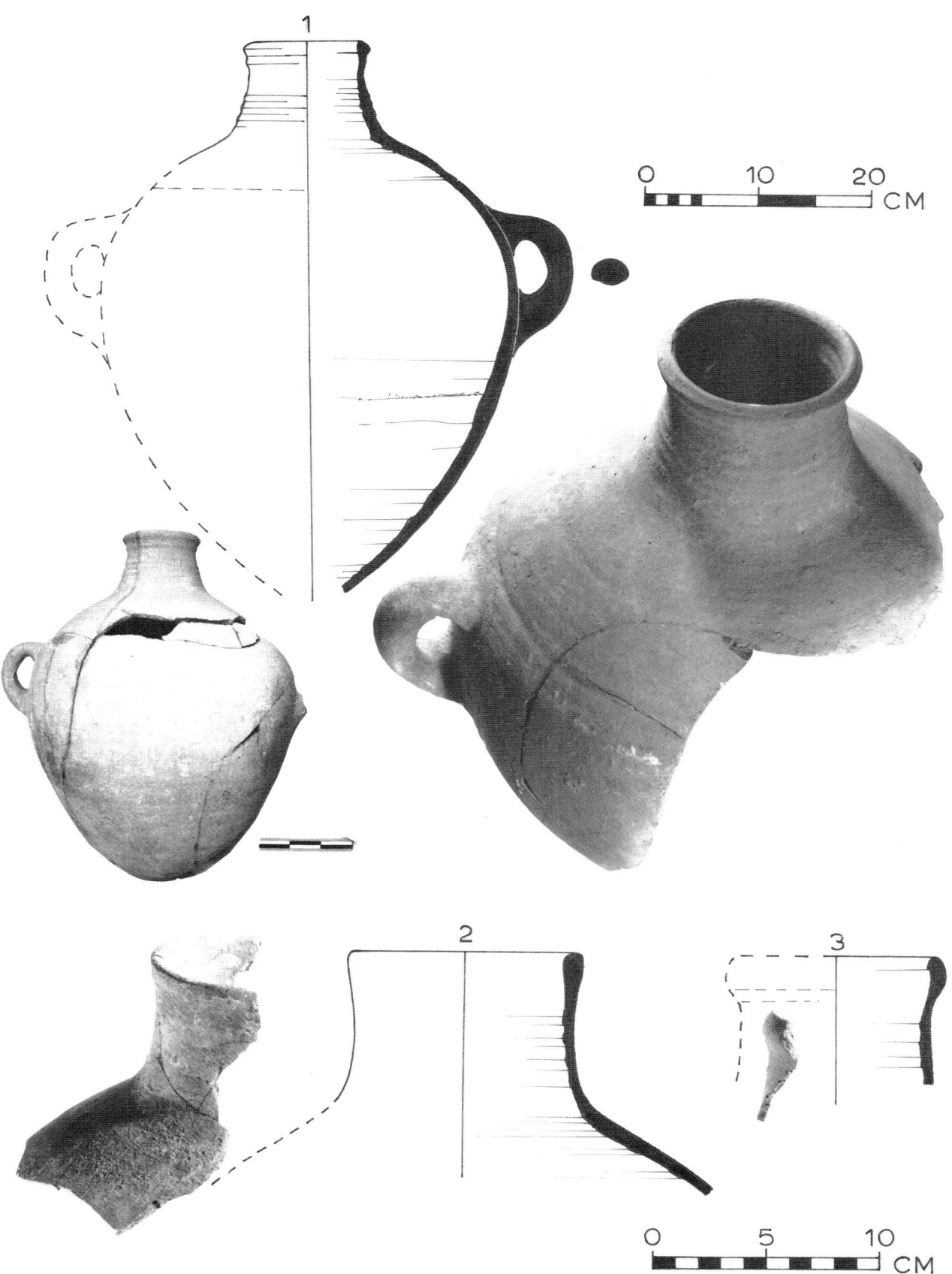

FIG. 21 POTTERY FROM SW 4-7, LOCUS 44 (PERIOD IIA)

1. Identification		2. Section						3. Surface	
a. Item	b. Square, Locus Basket	a. Fabric Color	b. Core		c. Non-Plastics			a. Exterior	b. Interior
			Color	Extent	Type	Size	Frequency	Density	Color, n-p, voids, forming, finishing features	Same
	SW 4-7									
1. Bowl Rim & Body	44.126	rd yl	dk rd gr	50%	lms	s,f	f	vlow	*Ex*: lt rd br, few n-p seen flaking, drag marks, some turning over wet-smoothing. *In*: dk pk, n-p protrude, wet-smoothing, rim trim is irreg.
2. Bowl Rim	44.128	rd yl	dk rd gr	50%	lms	s,f	f	vlow	*Ex & In*: dk pk gr, few n-p exposed, irreg fold-over ridge on rim. Formed as Nos. 1 & 3 except for deeper band below rim on *ex* and wet-smoothing.
3. Bowl Rim	44.126	rd yl	dk rd gr	50%	lms	s,f	f	vlow	As No. 1
4. Bowl Base	44.126	rd yl to br	gr	50% at ring base None body	lms bas	l,m,s m,s	s s	med	*Ex*: rd yl, n-p on surf, some lime spalls, many tiny pits, flaked and eroded, circular wipe marks. *In*: pitted, eroded, some n-p embedded, straw voids.
5. Cook Pot TT 864	44.127	rd br	gr	outer 25-50% body	cal	s,f	m	med	*Ex*: rd br to lt rd br, many small n-p visible, esp on rim and handles, turning marks on base, ridge seam at waist, straw voids on handle, wet-smoothing on rim also *In*: color as *ex* including heavy charcoal deposit, deep forming ridges on shoulder only, not below waist.

FIG. 22 POTTERY FROM SW 6-2, LOCUS 68 (PERIOD IIA)

1. Identification		2. Section						3. Surface	
a. Item	b. Square, Locus Basket	a. Fabric Color	b. Core		c. Non-Plastics			a. Exterior	b. Interior
			Color	Extent	Type	Size	Frequency	Density	Color, n-p, voids, forming, finishing features	Same
	SW 6-2									
1. Jar Rim	68.143	yl rd	dk rd gr	-50%	lms	l,m,s	s	low	*Ex & In*: dk pk, *in* more lm thus lt pk in part, small n-p protrude slightly, wet-smoothed.	
2. Jug Rim	68.139	br	lt gr	50%	lms	l,m,s	s-m	med	*Ex & In*: pk wh, many n-p, lime spalls, tiny pits, forming ridges *in* wet-smoothing both sides.	
3. Jug Rim	68.139	yl rd		none	lms bas	m,s s	s f	low	*Ex & In*: dk pk, tiny n-p protrude, lms encrustation, wet smoothing.	
4. Jug Rim	68.140	lt rd br	gr	50%	lms	s,f	m	med	*Ex & In*: rd yl to dk pk, n-p protrude often giving rough surface, crude horiz wipe lines, rim roughly finished with excess clay.	
5. Jug Rim	68.140	yl rd	gr	+50%	lms bas	s,f s	s f	low	*Ex & In*: pl rd, many n-p protruding and embedded, crude tooling under rim *in*, also *ex* rim, slight wet-smoothing.	
6. Juglet Base	68.140	rd br	gr	50%	lms	l,m,s	m	med	*Ex*: dk pk, many small n-p protrude, embedded, cloth wiped. *In* dk pk, forming ridges end in off-center pointed base plug.	
7. Crater Rim	68.143	yl rd	dk gr	75%	lms	l,m,s	m	med h	*Ex & In*: many n-p seen thru rd yl surf, some erosion on rim, few voids on *in*, wet-smoothing.	
8. Crater Rim	68.139	rd yl	lt gr	-50%	lms qrtz	l,f f	f s	low	*Ex & In*: rd yl, few n-p embedded on surf, wet-smoothed.	

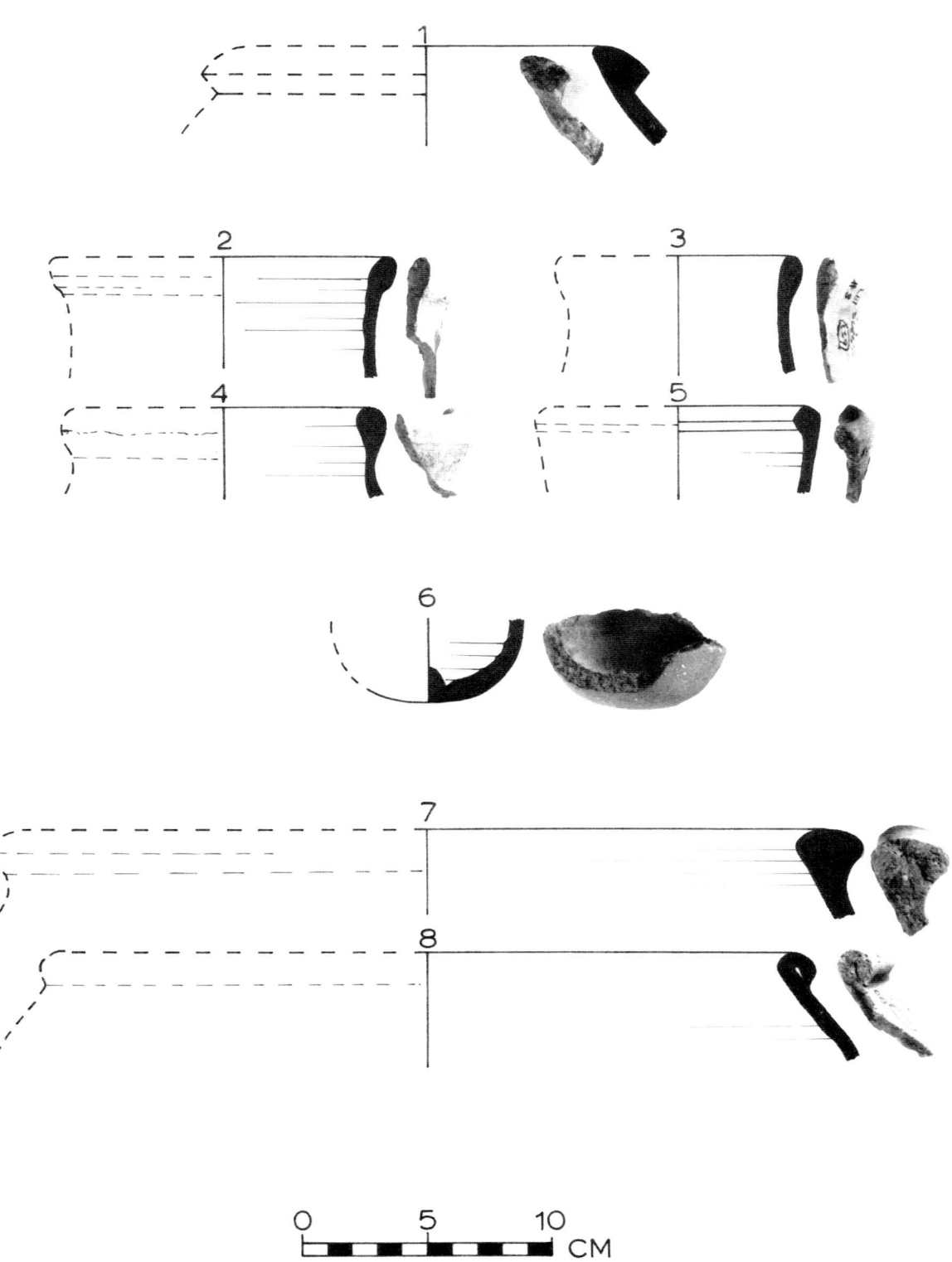

FIG. 23 POTTERY FROM SW 6-2, LOCUS 68 (PERIOD IIA)

1. Identification		2. Section						3. Surface	
a. Item	b. Square, Locus Basket	a. Fabric Color	b. Core		c. Non-Plastics			a. Exterior	b. Interior
			Color	Extent	Type	Size	Fre-quency	Density	Color, n-p, voids, forming, finishing features	Same
1. Bowl Rim	68.143	lt rd		none	qtz cal lms (sand?)	s,f s l,m,s	s f f	med	*Ex & In*: lt rd, many n-p embedded, wet-smoothing lines below horiz burnishing, almost to polish.	
2. Bowl Rim	68.139	lt rd br	dk gr	+50%	lms	l,m,s	s	med l	*Ex & In*: lt rd to rd, as No. 1 except that no wet-smoothing visible below generally cruder burnish.	
3. Bowl Rim	68.140	lt rd	lt gr	-50%	sand? As No. 1	l,m,s	m	med h	As No. 1.	
4. Bowl Rim	68.143	rd yl	lt gr	-50%	lms	l,m,s	f	vlow	*Ex & In*: dk pk, few n-p visible, shallow tooled ridges below rim, faint wet-smoothing lines.	
5. Bowl Rim	68.139	lt rd br	dk gr	-10%	sand? As No. 1	l,m,s	m	med h	As No. 2.	
6. Bowl Rim	68.139	lt rd br	dk gr	50%	sand? As No. 1	m,s	m	med	As No. 2 except that *ex* reg separated in bands of rd burnish, *in* more completely burnished in slightly tilted lines.	
7. Bowl Base	68.139	rd br	gr	+50%	lms	l,m,s	s	med	*Ex & In*: lt rd br, lightened on *in* and darkened on *ex* by 2ndary action; *Ex*: some n-p protrude, many drag marks in circular grooves to spiral center of base. *In*: some pits, irreg wipe lines.	
8. Bowl Base	68.140	rd yl to lt rd br	dk gr	outer 90%	sand? As No. 1	l,m,s	m	med h	*Ex*: lt rd br, some 2ndary charcoal deposit, some n-p protrude, covered, few drag marks, crude turning lines, some pits. *In*: lt to rd, many n-p embedded, shallow spalls and turning bands.	
9. Cook Pot Rim	68.143	rd br	dk gr	+50%	cal	l,m,s	s	med	*Ex & In*: lt rd br, few n-p protrude, tool depression at *in* rim base, irreg *ex* edge to rim fold-over. Wet-smoothing lines.	
10. Cook Pot Rim	68.139	lt rd to lt rd br	dk gr	75%	cal	m,s	m	med h	*Ex*: pk gr, eroded, spalls exposing many n-p, slight trace of smoothing. *In*: lt gr, wet-smoothing.	
11. Chalice Rim	68.143	rd yl	dk pk	30%	lms	l,s	f	low	*Ex & In*: dk pk, some n-p protrude, covered with pk slip as are wet-smoothing lines.	

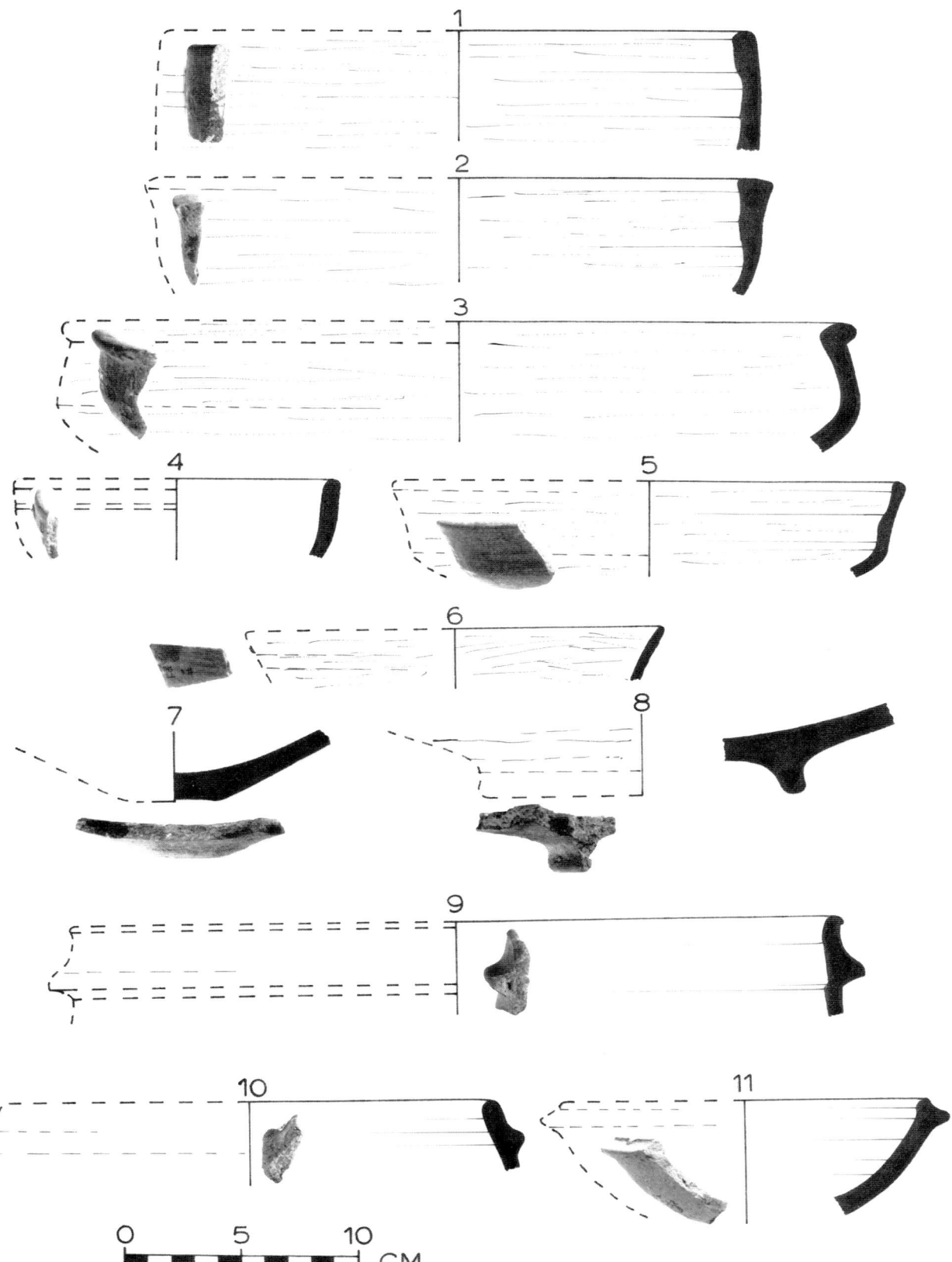

FIG. 24 POTTERY FROM SW 5-2, LOCI 60/61 (PERIOD IIA)

1. Identification		2. Section							3. Surface	
a.	b.	a.	b. Core		c. Non-Plastics				a. Exterior	b. Interior
Item	Square, Locus Basket	Fabric Color	Color	Extent	Type	Size	Frequency	Density	Color, n-p, voids, forming, finishing features	Same
1. Jar Handle	SW 5-2 60.111	lt rd	br	+75%	lms cal grog	l,m,s,f s s	m f f	med h	*Ex*: lt rd br, many lime spalls, excess clay crudely applied at lower handle attachment, wipe lines down handle, fingerprints interrupt. *In*: yl rd, many n-p protrude, few fissures, irreg surf also due to steam bubbles, horiz forming ridges and wet-smoothing lines.	
2. Jar Base	61.112	rd yl	dk gr	-75%	lms	s,f	f	vlow	*Ex*: lt br, some n-p seen, protrude, some spalling, forming ridges above base where wall thins, drag marks in circular turning lines, base smoothed laterally. *In*: dk pk, many tiny pits, color may be 2ndary.	
3. Jar Rim, Neck & Shoulder	61.112	lt rd	lt br	0-25%	lms bas	l,m,s l,m	s f	med	*Ex*: dk pk, few n-p, more on rim; some pits, flaking, straw voids. At point where shoulder thickens, shallow depression indicates flashing line; forming ridges on neck covered by shallow wet-smoothing. *In*: rd yl, some n-p visible beneath severe flaking; horiz forming lines on neck.	
4. Crater Rim	60.111	lt rd	gr	+50%	lms bas	m,s m,s	f f	low	*Ex*: dk pk, some n-p visible, drag marks, tooled trim to rim base, wet-smoothing lines. *In*: dk pk few protruding n-p, few straw voids, irreg smoothing lines.	
5. Crater Rim	60.111	lt br		none	lms bas	m,s m,s	s f	low	*Ex*: dk pk, few n-p embedded, some straw voids, rim base tooled undercut crudely closed, some wet-smoothing lines. *In*: lt pk many n-p visible, erosion at rim base, horiz straw voids, few pits.	
6. Bowl Rim	60.111	rd yl	gr	50%	lms	l,m,f	f	low	*Ex & In*: dk pk, some n-p, covered, some pop-outs, below rim *ex* forming ridges, horiz wet-smoothing lines, less clear on *in*.	
7. Bowl Rim	60.111	rd yl	lt gr	-50%	lms bas	l,m,s f	s s	low	*Ex*: lt rd, some embedded n-p visible, few drag marks R to L, wet-smoothing faint. *In*: rd yl, some n-p seen under flaking, wet-smoothing esp at and below rim.	
8. Bowl Rim	60.111	lt br	v lt gr	-25%	bas	m,s	s	low	*Ex & In*: dk pk, few n-p on *ex*, wet-smoothing.	
9. Cook Pot Rim	60.111	rd br	dk gr	+50%	cal	s,f	m	med	*Ex*: rd br, heavy deposit charcoal, tooled depression on upper rim and undercut below rim. *In*: lt rd br, narrow tooled line below rim, wet-smoothing.	
10. Chalice Rim	61.112	lt rd	lt br	50%	bas lms	s,f l,m,s	f f	low	*Ex & In*: lt rd, some n-p embedded, few drag marks, straw voids, horiz wet-smoothing lines.	

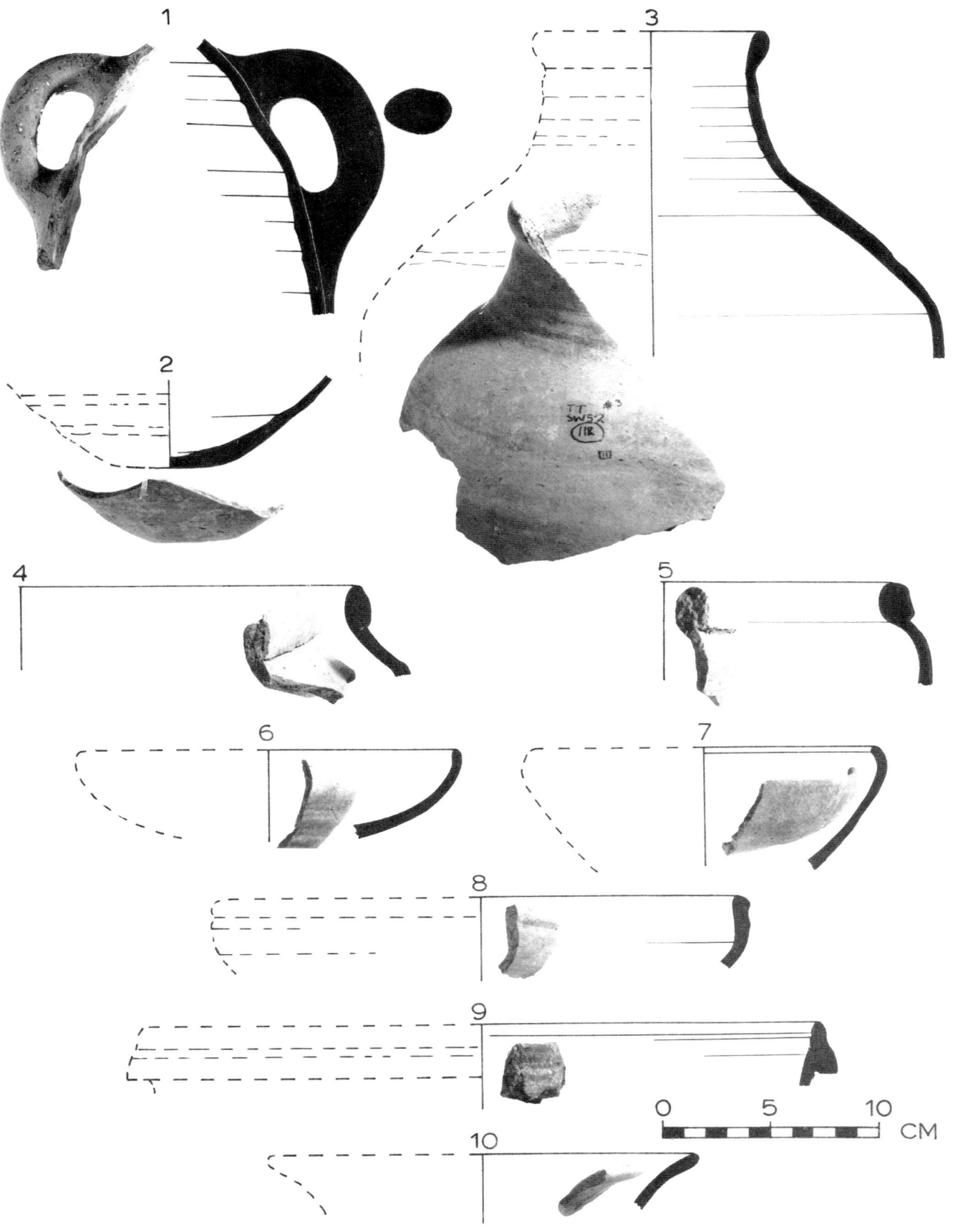

FIG. 25 POTTERY FROM SW 2-8, LOCUS 18 (PERIOD IIA)

1. Identification		2. Section						3. Surface	
a.	b.	a.	b. Core		c. Non-Plastics			a. Exterior	b. Interior
Item	Square, Locus Basket	Fabric Color	Color	Extent	Type	Size	Frequency	Density	Color, n-p, voids, forming, finishing features	Same
	SW 2-8									
1. Jar Handle & Body	18.63	lt pk to lt rd br	vlt gr	30%	lms bas	s,f s	f f	low	*Handle*: lt pk, few n-p embedded, straw voids along handle, wipe lines around join. *Body In*: dk pk, some n-p seen, horiz wet-smoothing.	
2. Jar Handle & Body	18.63	dk pk	gr dif gr	50% (handle) inner 60% (body)	lms grog	s,f f	f f	vlow	*Handle*: dk pk, few straw voids, vertical wet-smoothing, horiz at join. *Body In*: lt rd br, some n-p seen, flaking faint horiz smoothing.	
3. Jug Rim	18.63	rd yl	lt gr	-50%	lms bas grog	l,m,s s,f s	s f f	low	*Ex & In*: rd yl, some n-p protrude, few pits, shallow forming ridge, wet-smoothing lines.	
4. Jug Rim	18.63		rd gr	100%	lms grog	s,f f	s f	low	*Ex*: dk pk, protruding n-p roughen surface, crude ridging, shallow wipe lines. *In*: rd yl, few n-p protrude, crudely grooved forming ridges.	
5. Jug Handle & Fillet	18.63	yl rd	gr	50%	calc	s,f	m	med	Rd br, few n-p embedded, surf crudely finished, forming lines faint and irreg, clean break from body reveals fillet below handle join.	
6. Crater Rim	18.63	dk pk	gr	+50%	lms grog bas?	l,m,s m,s l,m,s	s s s	med h	*Ex & In*: dk pk, some n-p seen in pop-outs, many tiny pits on *in*, finishing lines clearest on rim *ex*.	
7. Bowl Rim	18.63	yl rd	lt br	50%	lms	l,s	f	vlow	*Ex & In*: rd yl, few n-p, covered, few straw voids *ex*, shallow wet-smoothing lines.	
8. Bowl Rim	18.63	yl rd	dk gr	50%	lms	l,m,s	m	med	*Ex*: dk pk, some n-p embedded, drag marks to r, circular wet-smoothing on base, vertical shaving on shoulder, horiz burnish below rim. *In*: lt rd, many n-p embedded, eroded burnish.	
9. Bowl Rim	18.63	lt br		none	lms	f	f	vlow	*Ex & In*: lt rd br, *in* has heavy charcoal deposit, n-p slightly protrude on *ex*, wet-smoothing, shallow tooled lines below rim.	
10. Bowl Rim	18.63	rd br		none	lms cal	l,m,s s	s vf	low	*Ex & In*: lt rd br, few n-p protrude, wet-smoothing burnish more on *ex* than *in*, horiz & spaced.	
11. Bowl Rim	18.63	rd yl		none	lms	l,m,s	s	low	*Ex & In*: dk pk, few n-p protrude slightly on *ex*, tiny pits *in*, crude finish below both sides of rim.	
12. Bowl Rim	18.63	rd yl	vlt gr	0-25%	lms cal	s,f m	f vf	vlow	*Ex & In*: dk pk, few n-p embedded on *in*, protrude on *ex*, wet-smoothed.	
13. Bowl Base	18.63	rd br	rd gr	inner +60%	lms bas	m,s s	f vf	low	*Ex & In*: lt rd br, few n-p covered and protrude from *ex*, many tiny pits *in*, shallow tooled lines around inside and outside edge of base, faint trace of wet-smoothing *ex*.	

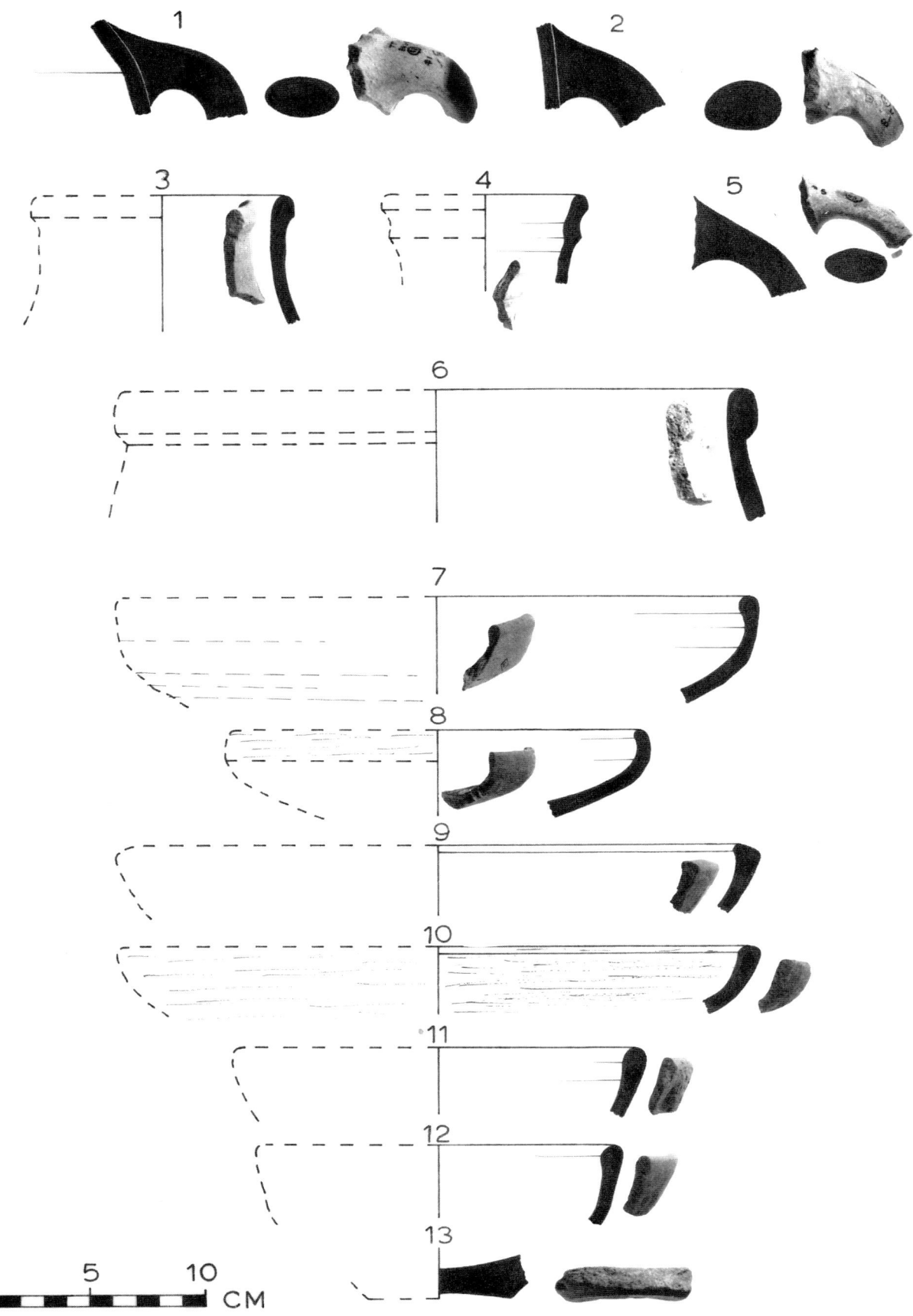

FIG. 26 POTTERY FROM SW 4-7, LOCI 57/60 (PERIOD IIA)

1. Identification		2. Section						3. Surface	
a. Item	b. Square, Locus Basket	a. Fabric Color	b. Core		c. Non-Plastics			a. Exterior	b. Interior
			Color	Extent	Type	Size	Frequency	Density	Color, n-p, voids, forming, finishing features	Same
1. Jar TT 834	Sw 4-7 60.102	rd yl	dk gr	inner 60%	lms	l,m,s	s	low	*Ex*: lt rd br, rd yl to pk gr. Some n-p embedded, few protrude, flashing line upper shoulder prominent forming ridges *in* and *ex* neck. Horiz turning ridges on body, one handle more crudely joined than other, excess clay deposit on top of one. Spout separated during firing. *In*: seems dk pk, no clear forming or finishing features remain. On *ex* upper shoulder is pk gr, lower being rd yl.	
2. Jug TT 631	57.95	lt rd	lt br	-50%	lms bas	l,m,s,f m,s	s f	med	*Ex*: lt rd, some n-p seen thru lime spalls below neck and on handle but on neck protrude and are covered, also below shoulder. Crude turning below shoulder; ring of base added after bottom formed, join visible in part. Straw voids on handle, 3 perforations on top of handle are not prominent. *In*: forming ridges up from omphalos in center of base; prominent forming ridges inside neck. Both *in* and *ex* show only faint trace of wet-smoothing.	

TT 834

TT 631

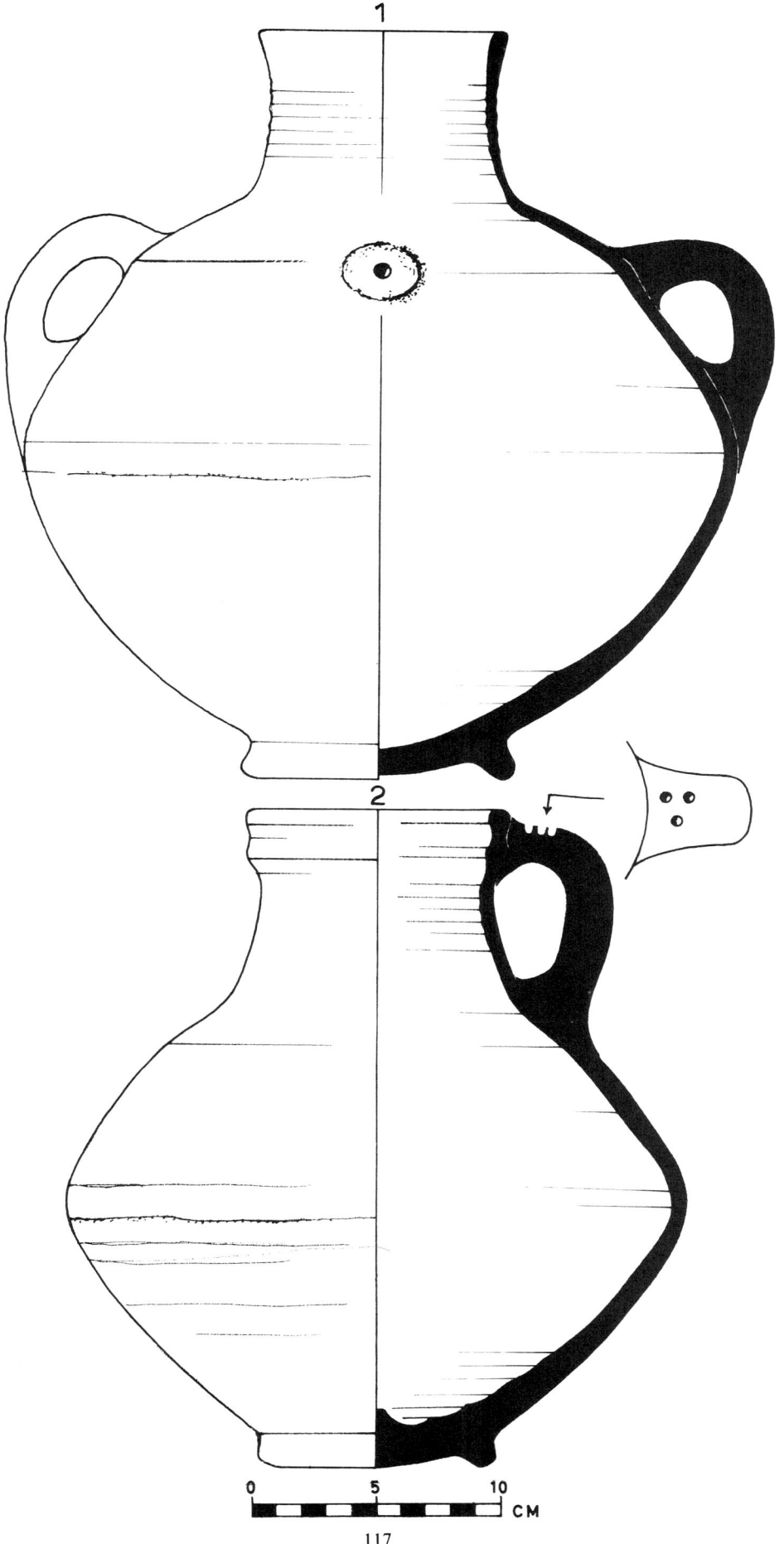

117

FIG. 27 POTTERY FROM SW 4-7, LOCI 57/60 (PERIOD IIA)

1. Identification		2. Section						3. Surface	
a.	b.	a.	b. Core		c. Non-Plastics			a. Exterior	b. Interior
Item	Square, Locus Basket	Fabric Color	Color	Extent	Type	Size	Frequency	Density	Color, n-p, voids, forming, finishing features	Same
1. Pyxis TT 621	SW 4-7 60.102	rd yl	lt br	inner 50%	lms	l,m,s	s	med l	*Ex*: lt rd br, many straw voids, some small pits, wet-smoothing is criss-cross. Bottom lm encrusted, also upper *in*. 5 rd br paint bands below lug handles. On *in* forming ridges above base to shoulder. Wide paint band rim down neck.	
2. Chalice TT 630	57.93	yl rd		none	lms	l,m,s	s-m	med	*Ex*: yl rd to rd yl, but generally badly affected by 2ndary charcoal deposit, also on *in*. Many n-p protrude, covered. Some pits. Forming ridges esp prominent on *in* of base, smoothing lines *ex* on base and dish. Drag marks most *in* dish. Surf crude & rough.	

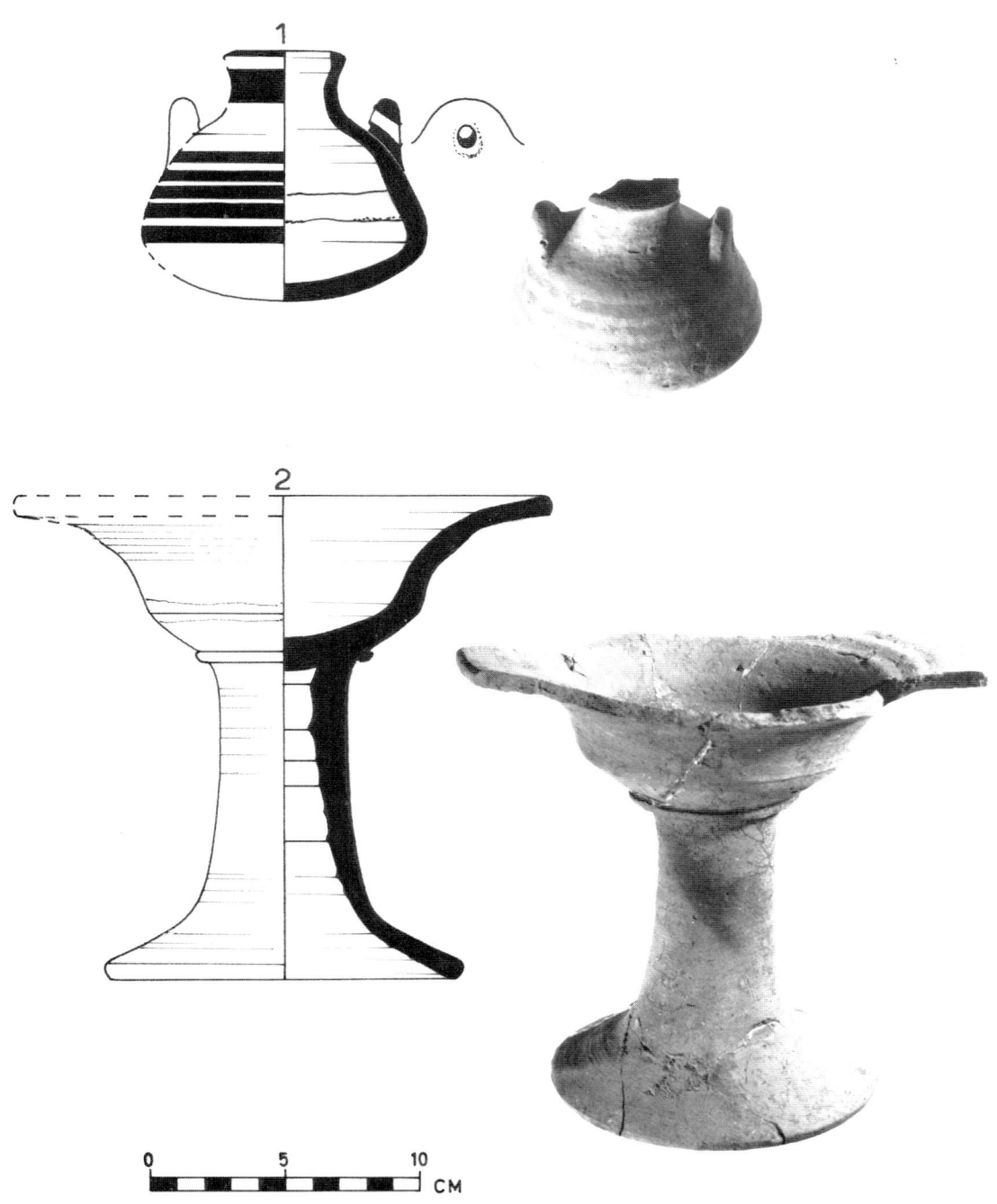

FIG. 28 POTTERY FROM SW 4-7, LOCUS 42 (PERIOD IIA)

1. Identification		2. Section						3. Surface	
		a.	b. Core		c. Non-Plastics			a. Exterior	b. Interior
a. Item	b. Square, Locus Basket	Fabric Color	Color	Extent	Type	Size	Frequency	Density	Color, n-p, voids, forming, finishing features	Same
1. Jar Handle	SW 4-7 42.68	yl rd to lt br	gr	50% (handle) 25% (body)	lms bas	s,f s	f f	low	*Handle*: rd yl, straw voids, some pits, wet-smoothing lines lateral at join, vert down handle, lm encrustation under. *Body in*: rd br, heavy lm encrustation.	
2. Crater Rim	42.68	lt br		none	lms bas	vl,m,s s	f f	low	*Ex & In*: lt rd br, few n-p protrude, covered, few pits, shallow forming or finishing depressions on rim & *in*, turning bands on *ex* body. Folded-over rim crudely trimmed at base.	
3. Crater Rim	42.68	rd yl		none	lms bas	l,m,s s	s f	low	*Ex & In*: dk pk, some n-p on surf, few pop-outs, wet-smoothing.	
4. Crater Rim	42.69	yl rd	lt gr	30%	lms grog	s s	f f	vlow	*Ex & In*: lt rd br, few n-p protrude, few straw voids, horiz wet-smoothing lines, fold-over rim tool trimmed, then sealed.	
5. Bowl Rim	42.68	rd yl		none	bas grog	s,f f	f vf	vlow	*Ex & In*: dk pk, deposit of charcoal, few pits, *in*, wet-smoothing, also rim, *ex* rubbed.	

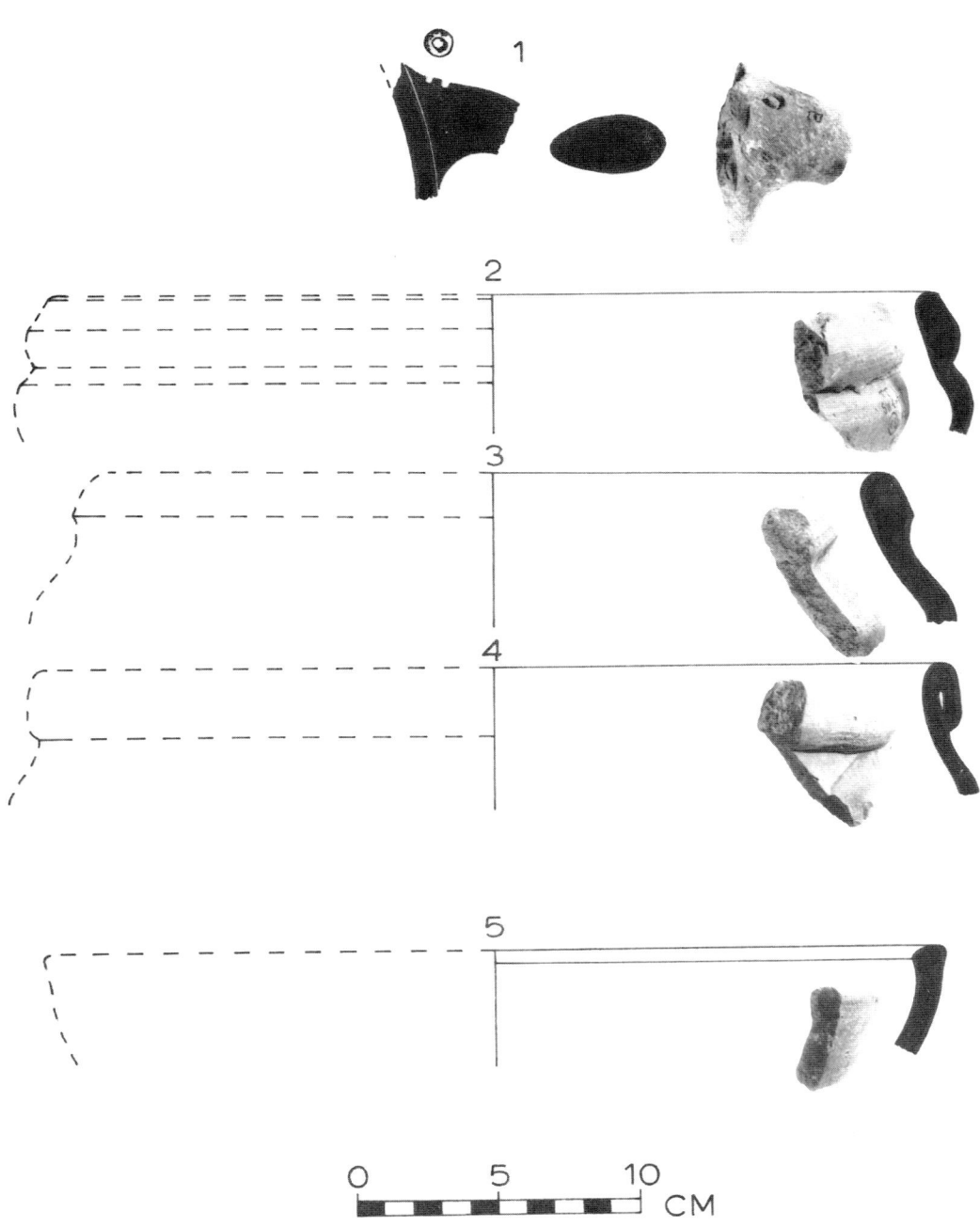

FIG. 29 POTTERY FROM SW 4-7, LOCUS 42 (PERIOD IIA)

1. Identification			2. Section						3. Surface	
a.	b.	a.	b. Core		c. Non-Plastics				a. Exterior	b. Interior
Item	Square, Locus Basket	Fabric Color	Color	Extent	Type	Size	Frequency	Density	Color, n-p, voids, forming, finishing features	Same
1. Cook Pot Rim	SW 4-7 42.68	br	gr	none inner 50% (bottom)	cal	s,f	m	low	*Ex & In*: rd br to dk gr, some n-p visible, few tiny voids, wet-smoothing is horiz.	
2. Cook Pot Rim	42.69	rd br		none	cal	l,m,s	m	med	*Ex & In*: rd br, many n-p protrude, rim base tool trimmed, wet-smoothing lines on *in*, some cracks, *ex* covered with what may be rd br slip.	
3. Cook Pot Rim	42.68	yl rd	dk gr	-50%	cal	s,f	m	med l	*Ex & In*: lt rd, *ex* grayed by fire, many tiny n-p protrude, covered, some lime spalls, drag marks, rim base undercut, wet-smoothing clearest *in*.	
4. Cook Pot Rim	42.68	yl rd	gr	-50%	cal lms	m,s l	m vf	low	*Ex*: rd br, below shoulder, dk gr, many tiny n-p protrude, esp *in*, few tiny pits, rim flange added as coil not well trimmed, undercut. *In*: rd yl, faint wet-smoothing.	
5. Cook Pot Rim	42.69	rd br	dk gr	+75%	cal	s,f	m	med l	*Ex*: dk rd, *In*: rd br, both burned gray below. Many tiny n-p protrude, few tiny pits; *ex* at shoulder coil seam left with irreg top edge. Wet-smoothing lines are faint.	

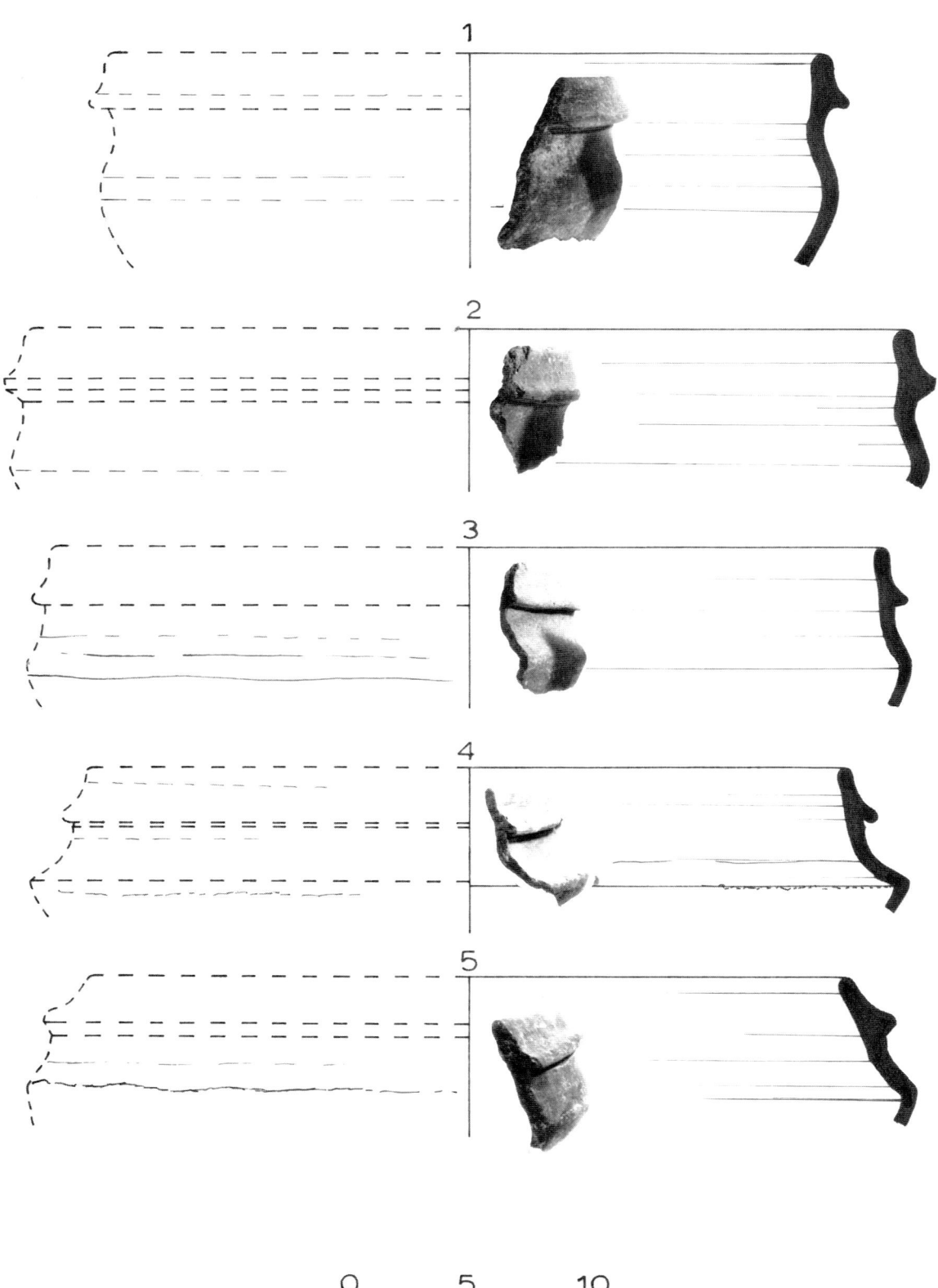

FIG. 30 POTTERY FROM THE CULTIC STRUCTURE (PERIOD IIB)

1. Identification		2. Section						3. Surface	
a.	b.	a.	b. Core		c. Non-Plastics			a. Exterior	b. Interior
Item	Square, Locus Basket	Fabric Color	Color	Extent	Type	Size	Frequency	Density	Color, n-p, voids, forming, finishing features	Same
1. Jar TT 478	SW 2-7 €1.339 €3.236	yl rd	gr	50%	lms	s,f	s	med	*Ex*: lt rd br, lm deposit lightens color, few n-p seen, some on handles, shallow depressions along horiz coil seams, finishing lines at base vertl, body criss-cross, at shoulder and neck, horiz. *In*: grayed by 2ndary burn, forming ridges more prominent, base criss-crossed, finger depressions.	
2. Jar TT 476	59.150	rd br	dk gr	50-90%	lms	l,m,s	s	med	*Ex*: lt rd br, lightened by lms deposit, slight depressions of coil seams, faint smoothing lines slant upwards L to R, horiz on shoulder and neck. As also in No. 3 the base of the rim is sharply tooled. *In*: build up of circular ridges, crudely wiped criss-cross, shoulder and neck as in No. 3.	
3. Jar TT 477	61.174	yl rd		none	lms bas	l,m,s m	m s	med h	*Ex*: dk pk, few small n-p protrude, few large n-p exposed in spalls, finish lines are faint and irreg, forming ridges only on upper shoulder but much more visible on *in* where the horiz flashing lines of coil buildup are not prominent but visible mid-body to base, more deeply grooved in upper shoulder & neck.	
4. Jar TT 36	13.20	lt rd br		none	lms	s,f	m	med	*Ex*: lt rd br, lms deposit lightens color, few n-p embedded, more near & on rim, some tiny pits, smoothing lines are slant upwards fr L to R. *In*: as others except for large blister swelling near base.	

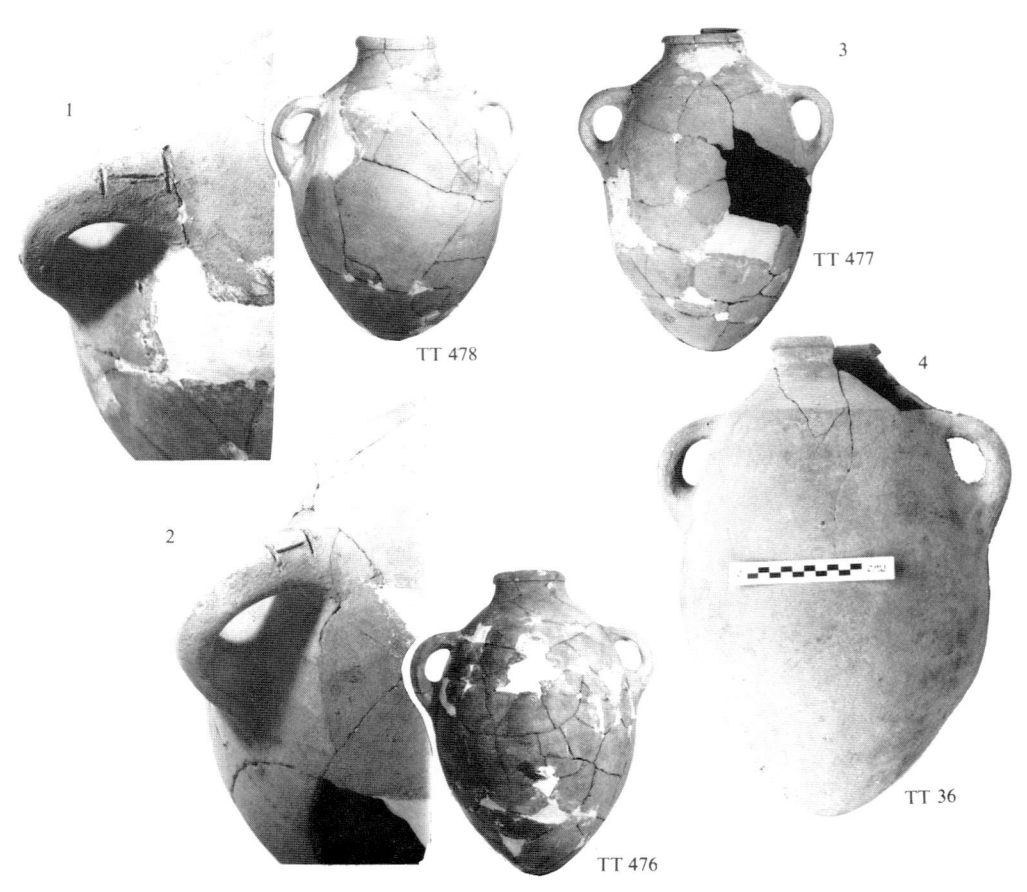

124

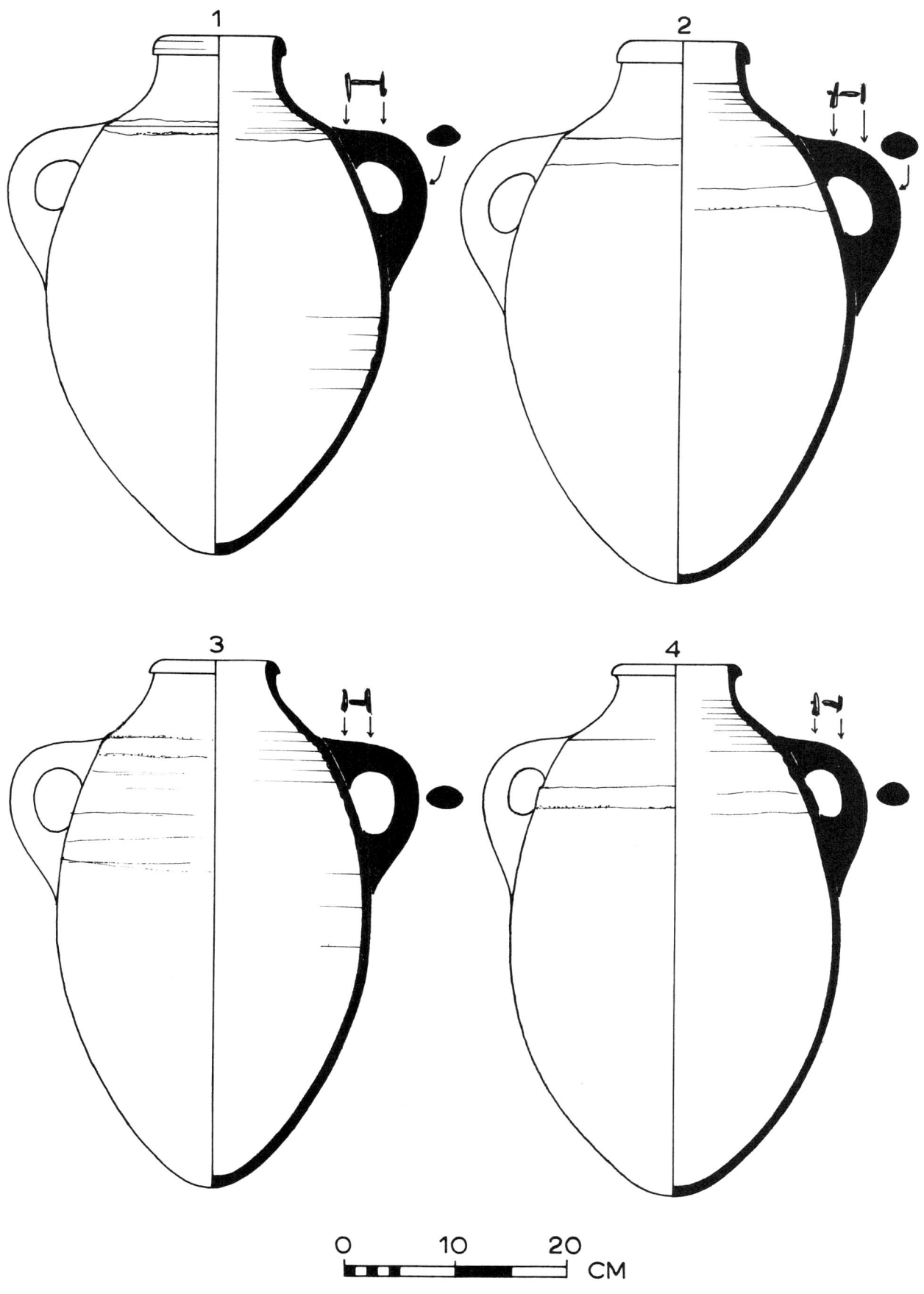

FIG. 31 POTTERY FROM THE CULTIC STRUCTURE (PERIOD IIB)

1. Identification		2. Section							3. Surface	
a. Item	b. Square, Locus Basket	a. Fabric Color	b. Core		c. Non-Plastics				a. Exterior	b. Interior
			Color	Extent	Type	Size	Frequency	Density	Color, n-p, voids, forming, finishing features	Same
1. Jar TT 474	SW 2-7 61.193	dk rd gr	lt gr	inner +50%	lms sand?	s,f s	s s	med	*Ex & In*: lt rd br, some n-p protrude, very few tiny voids, irreg wet-smoothing, handle join not as well-smoothed, rim base tooled, slightly undercut. *In*: twist at center of base and circular forming ridges up inner walls point to fast wheel, also forming ridges inside shoulder and neck.	
2. Jar TT 481	63.230	yl rd	vlt gr	only top or bottom ±25%	lms sand?	s,f s	s s	med	*Ex*: yl rd to lt rd, few n-p seen, finger marks, some flaking, irreg wet-smoothing. *In*: wheel forming lines from base up, coil added where neck formed from shoulder.	
3. Jar TT 469	61.205	rd br	gr	50% but also 25% or inner 60%	lms sand?	s,f s	s s	med	*Ex*: rd yl, many n-p embedded, some pop-outs, slight depressions mid-body to shoulder are forming ridges, visible also on *in*. *In*: dk gr, many more n-p protrude, forming ridges, bottom treated as items on Fig. 30.	
4. Jar Rim & Handle	48.127	rd br	gr	10-50% body +50% handle	lms	l,m,s	m	med h	*Ex*: rd br, discolored by dirt, charcoal. Some n-p seen, esp on rim & handle, in neck. Tiny voids in same areas, wet-smoothing lines not clear except around neck, rim. Potter's mark on handle interrupted by applied irreg seal of clay. *In*: rd br, n-p as *ex*, forming ridges clear.	
5. Jar Rim & Handle	57.228	br	vlt gr	rim 50% shoulder ±50%	lms	l,m,s	m	med h	*Ex*: lt rd br, some n-p on surf embedded, more on handle, straw voids and vert wet-smoothing also clearest on handle, horiz smoothing on shoulder, under rim tool trimmed. *In*: many n-p protrude, pop-outs, horiz forming lines, flashing line at neck.	
6. Jar Rim & Handle	61.165	st br		none	lms	l,m,s	m	med h	*Ex*: lt rd br, some n-p protrude, few deposits of excess clay, forming ridges on neck, finishing lines faint but horiz, handle punched at base and near top. Bottom of rim undercut, irreg overhang. *In*: lt rd br, forming ridges prominent on neck only, thumb-wide depression at neck base looks like coil seam. N-p seen thru many lime spalls. Pitting.	

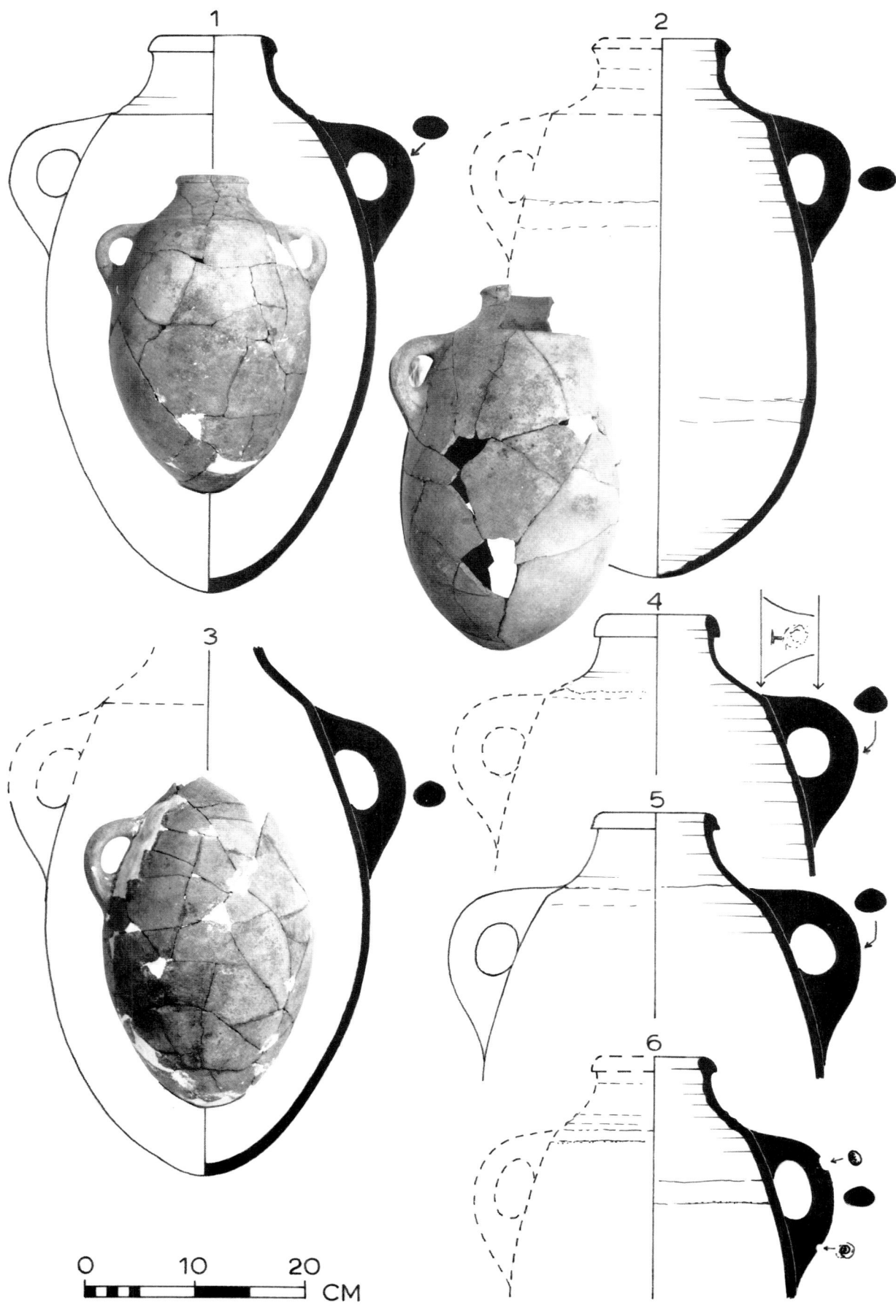

FIG. 32 POTTERY FROM THE CULTIC STRUCTURE (PERIOD IIB)

1. Identification		2. Section							3. Surface	
a.	b.	a.	b. Core		c. Non-Plastics				a. Exterior	b. Interior
Item	Square, Locus Basket	Fabric Color	Color	Extent	Type	Size	Frequency	Density	Color, n-p, voids, forming, finishing features	Same
1. Jar Rim & Handle	SW 2-7 48.119	rd br	dk gr vlt gr	75% handle +25% body	lms	m,s	s	med l	*Ex & In*: pk gr, lm encrusted, many n-p protrude, some pits, drag marks, *ex* wet-smoothing upper L to lower R, forming ridge on *ex* where shoulder curves in to neck above handle. *In*: forming ridges clearest at neck. Much as Figs. 30 & 31.	
2. Jar Handle	26.98	dk gr!	dk gr	-100%	lms	l,m,s	m	med	*Handle*: rd br, many n-p seen, straw voids, wet-smoothing vert, horiz at join. *In*: lt br, many lime spalls, horiz forming lines.	
3. Jar Handle	26.98	dk gr!	dk gr	-100%	lms grog	m,s m,s	s s	med h	*Handle*: lt gr & gr, many pop-outs, eroded, lms n-p seen under, vert wet-smoothing is faint. *Body*: some n-p protrude, more pop-outs *in*, horiz fingerprint lines.	
4. Jar Handle	27.45	lt br	gr-br	inner 50% body	lms	l,m,s	s	med	*Handle*: lt gr, some n-p protrude, some seen, straw voids, wet-smoothing vert. *Body In*: gr is probably 2ndary, some protruding n-p, forming lines seen thru dirt cover.	

FIG. 33 POTTERY FROM THE CULTIC STRUCTURE (PERIOD IIB)

1. Identification		2. Section							3. Surface	
a.	b.	a.	b. Core		c. Non-Plastics				a. Exterior	b. Interior
Item	Square, Locus Basket	Fabric Color	Color	Extent	Type	Size	Frequency	Density	Color, n-p, voids, forming, finishing features	Same
1. Jar TT 483	SW 2-7 59.143 61.197	rd yl		none	lms	l,m,s	m	high	*Ex*: lt rd br, lightened in general by lm deposit, some shallow n-p protrude, few lime spalls, embedded, few traces of finishing, irreg lines of smoothing. *In*: dk pk, base and shoulder plus neck show reg forming ridges, between these points body wall thicker, forming ridges less reg suggesting hand-building.	
2. Jar Rim & Handles	48.125-130	rd br to yl rd	vlt gr to gr br	+50%	lms grog	l,m,s l,m,s	s s	med	*Ex*: pl br to pk gr, many small n-p protrude, many large spalls, tiny pits, some shallow horiz ridges in body of irreg thickness suggest coil seams, flaking of what appears to be bloom, esp on rim. *In*: pk gr, much spalling, many more tiny pits, prominent & reg forming ridges on upper shoulder and neck. On body shallow & irreg coil flashing lines at 2.5cm intervals.	

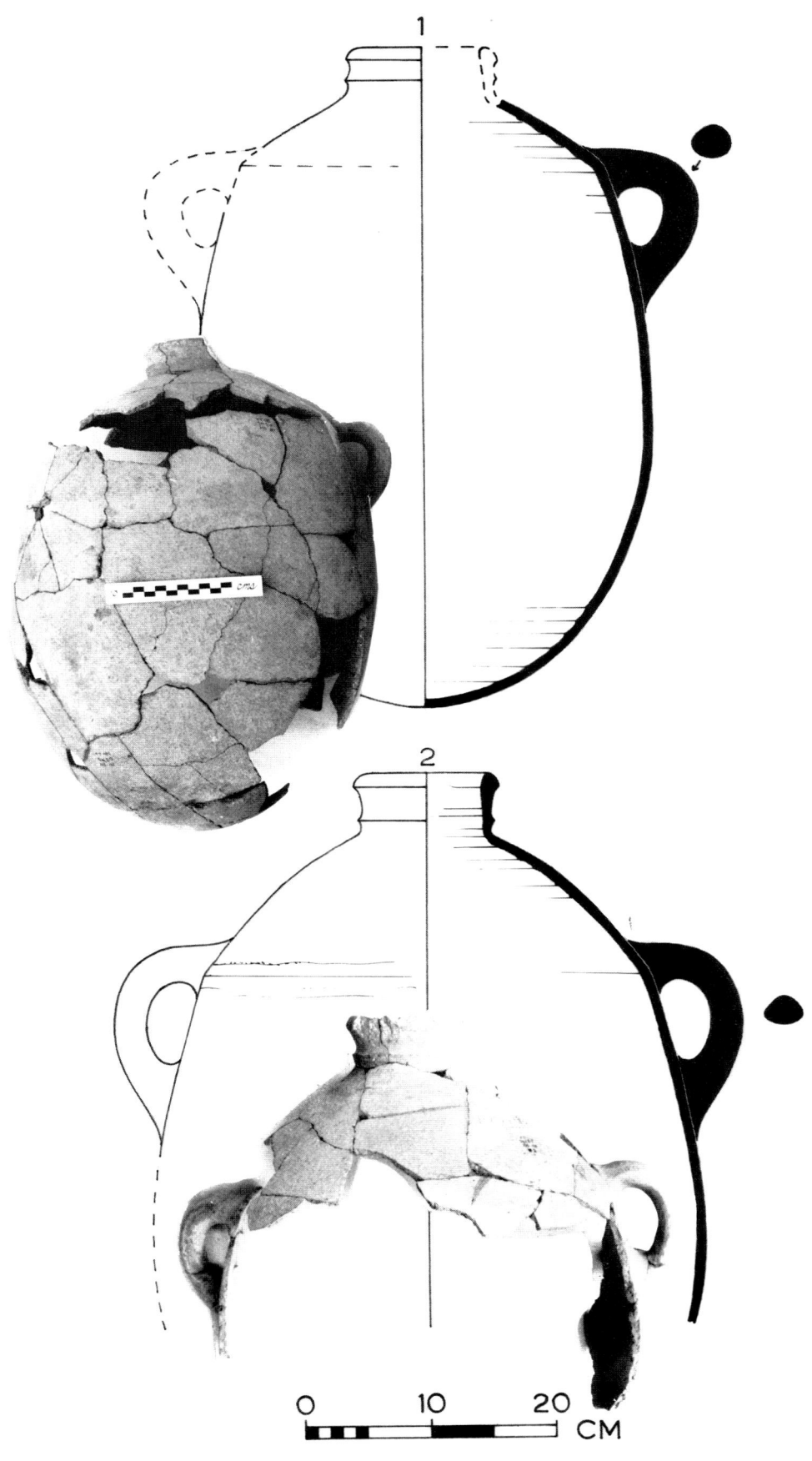

FIG. 34 POTTERY FROM THE CULTIC STRUCTURE (PERIOD IIB)

1. Identification		2. Section							3. Surface	
a.	b.	a.	b. Core		c. Non-Plastics				a. Exterior	b. Interior
Item	Square, Locus Basket	Fabric Color	Color	Extent	Type	Size	Frequency	Density	Color, n-p, voids, forming, finishing features	Same
1. Jar TT 482	SW 2-7 61.172. 173	str br	lt gr to gr	50% lower half; none upper half	lms grog bas	m,s l,m s	m s f	med l	*Ex*: dk pk to lt br; many n-p protrude, covered, few shallow lime spalls, mid-body shallow depressions indicate coil seams; area of upper body to R of handle flattened during drying; circular wet-smoothing on shoulder, neck, on body faint and irreg. *In*: rd yl; throwing ridges prominent to mid-body. Shallow forming ridges on upper shoulder and neck.	
2. Jar Rim	28.47, 51	wk rd to rd	dk gr	-100%	lms grog	f l,s	f f	low	*Ex*: rd yl, lime encrusted, some n-p protrude, covered; rim base and ridge tooled; wet-smoothing lines clear also *In*: rd yl, some n-p protrude, a little spalling, wet-smooth as *ex*.	
3. Jar Rim	28.47 32.60	rd br	wk rd	0-50%	lms bas	s,f m	s f	med l	*Ex & In*: gr; many n-p protrude, many tiny pits, pk white slip 90% flaked, trace of wet-smoothing over slip. Rim base tool-trimmed but inner edge irreg.	
4. Jar TT 475	61.191	lt rd br	lt gr	±50%	lms bas	s,f l,s	s vf	low	*Ex*: lt rd br, some n-p protrude, mostly covered, some tiny pits, smoothing lines on body faint, few horiz flashing lines. *In*: lt rd br, heavily lime encrusted, throwing ridges only on lower base & neck.	
5. Jar TT 459	61.192	rd yl	gr	inner 50%, lower half	lms bas grog	m s, s,	s s f	med	*Ex*: lt rd br, 2ndary graying, slight roughening of surf by covered n-p protruding, shallow turning on base, faint trace of wet-smoothing on shoulder & neck. *In*: lt rd br, some n-p protrude, shallow forming ridges at lower base spiral to center point. Reg horiz fingerprint lines and even thickness suggest body is wheel-formed. At shoulder depression ridges more prominent.	

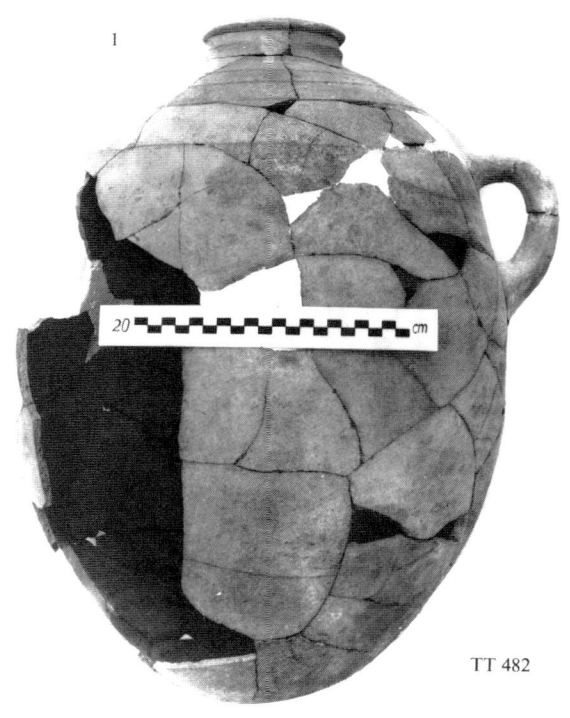

1

TT 482

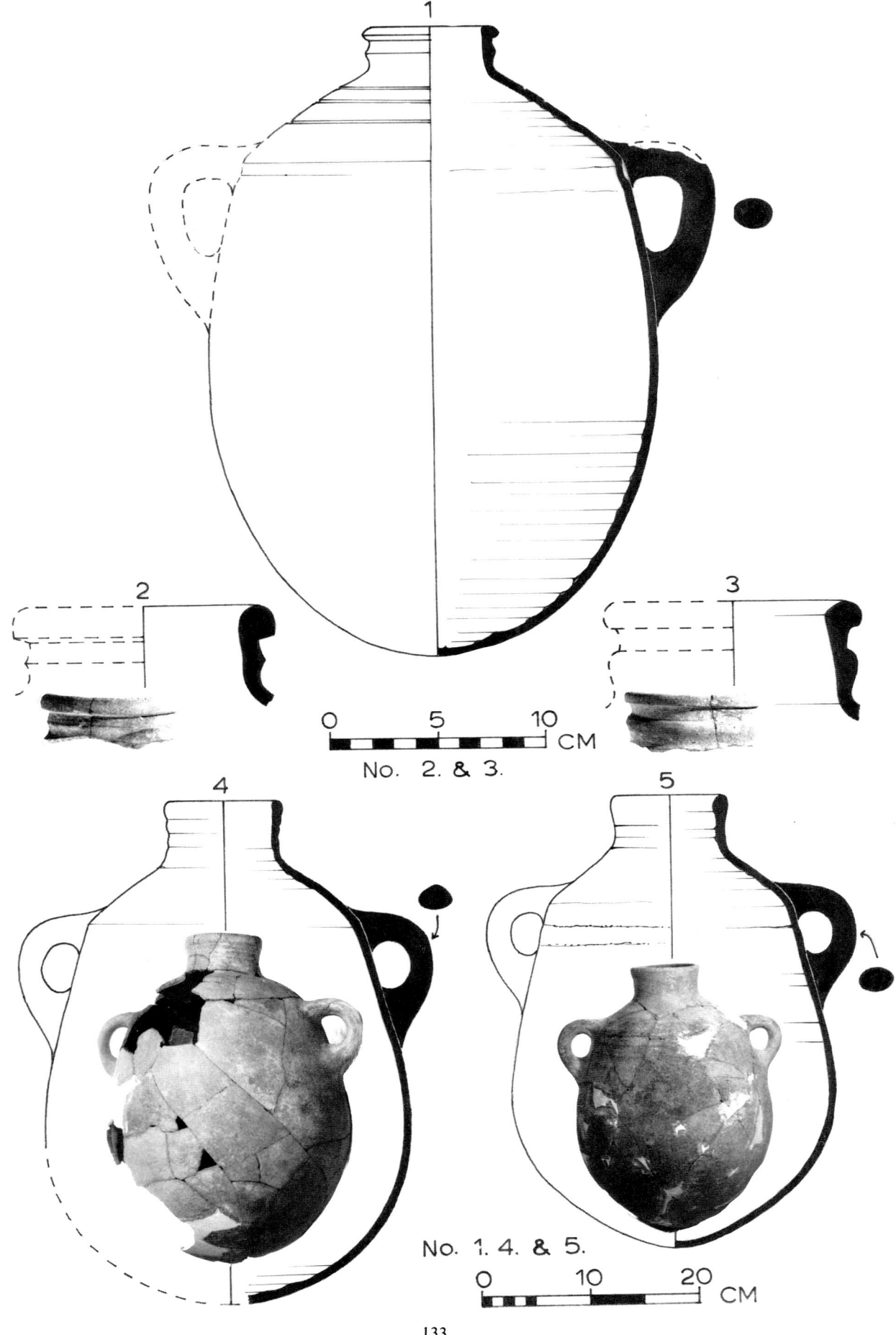

FIG. 35 POTTERY FROM THE CULTIC STRUCTURE (PERIOD IIB)

1. Identification		2. Section						3. Surface	
a.	b.	a.	b. Core		c. Non-Plastics			a. Exterior	b. Interior
Item	Square, Locus Basket	Fabric Color	Color	Extent	Type	Size	Frequency	Density	Color, n-p, voids, forming, finishing features	Same
1. Jar TT 1866	SW 2-7 59.146 152	st br	gr	inner lms +75%	l,m,s grog	l,m,s m,s	m s	med h	*Ex*: dk pk to lt br to gr; n-p seen in chipped area on body and in spalling at base; some visible on rim; wet-smoothing lines horiz over vert on lower portion, entirely horiz on shoulder. *In* n-p seen through many pits, spalling. Two widely separated slab seams on body, shallow ridges above shoulder & at neck.	
2. Jar TT 460	61.185	lt rd	lt gr	-50%	lms	l,m,s	m	med	*Ex*: lt rd to lt rd br; some n-p embedded, few lime spalls on body, most on rim, reg horiz forming lines rim to base, some vert finger finishing on shoulder. *In* lt rd to lt rd br; reg horiz forming ridges base to rim.	

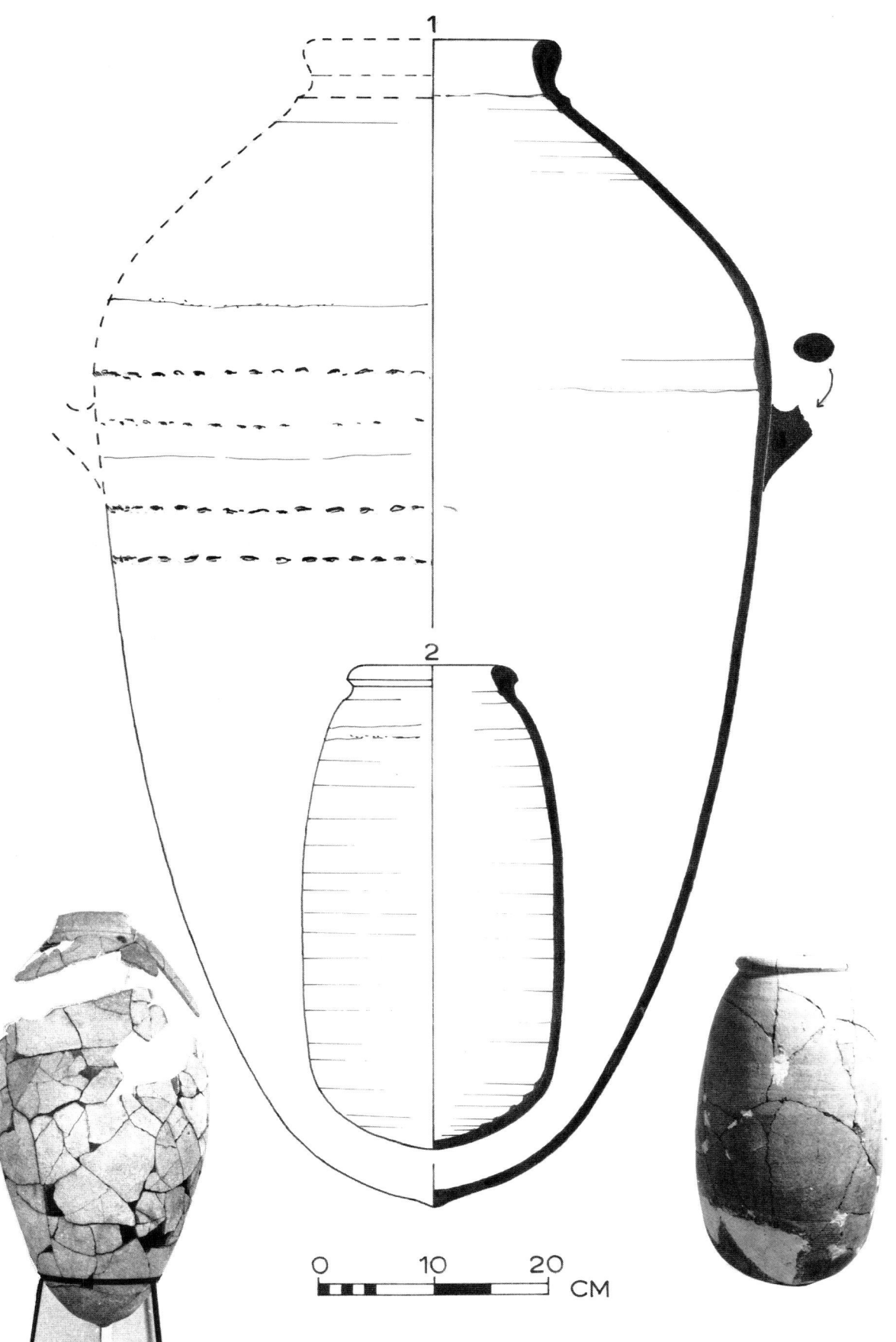

FIG. 36 POTTERY FROM THE CULTIC STRUCTURE (PERIOD IIB)

1. Identification		2. Section						3. Surface	
a. Item	b. Square, Locus Basket	a. Fabric Color	b. Core		c. Non-Plastics			a. Exterior	b. Interior
			Color	Extent	Type	Size	Frequency	Density	Color, n-p, voids, forming, finishing features	Same
1. Jar TT 467	SW 2-7 57.157	dk gr!	dk gr	-100%	lms	m,s	s	med l	*Ex*: rd; some n-p embedded, visible esp on handles. Entire surf burnished, shoulder bet handles in horiz strokes, below shoulder to base and neck, vert strokes; vert burnish on handles. *In*: dk gr, some n-p protrude; continuous shallow horiz forming lines, somewhat more deeply grooved near bottom and around neck.	
2. Jar TT 490	57.217	rd yl	lt gr	inner 75%	lms	l,m,s	m	med h	*Ex*: rd yl; discolored by lime deposit; many n-p protrude, some spalling; considerable layered flaking, many tiny pits, irreg faint wet-smoothing. *In*: br to gr; some spalling, few drag lines, prominent forming ridges from rim to spiral base center.	
3. Amphora TT 350	61.186	Section not available							*Ex*: lt rd br; some n-p visible in spalling; considerable pitting on handles and around neck; burnish is vert fr rim to base, horiz overlay burnish bet handles on upper shoulder.	
4. Amphora	57.218	dk gr! yl rd patch below handle	dk gr dk gr	100% 50%	lms	m,s,f	m	med	*Ex*: lt rd br, few n-p visible, some protrude, few tiny pits, continuous vert burnish, horiz on shoulder, near bottom becomes almost a polish, in rd br patch burnish has disappeared. *In*: dk gr, some n-p protrude, considerable flaking on body, reg horiz shallow forming ridges on upper shoulder & neck which is more crudely finished.	
5. Jar Rim & Handle	27.45, 49	rd yl		none	lms	l,m,s	s	med	*Ex*: rd, somewhat grayed by lms deposit, some lms embedded, what appears to be surface scraping is in fact vert (neck) & horiz (body, handle) burnishing which has lost its gloss. *In*: lt rd br, some n-p embedded, pitting on neck but many lime spalls on shoulder where forming ridges are much deeper than on neck. Lm deposit.	

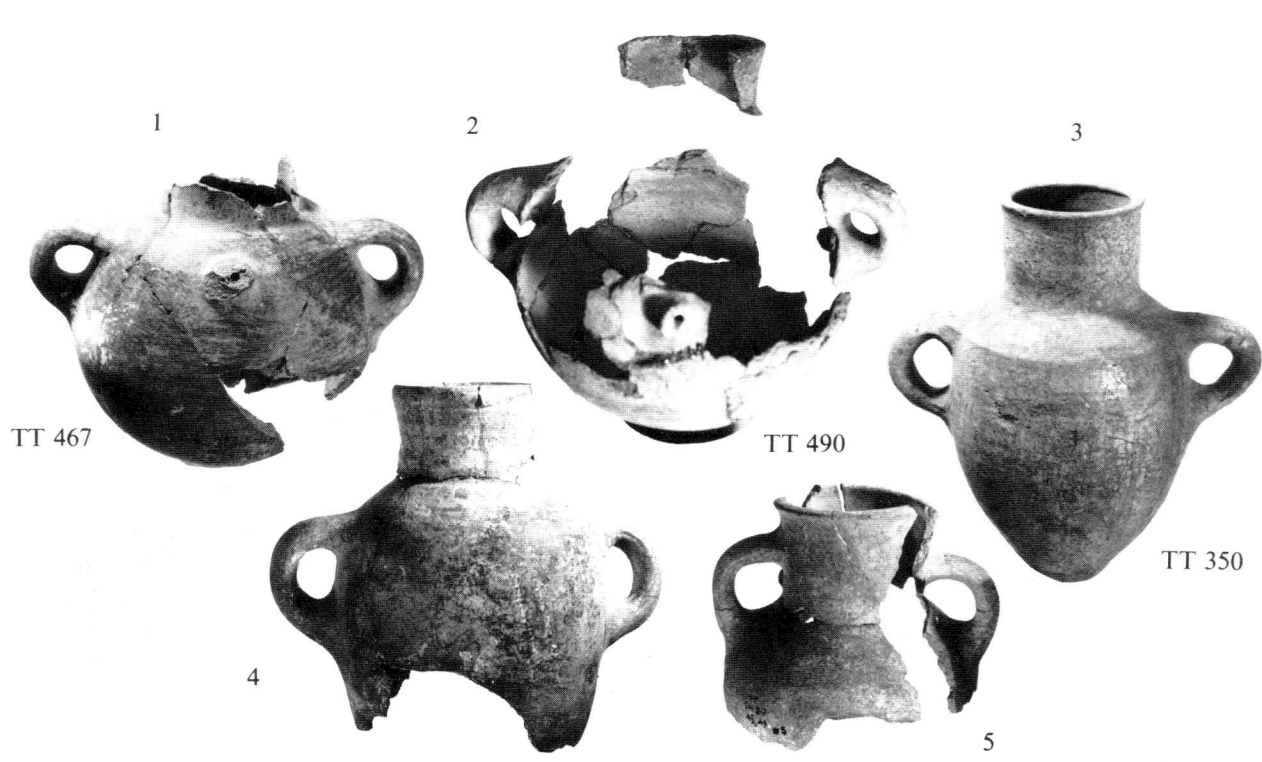

1 TT 467
2 TT 490
3 TT 350
4
5

136

FIG. 37 POTTERY FROM THE CULTIC STRUCTURE (PERIOD IIB)

1. Identification		2. Section						3. Surface	
a.	b.	a.	b. Core		c. Non-Plastics			a. Exterior	b. Interior
Item	Square, Locus Basket	Fabric Color	Color	Extent	Type	Size	Fre-quency	Density	Color, n-p, voids, forming, finishing features	Same
1. Jug TT 103	SW 2-7 27.45	lt br		none visible	lms	m,s	s	med h	*Ex*: lt rd, many n-p protrude covered, few exposed, some drag marks, wet-smoothing on body mostly slanting, neck horiz. Around and under base many straw voids. Slight indentation of seam mid-waist. *In*: lt rd, forming ridges around neck, some n-p protrude. Seam around *in* of base broken away in part.	
2. Jug TT 440	26.36-40	yl rd		none	lms cal bas	m,s m s	m f f	med h	*Ex*: yl rd, many n-p embedded, some protruding, most on the neck, some flaking, horiz burnish on body and vert on the neck has lost its gloss, base bottom eroded. *In*: rd yl, many n-p seen due to considerable flaking, forming ridges clear from rim to base, flashing line at neck bottom.	

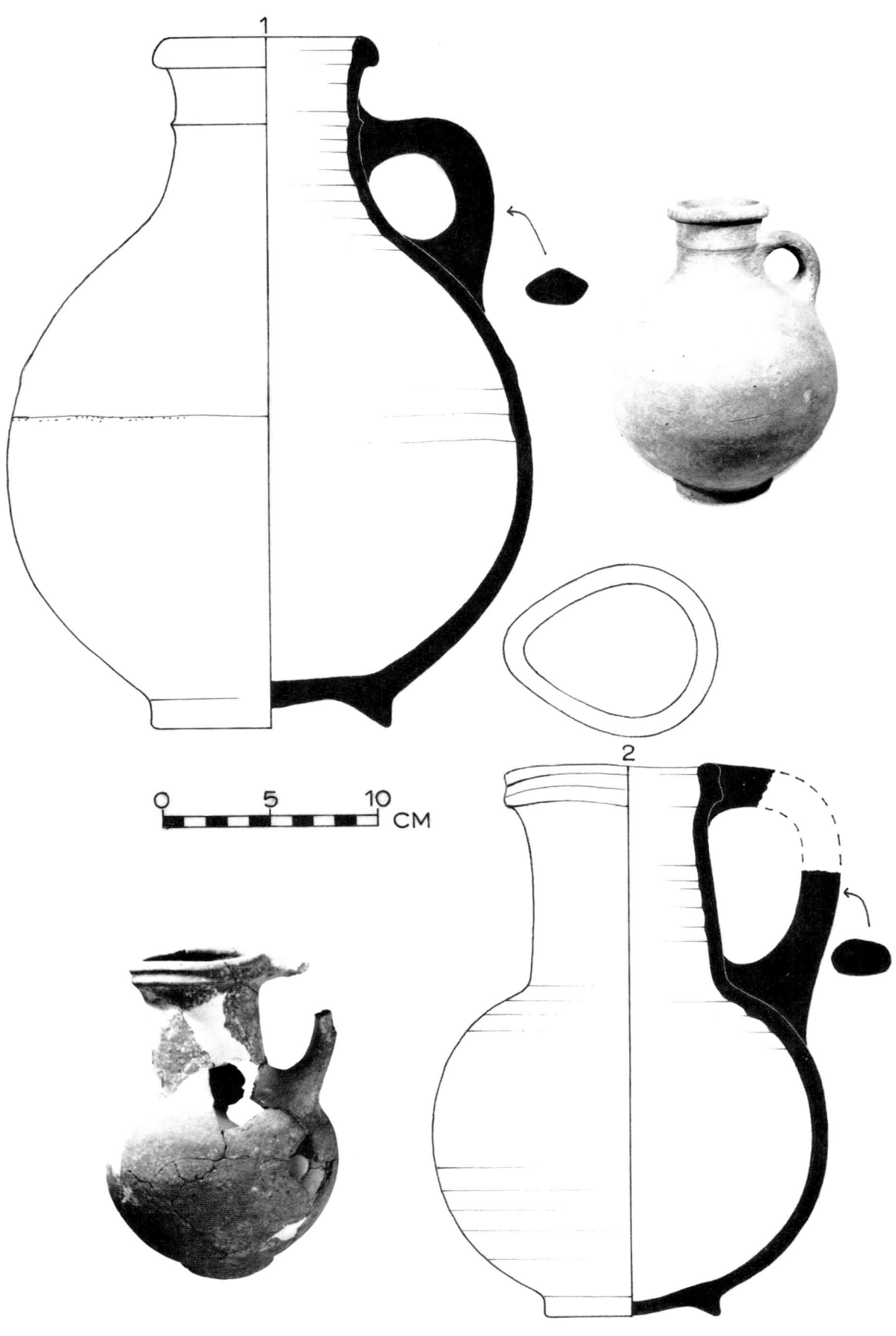

FIG. 38 POTTERY FROM THE CULTIC STRUCTURE (PERIOD IIB)

1. Identification		2. Section						3. Surface	
a.	b.	a.	b. Core		c. Non-Plastics			a. Exterior	b. Interior
Item	Square, Locus Basket	Fabric Color	Color	Extent	Type	Size	Frequency	Density	Color, n-p, voids, forming, finishing features	Same
1. Jug TT 454	SW 2-7 61.175	rd yl	lt br	75%	lms cal bas	m,s m m,s	s s s	med	*Ex*: rd br to rd yl, gray deposit 2ndary, many n-p protrude, covered, wet-smoothing lines are faint and generally horiz except handle where lines are vert. Forming ridges visible only on neck, also *in* where compression ridges reach to base which ends in slight omphalos. Body wall drops sharply before reaching base forming narrower basin inside the base.	
2. Jug TT 470	61.202	st br	lt gr	inner 50%	lms	m,s	s	med	*Ex*: lt rd br to pl rd, many n-p protrude, covered, roughen surf, esp clear on neck, rim, handle. Faint wet-smoothing usually horiz except handle. *In*: pl rd, forming lines reach base which curves smoothly in contrast to TT 454 above. *Ex*: base added as clay ring to earlier finished bottom of vessel.	

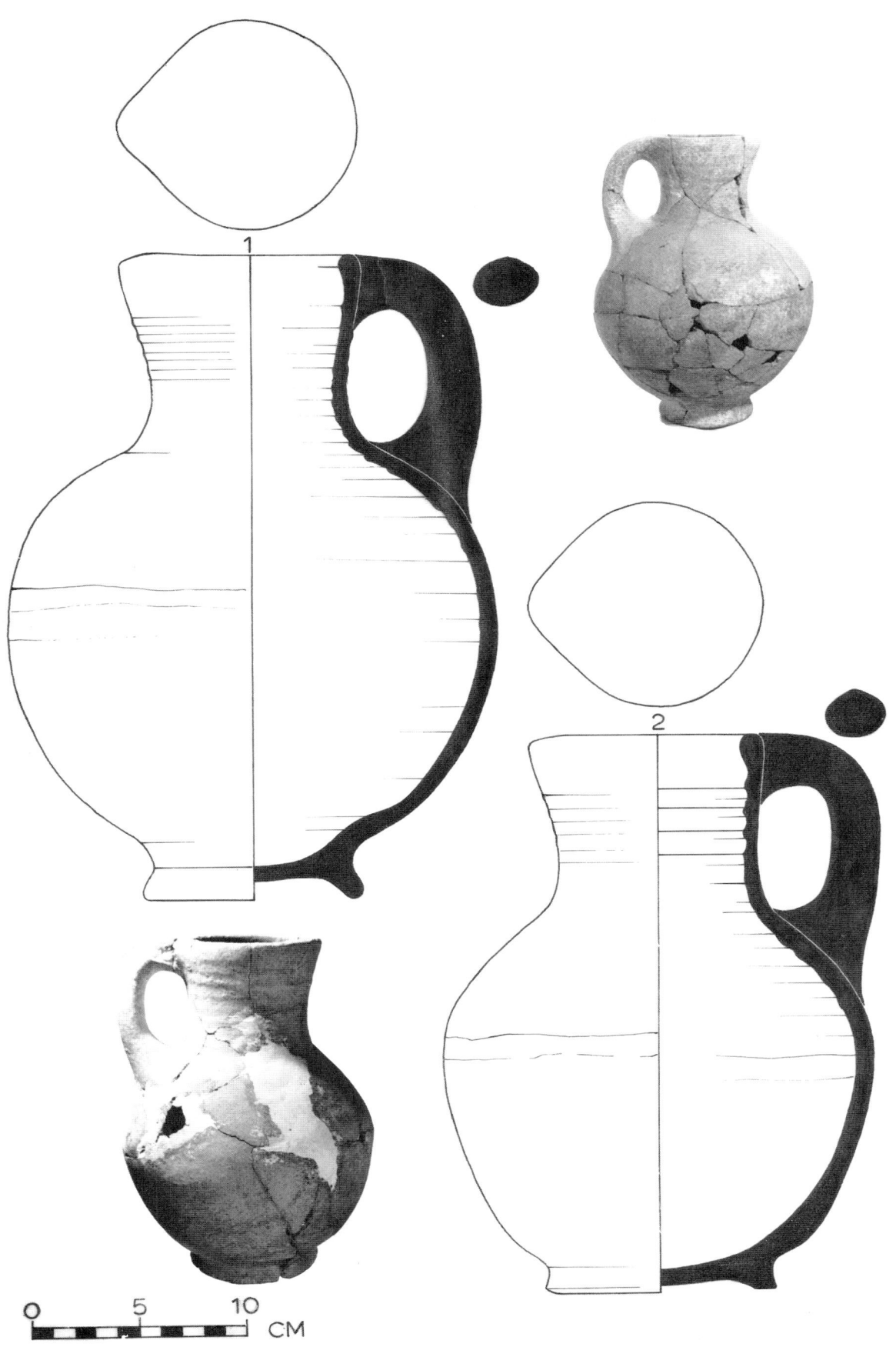

FIG. 39 POTTERY FROM THE CULTIC STRUCTURE (PERIOD IIB)

1. Identification		2. Section						3. Surface	
a. Item	b. Square, Locus Basket	a. Fabric Color	b. Core		c. Non-Plastics			a. Exterior	b. Interior
			Color	Extent	Type	Size	Frequency	Density	Color, n-p, voids, forming, finishing features	Same
1. Jug Rim & Handle	SW 2-7 57.226	br (body) rd br (handle)	lt gr	25% (handle)	cal (body) sand? (handle)	s,f s,f	s m	low	*Handle*: rd br, some n-p protrude, few embedded, drag marks, straw voids, vert finishing, low lump as clay patch. *Body in*: rd gr tiny n-p covered, protrude, horiz wet-smoothing.	
2. Jug TT 468	63.234	rd yl		none	lms (body) sand? (handle)	s,f s,f	vf f	vlow	*Ex*: lt rd under rd slip, vvfew n-p visible, vert and horiz burnishing rim to base except for four "windows" just above the base which are lt rd. *In*: rd yl lm encrusted, some n-p protrude, center base has forming spiral, some ridges can be seen.	
3. Jug? Base	36.106	rd yl		none	lms	m,s,f	f	low	*Ex & In*: lt rd br, vfew n-p on surf, many pits on inside, continuous burnish over *in* and *ex* so vessel is probably a "bowl" and not a "jug." Center of *ex* has trace of spiral twist.	
4. Jug TT 414	61.187	rd yl		none	lms	s,f	s	vlow	*Ex*: rd yl, some n-p embedded but visible, few horiz drag marks, flashing line just below handle around waist, forming ridges above and below slightly visible on *ex*, more on *In*: flaking has erased forming features below mid-body if indeed any had been seen. *In* neck has many tiny n-p protruding, wet-smoothing below rivets, burnish over. *Ex* is completely burnished to the point of polish, also over rim to *in* below "rivets." See Fig. 48: 15-19.	
5. Jug Base	61.229	rd br	gr	±50%	lms	m,s,f	m	med h	*Ex*: yl rd, chipped, very few n-p seen, burnished under and *ex* as No. 3. *In*: rd br, charcoal deposit, some n-p protrude, covered, slight trace of circular forming ridges.	
6. Jug TT 83	26.36	lt br	dk gr	inner 95%	lms	s,f	s	vlow	*Ex*: rd yl, some lms n-p seen thru shallow spalling, some pits, handle did not join body firmly, somewhat irreg forming ridges above base, flashing line at neck-body join is sharp, forming ridges on neck slight on *ex* but clear on *in*. *Ex* surf completely burnished after wet-smoothing which is only visible under broken handle.	

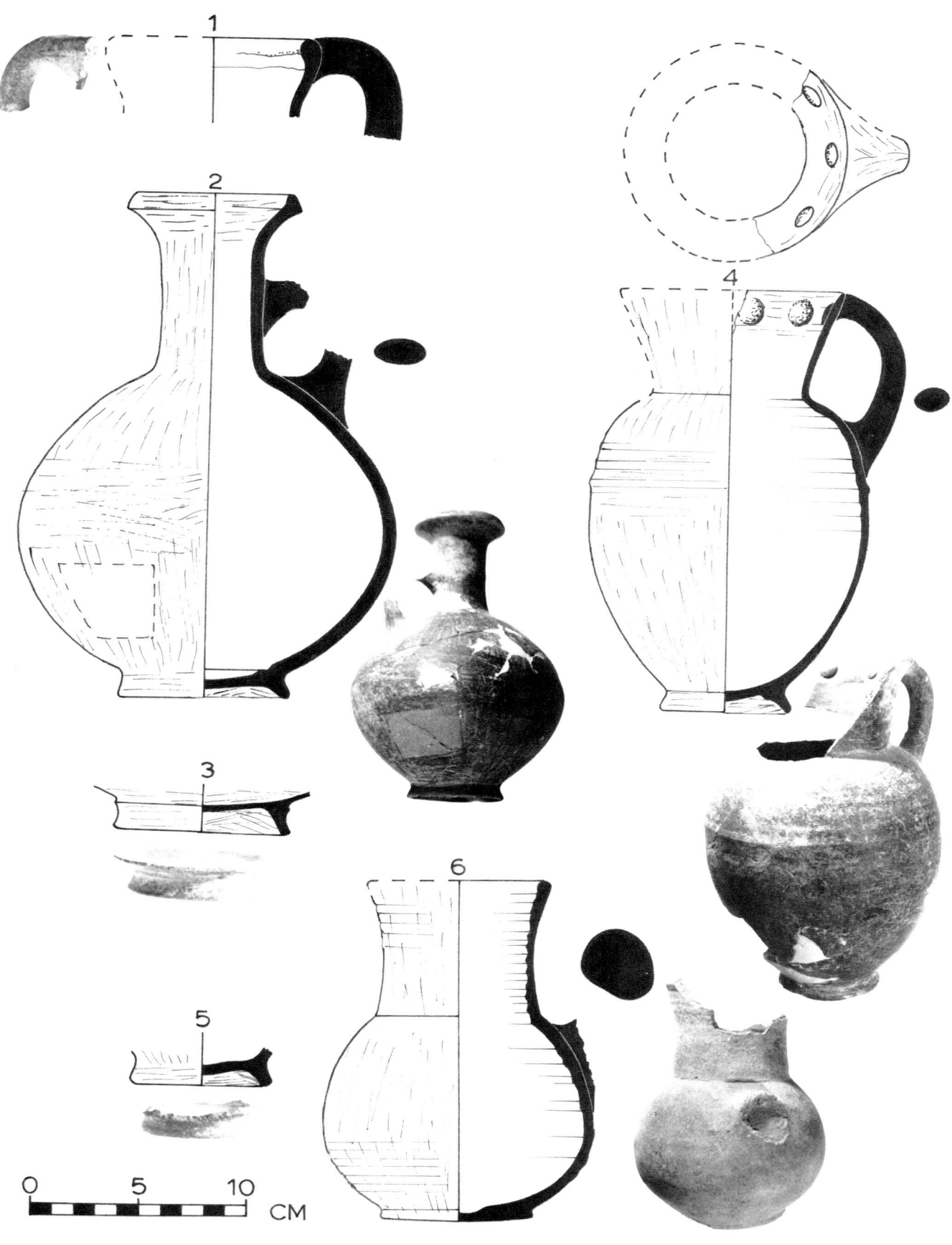

FIG. 40 POTTERY FROM THE CULTIC STRUCTURE (PERIOD IIB)

1. Identification		2. Section							3. Surface	
a.	b.	a.	b. Core		c. Non-Plastics				a. Exterior	b. Interior
Item	Square, Locus Basket	Fabric Color	Color	Extent	Type	Size	Frequency	Density	Color, n-p, voids, forming, finishing features	Same
1. Juglet TT 63	SW 2-7 26.38	not seen	same	same	lms bas	m,s l,m	s f	med	*Ex*: dk pk, n-p type judged from surf where some are exposed, esp lms on neck and rim, bas on body. Slightly irreg horiz forming depressions from base to waist, vert burnish covers surf except near base where it has been burned off. Rd br paint bands. *In*: tiny pits, some forming ridges but *in* not available.	
2. Juglet Neck & Handle	28.50	lt rd br	gr	inner 50%	lms bas	s,f s	f f	vlow	*Ex*: lt rd, some n-p seen thru spalling, vert burnish down neck to shallow grooved ring where burnishing begins to be horiz. *In*: pk gr, neck eroded, throwing ridges clear on body.	
3. Juglet TT 386	63.234	pk gr		none	lms bas	f s,f	s m	low	*Ex*: lt yl br beneath rd slip peeling off, dk br paint bands around waist below handle, continuous burnish over slip. *In*: lt gr, eroded, some slight sign of forming lines.	
4. Juglet TT 327	59.149	dk pk		not seen	lms bas	f s,f	s m	low	*Ex*: dk pk, n-p type seen from surf, embedded, few pits, continuous burnish partly eroded. *In*: not seen beyond inner lip.	
5. Juglet TT 306	18.25	dk gr	dk gr	-100%	none				*Ex*: gr covered with flaking dk gr to dk br burnished slip. Burnish becomes a polish. *In*: not seen beyond inner lip.	
6. Juglet TT 88	27.46	lt rd br	dk gr	75% inner?	none				*Ex*: dk pk under yl rd slip burnished to a polish but flaking on neck, 3 large chips out of body.	
7. Juglet TT 62	26.40	not seen	same	same	lms	l,m,s	s	low	*Ex*: lt pk, n-p seen from surf, burnished red slip pretty well flaked away. *In*: rd slip just over rim from which most is chipped away.	
8. Juglet Body & Base	61.205	lt rd br		none	lms bas	l,m m	s f	med	*Ex*: lt rd, many n-p seen thru shallow spalls, faint trace of horiz & vert smoothing. *In*: lt rd br, throwing ridges to 3cms above base where irreg compression ridges finish bottom.	
9. Juglet TT 458	61.204	br	dk gr	-50%	lms	l,m,s	m	med h	*Ex*: wk rd, many spalls expose n-p, neck and handle esp eroded. Traces of lt rd slip mostly eroded. *In*: same except that grooved throwing ridges are clear, end in spiral twist at base.	

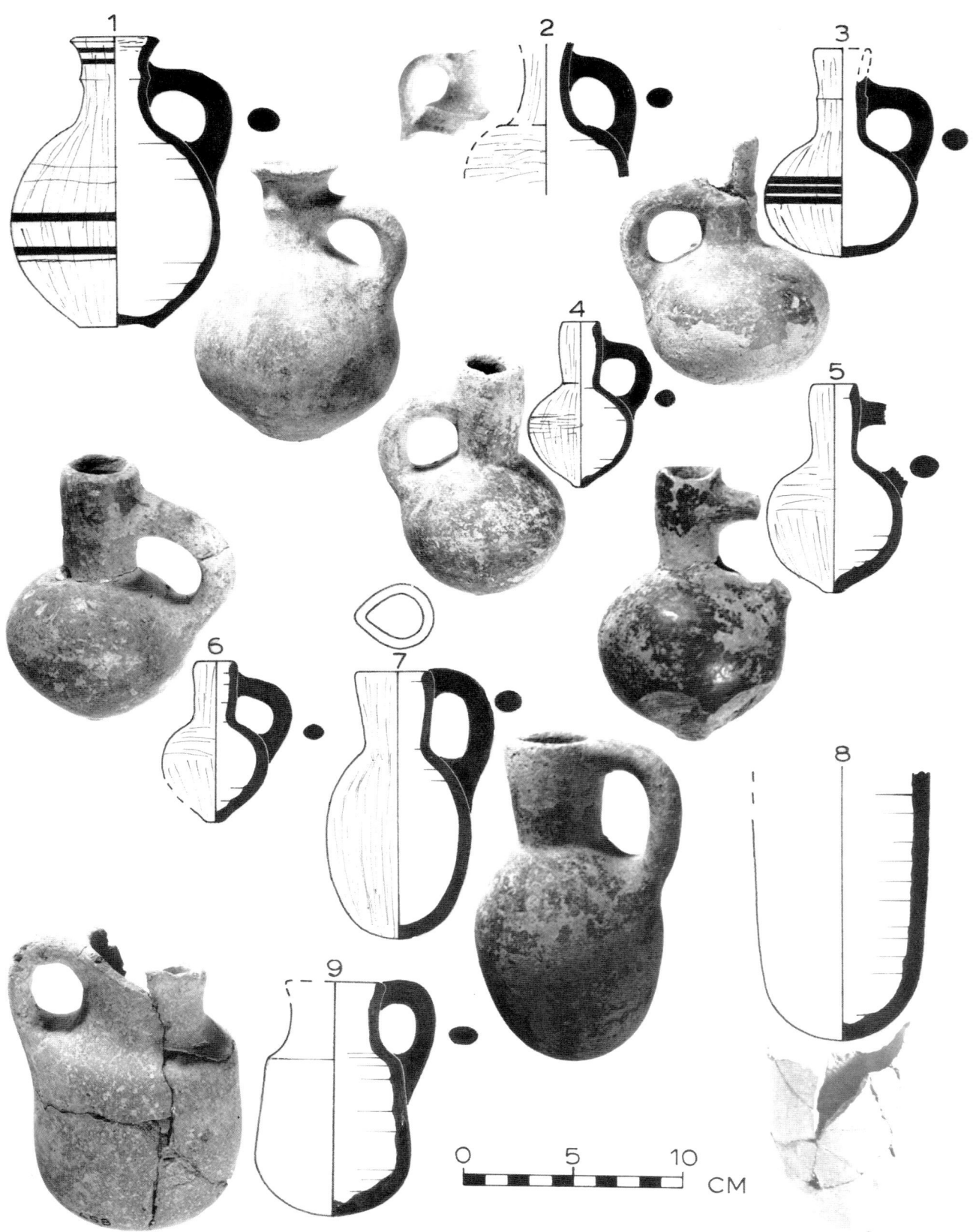

FIG. 40 (CONTINUED)

1. Identification		2. Section						3. Surface	
a.	b.	a.	b. Core		c. Non-Plastics			a. Exterior	b. Interior
Item	Square, Locus Basket	Fabric Color	Color	Extent	Type	Size	Fre-quency	Density	Color, n-p, voids, forming, finishing features	Same
10. Juglet TT 466	61.205	lt rd	lt rd br	25%	lms	l,m,s	s	med l	*Ex*: lt rd, surf badly eroded showing n-p, some pitting. *In*: same but for clear forming ridges reaching raised twist in center base.	
11. Juglet TT 484	28.53	rd br	dk gr	75%	lms	l,m,s	s	low	*Ex*: rd br, shallow spalling shows n-p, some embedded straw voids, pits, turning lines on upper shoulder and around neck. *In*: same but for forming ridges from rim to base ending in raised twist.	
12. Pyxis TT 488	27.45	vpl br		none	lms	s,f	f	vlow	*Ex*: vpl br, trace only of yl rd burnished slip. *In*: forming ridges near base which ends in spiral. Few tiny pits.	
13. Pyxis TT 372	61.208	rd br		none seen	none seen				*Ex*: br to yl rd, completely burnished surf, some horiz turning lines at base. *In*: same but not burnished. Forming ridges end in twist at center base.	
14. Pyxis TT 73	26.36	rd gr	rd gr	75%	sand?	s,f	s	low	*Ex*: dk pk to lt rd, br slip is burnished, extensively flaked, revealing some n-p. Many tiny pits. *In*: not clear, seems to be no forming ridges.	

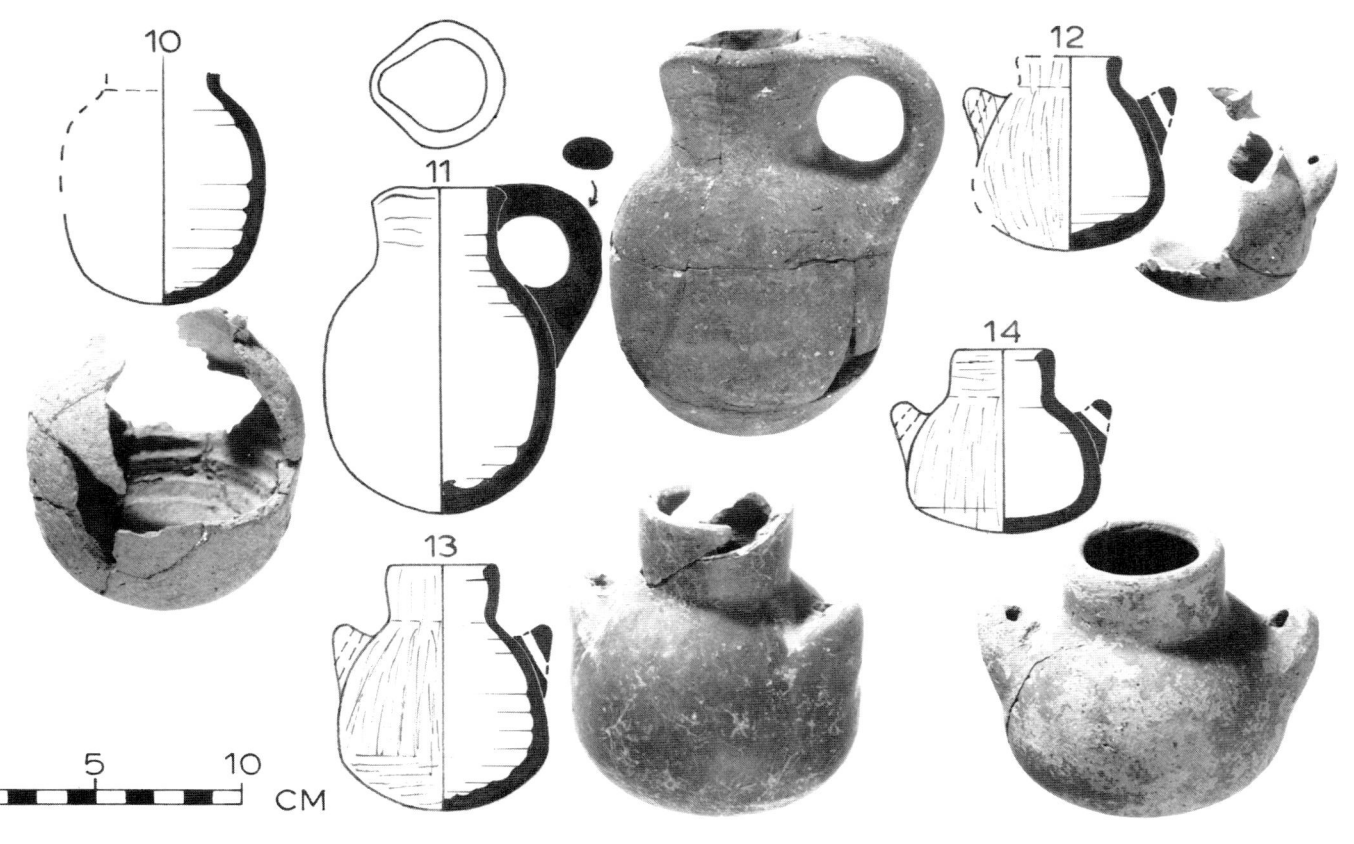

FIG. 41 POTTERY FROM THE CULTIC STRUCTURE (PERIOD IIB)

1. Identification		2. Section						3. Surface	
a.	b.	a.	b. Core		c. Non-Plastics			a. Exterior	b. Interior
Item	Square, Locus Basket	Fabric Color	Color	Extent	Type	Size	Fre-quency	Density	Color, n-p, voids, forming, finishing features	Same
1. Crater TT 489	59.155 61.189, 205	lt rd & br	gr	75% (where seen)	lms	l,m,s	m	med h	*Ex*: pk gr to rd br, n-p examined only on surf. Many straw voids, lms pop-outs, more on one side than the other. Surf smoothing by hand, vert grooves as kind of crude irreg combing below waist, more reg horiz incised lines in finish of center of vessel while above center to handles deeply grooved & slanting finger lines are topped by horiz smoothing lines. Base finished crudely by hand, coil ring added to previously finished bottom. *In*: much flaking and eroding, pitting but not many n-p seen nor forming ridges which are prominent only under shoulder. Irreg groove around outer edge of rim.	

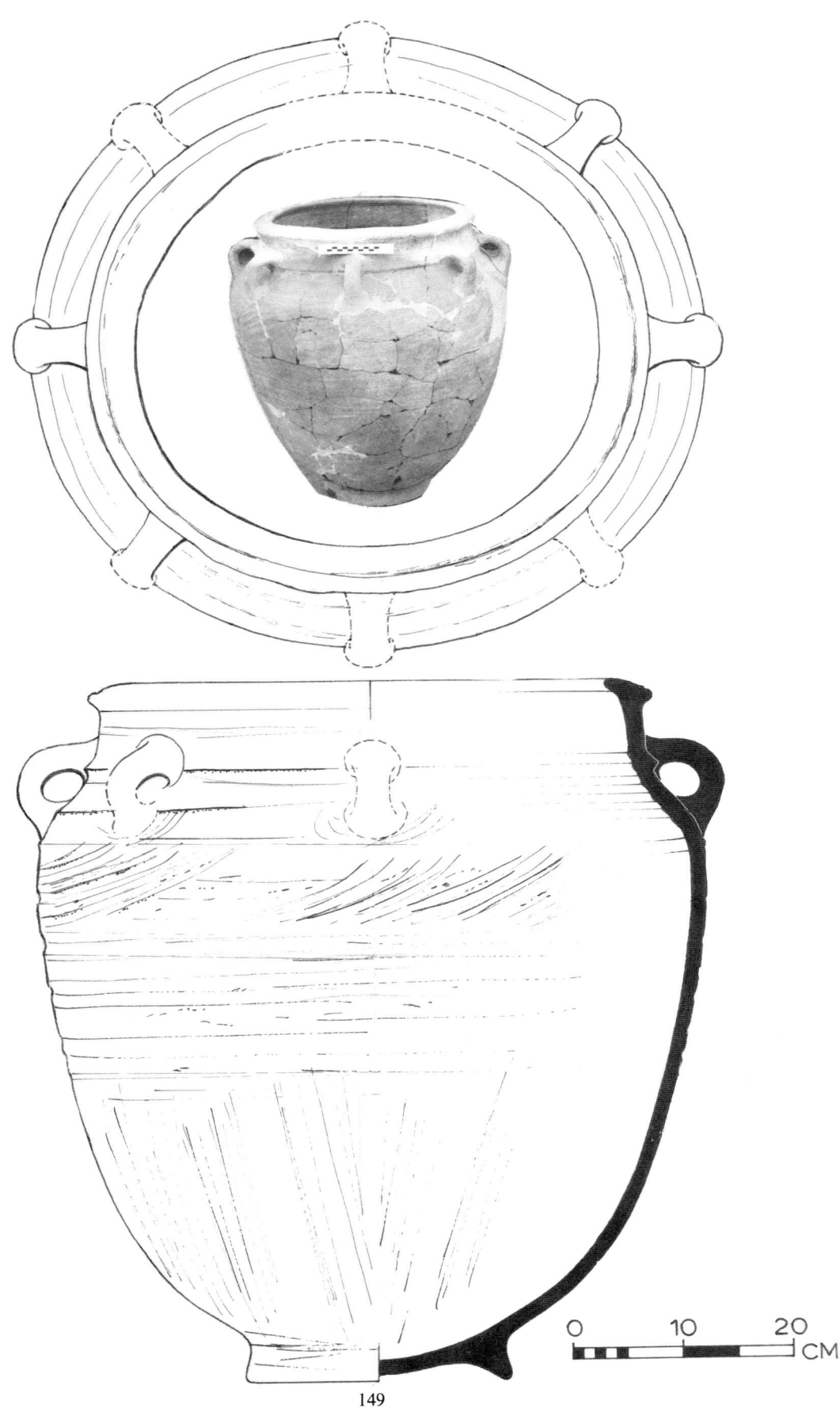

149

FIG. 42 POTTERY FROM THE CULTIC STRUCTURE (PERIOD IIB)

1. Identification		2. Section						3. Surface	
a. Item	b. Square, Locus Basket	a. Fabric Color	b. Core		c. Non-Plastics			a. Exterior	b. Interior
			Color	Extent	Type	Size	Frequency	Density	Color, n-p, voids, forming, finishing features	Same
1. Bowl TT 446	SW 2-7 27.45	rd yl	lt br	50%	lms bas	l,m,s l,m,s	m m	med h	*Ex*: lt rd br to rd br, many n-p visible thru shallow spalling, some erosion of upper shoulder where scraping opened rather than closed the surf, drag marks not common, turning depressions from base to shoulder, wet-smoothing shoulder to rim. Concentric forming ridges around center of base. Tool used to edge bottom of rim slowly. Burnish which covers *in* extends to outer rim edge. *In*: continuous burnish over rd slip, many n-p visible thru shallow spalling.	
2. Bowl TT 439	26.36-40	rd br	gr	±50%	lms	l,m,s	m	med	*Ex*: pl rd, many n-p seen in shallow spalling, tiny pits common, surf from shoulder edge to base smoothed with very fine, shallow & reg circular depressed lines. *In* of base the same with deeper groove around center. Some n-p protrude on shoulder and rim. As in No. 1 outer rim burnished as all of *in* though in center it has disappeared. Many n-p seen thru lime spalls which increase toward base. Break lines here as in No. 1 indicate seam at the shoulder.	
3. Bowl TT 480	61.182-188	st br		none	lms cal sand?	m,s m,s s	s s s	med h	*Ex*: lt rd br, some n-p seen, few drag marks, turning lines and smoothing reg horiz rim to base, base eroded but has convex center, ring is added clay coil after bottom had been finished, lms encrusted. Burnish only to just over rim edge. *In*: rd slip is burnished continuously, horiz to mid-way then vertically to center. N-p hardly seen thru shallow spalling.	
4. Bowl TT 479	61.172, 185.188, 201	rd yl		none	lms cal	m,s m	m f	med h	*Ex*: lt rd br, the general appearance and finish is as No. 3. Base is not as eroded, many protruding n-p. *In*: has a rd slip much eroded and not burnished. At 3cm intervals are reg depression ridges.	

3

TT 480

4

TT 479

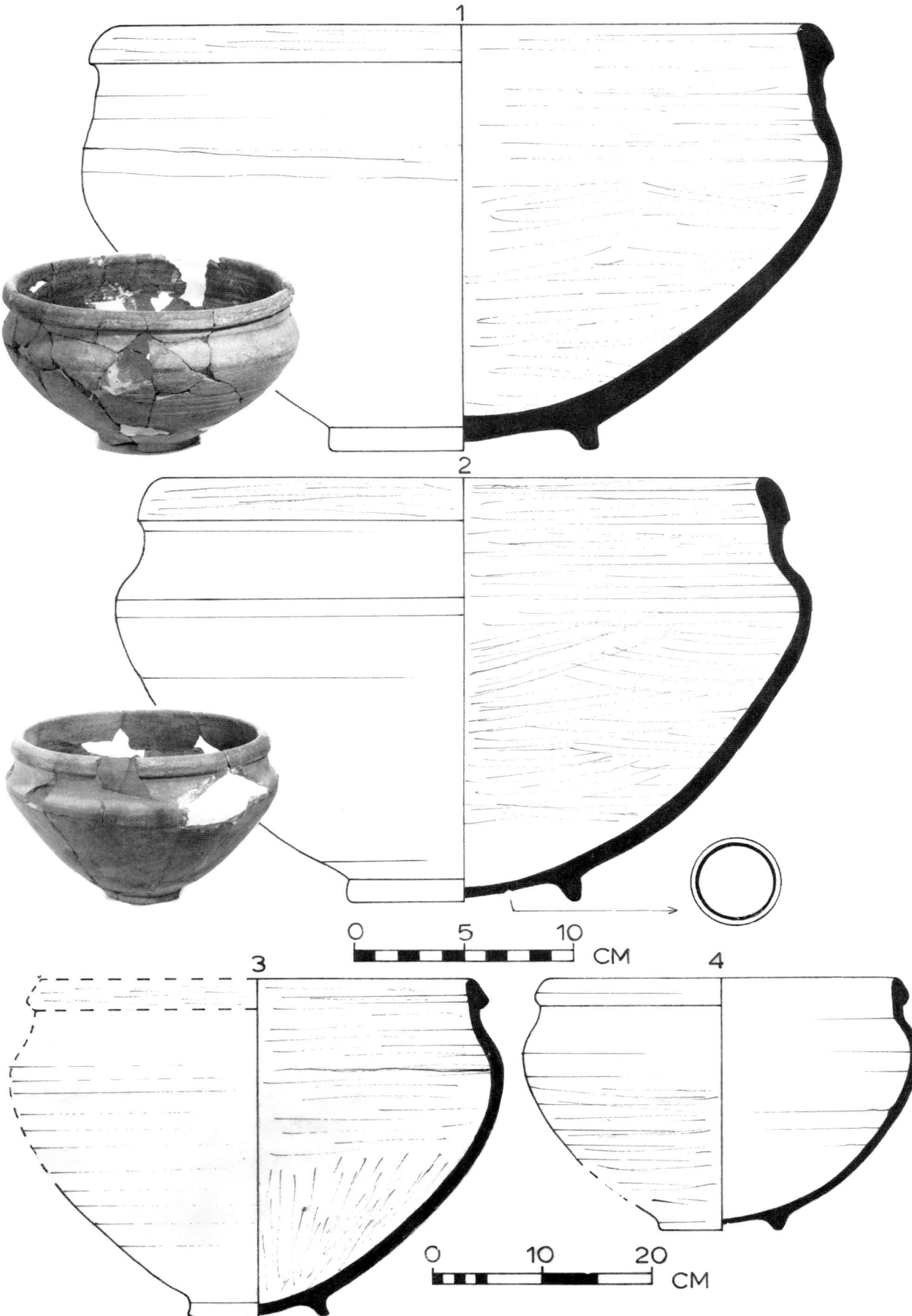

FIG. 43 POTTERY FROM THE CULTIC STRUCTURE (PERIOD IIB)

1. Identification		2. Section							3. Surface	
a.	b.	a.	b. Core		c. Non-Plastics				a. Exterior	b. Interior
Item	Square, Locus Basket	Fabric Color	Color	Extent	Type	Size	Frequency	Density	Color, n-p, voids, forming, finishing features	Same
1. Bowl TT 471	SW 2-7 28.57.59 57.157 59.148,150	rd yl		none	lms cal	l,m,s m,s	s s	med h	*Ex*: dk pk to rd br, many small lime spalls, faint wet-smoothing lines generally horiz, flashing line where shoulder begins, thickening, slight *ex* ridge, also indicated by break lines. 3 concentric ridges in center of base which is a turned ring added to preformed bottom. *In*: burnished rd slip mostly eroded leaving some erosion of surf revealing only some n-p. Break lines also suggest base extending 10cms from center formed separate from body and then shoulder added.	
2. Bowl TT 451	27.45	rd yl	g- br	50% lower body	lms cal	l,m,s m,s	s s	med	*Ex*: lt rd br, few protruding n-p, some spalling. Reg circular forming lines rim to base, base formed as No. 1, rim burnished on *ex* as all of *In*: rd, many lms spalls, esp toward the base, break lines suggest new clay at lower edge of shoulder.	
3. Bowl Rim & Body	57.147 59.152	dk br	dk gr	-100%	lms cal	l,m,s s	m vf	med h	*Ex*: dk br, some n-p seen protruding, covered, few pop-outs, rd spots, wet-smoothing, folded-over rim tooled to pointed edge. *In*: wk rd, ring burnished dk rd br, rim to body, some n-p visible thru tiny pits, 2cms below rim incised horiz line somewhat irreg.	
4. Bowl Rim & Body	57.147		All features exactly as in No. 3						Surf as No. 3.	

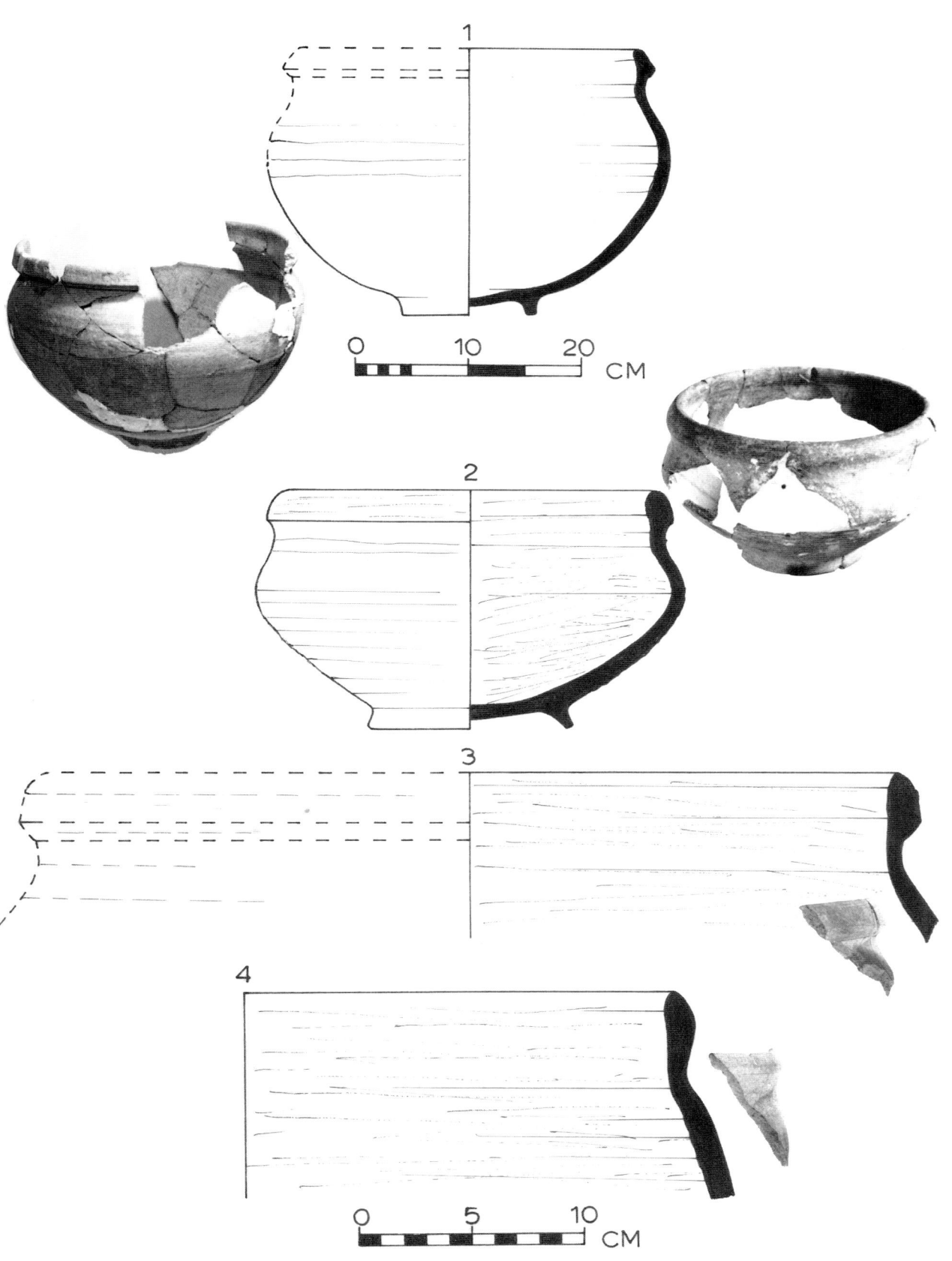

FIG. 44 POTTERY FROM THE CULTIC STRUCTURE (PERIOD IIB)

1. Identification		2. Section							3. Surface	
a.	b.	a.	b. Core		c. Non-Plastics				a. Exterior	b. Interior
Item	Square, Locus Basket	Fabric Color	Color	Extent	Type	Size	Frequency	Density	Color, n-p, voids, forming, finishing features	Same
1. Bowl Rim & Body	SW 2-7 48.127-130	rd yl	gr br	inner 50%	lms grog	l,m,s m,s	m s	med h	*Ex*: lt rd br, many n-p protrude, most covered, some wet-smoothing traces, turning just below shoulder bend, some drops of rd slip over rim in one place. *In*: rd slip, burnished but heavily encrusted, still some pits and pop-outs seen.	
2. Bowl Rim & Body	36.99	yl br	lt gr	inner 50%	sand? mostly lms	l,m,s	m	med	*Ex*: rd br discolored by lm encrustation, some n-p protrude, some visible, faint traces of smoothing on body, horiz lines on shoulder-rim. *In*: rd br slip burnished horiz on rim, vert on shoulder to center. Many n-p seen thru spalling, flashing line clear mid-shoulder.	
3. Bowl TT 461	61.194-195	st br		none	lms	l,m,s	s-m	med	*Ex*: lt br much discolored with lm encrustation, some lime spalls, many tiny pits, drag marks resulting in part from 1.5cm-wide turning bands, circular forming ridges on base, rim irreg smoothed, rd slip burnished 4-5cms *ex* rim. *In*: rd slip burnished, much eroded and covered, n-p seen esp on rim, thickening above flashing line at base of rim.	
4. Bowl TT 487	27.49	br	lt gr	50%-	lms	l,m,s	s	low	*Ex*: rd br, some n-p protrude covered, some spalling, many drag marks, circular forming ridges very shallow on base, straw voids on base, deep grooves 7.5 & 5cms from rim around shoulder, seems to mark a flashing line. *In*: dk gr, few n-p seen, surf color due to lm encrustation, thin but almost complete, finishing lines are very faint.	
5. Bowl Rim & Body	28.47	br		none	sand? mostly lms	l,m,s	m	med h	*Ex*: dk pk, many n-p visible thru shallow pop-outs drag marks, many tiny pits, above cm-wide depression br slip is burnished as is the case over all of *in* where it is also rd br in places. *In*: spalling increases to the point of causing flaking. Wet-smoothing lines most visible on rim.	

1

4

TT 487

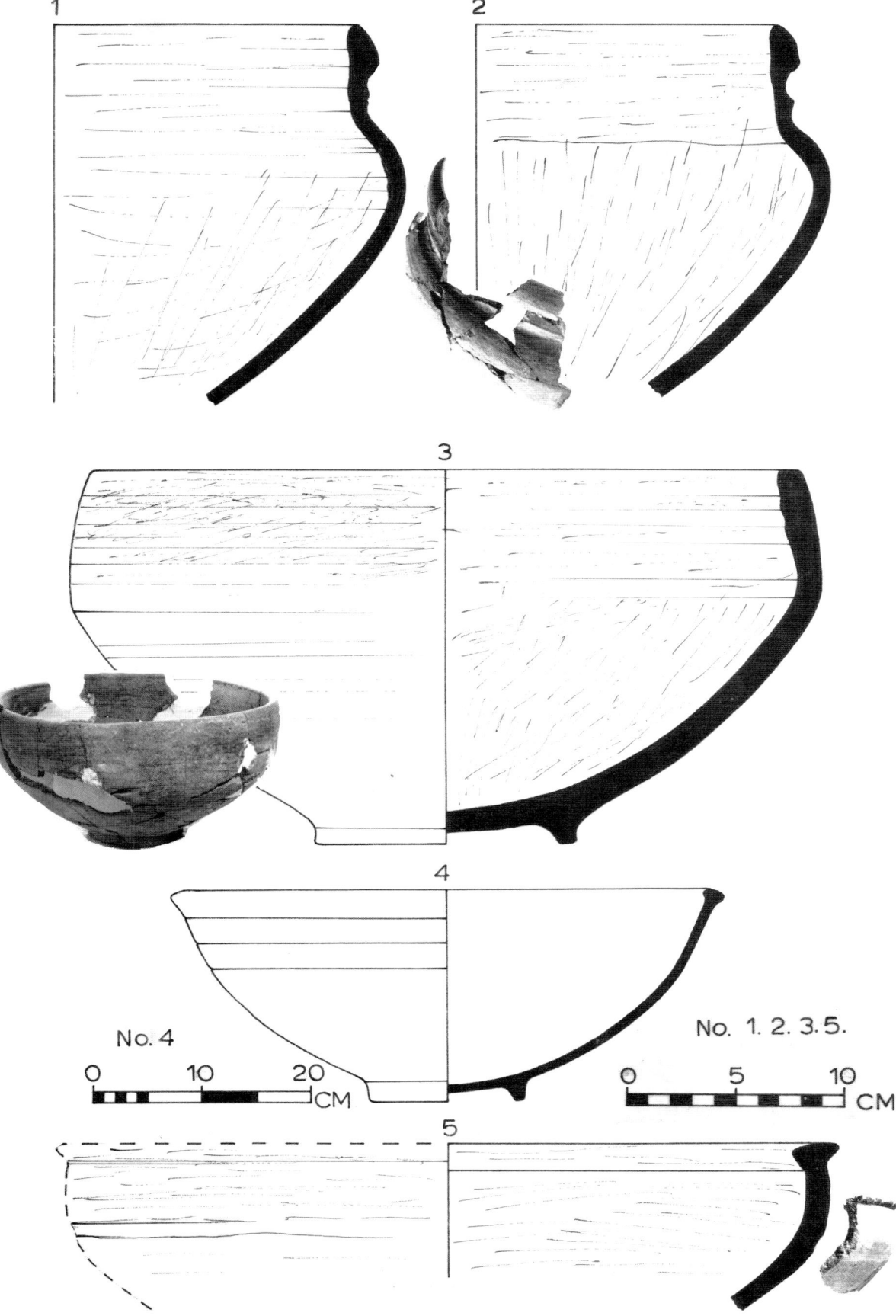

FIG. 45 POTTERY FROM THE CULTIC STRUCTURE (PERIOD IIB)

1. Identification		2. Section							3. Surface	
a.	b.	a.	b. Core		c. Non-Plastics				a. Exterior	b. Interior
Item	Square, Locus Basket	Fabric Color	Color	Extent	Type	Size	Frequency	Density	Color, n-p, voids, forming, finishing features	Same
1. Bowl TT 485	SW 2-7 28.47 35.68	rd br	dk gr	none to 100%	cal lms	m,s m	m f	med l	*Ex*: rd br, n-p seen thru shallow spalls, few tiny pits, circular smoothing lines around base to flashing depression just below shoulder where rd br slip is burnished as on *in* rim. *In*: rd br but not slip or burnish below rim which is coated with charcoal. Many tiny pits.	
2. Bowl TT 445	27.41, 44,45	lt rd	lt br	75%	lms bas	m,s m,s	s f	med l	*Ex*: lt rd, some n-p protrude, some exposed, tiny pits, drag marks esp on upper half of shoulder which is burnished in close horiz strokes. *In*: as *ex* except that flashing line where shoulder turns up to rim is sharply bent on *ex* also rim thins while *in* line is smooth. Entire bowl may have been rd-slipped.	
3. Bowl TT 416	27.101	dk gr!	dk gr	100%	lms	m,s	s	low	*Ex*: lt rd br to rd br, much covered with lm encrustation, some n-p protrude but are covered, depressed flashing line where shoulder bends up to rim, circular forming lines in and around base very reg, spiral to base center. Rim top is burnished, perhaps some of *in* but generally obscured by encrustation.	
4. Bowl TT 415	57.227	yl br to rd yl to br	lt gr to gr	0-40%	lms	l,m,s	s	low	*Ex*: lt rd br, heavy carbon deposit on bottom, many n-p protrude, some seen, drag marks, turning lines above ring base inside of which wet-smoothing is criss-cross. At shoulder bend to rim, flashing line, burnish begins to rim and inside, halfway to center of base. *In*: rd, horiz burnished slip, erosion in center reveals lms n-p.	
5. Bowl Rim & Body	27.45,49 61.169	br	gr	±50%	lms sand	l,m,s s	s s	med	*Ex*: dk pk, some n-p seen, embedded, some protrude, some drag marks, forming lines circular and reg, flashing line at shoulder bend, rim thins. *In*: n-p in shallow spalling, rd yl slip closely burnished in horiz strokes.	
6. Bowl TT 464	28.53, 55	lt br	dk gr	none (rim in part) 100%	lms sand	m,s s	s s	med	*Ex*: lt rd br, some n-p protrude, few seen in shallow spalls, flashing line at upper shoulder, wet-smoothing lines regular and circular. *In*: dk rd br slip burnished horiz rim to base, some lms n-p visible, base center has carbon deposit, lm encrustation is general.	
7. Bowl Rim	35.67	yl rd		none	cal lms	m,s l,m	m f	med	*Ex*: lt rd br, flashing line at fragment of upper shoulder preserved, excess clay overlaps rim which is slipped and horiz burnished as is *in* where few pits also reveal lms n-p.	
8. Bowl Rim	28.55	rd	dk gr	none -100% rim corner	lms cal bas	s,f s s	s s s	med l	*Ex & In*: except for lt rd color same as No. 7. Hand finish of rim wall more crude than No. 7.	
9. Bowl Rim & Body	26.98	br	gr	50%	lms	l,m,s	s	med l	*Ex*: lt rd, some n-p embedded, wet-smoothing, some flaking at flashing line where smoothing opened surf, some horiz strokes of burnish remain on upper rim. *In*: the same, except more pitting, even less burnish remains, base of rim line unevenly finished.	

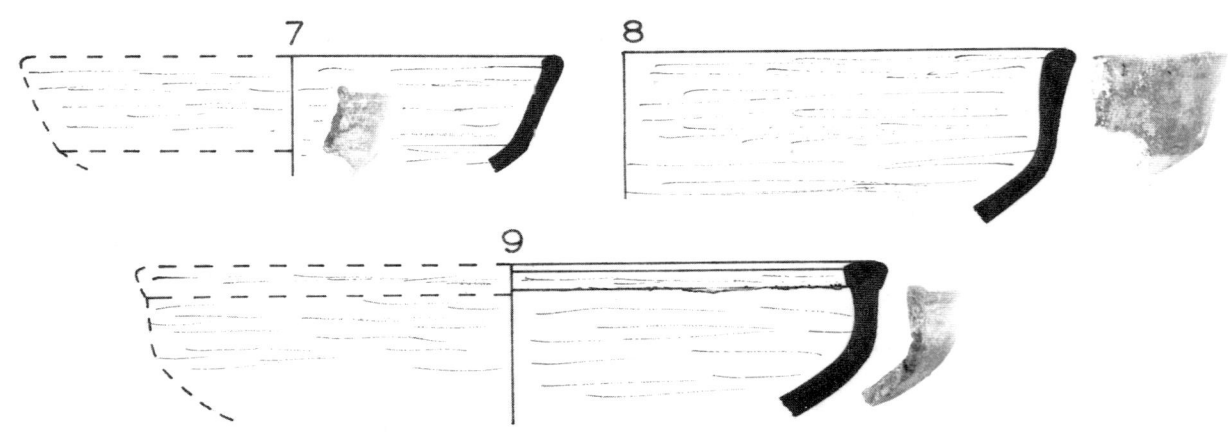

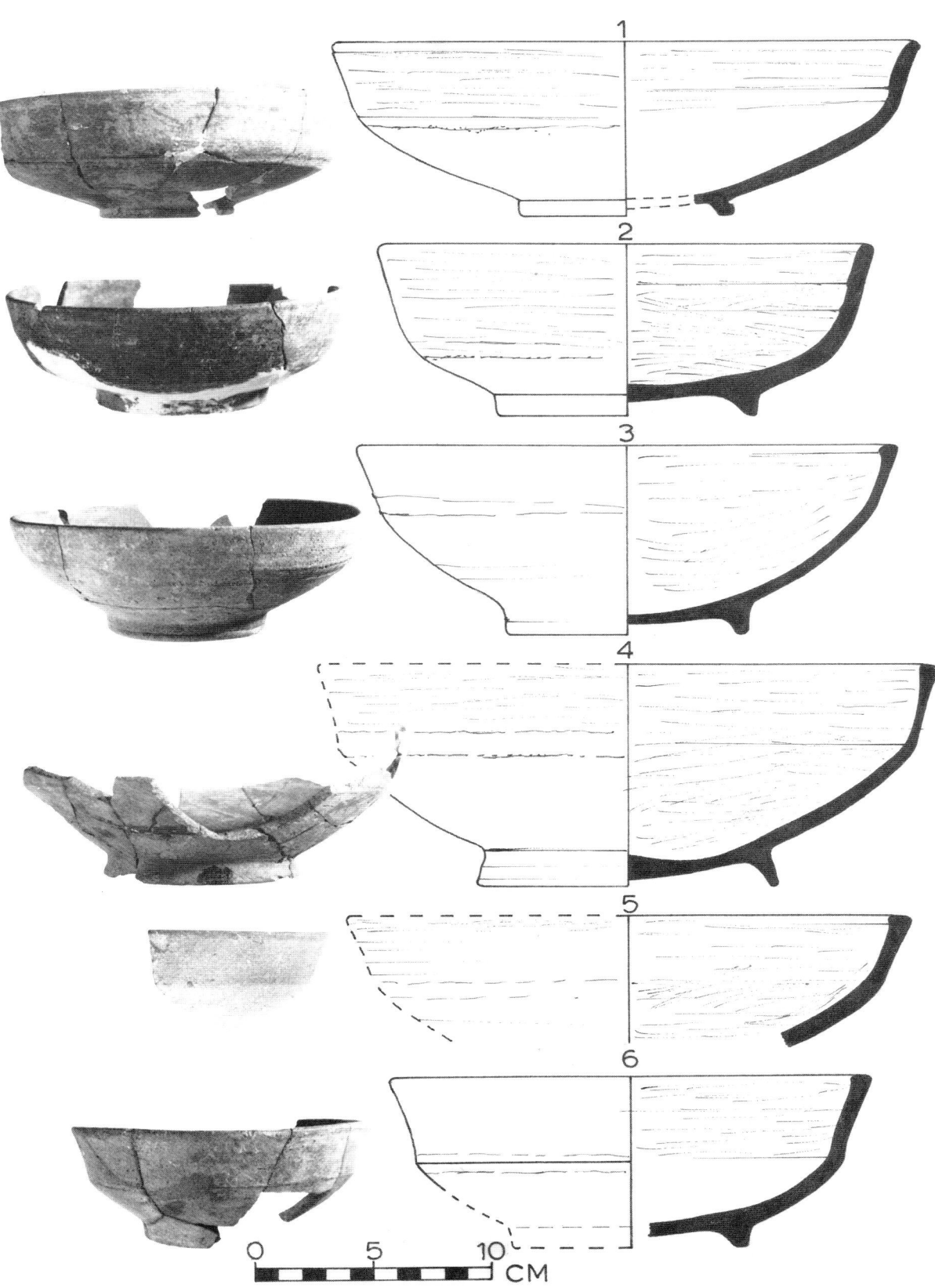

FIG. 46 POTTERY FROM THE CULTIC STRUCTURE (PERIOD IIB)

1. Identification		2. Section						3. Surface	
a. Item	b. Square, Locus Basket	a. Fabric Color	b. Core		c. Non-Plastics			a. Exterior	b. Interior
			Color	Extent	Type	Size	Fre-quency	Density	Color, n-p, voids, forming, finishing features	Same
1. Bowl TT 465	SW 2-7 60.162	rd yl	gr	50%	lms	l,m,s	s-m	med	*Ex*: lt rd br to lt rd, many n-p protrude, covered, visible at base, also section of rim has eroded due to prob 2ndary burning. Rough surf wet-smoothed, some drag marks, circular forming lines around base ring, edge of coil seam at shoulder laps over onto rim. *In*: lt rd br, some n-p protrude, few visible, 3 forming ridges down rim, surf lm encrusted. Trace of slip on rim and *ex* to shoulder prob covered all of *in*.	
2. Bowl TT 411	61.214	rd yl		none	cal lms	l,m,s m,s	m s	med h	*Ex*: lt rd, few n-p protrude, many embedded, irreg wet-smoothing to ring base inside which smoothing is circular. Rd slip on shoulder is burnished. *In*: rd slip prob. burnished at least on rim but now eroded.	
3. Bowl TT 453	27.45	yl rd		none	lms	m,s	s	low	*Ex*: rd br on base and shoulder, rd slip on rim. Many tiny n-p just under surf, drag marks in circular smoothing of bottom and base. Rim continuously burnished horiz as is *in* which is also rd. Most of area below rim has lost gloss if indeed it was ever burnished. Flashing line on *ex* in part laps over. Rim uneven at join with bottom. *In*: burnish strokes squared, qtr on each side, in each direction.	
4. Bowl TT 462	61.179	yl rd to lt br to br		none	lms sand?	l,m,s m,s	s s	low	*Ex*: lt rd br to a burned rd slip on shoulder-rim. Some n-p protrude, several drag marks in circular wiping bottom and base center, fine-line wet-smoothing on rim. Inside base sharply tooled, join visible on outside. *In*: rd slip burnished horiz on rim, vertically toward base center. Many lime spalls.	
5. Bowl TT 353	61.181 63.224	lt rd br to pk gr to much dk gr	lt gr to dk gr	inner 25% 100%	lms sand?	l,m,s m,s	s s	low	*Ex*: lt rd br on base to dk gr on rim prob due to 2ndary firing. Some n-p protrude, several drag marks in smoothing on bottom, circular forming lines around base end in point, coil seam clear at rim bottom. *In*: rd br to mostly dk gr, horiz burnishing on rim, cross-line on bottom. Pitting mostly on center, 3 forming ridges around rim.	
6. Bowl TT 457	61.179	rd yl		none	lms	l,m,s	s	low	*Ex*: rd br on base, rd slip on rim, many n-p protrude slightly, very few seen. Faint trace of wet-smoothing, horiz burnishing on rim to shoulder where flashing line is finished sharply but very smoothly. *In*: rd slip burnished rim to base as polished, some n-p protrude thru shallow spalling, some pitting.	
7. Bowl TT 450	27.45	yl rd		none	lms	m,s	s	low	*Ex*: lt rd bottom, base, rd slip on rim 95% eroded, some n-p protrude, few pits, circular smoothing around and in base causes some drag marks, burnish around rim is horiz. *In*: rd slip burnished, 80% eroded, lines are horiz on rim, criss-cross on bottom. Few n-p seen, some pits.	
8. Bowl TT 441	26.36 27.45	rd br	rd br to gr	50%	lms	l,m,s	s	med l	*Ex*: lt rd br bottom to lt rd rim, a much faded slip that has also lost its burnish. Flashing line more rounded than Nos. 6, 7, drag marks in smoothing, base center is raised point, ring added, join mostly rounded. *In*: rd slip on rim burnished, rd br in center, never burnished. Some n-p protrude on rim, many pits in center. Slight ridge mid-way down rim.	
9. Bowl Rim & Body	35.68 36.105 48.128	rd	yl rd	+75%	lms	s,f	s	vlow	*Ex* & *In*: rd to br, slip continuously burnished to polish, extremely smooth surf.	
10. Bowl Rim	27.45	rd	yl rd	60%	lms	m,s,?	s	low	*Ex* & *In*: rd slip, burnished with wide horiz strokes, few open spaces on *ex* where bottom & base are neither slipped nor burnished.	
11. Bowl TT 410	61.216	yl br to br	irreg gr br dk gr	50% -100%	lms	l,m,s	s	low	*Ex*: lt rd bottom & base, rd horiz burnished slip on rim, some straw voids in circular wipe lines, ring base and general craftsmanship as in No. 6. *In*: rd one side, rd br other side, all-over slip is burnished. Few n-p protrude, some pitting.	

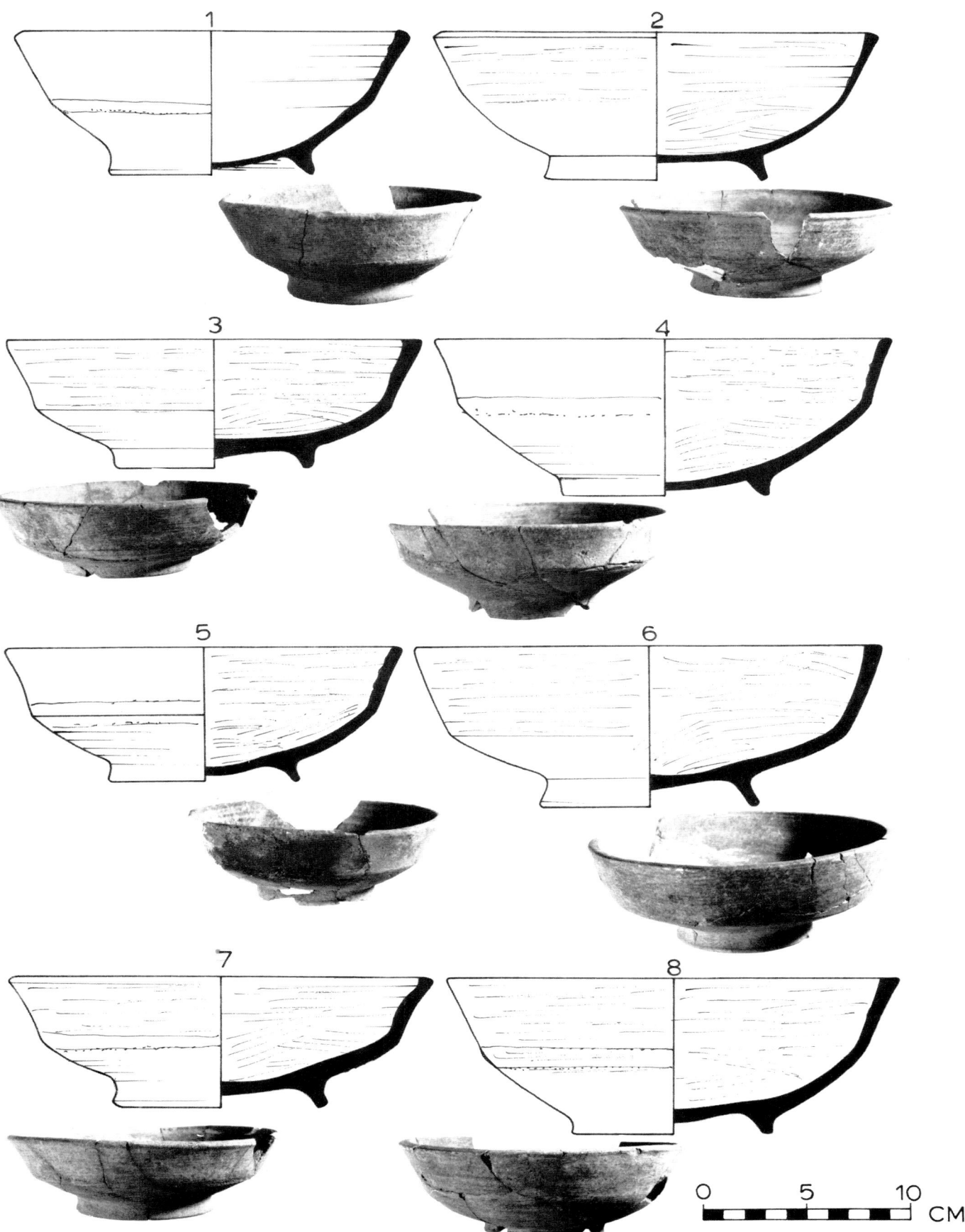

FIG. 46 (CONTINUED)

1. Identification		2. Section							3. Surface	
a.	b.	a.	b. Core		c. Non-Plastics				a. Exterior	b. Interior
Item	Square, Locus Basket	Fabric Color	Color	Extent	Type	Size	Frequency	Density	Color, n-p, voids, forming, finishing features	Same
12. Bowl TT 455	61.178	yl rd to lt br		none	lms cal	m,s m,s	s s	med	*Ex*: rd yl bottom & base, lt rd of rim is faded slip but there is no trace of burnish. Some n-p protrude, covered, few drag marks on shoulder, base ring smoothly finished, *in* base finishing lines spiral in fine lines to center. *In*: rd slip burnished though most of gloss is eroded, 3 forming ridges horiz spaced on rim, bottom pitted in part.	
13. Bowl TT 442	27.45.49	st br to lt br	gr br (base) dk gr (rim)	75% 100%	lms sand	l,m,s m,s	s s	med	*Ex*: dk pk to pk gr, lms spalling on upper shoulder & rim, some n-p protrude, few drag marks, wet-smoothing lines circular to center of base. Flashing ridge. *In*: mostly rd slip burnished, in part of rim dk gr burnished, latter color may be 2ndary because rim surf esp eroded revealing lms n-p. Some shallow spalling.	
14. Bowl TT 452	27.45.49	lt rd	yl rd	-100%	lms	l,m,s	s	low	*Ex*: rd br on base and shoulder, rd slip on rim. Smoothing of bottom and base has produced many drag marks in the circular grooves. Flashing line is thickened. Burnish has disappeared as in *in* which is also covered with eroded rd slip. 3 forming ridges on rim are shallow. Lm encrustation covers most other features.	
15. Bowl Rim & Body	27.45	st br & dk gr	same	each 100%!	lms sand	m,s s	s f	low	*Ex*: 3 of 5 pieces which did not experience severe refiring are rd slipped & burnished rim sherds, the other larger pieces are much darkened, n-p seen esp on bottom which was never burnished. Flashing line clear. *In*: the 2 refired sherds are dk gr, burnish gloss lost, while other 3 sherds are like *ex*.	
16. Bowl Base	27.45	rd y	br	75%	lms	m,s	f	vlow	*Ex*: lt rd br, some n-p seen in drag marks, few protrude. *In*: rd slip burnished, very few pits. Polish.	
17. Bowl Rim	35.68	rd yl		none	lms	f	f	vlow	As No. 9.	

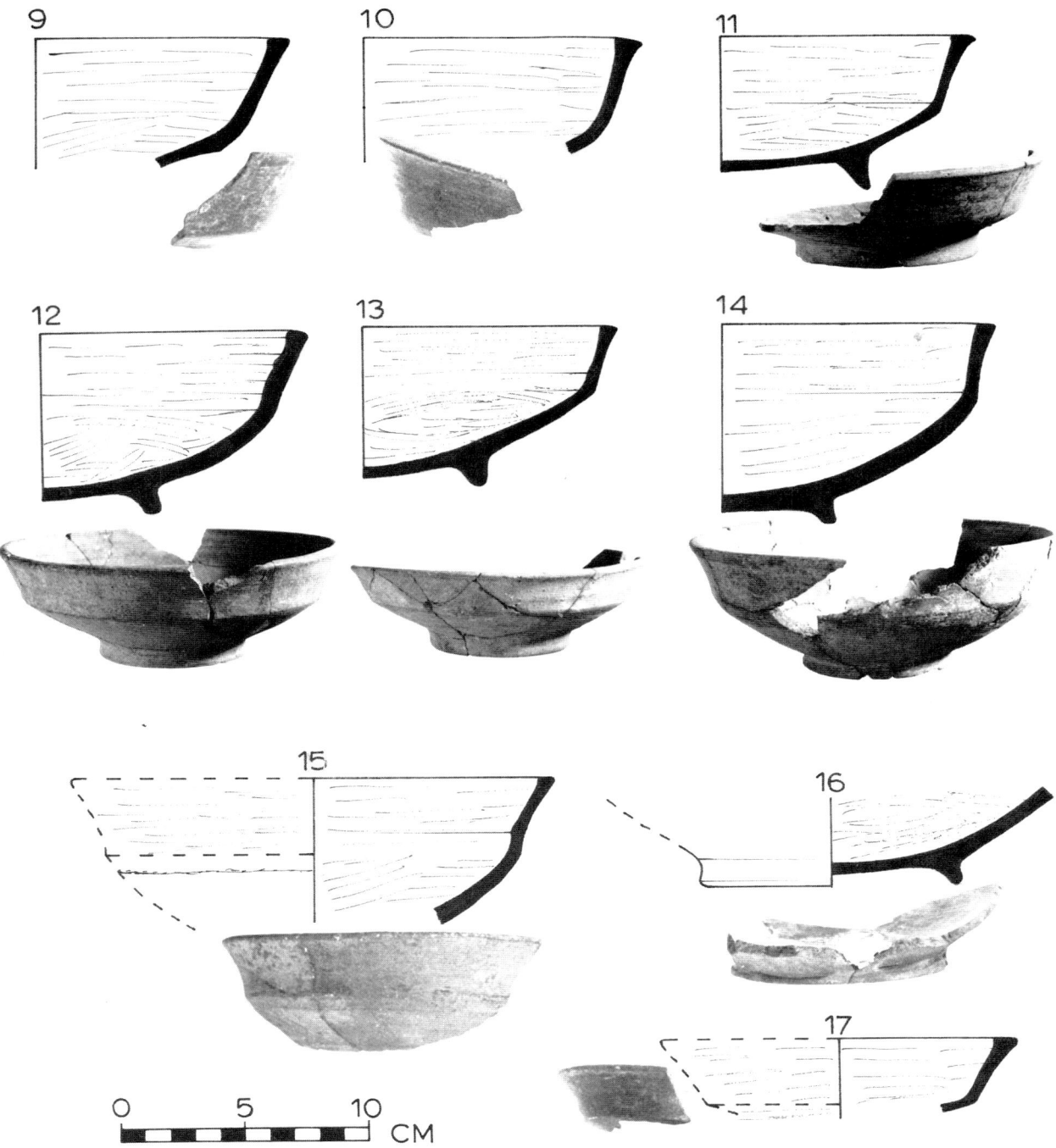

FIG. 47 POTTERY FROM THE CULTIC STRUCTURE (PERIOD IIB)

1. Identification		2. Section							3. Surface	
a.	b.	a.	b. Core		c. Non-Plastics				a. Exterior	b. Interior
Item	Square, Locus Basket	Fabric Color	Color	Extent	Type	Size	Frequency	Density	Color, n-p, voids, forming, finishing features	Same
1. Bowl TT 449	SW 2-7 27.45	yl rd	lt br	80%	lms bas	m,s m	s f	low	*Ex*: rd yl, bottom & base, rd slip on rim burnished. Many n-p protrude, few exposed, smoothing tool used on bottom has 1 cm-wide head, burnish tool narrower. Bar handle applied after rim had been formed & dried, very shallow circular wet-smoothing lines inside and outside base. *In*: rl slip burnished on rim in horiz strokes, vertical strokes toward center but this has largely eroded. N-p's seen thru some pits. On *ex* flashing line sometimes as sharp as on TT 457 (Fig. 46: 6).	
2. Bowl TT 352	61.176	lt br	dk gr lt br	80% only on base none on the rest	lms	s	f	vlow	*Ex*: lt br bottom & base, rd rim is burnished. Some n-p protrude, many exposed by shallow spalling, drag marks on bottom & base, circular finishing bands in base ends in spiral center. Flashing line sharp but smoothed. *In*: rd slip burnished, gloss is lost in much of *in*, burnish strokes consistently lateral. Some similarity to TT 453 (Fig. 46: 3).	
3. Bowl TT 412	61.215	rd yl	rd yl dk gr	rim almost 100% bottom & base	lms	m,s	s	med l	*Ex*: rd slip on rim, to some rd yl on bottom to dk gr most of bottom & base. N-p protrude under rim roughening surf, less so on bottom & base where few lms n-p seen thru spalls. Reg narrow circular turning grooves on bottom, fine line on base, more irreg burnish line on rim slip. *In*: rd slip on rim, turns dk rd br toward center which has been burned. Flashing line gives sharper *in* bend at rim base. *In* bottom burnish lines as No. 2, consistently lateral. Gloss lost in 80% of *in* below rim.	
4. Bowl TT 354	61.196	rd yl	dk gr	none but in 2 places 100% at rim bottom	lms bas	m,s m,s	f f	low	*Ex*: dk pk bottom & base, rd slip on rim. Flashing line more prominent than usual, more like TT 449 (No. 1 above). Tool marks much as No. 3 except that in center of base circular lines end in a spiral point, base is deeper. Forming lines more evident on rim. *In*: rd slip burnished, both much eroded thanks particularly to flaking on the rim. Some pits in center.	
5. Bowl Rim	63.237	pl br to gr	pl br to gr	75-100%	lms	m,s	s	low	*Ex*: lt gr bottom, br slip streaked with dk gr which may be produced by reduction. Effect is alternating br and blackish horiz bands burnished but gloss has disappeared. This is also on *in*. Many n-p protrude on *ex*, exposed on *in*. Fine lines of wet-smoothing visible on top of rim, *ex* bottom.	

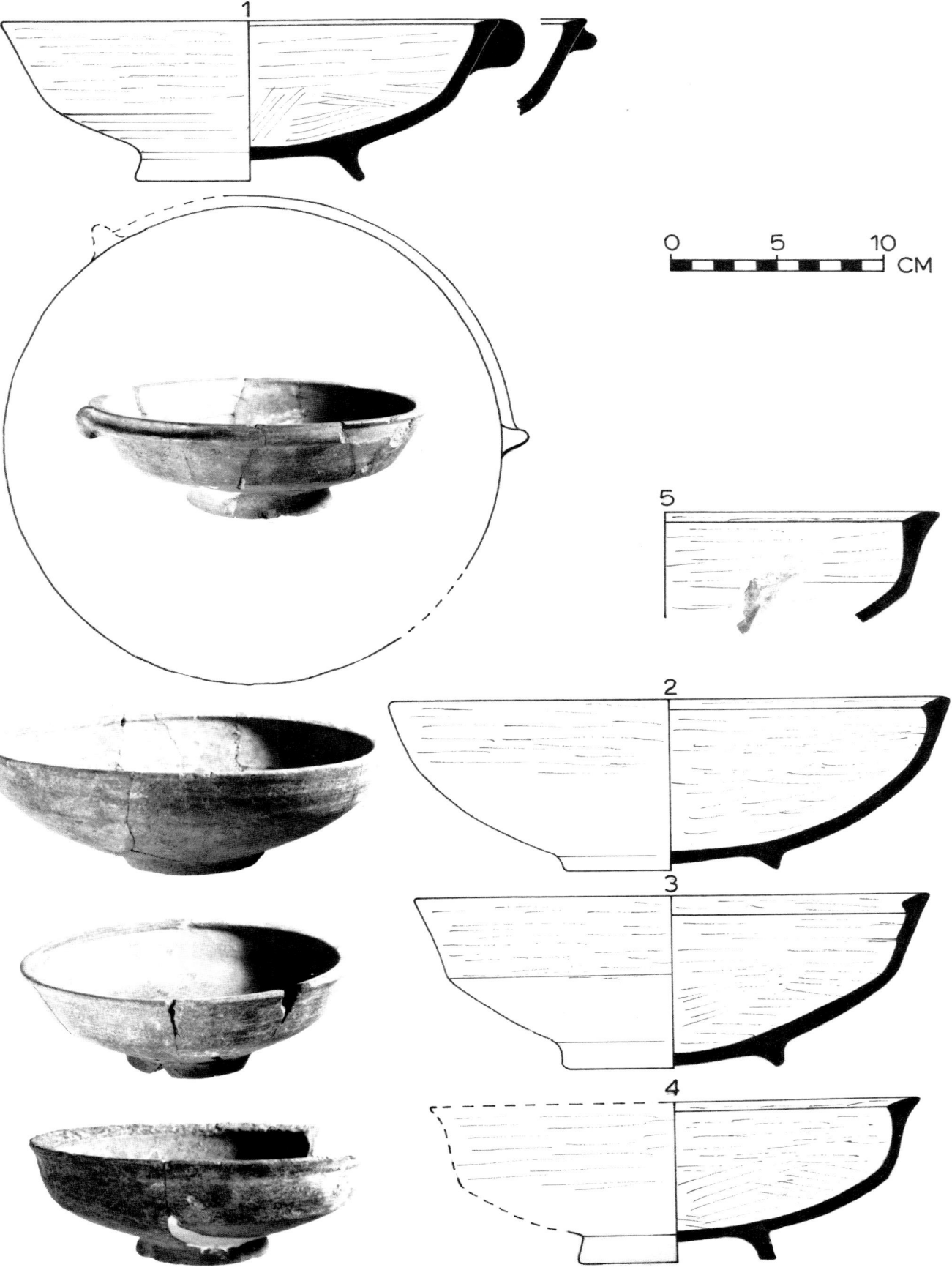

FIG. 48 POTTERY FROM THE CULTIC STRUCTURE (PERIOD IIB)

1. Identification		2. Section						3. Surface	
a. Item	b. Square, Locus Basket	a. Fabric Color	b. Core		c. Non-Plastics			a. Exterior	b. Interior
			Color	Extent	Type	Size	Frequency	Density	Color, n-p, voids, forming, finishing features	Same
	SW 2-7									
1. Bowl TT 486	36.105	rd yl	lt gr	some places ±50%	lms	l,m,s	s-m	med l	Ex: dk pk bottom, yl rd slip on rim, burnished. Reg circular forming lines meet at very slightly raised center. Pits, drag marks on bottom. On horiz burnished rim n-p embedded. In: yl rd slip burnished rim to bottom. Strokes on rim are mostly horiz, on bottom net-like. Some n-p seen in shallow lime spalls, pits on bottom. Ex flashing line in the tradition of Figs. 46-7.	
2. Bowl TT 448	26.40	gr	gr (where available)	-100%	lms	s,f	f	vlow	Ex: lt rd br bottom to yl rd slip on rim mostly turned gr. Few n-p embedded, visible, reg circular forming ridges center inside slight depression surrounded by very shallow rounded ring 3 cms across. Horiz burnish of rim begins at clear flashing line. In: yl rd slip on rim is burnished, in slip on bottom much eroded, as is burnish, pitted.	
3. Bowl TT 443	26.36-40	br	lt gr	-10%	lms sand	m,s,f m,s	m s	med	Ex: lt rd br, many small n-p protrude, many tiny pits, drag marks in reg circular forming lines end at slightly raised & flattened base in spiral. Flashing line at rim base is esp. crude. In: rd slip horiz burnished on rim, squared patterned on bottom, as TT 453, 455 (Fig. 46: 3, 12).	
4. Bowl Rim & Bottom	27.45	dk br dk gr		none 100% rim corner	lms shell	m,s l	s f	med	Ex & In: striking similarity to No. 2 except on ex base center more rounded, as is flashing line, walls heavier near bottom.	
5. Bowl Rim & Bottom	27.49	rd yl	br gr	100% 75% rim & bottom patch	lms cal	m,s,f s,f	s f	med l	Ex: dk pk, n-p protrude, some limes spalls, drag marks in circular forming/finishing lines on bottom, flashing line at rim base is sharp. In: rd yl slip, burnish has lost gloss, erosion at rim reveals n-ps, also many covered.	
6. Bowl Rim	26.98	dk gr!	dk gr	-100%	lms	s,f	s	vlow	Ex: wk rd on small bit of bottom preserved, rd slip burnished in separated horiz strokes on rim. Few pits. In: same except that bottom also burnished.	
7. Bowl Rim	27.45	st br	st br	100%	lms bas	m,s,f l	s vf	low	Ex: lt rd on bottom unslipped, rim is rd slipped, flashing line clear. Some pits. In: rd slipped & burnished, many pits, spalls.	
8. Bowl Rim	48.119	lt rd br to br	vlt gr	25%	lms sand	l,m,s m,s	s f	med	Ex & In: same as No. 3.	
9. Bowl Rim	35.68	yl rd		none	lms	m,s	f	vlow	Ex: lt rd br bottom, rd slip burnished on rim, sharp dividing line at flashing point, reg fine-line combing has some drag marks in its circular grooves, burnishing is continuous as on in: which is rd burnished, encrustation covers details.	
10. Bowl Rim & Bottom	36.99	rd br		none	lms	l,m,s	s	low	Ex & In: colors are as in No. 9. Differences are on ex: bottom a bit darker br, burnish covers flashing line which is less neatly and sharply edged. In burnish is identical.	
11. Bowl Rim & Bottom	48.119	yl rd		none	lms	m,s	s	low	As No. 10	
12. Bowl Rim & Bottom	27.41	lt rd	rd br mixed w/dk gr	+75%	lms	m,s,f	m	med	Ex: lt rd br bottom, rd on rim above even flashing line horiz burnished. Many lms spalls, bottom has shallow circular finish lines. In: rd slip burnished, gloss lost but many lime spalls as on ex.	
13. Bowl Rim & Bottom	26.36-40	(In all respects identical with No. 12)							Add gr to bottom due to 2ndary burning.	
14. Bowl Rim	33.66	st br		none	lms sand	m,s s,f	f s	low	As No. 10	
15. Bowl TT 447	27.45	rd	dk gr	50-100%	lms bas	s,f s,f	f f	vlow	Ex & In: rd slip burnished to high polish on eggshell thin body probably moulded. Burnish is so complete that no forming traces remain except for slight flashing line at bend to rim. Irreg dk gr due to 2ndary firing probably related to use. See Fig. 39: 4.	

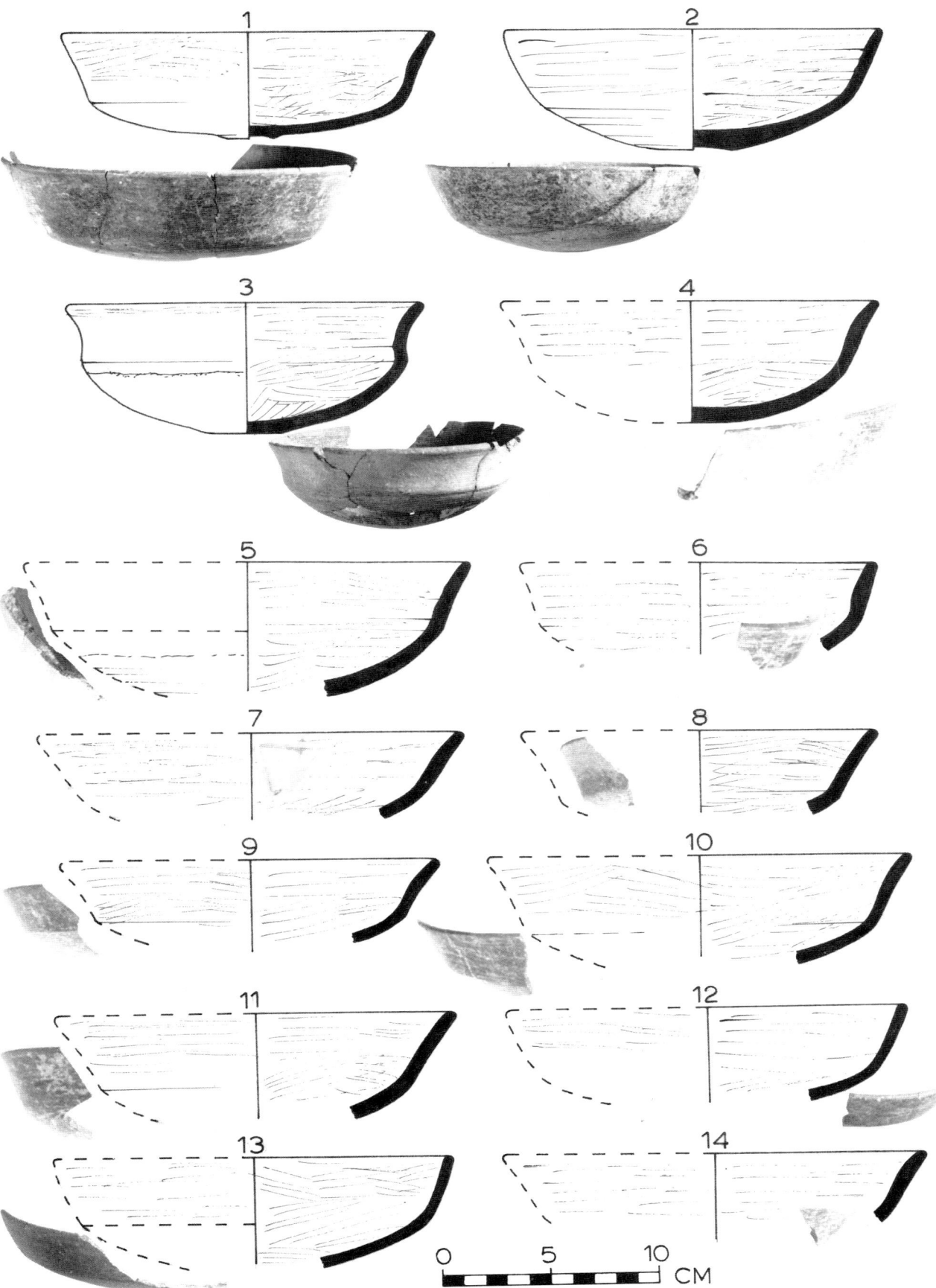

FIG. 48 (CONTINUED)

1. Identification		2. Section							3. Surface	
a.	b.	a.	b. Core		c. Non-Plastics				a. Exterior	b. Interior
Item	Square, Locus Basket	Fabric Color	Color	Extent	Type	Size	Fre-quency	Density	Color, n-p, voids, forming, finishing features	Same
16. Bowl TT 444	27.45	(In all respects identical with No. 15)								
17. Bowl TT 463	61.200				(As No. 15)				*In* has heavy lm encrustation, *ex* some. Burnishing is more grooved perhaps due to loss of gloss in 2ndary experience.	
18. Bowl Rim & Bottom	27.45				(As No. 15)					
19. Bowl Rim & Bottom	27.45				(As No. 15)					

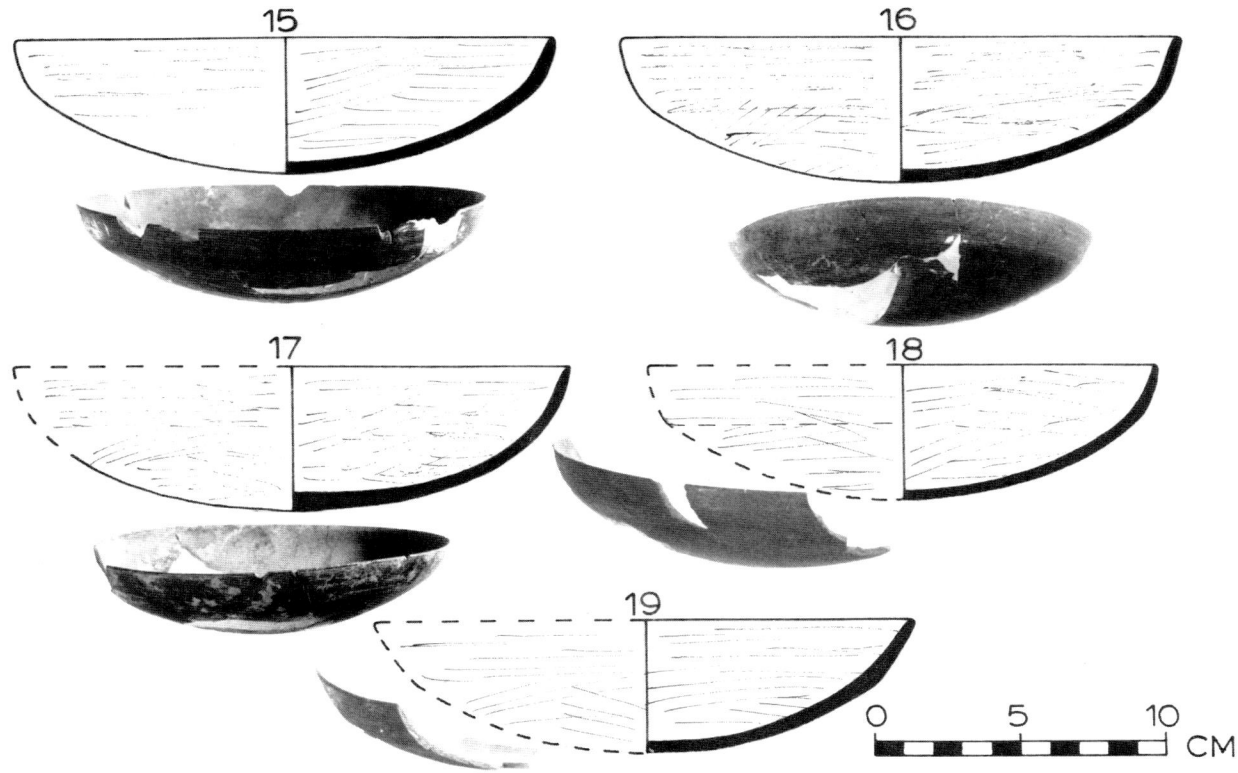

FIG. 49 POTTERY FROM THE CULTIC STRUCTURE (PERIOD IIB)

1. Identification		2. Section						3. Surface	
a.	b.	a.	b. Core		c. Non-Plastics			a. Exterior	b. Interior
Item	Square, Locus Basket	Fabric Color	Color	Extent	Type	Size	Frequency	Density	Color, n-p, voids, forming, finishing features	Same
1. Cook Pot Rim & Body	SW 2-7 59.146 61.208	yl rd	br	50-100%	cal	s.f	m	med h	*Ex*: rd br coated with lm in & around rim. Few pits & very few n-p seen. Flashing line mid-shoulder covered with excess clay but line is clean. Smoothing lines irreg & faint. *In*: rd br to br, the gr being due to use. Many tiny pits, some chips but very few n-p seen. Fine lines of wet-smoothing are horiz on rim & shoulder, vert on bottom.	
2. Cook Pot Rim	26.36	yl rd	br lt gr	100% patch is 50% inner	cal bas	s.f s	m s	med h	*Ex & In*: the same as No. 1 except that there are more n-p protruding on *ex* rim, more n-p seen thru pits *in*. On *ex* thin line under inner side of rim.	
3. Cook Pot Rim & Body	28.50 33.66	(In all respects identical to No. 1)							Finish lines a bit more crude than No. 1: flashing not as smooth *in* & *ex*; *ex* of flange of rim irreg finished, from sharper edge to rounded with overlap below.	

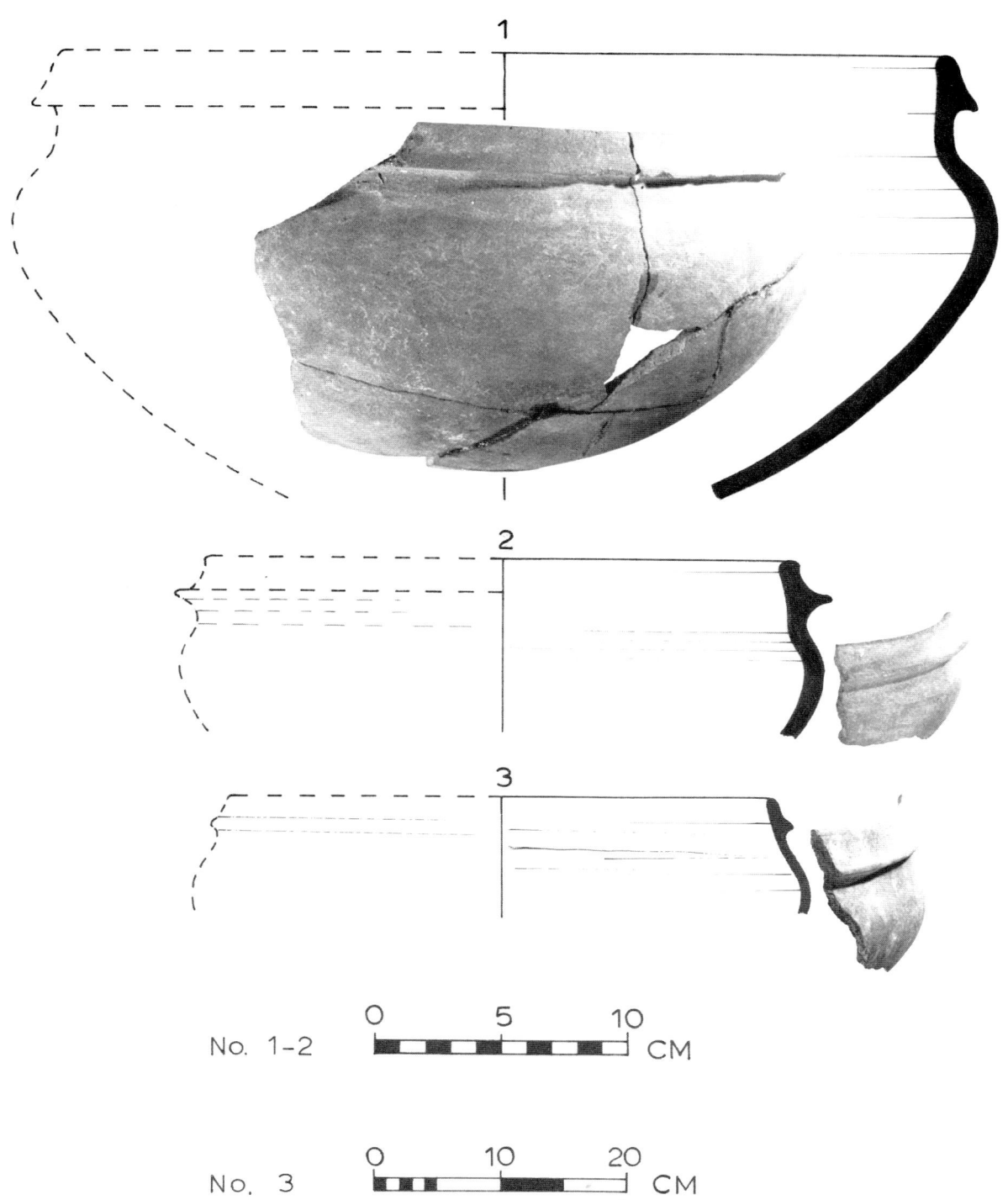

FIG. 50 POTTERY FROM THE CULTIC STRUCTURE (PERIOD IIB)

1. Identification		2. Section							3. Surface	
a.	b.	a.	b. Core		c. Non-Plastics				a. Exterior	b. Interior
Item	Square, Locus Basket	Fabric Color	Color	Extent	Type	Size	Frequency	Density	Color, n-p, voids, forming, finishing features	Same
1. Cook Pot TT 456	SW 2-7 60.160	yl rd to rd br	dk gr but often rd br	±50% 100%	cal	m,s,f	m	med l	Ex: rd br to gr due to use. Many tiny n-p protrude, straw voids on & around handle, some pits, wet-smoothing marks irreg over body. Flashing line mid-body generally smoothed, sharp in places. In: same as ex except that forming ridges prominent at body and neck flashing points.	
2. Cook Pot TT 472	57.226	rd br to br	gr	none inner 75%	cal	m,s,f	m	med l	Ex: rd gr to rd br, some pits, more voids on handle than elsewhere, some n-p protrude under surf heavy carbon deposit on shattered bottom, forming ridges clearest In: dk rd gr to gr, flashing lines at top and bottom of shoulder, smoothing lines, few pits, n-p.	
3. Cook Pot TT 65	27.41	yl rd to rd br	gr	none (rim) 50% (rim)	cal	s,f	m	low	Ex: rd br to rd gr to gr due to carbon deposit. For the rest see No. 2. Bottom in and ex rounded, prob in mould.	

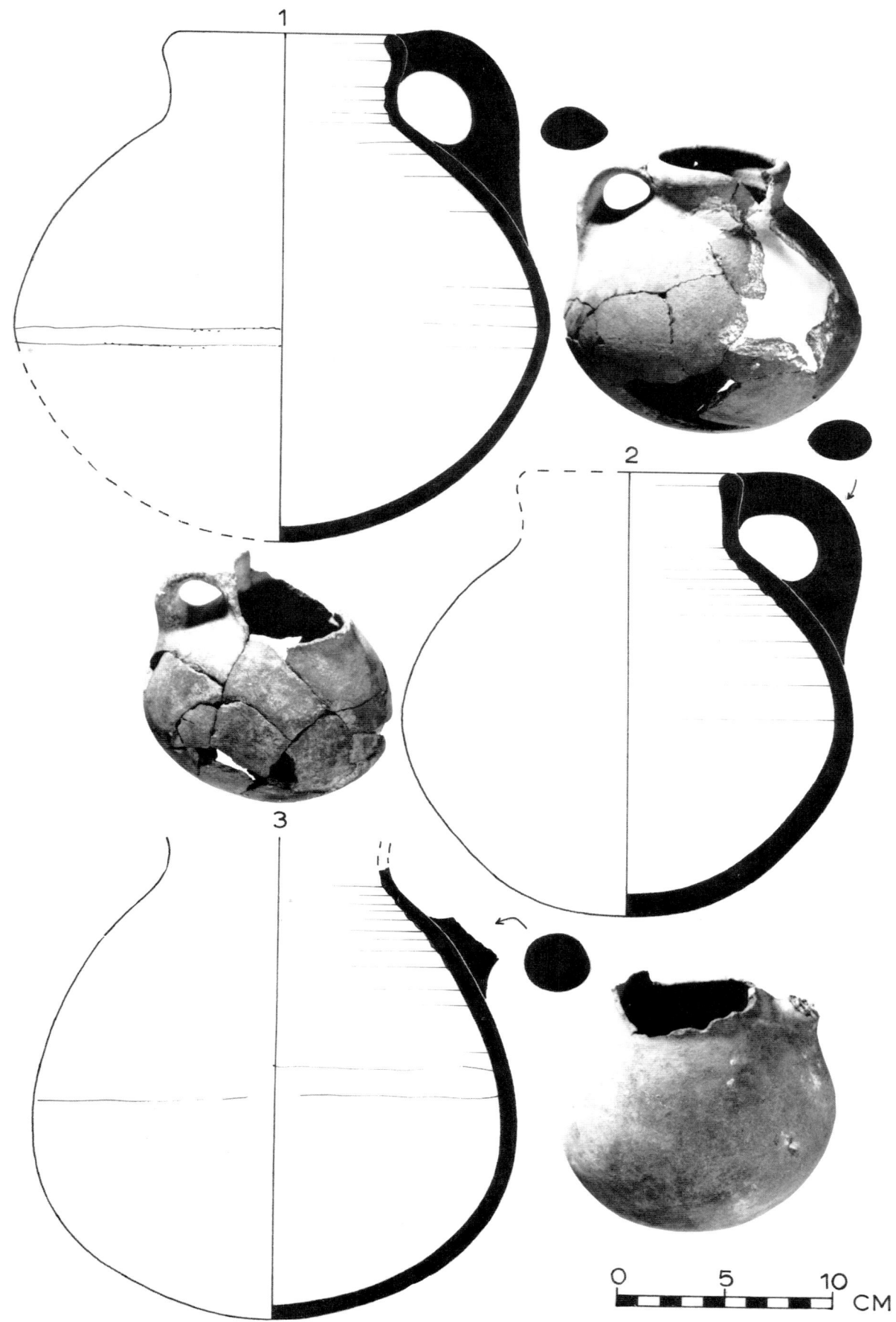

FIG. 51 POTTERY FROM THE CULTIC STRUCTURE (PERIOD IIB)

1. Identification		2. Section							3. Surface	
a.	b.	a.	b. Core		c. Non-Plastics				a. Exterior	b. Interior
Item	Square, Locus Basket	Fabric Color	Color	Extent	Type	Size	Frequency	Density	Color, n-p, voids, forming, finishing features	Same
1. Lamp TT 89	SW 2-7 27.45	lt rd br		none	lms	m,s,f	s	med l	*Ex*: rd br, many n-p protrude, wet-smoothing caused opening near lip, also some cracking. *In*: rd br, fine smoothing lines on edge rim, as also *ex*. Circular smoothing lines in dish, 3 pits, breaks at indentation near lip. Not used.	
2. Lamp TT 473	61.180	st br	gr br	none (rim) outer 75% (base)	lms	l,m,s	m	med	*Ex*: lt rd, many n-p embedded, some spalling, smoothing lines under rim, center groove, straw voids. *In*: lt br to lt rd br, otherwise as *ex*, *in* smoothing lateral, not as No. 1. No evidence of use.	
3. Censer TT 64	27.41	yl rd	dk gr (see under two legs)	-100%	lms	l,m,s	s	med l	*Ex*: rd yl but around top gr deposit. Lms n-p on surf all over, embedded horiz smoothing around neck and body, bottom is crudely criss-crossed, more pitted than elsewhere. Straw voids. *In*: color as *ex*, smoothing around rim, reg forming ridges to spiral twist at center.	
4. Stand TT 351	61.184	yl rd		none	cal	m,s,f	m	med l	*Ex*: lt rd br, many tiny n-p protrude, few larger lime spalls, circular smoothing caused drag marks, flashing line at level of bottom of window, also at top of window. *In*: lt rd br, n-p seen on rim, smoothing lines very faint but forming ridges inside stand are deep, windows cut in, slight bit of excess clay only *ex*.	

TT 64   TT 351

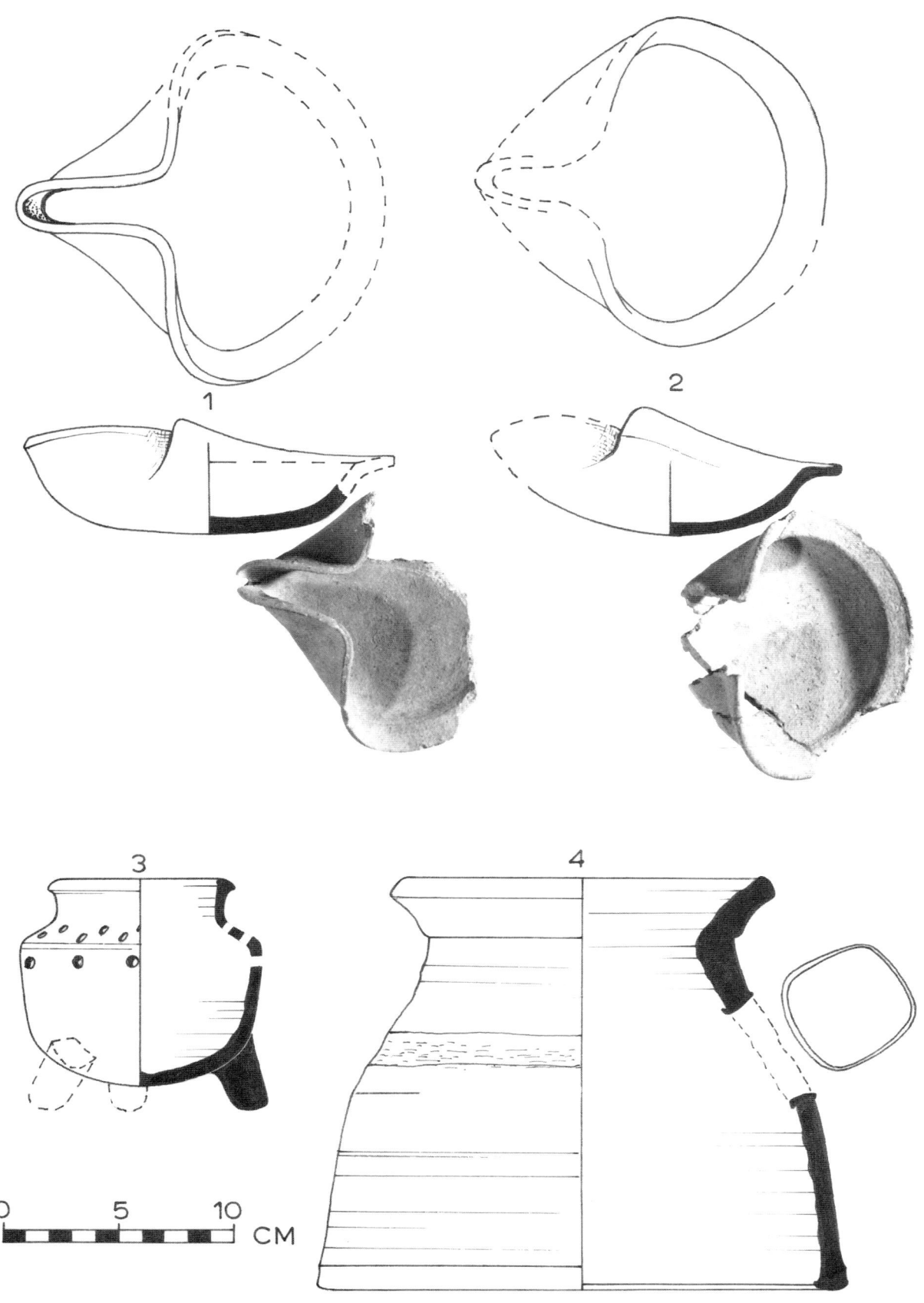

FIG. 52 POTTERY FROM CISTERN 69 (PERIOD IIB)

1. Identification		2. Section						3. Surface	
a. Item	b. Square, Locus Basket	a. Fabric Color	b. Core		c. Non-Plastics			a. Exterior	b. Interior
			Color	Extent	Type	Size	Frequency	Density	Color, n-p, voids, forming, finishing features	Same
1. Jar Rim	SW 2-8 171.366	lt rd	lt br to gr	±50%	lms	l,m,s	m	med l	*Ex*: dk pk, many n-p protrude, some spalling, fine line wet-smoothng, also on *In*: where color & n-p the same as *ex*. Some irreg smoothing down rim lip opens surf, exposes n-p.	
2. Jar Rim	171.366	lt rd	lt br to lt gr	±50%	lms	m,s,f	f	low	*Ex & In*: lt rd, some n-p protrude, some exposed, fine line wet-smoothing on neck but criss-cross below on shoulder. 2 flashing lines clearer on *in* at base and top of shoulder, forming ridges on neck are shallow & smoothed, lm encrustation, bits of excess clay adhere to *in*.	
3. Bowl TT 1855	163.326	st br	lt gr	none 50% (base)	lms bas sand?	l,m,s m,s m,s	s s m	med h	*Ex*: rd yl, many n-p protrude, more above first flashing line below handle, some pits and drag marks in circular finishing lines from handle to base center which ends in a spiral. Grooved flashing line below handle, 2nd lines with sharp *ex* edge just above handle base. *In*: rd yl, many n-p seen thru spalling, shallow circular finishing from rim to base where it ends in grooved circle. 2 vlarge n-p exposed.	
4. Bowl Rim & Bottom	156.320	lt rd	dk gr	90%	lms	m,s	s	low	*Ex*: lt rd bottom to rd slip burnished on rim and all of *in*. cm-wide turning bands on bottom expose some n-p, few drag marks, burnish horiz and mostly continuous, *in* is the same except bottom is a bit more criss-crossed. Flashing line is neatly finished.	
5. Bowl Rim & Bottom	156.320	yl rd	dk gr	±75%	lms	l,m,s	m	med h	*Ex*: lt rd br bottom with a bit of lt rd slip on rim mostly eroded. Circular turning bands on bottom produce some drag marks, many n-p exposed, flashing line at rim bottom. *In*: rd slip burnished, horiz on rim, bottom box burnished. Many n-p seen thru shallow spalling.	
6. Bowl Rim to Base	171.384	dk br	dk gr	75%	lms	l,m,s	s	med l	*Ex*: dk pk much grayed by carbon deposit, Many n-p protrude, many drag marks due to turning, also on bottom of base, irreg circular grooves. Fine-line smoothing on rim. *In*: rd br slip rim to base but only fraction of gloss remains on upper rim. Bottom has carbon deposit.	
7. Bowl Rim to Base	170.350	rd yl	lt gr br	25%	lms	s	f	vlow	*Ex*: lt rd slip burnished in criss-cross pattern, partly eroded, drag marks more common than exposed embedded n-p, some pits. Button base is added clay ring, seal line at base visible. *In*: lt rd, slip & burnished 95% eroded, dk gr carbon deposits in center. Possible flashing just below rim.	
8. Bowl Rim & Base	156.320	br	lt gr	-40% mid-bottom	lms bas	l,m,s m,s	s s	med	*Ex & In*: same as No. 5 except that lt rd slip on *ex* rim better preserved and enough of center bottom to show 3 deeply grooved concentric circles.	
9. Bowl TT 1854	175.406	lt br		none	lms bas	m,s,f m,s	s s	med	*Ex*: rd yl, many n-p embedded on surf, many pits, drag marks on bottom, circular smoothing lines are faint, less so on rim, base is joined ring, sharply edged, ends in circular twist in center. Flashing line at carination. *In*: rd yl, n-p & smoothing as *ex*, base slightly cupped, shallow forming depressions in upper rim half.	

3 8 9
TT 1855 TT 1854

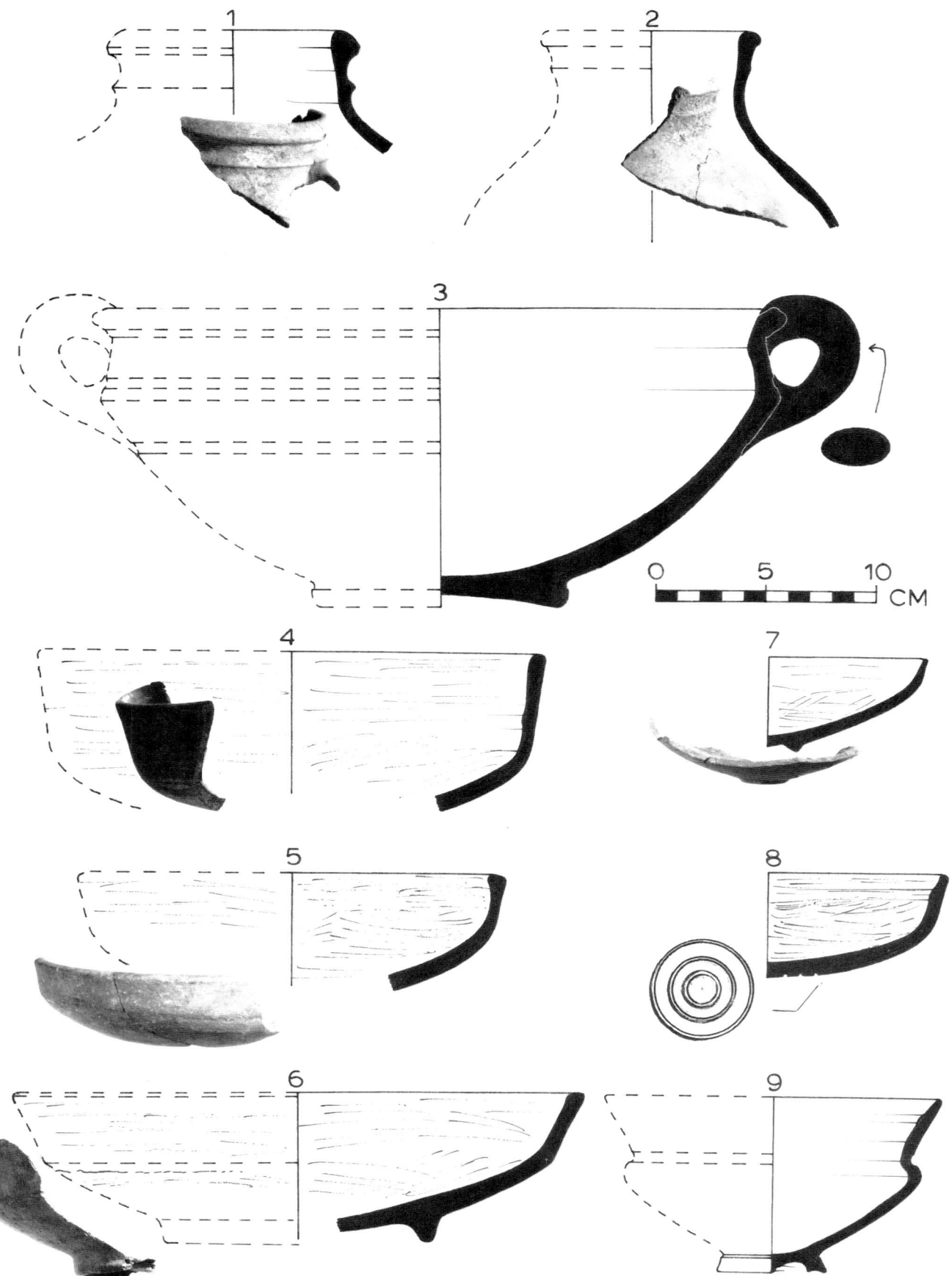

FIG. 53 POTTERY FROM CISTERN 69 (PERIOD IIB)

1. Identification		2. Section						3. Surface	
a.	b.	a.	b. Core		c. Non-Plastics			a. Exterior	b. Interior
Item	Square, Locus Basket	Fabric Color	Color	Extent	Type	Size	Frequency	Density	Color, n-p, voids, forming, finishing features	Same
1. Cook Pot Rim & Body	SW 2-8 171.390	yl rd	dk gr	75%	cal	m,s,f	m	med l	*Ex*: rd br, some n-p protrude, only few visible, smoothing on shoulder & rim is faint, below flashing line turning bands give surf irreg appearance, carbon deposit on bottom. Base of rim sharply tooled. *In*: rd br, many n-p protrude, some seen, flashing line irreg grooved, wet-smoothed in fine line horiz strokes, sometimes irreg, slight depression just inside *ex* rim flange.	
2. Cook Pot Rim	156.313		Identical with No. 1						Same as No. 1 with exception that lms n-p break thru surf giving salty appearance, *in* is pk gr while *ex* still is more rd br.	
3. Cook Pot Rim	156.314		Identical with No. 1						Same as No. 1 but color is lt rd br, *ex* rim flange deeply grooved also on side and above, eroded rim reveals many n-p just under the surf.	
4. Cook Pot Rim & Body	156.313		Identical with No. 1						Same as No. 1	
5. Chalice TT 1853	156.313	lt rd	gr	inner 90% in bowl 75% base	lms	l,m,s	s-m	med	*Ex*: lt rd (slip?), many n-p protrude, at surf, some pits, wet-smoothing, flashing line below bowl. *In bowl*: heavy carbon deposit, circular smoothing around rim, lateral across bowl bottom. Slight depression half-way up to rim bend from base center. *In base*: same as *ex* except that surf is more rough due to protruding n-p, throwing ridges up from very center which shows compression twist.	
6. Chalice Base	156.313	rd yl	gr to lt gr	± 50%	lms cal	l,m,s m,s	m s	med h	*Ex & In*: rd yl, many n-p seen thru shallow spalling some embedded, wet-smoothing circular has left some drag marks, flashing lines clear on *in* where base begins to narrow, above 2nd ridge in drawing. *In* surf becomes rougher above this point.	
7. Lamp Rim, Lip & Base	171.401	yl rd	dk gr	75%	lms	l,m,s	s	med l	*Ex*: yl rd, carbon on lip, many n-p embedded, seen, many cracking fissures, fine-line smoothing only around edge. *In*: same color, other features same except less cracking, fewer n-p seen.	

5

TT 1853

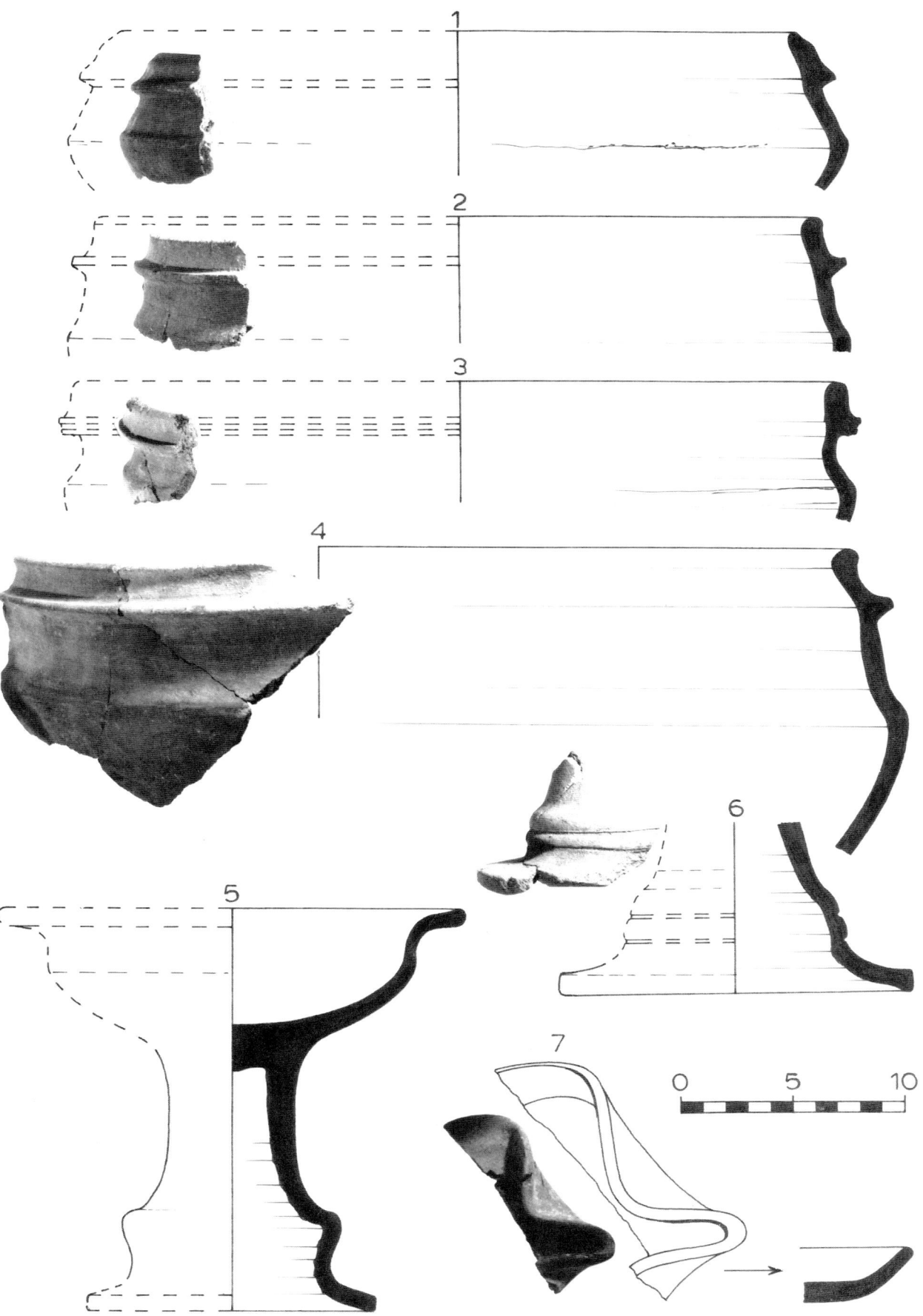

FIG. 54 POTTERY FROM CISTERN 69 (PERIOD IIB)

1. Identification		2. Section						3. Surface	
a.	b.	a.	b. Core		c. Non-Plastics			a. Exterior	b. Interior
Item	Square, Locus Basket	Fabric Color	Color	Extent	Type	Size	Frequency	Density	Color, n-p, voids, forming, finishing features	Same
1. Offering Stand TT 1830	SW 2-8 156.320	rd yl	dk gr	+50%	lms	l,m,s	s	med l	*Ex*: lt rd, many n-p protrude, some embedded, horiz wipe lines cause drag marks, esp in lower part below 2nd line of leaves, traces of two tabs at very top ridge, straw voids on existing tabs, ridge above base has untrimmed excess clay on both top & bottom edge. Tabs applied very much as handles on jars. *In*: lt rd, n-p as *ex* but forming ridges more prominent, esp two deep flashing lines behind ridge above base on *ex* and behind 2nd line of tab leaves. Entire surf is covered with the very fine horiz lines associated with wet-smoothing.	

TT 1830

FIG. 55 POTTERY FROM CISTERN 74 (MOSTLY PERIOD IIB)

1. Identification		2. Section						3. Surface	
a.	b.	a.	b. Core		c. Non-Plastics			a. Exterior	b. Interior
Item	Square, Locus Basket	Fabric Color	Color	Extent	Type	Size	Frequency	Density	Color, n-p, voids, forming, finishing features	Same
1. Jar Rim	SW 6-2 74 Cist. I No.44	lt rd	pk gr	75%	grog bas lms shell	l,m m,s m,s,f	s s s	med h	*Ex*: lt br gr, many lime spalls and pits yet few n-p seen, smoothing is crude perhaps because clay was too plastic; some dripping. *In*: pk gr but otherwise much the same.	
2. Jar TT 380	74.163	rd yl	dk gr	± 50%	lms	l,m,s	s	low-med l	*Ex*: dk pk, many large n-p exposed on surf, horiz wiping interrupted by vert swipes, considerable erosion & cracking reveals many lms n-p just below surf. Prominent depression somewhat below handle is flashing line, less clear on *in*. Forming ridges as irreg shallow depressions can be traced from top to base, even more clear on the *in* where the ridges spiral down to a center twist. Some lms deposit.	

TT 380

180

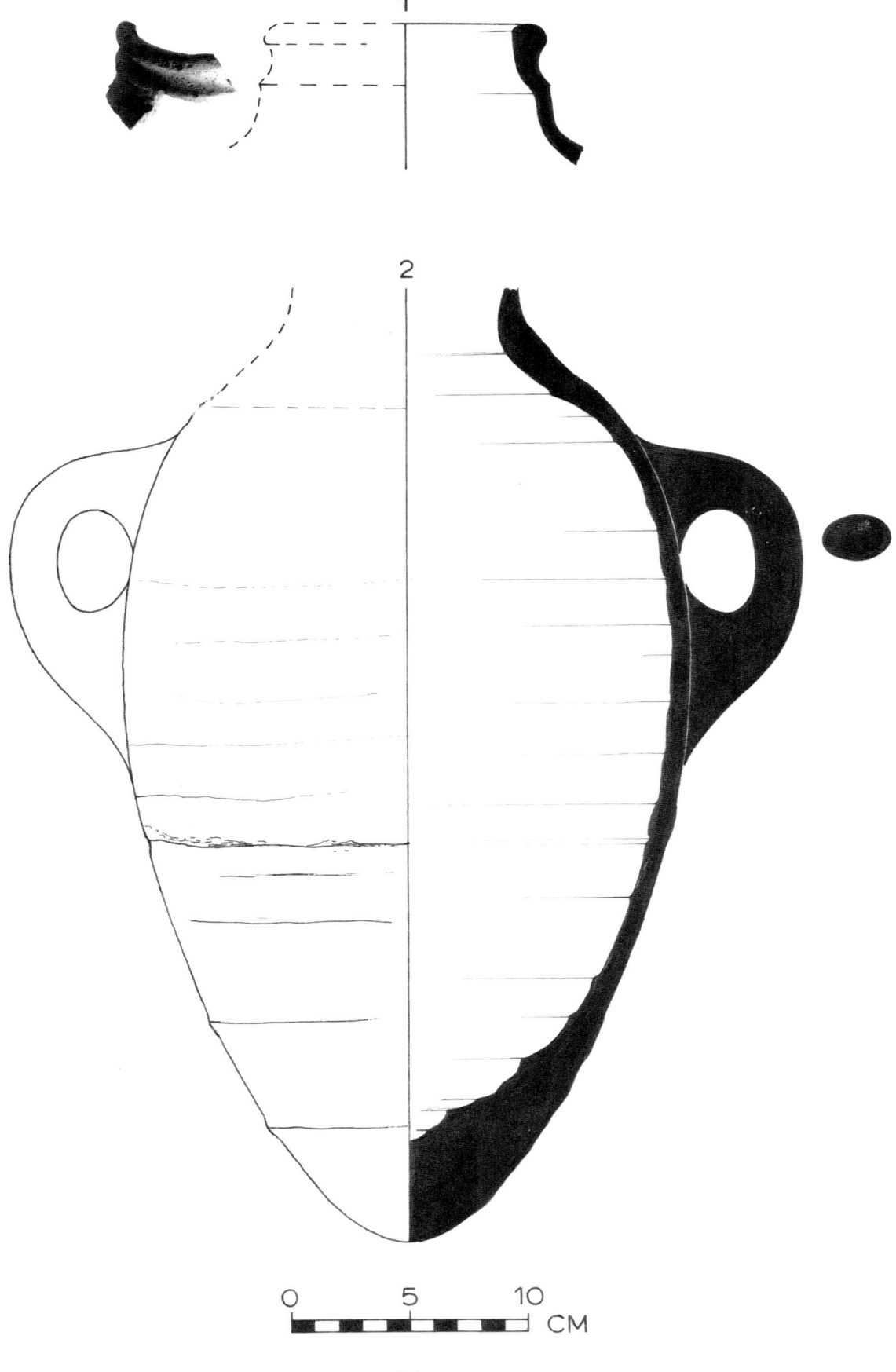

FIG. 56 POTTERY FROM CISTERN 74 (MOSTLY PERIOD IIB)

1. Identification		2. Section							3. Surface	
a. Item	b. Square, Locus Basket	a. Fabric Color	b. Core		c. Non-Plastics				a. Exterior	b. Interior
			Color	Extent	Type	Size	Frequency	Density	Color, n-p, voids, forming, finishing features	Same
1. Jar Base	SW 6-2 74. Cist 1 No. 1	st br	dk gr	inner 75%	lms	l,m,s	s	med	*Ex*: dk pk to pk gr, many n-p protrude, many pits, crude wipe lines cover entire surf, appears much like TT 380 (Fig. 55: 2), 2 flashing lines appear as grooves irreg. *In*: pk gr, deep forming ridges esp in lower half, bottom fill is deeply fissured. N-p appear as on *ex*.	
2. Jar Base	same No. 22	rd yl	lt br	+50%	lms	l,m,s	s-m	med h	*Ex*: rd yl, many n-p seen thru shallow spalling, surf smoothed but horiz fine lines hardly visible. Forming ridges also faint. Center of base has been neatly perforated with chips on. *In*: horiz smoothing lines more visible, many n-p as *ex*, center bottom has been smoothed criss-cross. No. 4 below is approx likeness.	
3. Jar Base	same No. 21	lt rd br	gr	+50%	lms	l,m,s	s	med l	*Ex*: dk pk, many large n-p on surf embedded, shallow wipe lines give firm smooth surf, but *In*: dk pk, deep regularly spaced grooves of forming ridges, flashing line just above base. At this point walls thicken considerably.	
4. Jar Base	same No. 20	rd yl	gr	±50%	lms	l,m,s	s	low	*Ex*: dk pk, several large n-p break surf, fine wet-smoothing lines end up in swirl at center base, some covered n-p protrude. *In*: dk pk, forming ridges cover preserved element, ends in spiral to base center which is broken, long wipe marks. Flashing depression near top of preserved feature.	

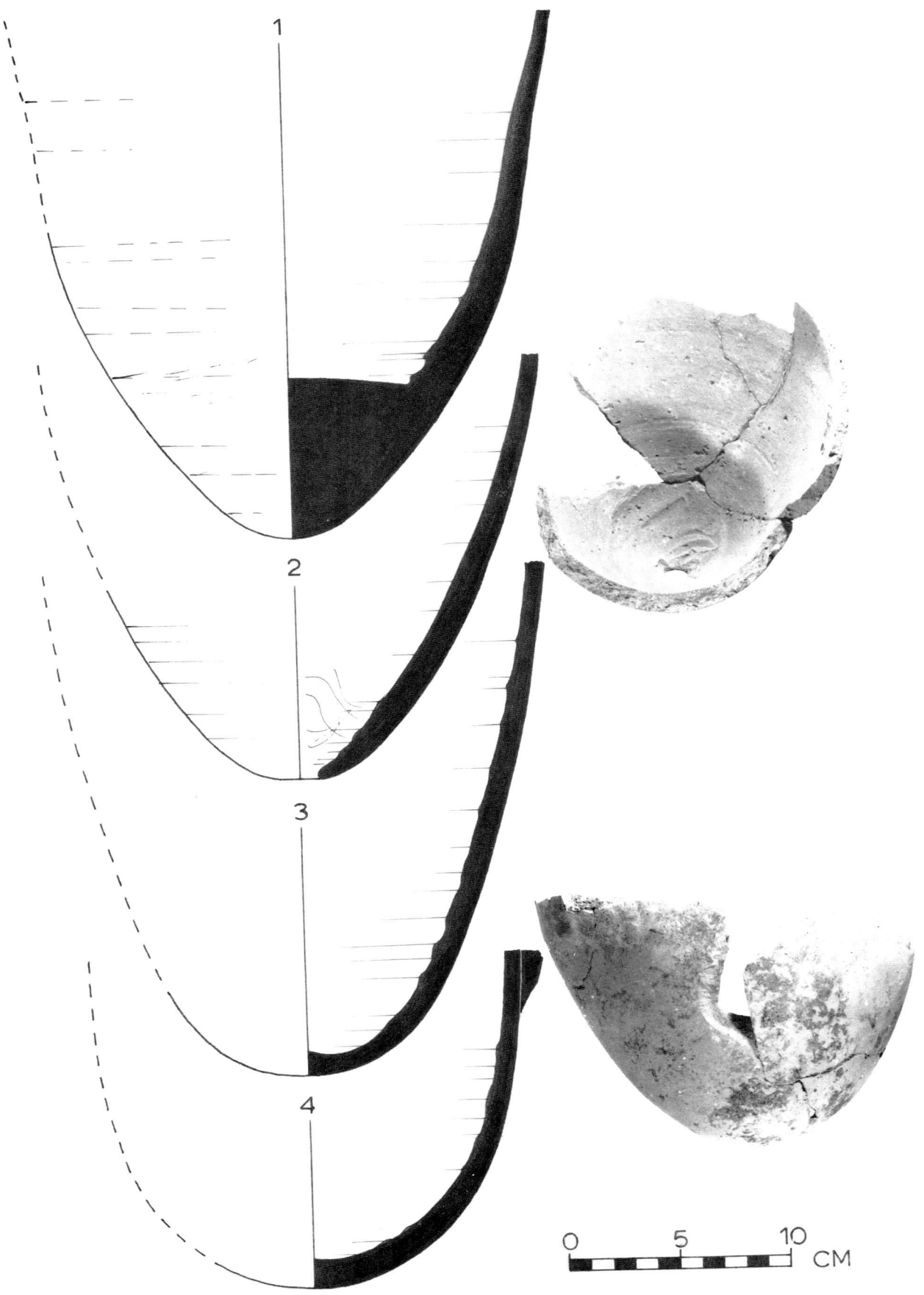

FIG. 57 POTTERY FROM CISTERN 74 (MOSTLY PERIOD IIB)

1. Identification		2. Section						3. Surface	
a.	b.	a.	b. Core		c. Non-Plastics			a. Exterior	b. Interior
Item	Square, Locus Basket	Fabric Color	Color	Extent	Type	Size	Frequency	Density	Color, n-p, voids, forming, finishing features	Same
1. Jar TT 383	SW 6-2 74. Cist 1 Bas 165	lt rd br	dk gr	none (rim) 50% (handle)	lms	l,m,s	s	low	*Ex*: lt rd br slip to dk pk. Some n-p protrude, covered, many pop-outs, pits, turning lines on lower body cause some drag marks, base closed with disk base, circular forming ridges are faint, wipe marks cut across. Flashing line below handle marked by more pits and drag marks than usual, body bends upward & inward. 2nd flashing line is at level of top of handles in form of raised ridge as wall bends toward absent neck. Surf above midpoint is smoother than below. *In*: blackish spots on bottom half walls, between spout and R handle on *ex* are two holes penetrating from *ex* to *in*; on *in* at line of 2nd hole is a groove. To the L of the spout is another deep chip, as around the holes, the beginning of a long crack reaching to the neck, located on the *ex* by a small chip.	
2. Jar TT 1856	same No. 27	rd br	gr	inner 50-100%	lms	vl,m, s,f	m	high	*Ex*: very little lt rd slip remains, most of surf is pk gr. Many protruding lime spalls giving very marred, scabby appearance; the disk base has many straw voids, from crude smoothing, only faint traces of fine-line surf smoothing remain, more on the neck. *In*: dk pk, reg narrow horiz forming lines begin at mid-point, apparent flashing line just below handle on *ex*.	

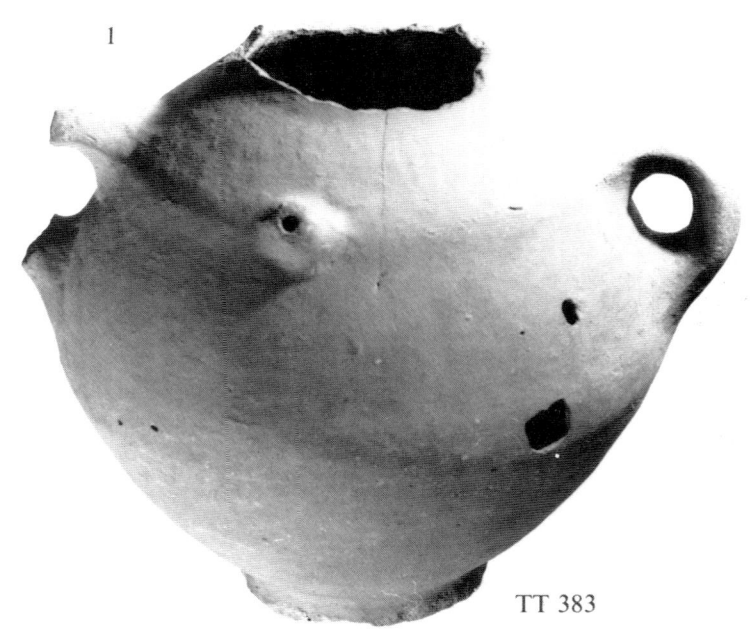

1

TT 383

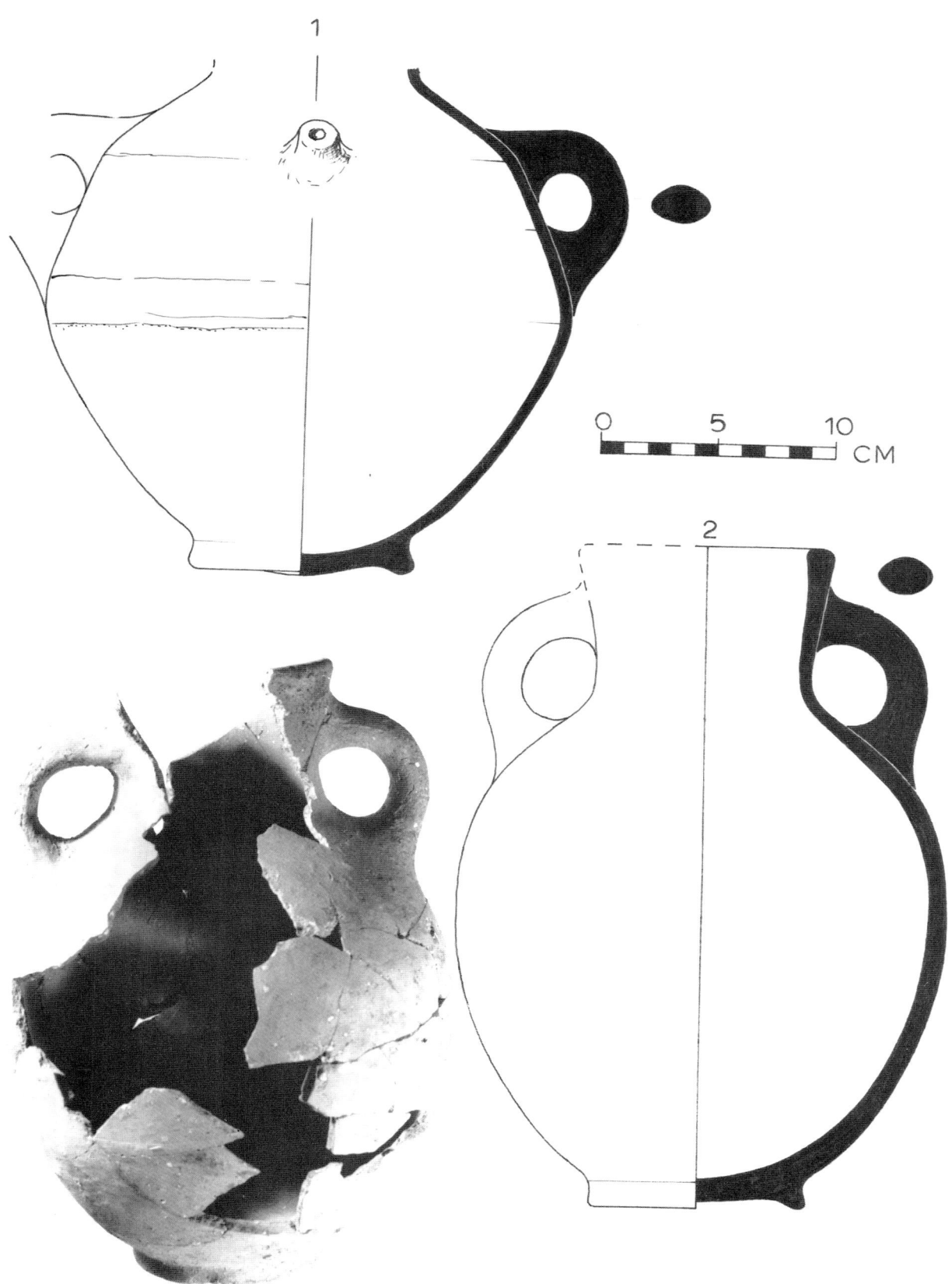

FIG. 58 POTTERY FROM CISTERN 74 (MOSTLY PERIOD IIB)

1. Identification		2. Section							3. Surface	
a.	b.	a.	b. Core		c. Non-Plastics				a. Exterior	b. Interior
Item	Square, Locus Basket	Fabric Color	Color	Extent	Type	Size	Frequency	Density	Color, n-p, voids, forming, finishing features	Same
1. Jug TT 382	SW 6-2 74 Cist 1 No. 28	rd yl	v vlt gr	10% rim	lms	m,s,f		low	*Ex*: pk gr surf covered with lt rd slip burnished in spaced vert lines from rim to base, entirely eroded around handle, none on base. Base ring sealed by *ex* circular smoothing, irreg circular inside 5mm-wide 7cms from base. *In*: lt rd br, center circle evenly depressed, not round bottomed, forming ridges are even, reg and shallow, flashing line abrupt at neck base, grooved forming ridges up the neck become shallower near top. Excess clay from handle join to rim untrimmed leaving excess overfold. Few protruding but covered n-p on neck.
2. Jug Rim	same No. 4	rd yl to rd br	lt gr	25% rim only	lms	l,m,s	f	low	*Ex & In*: dk pk, few n-p protrude, some straw voids, shallow horiz smoothing lines on *ex*, forming grooves on *in*.
3. Jug Rim	same No. 14	rd yl	dk gr	50% rim 25% body	lms bas	l,s,f s	f f	low	*Ex & In*: dk pk, few n-p protrude, fewer exposed, wet-smoothing, flashing line at rim base.
4. Jug Rim	same No. 8	pk gr		none	lms cht	s,f s	f vf	low	*Ex & In*: pk gr to dk pk, few n-p protrude, wet-smoothing, rd yl paint bands on *ex* eroded.
5. Jug Rim	same No. 48	dk pk to lt br		none	lms bas	l,m,s s	s s	med	*Ex & In*: like No. 2, except no straw voids, *in* has more n-p protruding than *ex*.
6. Jug Rim	same No. 46	lt br	vlt gr	25% rim	lms cht	s,f l	s vf	low	*Ex & In*: pk gr, many tiny n-p protrude, some covered. Wet-smoothing lines.
7. Jug Rim	same No. 17	lt rd br to rd yl	gr	-50% rim only	lms	l,s,f	f	low	*Ex & In*: rd yl, some n-p protrude, few seen, forming ridges shallow, even, reg, wet-smoothed.
8. Jug Rim	same No. 51	vpl br		none	lms cht	s,f s	f f	low	*Ex & In*: some n-p protrude, covered, vpl br color, wet-smoothed.
9. Jug Rim	same No. 50	pk	pk gr	50%	lms cht	l s,f	vf s	low	*Ex & In*: pk, some n-p seen, some protrude, wet-smoothing not as even as usual in this series.
10. Jug Rim	same No. 49	pk	vlt gr	50% rim only	lms cht	s,f s,f	f f	low	*Ex & In*: dk pk, n-p protrude, mostly *in*, wet-smoothed.
11. Jug Rim	same No. 53	pk	dk gr	75%	lms bas	m,s m,s	f s	low	*Ex & In*: many n-p protrude rd yl surf, wet-smoothing on *ex*, forming ridges on *in*, crude finish.
12. Jug Rim	same No. 47	pk	vlt gr	-50%	lms cht	s m,s	vf f	low	*Ex & In*: pk to lt br, some n-p protrude, many tiny pits *ex*, few *in*, wet-smoothed.
13. Jug Base to Body	same No. 38	lt rd to lt br	vlt gr	25%	lms cht	m,s,f s,f	s s	low	As No. 1, general *ex & in*, more n-p visible on *in*.
14. Jug TT 1858	same No. 32	lt br	gr	50% but none at rim	lms cht	s m,s	vf f	low	As No. 1, except on *ex* more erosion of color, faint depression of forming grooves visible, at center of body wide horiz wh paint band between 2 gr br bands. On *In* lower half smoothed so that forming lines are erased. Above this the upper 2/3 of body has clear forming lines.

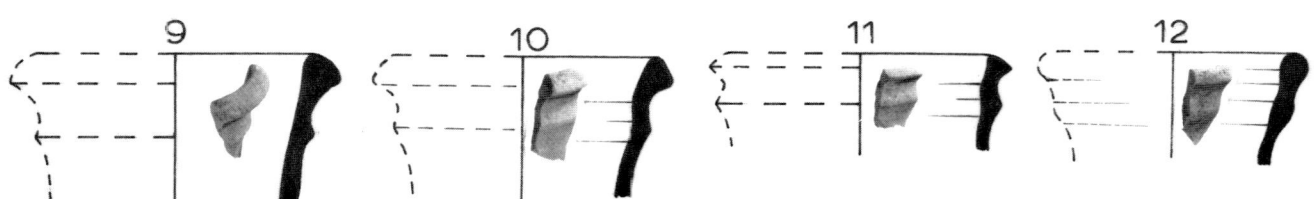

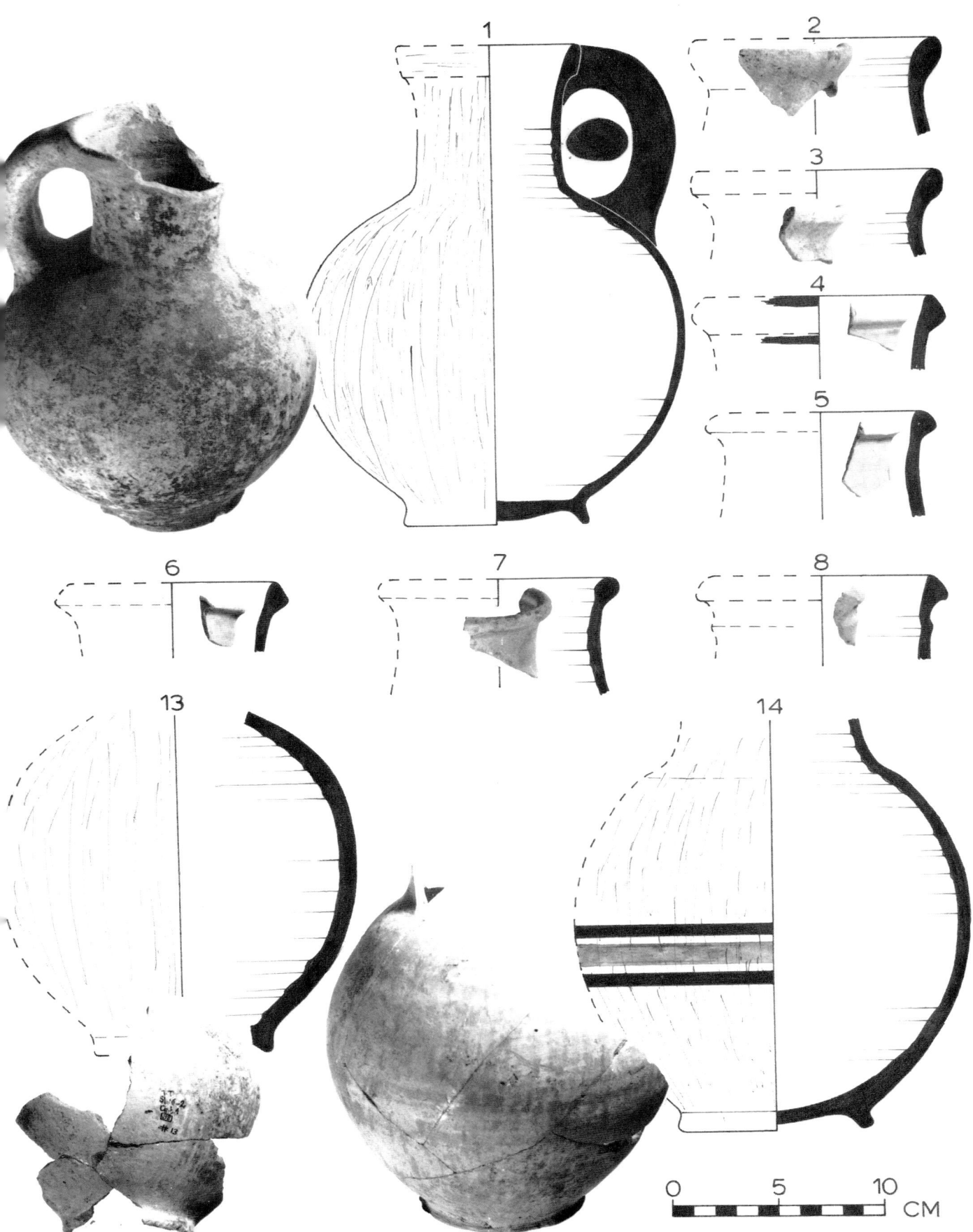

FIG. 59 POTTERY FROM CISTERN 74 (MOSTLY PERIOD IIB)

1. Identification		2. Section						3. Surface	
a.	b.	a.	b. Core		c. Non-Plastics			a. Exterior	b. Interior
Item	Square, Locus Basket	Fabric Color	Color	Extent	Type	Size	Frequency	Density	Color, n-p, voids, forming, finishing features	Same
1. Jug Base & Body	SW 6-2 74 Cist 1 No. 35	lt br	vlt gr	50%	lms	l,m,s	s	med	*Ex*: dk pk slip, burnished vertically to base, flashing line mid-way between base and br horiz paint band, reg horiz forming ridges below flashing line, many n-p protrude, some seen, esp around edge of base. Circular forming lines in ring of base, burnished. *In*: lt br, considerable pitting, spalling, n-p seen thru, base disk sunken into separate dish, centered by depressed twist. Forming lines clearest above flashing line.	
2. Jug TT 1860	same No. 34	rd yl		none	lms bas	l,m,s s,f	s f	vlow	*Ex*: some n-p seen embedded, straw voids in horiz wipe lines, tiny pits, vpl br slip under horiz smoothing lines, dk pk vert burnish lines much eroded. Brown paint net pattern above horiz bands on body center. *In*: lt br, some n-p on surf embedded, throwing ridges base to rim, flashing lines just above base & top of shoulder.	
3. Jug TT 384	same No. 31 Bas. 165	rd yl	yl rd to br dk gr	100% at rim 50% handle	lms	l,m,s	m	med h	*Ex*: pl br, many n-p protrude, covered, some exposed, reg forming ridges from base to neck bottom, flashing lines just above center and at base of neck, former a shallow depressed line, latter a slight ridge. Center of base has series of wide concentric circles ending in slightly raised point. Burnish on body in both vert and slant lines is largely eroded, some remains of vert burnish on neck. *In*: dk pk, many n-p protrude giving coarse finish, some forming ridges on neck, below shoulder to base, upper flashing line a felt depression.	
4. Jug TT 385	same No. 29	lt rd br		none	lms	s,f	f	vlow	*Ex*: very pl br slip, lt rd regularly spaced horiz burnish lines to neck with vert burnish strokes. Band of white paint just above flashing line near base. Base also burnished in concentric circles. *In*: lt rd br, horiz reg forming ridges mid-neck to base where it centers in crude twist.	
5. Jug Rim	same No. 54	rd yl	lt gr	50%	lms	s,f	f	low	*Ex & In*: lt rd, some burnish remains below *ex* rim flange, n-p seen esp on *ex*, burnish is vert, wet-smoothing is horiz.	
6. Jug Rim	same No. 52	rd	br	+50%	lms	s,f	s	low	*Ex*: lt rd slip, n-p protrude on *ex*, seen on *in*, horiz wet-smoothing.	
7. Jug Base & Body	same No. 36	yl rd	dk gr	+50%	lms	m,s,f	m	med	*Ex*: yl rd, wide bands of spaced horiz burnish. Streaks of lm deposit between burnish lines. Few pits, what n-p protrude are on base which is unburnished but has wide-spaced forming ridges ending in raised center point. *In*: yl rd, many lms n-p seen and protrude, forming ridges end in depressed center.	

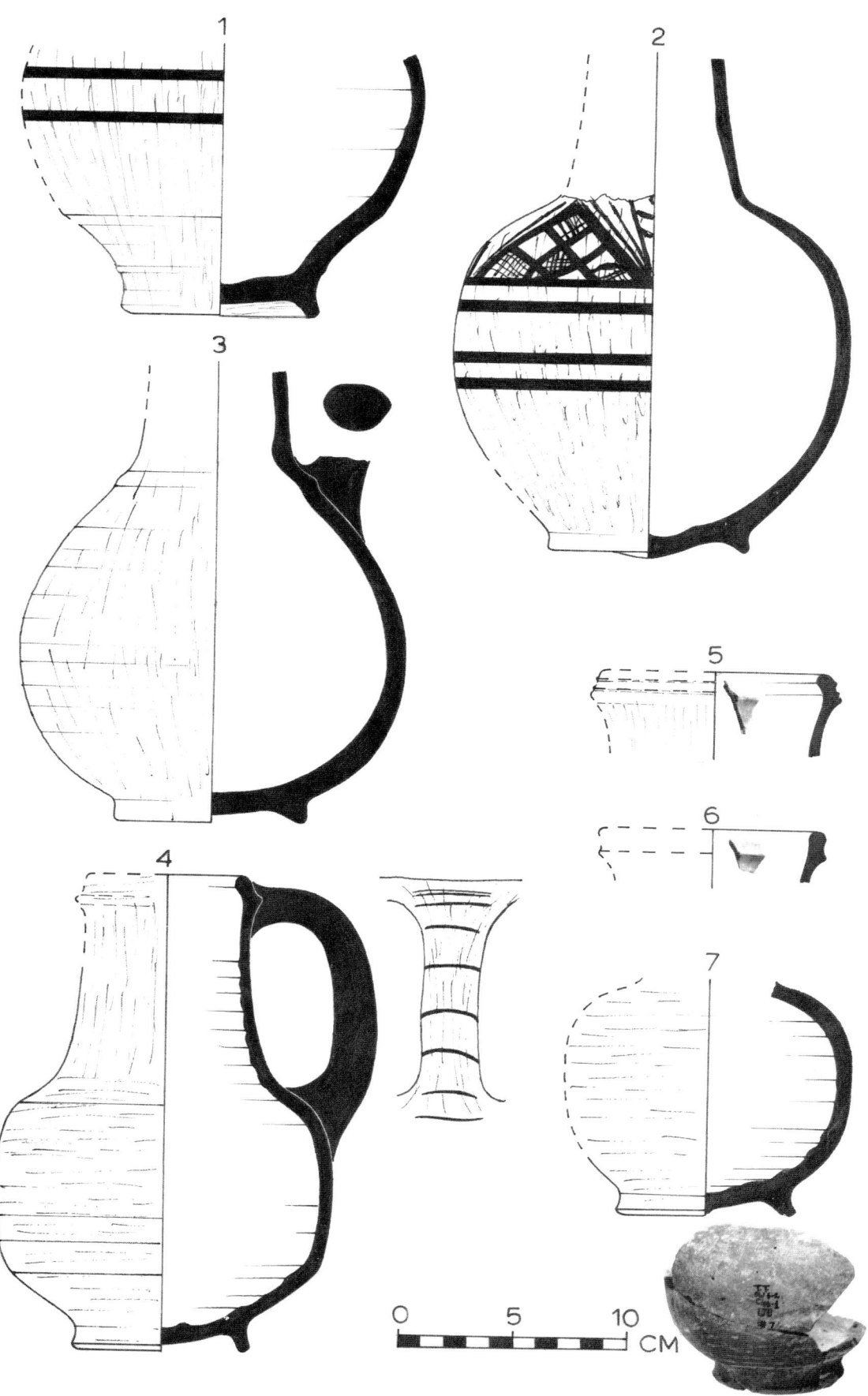

FIG. 60 POTTERY FROM CISTERN 74 (MOSTLY PERIOD IIB)

1. Identification		2. Section						3. Surface	
a.	b.	a.	b. Core		c. Non-Plastics			a. Exterior	b. Interior
Item	Square, Locus Basket	Fabric Color	Color	Extent	Type	Size	Frequency	Density	Color, n-p, voids, forming, finishing features	Same
1. Jug TT 381	SW 6-2 74 Cist 1 No. 33 Bas. 170	rd yl	br lt gr	100% rim 50% handle	lms	l,m,s	s-m	med h	*Ex:* dk pk, some n-p seen, in large area erosion & spalling expose large n-p, hand-smoothing irreg over body, base center has many circular forming ridges. Neck smoothed with overlapping horiz lines. *In:* lt rd br, forming ridges on neck, flashing line at join with body, n-p visible but other features are not clear.	
2. Jug Rim	same No. 24	rd yl to rd br	gr	±50%	lms bas	m,s m,s	s s	med	*Ex:* rd yl, discolored by ferric oxide, many n-p seen thru shallow spalling, protrusions, horiz wet-slipping on rim interrupted by vert wiping of neck. Flashing line at neck base. *In:* lt rd br, n-p protrude, covered, horiz forming ridges. Possibly part of No. 4 below.	
3. Jug Rim	same No. 45	lt rd	lt rd br	50%	lms	l,m,s	s-m	med l	*Ex:* lt rd br, some lm n-p seen, embedded, few pits, shallow horiz wipe lines indented by tooled grooves. *In:* lt rd br, n-p as *ex* few more protruding. Forming ridges.	
4. Jug TT 1857	same	rd yl to rd br	gr	±50%	lms	l,m,s	s	med l	*Ex:* rd yl, many n-p protrude, some spalling, many tiny pits, wiping tends to be generally horiz, not reg, causing a few drag marks toward bottom, forming depressions slight, clearer mid-body, base has circular forming lines spiraling from center. *In:* lt rd br, above flashing line, mid-body wide bands of comb-like forming ridges to neck. Bottom is wiped in broad criss-cross bands erasing any forming lines.	

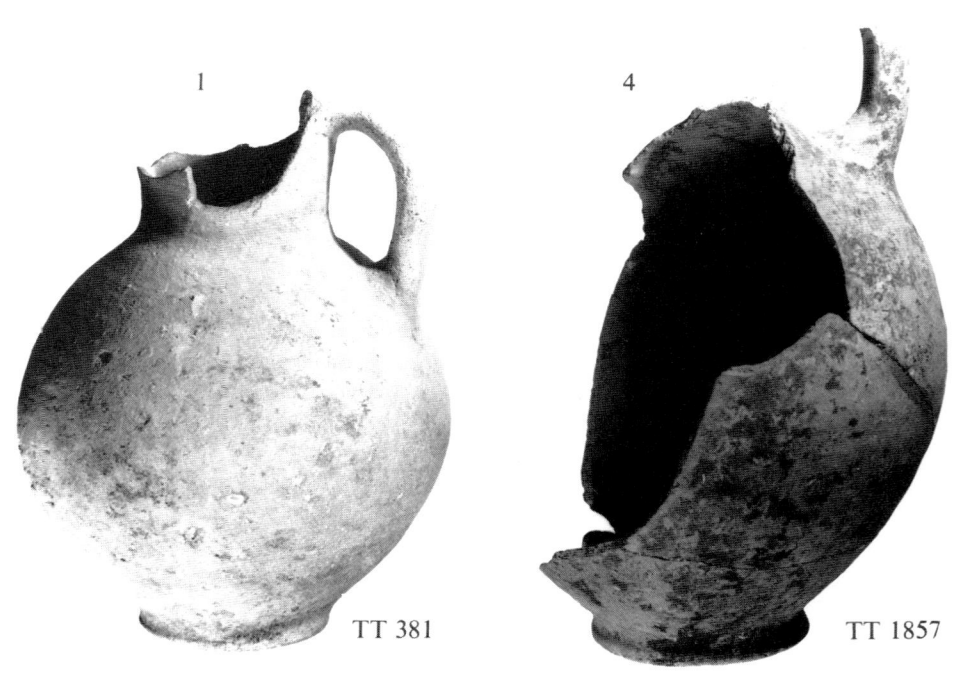

1   4

TT 381   TT 1857

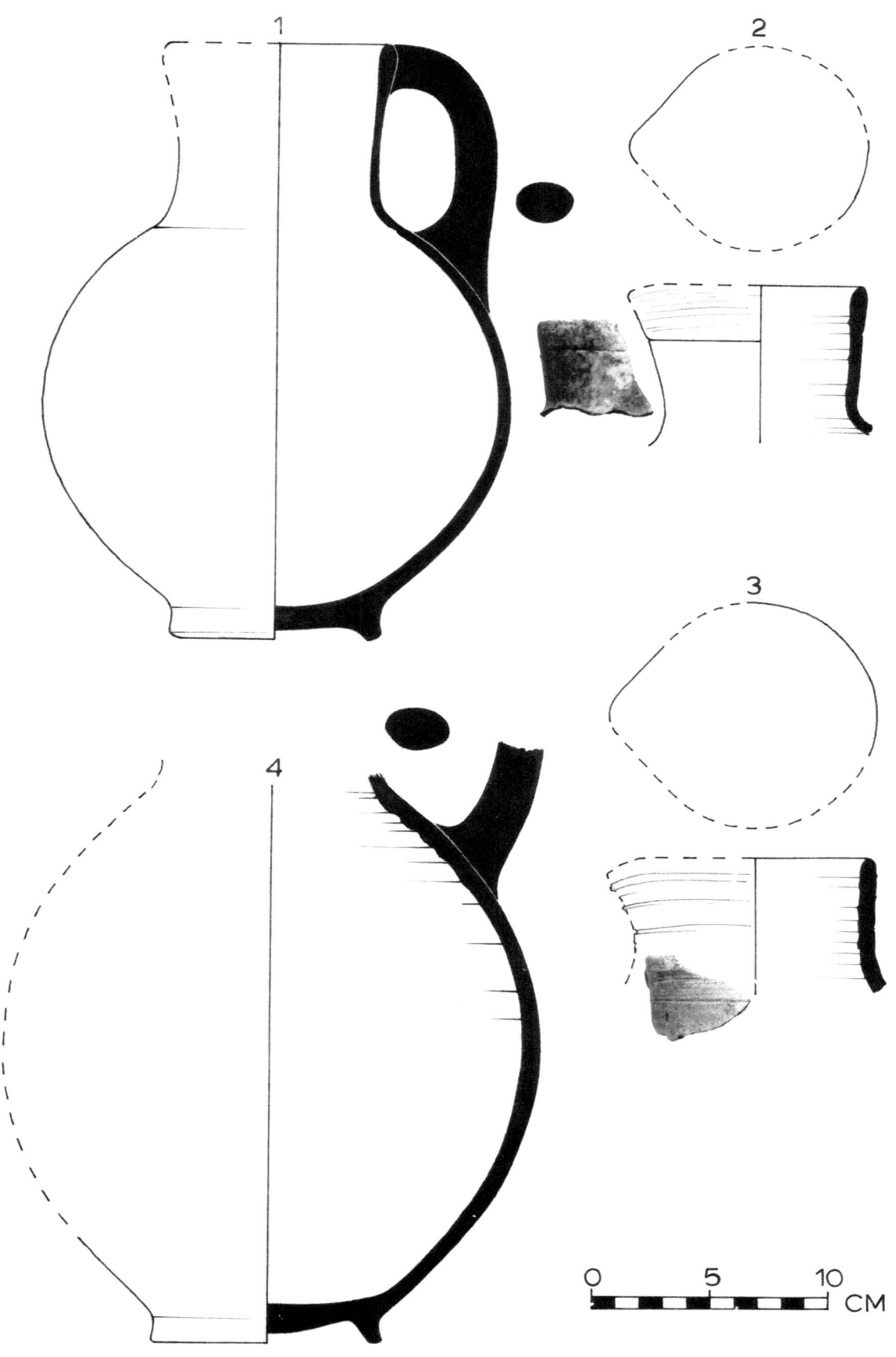

FIG. 61 POTTERY FROM CISTERN 74 (MOSTLY PERIOD IIB)

1. Identification		2. Section						3. Surface	
a. Item	b. Square, Locus Basket	a. Fabric Color	b. Core		c. Non-Plastics			a. Exterior	b. Interior
			Color	Extent	Type	Size	Frequency	Density	Color, n-p, voids, forming, finishing features	Same
1. Jug Base & Body	SW 6-2 74 Cist 1 No. 37	rd yl	lt br	±50%	lms	l,m,s	s-m	med h	*Ex*: rd yl, many n-p protrude, some seen, few spalls, 2ndary deposit makes surf green, small voids criss-cross wipe lines, forming ridges on base spiral from center point, base ring sealed with horiz wipe lines. *In*: rd yl, very much spalling, lms seen, faint trace of criss-cross wipe lines break lines around base edge.
2. Jug Base & Body	same No. 41	rd yl to rd br	gr	±50%	lms	m,s	s	med l	*Ex*: pk gr, many lms n-p seen thru shallow spalling, some drag marks L to R esp in heavy wiping to smooth flashing line 3cm above base, most clear on *in*. Circular finishing/forming ends in raised point at base bottom. *In*: pk gr, many n-p protrude, some seen, criss-cross wipe marks pass over flashing line to base concave center.
3. Jug Base & Body	same No. 25	rd yl	dk gr	±50%	lms	l,m,s	s-m	med	*Ex*: dk pk, many n-p protrude, covered, slanting criss-cross wipe lines, some voids, pits, circular forming ridges on base end in raised point, single slight depression indicating forming ridge. *In*: lt br, many n-p seen, criss-cross wipe lines link base & body.
4. Jug Base & Body	same No. 42	rd yl	dk gr	+50%	lms	l,m,s	s-m	med h	*Ex*: rd yl, many n-p protrude, some visible thru shallow spalling, circular wet-smoothing around *ex* of base ring and *in*, reaching rounded peak in center. *In*: lt br, many n-p seen thru spalling, wipe marks as in No. 2 though more completely obscuring the flashing line, bottom somewhat flat with roughly defined edge ca 5cms in diameter.
5. Jug TT 1859	same No. 26	lt rd	lt br	inner 75%	lms	l,m,s	s-m	med h	*Ex*: vpl br slip, pk in places, many lms spalls & protrusions, erosion on handles, shoulder, base reveals n-p clearly. Flashing line just above center wipe lines clearest around neck, interrupted by handle joining. *In*: lt rd many n-p on surf, mostly tiny, bottom wipes criss-cross to just above base where horiz forming ridges become common. Vert wipe lines cross horiz forming ridges on neck. General similarity to TT 1856 (Fig. 57:2).
6. Jug Rim	same No. 18	lt rd	dk gr	75% rim none neck	lms	l,m,s	s	med l	*Ex & In*: lt rd, many n-p seen embedded, some shallow spalling, fewer *in*; horiz wipe lines interrupted on rim by bits of excess clay, some vert wiping at bottom *in*.
7. Jug Rim	same No. 13	yl rd		none	lms	l,m,s	s	low	*Ex & In*: pk slip, n-p protrude slightly, some seen, few pits, wet-smoothed.
8. Jug Rim	same No. 12	rd yl	gr	50%	lms	m,s,f	m	med l	*Ex*: lt rd br to gr from 2ndary burning, many n-p seen, protrude, horiz forming ridges below smoothing lines, fold over of rim on *in* has irreg edge.
9. Jug Rim	same No. 9	rd yl to lt br	lt gr	trace	lms	l,m,s	s	low	*Ex*: some n-p on surf, wet-smoothing lines, rim folded *in* but well-smoothed. *In*: same as *ex*.
10. Jug Rim	same No. 7		Identical with No. 9						See No. 9, fewer n-p seen on *in*.
11. Jug Rim	same No. 11	lt rd	dk gr	inner +75%	lms	l,m,s	s	low	*Ex*: lt rd br, few n-p protrude, many tiny n-p seen, wet-smoothing, also on *In*: which is dk gr below rim where also smoothing lines cease and some rough vert wiping at what may be flashing line fr neck to shoulder.

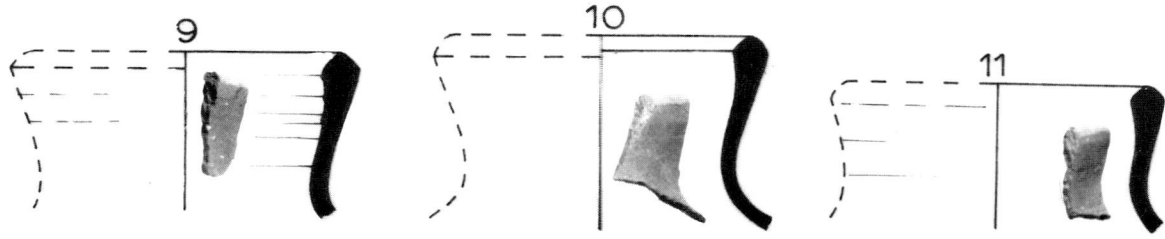

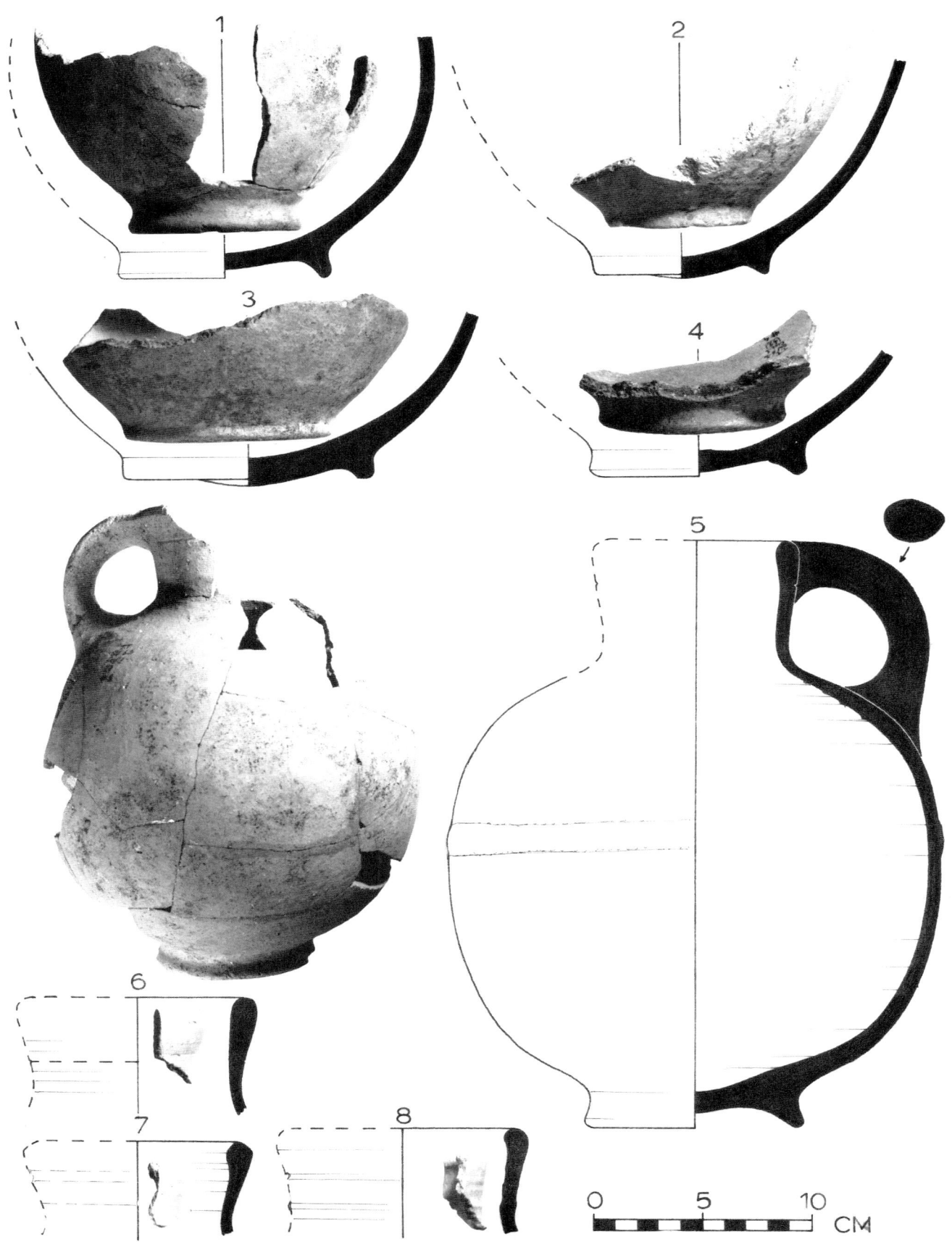

FIG. 62 POTTERY FROM CISTERN 74 (MOSTLY PERIOD IIB)

1. Identification		2. Section							3. Surface	
a.	b.	a.	b. Core		c. Non-Plastics				a. Exterior	b. Interior
Item	Square, Locus Basket	Fabric Color	Color	Extent	Type	Size	Frequency	Density	Color, n-p, voids, forming, finishing features	Same
1. Jug Rim	SW 6-2 74 Cist 1 No. 43	yl rd	lt gr	none (rim) inner 50% shoulder	lms	l,m,s	s	med	Ex & In: lt rd, many lms n-p seen, small spalls, wet-smoothing around rim; section of ex rim vpl br due to lack of oxygen.	
2. Jug Rim	same No. 5	rd yl		none	lms bas	m,s m,s	s s	low	Ex & In: rd yl, n-p protrude on surf, some are visible, few drag marks, wet-smoothing lines reg, on in folded over rim edge smoothed, flashing line at bottom of rim clearest on in.	
3. Jug Rim	same No. 10	yl rd		none	lms	l,m,s	s	med	Ex & In: rd yl, lms n-p visible in shallow spalling, some protrude covered, wet-smoothing more clear on ex than in.	
4. Jug Rim	same No. 16	st br		none	lms	l,m,s	s	med	Ex & In: rd yl, n-p sub-surf covered but many visible giving salty look, reg finishing lines, trim of folded-over rim a bit crude.	
5. Jug Rim	same No. 19	rd yl		none	lms	l,m,s	s	low	Ex & In: rd yl, few n-p visible, few pits, wet-smoothing reg fine-lined, folded-over rim trimmed with tool on in.	
6. Jug Base, Body & Neck	same No. 32	yl rd	dk gr	50%	lms cal	m,s,f s	s f	med	Ex: lt rd mostly, section is dk pk, dividing line is quite apparent. Many n-p seen, some protrude, forming lines clearest at mid-body just below flashing line, smoothing covers forming ridges, drag marks; base ring sealed with horiz smoothing, circular ridges inside base ring end in slightly raised center. In: irreg smoothing lines below center flashing line; above to neck forming ridges are reg.	
7. Jug Base & Body	same No. 39	lt br		none	lms	s,f	f	vlow	Ex: dk pk, lt yl br slip almost all gone, horiz smoothing does not entirely cover forming ridges, some pits, base ring not evenly attached, i. e., in part sealed, in part deeply undercut, inside base are crude spirals ending in raised point. In: dk pk deeply grooved forming ridges spiral to center of base ending in small raised point. Neater than the usual.	
8. Jug Neck & Handle	same No. 40	lt rd to lt br	lt gr	50%	lms	m,s	f	vlow	Ex: lt rd, faded slip vertically burnished in close strokes, begins below rim lip. Some few n-p seen on surf. In: dk pk forming lines clear, also deep flashing line opposite ex ridge at top of handle, probably a 2nd at bottom of preserved feature. Paint is dk gr.	
9. Juglet TT 690	same Bas. 222	rd yl (rim)	gr	inner +50%	lms	l,m,s	s	med l	Ex: rd yl in area of handle, rest is dk pk. Many n-p embedded, seen, irreg smoothed, esp bottom, handle double grooved, flashing line at neck base is erased, also on In: color of in neck and rim is rd yl, forming ridges also on neck, base is pointed; just above is a heavy ridge before rest of body emerges. Drawing not sufficiently detailed.	
10. Juglet TT 691	same Bas. 221	dk gr! (rim)		none	lms cht	l,m,s l	s-f f	low	Ex: dk pk, some n-p seen, several pits, vert straw voids, horiz on neck, flashing line at base of neck, clearer on In: pk gr, but in generally not available. Base is pointed more than drawing shows.	
11. Juglet Rim & Handle	same No. 57	rd	dk gr	inner 75%	lms	l,m,s	s	low	Ex: rd yl, some n-p visible, embedded, straw voids along vert smoothing lines. In: rd yl at rim to dk gr lower neck & shoulder. Some n-p visible forming ridges fade up neck near rim.	
12. Juglet Rim & Handle	same No. 56	rd yl	lt br lt gr	inner 50% neck inner 25% body	lms	l,m,s	s	low	Ex & In: lt br, more n-p visible in than ex, smoothing lines vert along handle, tiny pits, forming lines on in best seen under shoulder, wiped clean from neck in.	
13. Juglet	same No. 55	lt br		none	lms	l,m,s	s	low	Ex: lt yl br, few n-p seen, many straw voids, circular forming lines on disk base, slightly asymmetrical. In: not clearly available.	

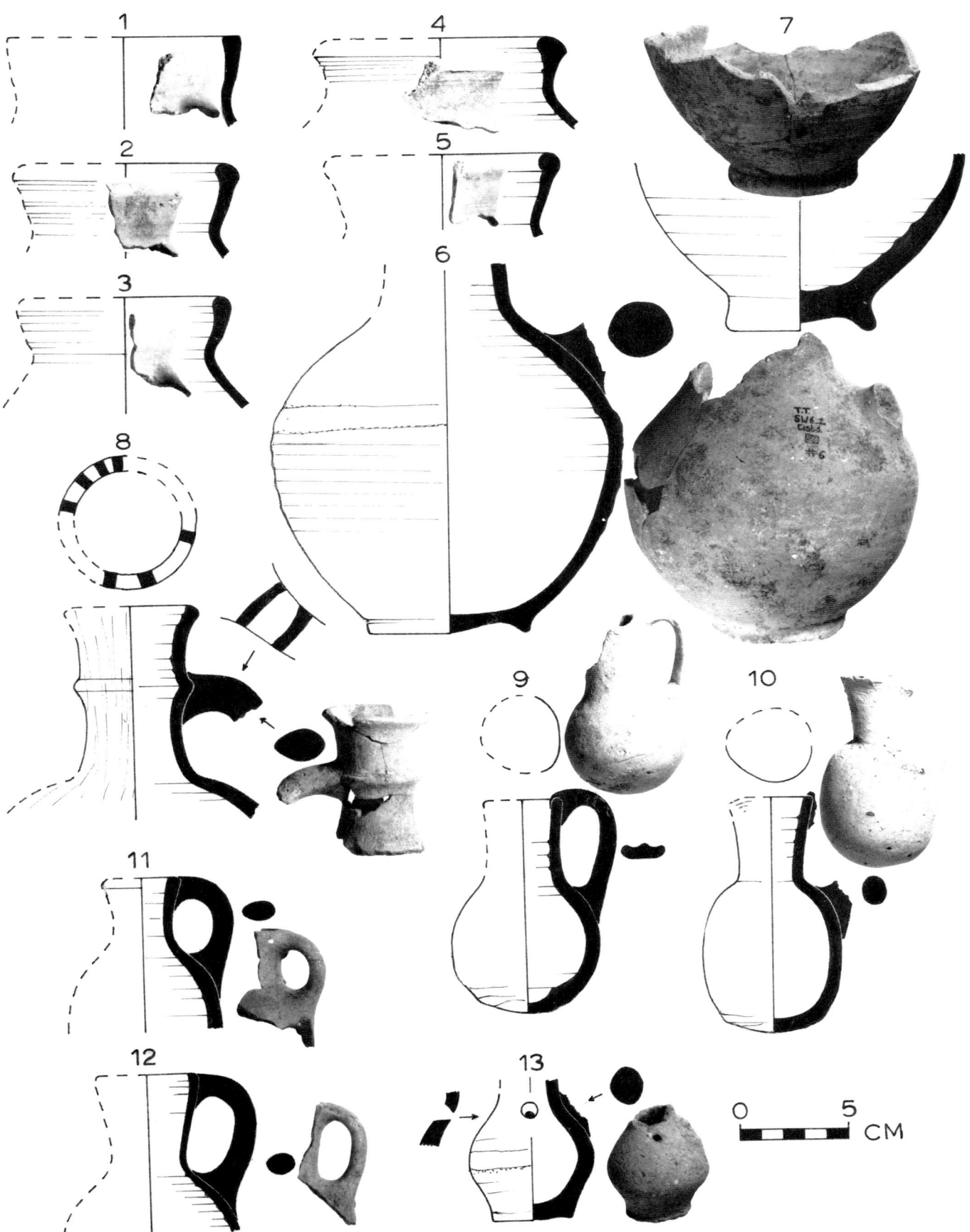

FIG. 63 POTTERY FROM CISTERN 74 (MOSTLY PERIOD IIB)

1. Identification		2. Section						3. Surface	
a. Item	b. Square, Locus Basket	a. Fabric Color	b. Core		c. Non-Plastics			a. Exterior	b. Interior
			Color	Extent	Type	Size	Frequency	Density	Color, n-p, voids, forming, finishing features	Same
1. Crater Rim	SW 6-2 74 Cist 1 No. 1	rd yl	dk gr	80%	lms dung? See Fig. 23:7	m,s,f m,s,f	s s	low	*Ex & In*: rd yl, some n-p visible, some protrude covered, irreg edge to .5cm-wide shallow depression under *ex* rim, wet-smoothing lines may be reflection of forming, slight fold over on *in* of rim, some horiz voids.	
2. Crater Rim	same No. 2	rd yl	dk gr	80%	lms	l,m,s	s	med l	*Ex & In*: dk pk, eroded surf reveals lms n-p, horiz wet-smoothing, some drag marks, lime spalling.	
3. Crater Rim	same No. 83	rd yl to lt br	gr	±50% rim	lms	l,m,s	s	low	*Ex & In*: dk pk, few n-p protrude, covered, few seen, fold over rim sealed to body, wet-smoothing in fine-line horiz bands.	
4. Crater Rim	same No. 89		(Identical to No. 3)						Same as No. 3, except color is rd yl, *ex* rim bottom not as sealed, tooled edge.	
5. Crater Rim	same No. 90		(Identical to No. 3 but fabric has more rd yl, core is darker gr)						Same as No. 3, except as No. 4 but more so, *ex* rim bottom is undercut.	
6. Crater Rim	same No. 84	rd	dk gr	75%	lms	l,m,s	s	med	*Ex & In*: lt rd, some n-p protrude, few visible, reg wet-smoothing, flashing line just below rim where shoulder begins.	
7. Crater Rim	same No. 86	lt br	gr	none streak outer edge	lms	l,m,s	s	low	*Ex & In*: dk pk grayed by carbon deposit on *ex*, few n-p protrude *in*, wet-smoothing.	
8. Crater Rim	same No. 85		(Identical with No. 6 except that core edge is diffuse, core larger)						Same as No. 6, except rim edge *ex* has more covered n-p; flashing line at shoulder is preserved, more pit voids *in*.	
9. Crater Rim	same No. 91		(Identical with No. 3, except down to 25% core at rim)						Same as No. 3, slight trace of flashing line at bottom edge.	
10. Crater Rim	same No. 88		(Identical with No. 6, except core is 95%)						Same as No. 6, *ex* rim edged.	
11. Crater Rim	same No. 87		(Identical with No. 3, except no core and fabric is all lt br)						Same as No. 3.	

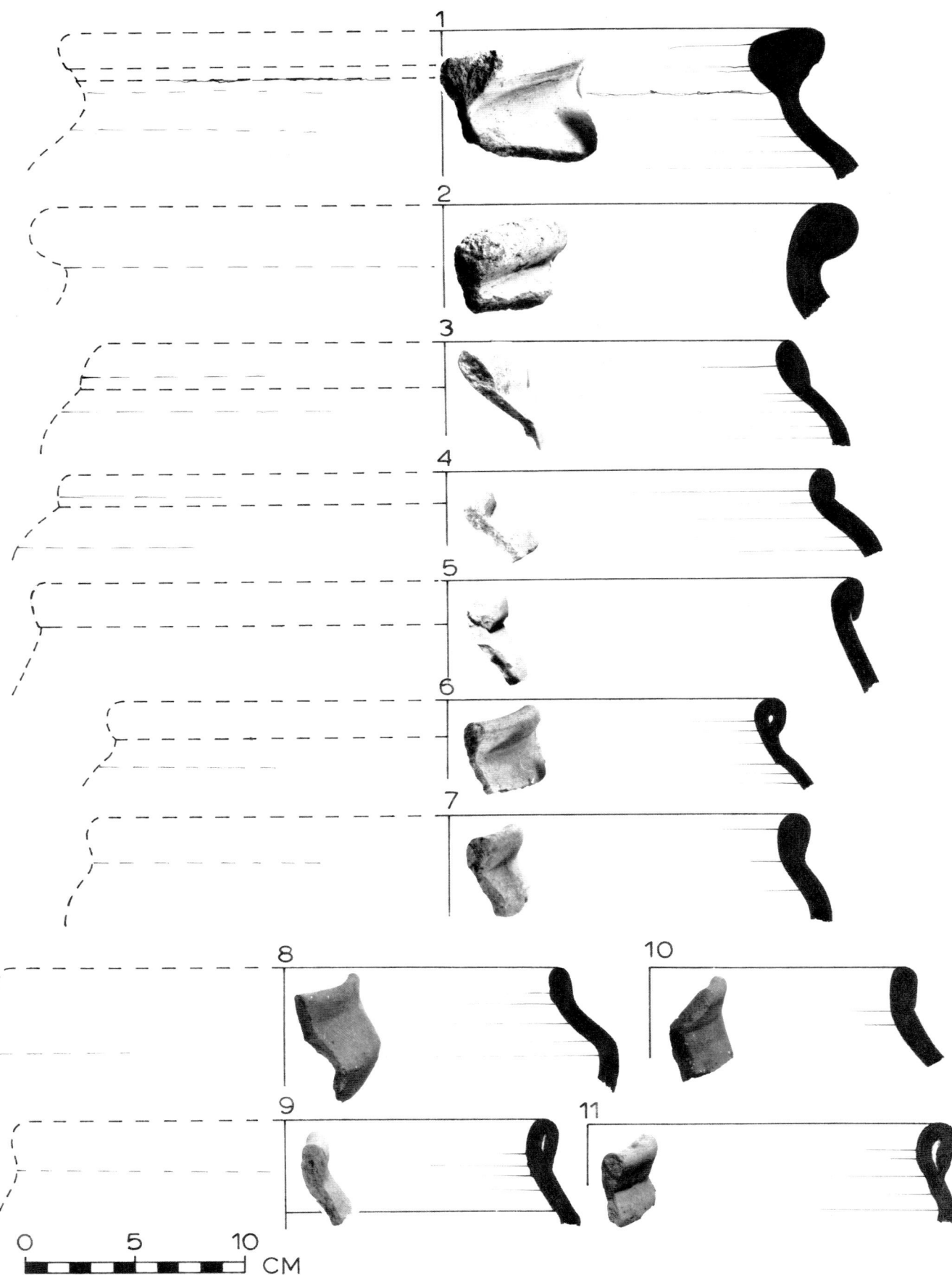

FIG. 64 POTTERY FROM CISTERN 74 (MOSTLY PERIOD IIB)

1. Identification		2. Section							3. Surface	
a.	b.	a.	b. Core		c. Non-Plastics				a. Exterior	b. Interior
Item	Square, Locus Basket	Fabric Color	Color	Extent	Type	Size	Frequency	Density	Color, n-p, voids, forming, finishing features	Same
1. Bowl Rim	SW 6-2 74 Cist 1 No. 63	pk gr	vlt gr	75%	lms	s,f	vf	vlow	*Ex & In*: dk pk, burnished slip, wide horiz band below rim *ex* unburnished, firm surf.	
2. Bowl Rim	same No. 82	lt br	gr	40%	lms cht	s,f s,f	f s	low	*Ex & In*: dk pk, few n-p protrude, covered, few straw voids *ex*, somewhat irreg combed horiz shallow grooves.	
3. Bowl Rim	same No. 62	pk gr	vlt gr	25%	lms cht	l,s s,f	f s	med l	*Ex & In*: dk pk, 1 lms n-p visible, embedded, wet-smoothing.	
4. Bowl Rim	same No. 70	lt br	gr	-100%	lms	l,m,s	s	med l	*Ex & In*: rd yl, some n-p visible thru shallow spalling, thin slip cover eroded 80%.	
5. Bowl Rim	same No. 60	pk gr		none	lms	s,f	s-m	med	*Ex & In*: lt br, few n-p visible embedded, tiny pits below rim bend on *ex* which is smooth compared to horiz forming lines of *in*.	
6. Bowl Rim	same No. 61	lt rd	lt br	40%	lms	m,s f	s	med	*Ex & In*: lt rd br, some tiny n-p protrude, some visible, wet-smoothing lines, rougher below bend on *ex*, perhaps flashing line.	
7. Bowl Rim	same No. 77	lt rd to rd br	gr	50%	lms	s,f	s	med	*Ex & In*: lt rd, some tiny n-p protrude, one large n-p as thick as wall, rd slip on rim to just below bend on *ex*, faded.	
8. Bowl Rim	same No. 76	rd yl to lt br	lt gr	-25%	lms cht	s,f s,f	f s	med l	*Ex & In*: lt pk with horiz burnish producing dk pk, tiny n-p visible, esp *ex*, some drag marks *ex*.	
9. Bowl Rim	same No. 58	lt br	lt gr dk gr	100% rim top, 75% outer wall patch	lms cht	l,m,s m,s	s m	med h	*Ex & In*: dk pk darkened by carbon, many tiny n-p protrude, some visible, horiz thin-line finish below rim, *ex* upper and *in* lower edges unevenly trimmed, at bend of wall on *ex* bottom, rougher.	
10. Bowl Rim	same No. 72	(Identical to No. 7, except that core is +75% with 100% at tip of rim)							*Ex & In*: lt rd *ex* bottom but rest covered with rd slip burnished, rim top dk gr. Many n-p protrude, some exposed. Burnish is horiz at rim, flashing line on *ex* has long drag voids, fine combine below. *In* bottom burnish is slanted.	
11. Bowl Rim	same No. 73	lt rd to lt rd br	gr	50%	lms cht	m,s,f f	s f	low	*Ex & In*: rd slip burnish continuous, broken with tiny pits.	
12. Bowl Rim	same No. 71	lt br	lt gr	75%	lms cht	m,s l,m,s	f s	med l	*Ex & In*: rd yl slip burnished on *in* spaced horiz strokes, on *ex* with closely spaced strokes. Most of *ex* has been grayed by carbon deposit. Some n-p protrude, appear esp on rim.	

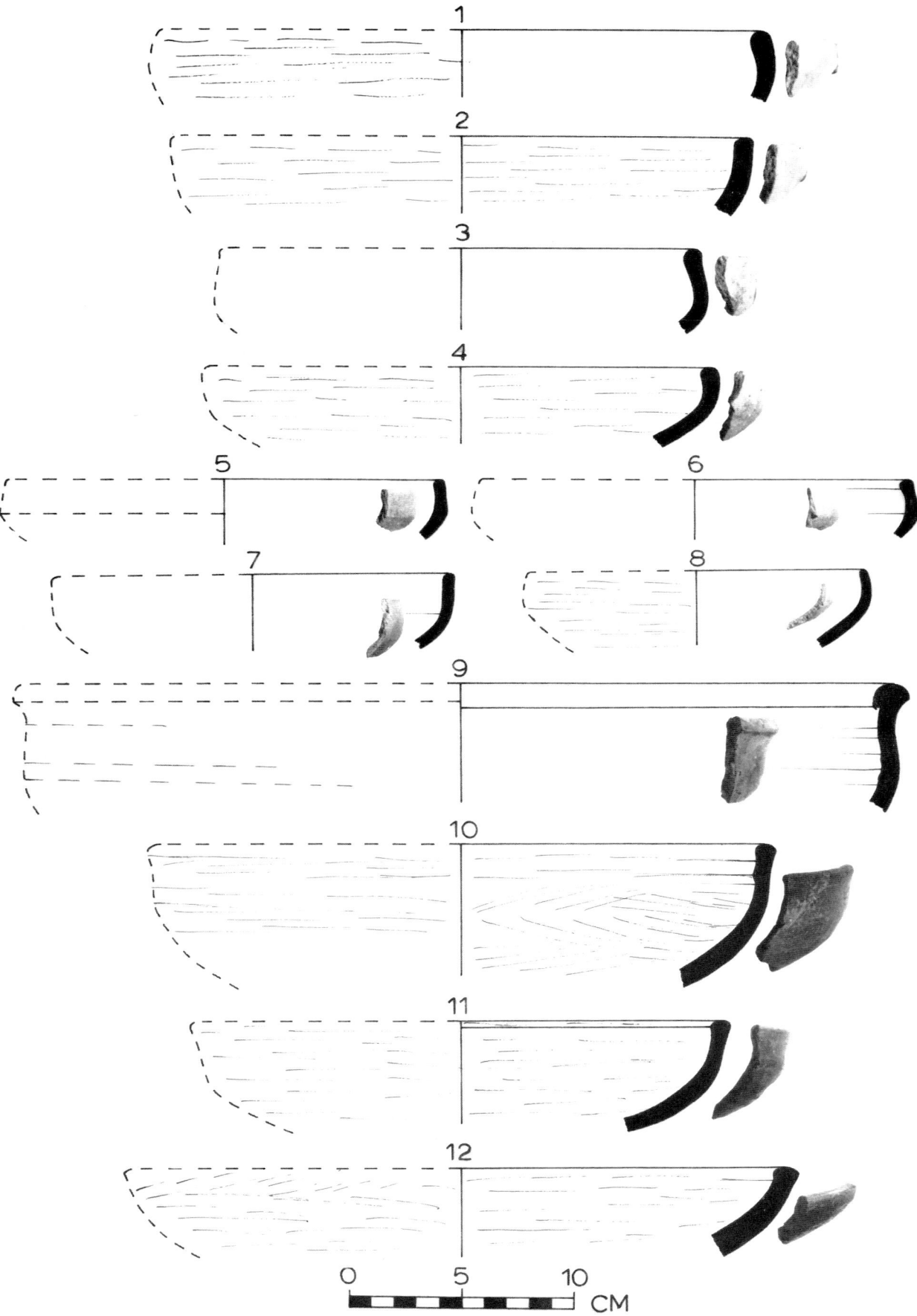

FIG. 65 POTTERY FROM CISTERN 74 (MOSTLY PERIOD IIB)

1. Identification		2. Section							3. Surface	
a.	b.	a.	b. Core		c. Non-Plastics				a. Exterior	b. Interior
Item	Square, Locus Basket	Fabric Color	Color	Extent	Type	Size	Fre-quency	Density	Color, n-p, voids, forming, finishing features	Same
1. Bowl TT 402	SW 6-2 74 Cist 1 Bas. 155	rd yl	dk gr	+30%	cal bas lms	m,s s s	f f s	low	*Ex*: lt rd to pk gr, part of base dk gr from carbon deposit, forming ridges on walls, some drag marks, some n-p protrude, circular forming lines in base end in spiral, one deep fissure in base. Faint trace of horiz burnish lines widely spaced. *In*: lt rd, vert burnish lines separated from rim to bowl center. Below burnish are horiz wipe lines.	
2. Bowl Rim	same No. 80	lt rd br	gr	50%	lms cht	s,f s	s f	low	*Ex & In*: lt rd br, bottom rd burnished slip rim & all of *In*. Burnish is horiz and covers *ex* bottom which is unslipped. Some n-p seen, drag marks, rim folded to *in*, thin irreg line.	
3. Bowl Rim	same No. 75			(Identical with No. 2)					Same as No. 2, except bottom is not burnished.	
4. Bowl Rim	same No. 81			(Identical with No. 2)					Same as No. 2, bottom as No. 3.	
5. Bowl Rim	same No. 59	lt gr		none	lms	s,f	m	med	*Ex & In*: lt rd br, slip burnished, some n-p seen in drag marks where burnishing opened the surf.	
6. Bowl Rim	same No. 66	br	gr	+80% diffuse	lms	s,f (Same as No 5)	m	med	*Ex & In*: br slip burnished only on inside of bowl. Few pits, horiz straw voids, carbon deposit.	
7. Bowl Rim	same No. 67	lt br	pl br	inner 90%	lms cht	l,m,s l,f	s f	med l	*Ex & In*: vpl br, n-p seen on rim, some protrude, wipe lines *in*, excess clay untrimmed from rim, *ex* finish leaves roughened surf.	
8. Bowl Rim	same No. 74			(Identical with No. 2)					Same as No. 2, except rim trim is smooth.	
9. Bowl Rim	same No. 64	dk pk	gr	none outer 10% patch	lms	m,s,f	s	low	*Ex & In*: dk pk, gr patch below *ex* rim, few n-p visible, few pits, horiz wipe lines, interrupted by swipes of excess clay on *ex*.	
10. Bowl Rim	same No. 69	dk pk	pk gr	75%	lms	m,s,	s	low	*Ex & In*: dk pk, some n-p seen, few pits *in*, even wipe lines horiz.	
11. Bowl Rim	same No. 79	br gr	lt gr	50%	lms	t	m	vlow	*Ex*: lt br covered with few separated bands of yl rd burnished slip. *In*: rd slip burnished.	
12. Bowl Rim	same No. 92	lt rd	dk pk with some vlt gr	±50%	lms bas cht	l,m,s s s	f s f	med	*Ex & In*: pl br, trace of rd yl slip, *in* only, some large n-p protrude, covered, wet-smoothing, rim fold line on *ex* well smoothed.	
13. Bowl Rim	same No. 78	lt rd	gr	50%	lms	s	vvf	vvlow	*Ex & In*: rd slip burnished, 2 shallow fine-line grooves below *ex* rim. See Fig. 48:15-19.	

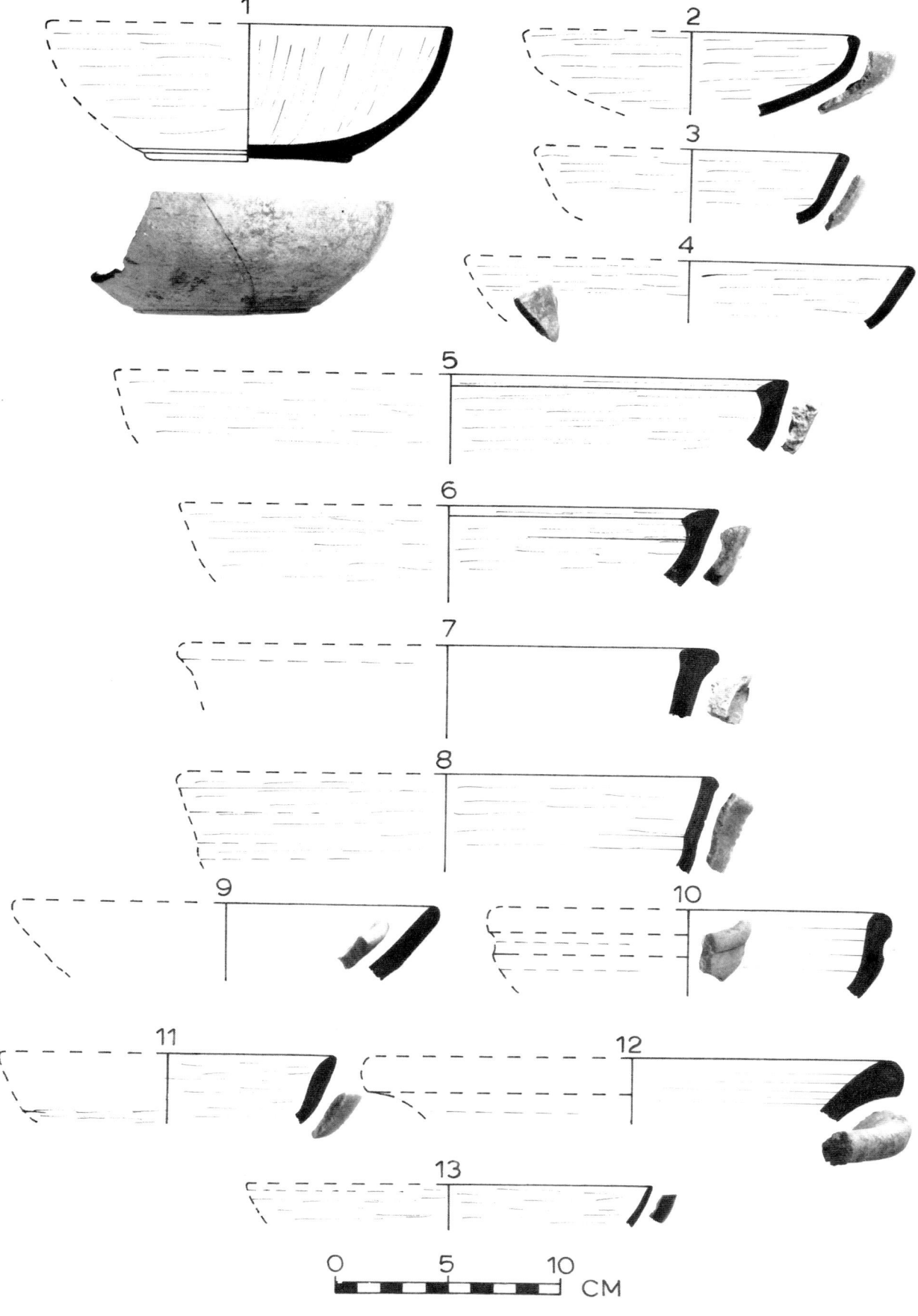

FIG. 66 POTTERY FROM CISTERN 74 (MOSTLY PERIOD IIB)

1. Identification		2. Section							3. Surface	
a.	b.	a.	b. Core		c. Non-Plastics				a. Exterior	b. Interior
Item	Square, Locus Basket	Fabric Color	Color	Extent	Type	Size	Frequency	Density	Color, n-p, voids, forming, finishing features	Same
1. Cook Pot Rim	SW 6-2 74 Cist 1 No. 107	yl rd	gr (Cut section shows dk gr · rd br · gr)	50%	cal	s,f	m	med h	*Ex & In*: rd br to dk gr, many tiny n-p protrude, some seen, sharp line under flange of *ex* rim, excess clay folded over to outside of rim.	
2. Cook Pot Rim	same No. 108	br	dk gr	50%	cal	m,s,f	m	med h	*Ex*: dk gr, many n-p protrude, covered, rim base undercut, double depression above flange, some trace of wet-smoothing, few straw voids. *In*: pk gr, some n-p visible, wet-smoothing.	
3. Cook Pot Rim	same No. 112	yl rd	dk gr	50%	cal	s,f	m	med h	*Ex*: rd gr, *In*: rd br, many tiny n-p protrude, on *ex* covered, on *in* some visible, wet-smoothing, *ex* rim flange undercut.	
4. Cook Pot Rim	same No. 124	yl rd	gr	50%	cal	m,s,f	m	med h	*Ex*: dk br, many tiny n-p protrude, rim base tooled also flange edge, wet-smoothed. *In*: pk gr rim edge overfolded, join line slightly irreg, wet-smoothing over many tiny protruding n-p.	
5. Cook Pot Rim	same No. 180	dk br	dk gr	50%	cal	m,s,f	m	med h	*Ex*: dk gr, many protruding n-p, covered, flange is added coil, seal along top edge not completely covered, tooled undercut has left untrimmed edge to *ex* flange, wet-smoothed *In*: gr, wet-smoothed rim edge bent inward, untrimmed.	
6. Cook Pot Rim	same No. 131	lt rd br	dk gr	inner 75%	cal	m,s,f	m	med h	*Ex*: pk gr, many n-p protrude, some seen, erosion & cracking, smoothing is faint. *In*: gr, many protruding n-p, some seen, vert cracks.	
7. Cook Pot Rim	same No. 140	rd br	dk gr	+50%	cal	m,s,f	m	med h	*Ex*: dk br, many n-p protrude, rim undercut. *In*: br, both sides wet-smoothed.	
8. Cook Pot Rim	same No. 109	rd br	dk gr	outer 75%	cal	m,s,f	m	med h	*Ex*: br, many n-p protrude covered, some visible, flange smoothly joined, trimmed, wet-smoothed, also *in* otherwise like *ex* except it is rd br.	
9. Cook Pot Rim	same No. 110	yl rd to lt br	gr	-50%	cal	m,s,f	m	med h	*Ex*: br, *In*: rd br, bottom edge of rim flange flatted with tool, as No. 4, 18-20.	
10. Cook Pot Rim	same No. 111	rd br	dk gr	50%	cal	m,s,f	m	med h	*Ex*: rd br to gr, *In*: lt rd br, many tiny n-p protrude, on *ex* flange neatly joined, undercut, wet-smoothing *ex & in*.	
11. Cook Pot Rim	same No. 113	rd br	dk gr	+50%	cal	m,s,f	m	med h	*Ex*: rd br, *In*: lt rd br, few n-p visible, most protrude covered, *ex* rim top folded over, flange pushed up against thin-bladed tool allowing slight over-fold.	
12. Cook Pot Rim	same No. 114	yl rd	gr	outer 50%	cal	m,s,f	m	med h	*Ex*: rd br to gr, *In*: lt rd br. Many n-p protrude, more visible on *in*, rim flange slightly tooled under, wet-smoothed.	
13. Cook Pot Rim	same No. 116	yl rd	dk gr	50%	cal	m,s,f	m	med h	*Ex*: dk gr, many n-p protrude, few only seen, flashing line at shoulder join. *In*: rd gr to gr, n-p & smoothing as *ex*.	
14. Cook Pot Rim	same No. 117	yl rd	gr	50%	cal	m,s,f	m	med h	*Ex*: dk rd br, n-p protrude, rim undercut with sharp tool, slight ridge at top of flange. *In*: lt rd br, 7mm-wide grooved depression below rim. N-p protrude, some visible.	
15. Cook Pot Rim	same No. 119	br	dk gr	+50%	cal	m,s,f	m	med h	*Ex*: pk gr to gr, many n-p protrude, many visible, rim folded over, at flashing line wall thickens esp before thinning to rim. Fold void at upper part of rim. *In*: rd gr, other surf as *ex*.	
16. Cook Pot Rim	same No. 136	yl rd	dk gr	75%	cal	s,f	m	med h	*Ex & In*: pk gr to gr, erosion reveals many n-p below the surf.	
17. Cook Pot Rim	same No. 138	yl rd	dk gr	+50%	cal	m,s,f	m	med	*Ex & In*: lt rd br, many n-p protrude, some seen, wet-smoothing is horiz. *Ex*: flange broken off, tooled groove above it.	
18. Cook Pot Rim	same No. 120	dk rd br	dk gr	50%	cal	m,s,f	m	med h	*Ex*: dk br to gr, otherwise as No. 15.	
19. Cook Pot Rim	same No. 121	rd br	gr	-50%	cal	m,s,f	m	med h	*Ex*: rd br to gr, n-p protrude, some visible, flange edge partly eroded. *In*: lt rd br, many n-p protrude, some visible, wet-smoothing.	

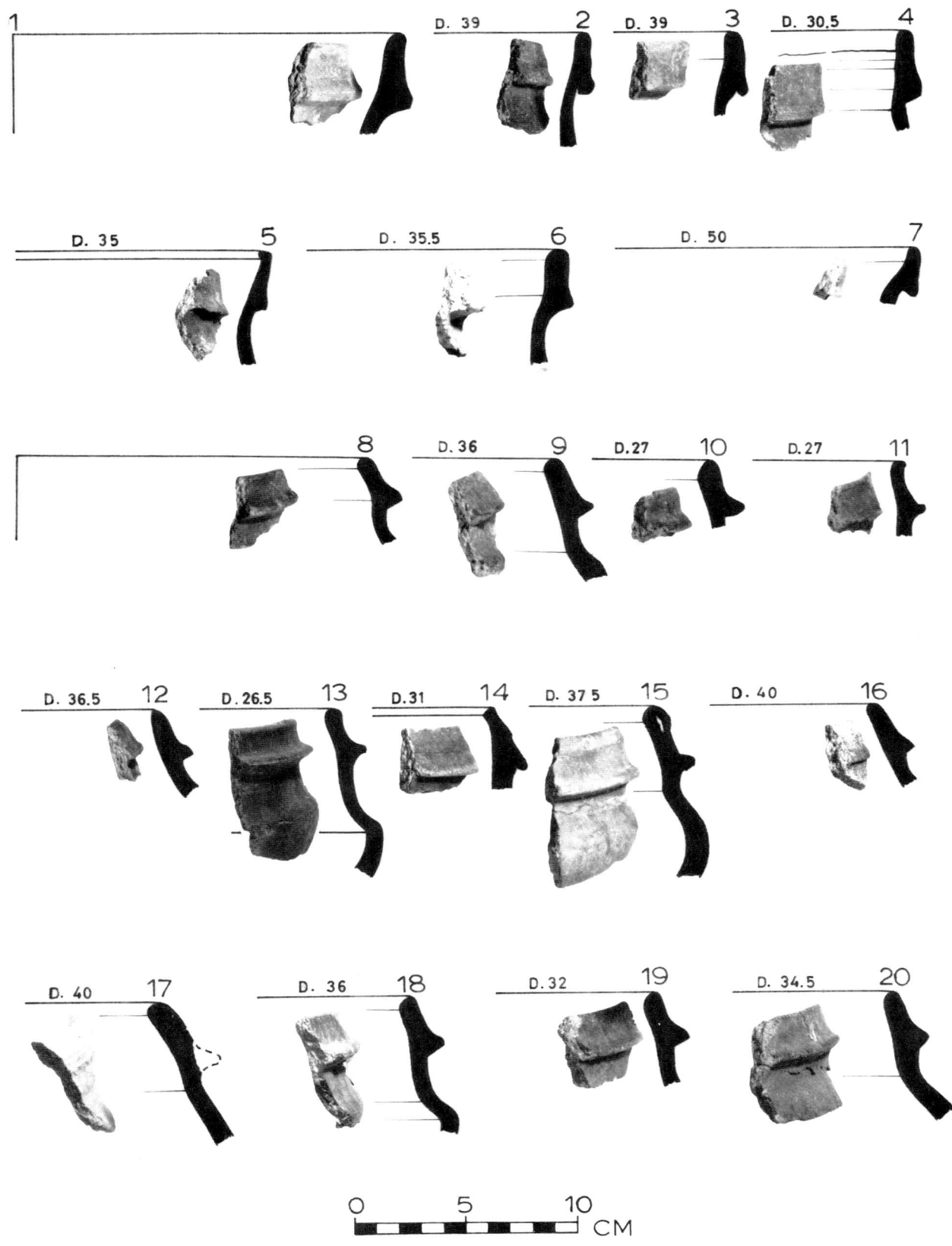

FIG. 66 (CONTINUED)

1. Identification		2. Section						3. Surface	
a. Item	b. Square, Locus Basket	a. Fabric Color	b. Core		c. Non-Plastics			a. Exterior	b. Interior
			Color	Extent	Type	Size	Frequency	Density	Color, n-p, voids, forming, finishing features	Same
20. Cook Pot Rim	same No. 126	rd br to br	dk gr	+50%	cal	m,s,f	m	med	*Ex*: rd br to gr, many n-p protrude, some seen, wet-smoothing, flange treated as No. 18. *In*: lt rd br, many n-p protrude, few seen, wiping is horiz.	
21. Cook Pot Rim	same No. 127	yl rd	dk gr	+50%	cal	m,s,f	m	med	*Ex & In*: lt rd br, many n-p protrude, seen, wet-smoothing.	
22. Cook Pot Rim	same No. 132	yl rd	gr	outer 75% rim 50% body	cal	m,s,f	m	med	*Ex*: br to gr, many n-p protrude, upper line of flange not fully sealed. *In*: lt rd br, some n-p protrude, many visible, wet-smoothing.	
23. Cook Pot Rim	same No. 133	yl rd	gr	30%	cal cht	s,f m	m f	med	*Ex & In*: pk gr to gr, some n-p protrude, rim eroded, wet-smoothed.	
24. Cook Pot Rim	same No. 134	yl rd	dk gr	+50%	cal	m,s,f	m	med h	*Ex & In*: lt rd br, n-p visible *ex*, most protrude *in*, rim tooled to give slight overhang on bottom of outer flange edge, wet-smoothed.	
25. Cook Pot Rim	same No. 135	yl rd	gr	50%	cal	m,s,f	m	med h	*Ex*: rd br, tiny n-p protrude, some seen, flange tooled with rounded edge. *In*: pk gr, surf as *ex*.	
26. Cook Pot Rim	same No. 139	yl rd	dk gr	+50%	cal	m,s,f	s-m	med	*Ex*: br to gr, many n-p protrude, some seen, wet-smoothing, flange as No. 19, better sealed.	
27. Cook Pot Rim	same No. 141	rd br	gr	+50%	cal	l,m,s f	s	med l	*Ex*: rd br to gr, flange slightly undercut. *In*: pk gr to gr, otherwise both sides as usual.	
28. Cook Pot Rim	same No. 115	br	gr	-50%	cal	m,s,f	m	med	*Ex*: pk gr, n-p protrude, wet-smoothing, *In*: rd br, some n-p protrude, seen, wet-smoothing.	
29. Cook Pot Rim	same No. 118	rd br	lt gr	50%	cal	l,m,s,f	m	med h	*Ex*: br, many n-p protrude many visible, finishing is a bit coarse, excess clay remaining to roughen rim edge, also deep groove under flange irreg depth. *In*: pk gr, many n-p protrude, seen, wet-smoothing approx horiz.	
30. Cook Pot Rim	same No. 122	yl rd	dk gr	+50%	cal	m,s,f	m	med h	*Ex*: rd br to gr, many n-p protrude, some seen, some pit voids, horiz wipe lines, groove under flange tooled but irreg in depth varying from 4-10mm. *In*: lt rd br, many n-p protrude, some visible, horiz wet-smoothing, *in* of rim has 3 shallow grooves.	
31. Cook Pot Rim	same No. 137	br-gr	dk gr	+50%	cal	m,s,f	m	med h	*Ex & In*: lt gr, few n-p protrude, none seen (surf is encrusted), forming lines *in*, *ex* bottom of flange tooled.	
32. Cook Pot Rim	same No. 125	yl rd	dk gr	50% rim +10% inner Body inner 30%	cal	l,m,s,f	m	med h	*Ex*: rd br, many n-p protrude, some seen, flange bottom tooled flat, edge squared by slight depression, on rim excess rolled over to *ex*. *In*: rd gr, many n-p protrude, seen, wet-smoothed, few lime spalls.	
33. Cook Pot Rim	same No. 128	dk gr	dk gr	100%	cal	s,f	m	med	*Ex*: dk gr, n-p protrude, light smoothing, top of rim slightly rolled to *ex*. *In*: many pits, n-p seen, forming lines horiz.	
34. Cook Pot Rim	same No. 129	rd yl	dk gr	+50%	cal	m,s,f	s	med l	*Ex & In*: rd br, many n-p visible, some protrude covered, wet-smoothing seen best on *in*, rim flange on *ex* undercut.	
35. Cook Pot Rim	same No. 123	rd br	dk gr	+50% rim +25% body	cal	m,s,f	s	med	*Ex & In*: rd br, *ex* rim 2ndary burn dk gr, many n-p seen, some protrude, wet-smoothing lines. Rim folded over (fold void visible), followed by top fold-over.	

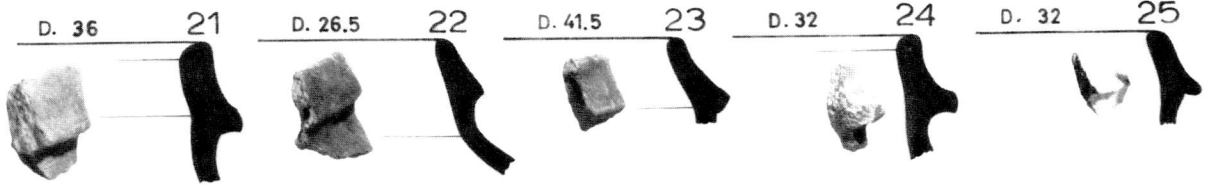
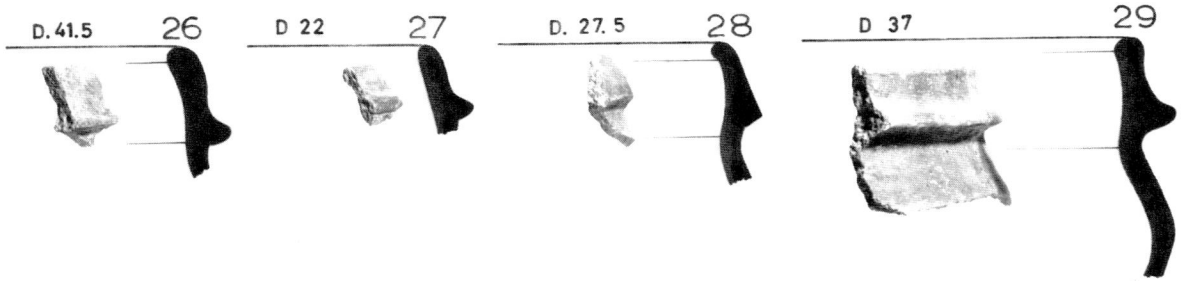
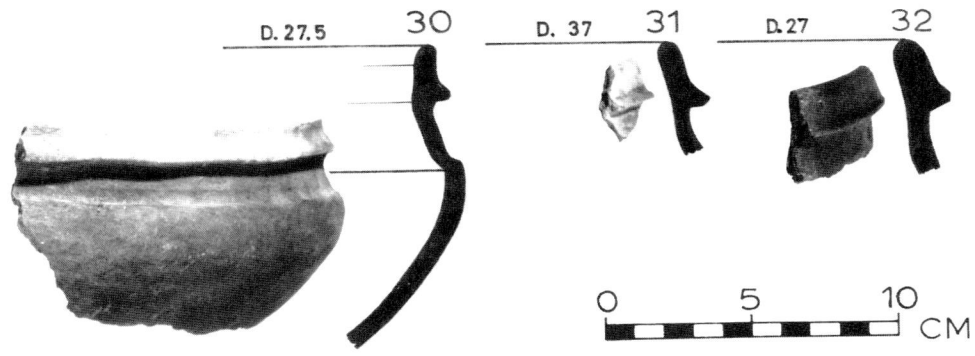
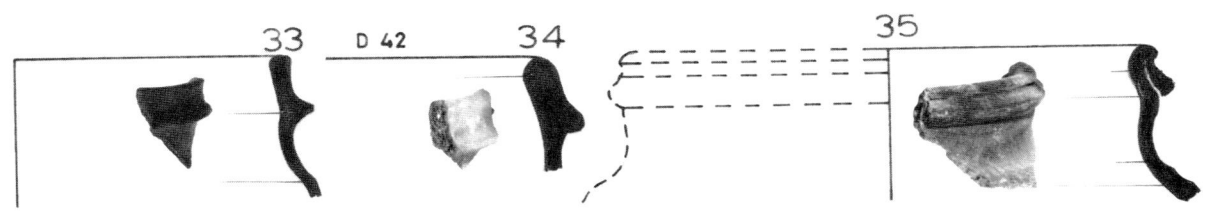

205

FIG. 67 POTTERY FROM CISTERN 74 (MOSTLY PERIOD IIB)

1. Identification		2. Section						3. Surface	
a.	b.	a.	b. Core		c. Non-Plastics			a. Exterior	b. Interior
Item	Square, Locus Basket	Fabric Color	Color	Extent	Type	Size	Frequency	Density	Color, n-p, voids, forming, finishing features	Same
1. Jar? Rim	SW 6-2 74 Cist 1 No. 3	lt rd to lt br	dk gr	+60%	lms bas	l,m,s m,s	s s	med	Ex: lt br, some n-p seen, chipping, fissures, straw voids, spalling, wet-smoothing. In: many n-p seen and many pits, spalls in lt br surf, wipe lines near top of rim.	
2. Cook Pot Rim	same No. 106	yl rd		none	cal bas	m,s s	m f	med	Ex: yl rd, many n-p protrude, seen mostly on rim, tooled undercut to rim, smoothing but voids at seam line seen ex. In: lt rd br, many n-p protrude, smoothing lines are horiz.	
3. Cook Pot TT 692	same Bas. 218	rd yl			(Not Available)				Ex: yl rd, many n-p protrude like fine sandpaper, criss-cross wipe lines at bottom but generally horiz, seam line smoothly finished, not quite so neat at rim. In: horiz smoothing lines around yl rd rim. Inside encrusted but seam line at midbody can be felt as raised sharp ridge. Neck join smoothed.	
4. Cook pot Rim & Body	same No. 97	rd	dk gr dk gr	50% patch 100%	cal	m,s,f	m	med h	Ex: yl rd in few places but most of surf is eroded reveals very many n-p, very salty look. Further heavy carbon deposit bottom and shoulder in patches, midbody seam line preserved. In: yl rd color more common, many pits on one side, many n-p visible on the other, reg horiz forming lines to rim, below handle point seam line has deeper than usual groove. Brittle.	
5. Cook Pot Rim & Handle	same Bas. 218	yl rd	br	25%	cal	m,s	s	low	Ex: rd mostly, dk pk around handle, n-p seen only on rim, handle, most are covered. Smoothing is generally horiz except handle which has few voids. In: rd, as ex except that forming depressions are very clear, also patch of 2cm-wide hole not detectable on ex.	
6. Cook Pot Rim & Handle	same No. 99	yl rd	dk gr	50-75%	cal	m,s,f	m	med l	See No. 3. Ex: rd br, some n-p seen, more on handle and rim; seam lines at neck and midbody prominent, shoulder smoother than bottom. In: rd br forming ridges covered with fine-line horiz grooves, seam line at neck join shows more protruding but covered n-p than is usual.	

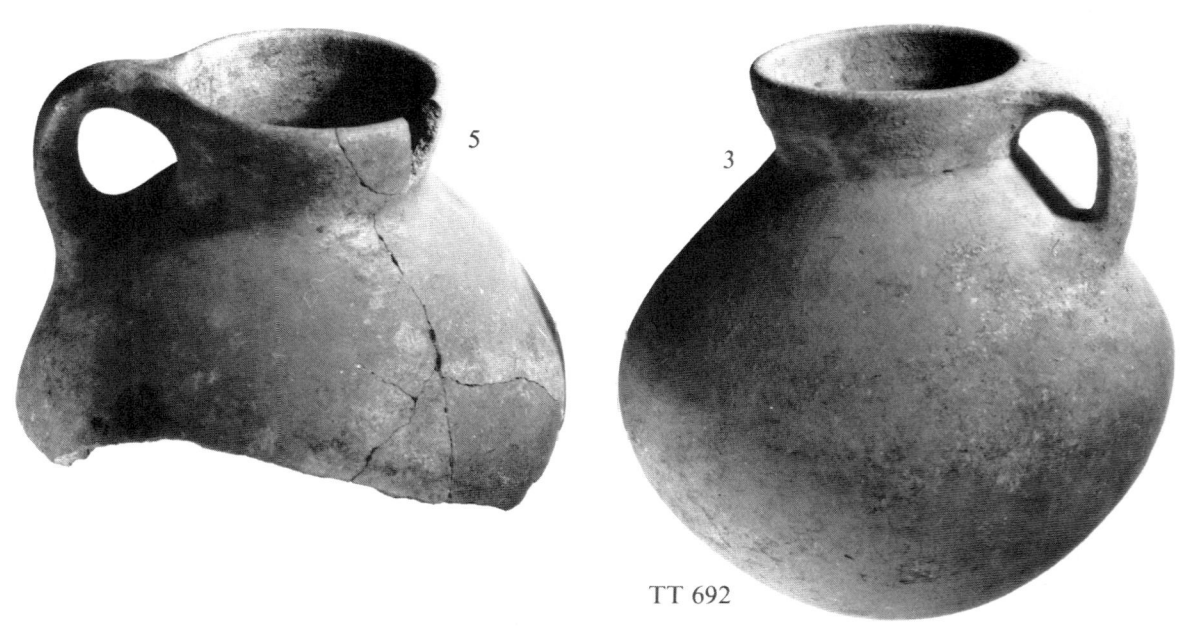

TT 692

206

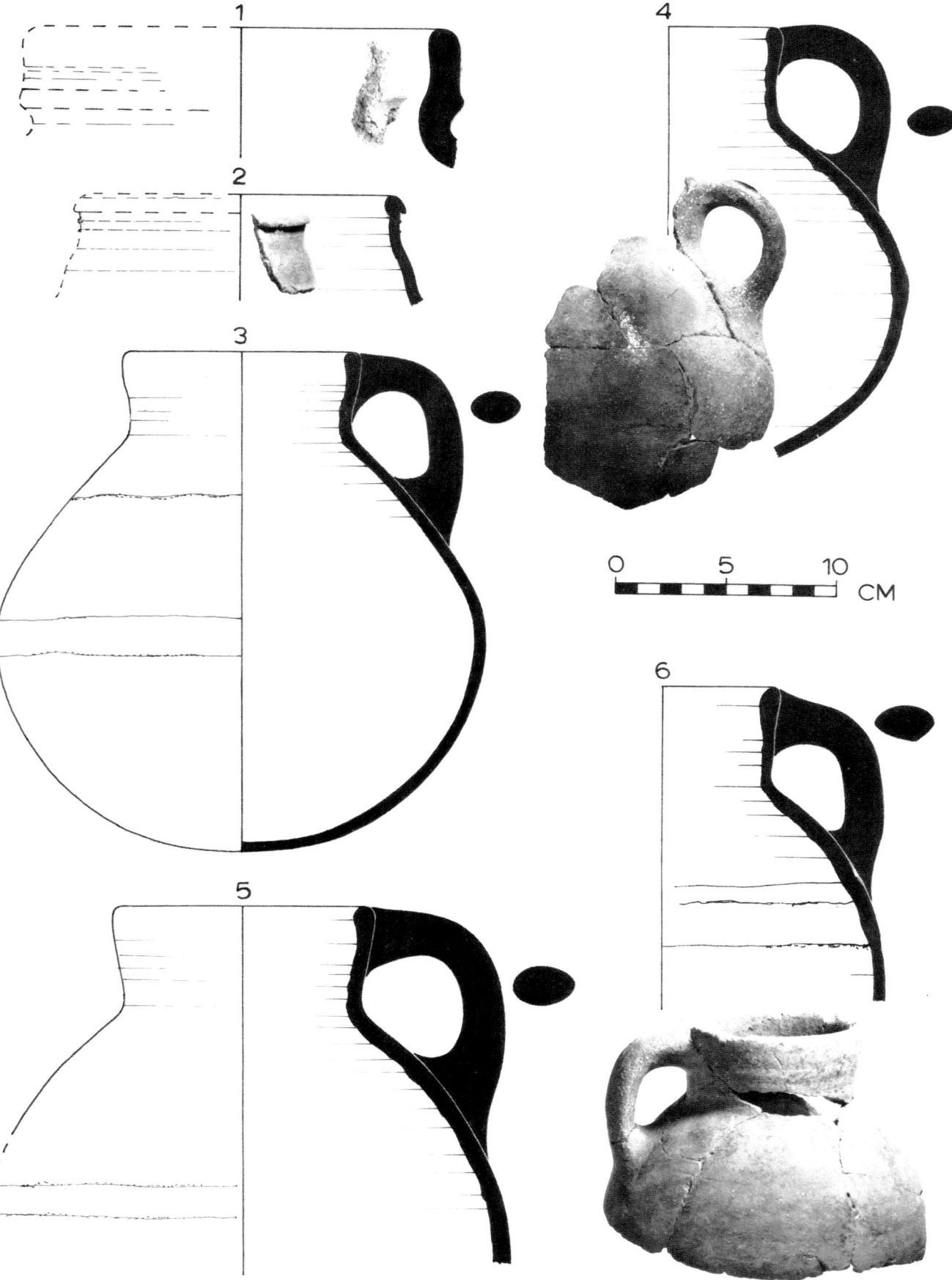

FIG. 68 POTTERY FROM CISTERN 74 (MOSTLY PERIOD IIB)

1. Identification		2. Section							3. Surface	
a.	b.	a.	b. Core		c. Non-Plastics				a. Exterior	b. Interior
Item	Square, Locus Basket	Fabric Color	Color	Extent	Type	Size	Frequency	Density	Color, n-p, voids, forming, finishing features	Same
1. Cook Pot Rim & Handle	SW 6-2 74 Cist 1 No. 101	yl rd	dk gr	50% body 80% handle	cal	m,s,f	m	med	*Handle*: many n-p protrude on rd br surf, more are visible, straw voids, wet-smoothing vert, horiz at rim join. *Body in*: rd br, n-p as handle, smoothing lines interrupted by fingerprints. Forming ridges clear as shoulder begins.	
2. Cook Pot Rim & Handle	same No. 98	yl rd	lt gr	0-50%	cal	m,s,f	m	med h	*Ex*: rd br, many n-p seen upper shoulder, rim, many protruding covered. Forming ridges fainter than wet-smoothing lines on neck, flashing line patch at neck base. *In*: rd br, reg shallow horiz forming ridges to neck where flashing line is coarsely finished, wet-smoothing is horiz.	
3. Cook Pot Rim	same No. 15	yl rd	lt br gr	50% body 50% rim	cal	s,f	s-m	low	*Ex & In*: rd br, many n-p protrude, some seen, horiz smoothing *ex*, forming lines *in*, vert wipe lines on *ex*.	
4. Cook Pot Rim	same No. 103	yl rd		none	cal	s,f	s-m	low	*Ex & In*: yl gr to dk gr due to 2ndary firing, many n-p protrude, slight over fold of rim to *ex*, wet-smoothing.	
5. Cook Pot Rim	same No. 104	yl rd	ck gr	40%	cal	m,s,f	s-m	med l	*Ex*: rd, many n-p protrude, some visible, horiz wet-smoothing, same true for *in* which is rd br, lower rim difficult to explain. *Ex* rim & neck burned dk gr on L.	
6. Cook Pot Rim & Handle	same No. 100	yl rd	dk gr	90% handle 50% body	cal	s,f	s-m	low	*Handle & Body*: rd br, n-p protrude, more are seen, forming ridges prominent on *in*, *ex* join smoothed horiz above & below.	
7. Cook Pot Rim & Handle	same No. 102	yl rd rd br	dk gr	50-75%	cal	m,s,f	s-m	med l	*Ex*: rd br, neck dk gr, also part of body, many n-p protrude, some seen, criss-cross smoothing on body horiz on neck, flashing line below shoulder. *In*: lt rd br, horiz forming ridges, join at flashing point, many tiny pit and straw voids.	
8. Cook Pot Rim	same No. 105	br		none	cal	m,s,f	s-m	low	*Ex & In*: rd br, on *ex* dk rd br due to 2ndary firing. Some protruding n-p, few visible, esp on *in*. Excess clay unsmoothed on *in*, i.e., appears over wet-smoothing lines.	

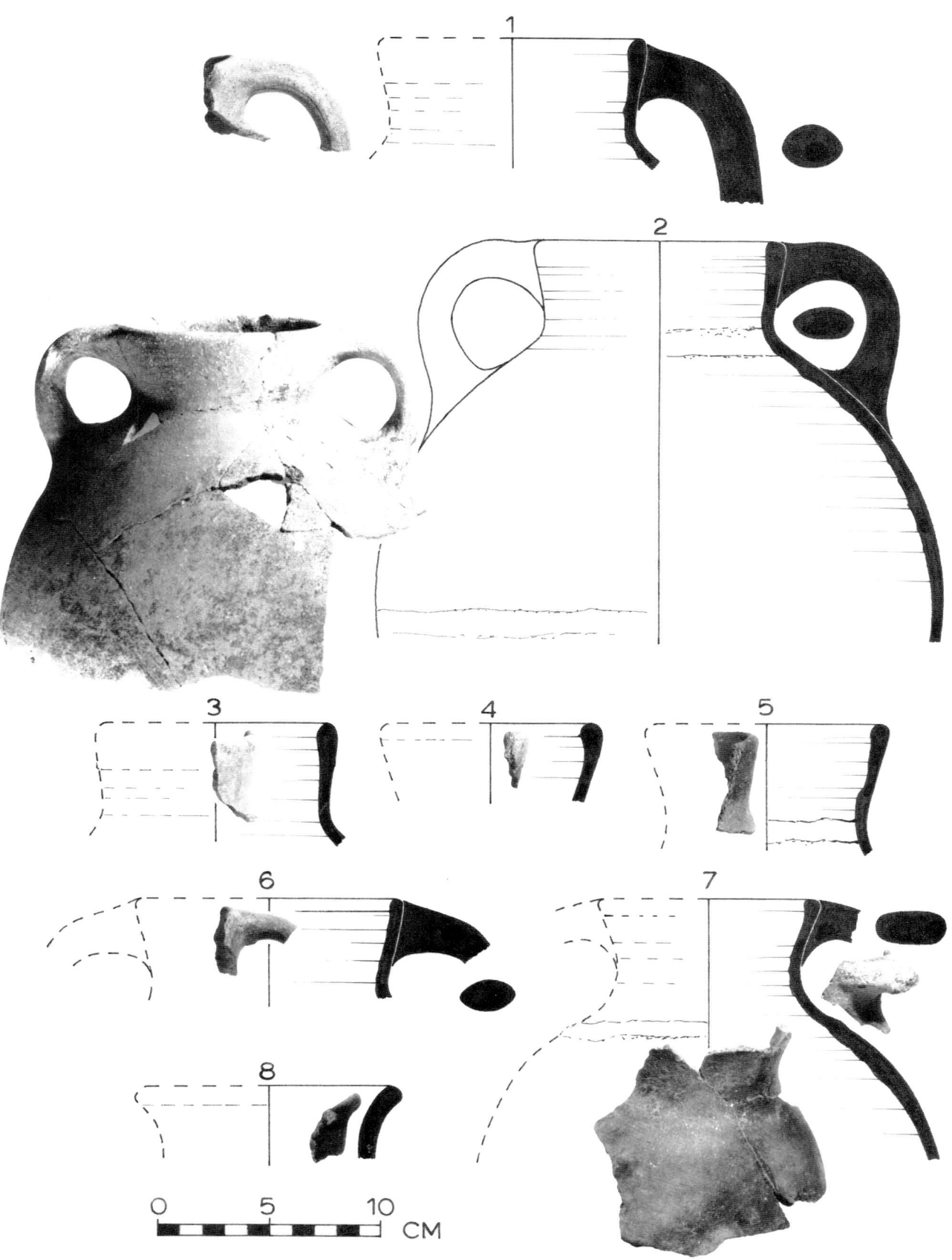

FIG. 69 POTTERY FROM CISTERN 74 (MOSTLY PERIOD IIB)

1. Identification		2. Section							3. Surface	
a.	b.	a.	b. Core		c. Non-Plastics				a. Exterior	b. Interior
Item	Square, Locus Basket	Fabric Color	Color	Extent	Type	Size	Frequency	Density	Color, n-p, voids, forming, finishing features	Same
1. Baking Tray	SW 6-2 74 Cist 1 No. 95	br	dk gr	+25% rim inner +50% bottom	sand	m,s,f	s-m	low	*Ex*: rd br, some n-p protrude, many drag marks L to R. wide groove near rim, narrow incised line lower, few larger random pits circular wet-smoothing lines are faint. *In*: many n-p protrude, some visible, generally horiz wet-smoothing crossed with slant lines, rim edge slightly folded over inward.	
2. Baking Tray	same No. 96	rd br	dk gr	inner 75%	sand	m,s,f	s-m	low	*Ex*: dk br to gr due to carbon, circular smoothing, many drag marks, several shallow punch marks made with blunt instrument from R slanting to L.	
3. Chalice Foot	same No. 93	pk to lt br	dk gr dk gr	none bottom 100% bowl 50% stem	lms cal	l,m,s m,s	s s	med	*Ex*: dk pk, some n-p seen, some protrude, straw voids common, circular wet-smoothing. *Ex*: bowl, heavy carbon deposit on most, many n-p protrude, covered. *In*: foot, dk pk, forming ridges wide & deep at bottom third.	
4. Chalice Foot	same No. 94	lt rd	dk gr	75%	lms	l,m,s	s-m	med	*Ex*: lt rd to pk, many n-p visible, also covered & protruding, straw voids, horiz wipe marks. *In*: same as ex except for forming ridges, visible in upper half. See Fig. 53:5.	
5. Chalice Bowl Rim	same No. 65	lt br	lt gr	75%	lms cht	m,s,f s,f	s s	med	*Ex*: dk pk, many tiny lms spalls, circular forming lines around outer edge, smoothing inside. *In*: lt br, chipping, pits but fewer n-p visible.	
6. Lamp Lip	same No. 142	pk gr	lt gr	75%	lms	l,m,s	s	med	*Ex & In*: lt rd br to pk gr, many n-p visible, some protrude, shallow smoothing lines along flattened *in* rim folded to lip which is dk gr with carbon deposit.	

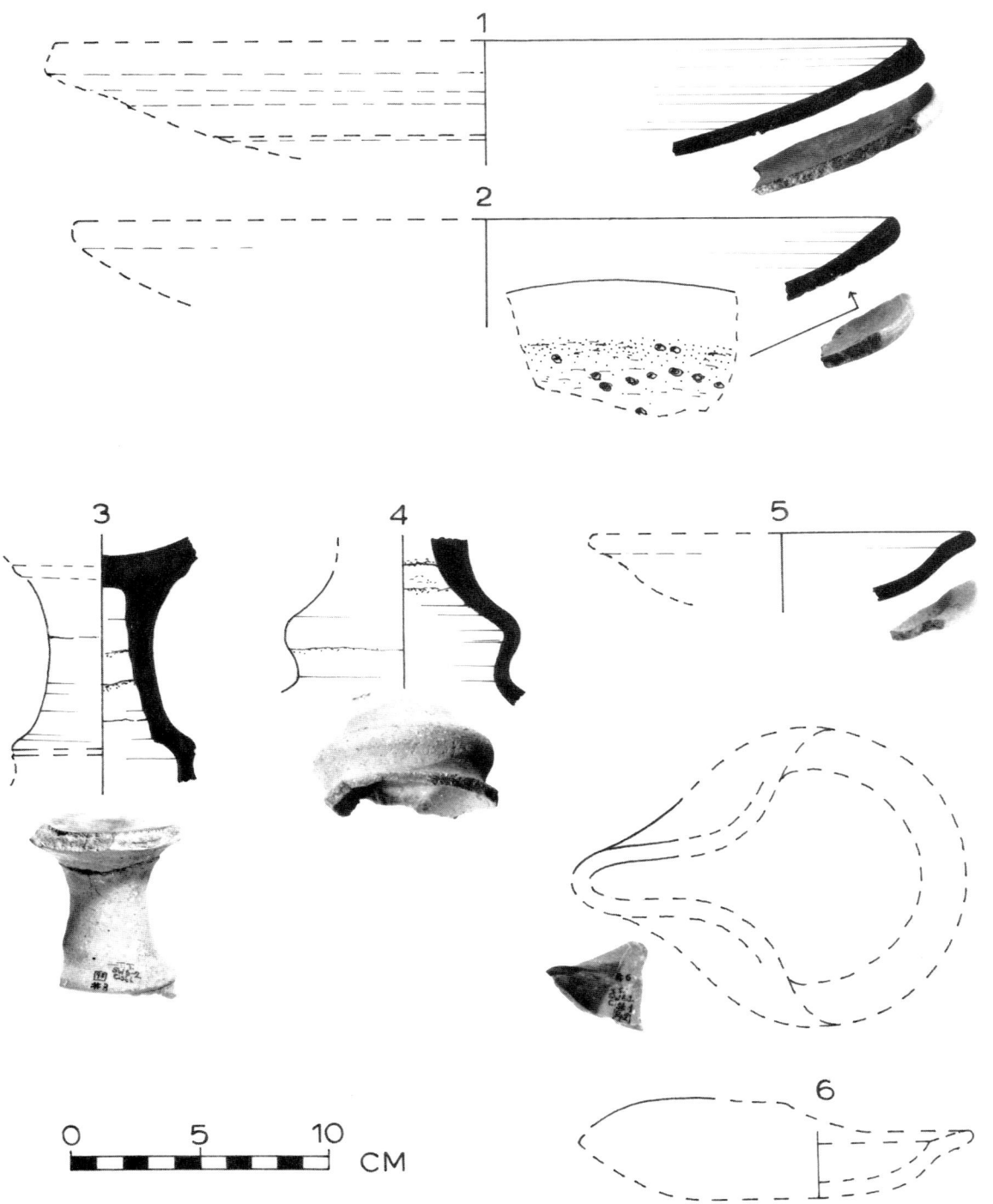

FIG. 70 POTTERY FROM SW 4-7, LOCUS 41 (PERIOD III)

1. Identification		2. Section							3. Surface	
a.	b.	a.	b. Core		c. Non-Plastics				a. Exterior	b. Interior
Item	Square, Locus Basket	Fabric Color	Color	Extent	Type	Size	Frequency	Density	Color, n-p, voids, forming, finishing features	Same
	SW 4-7									
1. Jug Rim	41.67	dk pk	lt br	inner 50%	lms	l,m,s	s	med l	*Ex & In*: pk, large n-p seen embedded, horiz finishing lines interrupted by fingerprint. *In* encrusted with lms.	
2. Jug Rim	41.67	rd to lt br	lt gr	+50%	lms	m,s,f	s	med	*Ex & In*: dk pk, some n-p seen, wet-smoothing, spalling, lm encrustation.	
3. Crater Rim	41.67	lt br	gr	+50%	lms	m,s	s	low	*Ex & In*: dk pk, few n-p seen but protrude *in* only; wet-smoothing.	
4. Crater Rim	41.67	rd yl to lt br	dk gr	-75%	lms See 23:7	s,f	f	low	*Ex & In*: rd yl, some n-p protrude, covered, few seen, somewhat irreg but horiz smoothing line. Many horiz voids, perhaps straw voids.	
5. **Bowl** Rim	41.67	dk pk	lt br	outer 75%	lms	l,m,s	s	med l	*Ex*: lt pk, some n-p protrude, covered, some visible, smoothing lines, drag marks. *In*: rd yl, few large n-p seen, spalling, wet-smoothing.	
6. Cook Pot Rim	41.67	yl rd	dk gr	75%	cal	m,s,f	s-m	med l	*Ex & In*: rd br, many tiny n-p protrude, covered, fine-line smoothing.	

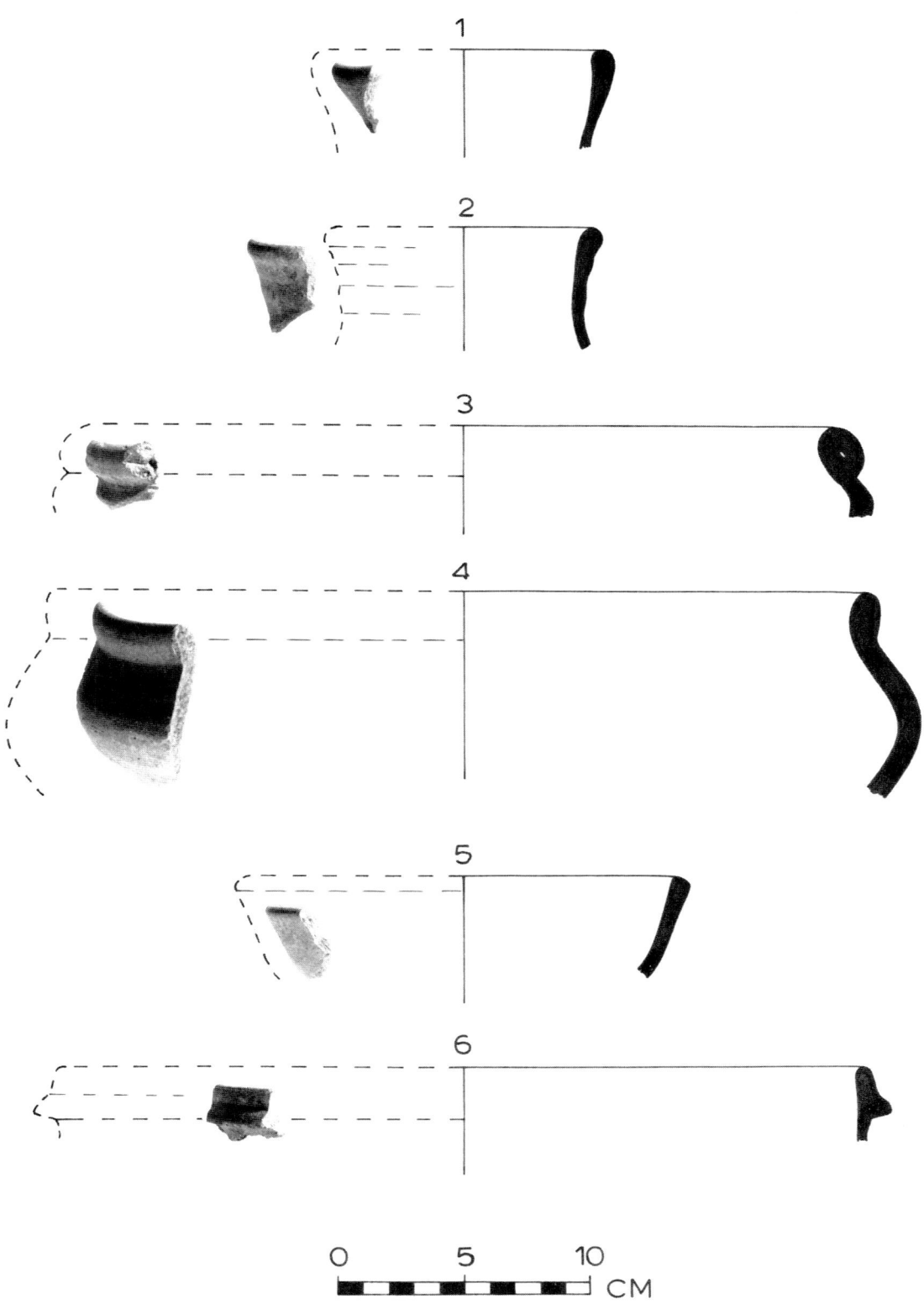

FIG. 71 POTTERY FROM THE NORTHEAST OUTWORK, NEO-2 (PERIOD III)

1. Identification		2. Section						3. Surface	
a.	b.	a.	b. Core		c. Non-Plastics			a. Exterior	b. Interior
Item	Square, Locus Basket	Fabric Color	Color	Extent	Type	Size	Frequency	Density	Color, n-p, voids, forming, finishing features	Same
	Neo-2									
1. Bowl Rim	3.61	lt rd	lt rd br	+50%	lms	l,m,s	s	med l	*Ex* & *In*: lt rd, few n-p visible thru shallow spalling, few tiny pits, reg smoothing lines clearest on rim top.	
2. Bowl Rim	36.70	rd yl		none	cal lms	m,s m,s	m f	med	*Ex* & *In*: rd yl, some n-p protrude, few visible, wet-smoothing lines horiz, reg, *ex* encrusted.	
3. Bowl Rim	3.61	st br		none	bas brown?	l,m,s l,m,s	m s	med	*Ex* & *In*: rd br, many n-p visible, continuous horiz burnish, encrusted.	
4. Bowl Rim	36.70	rd to lt br	dk gr	+50%	lms bas	l,s,f m,s	s f	low	*Ex* & *In*: lt rd with rd separated burnished bands. From rim it appears burnished slip has chipped revealing many protruding n-p.	
5. Bowl Rim	36.70	yl rd to rd br	dk gr	+50%	lms bas	s,f l	s vf	low	*Ex* & *In*: continuous burnish over lt rd *in* and rd *ex* slip. Encrusted.	
6. Bowl Rim	3.61	yl rd	vlt gr	-25%	bas lms	m,s m	f f	low	*Ex* & *In*: burnished rd slip in separated bands, few n-p protrude.	

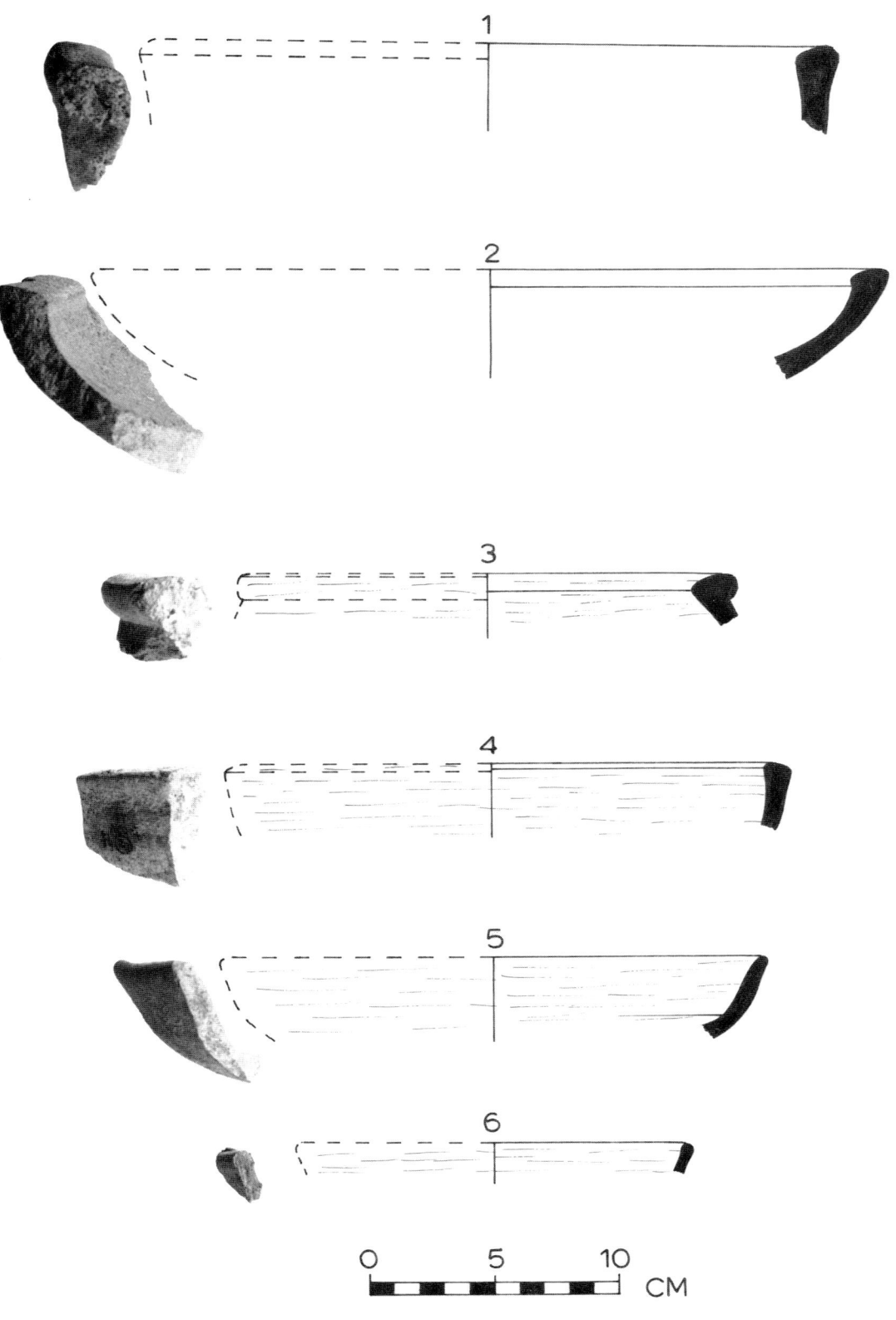

FIG. 72 POTTERY FROM SW 4-7, LOCUS 36 (PERIOD IV)

1. Identification		2. Section							3. Surface	
a.	b.	a.	b. Core		c. Non-Plastics				a. Exterior	b. Interior
Item	Square, Locus Basket	Fabric Color	Color	Extent	Type	Size	Frequency	Density	Color, n-p, voids, forming, finishing features	Same
1. Jug Rim	SW 4-7 36.61	lt br		none	lms	l,m,s	f	low	*Ex*: pk gr, some n-p seen embedded, few protrude covered *in*, irreg horiz smoothing grooves. *In*: dk pk, otherwise as *ex*. Slip *ex* and *in*.	
2. Jug Rim	same	lt br		none	lms	m,s	f	low	*Ex & In*: dk pk, wet-smoothing irreg over many n-p covered, protruding. Grayed with carbon cover.	
3. Juglet Rim & Handle	same	yl rd to lt br	gr	none (body) 40% (handle)	lms cal	s,f m,s	f f	low	*Handle*: lt rd br, many protruding n-p, covered, many straw voids, slight trace of smoothing down handle. *Body In*: lt rd br, forming ridges, some n-p protrude covered, fold-over of rim edge untrimmed.	
4. Crater Rim	same	rd yl	lt br	90%	lms	l,s	vf	vlow	*Ex & In*: rd yl, few forming lines *in* below rim, finishing lines on rim *ex*. Tooled fine-line edge to *ex* rim fold-over. Lm encrusted.	
5. Crater Rim	same	rd yl	d< gr	75%	lms	s,f	s	vlow	*Ex*: dk gr, some spalling, some horiz fissures; bottom edge of fold-over rim tooled. *In*: rd br, much deep pitting, very few seen.	
6. Bowl Rim	same	lt br		none	lms	l,m,s	s	med l	*Ex*: dk pk, some n-p seen on surf embedded, erosion of rim surf, irreg rim smoothing leaves shallow ridge just above base. *In*: dk pk, n-p embedded on surf, faint traces of smoothing.	
7. Bowl Rim	same	rd yl to br	lt gr	50%	lms	m,s,f	f	low	*Ex & In*: lt rd br, many tiny n-p slightly protrude, covered, tiny drag marks seen thru wet-smoothing lines.	
8. Cook Pot Rim	same	rd yl		none	cal	s,f	m	med	*Ex & In*: rd br, many n-p protrude, covered, wet-smoothing, encrusted.	
9. Cook Pot Rim	same	br		none	cal	s,f	m	med l	*Ex & In*: rd br, some n-p protrude, covered, wet-smoothing, tooled rim base on *ex*, some carbon on rim *ex*.	

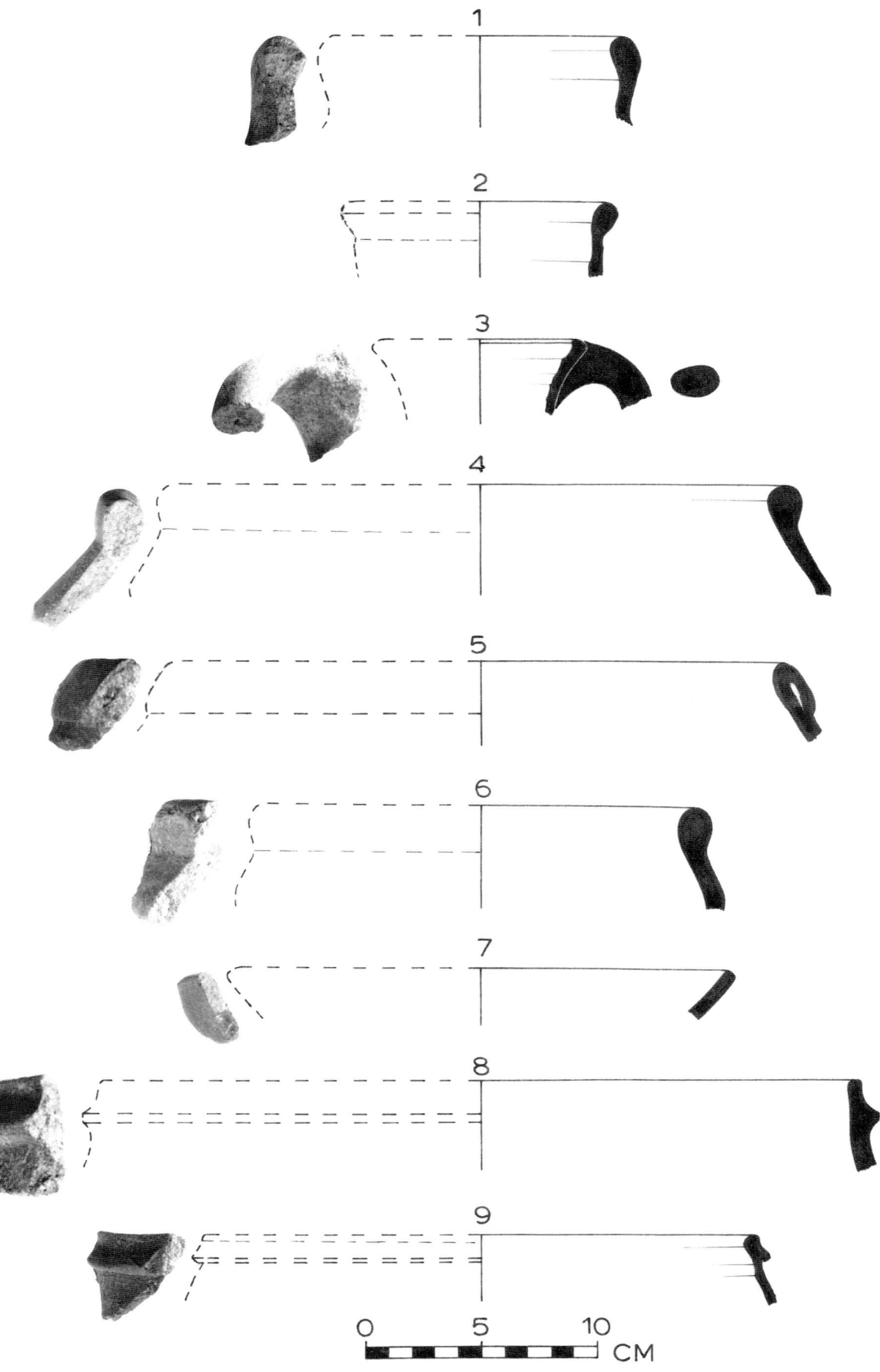

FIG. 73 POTTERY FROM SW 4-7, LOCUS 37 (PERIOD IV)

1. Identification		2. Section							3. Surface	
a.	b.	a.	b. Core		c. Non-Plastics				a. Exterior	b. Interior
Item	Square, Locus Basket	Fabric Color	Color	Extent	Type	Size	Frequency	Density	Color, n-p, voids, forming, finishing features	Same
1. Jar Handle	SW 4-7 37.62	dk pk to st br		none body 50% handle	lms	l,m,s	s	low	*Handle*: dk pk, some protruding, some visible n-p, straw voids in vert wiping. *Body In*: lt br, few tiny pits, n-p protrude and some seen, horiz wiping.	
2. Jug Rim	same	rd yl	lt br	inner 75%	lms grog	s,f l	s vf	low	*Ex & In*: rd yl, v few n-p protrude, smoothing, bits of excess clay pasted over smoothing on *in*.	
3. Bowl Rim	same	yl rd	lt br	outer 60%	sand	vf	m	low	*Ex*: pk gr, few n-p protrude, wet-smoothing on rim, covered below rim with pk gr slip. *In*: pk, pitting thru reg horiz wet-smoothing lines.	
4. Bowl Rim	same	rd yl to lt br	dk gr	-50%	lms bas cal	s s s	vf vf vf	vlow	*Ex & In*: pk, 3 spaced horiz burnish lines *in* continuous on *ex* over forming grooves.	
5. Bowl Rim	same	rd to yl br (rim)	dk gr	50% below rim	lms	s,f	f	vlow	*Ex & In*: lt rd br, few n-p seen, *ex* spalling, wet-smoothing, drag marks on *ex* bottom.	
6. Bowl Rim	same	rd yl	lt br	90%	lms	l,m,s	f	low	*Ex & In*: rd yl, some n-p protrude, covered, wet-smoothing lines clear, *ex* not cleanly trimmed.	

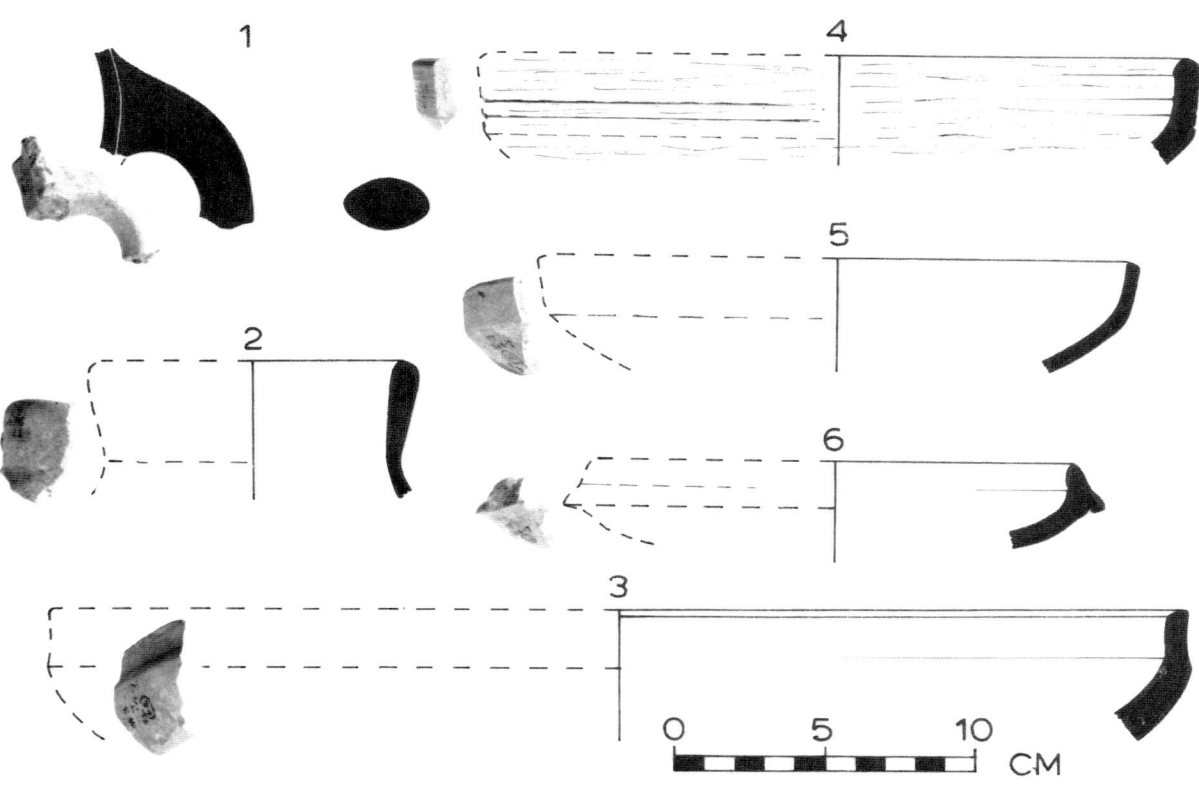

FIG. 74 POTTERY FROM SW 4-7, LOCUS 38a (PERIOD IV)

1. Identification		2. Section							3. Surface	
a.	b.	a.	b. Core		c. Non-Plastics				a. Exterior	b. Interior
Item	Square, Locus Basket	Fabric Color	Color	Extent	Type	Size	Frequency	Density	Color, n-p, voids, forming, finishing features	Same
1. Jug Rim	SW 4-7 38a. 63	rd yl	lt br	90%	lms	l,m,s	s	med l	*Ex*: rd yl, many n-p seen, lime spalls, slanting lines of wet-smoothing. *In*: rd yl, few n-p, pits, horiz smoothing, rim trim later.	
2. Crater Rim	same	lt br		none	lms	l,m,s	f	low	*Ex & In*: rd yl, few n-p protrude, covered, wet-smoothing more reg on rim than elsewhere. *Ex* rim base tool trimmed.	
3. **Bowl** Rim	same	lt rd to lt br		none	lms	m,s,f	f	vlow	*Ex & In*: lt rd, few n-p protrude, covered, pit voids *ex*, base of rim *in* over-fold is irreg. Wet-smoothed.	
4. **Bowl** Rim	same	rd to pl br	lt gr	10%	lms bas cal	s,f s s	f f vf	low	*Ex*: lt br, continuous burnish to 2.5cm below rim, partly eroded. *In*: rd slip burnished with 2 reserve bands below the rim. The burnish gloss has been eroded.	

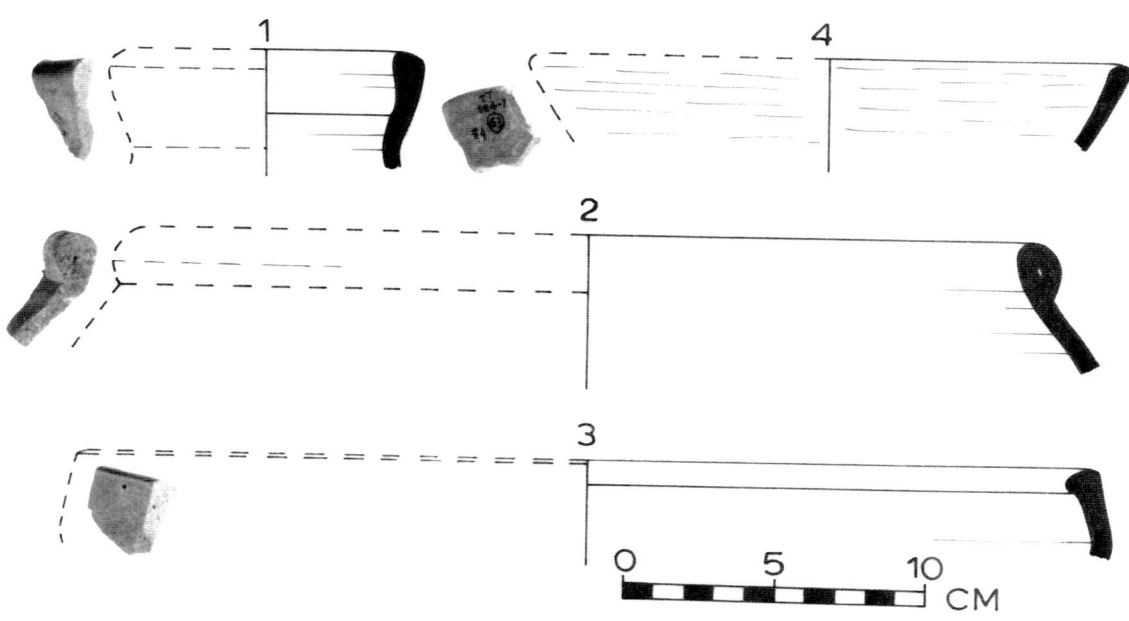

FIG. 75 POTTERY FROM SW 5-6, LOCUS 16 (PERIOD V)

1. Identification		2. Section						3. Surface	
a.	b.	a.	b. Core		c. Non-Plastics			a. Exterior	b. Interior
Item	Square, Locus Basket	Fabric Color	Color	Extent	Type	Size	Frequency	Density	Color, n-p, voids, forming, finishing features	Same
1. Jar Rim & Handle*	SW 5-6 16.36	lt rd	dk gr	-100%	lms	m,s,f	f	low	*Ex:* wk rd to rd gr, some spalls, few n-p seen, some protruding, covered, smoothing faint, prominent dent on L of handle on shoulder, flashing line in middle of upper join of handle. *In:* lt rd, forming ridges prominent, patch behind bottom handle join. Some n-p protrude, covered, few pits, flashing line is clean join.	
2. Jar TT 1861	16.30	rd to rd br	gr	inner 50%	lms	f	s	vlow	*Ex:* pl rd, some tiny n-p protrude, covered, wet-smoothing faint lines rim to base, forming ridges at base, sharp ridge to flashing line on bottom of shoulder. *In:* pk gr to gr, shallow forming ridges end in squeezed off bottom point. Slight protruding ridge at flashing line under shoulder bottom.	
3. Jar Rim	same	rd	gr br	25%	grog	s,f	s	low	*Ex:* lt rd br, many n-p protrude below surf, many tiny pits, slip over faint wet-smoothing lines.	
4. Jar Handle & Body	same	lt rd	dk gr	80% handle inner 80% body	lms	s,f	f	low	*Ex:* lt rd, some n-p seen, embedded, some straw voids. *In:* pk some spalls, few pits, few shallow forming ridges.	
5. Jar Handle & Body	same	br	dk gr	75%	lms	m,s,f	s	low	*Ex:* dk pk, tiny n-p protrude, some chipping, uneven joins with shallow ridges. *In:* dk pk, some protruding covered n-p, forming ridges.	
6. Jar Handle	same	st br	dk gr	75%	lms	l,m,s	s	low	Dk pk to lt br, some n-p seen embedded, many straw voids vert. Bottom of handle completely detached from wall.	
7. Juglet Body & Handle	16.35	rd yl	lt gr br	+25% inner	bas cal	m,s s	s f	low	*Ex:* pl rd slip, covers some n-p, flashing line just above bottom. *In:* rd yl forming ridges become progressively faint toward neck, sharp ridge at flashing line.	
8. Jug Rim	16.30	rd yl		none	lms	l,f	s	low	*Ex & In:* dk pk, some n-p seen, faint wet-smoothing slanted.	

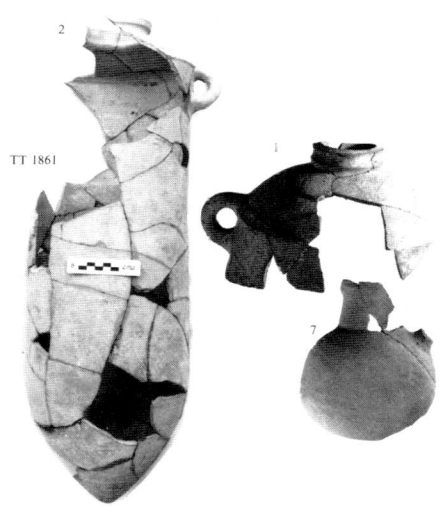

*TT 1865, SW 5-6, 16.34 is an unpublished parallel with more of body preserved.

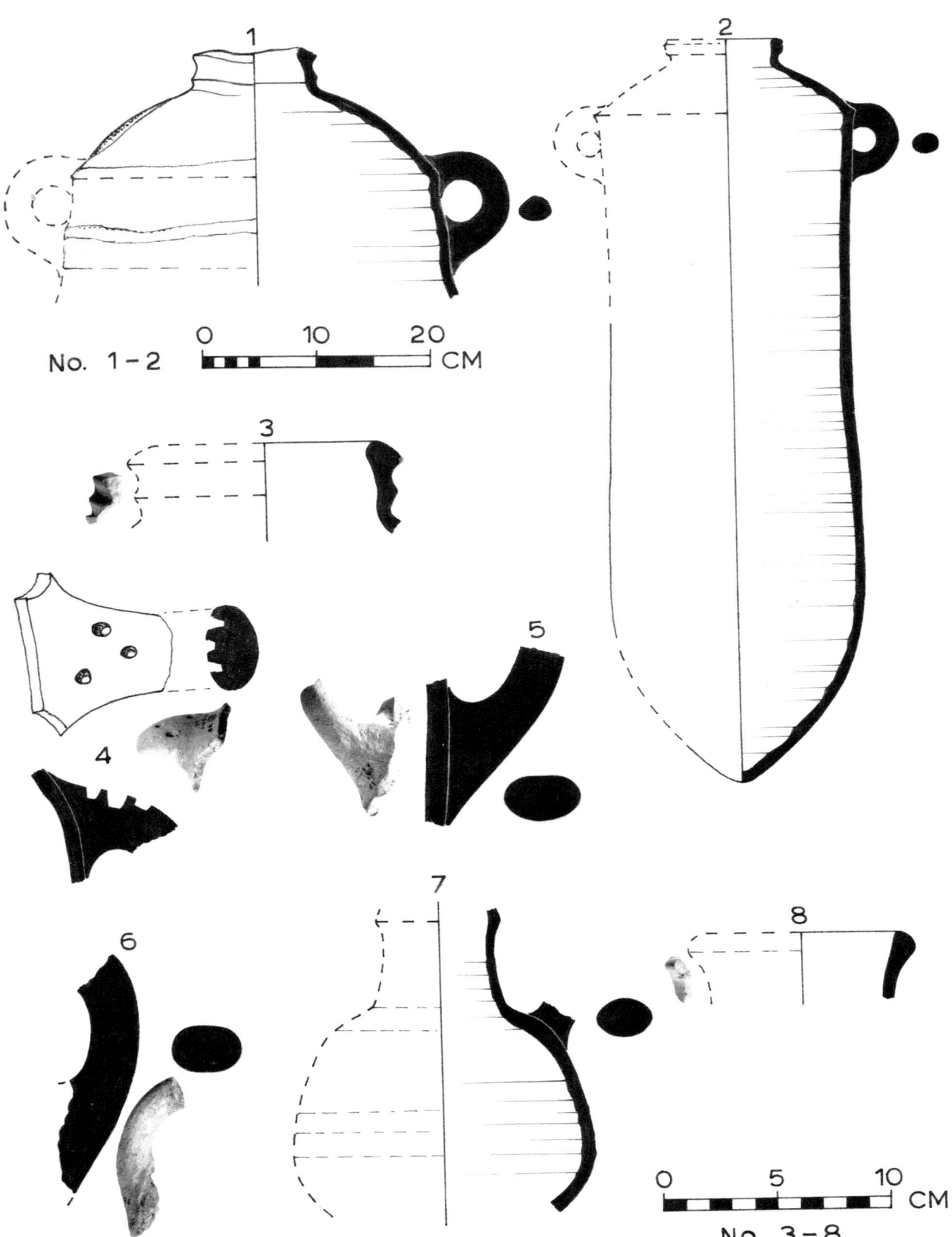

FIG. 76 POTTERY FROM SW 5-6, LOCUS 16 (PERIOD V)

1. Identification		2. Section						3. Surface	
a. Item	b. Square, Locus Basket	a. Fabric Color	b. Core		c. Non-Plastics			a. Exterior	b. Interior
			Color	Extent	Type	Size	Frequency	Density	Color, n-p, voids, forming, finishing features	Same
1. Crater Rim	SW 5-6 16.30	rd yl	gr br	50%	bas lms	l,f l,s	s s	low	*Ex & In*: dk pk, many tiny n-p protrude roughening surf, some lms seen, wet-smoothing lines *ex*, erosion on *in*.
2. Bowl Rim	same	lt gr	dk gr	90%	lms	m,s,f	f	vlow	*Ex & In*: lt gr, few n-p protrude, covered, wet-smoothing lines.
3. Bowl Rim	same	lt br		none (rim) 50% (bottom)	lms	m,f	f	vlow	*Ex & In*: dk pk, few n-p protrude, covered, few drag marks in circular smoothing *in*, some erosion and roughness due to unsmoothed excess clay on bottom. Slip.
4. **Bowl** Rim	same	rd yl	vlt gr	10%	lms bas	s,f s,f	f f	low	*Ex & In*: rd yl, some protruding, covered n-p, wet-smoothing more reg on *in* than *ex*. Slip.
5. Bowl Base	same	rd yl		none	lms bas	f s,f	s s	vlow	*Ex & In*: rd yl, slip, few n-p protrude, covered & visible on bottom, *In* has many tiny pits. Circular reg forming ridges on base bottom.
6. Cook Pot TT 1863	16.32	rd to yl rd	dk gr	+60% outer bottom	cal	m,s,f	m	med	*Ex*: wk rd to rd br, many n-p protrude, covered, wet-smoothed on shoulder. But bottom is much more rough with protruding n-p below flashing line, some fine-line smoothing near bottom. Moulded. *In*: lt rd br, many pits on shoulder and rim, n-p seen, below seam on bottom wipe lines are criss-cross but much more smoothed than *ex*. Some carbon deposit at bottom center.
7. Cook Pot Handle	same			(Identical with No. 6)					Same as no. 6, probably the same vessel.
8. Cook Pot Rim	16.30	rd br	dk gr	10%	cal	m,s	m	med	*Ex & In*: gr to dk gr, many n-p protrude, some seen, wet-smoothing lines faint. Carbon deposit.
9. Cook Pot Rim	same	rd br	dk br	+50%	cal	s,f	s	med l	*Ex & In*: rd br with carbon on *ex* flange & below. Some n-p protrude, few seen, faint smoothing.
10. Lamp Lip	same	rd yl	lt br dk gr	40% bottom 90% lip	lms	m,s,f	f	vlow	*Ex & In*: lt rd, carbon deposit at lip, mostly *in*. Smoothing lines before folding *ex* and *in*.

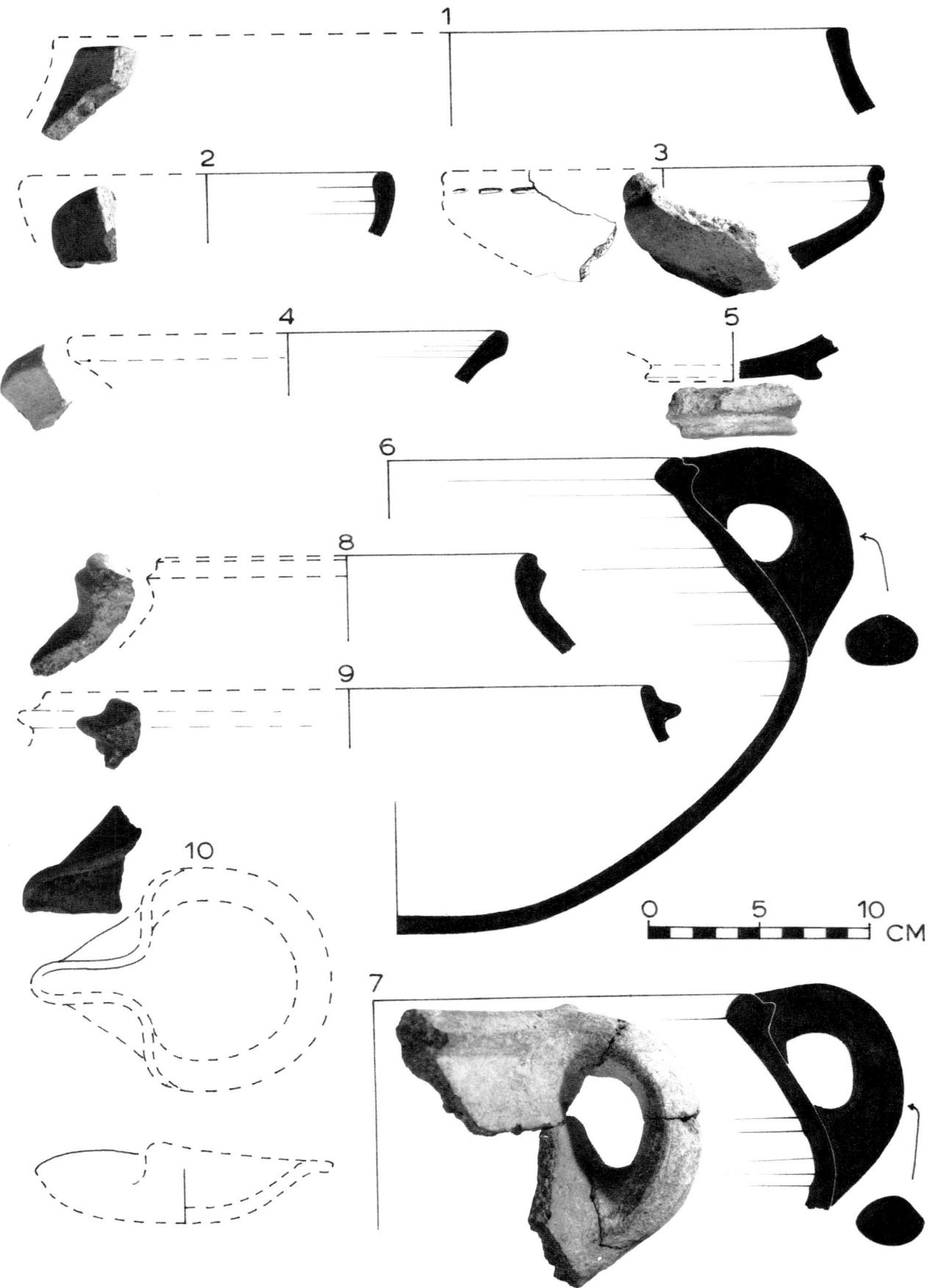

FIG. 77 POTTERY FROM SW 4-7, STONE-LINED PIT 7 (PERIOD VIA)

1. Identification		2. Section							3. Surface	
a.	b.	a.	b. Core		c. Non-Plastics				a. Exterior	b. Interior
Item	Square, Locus Basket	Fabric Color	Color	Extent	Type	Size	Frequency	Density	Color, n-p, voids, forming, finishing features	Same
1. Jar Rim	SW 4-7 7.79	gr	gr	100%	lms grog	m,s,f m,s	s f	low	*Ex & In*: dk pk to rd yl, gr carbon on *in*, many spalls, n-p seen, wet-smoothing on *in*, also *ex* but more faint.	
2. Jar Rim	same	rd	gr	+60% inner	lms	m,s,f	s	vlow	*Ex*: rd yl, some n-p protrude, covered, more seen, fine-line horiz wet-smoothing. *In*: vpl br, more n-p covered, fewer seen, forming ridges shallow.	
3. Jar Rim	same	yl rd		none	lms	m,s,f	vf	vlow	*Ex & In*: rd yl, irreg pitting, erosion yet few n-p seen.	
4. Jug Rim	same	rd	some dk gr	inner 50%	lms	l,m,s	f	vlow	*Ex*: rd gr, few n-p protrude, covered smoothing lines near top. *In*: rd, as *ex* but not as smooth.	
5. Juglet Handle	same	vpl br		none	grog bas	m,s s	f f	vlow	*Ex & In*: vpl br, vert wet-smoothing down handle, horiz *in* body. Paint is wk rd. Slip.	
6. Crater Rim	same	rd yl	gr	50%	lms bas	l,s,f m,s	s s	low	*Ex*: dk pk, many lms n-p seen both embedded and in spalling, tooled edge under rim. *In*: rd yl, some lime spalls, lms n-p, flat-bottom depressions at base of shoulder.	
7. Mortarium Rim	7.78	vpl br		none	sand	vf	s	vlow	*Ex & In*: vpl br to wh slip, somewhat pitted, esp *in*, circular forming ridges on *ex* esp. Tooled ridge under *ex* rim.	
8. Mortarium Rim	7.79	vpl br	rd yl	90%	sand lms	vf s	s f	vlow	Same as No. 7 except that slip is more vpl br.	
9. Mortarium Base	7.78	vpl br	rd yl	95%	sand	vf	s	vlow	Same as No. 8.	
10. Bowl Rim	same	dk pk	lt yl br	-100%	lms bas	m,s s,f	s s	low	*Ex & In*: lt rd, near *ex* rim, rd yl, some protruding n-p seen, some pits, some embedded, smoothing circular but faint on *in*, also *ex* where there is some chipping.	
11. Bowl Rim	7.79	vpl br	lt gr	rim none 90% body	lms bas	l,m s	s s	low	*Ex & In*: vpl br slip, many voids due to erratic pressures, the form is crudely handmade. Voids occur after basic smoothing which has not left the usual fine-line impressions.	

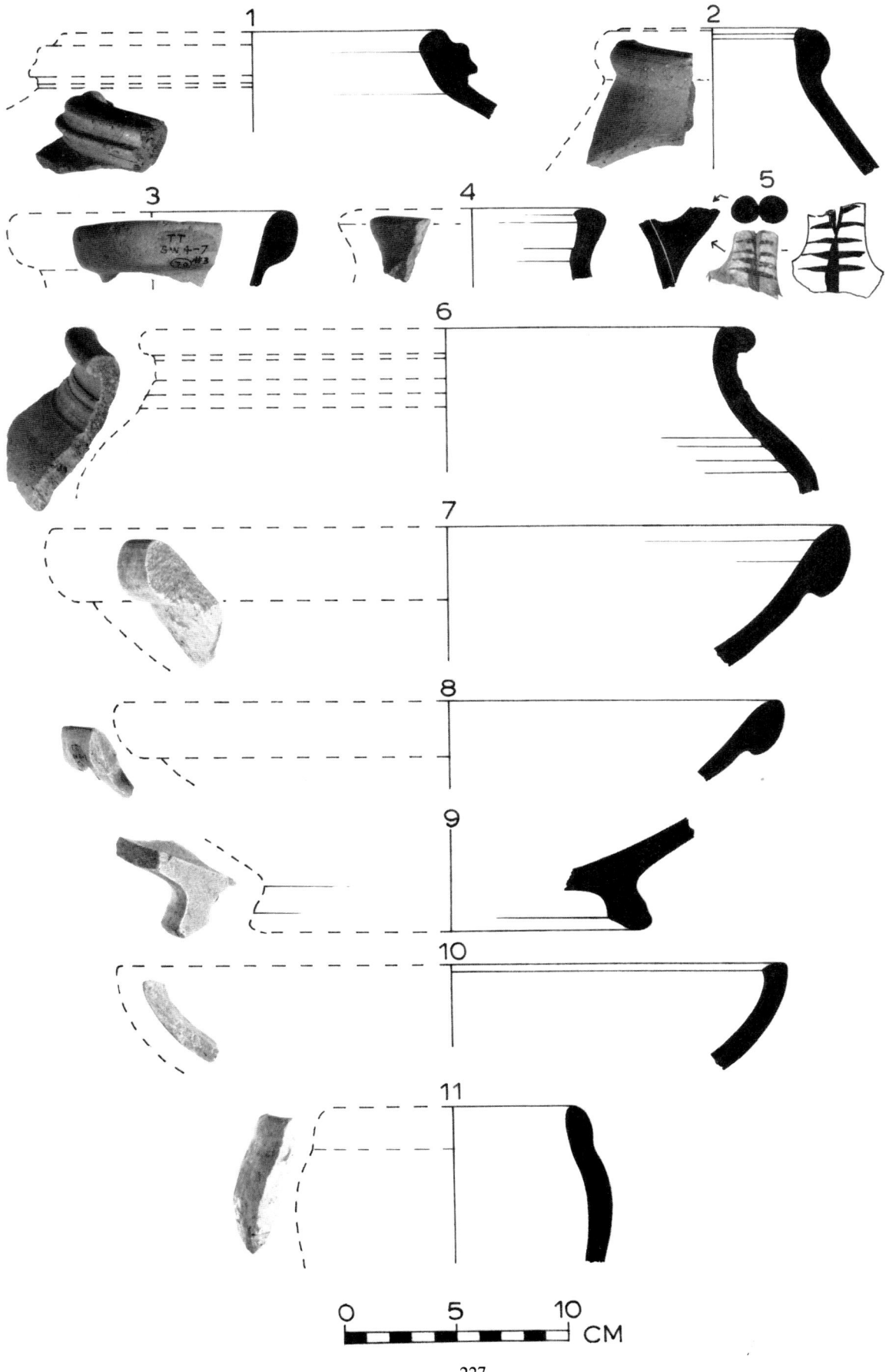

FIG. 78 POTTERY FROM SW 4-7, STONE-LINED PIT 7 (PERIOD VIA)

1. Identification		2. Section						3. Surface	
a.	b.	a.	b. Core		c. Non-Plastics			a. Exterior	b. Interior
Item	Square, Locus Basket	Fabric Color	Color	Extent	Type	Size	Frequency	Density	Color, n-p, voids, forming, finishing features	Same
1. Lamp Rim	SW 4-7 7.79	rd yl		none	sand	s,f	f	vlow	*Ex* & *In*: rd yl, very few n-p protrusions covered under wet-smoothing, wider lines on *ex* rim than *in*. Traces of burnish on *in*. Fingerprints interrupt *ex* finish. Bottom is shaved.
2. Lamp Lip	same	rd yl		none	sand +shell	m,s,f	f	vlow	Same as No. 1, but more n-p protrude, covered, sub-surf, some carbon deposit at lip, bottom of lip chipped as TT 1 (Fig. 95:10).
3. Lamp Rim	same	rd yl		none	sand	f	f	vvlow	Same as No. 1, fabric & shaved bottom identical to TT 1 (Fig. 95:10). *In* finished with fine-line circular smoothing in bowl.

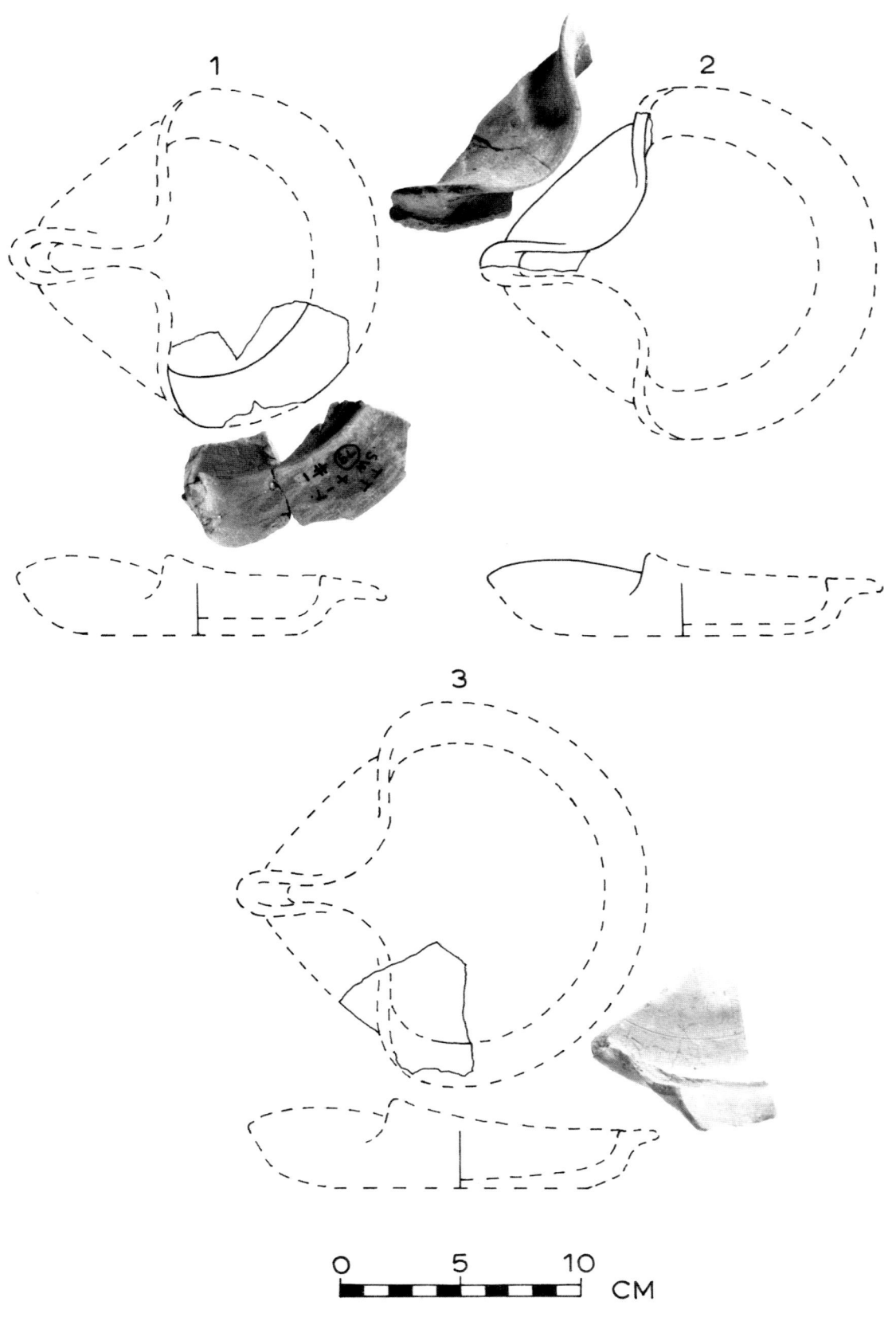

FIG. 79 POTTERY FROM SW 5-7, STONE-LINED PIT 11 (PERIOD VIA)

1. Identification		2. Section							3. Surface	
a.	b.	a.	b. Core		c. Non-Plastics				a. Exterior	b. Interior
Item	Square, Locus Basket	Fabric Color	Color	Extent	Type	Size	Frequency	Density	Color, n-p, voids, forming, finishing features	Same
1. Jar Rim	SW 5-7 15.24	rd br	gr	-100%	lms grog	l,m,s m,s	s-m s	med	*Ex & In*: dk pk, many lms spalls, much bloating, also numerous large voids in section indicate fast firing of wet-clay not adequately wedged; many protruding n-p covered give rough surf. Wet-smoothing lines shallow.	
2. Jar Handle	same	lt rd	dk gr lt gr	50% handle 40% body	lms	m,s,f	s	med l	*Handle*: lt rd br, few n-p embedded, few pits, wipe lines down handle. *In Body*: lt rd br, protruding n-p, covered, no wiping.	
3. Jar Handle	same	lt rd		none	lms	s,f	vf	vlow	Lt rd br, few n-p seen, few tiny pits, some erosion but very shallow, vert wiping very faint.	
4. Crater Rim	same	rd yl		none	cal lms bas	m,s l,s s,f	s s s	med	*Ex & In*: pk, ex & rim wet-smoothed, *in* much pitted & eroded.	
5. Mortarium Base	same	lt rd		none	sand?	s,f	m	low	*Ex*: rd yl, many tiny n-p protrude, covered, sandpaper finish, some circular smoothing lines above base, also inside base ring. *In*: rd yl, much pitting, finish lines all gone.	
6. Cook Pot Rim & Handle	same	rd br	yl rd	-100%	cal	s,f	s	low	*Ex*: rd br to gr, carbon deposit around handle. No n-p seen, except on handle. *In*: rd br, forming ridges below flashing line at base of rim. Very tiny protrusions probably fr n-p.	

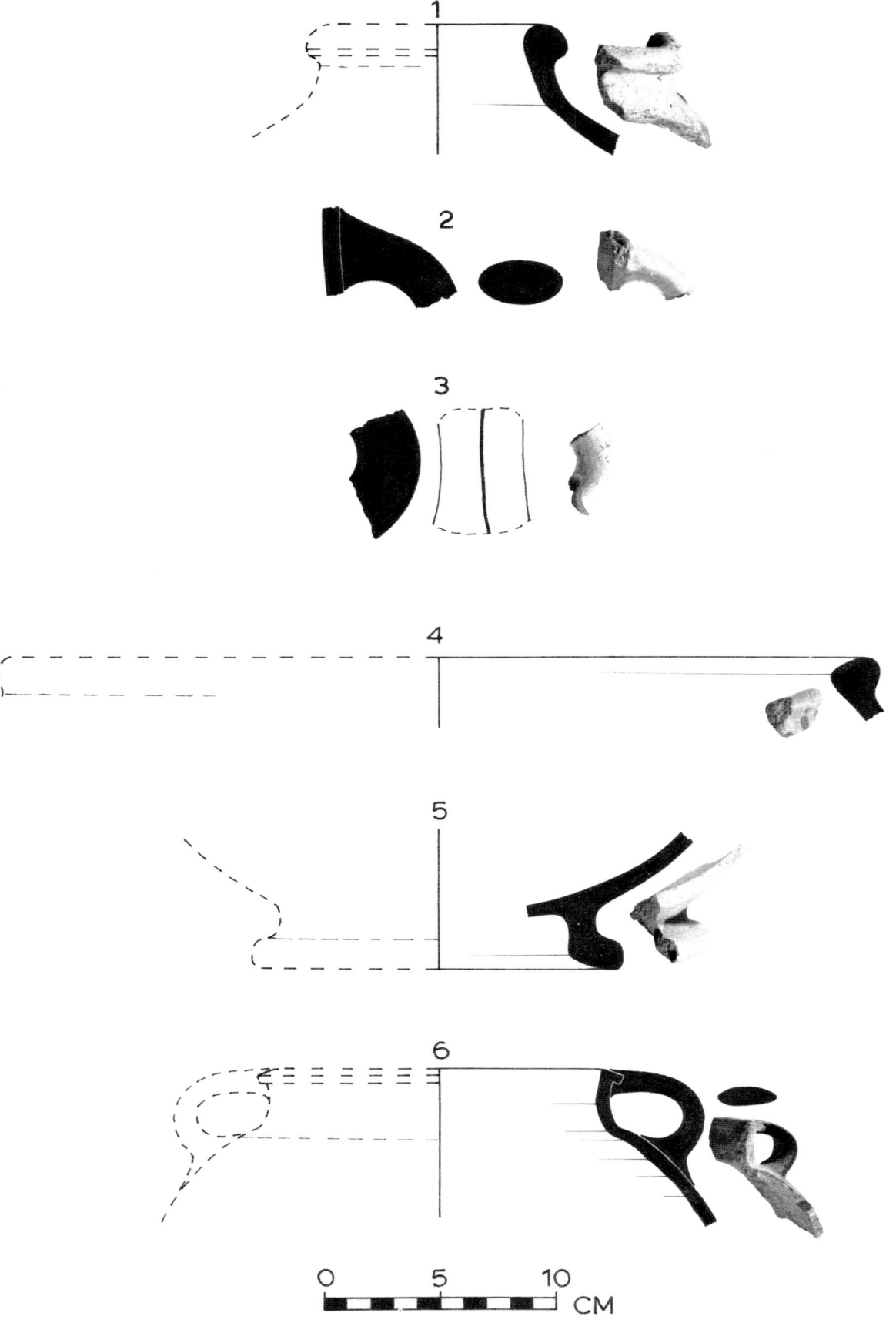

FIG. 80 POTTERY FROM PIT 74 (PERIOD VIA)

1. Identification		2. Section							3. Surface	
a.	b.	a.	b. Core		c. Non-Plastics				a. Exterior	b. Interior
Item	Square, Locus Basket	Fabric Color	Color	Extent	Type	Size	Frequency	Density	Color, n-p, voids, forming, finishing features	Same
1. Jar Rim	SW 6-2* 19.37 PP4	lt br	gr	±75%	lms	l,m,s	s	med	*Ex & In*: pk to gr, many lime spalls, many protruding n-p covered, smoothing lines irreg along rim which is entirely preserved but very uneven. The fabric and firing much resemble Fig. 79:1.	
2. Jar Rim	same PP2	rd	lt gr	±50%	lms bas	l,m m,s	s s	med	*Ex*: rd br with gr carbon deposit, many protruding n-p covered, slight depression at rim base, tooled, rim depression not finished by clearing excess clay. *In*: lt rd, some spalling, some protruding n-p. Wet-smoothing.	
3. Jar Rim	same PP3	rd	dk gr	inner 75%	lms	m,s,f	s	med l	*Ex*: rd, many tiny n-p protrude, some chips, few spalls, light wet-smoothing. *In*: rd gr mostly, many tiny pits, one large lateral fissure, chipping on shoulder.	
4. Jar Rim & Handle	same PP1	gr!	gr	100%	lms	l,m,s	s	low	*Ex*: rd to pk gr, many n-p protrude, covered, few seen, smoothing lines obscured by lm encrustation. Pulled handle. *In*: lt rd to rd br, forming ridges, esp on upper shoulder above flashing line which is neatly joined, many n-p protrude, covered. Both sides coarse.	
5. Jar Rim & Handle	same PP5	rd yl		none	lms See Fig. 79:3	m,f	vvf	vvlow	*Ex*: rd yl, excess clay in unsmoothed globs, beads all over shoulder & body handle very crudely attached, smearing rather than smoothing, 3 depressions between top & bottom of handle form flat rings around body. *In*: rd yl deep widely-spaced forming ridges, lime deposit between ridges.	

*Pit 74 was located in SW 6-1, but recorded as SW 6-2.

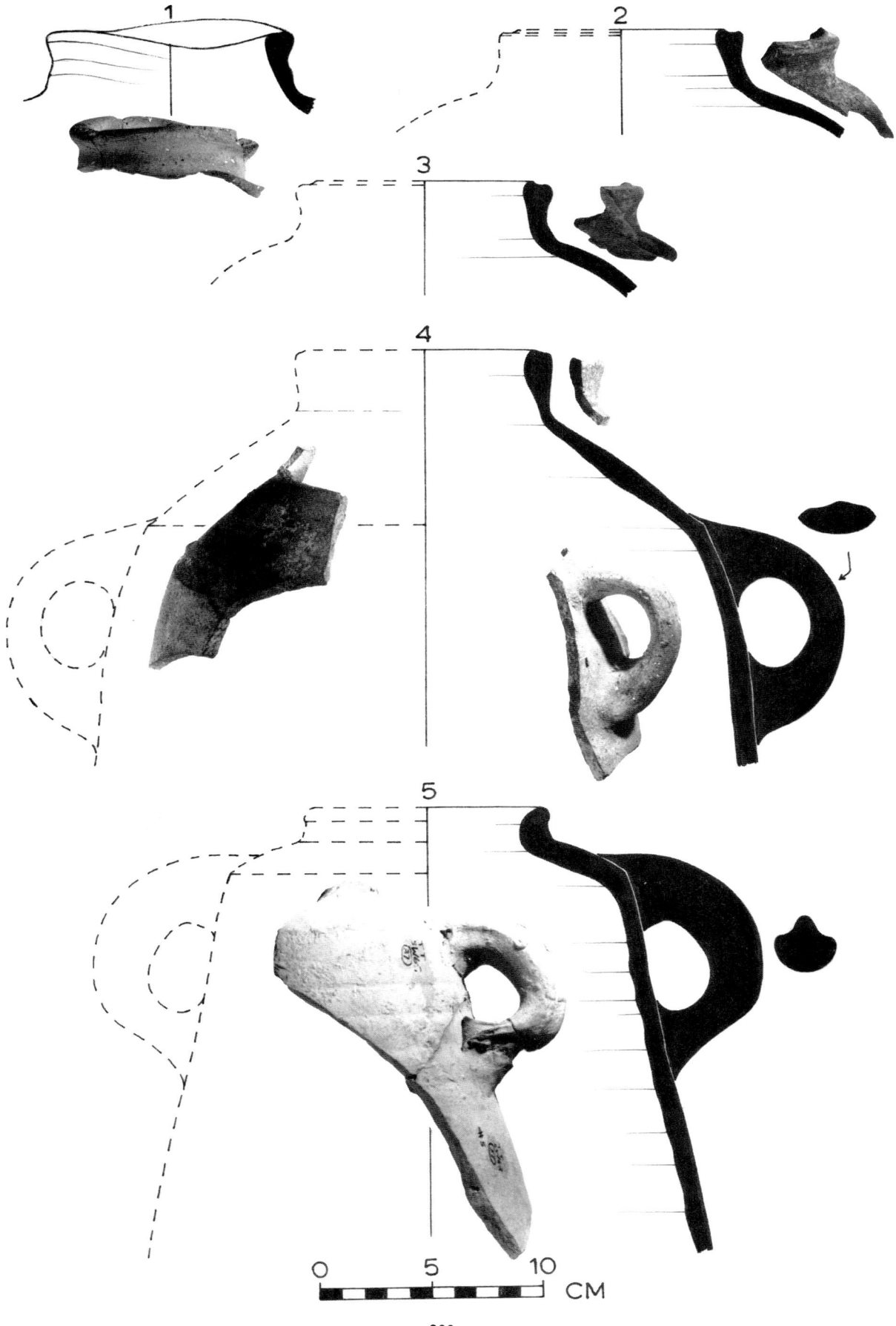

FIG. 81 POTTERY FROM PIT 74 (PERIOD VIA)

1. Identification		2. Section							3. Surface	
a.	b.	a.	b. Core		c. Non-Plastics				a. Exterior	b. Interior
Item	Square, Locus Basket	Fabric Color	Color	Extent	Type	Size	Frequency	Density	Color, n-p, voids, forming, finishing features	Same
	SW 6-2*									
1. Jar Rim & Handle	19.37 PP6	yl rd	rd br	75%	sand	s,f	m	low	*Ex*: vpl br under rd slip, many tiny pits but only a few n-p seen, flashing line ridge at handle top is prominent, wet-smoothing over few forming depressions below handle. *In*: rd br, many tiny pits, more n-p seen, lm encrusted, forming ridges all over.	
2. Jar Rim	same PP7	lt rd	lt br	50%	lms	s,f, vf	m	vlow	*Ex*: lt rd, shallow pitting & eroding, ridged flashing line, coarsely finished body. *In*: lt rd, considerable erosion, forming lines are reg & circular, shallow.	
3. Jar Rim	same PP8	rd yl		none	lms grog	s,f s	f vf	vlow	*Ex*: rd yl on rim, pk on shoulder, very few pits & covered, protruding n-p. Wet-smoothing lines are shallow, rim lines interrupted with erratic dents.	
4. Jug Rim	same PP10	yl rd	gr br	40-60% inner & center	lms grog	s,f s	f f	vlow	*Ex & In*: rd, some tiny pits on rim, few protruding n-p covered below, fine-line wet-smoothing. *In*: rd, wet-smoothed, lm encrusted.	
5. Juglet Rim	same PP23	rd yl		none	lms grog	s,f s	f vf	vlow	*Ex & In*: rd yl, decorated rim, animal head and tree (?) in relief, rim top is uneven. Irreg folds *in* indicate handwork.	
6. Bottle Base	same PP12	rd yl	dk gr	inner 90%	lms grog	m,s,f s	s f	low	*Ex*: rd yl in small part, mostly rd br and gr, many tiny pits, protruding n-p tiny, some seen, slight chipping, faint circular smoothing to base. *In*: pk gr, n-p seen, few protrude, some encrustation.	
7. Juglet Body & Base	same PP11	rd	wk rd	inner 25% body 50% base center	lms	f	s	vlow	*Ex*: many tiny voids in lt rd, no n-p seen, slight depressions indicating forming ridges. *In*: lt rd, mostly covered with lm, forming ridges clear, top to bottom which ends in pulled out twist.	
8. Mortarium Rim	same PP14	vpl br	dk pk	50%	lms	f	s	vlow	*Ex & In*: vpl br, some tiny pits, smoothing across rim, thumb-wide forming ridges are clear on ex below rim.	
9. Mortarium Base	same PP18	lt gr	yl	-100%	none!				*Ex*: lt gr, forming ridges on body, base crudely finished, couple of swirls of wet-smoothing, base edge smoothed leaving untrimmed edge. *In*: lt gr, even surf of many small & tiny pits, no lines.	

*Pit 74 was located in SW 6-1, but recorded as SW 6-2.

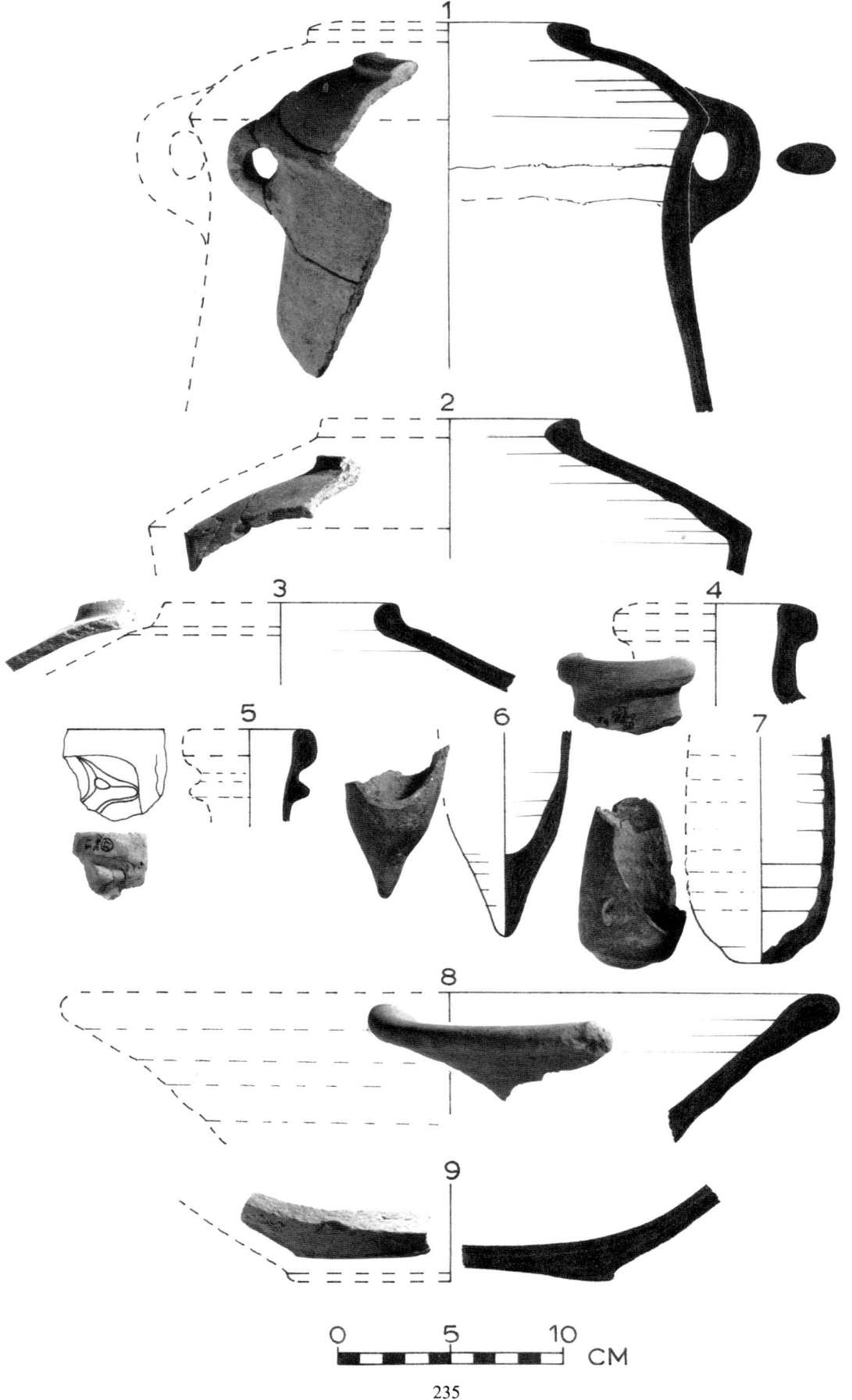

FIG. 82 POTTERY FROM PIT 74 (PERIOD VIA)

1. Identification		2. Section							3. Surface	
a.	b.	a.	b. Core		c. Non-Plastics				a. Exterior	b. Interior
Item	Square, Locus Basket	Fabric Color	Color	Extent	Type	Size	Frequency	Density	Color, n-p, voids, forming, finishing features	Same
1. Bowl (Jar?) Rim	SW 6-2* 19.37 PP9	rd yl	gr	75%	fine sand	vvf	m	vvlow	*Ex & In*: dk pk, irreg surfaces of crudely hand-built jar, continuous turning lines slant on *ex* around broken handle, *in* surf irreg, some horiz wet-smoothing covered by numerous fingerprints, bits of excess clay.	
2. Bowl Rim	same PP15	lt rd		none	lms	vvf	s	vvlow	*Ex*: lt rd, some tiny pits, few covered n-p protrude horiz smoothing faint. *In*: dk pk, forming lines under smoothing.	
3. Cook Pot Rim & Handle	same PP13	rd to rd br	dk gr	±50%	lms bas grog	vf f s	f s f	vlow	*Ex & In*: rd to rd br, many tiny n-p protrude, reg horiz smoothing on *in*, handle finished with some irregularities, i. e., excess clay remains, few dents, but not below standard. Forming lines on lower *in*.	
4. Cook Pot Rim†	same PP16	st br	st br	inner 50%	sand	s	m	low	*Ex*: dk pk, slip, horiz burnish lines on shoulder have lost gloss, many tiny pits, reg smoothing lines, flashing line at shoulder base. *In*: pl br to dk pk, many tiny pits, fine-line wet-smoothing.	
5. Lamp TT 1868	same PP18	rd		none	lms	m,s	s	low	*Ex*: rd, flaking, lms n-p seen, rim finished in fine-line smoothing along edge before folding lip. Much lm encrusted.	
6. Lamp Rim, Lip & Base	same PP19	yl rd		none	lms	f	s-m	low	*Ex & In*: yl rd, much shallow erosion, lms encrusted, lip has carbon deposit, bottom shaved, not as sharply as Fig. 78:3.	
7. Painted Body Sherd	same PP20	lt rd		none	sand	s,f	m	med l	*Ex*: vpl br, many tiny protruding n-p, wk rd paint for concentric circles, also rim (?) bottom, rd br paint. *In*: lt rd, many tiny n-p protrude, some pits, wet-smoothing over faint forming lines.	

*Pit 74 was located in SW 6-1, but recorded as SW 6-2.
†Could be "Jar"

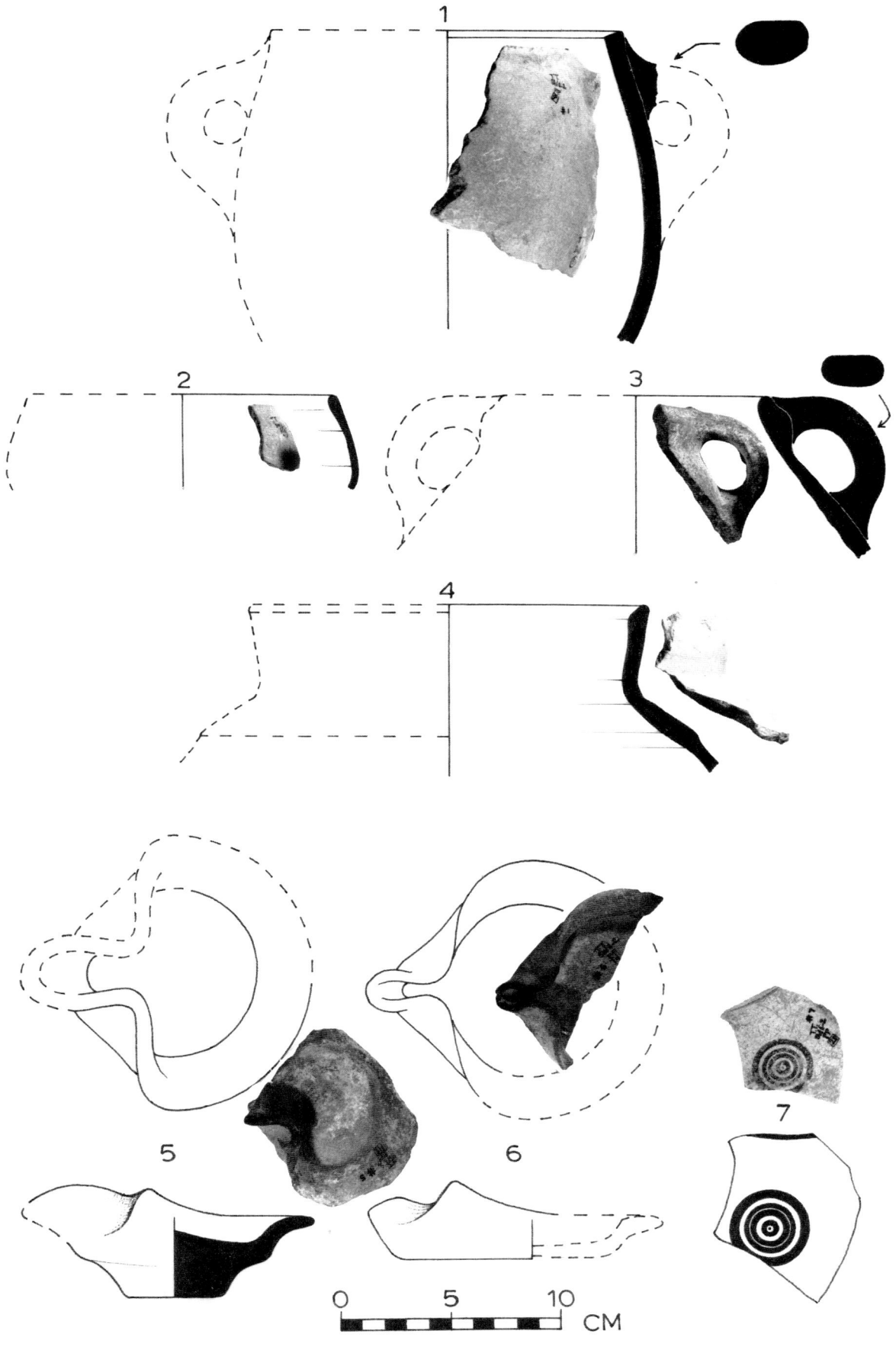

FIG. 83 POTTERY FROM SW 2-25, STONE-LINED PIT 125 (PERIOD VIB)

1. Identification		2. Section						3. Surface	
a.	b.	a.	b. Core		c. Non-Plastics			a. Exterior	b. Interior
Item	Square, Locus Basket	Fabric Color	Color	Extent	Type	Size	Frequency	Density	Color, n-p, voids, forming, finishing features	Same
1. Jar Rim	SW 2-25 125.238	lt rd		none	lms	l,f	f	vlow	*Ex*: lt pk slip, rough surf, unsmoothed clay lump, droplets, rim edge only partly trimmed. *In*: rd yl, 2 large lime spalls, one airhole protrudes (!), reg circular forming line under rim.	
2. Jar Rim	125.239	rd	dk gr	-50%	bas grog (See Fig. 82:3)	f f	m s	low	*Ex & In*: rd br, some tiny n-p protrude, covered, some erosion at rim, wet-smoothing deeper line on *in* than *ex*.	
3. Jar Rim	same	rd yl to lt br	dk gr	50%-	lms bas grog	s,f s f	f s vf	vlow	*Ex*: rd yl, many pits, some n-p seen embedded, smoothing lines eroded. *In*: pk, few pits, forming ridges are wide shallow depressions on body, at flashing line becomes narrower & deeper. Flaking.	
4. Jug Rim & Handle	145.262, 263	lt rd br	gr	100%	lms	m,s,f	s	low	General brittleness and fabric resemble Figs. 75:1; 80:1,4. *Ex*: pk slip, many n-p protrude, covered, much bloating on *ex & in*. which is dk pk to gr. Both sides have fine-line wet-smoothing. Few n-p seen on *in*. Some tiny pits, look deep on *ex*, some spalling on *in*.	
5. Jug Rim & Handle	144.261	lt rd	dk gr	75%	lms	m,s,f	s	low	*Ex & In*: lt rd, many n-p protrude, covered, some seen, some deep pits, straw voids on *ex* rim, bits of excess clay untrimmed, esp on handle, glob on *in*; wet-smoothing even all over.	

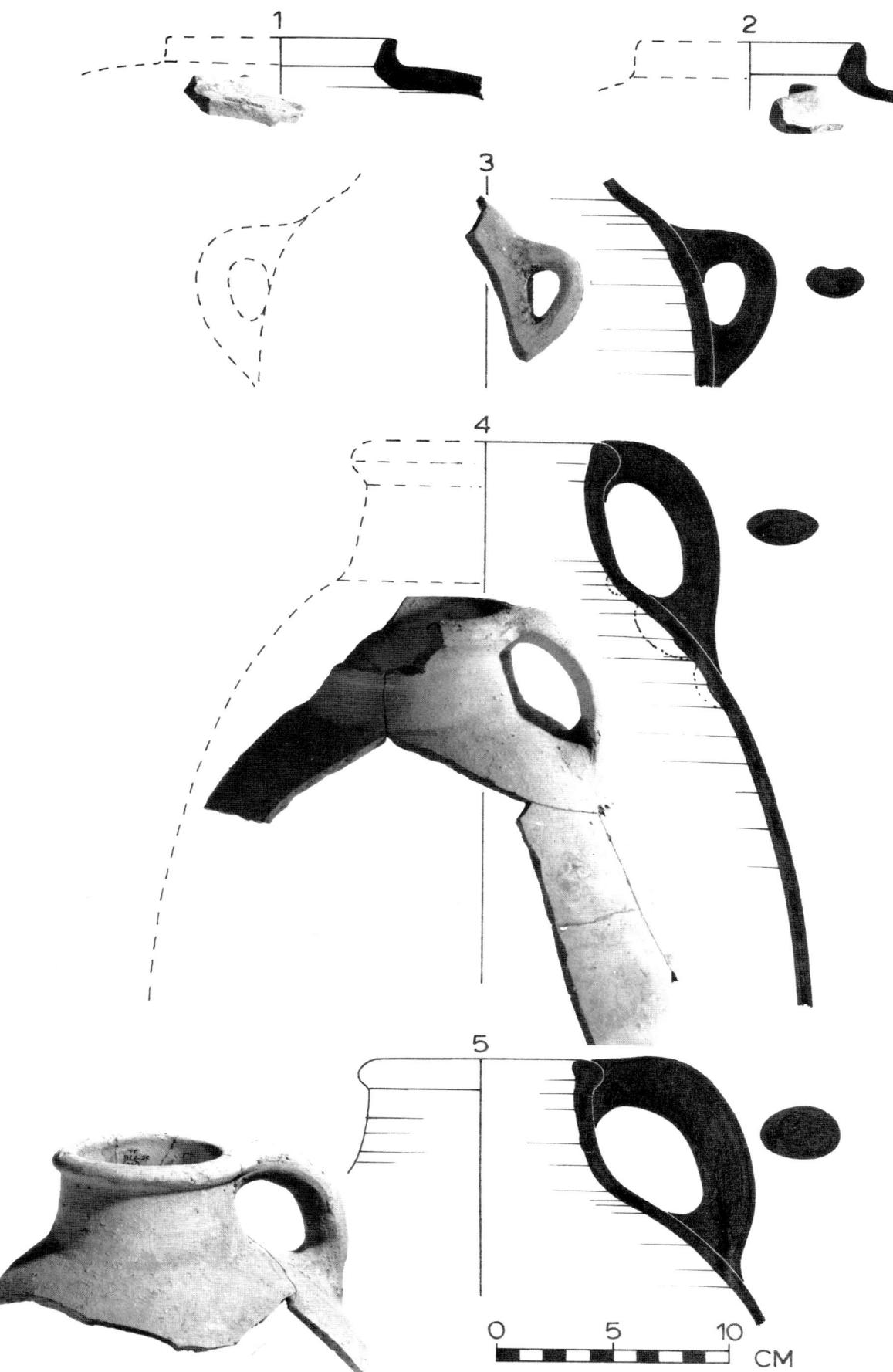

FIG. 84 POTTERY FROM SW 2-25, STONE-LINED PIT 125 (PERIOD VIB)

1. Identification		2. Section						3. Surface	
a.	b.	a.	b. Core		c. Non-Plastics			a. Exterior	b. Interior
Item	Square, Locus Basket	Fabric Color	Color	Extent	Type	Size	Frequency	Density	Color, n-p, voids, forming, finishing features	Same
	SW 2-25									
1. Juglet Rim	125.238	pk gr	dk gr	100% body outer 50% rim	lms grog	l,m,s s	vf s	low	*Ex & In*: pk gr, many n-p protrude, covered, few pits, wet-smoothing. Some n-p seen on rim.	
2. Mortarium Rim to Base	144.261	wh	dk pk	±75%	none!	(See Fig. 81:9)			*Ex & In*: pk on rim, wh *in* & *ex* otherwise, some tiny pits *ex*, fold-over rim tool-trimmed at outer edge but irreg length; forming ridges wide and shallow on rim and body. *In* has been used as a grinding bowl, mortar, bottom is now 4mm thick, wall averages 12mm. Pits are round above bottom, long fissures at bottom where wear is greatest. The pk at rim *in* is slip.	
3. Cook Pot Rim & Handle	125.238	rd	gr	none outer 25% body spot	cal	s,f	s	low	*Ex & In*: dk rd, dk gray patch *ex*, very tiny n-p protrude; many faint horiz smoothing lines, deep depression at rim base may be flashing line. *In*: rd br, many tiny n-p protrude, etc, shallow forming depressions.	
4. Cook Pot Rim?	same	rd		none	cal bas	m,s,f s	s f	low	*Ex*: rd gr, few n-p seen, wet-smoothing, rim groove interrupted by protruding n-p. *In*: rd br, n-p protrude, covered, wet-smoothed.	
5. Lamp Lip	same	rd yl		none	bas grog	f s	f vf	vvlow	*Ex & In*: rd yl, *ex* rim has usual wet-smoothing lines along the edge.	
6. Kylix TT 848	144.261	rd yl		none	lms	f	vvf	vvlow	*Ex*: yl rd, some pits, few lime spalls, hard finish with thin-incised lines irregularly spaced, band of irreg smoothing 1.5cm below rim interrupted by sponge marks near one handle prob due to slip drip. Paint is rd br to black. *In*: lt rd slip, few chips, regular circular lines of wet-smoothing. Paint is rd br to bl.	

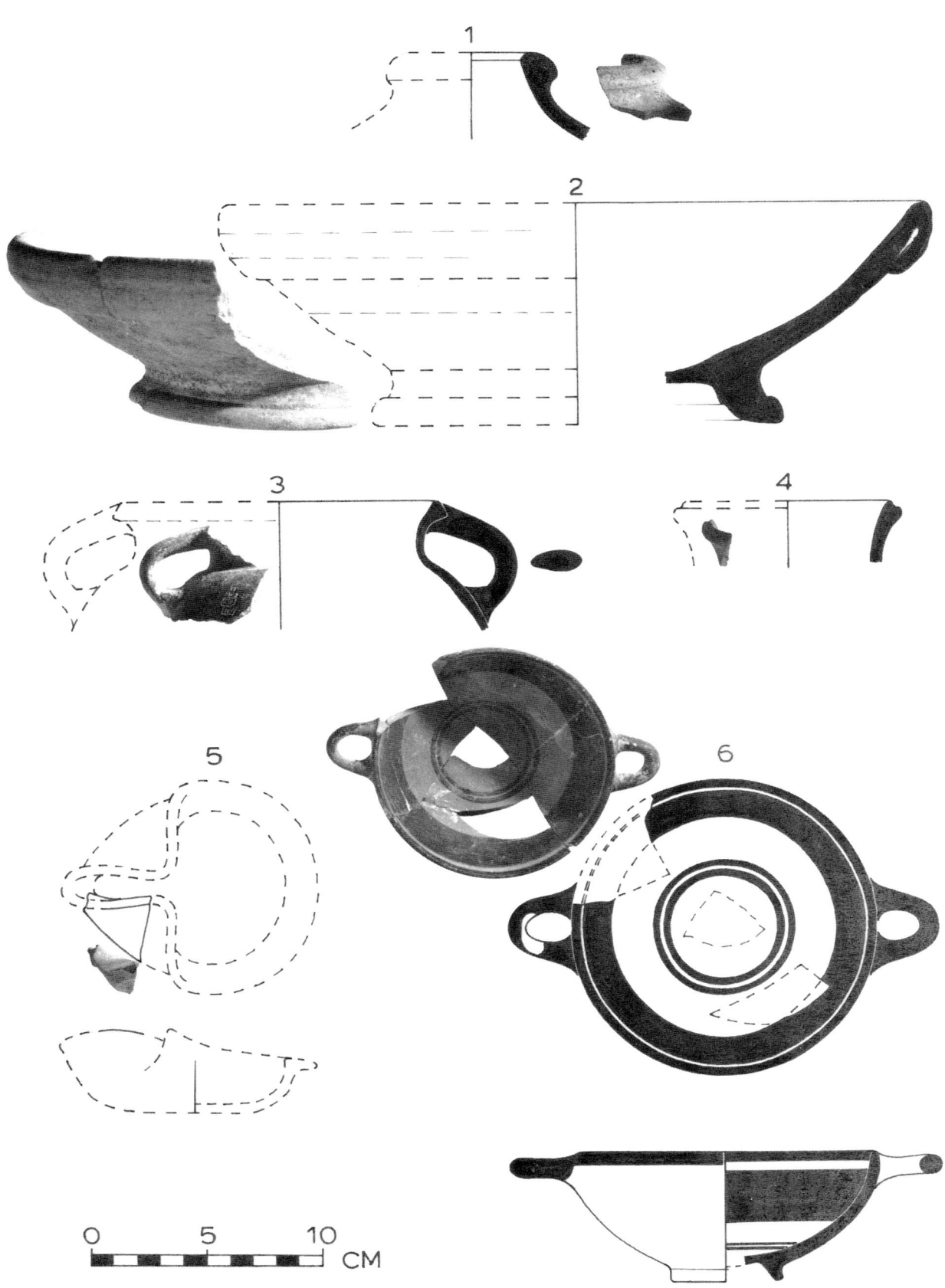

FIG. 85 POTTERY FROM SW 3-25, STONE-LINED PIT 22 (PERIOD VIB)

1. Identification		2. Section						3. Surface	
a.	b.	a.	b. Core		c. Non-Plastics			a. Exterior	b. Interior
Item	Square, Locus Basket	Fabric Color	Color	Extent	Type	Size	Frequency	Density	Color, n-p, voids, forming, finishing features	Same
	SW 3-25									
1. Jug Rim	22.31	rd to lt rd	dk gr	inner +60%	lms bas	l,m,s s	f s	low	Ex: lt rd, some n-p seen, some small n-p protrude, covered, light line wet-smoothing, as In: lt rd, few small n-p seen, n-p protrude, covered.	
2. Jug Rim	same	lt rd		none	grog cal	f f	vf vf	vvlow	Ex: pk some very tiny n-p protrude, covered, wet-smoothed. Same for lt rd in.	
3. Jar Handle	same	dk pk	vpl br	-100%	grog	f	vf	vvlow	Handle: pk, crudely twisted from top to bottom where join with body left thin vertical void. Dents on top and side. Very tiny voids. Body in: vpl br, forming ridges, wet-smoothing.	
4. Jar Handle	same	lt rd	gr	+75% handle 40% body	lms grog	m,s,f s	s s	low	Handle: lms n-p seen in spalling embedded, join with long vert wipe lines, some depressions along wipe lines. In: lt rd; lms n-p seen thru shallow spalls, some crazing, flashing line mid-handle join. Some forming ridges.	
5. Jar Handle	same	rd yl	gr	90% handle inner 90% body	lms grog bas	l,m,s s,f f	s s f	med l	Ex: handle: dk pk, some n-p seen thru lime spalling, many tiny pits, wipe over join left unsmoothed horiz ridges. In: lt gr, many tiny protruding n-p, some seen embedded, horiz wipe lines in cm-wide comb bands.	
6. Jug Handle	same	rd yl		none	grog bas	s m	vf vvf	vvlow	Handle: lt rd, horiz ridges at join are deep, ex particularly crude. In: rd yl, horiz wipe lines cover vfew protruding n-p.	
7. Jug Handle	same	lt rd	dk gr	+50% handle +75% inner body	lms grog	s,f f	f f	low	Handle: pk, some pits, n-p seen on surf, wipe lines are horiz on top of handle at join. Body: pk, many protruding n-p covered, forming ridges, wipe lines circular.	
8. Mortarium Rim	same	lt rd		none	lms	f	f	vlow	Ex: dk pk, some n-p protrude, covered, horiz wet-smoothing gives drag to feel, rim edge bottom undercut. In: dk pk, hard smooth; wet-smoothing lines have been depressed.	
9. Mortarium Rim	same	rd yl	lt br	+50%	sand	m,s	m	med l	Ex: vpl br, many protruding n-p, covered, coarse wet-smoothing, untrimmed excess clay, In: vpl br, many tiny pits at bottom of sherd, traces of wet-smoothing lines over protruding tiny n-p.	
10. Mortarium Base	same	vpl br		none	bas	s,f	m	vlow	Ex & In: vpl br, many tiny n-p seen, on ex covered, faint wet-smoothing on ex, none on bottom of bowl.	

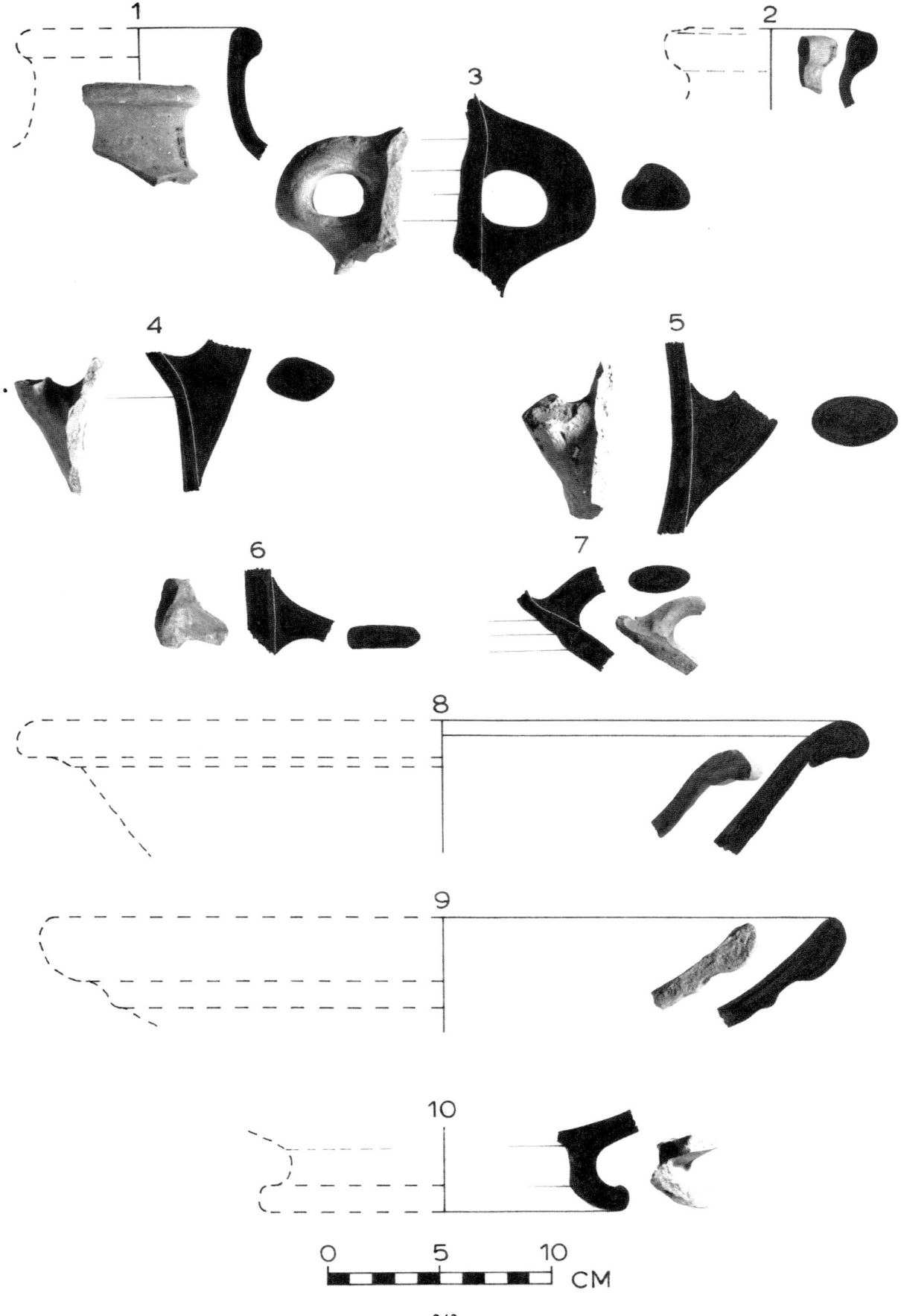

FIG. 86 POTTERY FROM SW 3-25, STONE-LINED PIT 22 (PERIOD VIB)

1. Identification		2. Section						3. Surface	
a.	b.	a.	b. Core		c. Non-Plastics			a. Exterior	b. Interior
Item	Square, Locus Basket	Fabric Color	Color	Extent	Type	Size	Frequency	Density	Color, n-p, voids, forming, finishing features	Same
1. Mortarium Base	SW 3-25 22.29	vdk gr to br		none	lms bas	m,s,f m,s,f	s s-m	med	*Ex*: gr to gr br, many pits with n-p showing, deep v-groove in base and lower body tooled and reg slight depression 2cms above upper groove. *In*: gr to yl br, many bas n-p visible, with lms embedded. Very hard, could be carved rather from bas.	
2. Crater Rim	22.31	lt rd	dk gr	inner 90%	lms	l,m,s	m-s	med l	*Ex*: pk slip, many spalls show n-p, some bloating. Deeper wet-smoothing lines around upper rim. *In*: pk slip many n-p protrude, some lime spalls, horiz wet-smoothing lines. Fig. 79:1 *et al.*	
3. Lamp Lip	22.31	rd yl		none	grog lms	s f	f f	vlow	*Ex & In*: dk pk, vfew n-p protrude, covered, smoothing lines on rim, fainter on *ex*, bottom near lip.	
4. Lekythos Body	22.29	rd yl		none	none!				*Ex*: paint polished glossy black, dk rd br edges, other surf is dk pk paint. *In*: rd yl, several forming depressions.	

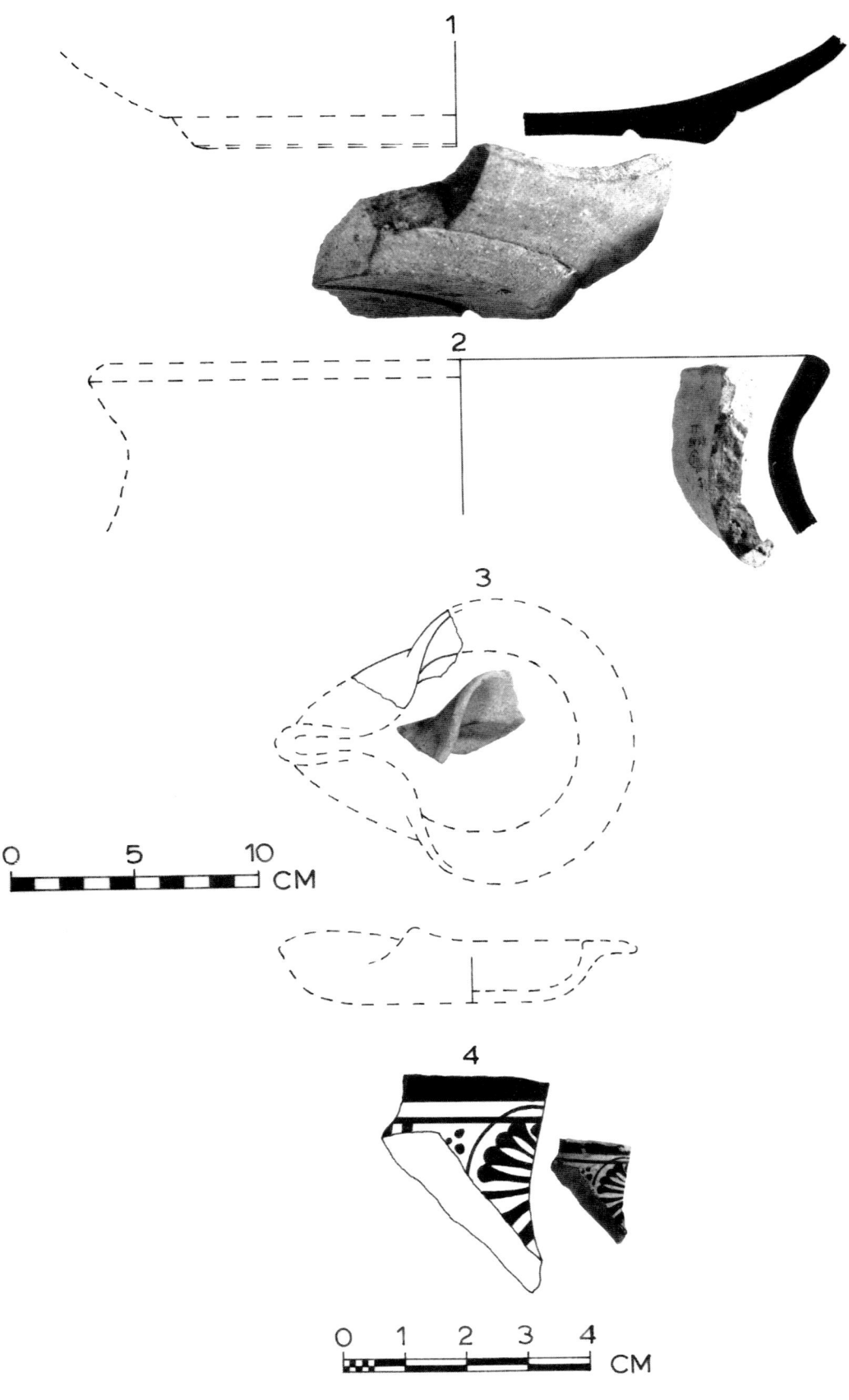

FIG. 87 POTTERY FROM SW 2-25, LOCUS 19 (PERIOD VIB)

1. Identification		2. Section						3. Surface	
a. Item	b. Square, Locus Basket	a. Fabric Color	b. Core			c. Non-Plastics			a. Exterior	b. Interior
			Color	Extent	Type	Size	Frequency	Density	Color, n-p, voids, forming, finishing features	Same
1. Jug Rim	SW 2-25 19.59	rd	lt gr	inner -50%	lms	l,m,s	s-m	med	*Ex*: pk white slip, several spalls, many tiny pits, wet-smoothing. *In*: dk pk, many spalls showing lms n-p, other pits; wet-smoothing lines eroded. See 82:2 *et al*.	
2. Mortarium Rim	same	vpl br	dk pk	75%	none!				*Ex & In*: vpl br, wet-smoothing reg. See Fig. 81:8.	
3. Jar Rim & Body	same	rd yl		none	lms grog	l,m,s,f m,s	s f	low	*Ex*: lt pk, some tiny n-p protrude, join is extremely crude, fold ridges on handle and body. Some wet-smoothing. *In*: dk pk, some n-p in shallow spalls wet-smoothing.	
4. Jar Handle	same	vpl br	dk pk	inner 50-75%	sand	m,s f	s	low	*Handle*: pl br, some small pitting, long vert wipe lines, over join as preserved. *In*: dk pk, many tiny n-p protrude, covered, horiz forming ridges are shallow, one very deep vert forming ridge behind join, one more shallow.	

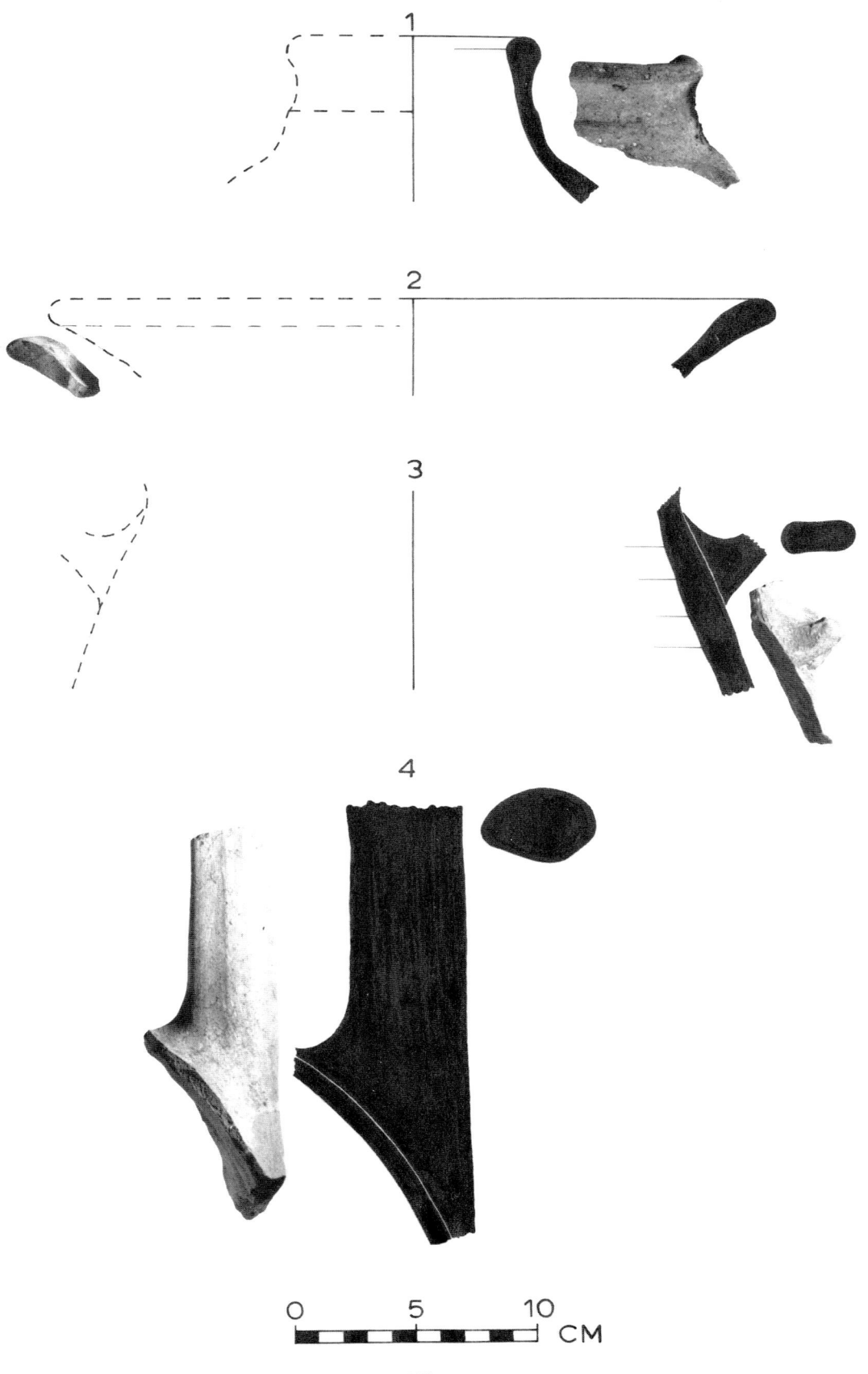

FIG. 88 MISCELLANEOUS POTTERY (PERIOD IA)

1. Identification		2. Section						3. Surface	
a. Item	b. Square, Locus Basket	a. Fabric Color	b. Core		c. Non-Plastics			a. Exterior	b. Interior
			Color	Extent	Type	Size	Frequency	Density	Color, n-p, voids, forming, finishing features	Same
1. Jar Rim, Handle & Body TT 1862	SW 2-8 46.124	lt br		none	lms	l,m,s	s	low	Ex: dk pk, rope impression on waist, wet-smoothing, on top of these lines handle joins smoothed, n-p few but depressed and smoothed; In: forming ridges on neck but below surf eroded, pitted with lms spalls.	
2. Jug Rim to Base Complete TT 1430	SW 7-27 20.33	lt rd	lt gr	25-50%	lms bas	s,f s	f vf	vlow	Ex: dk pk where visible below lime encrustation, wet-smoothing on rim and neck before handle added. Coil ridges just above waist to neck, ring base added after bottom formed. Pot does not sit evenly. In: dk pk, also encrusted, forming ridges only seen on neck.	
3. Jug Rim to Base Complete TT 1281	SW 8-26 12.65	rd yl	gr to lt gr	50%	lms	m,s,f	s	vlow	Ex: dk pk, some n-p seen & protrude, wet-smoothed with straw burned out leaving pits. In: dk pk, forming ridges on neck, join at shoulder smoothed. Many n-p protrude but covered.	

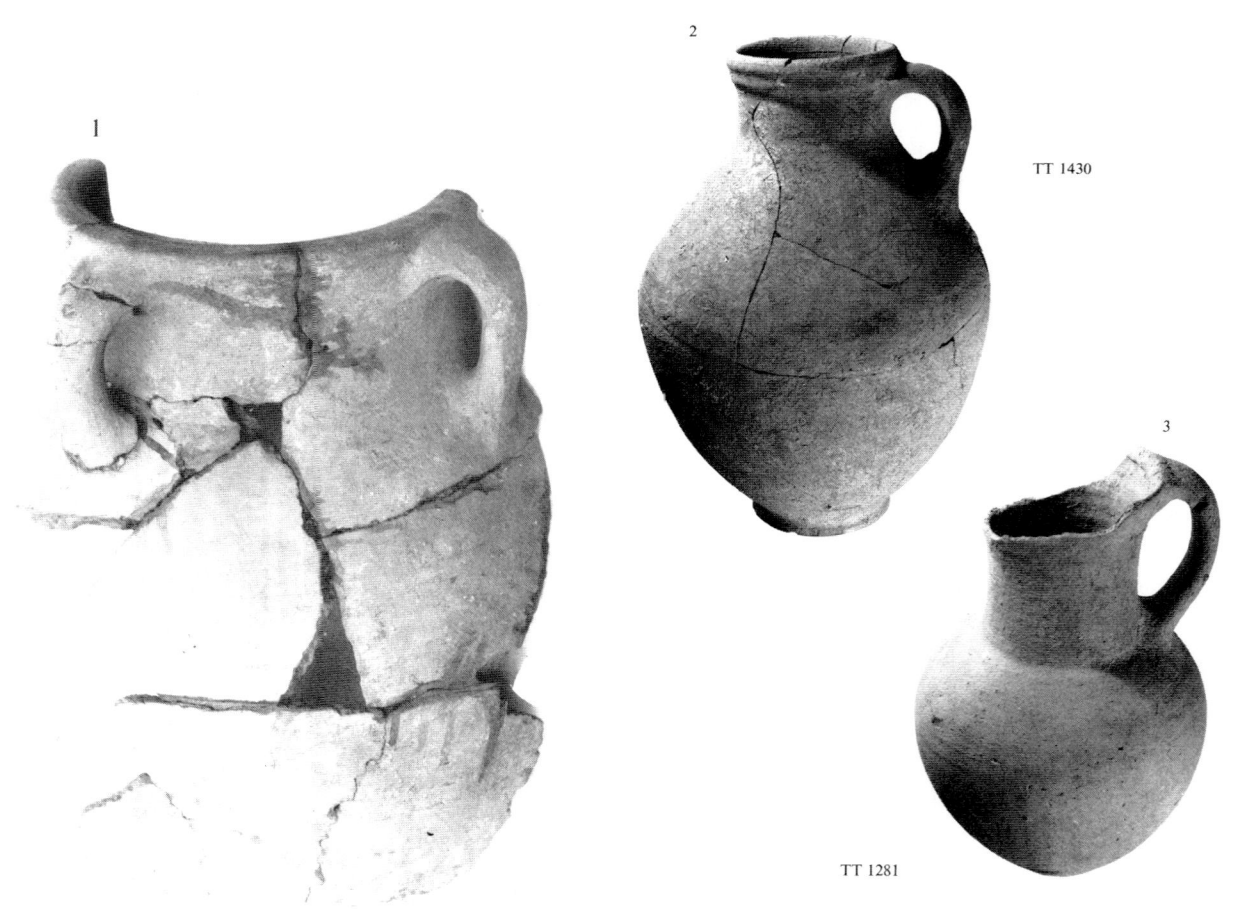

248

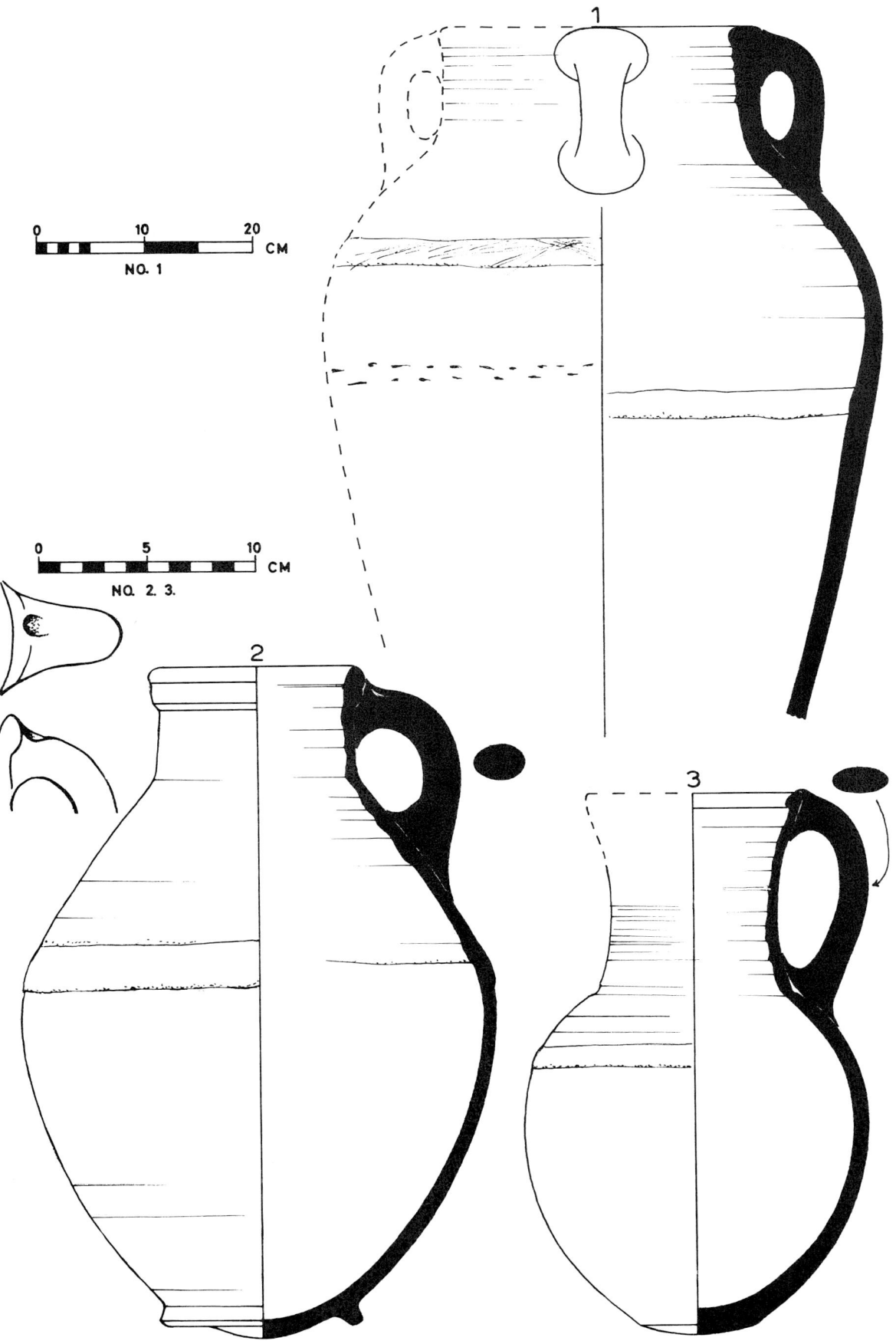

FIG. 89 MISCELLANEOUS POTTERY (PERIOD IA)

1. Identification		2. Section							3. Surface	
a.	b.	a.	b. Core		c. Non-Plastics				a. Exterior	b. Interior
Item	Square, Locus Basket	Fabric Color	Color	Extent	Type	Size	Frequency	Density	Color, n-p, voids, forming, finishing features	Same
1. Crater Rim to Base Complete TT 832	SW 2-8 50.135	dk pk	lt gr to	50% none	lms	l,m,s	m	med h to h	*Ex*: dk pk, many n-p seen in lms spalls, drag marks, pits, rim base edge irreg tooled, shoulder irreg width, lms patch inside and outside below shoulder, roundish hole thru base left wide fracture on *ex*. *In*: dk pk, somewhat fewer n-p, slanting smoothing lines.	
2. Bowl Rim to Base Complete TT 1431	SW 7-27 20.31, 33	rd yl	lt br	50%	lms bas	s f	f f	vlow	*Ex & In*: rd yl under lm encrustation. *In* few but on *ex* some n-p seen, drag marks R to L, pit voids, spiral forming lines on *ex* of base, rim ridge irreg, depression below rim irreg, as rim line itself. *In*: wet-smoothing. Clay patch below rim.	
3. Chalice Rim to Base Complete TT 988	SW 5-7 131.203	lt pk	rd yl	50%	lms	m,s	m	med h	*Ex*: lt to dk pk, n-p commonly bulge fr surf but no drag marks; surplus clay roughens surf. Forming ridges inside trumpet base. *In*: dk pk, n-p bulge, wet-smoothed to spiral center. No. 4 is cruder version of No. 3.	
4. Chalice Rim to Base Complete TT 1356	SW 7-27 20.31	rd yl	gr	25% (base)	lms cal	m,s m	s f	med	*Ex*: lt pk, many n-p seen protruding, but few drag marks, several med pit voids, rougher *ex* surf than *in*: dk pk, most n-p at rim, some pits, crude horiz finish lines. Lms encrustation *ex* and *in*.	
5. Chalice Rim to Base Complete TT 1146	SW 5-7 117.208	rd yl	dk pk	+50%	lms	m,s	f	low	*Ex*: dk pk, some n-p protrude, few extra clay discs, light wet-smoothing, lime encrusted. *In*: lt pk grayed with charcoal burn, few n-p protrude, approx horiz smoothing lines.	

TT 832

TT 1431

TT 1356

TT 988

TT 1146

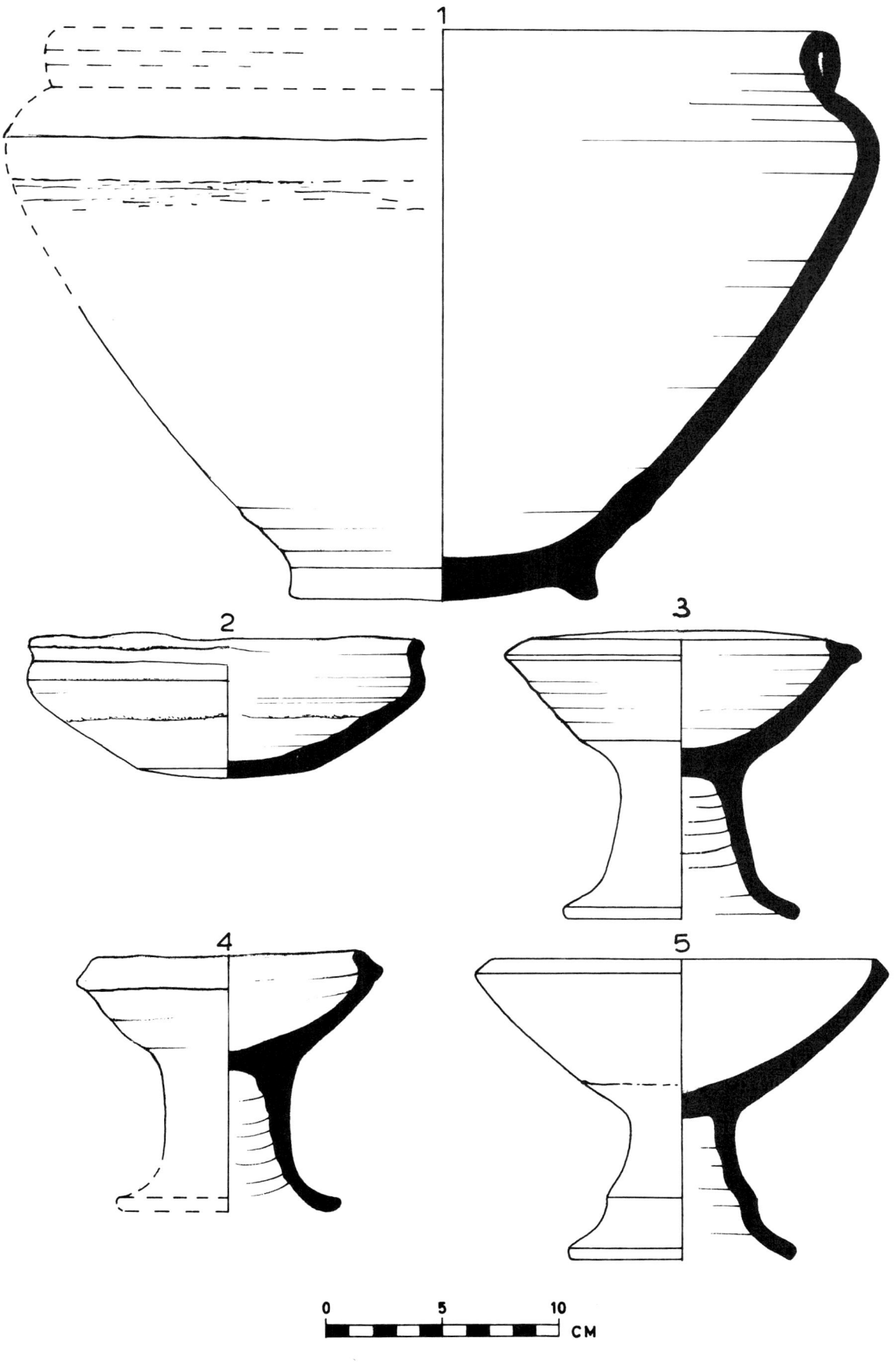

FIG. 90 MISCELLANEOUS POTTERY (PERIOD IA)

1. Identification		2. Section							3. Surface	
a.	b.	a.	b. Core		c. Non-Plastics				a. Exterior	b. Interior
Item	Square, Locus Basket	Fabric Color	Color	Extent	Type	Size	Frequency	Density	Color, n-p, voids, forming, finishing features	Same
1. Cup & Saucer TT 1157	SW 1-9 128.230	rd yl	gr	-20% (edge) to 50% (base)	bas cal lms	m,s s s	s vf f	low	*Ex & In*: lt rd br penetrates section, some n-p on surf, cup surf *in* flaked, *ex* ridges crudely hand-formed. Saucer somewhat more smoothed than cup.	
2. Lamp Complete TT 1054	SW 2-8 77.185				not visible				*Ex*: lt rd br, smoothing horiz on outer edge, then criss-cross, some n-p, pit voids. *In*: lms & bas n-p smoothed, circular smoothing lines; lms encrustation *ex & in*.	
3. Lamp TT 945	SW 5-7 27.194	lt rd br	lt gr	+25%	lms bas	l,s f	s s	low	*Ex & In*: dk pk. Remainder of surf as No. 2 except *ex* scaling near lip. Some evidence of use as also in No. 2.	

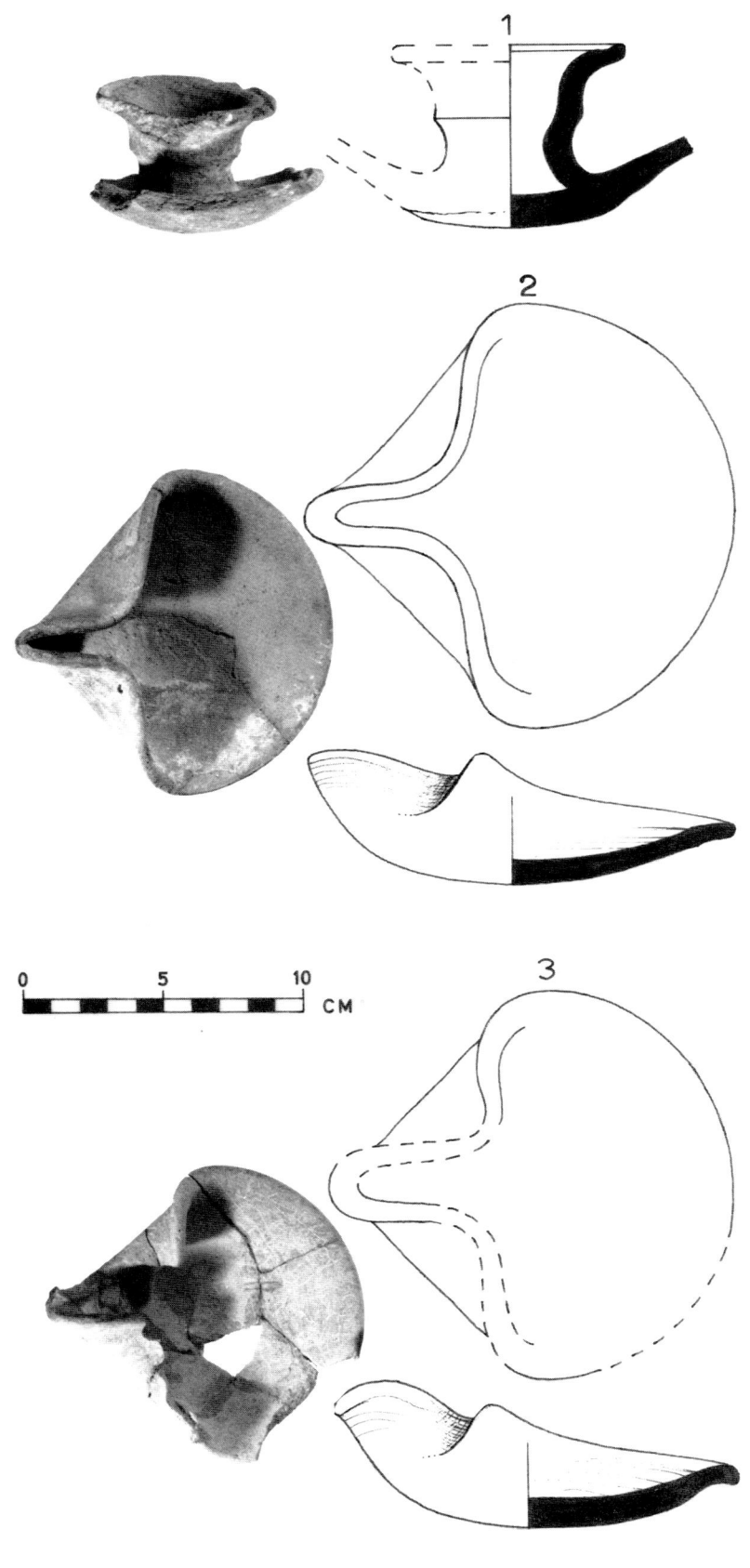

FIG. 91 MISCELLANEOUS POTTERY (PERIOD IB)

1. Identification		2. Section							3. Surface	
a.	b.	a.	b. Core		c. Non-Plastics				a. Exterior	b. Interior
Item	Square, Locus Basket	Fabric Color	Color	Extent	Type	Size	Frequency	Density	Color, n-p, voids, forming, finishing features	Same
1. Cook Pot TT 753	SW 2-8 27.97	yl rd	lt gr	50%	cal	s,f	m	low	*Ex*: rd br, very shallow ridges round bottom and shoulder perhaps from basket mould(s), turning lines just below waist (join). *In*: rd br, criss-cross smoothing on bottom, center slightly raised, knuckle ridges on shoulder above waist.	
2. Cook Pot TT 891	SW 5-8 100.144	dk br	gr	none (1/3 of Neck) 100% (2/3 of neck)	cal	f	m	med	*Ex*: rd yl to rd br to dk gr over 3/4 *ex*, charcoal deposit. Very few n-p seen, some horiz straw voids, some pits, irreg scraping at waist join, on shoulder near single handle is 1cm wide perforation, another 1.5cm wide below waist on opposite side. *In*: horiz wipe lines visible on extant neck.	
3. Bowl TT 564	SW 5-2 96.194	rd yl	dk gr	+50%	lms	l,m,s	f	low	*Ex*: dk pk, some n-p covered, many drag marks, many prominent turning ridges on both sides of flashing, turn mark inner edge of ring base, heavy lm encrustation. *In*: rd yl, some n-p seen thru lms spalls, many horiz finishing lines, fainter toward center base, over slip.	
4. Chalice TT 800	SW 5-8 88.115	dk pk	gr	±50%	lms	l,ms	s	low	*Ex*: lt rd, many n-p seen, some protruding, some lime spalling, many tiny pits, some straw voids, irreg body many mean pinching, some scraping, wet-smoothing at neck. Some lm encrustation, more on *In*: covering entire surf. Center depression.	

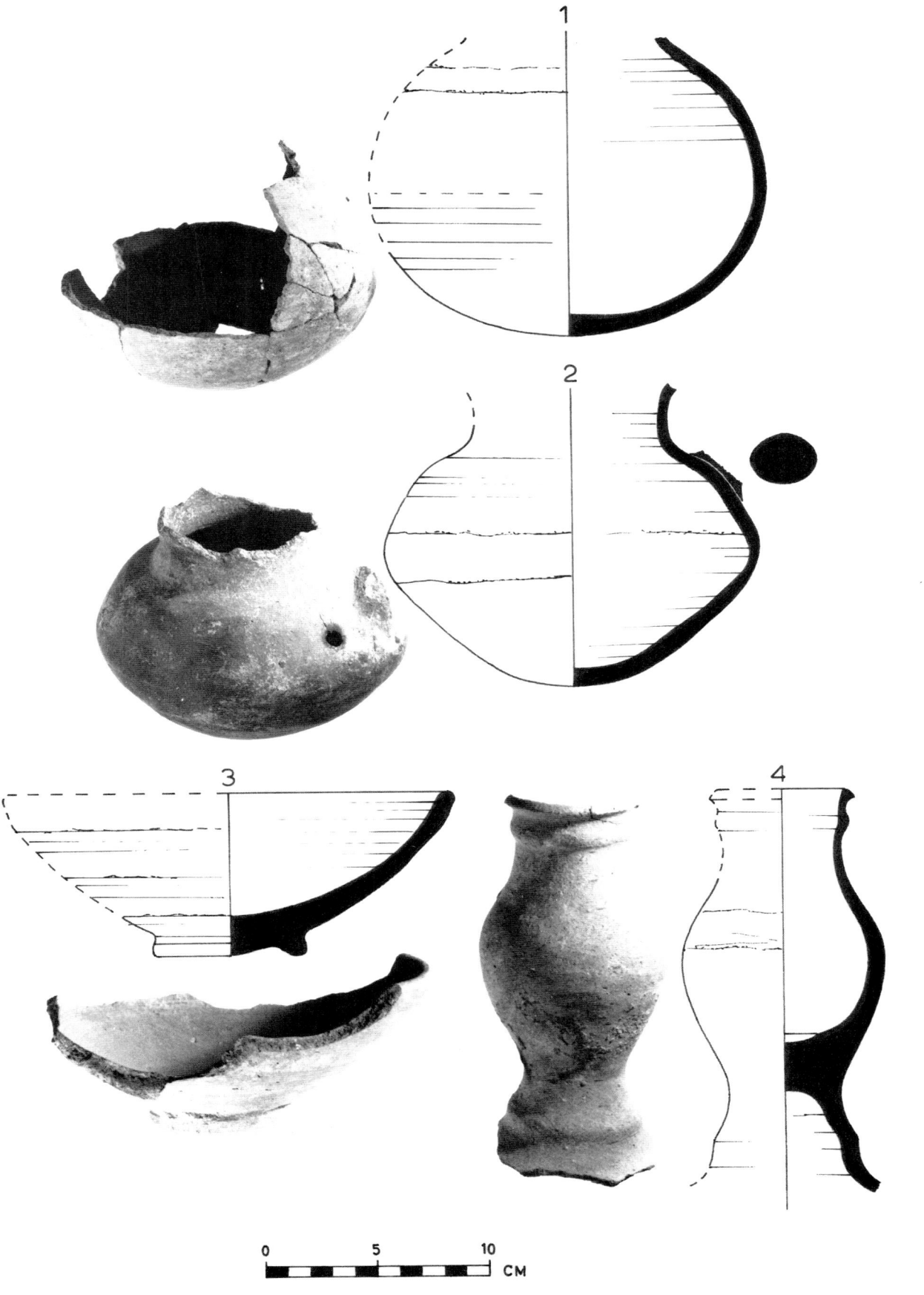

FIG. 92 MISCELLANEOUS POTTERY (PERIOD IIB)

1. Identification		2. Section							3. Surface	
a.	b.	a.	b. Core		c. Non-Plastics				a. Exterior	b. Interior
Item	Square, Locus Basket	Fabric Color	Color	Extent	Type	Size	Frequency	Density	Color, n-p, voids, forming, finishing features	Same
1. Jug TT 845	SW 1-9 52.94	rd br	lt br	-90%	lms	l,m,s	s-m	med	*Ex*: lt rd br, many lms n-p visible thru shallow spalls, many tiny pits near bottom, smoothing lines slant, mid-body sometimes rounded, sometimes sharper ridge, straw voids on base, finish lines circular and crossing. *In*: lt rd br, circular forming ridges on neck, neck-shoulder join felt, forming ridges down shoulder, base is much narrower than *ex*, thus heavier than drawing indicates.	
2. Juglet TT 635	SW 2-7 87.302	lt rd	lt br	not clear	lms	l,m,s	s	low	*Ex*: lt rd, n-p available only on surf, many protruding, covered, esp on neck, wet-smoothing on body is criss-cross, on neck is horiz. *In*: lt rd, forming ridges on lower neck, rest not available.	
3. Juglet TT 127	SW 3-7 28.54	pk gr	lt br	not clear	Not Available				*Ex*: mostly dk gr, br in spots, continuously burnished, some pits and general irreg in wall shaping.	
4. Juglet TT 35	SW 3-7 25.26	dk pk	gr	-100% bottom none at top body	lms grog	m,s,f s,f	s s	low	*Ex*: rd yl to br gr, many tiny pits, some larger; surf is firm, finish lines erased. *In*: lt br but encrusted with gray, forming ridges on bottom end, spiral twirl at center base. Some forming lines just inside rim.	
5. Juglet TT 128	SW 3-7 29.51	pl br	dk gr	inner -100%	Not Available				*Ex*: rd yl slip burnished, vert on neck and lower body, horiz on upper body. Burnish 25% eroded. *In*: reg ridged forming lines converge at point of depressed swirl, pinched off.	
6. Pyxis TT 272	SW 5-2 42.103				Not Available				*Ex*: yl br upper, lt br lower, some lms n-p seen on shoulder, inside rim, many straw voids, untrimmed excess clay beads, turning of bottom quite uneven, ring base off center, depressed band below handle wider on one side than other. *In*: forming ridges clear, center more depressed than drawing shows.	
7. Pyxis TT 66	SW 3-7 24.44	lt br to gr br	dk gr	-100%	lms	s,f	s	vlow	*Ex*: st br to dk gr, burnished slip, continuous horiz strokes. *In*: dk gr carbon deposit, no forming ridges visible.	

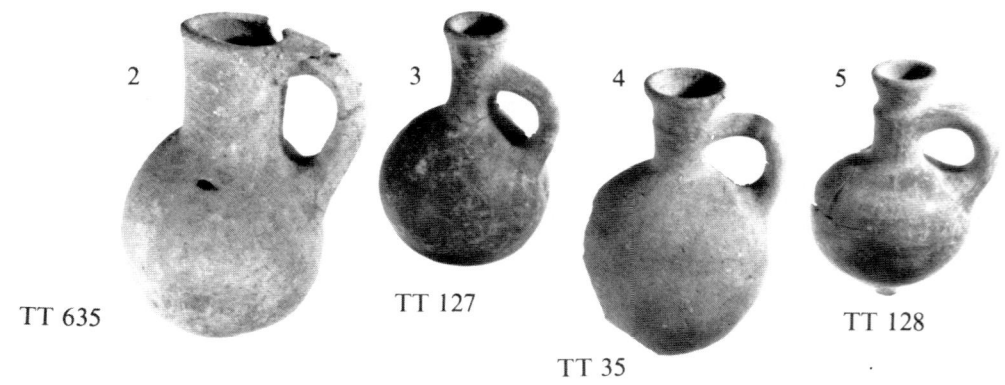

2 TT 635   3 TT 127   4 TT 35   5 TT 128

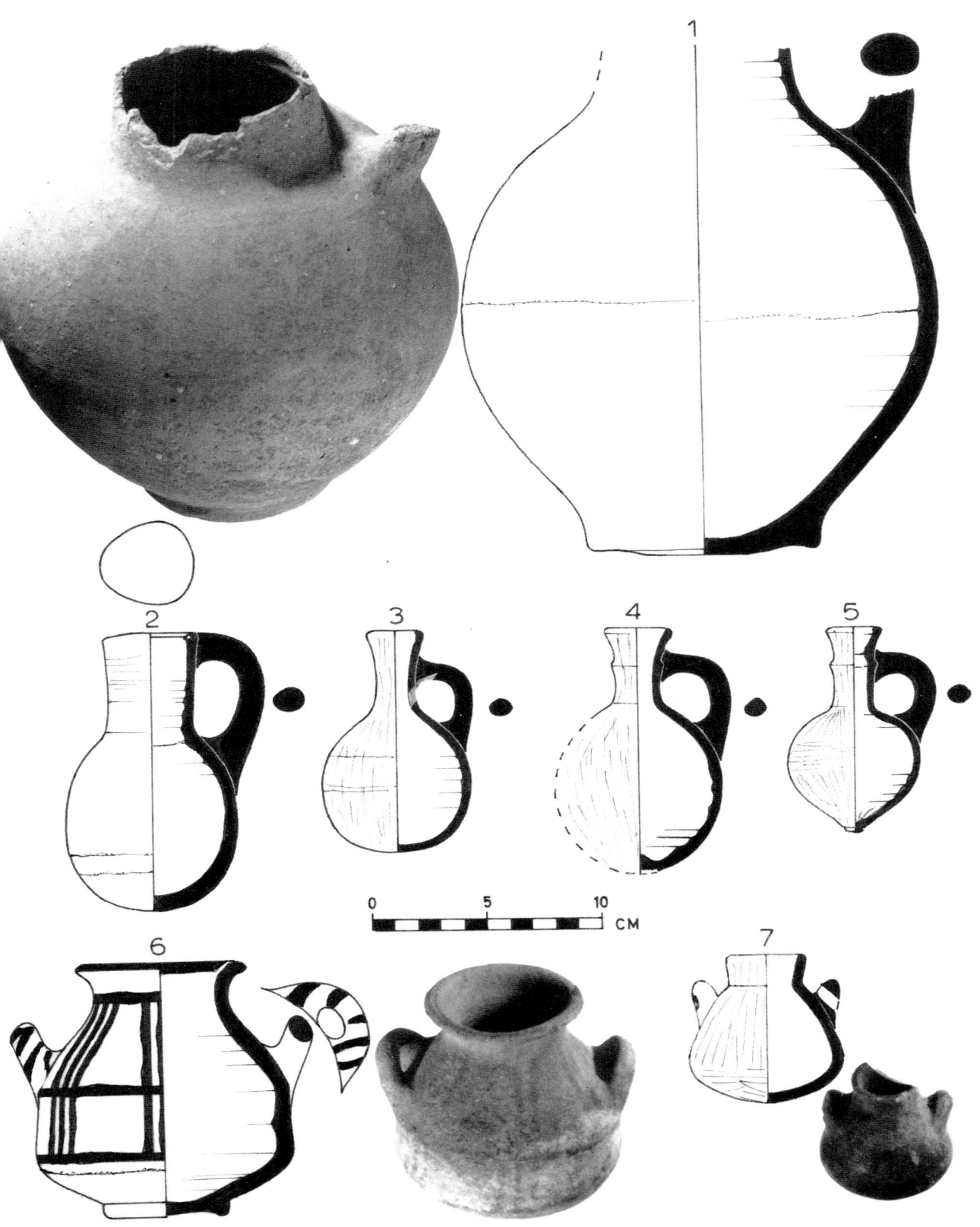

257

FIG. 93 MISCELLANEOUS POTTERY (PERIOD IIB)

1. Identification		2. Section							3. Surface	
a.	b.	a.	b. Core		c. Non-Plastics				a. Exterior	b. Interior
Item	Square, Locus Basket	Fabric Color	Color	Extent	Type	Size	Frequency	Density	Color, n-p, voids, forming, finishing features	Same
1. Bowl TT 115	SW 3-7 29.55	br		none	lms bas	l,m,s m,s	s f	med l	*Ex:* rd & dk pk on bottom & base, rd slip burnished on rim. Many pits, spalls, drag marks. Circular turning grooves on bottom and base covered on rim by burnish. *In:* rd slip is much eroded, burnish remains on small part of rim, much pitting, some lms spalling.	
2. Bowl TT 681	SW 6-7 4.13	lt rd	ck gr	+75%	lms	m,s,f	s	low	*Ex:* lt rd bottom, base, rd slip on rim, some n-p protrude, few seen, forming ridges are reg, circular, covered with fine-line combing on rim and with slip. *In:* rd slip, burnished horiz on rim, bottom in box burnish. Few n-p seen, much encrusted, slightly burned on bottom, *in* & *ex*.	
3. Bowl Rim & Bottom	SW 5-7 21.71	yl rd	rd yl	50%	lms	l,m,s	s	med l	*Ex:* lt rd, rd slip burnished on rim, many n-p seen on bottom, circular forming lines covered with smoothing. The rim on most of *in* slip has covered the n-p, some protrude, covered. *In:* rd slip burnished, horiz on top of rim, lateral on bottom. One large (9mm) bas n-p protrudes slightly on bottom.	
4. Lamp TT 551	SW 5-7 20.33	lt rd br	dk gr	90%	lms	l,s,f	s	low	*Ex:* lt rd br to rd gr, many n-p seen, much encrusted, some carbon on bottom. *In:* lt rd br to rd gr, carbon on bottom and lip, many n-p seen on rim thru shallow erosion, in bowl some protrude, covered, some pitting, faint trace of fine-line smoothing on outer edge of rim.	
5. Juglet TT 604	SW 1-9 19.67	rd yl	gr	not clear	Not Available				*Ex:* rd yl slip, neatly burnished in horiz strokes. On base bottom circular lines end in reg focal spiral. Paint is mostly vdk gr to bk. The 3 middle lines in the 5 horiz bands are dusky rd (2.5YR 3/2). *In:* not available. Few pits.	
6. Juglet TT 605	SW 2-8 21.73	rd yl		none (rim chip)	Not Available				*Ex:* burnished rd slip, not burnished under handle, bottom has circular forming lines ending in center point, forming lines on inside rim. Paint is bk, some pits.	

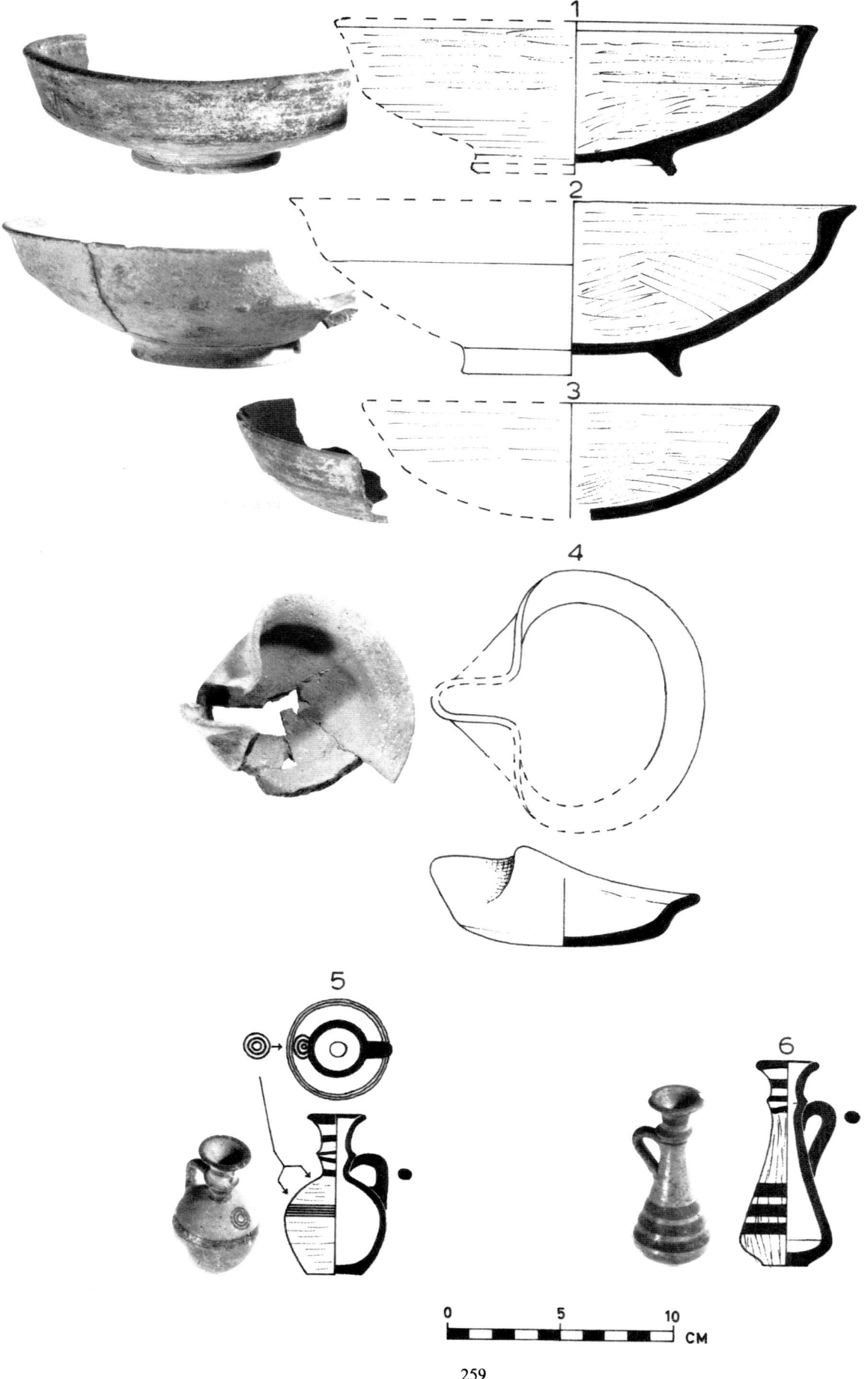

FIG. 94 MISCELLANEOUS POTTERY (PERIOD III-VI)

1. Identification		2. Section						3. Surface	
a.	b.	a.	b. Core		c. Non-Plastics			a. Exterior	b. Interior
Item	Square, Locus Basket	Fabric Color	Color	Extent	Type	Size	Fre-quency	Density	Color, n-p, voids, forming, finishing features	Same
1. Jar Rim	SW 6-6 16.77	rd	dk gr	-75%	lms	l,m,s	s	low	*Ex*: lt rd br to gr, many n-p protrude, covered, some exposed, wet-smoothing around rim & body is horiz generally. *In*: same colors, shallow reg forming ridges from rim to edge of extant piece. Much encrusted. Many n-p seen protruding, covered, fine-line smoothing is very reg. Hard, brittle.	
2. Jar Rim & Handle	SW 5-7 8.12	rd	gr	+75%	lms	l,s,f	s	med l	*Ex*: lt br to gr, many n-p protrude, many exposed thru lime spalls, circular fine-line finish, flashing line at top of handle. *In*: rd, encrusted, many lms n-p protrude, covered, some seen, forming lines reg but shallow, many fine-line finishing bands, many n-p protrude, some pitting.	
3. Jar Rim & Body	SW 6-7 28.52	rd yl	dk gr	+75%	lms	m,s	s	med l	*Ex*: rd yl to gr, many n-p protrude, covered, few seen, slanting wipe lines on shoulder, horiz on rim, drag marks and crude finish to neck. *In*: same colors, forming lines as No. 2 but not quite so reg. Many n-p protrude, some pitting. Very shallow, forming depressions on *ex* shoulder. Base also has forming ridges ending in a depressed twist. Many lms n-p seen in shallow spalls. On *ex* same except that smoothing is in long criss-cross bands.	
4. Jug Handle TT 910	SW 5-7 34.64	rd yl		none	lms	m,s	vvf	vvlow	*Ex*: rd yl, few n-p protrude, covered, none seen, circular horiz wet-smoothing, paint is dk rd br with yl rd halo, handle rather crudely joined to shoulder, seal not smoothed. *In*: rd yl, forming lines clear on shoulder up to depression mid-way between handle and neck joins. Circular forming lines inside neck.	

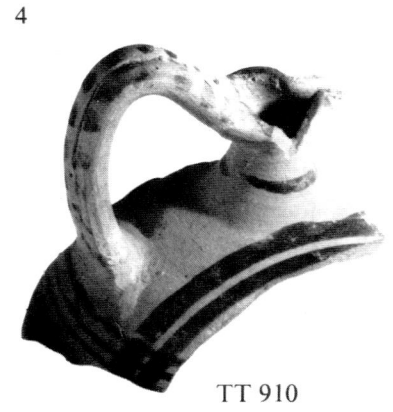

4

TT 910

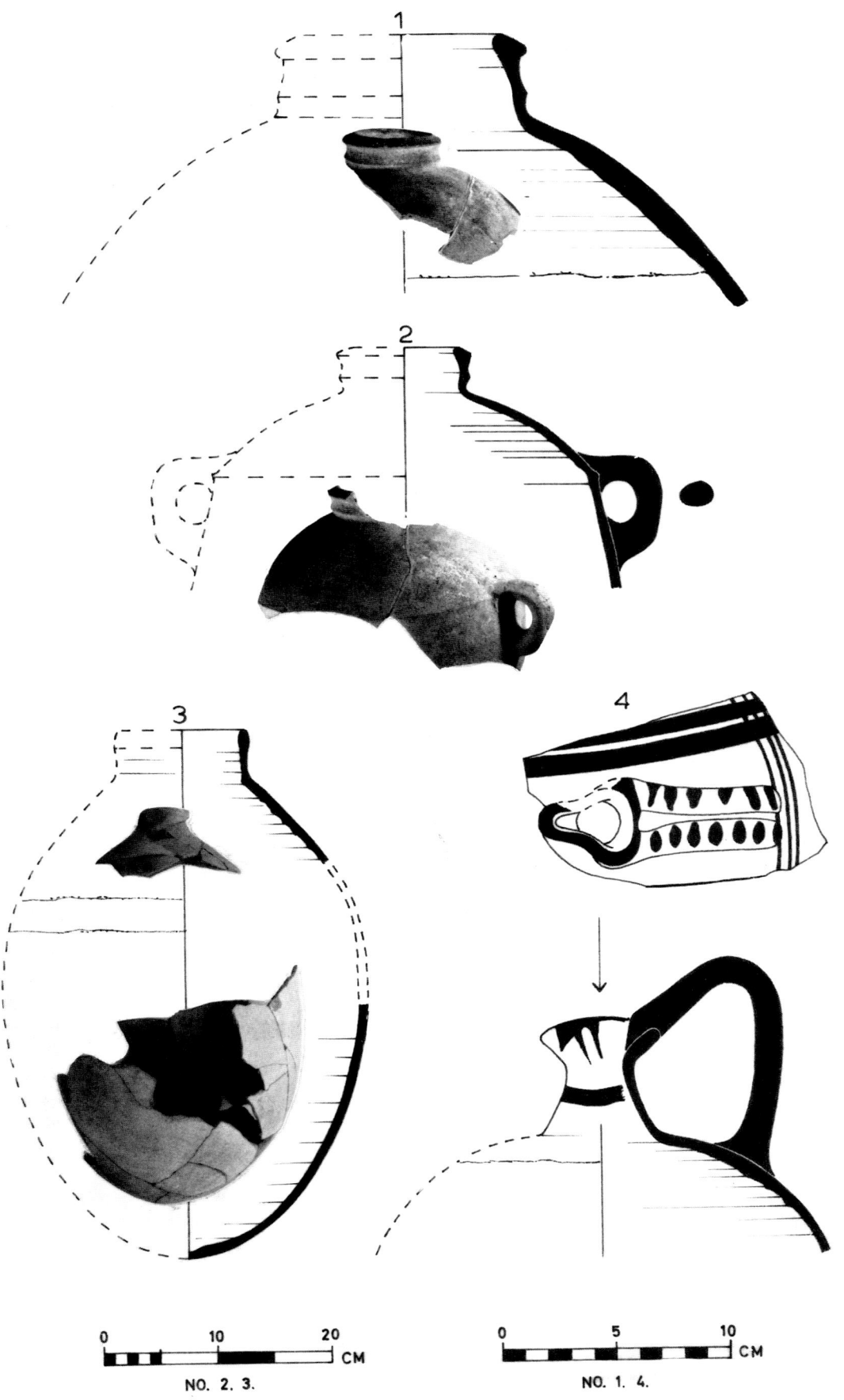

FIG. 95 MISCELLANEOUS POTTERY (PERIODS III-VI, except NO. 2, PERIOD IA)

1. Identification		2. Section							3. Surface	
a.	b.	a.	b. Core		c. Non-Plastics				a. Exterior	b. Interior
Item	Square, Locus Basket	Fabric Color	Color	Extent	Type	Size	Frequency	Density	Color, n-p, voids, forming, finishing features	Same
1. Juglet TT 60	SW 3-7 24.43	lt rd br (rim chip)		none	lms bas	l,m,s s,s	f f	low	*Ex*: rd slip, n-p judged from surf, some seen, embedded, many tiny pits, some n-p protrude, covered, straw voids few, lime encrustation on one side. *In*: same color at lip, neck, rim overfold untrimmed, some covered n-p protrude, some forming ridges felt inside.	
2. Juglet TT 48	SW 9-1 5.21	dk pk	dk gr	90% handle only visible	bas lms	l,m,s m,s	s f	med l	*Ex*: pk, many n-p on surf, embedded, some spalling, straw voids common, forming ridges on base, smoothing on neck, irreg smoothing on body, excess clay from handle attachment to lip untrimmed. *In*: also pk, slight ridging visible inside neck, remainder not visible.	
3. Juglet TT 519	SW 5-7 8.11	rd yl	dk pk	-50%	lms	m,s,f	s	low	*Ex*: lt rd slip but so heavily encrusted not much is available; horiz forming ridges on vert section of wall, some n-p seen on surf, crudely finished. *In*: dk pk, forming ridges down in ending in crude twist raised, base is heavy.	
4. Juglet TT 143	SW 2-25 54.97	rd yl	lt br	none rim +50% handle	lms cal	l,s m,s	s s	med	*Ex*: lt br, many n-p embedded, many fingerprints, few pits, flashing line at shoulder above handle. *In*: lt br, prominent forming ridges lead to irreg depression in the center.	
5. Juglet TT 801	SW 3-7 64.151	rd yl	lt br	inner 75%	bas lms	m,s m,s,f	s s	med l	*Ex*: rd slip, encrusted, few n-p seen embedded, some straw voids, crazing. *In*: lt br, encrusted, few forming ridges near bottom leading to pointed depression with slight twist.	
6. Juglet TT 546	SW 6-7 17.25	vpl br		none	lms	s,f	f	vlow	*Ex*: rd yl, many tiny pits, irreg shaping esp at base, encrusted. *In*: vpl br, reg forming ridges end in raised twist at base center.	
7. Juglet TT 802	SW 3-7 64.151				Not Available				*Ex*: rd br to dk gr, much eroded and pitted, some bits of grog and lms n-p seen, bit of handle is burnished. *In*: same, as seen on in neck.	
8. Juglet TT 120	SW 6-5 12.39	rd yl		none	none				*Ex*: rd yl, forming ridges visible, deeper depression at bottom of handle, base has off-center twirl of string cut.	
9. Cook Pot TT 823	SW 1-9 43.119	rd br	dk gr	25% rim parts only	cal lms	m,s m,s	s-m f	med	*Ex*: rd br, many n-p protrude, covered, some seen, straw voids on handle, center protrusion at base is off-center, some forming depression above mid-body, fine-line smoothing around rim. *In*: rd br, forming lines only at lower part of neck, flashing line at mid-body covered well.	
10. Lamp TT 1	SW 6-5 1.1	rd yl		none	none	(See TT 120, Fig.95:8)			*In*: rd yl, rim edge opposite lip is sharply cornered, inner half of rim is slightly depressed, circular finishing to both dish and rim, only slight carbon deposit on lip. *Ex*: rd yl, bottom is shaved flat, too much near lip end. Some pitting.	

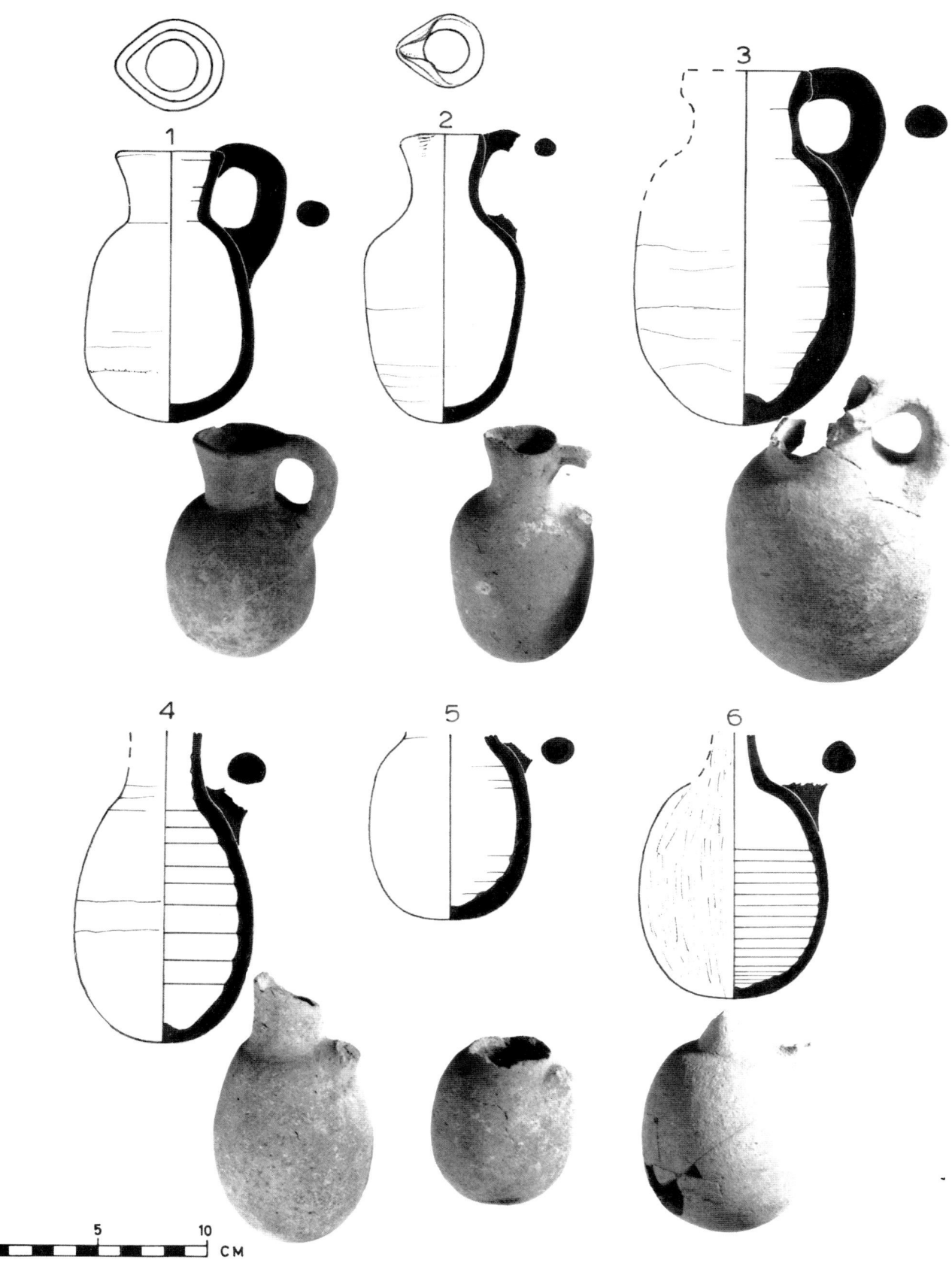

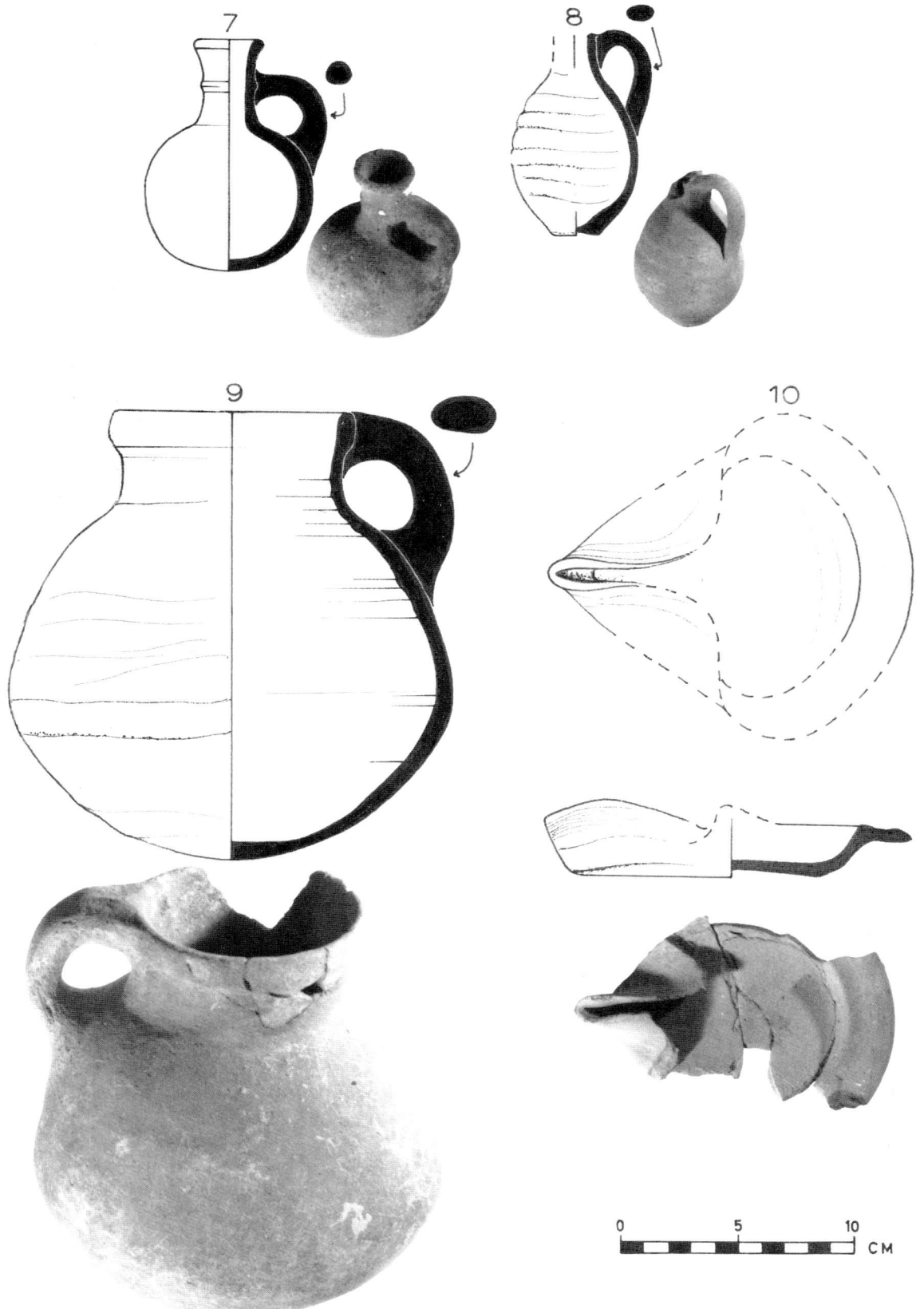

FIG. 96a DRAINPIPE STRUCTURE

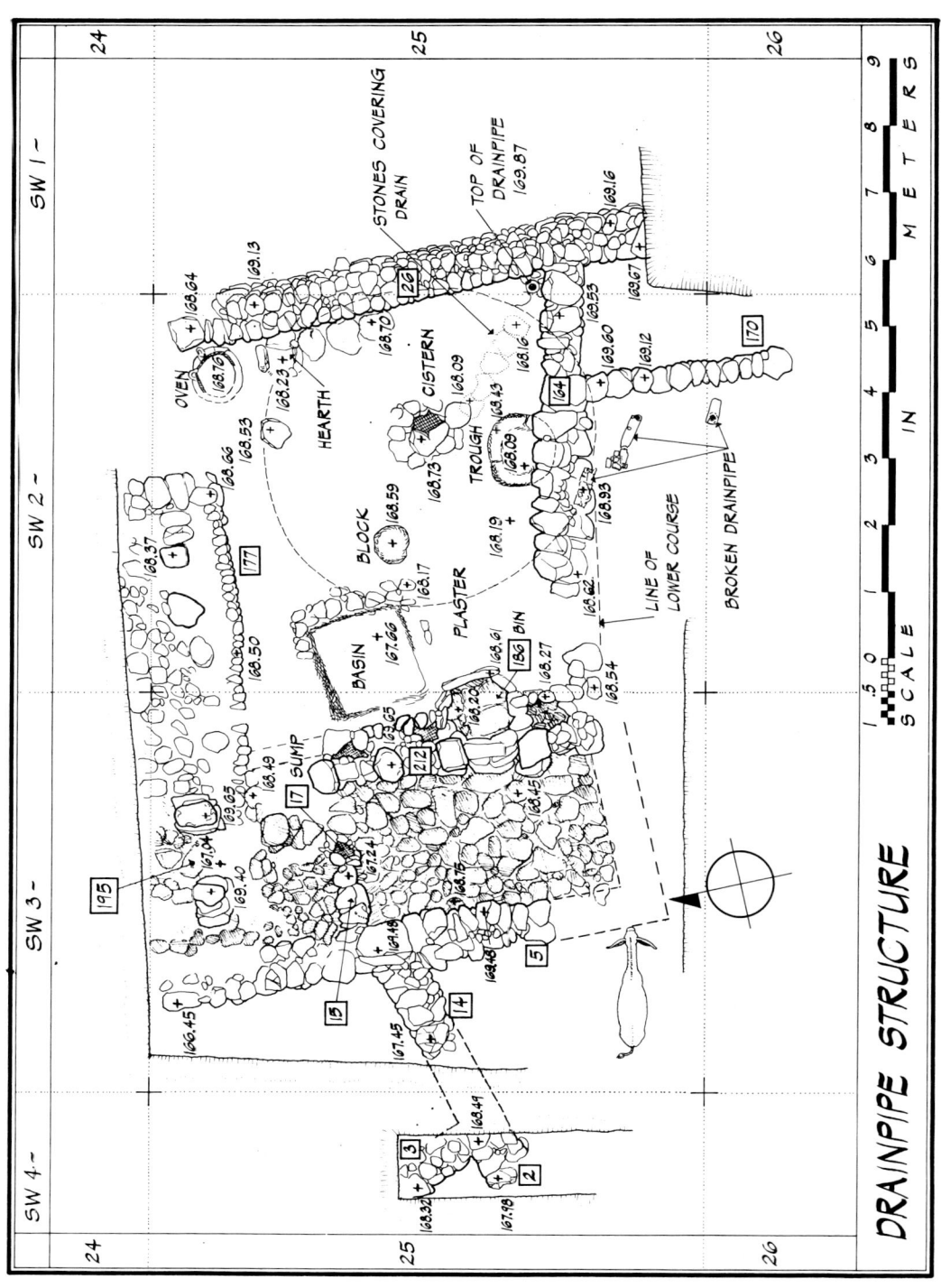

DRAINPIPE STRUCTURE

FIG. 96b TABLET BUILDING

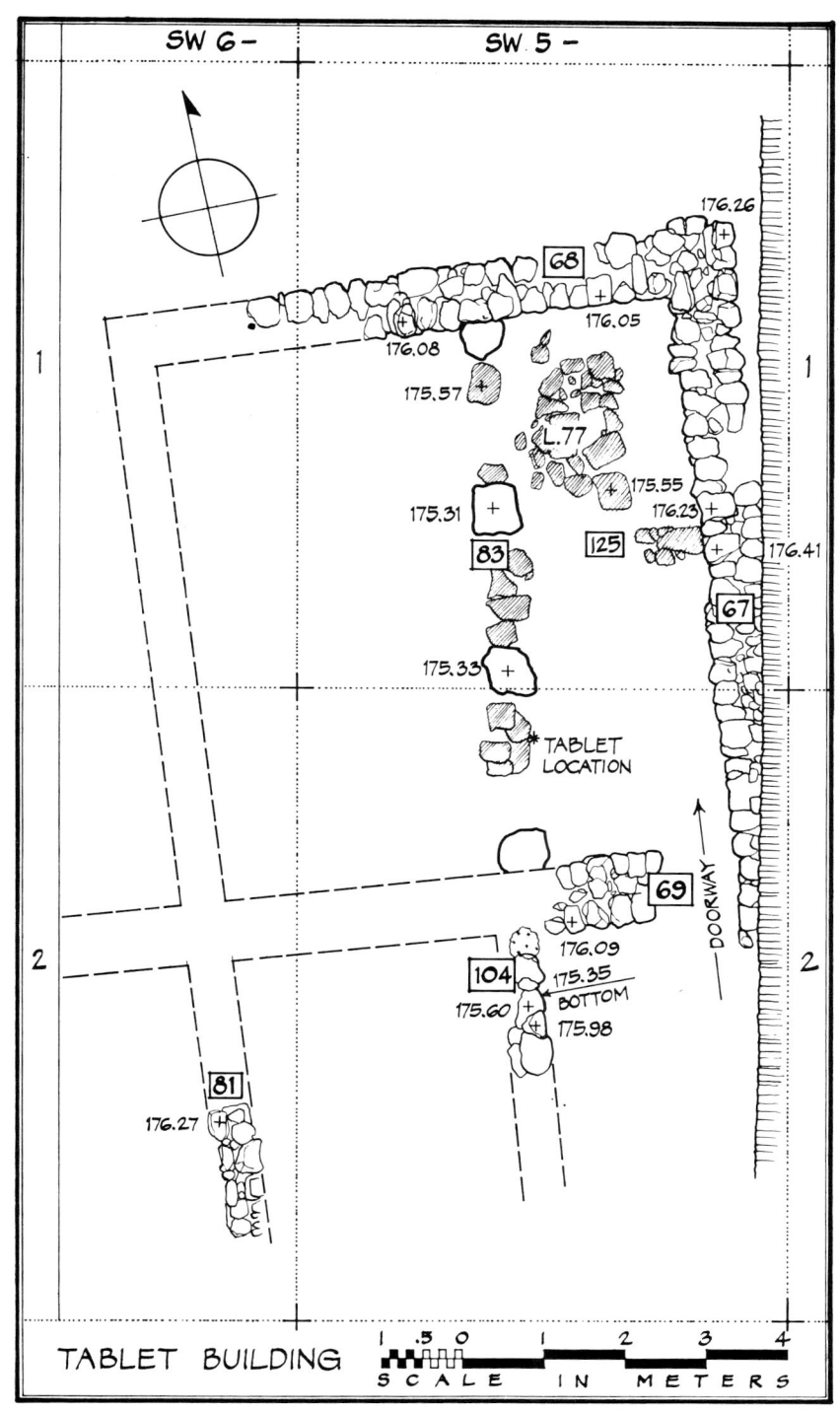

FIG. 96c TWELFTH-CENTURY HOUSE

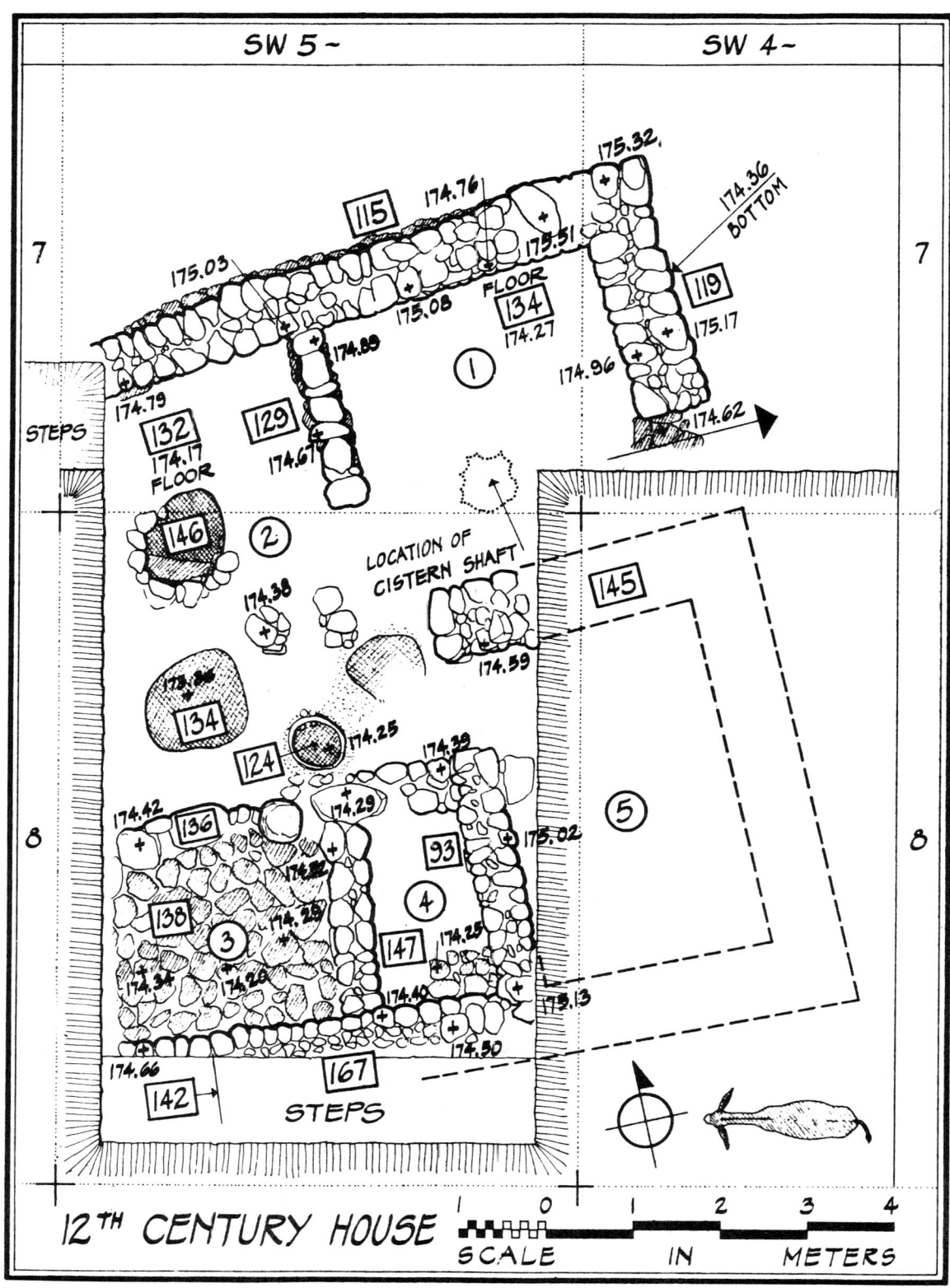

FIG. 97a CULTIC STRUCTURE

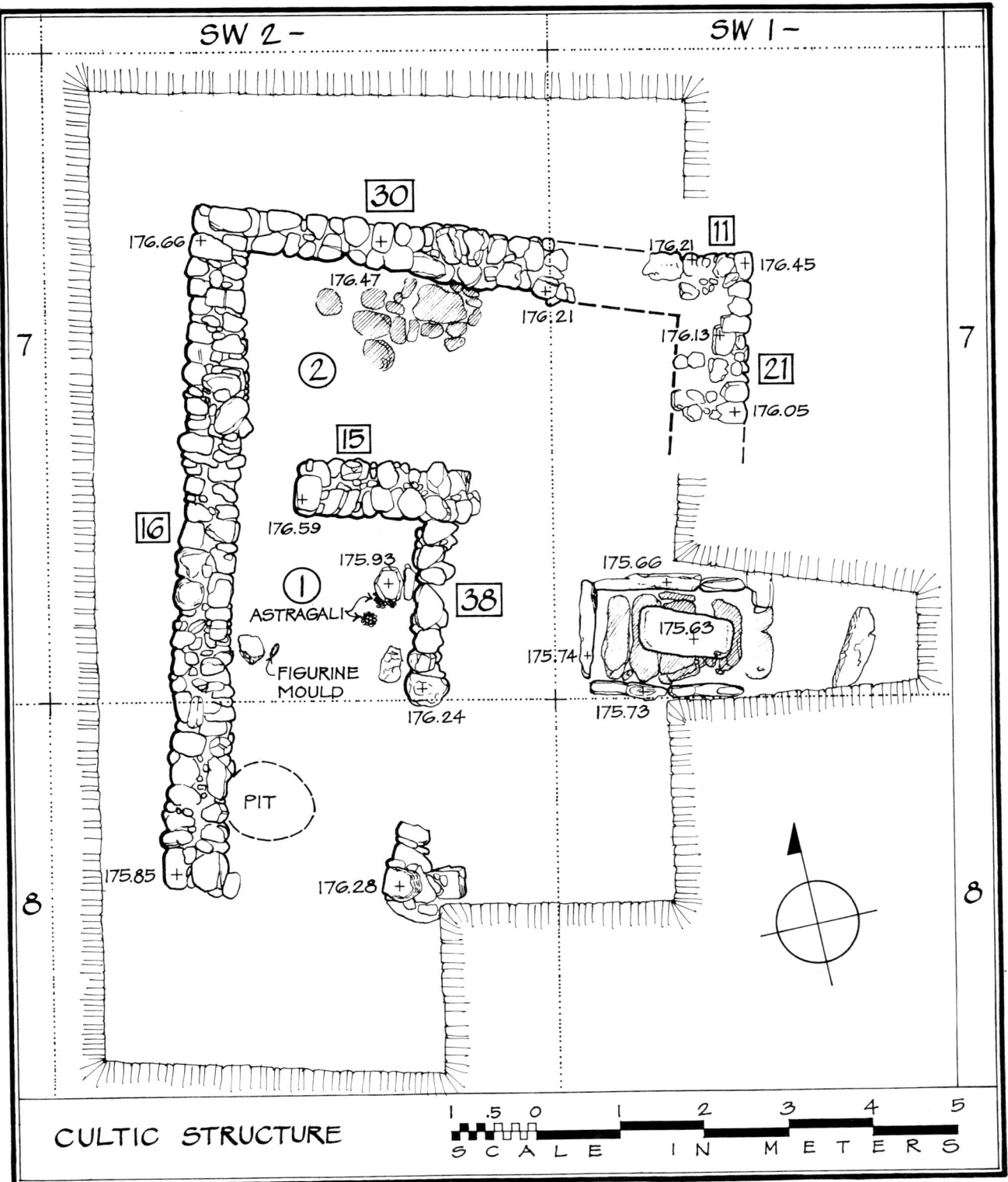

CULTIC STRUCTURE

FIG. 97b SECTION THROUGH SW 2-7, LOOKING SOUTH

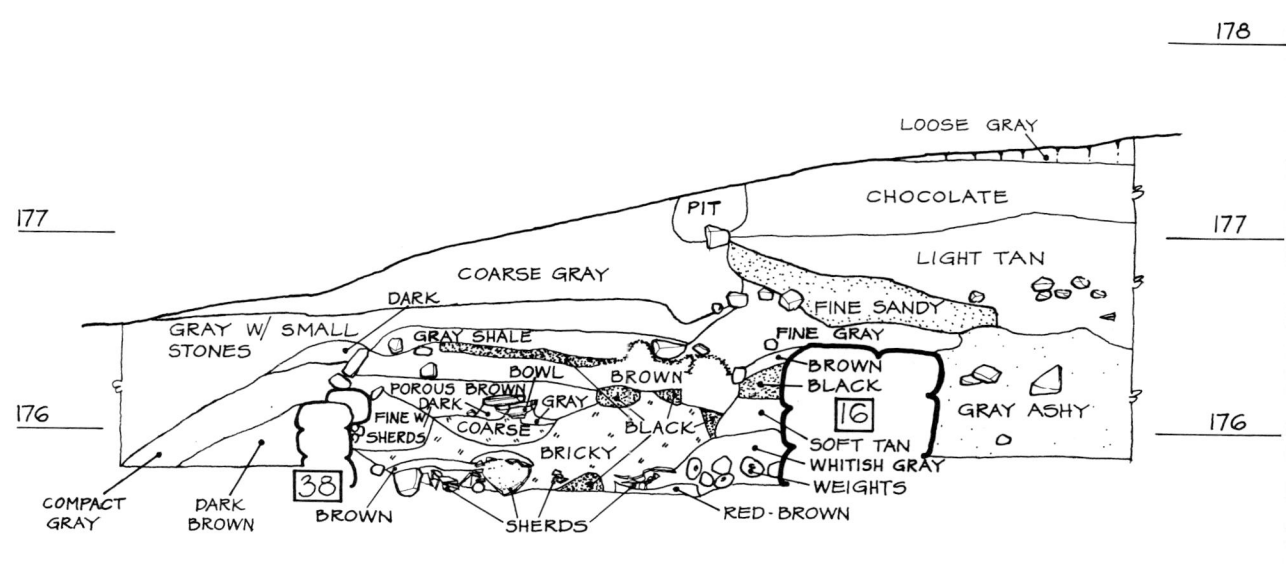

TELL TA'ANNEK
SECTION C - C

INDEXES

GENERAL INDEX

A

Abu Hawām, Tell	5, 9, 18, 26, 30, 33, 48
Abu Qudeis, Tell	26
Afrit, Wadi	33
ᶜAfula	5, 9, 18, 26, 48
Aharoni, Y.	5, 10, 24, 55
ᶜAi (see et-Tell)	
ᶜAin Shems	5, 9, 13, 18, 20, 21, 30, 32, 33, 35, 49, 53
Alabastron	49, 51
Albright, W. F.	4, 9, 10, 15, 24, 25, 26, 27, 55
ᶜAmal, Tell	5, 18, 25-28
Amphorae	28
ᶜAmuq	21
Arad	26, 37
Ashdod	5, 9
ᶜAthlit	48

B

Baking Trays	38
Beit Mirsim, Tell	4, 9, 18, 21, 26, 28, 30, 32, 35, 42
Bethel	5, 8, 9, 18
Beth Shan	5, 26
Beth-zur	29, 33
Bible, References to	
Amos 1:1	42
2 Chr 12:9	26
2 Chr 16:4	42
Josh 12:21	15
Josh 17:11-12	15
Judg 1:27	15
Judg 4-5	15, 55
1 Kgs 14:25, 26	26
1 Kgs 15:20	42
Zech 14:5	42
Bottles	49
Bowls	12-13, 15, 20, 21, 30-33, 35, 38, 43, 44, 45, 50, 51, 53
Bar-handled	13, 31-32
Burnishing, Hand-	6, 12, 14, 19, 20, 21, 28, 29, 30, 31, 32, 33, 37, 38-39, 43, 45, 54
Buhl, M.	5, 9

C

Canaanites	15, 55
Callaway, J.	5, 9, 10
Censers	33, 35
Chalices	14, 20-21, 35, 38, 53
Chronology Summaries	6, 26-27, 42, 48
Cistern L. 69 (SW 2-8)	23, 35, 36, 38
Cistern L. 74 (SW 6-2)	19, 23-24
	29, 35-39
Cooking Pots	13-14, 15, 20-21, 33, 35, 38, 43, 44, 50, 53, 54
Cooley, R.	10
Craters	12, 19, 30 37, 43, 49-50, 51, 53
Cross, F.	10
Crowfoot, G.	35
Cultic Stand	23, 36
Cultic Structure	1, 3, 4, 10, 13, 17, 19, 23-39 passim.
Cuneiform Tablet Building	1, 3, 4, 7, 8, 15, 17, 24
Cup, Tripod	33, 35
Cyprus (Cypriote Pottery)	29, 35, 50, 54

D

David	5, 21, 55
Deborah	15, 55
Deir ᶜAllā	5-6, 9, 10, 18, 26, 27, 30, 31, 32, 33, 38, 42
Dever, W.	5, 8, 26
Dothan, M.	5
Dothan, T.	4, 5
Drainpipe Structure	3, 7, 8, 15, 47

E

Esdraelon Plain	15, 21, 55

F

Fârᶜah (N), Tell el-	26, 28, 29, 30, 31, 33, 38, 42

Franken, H.	6		
Freedman, D. N.	10, 27		
Fûl, Tell el-	18		

M

Macalister, R.	24
Maisler, B. (see Mazar, B.)	
May, H.	36
Mazar, B.	4, 5, 26
Medinet Habu	4
Megadim	48, 51
Megiddo	1, 4, 8, 10, 14, 15, 18, 24-25, 27-39 *passim*, 42, 48, 55
Mersin	51
Mortaria	50, 51
Munshara	28-29, 37
Mycenean Imports	30

G

Gezer	5, 9, 18, 24, 26
Gibeon (see el-Jib)	
Goren, Tel	48

H

Hazor	4-5, 9, 18, 24, 25, 28-39 *passim*, 42, 47-48
Ḥesi, Tell el-	48
Holm-Nielsen, S.	5, 9

N

Naṣbeh, Tell en-	12, 26, 28, 30, 31, 48, 49, 50
Northeast Outwork (NEO)	41, 45, 47, 49

I

Ibrahim, M.	10
Iron I Court	3
Israelites	21, 55

O

Oenochoe	28
Offering Stand	36

J

James, F.	5, 26
Jars	9-10, 18, 21, 27-28, 35, 36, 44, 45, 48-49, 51, 53, 54
Collared-Rim	5, 9, 15, 21, 27-28, 55
"Sausage"	44, 45, 48, 49, 51
Jar Stand	35
Jericho	26, 30
Jib, el- (Gibeon)	5, 9
Juglets	10-12, 18-19, 29-30, 37, 49, 51, 53, 54
Jugs	10-12, 15, 18-19, 21, 28-29, 36-37, 38, 42, 43, 44, 49, 51, 53, 54

P

Philistines	4, 5, 6, 12, 13
Pit L. 74 (SW 6-2)	47
Potters' Marks	27
Pritchard, J.	5, 9
Pyxis	19, 29-30, 53

Q

Qasile, Tell	5, 9, 14, 18, 28

R

Raddana, Khirbet	10
Rumeith, Tell er-	33, 45

K

Kalsbeek, J.	6
Kamid el-Loz	35
Kelso, J.	5, 8, 9
Kenyon, K.	4
Kylix	48, 51

S

Sahab	10
Samaria	26, 28, 33, 42
Sauer, J.	33, 45
Sellin, E.	10, 23, 41, 45
Shechem	50
Shiloh	5, 9
Shishak I	4, 5, 26-27
Slip, Red	19, 20, 21, 28, 29, 30, 31-33, 38, 39, 54
Solomon(ic)	5, 21, 24, 25, 26, 42, 44
Syria	21

L

Lachish	18, 26, 28, 30, 35, 36, 48
Lamps	33, 35, 38, 44, 50, 51, 53, 54
Lapp, P.	1, 3, 6, 7, 15, 55
Lekythoi	48, 51
Loci, Primary Comparative (PCL)	1, 4-6, 8-9, 18, 24-26, 41-42, 47-48

INDEX

T

Tell, et- (ʿAi)	5, 9-10
Transjordan	33, 55
Twelfth-Century House	3, 7, 8

U

Umm el-Biyara	48

W

Wright, G. E.	4, 5, 24, 25, 32, 35

Y

Yadin, Y.	4, 5, 9, 24, 25, 27

Z

Zeror, Tell	5, 26

INDEX TO FIGURES
AND RELATED DISCUSSION IN TEXT

Fig. No.	Discussion Page	Figure No.	Discussion Page
1	9-13, 53	40	19, 29-30, 53, 54
2	12-14	41	19, 30, 37
3	10-14, 21, 36, 53	42	30, 37
4	9-13, 53	43	30, 37
5	12, 13	44	31
6	9-11, 36	45	13, 20, 31-33
7	12, 19		38, 43, 54
8	12-13, 14	46	13, 31-33, 38, 44
9	9-10	47	13, 31-33, 38, 54
10	9-10	48	13, 20, 29, 31-33
11	10-11, 36		38, 43, 54
12	12, 19	49	33, 38
13	12-13, 44, 53	50	20, 33, 38
14	12-14, 20	51	33, 35, 38, 54
15	9-12	52	35, 43
16	12	53	35, 38
17	12-14, 20, 21	54	36
18	18-20, 37	55	36
19	18-20, 37	56	36
20	18-19	57	36, 39
21	20	58	19, 36-37, 38
22	18-19, 37	59	19, 28, 36-37
23	20-21	60	29, 36-37
24	18-21, 37	61	19, 29, 36, 43, 53
25	12, 13, 18, 20	62	19, 29, 37, 53
26	18-19, 28, 36	63	12, 19, 37, 39
27	19, 21	64	37, 39
28	18-20, 37	65	37
29	20	66	33, 38, 43
30	27-28, 36, 54	67	29, 38
31	27-28, 54	68	38
32	27-28, 44	69	38
33	27-28	70	12, 19, 37, 42, 43
34	27-28	71	42-43
35	27-28	72	12, 19, 43
36	28-29, 36	73	27, 43
37	19, 28, 37	74	12, 19, 43, 49
38	29, 37	75	43-44, 54
39	29, 43	76	43-44

Figure No.	Discussion Page	Figure No.	Discussion Page
77	48, 50, 51	87	48-50, 51
78	50	88	53
79	48-50	89	53
80	44, 48	90	53
81	44, 48-50, 51	91	53
82	44, 50, 51	92	19, 30, 53-54
83	44, 48-49	93	29, 53-54
84	49-50, 51	94	49, 54
85	48-50	95	54
86	48, 49-50, 51		

INDEX TO TAANACH LOCI MENTIONED IN TEXT AND FIGURES

NEO-2
  Locus 3 — 41, 42, Fig. 71
  Locus 5 — 41, 42
  Locus 36 — 41, 42, Fig. 71

SW 1-9
  Locus 19 — Fig. 93
  Locus 43 — Fig. 95
  Locus 52 — Fig. 92
  Locus 128 — Fig. 90

SW 2-7
  Locus 13 — 23, Fig. 30
  Locus 14 — 23
  Wall 15 — 23
  Wall 16 — 23
  Locus 18 — Fig. 40
  Locus 25 — 23
  Locus 26 — 23, Figs. 32, 37, 39, 40, 42, 45, 46, 48, 49
  Locus 27 — 23, Figs. 32, 36, 37, 40, 42, 42-48, 50, 51
  Locus 28 — 23, Figs. 34, 40, 43, 44, 45, 49
  Wall 30 — 23
  Locus 32 — Fig. 34
  Locus 35 — 23, Figs. 39, 44, 46, 48
  Locus 36 — 23, Figs. 39, 44, 46, 48
  Wall 38 — 23
  Locus 48 — 23, Figs. 31, 32, 33, 44, 46, 48
  Locus 57 — 23, Figs. 31, 36, 39, 43, 45, 50
  Locus 59 — 23, Figs. 30, 33, 35, 40, 41, 43, 49
  Locus 60 — Figs. 46, 50
  Locus 61 — 23, Figs. 30, 31, 34, 35, 36, 38, 39, 40, 41, 42, 44, 46, 47, 48, 49, 51
  Locus 63 — 23, Figs. 30, 31, 39, 40, 46, 47
  Locus 87 — Fig. 92
  Room 1 — 23, 27
  Room 2 — 23, 27

SW 2-8
  Locus 12 — 17
  Locus 18 — 17, Fig. 25
  Locus 21 — Fig. 93
  Locus 27 — Fig. 91
  Locus 38 — 17
  Locus 46 — Fig. 88
  Locus 50 — Fig. 89
  Cistern 69 — 23, 38, Figs. 52, 53, 54
  Locus 77 — Fig. 90
  Locus 156 — 23, Figs. 52, 53, 54
  Locus 163 — Fig. 52
  Locus 170 — Fig. 52
  Locus 171 — Figs. 52, 53
  Locus 175 — Fig. 52

SW 2-25
  Wall 5 — 3, 7
  Pit 19 — 47, 48, Fig. 87
  Pit 22 — 47
  Wall 26 — 7
  Locus 44 — 8, Fig. 9
  Locus 45 — 7, 8, Fig. 3
  Locus 49 — 8, Figs. 11, 13, 14
  Locus 54 — Fig. 95
  Locus 59 — Fig. 14
  Locus 61 — 8, Fig. 10
  Locus 62 — 8, Fig. 12
  Locus 124 — 8, Fig. 10
  Pit 125 — 47, 48, Figs. 83, 84
  Locus 144 — Figs. 83, 84
  Locus 145 — Fig. 83
  Locus 158 — 8, Figs. 10, 11, 12, 13, 14
  Locus 160 — 8, Figs. 10, 11, 13, 14
  Locus 162 — 8, Fig. 10
  Wall 164 — 3, 7
  Locus 171 — 8, Figs. 10, 11, 13, 14
  Locus 180 — 8, Fig. 11
  Locus 186 — 8, Figs. 10, 11, 12, 13, 14
  Locus 195 — 7
  Locus 208 — 8, Figs. 11, 14
  Locus 212 — 7

SW 3-7		SW 5-7		
Locus 24	Figs. 92, 95	Wall 3	47	
Locus 25	Fig. 92	Locus 8	Figs. 94, 95	
Locus 28	Fig. 92	Locus 11	48	
Locus 29	Figs. 92, 93	Locus 15	47, Fig. 79	
Locus 64	Fig. 95	Locus 20	Fig. 93	
SW 3-25		Locus 21	Fig. 93	
Pit 22	47, 48, Figs. 85, 86	Locus 34	Fig. 94	
SW 4-7		Locus 66	47	
Locus 4	47	Locus 117	Fig. 89	
Pit 6	17, 41	Locus 127	Fig. 90	
Pit 7	47, 48, Figs. 77, 78	SW 5-8		
Wall 9	41	Pit 11	8	
Wall 19	17	Locus 88	Fig. 91	
Locus 31	41	Locus 100	Fig. 91	
Locus 32	41	Wall 119	8	
Locus 36	41, 42, Fig. 72	*Tabun* 124	8, Figs. 6, 7, 8	
Locus 37	41, 42, Fig. 73	Wall 136	7, 8	
Wall 38	17	Locus 138	8, Figs. 6, 8	
Locus 38a	41, 42, Fig. 74	Wall 142	8	
Locus 40	18, 41	Wall 147	8	
Locus 41	41, 42, Fig. 70	Locus 152	8	
Locus 42	18, Figs. 28, 29	Locus 153	8, Figs. 6, 7, 8	
Locus 44	17, Figs. 20, 21	*Tabun* 155	8, Figs. 4, 5	
Locus 53	17, Fig. 19	Locus 157	8, Figs. 4, 5	
Locus 56	17	Room 2	7, 8	
Locus 57	17, Figs. 26, 27	Room 3	7, 8	
Locus 58	17	SW 6-2		
Locus 59	17	Locus 142	17, 24	
Locus 60	17, Figs. 26, 27	Locus 45	24	
Wall 64	17, 18	Locus 68	4, 17, Figs. 22, 23	
Locus 65	41	Locus 71	17	
Locus 68	17, Fig. 18	Cistern 74	23, 36, 39, Figs. 55, 56,	
Locus 69	47		57, 58, 59, 60, 61, 62, 63,	
Wall 74	18		64, 65, 66, 67, 68, 69	
Locus 76	17	Pit 74	47, 48, Figs. 80, 81, 82	
Wall 119	3	Locus 103	7, 8, Figs. 15, 16, 17	
SW 5-2		Locus 104	7, 8, Figs. 15, 16, 17	
Locus 42	Fig. 92	Locus 106	7, 8, Figs. 15, 17	
Locus 48	17	Locus 116	3	
Locus 60	4, 17, Fig. 24	SW 6-6		
Locus 61	4, 17, Fig. 24	Locus 16	Fig. 94	
Wall 67	7	SW 6-7		
Wall 68	7	Locus 4	Fig. 93	
Wall 69	7, 17	Locus 17	Fig. 95	
Locus 76	24	Locus 28	Fig. 94	
Locus 77	7, 24	SW 7-27		
Locus 80	3, 7, 8, Figs. 1, 2	Locus 20	Figs. 88, 89	
Locus 81	7, 8, Figs. 1, 2	SW 8-26		
Locus 96	Fig. 91	Locus 12	Fig. 88	
SW 5-6		SW 9-1		
Locus 14	41	Locus 5	Fig. 95	
Locus 16	41, 42, Figs. 75, 76			
Locus 17	41			

INDEX TO REGISTERED POTTERY VESSELS

Registration Number	Form	Square & Locus	Figure Number	Discussion Page
TT 1	Lamp	SW 6-5 L. 1	95:10	54
TT 35	Juglet	SW 3-7 L. 25	92:4	53
TT 36	Jar	SW 2-7 L. 13 (Cultic Structure)	30:4	27
TT 48	Juglet	SW 9-1 L. 5	95:2	54
TT 60	Juglet	SW 3-7 L. 24	95:1	54
TT 62	Juglet	SW 2-7 L. 26 (Cultic Structure)	40:7	30
TT 63	Juglet	SW 2-7 L. 26 (Cultic Structure)	40:1	29
TT 64	Censer	SW 2-7 L. 27 (Cultic Structure)	51:3	33, 35
TT 65	Cook Pot	SW 2-7 L. 27 (Cultic Structure)	50:3	33
TT 66	Pyxis	SW 3-7 L. 24	92:7	30, 54
TT 73	Pyxis	SW 2-7 L. 26 (Cultic Structure)	40:14	19, 30
TT 83	Jug	SW 2-7 L. 26 (Cultic Structure)	39:6	29
TT 88	Juglet	SW 2-7 L. 27 (Cultic Structure)	40:6	29
TT 89	Lamp	SW 2-7 L. 27 (Cultic Structure)	51:1	33, 38, 44
TT 103	Jug	SW 2-7 L. 27 (Cultic Structure)	37:1	19, 28, 36
TT 115	Bowl	SW 3-7 L. 29	93:1	54
TT 120	Juglet	SW 6-5 L. 12	95:8	54
TT 127	Juglet	SW 3-7 L. 28	92:3	53
TT 128	Juglet	SW 3-7 L. 29	92:5	53
TT 143	Juglet	SW 2-25 L. 54	95:4	54
TT 272	Pyxis	SW 5-2 L. 42	92:6	53
TT 306	Juglet	SW 2-7 L. 18 (Cultic Structure)	40:5	29, 53
TT 327	Juglet	SW 2-7 L. 59 (Cultic Structure)	40:4	29, 53
TT 350	Amphora	SW 2-7 L. 61 (Cultic Structure)	36:3	28
TT 351	Stand	SW 2-7 L. 61 (Cultic Structure)	51:4	35
TT 352	Bowl	SW 2-7 L. 61 (Cultic Structure)	47:2	32, 38
TT 353	Bowl	SW 2-7 L. 61, 63 (Cultic Structure)	46:5	32, 38
TT 354	Bowl	SW 2-7 L. 61 (Cultic Structure)	47:4	33
TT 372	Pyxis	SW 2-7 L. 61 (Cultic Structure)	40:13	19, 30
TT 380	Jar	SW 6-2 L. 74 (Cistern)	55:2	36
TT 381	Jug	SW 6-2 L. 74 (Cistern)	60:1	37
TT 382	Jug	SW 6-2 L. 74 (Cistern)	58:1	36
TT 383	Jar	SW 6-2 L. 74 (Cistern)	57:1	36, 38
TT 384	Jug	SW 6-2 L. 74 (Cistern)	59:3	37
TT 385	Jug	SW 6-2 L. 74 (Cistern)	59:4	19, 37
TT 386	Juglet	SW 2-7 L. 63 (Cultic Structure)	40:3	29, 53, 54
TT 402	Bowl	SW 6-2 L. 74 (Cistern)	65:1	38
TT 410	Bowl	SW 2-7 L. 61 (Cultic Structure)	46:11	32
TT 411	Bowl	SW 2-7 L. 61 (Cultic Structure)	46:2	32
TT 412	Bowl	SW 2-7 L. 61 (Cultic Structure)	47:3	32
TT 414	Jug	SW 2-7 L. 61 (Cultic Structure)	39:4	29
TT 415	Bowl	SW 2-7 L. 57 (Cultic Structure)	45:4	31

Registration Number	Form	Square & Locus	Figure Number	Discussion Page
TT 416	Bowl	SW 2-7 L. 27 (Cultic Structure)	45:3	31
TT 439	Bowl	SW 2-7 L. 26 (Cultic Structure)	42:2	30-31
TT 440	Jug	SW 2-7 L. 26 (Cultic Structure)	37:2	19, 28, 37
TT 441	Bowl	SW 2-7 L. 26, 40, 41 (Cultic Structure)	46:8	32, 44
TT 442	Bowl	SW 2-7 L. 27 (Cultic Structure)	46:13	32
TT 443	Bowl	SW 2-7 L. 26 (Cultic Structure)	48:3	33, 43
TT 444	Bowl	SW 2-7 L. 27 (Cultic Structure)	48:16	38
TT 445	Bowl	SW 2-7 L. 27, 44 (Cultic Structure)	45:2	31, 35
TT 446	Bowl	SW 2-7 L. 27 (Cultic Structure)	42:1	31
TT 447	Bowl	SW 2-7 L. 27 (Cultic Structure)	48:15	38
TT 448	Bowl	SW 2-7 L. 26 (Cultic Structure)	48:2	43
TT 449	Bowl	SW 2-7 L. 27 (Cultic Structure)	47:1	32
TT 450	Bowl	SW 2-7 L. 27 (Cultic Structure)	46:7	32
TT 451	Bowl	SW 2-7 L. 27 (Cultic Structure)	43:2	30
TT 452	Bowl	SW 2-7 L. 27 (Cultic Structure)	46:14	32, 44
TT 453	Bowl	SW 2-7 L. 27 (Cultic Structure)	46:3	32
TT 454	Jug	SW 2-7 L. 61 (Cultic Structure)	38:1	29, 37
TT 455	Bowl	SW 2-7 L. 61 (Cultic Structure)	46:12	32
TT 456	Cook Pot	SW 2-7 L. 60 (Cultic Structure)	50:1	33, 38
TT 457	Bowl	SW 2-7 L. 61 (Cultic Structure)	46:6	32
TT 458	Juglet	SW 2-7 L. 61 (Cultic Structure)	40:9	30
TT 459	Jar	SW 2-7 L. 61 (Cultic Structure)	34:5	27, 28
TT 460	Jar	SW 2-7 L. 61 (Cultic Structure)	35:2	18, 28
TT 461	Bowl	SW 2-7 L. 61 (Cultic Structure)	44:3	31
TT 462	Bowl	SW 2-7 L. 61 (Cultic Structure)	46:4	32
TT 463	Bowl	SW 2-7 L. 61 (Cultic Structure)	48:17	33, 38
TT 464	Bowl	SW 2-7 L. 27, 61 (Cultic Structure)	45:6	31
TT 465	Bowl	SW 2-7 L. 60 (Cultic Structure)	46:1	32
TT 466	Juglet	SW 2-7 L. 61 (Cultic Structure)	40:10	30
TT 467	Jar	SW 2-7 L. 57 (Cultic Structure)	36:1	18, 28
TT 468	Jug	SW 2-7 L. 63 (Cultic Structure)	39:2	29, 43
TT 469	Jar	SW 2-7 L. 61 (Cultic Structure)	31:3	27
TT 470	Jug	SW 2-7 L. 61 (Cultic Structure)	38:2	29, 37
TT 471	Bowl	SW 2-7 L. 28, 57, 59 (Cultic Structure)	43:1	31
TT 472	Cook Pot	SW 2-7 L. 57 (Cultic Structure)	50:2	33
TT 473	Lamp	SW 2-7 L. 61 (Cultic Structure)	51:2	33, 54
TT 474	Jar	SW 2-7 L. 61 (Cultic Structure)	31:1	27
TT 475	Jar	SW 2-7 L. 61 (Cultic Structure)	34:4	27, 28
TT 476	Jar	SW 2-7 L. 59 (Cultic Structure)	30:2	27
TT 477	Jar	SW 2-7 L. 61 (Cultic Structure)	30:3	27, 36
TT 478	Jar	SW 2-7 L. 61, 63 (Cultic Structure)	30:1	27
TT 479	Bowl	SW 2-7 L. 61 (Cultic Structure)	42:4	30
TT 480	Bowl	SW 2-7 L. 61 (Cultic Structure)	42:3	31
TT 481	Jar	SW 2-7 L. 63 (Cultic Structure)	31:2	27
TT 482	Jar	SW 2-7 L. 61 (Cultic Structure)	34:1	27, 35
TT 483	Jar	SW 2-7 L. 59, 61 (Cultic Structure)	33:1	27
TT 484	Juglet	SW 2-7 L. 28 (Cultic Structure)	40:11	30
TT 485	Bowl	SW 2-7 L. 28, 35 (Cultic Structure)	45:1	31
TT 486	Bowl	SW 2-7 L. 36 (Cultic Structure)	48:1	43
TT 487	Bowl	SW 2-7 L. 27 (Cultic Structure)	44:4	31
TT 488	Pyxis	SW 2-7 L. 27 (Cultic Structure)	40:12	19, 30, 54
TT 489	Crater	SW 2-7 L. 59, 61 (Cultic Structure)	41:1	30, 37
TT 490	Jar	SW 2-7 L. 57 (Cultic Structure)	36:2	18, 28
TT 519	Juglet	SW 5-7 L. 8	95:3	54
TT 546	Juglet	SW 6-7 L. 17	95:6	54

INDEX

283

Registration Number	Form	Square & Locus	Figure Number	Discussion Page
TT 551	Lamp	SW 5-7 L. 20	93:4	54
TT 564	Bowl	SW 5-2 L. 96	91:3	53
TT 604	Juglet	SW 1-9 L. 19	93:5	30, 54
TT 605	Juglet	SW 2-8 L. 21	93:6	54
TT 621	Pyxis	SW 4-7 L. 60	27:1	19
TT 630	Chalice	SW 4-7 L. 57	27:2	19, 21
TT 631	Jug	SW 4-7 L. 57	26:2	19
TT 635	Juglet	SW 2-7 L. 87	92:2	53
TT 681	Bowl	SW 6-7 L. 4	93:2	54
TT 690	Juglet	SW 6-2 L. 74 (Cistern)	62:9	37, 53
TT 691	Juglet	SW 6-2 L. 74 (Cistern)	62:10	37
TT 692	Cook Pot	SW 6-2 L. 74 (Cistern)	67:3	37, 38
TT 753	Cook Pot	SW 2-8 L. 27	91:1	53
TT 800	Chalice	SW 5-8 L. 88	91:4	53
TT 801	Juglet	SW 3-7 L. 64	95:5	54
TT 802	Juglet	SW 3-7 L. 64	95:7	54
TT 823	Cook Pot	SW 1-9 L. 43	95:9	54
TT 832	Crater	SW 2-8 L. 50	89:1	53
TT 834	Jar	SW 4-7 L. 60	26:1	18
TT 845	Jug	SW 1-9 L. 52	92:1	53
TT 848	Kylix	SW 2-25 L. 144 (Pit)	84:6	48, 51
TT 864	Cook Pot	SW 4-7 L. 44	21:5	20
TT 891	Cook Pot	SW 5-8 L. 100	91:2	53
TT 910	Jug	SW 5-7 L. 34	94:4	49, 54
TT 928	Chalice	SW 2-25 L. 160 (Drainpipe Structure)	14:14	14, 53
TT 945	Lamp	SW 5-7 L. 127	90:3	53
TT 988	Chalice	SW 5-7 L. 131	89:3	53
TT 990	Chalice	SW 5-8 L. 124 (12th-Century House)	8:14	14, 53
TT 1054	Lamp	SW 2-8 L. 77	90:2	53
TT 1146	Chalice	SW 5-7 L. 117	89:5	53
TT 1157	Cup & Saucer	SW 1-9 L. 128	90:1	53
TT 1281	Jug	SW 8-26 L. 12	88:3	53
TT 1356	Chalice	SW 7-27 L. 20	88:2	14, 53
TT 1430	Jug	SW 7-27 L. 20	89:4	53
TT 1431	Bowl	SW 7-27 L. 20	89:2	53
TT 1793	Lekythos	SW 6-5 L. 23, 25, 45	–	48
TT 1794	Lekythos	SW 6-5 L. 20	–	48
TT 1810	Jar	SW 2-25 L. 44 (Drainpipe Structure)	9:1	9
TT 1830	Offering Stand	SW 2-8 L. 156 (Cistern 69)	54:1	36
TT 1853	Chalice	SW 2-8 L. 156 (Cistern 69)	53:5	35, 38
TT 1854	Bowl	SW 2-8 L. 175 (Cistern 69)	52:9	35
TT 1855	Bowl	SW 2-8 L. 163 (Cistern 69)	52:3	35
TT 1856	Jar	SW 6-2 L. 74 (Cistern 74)	57:2	36
TT 1857	Jug	SW 6-2 L. 74 (Cistern 74)	60:4	37
TT 1858	Jug	SW 6-2 L. 74 (Cistern 74)	58:14	37
TT 1859	Jug	SW 6-2 L. 74 (Cistern 74)	61:5	37
TT 1860	Jug	SW 6-2 L. 74 (Cistern 74)	59:2	37
TT 1861	Jar	SW 5-6 L. 16	75:2	44
TT 1862	Jar	SW 2-8 L. 46	88:1	53
TT 1863	Cook Pot	SW 5-6 L. 16	76:6	44
TT 1864	Jar	SW 4-7 L. 44	20:1	18
TT 1865	Jar	SW 5-6 L. 16	75:n	(44)
TT 1866	Jar	SW 2-7 L. 59	35:1	9, 10, 27
TT 1868	Lamp	SW 6-2 L. 74 (Pit)	82:5	50, 51